Teacher's Edition

AGS

Basic English Grammar

by

Bonnie L. Walker

AGS®
American Guidance Service, Inc.
Circle Pines, Minnesota 55014-1796
800-328-2560

About the Author

Bonnie L. Walker taught for sixteen years in secondary schools and college. She holds a Ph.D. in curriculum theory and instructional design from the University of Maryland, an M.Ed. in secondary education, and a B.A. in English. She studied psycholinguistics at the University of Illinois Graduate School, and was a curriculum developer at the Model Secondary School for the Deaf at Gallaudet University. She is the author of *Life Skills English*, *Basic English Composition*, and numerous workbooks, learning packages, and sound filmstrips in written expression, grammar, and usage. She was a member of Project EduTech, which investigated promising technologies to improve the delivery of special education services. Dr. Walker has written several papers on the applications of personal computers, video technology, and cable television in education. She has been the director for research and development projects funded by the U.S. Department of Education, the U.S. Department of Agriculture, and the Administration on Youth, Children, and Families. Since 1986, Dr. Walker has been president of a research and development company specializing in development of training and educational materials for special populations.

The publisher wishes to thank the following educators for their helpful comments during the review process for *Basic English Grammar.* Their assistance has been invaluable.

Dr. William B. Whitaker
Director of Adult High School and GED Programs
Rowan Cabarrus Community College
Salisbury, NC

Beverly C. Allen
Coordinator, Learning Disabilities
L.D. Office, Norman Center
Kansas City, MO

Marie Ramey
Department Chairperson
West Side High School
Newark, NJ

Virginia Malling
Special Education Teacher
Oak Ridge High School
Oak Ridge, TN

Cathy Guzzo
Transition/Special Education Coordinator
Penn Hills Senior High School
Pittsburgh, PA

Ms. Cecilia Lozano
ESL Teacher
Douglas High School
Oklahoma City, OK

Susan Harrington
Special Education Teacher—Option III
Salamanca Middle School
Salamanca, NY

Printed in the United States of America
ISBN 0-7854-2309-5 (Previously ISBN 0-7854-0497-X) Product Number 91382
A 0 9 8 7 6 5 4 3 2

Table of Contents

Overview

Lesson Plans

Teacher's Resources

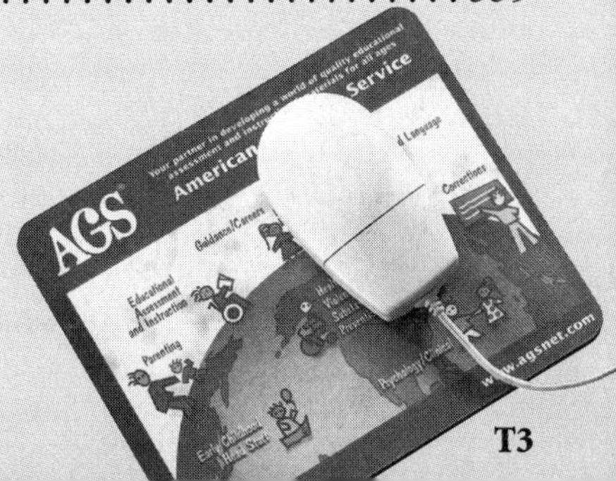

Basic English Grammar

BASIC ENGLISH GRAMMAR is designed to meet the needs of secondary students and adults who read well below grade level. Prior to the book being written, a series of interviews was conducted with teachers, supervisors, and students across the United States. A need was identified for a textbook that would present grammatical rules and concepts one at a time and provide sufficient opportunities for appropriate practice.

All aspects of the text are carefully controlled, including instruction, examples, directions, and exercises. The sentence structure and vocabulary are clear and straightforward, which helps reluctant readers access the material more easily than they could with traditional grammar textbooks. In addition, the high-interest content of the activities appeals to older students.

Particular attention is given to subdividing the instruction so that only a single rule or a single concept is presented at one time, each accompanied by at least one practice exercise. The numerous practice exercises allow frequent review of students' understanding so that teachers can provide appropriate instructional intervention. Lessons are constructed so that succeeding activities incorporate previous instruction. Concepts introduced earlier are reinforced and assimilated in combination with new material.

Grammar and usage are integrated in each lesson to facilitate understanding of rules and their practical application to the patterns of written and spoken English. Students practice and apply each language skill in a variety of ways, taking the student from identification and classification through application and evaluation. These skills are essential if students are to apply grammar and usage to everyday writing.

The ability to communicate in clear, correct language is important in virtually every job and situation. *Basic English Grammar* provides the English grammar and usage skills students need to help them succeed when they make the transition from school to the workplace.

AGS Worktexts

CHECK OUT AGS WORKTEXTS! AGS offers additional language arts materials to help you tailor instruction to meet the diverse needs of your students. Each worktext contains 96 pages of up-to-date information and motivating skill lessons with lots of opportunities for practice and reinforcement. These may be used to accompany a basal program or as the core instructional tool.

AGS Grammar and Composition Skills

AGS Practical English Skills

For more information on AGS Worktexts, call 1-800-328-2560.

AGS English Textbooks

Basic English Composition

Basic English Composition is designed to help secondary students and adults develop practical writing skills. Throughout the text, comprehension is enhanced through the use of simple sentence structure and low-level vocabulary. To add motivational interest, the instruction and activities revolve around a group of high school students experiencing a typical school year.

Prior to development of this text, the author conducted a series of interviews with teachers, curriculum supervisors, and students across the country. As a result, *Basic English Composition* reflects these needs by emphasizing writing sentences, then paragraphs, followed by reports and other projects. All are identified as important skills to be taught.

Reading Level: 3.8 Spache
Interest Level: Grades 6-12, ABE, ESL

Life Skills English

The major goal of *Life Skills English* is to develop language skills that young people and adults need in their everyday lives. The development of this textbook is based on a series of interviews with teachers, supervisors, and students across the country. Topics included in the text are based on these findings.

The primary focus of *Life Skills English* is seeking and evaluating information. The text first emphasizes the skills needed to find information. Students learn how information is organized and how to use reference tools to locate information. The text teaches students how to use and develop skills that they will apply in other subjects and everyday life.

To motivate students, both the sentence structure and the vocabulary are controlled throughout the text, including the directions, examples, and exercises. This allows students to concentrate on content mastery. Chapter openers, examples, and exercises focus on relevant and practical applications. For example, students are taught how to read a food label, read the yellow pages, follow recipe directions, and read the want ads.

Reading Level: 3.7 Spache
Interest Level: Grades 6-12, ABE, ESL

For more information on AGS Textbooks, call 1-800-328-2560.

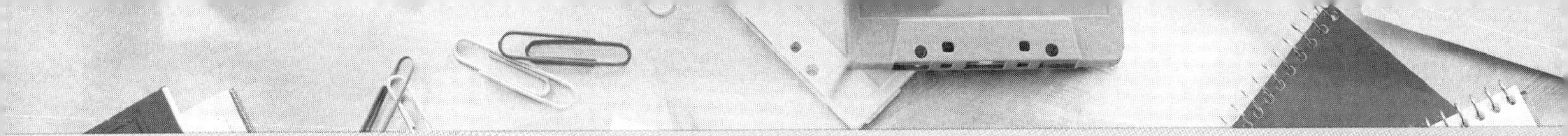

English for the World of Work

English for the World of Work develops communication skills that are essential for deciding upon a career, obtaining a job, keeping a job, and being prepared for promotions. Students prepare a career portfolio that can be used later during their job searches. This textbook is intended for secondary students and adults who are planning to enter the world of work soon after the course.

This text is designed to be practical and relevant. Activities and exercises are patterned after situations in the working world and are designed to develop better reading, writing, speaking, and listening skills. Effort has been made to keep the reading level below the fourth grade. Some concepts are dealt with at a slightly higher level than others. Suggestions are provided in the Teacher's Edition for directing the students' reading to help them achieve full comprehension.

Reading Level: 3.6 Spache
Interest Level: Grades 6-12, ABE, ESL

English to Use

English to Use is designed to meet the communication needs of secondary students and adults who are reading below grade level or learning English as a second language. Grammar and usage are integrated into each lesson to facilitate an understanding of rules and their practical application to the patterns of written and spoken English. Students practice and apply each language skill in a variety of settings, from identification and classification to evaluative thinking and application.

The instructions, examples, directions, and exercises are presented in a systematic, discrete manner. Particular attention is given to organizing the instruction so that only a single rule or a single concept is presented at one time. Numerous exercises allow the teacher frequent review of students' understanding. Lessons build upon each other throughout the book.

Sign language is featured throughout *English to Use.* By including these illustrations, we hope to connect the spoken word and signing. It is not the intention of this text to provide a total program in signing—only an awareness.

Reading Level: 3.3 Spache
Interest Level: Grades 6-12, ABE, ESL

Student Text Highlights

The student texts are designed to motivate even the most reluctant learner. Concise, targeted lessons allow students to focus on a single concept and experience success. Students will demonstrate increased comprehension with the text written at 3.0 reading level.

- Each chapter opens with an engaging photo that relates the chapter content to real-life application.
- Background information is provided to set the stage for learning and to make the material relevant for students.
- *Goals for Learning* are identified at the beginning of each chapter to help students understand the main ideas they will be learning.

Chapter 10

Sentences: Subjects and Predicates

When you tell a story, you express complete ideas so that listeners can picture the characters in the story and what happens to them. You break the ideas in your story into units of meaning called sentences.

A sentence is a group of words that expresses a complete thought. Every sentence has two parts. They are the subject and the predicate. The subject of a sentence is who or what the sentence is about. The predicate tells what the subject did or what happened to the subject.

Each lesson in Chapter 10 focuses on what a sentence is and how subjects and predicates work in different types of sentences.

Goals for Learning

- To identify a sentence
- To identify the subject and predicate in simple sentences
- To identify the noun or pronoun in subjects
- To identify the verb or verb phrase in predicates
- To identify different types of sentences
- To identify the subject and predicate in compound sentences

199

Lesson 1

What Is a Sentence?

Sentence
A group of words that expresses a complete thought. A sentence always begins with a capital letter and ends with a period, question mark, or exclamation point.

A **sentence** is a group of words that expresses a complete thought. Every sentence begins with a capital letter and ends with a punctuation mark.

EXAMPLES
Mrs. Johnson sold her old car to Rafael.
What did he pay for the car?
Stop right there!

A group of words may look like a sentence, but if it does not express a complete thought, it is not a sentence.

EXAMPLES

Not a sentence:	The car with the red top. (This group of words does not express a complete thought. What about the car with the red top?)
Sentence:	The car with the red top belongs to her friend.
Not a sentence:	Looked all over town for a car. (This group of words does not express a complete thought. Who looked all over town for a car?)
Sentence:	Rafael looked all over town for a car.
Not a sentence:	Before Rafael bought the car. (This group of words does not express a complete thought. What happened before Rafael bought the car?)
Sentence:	Before Rafael bought the car, his father looked it over.

200 Chapter 10 Sentences: Subjects and Predicates

Activity A For each item below, write *S* on your paper if the group of words is a sentence. Write *NS* if the group of words is not a sentence.

1) Stop for the red light!
2) Before the storm was over.
3) In the house across the street.
4) That's nice.
5) Where does she live?
6) Searching for a new job.
7) She laughed.
8) Jack went fishing.
9) Because of the cold weather.
10) Each day before the sun rises.
11) You can leave now.
12) Everyone at the party had a good time.
13) Chen moved to town in March.
14) On the day of the party for Mrs. Williams.
15) Afterwards, they all helped clean up.

Activity B Copy each group of words from Activity A that you marked *NS* onto your paper. Add words to each item to make it a complete sentence. Check that each sentence begins with a capital letter and ends with a period, question mark, or exclamation point.

Sentences: Subjects and Predicates Chapter 10 201

- Each lesson is clearly labeled to help students focus on main ideas.
- Graphs and charts present concepts visually to reinforce and clarify instruction.
- Glossary words are boldfaced the first time they appear in the text. In addition to being defined in context, they are also defined in a special vocabulary box in the side column. This provides a quick review for students.

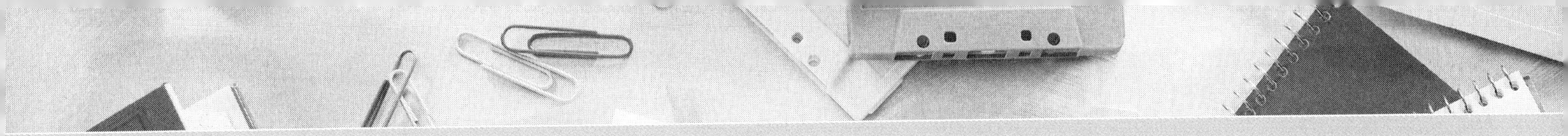

■ Examples are clearly labeled and illustrate new skills.

■ Frequent exercises offer teachers opportunities to check students' understanding.

■ Exercises focus on practical, real-life applications.

Lesson 3 Participles and Participial Phrases

Participle
A verb form that is used like an adjective.

A **participle** is another verb form. Participles are used in sentences as adjectives. A participle may be in the present tense or in the past tense.

EXAMPLES

Present tense:	The **running** deer was beautiful.
Past tense:	The house looks larger **painted** white.
	He picked up the pieces of **broken** glass.

Activity A Write the participles in each of these sentences on your paper.

1) The setting sun turned the sky red and purple.
2) Those cooked carrots are mushy.
3) The girl reading that book is my sister.
4) Will you help that lost child find her mother?
5) My rumbling stomach told me I was hungry.
6) The cracked glass hid the details of the painting.
7) Steamed vegetables are good for you.
8) The hikers climbed over the fallen log.
9) What a frightening movie that was!
10) Fish jumped in the bubbling brook.

Do not confuse a participle used as an adjective with a participle that is part of a verb phrase.

EXAMPLES

Participle:	The deer **running** through the woods was beautiful.
Verb phrase:	The deer **was running** through the woods.

310 Chapter 14 The Verbal and the Verbal Phrase

Activity B Write on your paper whether the words in bold in these sentences are participles used as *adjectives* or are part of the *verb phrase.*

Example The **barking** dog scared the child. **adjective**
The dog was **barking** at the child. **verb phrase**

1) Your cold is probably **catching.**
2) We will be **catching** the train.
3) The newly **painted** room was bright and cheery.
4) They have **painted** the room a bright yellow.
5) The wind was **howling** all night.
6) The **howling** wind kept us awake all night.

Participial phrase
A phrase that includes the participle and all the words and phrases related to it.

A **participial phrase** is a participle plus any words that complement or describe it. A participle comes right before or right after the noun or pronoun it describes.

EXAMPLE **Running at full speed,** she caught the bus.
(The participial phrase *Running at full speed* describes *she.*)

Activity C Write these sentences on your paper. Underline each participial phrase. Draw a line to the noun or pronoun it describes.

1) Howling wildly, the wind frightened the child.
2) Dana lent her book to the girl sitting in the first row.
3) Expecting the worst, Julian was pleasantly surprised with his grade.
4) The keys locked inside the car were of little use.
5) Concentrating on her notes, Mrs. Agnello did not hear Julian enter the room.
6) Mr. Agnello has mailed the letter addressed to the bank.
7) Recommended by his teachers, Chan was given the award.
8) Dinner cooked by her sons was a special treat for Mrs. Agnello.

The Verbal and the Verbal Phrase Chapter 14 311

■ *Chapter Reviews* appear in the student text and allow students and teachers to check skill mastery.

■ The *Chapter Reviews* directly reflect the chapter *Goals for Learning.*

Chapter 11 Review

Part A Decide whether the verb in bold in these sentences is transitive or intransitive. Write *transitive* or *intransitive* on your paper.

1) One day Mr. Ellis **bought** a computer.
2) He **called** it an investment in their future.
3) The younger children **clapped** with glee.
4) He **plugged** a modem into the computer.
5) The puppy just **stared** at the computer screen.
6) **Can** we **use** it?
7) They **could play** video games.
8) Mrs. Ellis **keeps** a daily journal on the computer.
9) They **used** it for their tax records.
10) That computer **ran** all evening!

Part B Write the words in bold in these sentences on your paper. Beside each word, write whether it is the *subject, verb or verb phrase, direct object, indirect object, object of the preposition,* or *objective complement.*

1) We gave **Jiro** a CD for his **birthday.**
2) The **Rolling Stones recorded** that song.
3) **Some** of us are going to the movies.
4) **Have** you **read** that book?
5) **Hand me** that hammer, please.
6) The **band** raised **money** for the trip.
7) We elected **John president.**
8) Where are **you** and **Jackie** sitting?
9) **Which** of **these** do you want?
10) Will **you** give **us** a ride?

252 Chapter 11 Sentence Patterns

Part C Write two sentences on your paper for each of the four patterns. Follow the examples.

Pattern 1:	Subject + Verb The frightened girl screamed.
Pattern 2:	Subject + Verb + Direct Object Mary read her report to the class.
Pattern 3:	Subject + Verb + Indirect and Direct Objects Paco gave the puppy a bath.
Pattern 4:	Subject + Verb + Direct Object + Objective Complement Connie considers raw vegetables a healthy snack.

Part D Diagram the following sentences.

1) Which of these do you want?
2) Kevin writes music and lyrics.
3) Kevin's music has variety, and his lyrics have real meaning.
4) He named it "Melody" and sang it for Julia.
5) We can make our own birthday cards on the computer.
6) He has been at the computer for hours.
7) They named their computer "The Whiz."
8) Try it yourself.
9) I can add fast, but the computer adds faster.
10) Walter and Andrea asked their mom a question about the computer.

Test Taking Tip Before you answer any questions on a test, skim through the whole test to find out what is expected of you.

Sentence Patterns Chapter 11 253

■ Each *Chapter Review* includes a *Test Taking Tip.* These tips will help students prepare to take tests of all types.

Test Taking Tip Before you answer any questions on a test, skim through the whole test to find out what is expected of you.

Teacher's Edition Highlights

The comprehensive, wraparound teacher's edition provides instructional strategies at point of use. Everything from preparation guidelines to teaching tips and strategies are included in an easy-to-use format. Activities are featured at point of use for teacher convenience.

- Quick overview of the lesson saves time.
- Lesson objectives are listed for easy reference.
- Page references are provided for convenience.
- Instructional resources are clearly identified.
- An introductory discussion or activity opens each lesson by activating prior knowledge and setting the stage for learning.
- Suggestions are given for introducing and teaching the learning activities.
- Teachers are given suggestions for reviewing skills needed for success in the lesson.
- The *Global Connection* features will help students connect the lesson to the world community at large. Multicultural issues are emphasized as students view the world as a community.

Lesson at a Glance

Chapter 10 Lesson 4

Overview This lesson presents different types of sentences and explains their purposes.

Objectives

- To identify types of sentences.
- To write different types of sentences.

Student Pages 212–214

Teacher's Resource Library

Activity 30

Workbook Activities 43–44

Reading Vocabulary

request (6)

Teaching Suggestions

Introducing the Lesson Discuss each type of sentence presented in the text. Ask students for additional examples of each type and write them on the board. Have students tell you what end punctuation to use for each sentence.

Reviewing Skills Review the definition of a sentence.

Teacher Alert

You may wish to point out that sentences that show strong feeling are often called *exclamatory sentences* or *exclamations*.

Lesson 4 Kinds of Sentences

Every sentence has a purpose. A sentence can make a statement. A sentence can ask a question. A sentence can give a command or make a request. A sentence can show strong feelings.

Examples

Statement:	They went to the concert.
Question:	Are you going to the concert?
Command:	Go to the concert with them.
Strong feeling:	What a great concert that was!

A sentence that makes a statement usually begins with the subject. A statement ends with a period.

Example The **concert** began at eight o'clock.

A sentence that asks a question begins with either a helping verb or an interrogative pronoun or adverb. A question ends with a question mark.

Examples

Are you ready yet?	**Who** is she?
Did you like the music?	**Where** are my shoes?

A sentence that makes a command or request begins with a verb. The subject is understood to be the person spoken to. A command usually ends with a period. A strong command may end with an exclamation mark.

Examples

(You) Please **give** me two tickets.

(You) **Take** your medicine.

(You) **Do** it now!

212 *Chapter 10 Sentences: Subjects and Predicates*

Global Connection

In Spanish, an inverted question mark comes at the beginning of a question and an inverted exclamation point comes at the beginning of an exclamation. Regular end punctuation appears at the end of each type of sentence. To illustrate, write these sentences on the board or invite a student fluent in Spanish to do so: ¿Qué podemos hacer? (*What can we do?*) / ¡Claro que podrás! (*Of course you can!*)

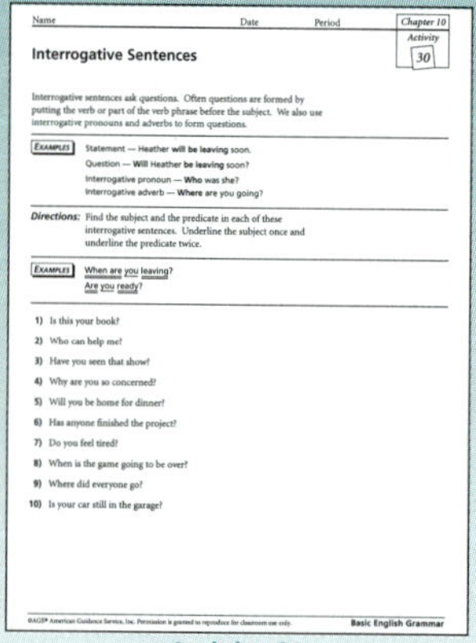
Name Date Period Chapter 10 Activity 30

Interrogative Sentences

Interrogative sentences ask questions. Often questions are formed by putting the verb or part of the verb phrase before the subject. We also use interrogative pronouns and adverbs to form questions.

Examples: Statement — Heather **will be leaving** soon. Question — **Will** Heather **be leaving** soon? Interrogative pronoun — **Who was she?** Interrogative adverb — **Where are** you going?

Directions: Find the subject and the predicate in each of these interrogative sentences. Underline the subject once and underline the predicate twice.

Examples: When are you leaving? Are you ready?

1) Is this your book?
2) Who can help me?
3) Have you seen that show?
4) Why are you so concerned?
5) Will you be home for dinner?
6) Has anyone finished the project?
7) Do you feel tired?
8) When is the game going to be over?
9) Where did everyone go?
10) Is your car still in the garage?

©AGS® American Guidance Service, Inc. Permission is granted to reproduce for classroom use only. Basic English Grammar

Activity 30

212 *Chapter 10 Sentences: Subjects and Predicates*

A sentence that shows strong feeling or excitement ends with an exclamation mark.

EXAMPLES I can't believe our team won!
What a great game that was!

Activity A Decide the purpose of each of these sentences. Write *S* on your paper if the sentence makes a statement. Write *Q* if the sentence asks a question. Write *C* if the sentence makes a command or request. Write *SF* if the sentence shows strong feelings or excitement.

1) Are you hungry?

2) I am starved!

3) We can eat at this restaurant.

4) Melissa and her parents had lunch here last week.

5) Do you know what you want?

6) Please order something for both of us.

7) I'm having the soup and sandwich special.

8) That sounds good to me.

9) What kind of sandwich would you like?

10) Decide quickly!

11) I'll have the tuna on dark rye.

12) Here is your check.

13) Has someone made a mistake?

14) This can't be the right amount!

15) Next time, we'll eat at my house.

Sentences: Subjects and Predicates *Chapter 10* **213**

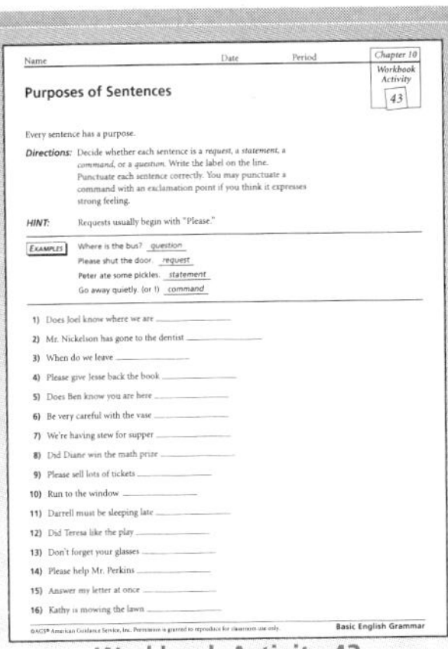
Name Date Period — Chapter 10 Workbook Activity 43

Purposes of Sentences

Every sentence has a purpose.

Directions: Decide whether each sentence is a *request*, a *statement*, a *command*, or a *question*. Write the label on the line. Punctuate each sentence correctly. You may punctuate a command with an exclamation point if you think it expresses strong feeling.

HINT: Requests usually begin with "Please."

EXAMPLES Where is the bus? question
Please shut the door. request
Peter ate some pickles. statement
Go away quietly. (or !) command

1) Does Joel know where we are _____
2) Mr. Nickelson has gone to the dentist _____
3) When do we leave _____
4) Please give Jesse back the book _____
5) Does Ben know you are here _____
6) Be very careful with the vase _____
7) We're having stew for supper _____
8) Did Diane win the math prize _____
9) Please sell lots of tickets _____
10) Run to the window _____
11) Darrell must be sleeping late _____
12) Did Teresa like the play _____
13) Don't forget your glasses _____
14) Please help Mr. Perkins _____
15) Answer my letter at once _____
16) Kathy is mowing the lawn _____

 Basic English Grammar

Workbook Activity 43

Reading Vocabulary

restaurant (5) tuna (6)
rye (6)

■ Presenting Activity A

Before having students do Activity A on their own, invite volunteers to read each item aloud. Encourage readers to think about the words and use good oral expression as they read. Listeners should pay attention to the meaning of the words and the expression. This should help them determine the purpose of each sentence.

Activity A Answers

1) Q 2) SF 3) S 4) S 5) Q 6) C 7) S 8) S 9) Q 10) C/SF 11) S 12) S 13) Q 14) SF 15) S

APPLICATION

In the Community
Students who feel they have a good understanding of sentence structure and sentence purpose may enjoy sharing their knowledge with younger people in the community. Encourage students to volunteer at youth centers, daycare centers, and other organizations where they might work with school-age children to help them write short stories, letters, and simple articles. Students can also help review younger children's school writing assignments to check for complete sentences and correct capitalization and end punctuation.

Sentences: Subjects and Predicates *Chapter 10* **213**

■ Reading vocabulary classified above fourth grade level is listed on each page. Grade levels are shown in parentheses. Nongraded words show no number.

■ Answers are provided in the teacher's edition for all exercises in the student text.

■ Special helps will assist ESL students with lesson content.

■ *Application:* There are three kinds of applications—At Home, Career Connection, and In the Community. Relating lessons to the world outside of the classroom helps motivate students and makes learning relevant.

■ Community participation and environmental awareness are encouraged with activities in the teacher's edition as extensions of various lessons.

■ Activity and Workbook Activity pages are shown at point of use. The Teacher's Resource Library contains all reproducible activities. Emphasis is placed on including learning activities for reaching a diverse range of learning styles. A variety of teaching and student activities are included at the point of use.

Teacher's Resource Library

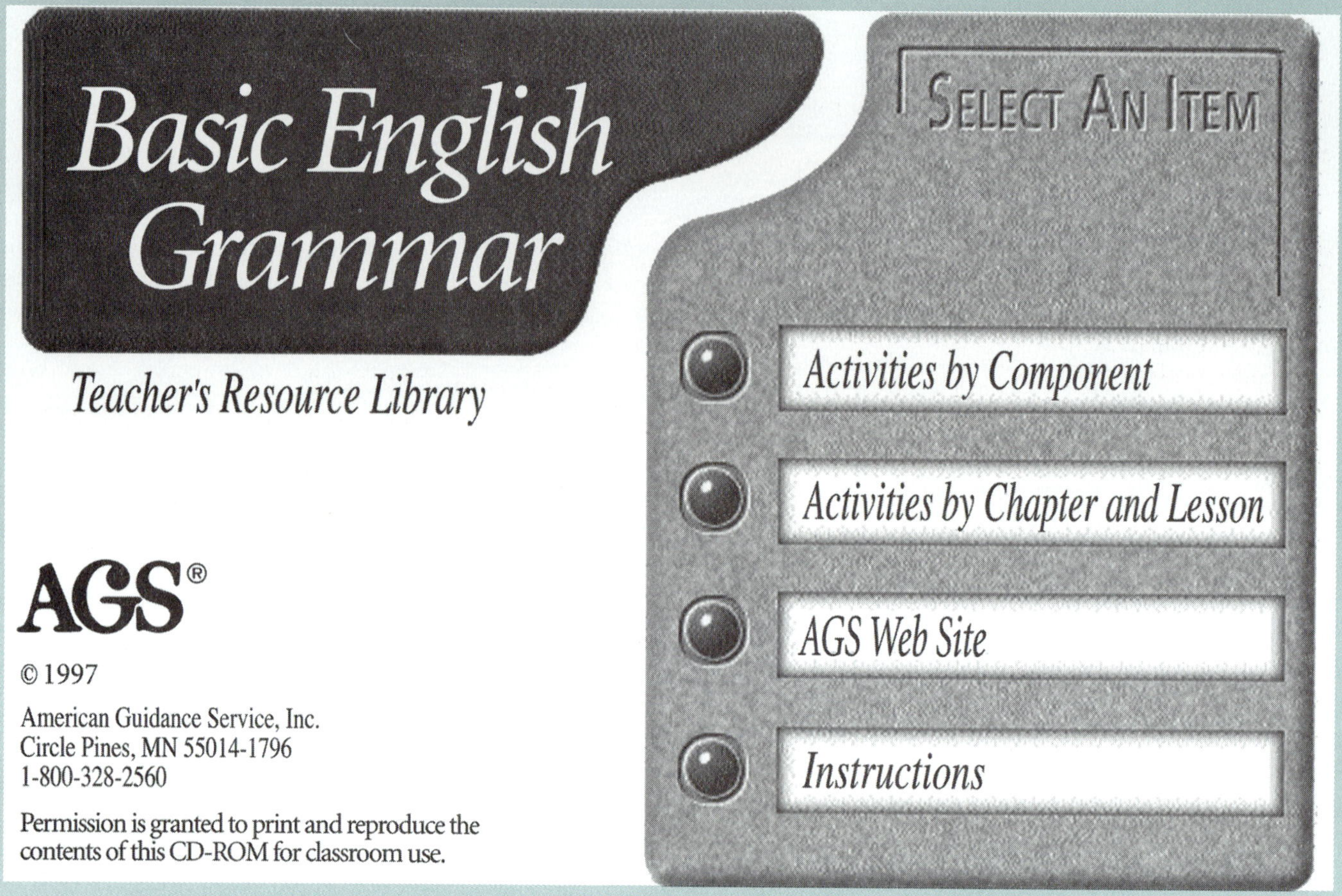

TRL All of the activities you'll need to reinforce and extend the text are conveniently located on the AGS Teacher's Resource Library (TRL) CD-ROM. The reproducible activities featured in the Teacher's Edition are ready to review, select, and print. Additionally, you can preview other materials by directly linking to the AGS web site.

Activities
Lesson activities reinforce the concepts taught in the lesson. Activities are designed to help students see the relevance of the skills being taught. A variety of activities provide additional motivation.

Workbook Activities
Workbook activities may be reproduced as added reinforcement and practice for lessons. These activities are also available in a workbook format.

Community Connections
Relevant activities help students apply their new knowledge in the community and reinforce concepts covered in class.

Diagramming Activities
Additional diagramming exercises are included to give students extra practice.

Self-Study Guide
Assignment guides with student/teacher contracts are provided for the entire text. These are suggested lesson plans from the text and workbook. This provides teachers with the flexibility of individualized instruction or independent study.

Mastery Tests
Chapter, midterm, and final mastery tests are conveniently referenced as assessment options.

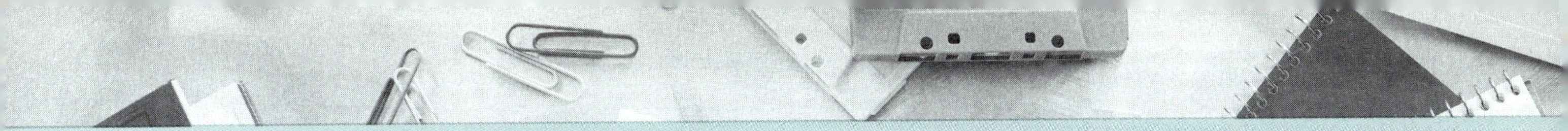

Self-Study Guide
Assignment guides with student/teacher contracts are provided for the entire text. These guides outline suggested lessons from the text and workbook. This provides teachers with the flexibility of individualized instruction or independent study.

SELF-STUDY GUIDE

Name ______________

CHAPTER 2: The Pronoun

Goal 2.1 To identify pronouns and personal pronouns in a sentence

Date	Assignment	Score
______	1: Read pages 27-30. Complete Activity A on page 30	______
______	2: Complete Workbook Activities 6-7.	______
______	3: Complete Activities B-C on page 31 and Activity D on page 32.	______
______	4: Complete Workbook Activity 8.	______
______	5: Read page 33. Complete Activity E on page 33.	______
______	6: Complete the Lesson 1 Review, Parts A-B on page 34.	______

Comments:

Goal 2.2 To identify the correct usage of relative pronouns

Date	Assignment	Score
______	7: Read page 35. Complete Activity A on page 35.	
______	8: Complete Activities B-C on page 36.	
______	9: Complete Activities D-F on page 37.	
______	10: Complete the Lesson 2 Review, Parts A-B on page 38.	

Comments:

Goal 2.3 To identify the correct usage of interrogative pronouns

...tivity A on page 39.
...tivity B on page 40 and Activity C on page 41.
...iew, Parts A-B on page 42.

...o reproduce for classroom use only. Basic Engli...

Tests
Teachers are provided with a complete testing program. Tests are provided for each chapter, forms A and B. A midterm and final test provide additional assessment options.

Name ______ Date ______ Period ______ Chapter 6 Mastery Test B page 1

Chapter 6 Mastery Test B

Part A Write the word that each bold adverb answers questions about.

1) Jessye Norman sings **beautifully**. ______
2) The plumber turned the wrench **slowly**. ______
3) The stars glistened **brilliantly** in the dark sky. ______
4) We retreated **hastily** from the bear's path. ______
5) Using a computer is **extremely** easy. ______
6) Toby walks **too** slowly for the dog. ______
7) Bea was **totally** exhausted by day's end. ______
8) We went on a five-mile hike **yesterday**. ______
9) Sondra ran **downstairs**. ______
10) **Later** we will talk about the book. ______
11) I exercise **early**. ______
12) Wayne Gretzky plays hockey **very** well. ______
13) We can **almost** see through the fog. ______
14) Everyone here works **fairly** well together. ______
15) The lakes were frozen **solid**. ______

Part B Write the correct form of the adverb in parentheses to complete each sentence.

1) Manuel writes quite ______. (clearly)
2) They greeted all of the guests very ______. (warmly)
3) This shoe fits ______ than that one. (comfortably)
...ers swam ______? (fast)
...akes to strangers ______. (easily)

...is granted to reproduce for classroom use only. Basic English Grammar

Name ______ Date ______ Period ______ Chapter 4 Activity 11

Verb Tense

A verb can have six regular tenses. They are: present, past, future, present perfect, past perfect, and future perfect. Use the helping verb *have* to form the perfect tense. Use the helping verb *will* to form the future tense.

EXAMPLE cook
Present: She cooks. (or) They cook.
Past: She cooked.
Future: She will cook.
Present perfect: She has cooked. (or) They have cooked.
Past perfect: She had cooked.
Future perfect: She will have cooked.

Directions: In the following sentences, name the tense of the verb in bold print.

EXAMPLE Alex **cooked** dinner for the family past

1) Sally **wrote** a letter to Aunt Marie. ______
2) The loud thunderstorm **terrified** the cat. ______
3) Rita **has run** the mile in five minutes. ______
4) **Give** me your name, please. ______
5) Some people **eat** whatever they want. ______
6) Nikki **has gone** to Canada on a fishing trip. ______
7) The quarterback **had thrown** a long pass. ______
8) Yesterday we **returned** home from Nashville. ______
9) Maya **writes** very well. ______
10) We **will have completed** this assignment on time. ______
11) Everyone **will have helped** with dinner. ______
12) Jamal **has written** his term paper. ______
13) The trial **lasted** for three weeks. ______
14) Paul **will travel** to China next summer. ______
15) Last year Karen **visited** Montana. ______

Name ______ Date ______ Period ______ Chapter 11 Workbook Activity 47

Transitive and Intransitive Verbs

A transitive verb has a direct object. An intransitive verb does not.

EXAMPLES Transitive: Janet bought a new coat. (direct object)
Intransitive: She **went** to the store.

Directions: The verb in each sentence is in bold print. Decide whether it is transitive or intransitive. Underline the objects of the transitive verbs. Circle the type of verb that is in the sentence.

1) The book **fell** off the shelf. Transitive Intransitive
2) The audience **cheered** loudly. Transitive Intransitive
3) **Stop** that noise! Transitive Intransitive
4) You **should see** that movie! Transitive Intransitive
5) The band **will win** the contest. Transitive Intransitive
6) Darleen **laughed** at Tiny. Transitive Intransitive
7) **Write** your aunt a letter. Transitive Intransitive
8) They **named** the puppy Spot. Transitive Intransitive
9) **Give** Herman this message. Transitive Intransitive
10) The hard work **made** us tired. Transitive Intransitive
11) **Have** you **read** that book? Transitive Intransitive
12) **Spend** your money wisely. Transitive Intransitive
13) My aunt **left** in July. Transitive Intransitive
14) They **will stay** after school to work. Transitive Intransitive
15) Anne **listened** carefully. Transitive Intransitive
16) **Have** you **seen** my book? Transitive Intransitive
17) The book **is** over there. Transitive Intransitive
18) Bob **rode** the bus today. Transitive Intransitive
19) Tomorrow Bob **is walking** to school. Transitive Intransitive
20) Hey, **give** me a ride! Transitive Intransitive

 Basic English Grammar

Activities
These activities will help you reinforce the concepts taught in the lesson.

Activities are designed to help students see the relevance of the skills being taught. A variety of activities will provide additional motivation.

Workbook Activities
Students are encouraged to practice skills and apply knowledge in relevant and real-life situations.

Skills Chart

Basic English Grammar

Identification Skills	Chapter													
Parts of Speech														
Nouns	1	2	3	4	5	6	7	8		10	11	12	13	14
Pronouns		2	3	4	5	6	7	8		10	11	12	13	14
Adjectives			3			6	7			10	11	12	13	14
Verbs				4	5	6	7	8		10	11	12	13	14
Adverbs						6	7	8		10	11	12	13	14
Prepositions							7	8		10	11	12	13	14
Conjunctions								8		10	11	12	13	
Interjections									9					
Phrases														
Noun													13	
Adjective											11		13	
Verb				4						10	11			14
Adverb							7				11		13	14
Prepositional							7			10	11	12	13	14
Infinitive														14
Gerund														14
Participial														14
Clauses														
Noun													13	
Adjective													13	
Adverb													13	
Dependent								8					13	
Independent								8		10			13	
Sentences														
Subject				4	5					10	11	12	13	14
Predicate										10	11	12		14
Complete												12		
Incomplete/Fragments												12		
Compound										10	11	12		
Complex													13	
Compound-complex													13	
Patterns											11	12		
Purposes										10			13	

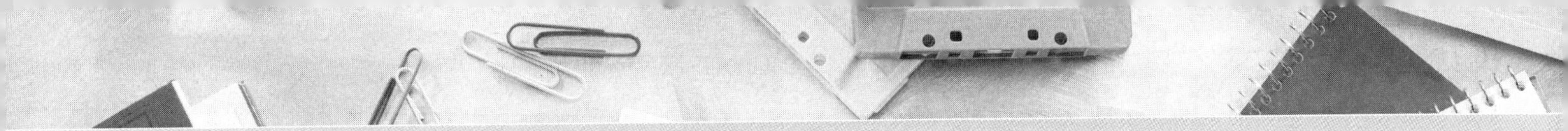

	Chapter													
	1	2	3	4	5	6	7	8	9	10	11	12	13	14
Antecedents		2												
Appositives													13	14
Articles			3											
Degrees of Comparison			3			6								
Direct Object											11	12	13	
Genders		2												
Indirect Object											11			
Intransitive Verbs											11	12		
Person		2									11			
Transitive Verbs											11			
Verb Forms														14
Verb Tenses				4	5	6								
Voice				4	5									
Diagramming Skills														
Diagramming											11	12		
Writing Skills														
Sentences	1	2	3	4	5	6	7	8	9	10	11	12	13	14
Punctuation Skills														
Capitalization	1		3						9	10				
Period										10				
Question Mark									9	10				
Exclamation Mark									9	10				
Comma								8	9	10				
Quotation Marks													13	
Semicolon								8						

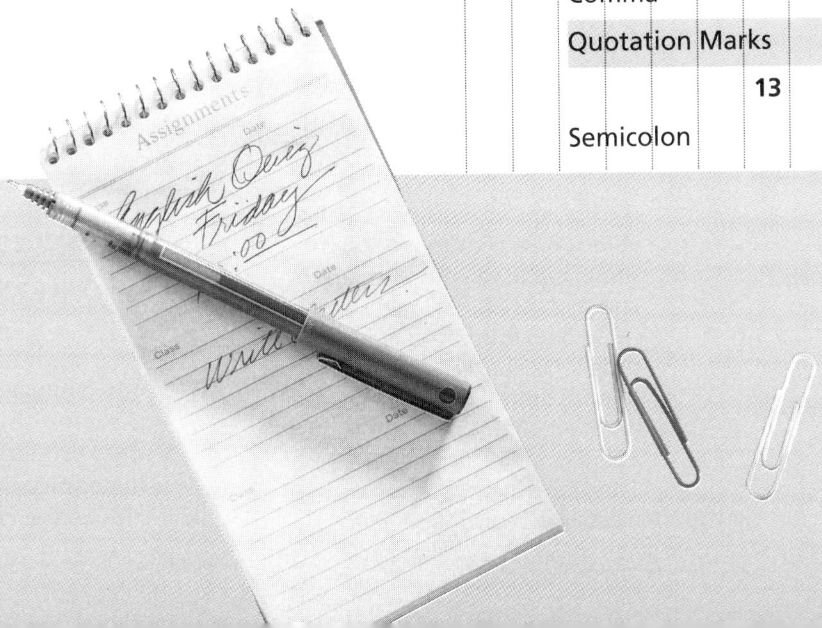

Adapting Activities for Diverse Learning Styles

The learning style activities in the *Basic English Grammar* Teacher's Edition provide activities to help students with special needs understand the lesson. These activities focus on the following learning styles: Visual/Spatial, Auditory/Verbal, Body/Kinesthetic, Logical/Mathematical, Interpersonal/Group Learning, LEP/ESL. These styles reflect Howard Gardner's theory of multiple intelligences. The writing activities suggested in this student text are appropriate for students who fit Gardner's description of Verbal/Linguistic Intelligence.

The activities are designed to help teachers capitalize on students' individual strengths and dominant learning styles. The activities reinforce the lesson by teaching or expanding upon the content in a different way.

Following are examples of activities featured in the *Basic English Grammar* Teacher's Edition:

Interpersonal/Group learners benefit from working with at least one other person on activities that involve a process and an end product.

Learning Styles

Interpersonal/ Group Learning
Divide the class into groups of four. Invite each group to create a short story using the four demonstrative pronouns—*this, that, these,* and *those.* Then ask each group to read its story to the class. As each group reads, have the rest of the students raise their hands when they hear one of the demonstrative pronouns.

Body/Kinesthetic learners benefit from activities that include physical movement or tactile experiences.

Learning Styles

Body/Kinesthetic
Invite partners to use their bodies to present a "snapshot" of something. (For example, two students might pose silently in front of the room as if they are riding a bike together. Or they might stand silently as if one is singing into a microphone and the other is playing a guitar.) After each set of partners "poses," have the class use the five interrogative pronouns—*who, whom, which, what,* and *whose*—to ask the partners questions about their snapshot. Challenge the class to use all five pronouns to ask questions of each set of partners.

Logical/Mathematical students learn by using logical/mathematical thinking in relation to the lesson content.

Learning Styles

Logical/Mathematical
Challenge the class to create a set of icons for the six relative pronouns *who, whom, whose, which, what,* and *that.* First, invite a student to print them in alphabetical order on the chalkboard. Then divide the class into six groups. Assign a relative pronoun to each group. Encourage each group to create an icon or symbol that will help the class remember the pronoun. Afterward, have a volunteer make a poster of the six icons and post it in the classroom for ready reference.

Auditory/Verbal students benefit from having someone read the text aloud or listening to the text on audiocassette. Musical activities appropriate for the lesson may help auditory learners.

Learning Styles

Auditory/Verbal
Divide the class into two equal teams. Have them stand facing one another. Invite the first student in Team 1 to look at the objects around the classroom and to call out the name of a common noun. Invite the first student in Team 2 to name a proper noun for that common noun. Continue until all the students on both teams have named a common or a proper noun. Then have the two teams trade places and repeat the activity.

Visual/Spatial students benefit from seeing illustrations or demonstrations beyond what is in the text.

Learning Styles

Visual/Spatial
Divide the class into pairs. Give each pair a colorful magazine picture. On the chalkboard, print the following categories: 1) sentence with a singular noun; 2) sentence with a plural noun; 3) sentence with a singular possessive; 4) sentence with a plural possessive. Encourage the partners to use their magazine picture to create a sentence for each of the four categories. Afterward, ask each set of partners to read one sentence aloud. Have the class name the sentence category. Note: Keep the magazine pictures for use with the Learning Styles activity on page 47.

LEP/ESL students benefit from activities that promote English language acquisition and interaction with English-speaking peers.

Learning Styles

LEP/ESL
Invite students for whom English is a second language to explain to the class how they form plurals in their primary language. Encourage them to print examples on the chalkboard.

AGS

Basic English Grammar

by
Bonnie L. Walker

AGS®
American Guidance Service, Inc.
Circle Pines, Minnesota 55014-1796
800-328-2560

About the Author

Bonnie L. Walker taught for sixteen years in secondary schools and college. She holds a Ph.D. in curriculum theory and instructional design from the University of Maryland, an M.Ed. in secondary education, and a B.A. in English. She studied psycholinguistics at the University of Illinois Graduate School and was a curriculum developer at the Model Secondary School for the Deaf at Gallaudet University. She is the author of *Basic English Composition, Life Skills English,* and numerous workbooks, learning packages, and sound filmstrips in written expression, grammar, and usage. She was a member of Project EduTech, which investigated promising technologies to improve the delivery of special education services. Dr. Walker has written several papers on the applications of personal computers, video technology, and cable television in education. She has been the director for research and development projects funded by the U.S. Department of Education, the U.S. Department of Agriculture, and the Administration on Youth, Children, and Families. Since 1986, Dr. Walker has been president of a research and development company specializing in development of training and educational materials for special populations.

Photo Credits: pp. viii, 190—James L. Shaffer; pp. 2, 26, 78, 110, 152, 196—Patterson Graphics; p. 52—Eugen Gebhardt/FPG International; p. 92—John Terence Turner/FPG International; pp. 128, 254—Cathlyn Melloan/Tony Stone Images; pp. 172, 198, 298—Superstock; p. 220—Jim and Mary Whitmer; p. 274—David Young-Wolff/Tony Stone Images

Printed in the United States of America

ISBN 0-7854-2308-7 (Previously ISBN 0-7854-0495-3)
Product Number 91380

A 0 9 8 7 6 5 4 3 2 1

Contents

Basic English Grammar *Contents* iii

iv *Contents Basic English Grammar*

Basic English Grammar *Contents* v

vi Contents Basic English Grammar

Part
1

Why Study Grammar?

No matter what kind of writing you do, you need to know how words work in sentences. In other words, you need good grammar skills. Studying grammar teaches you the rules about putting the right words in the right places in sentences.

Knowing grammar will help you write clearly so that your reader will understand exactly what you are trying to say. Once you know the rules about how to use words, writing will become much easier. You won't have to think about whether your words are right. Just like riding a bicycle or driving a car, your use of words will become automatic.

When you study grammar, you will learn that every word in a sentence has a purpose. The English language has thousands of words. Each of these words can be put into at least one of eight main groups. These groups are called parts of speech.

Parts of Speech

Nouns	Words that name people, places, things, and ideas.
Pronouns	Words that replace nouns.
Adjectives	Words that describe nouns or pronouns.
Verbs	Words that express action or a state of being in a sentence.
Adverbs	Words that tell about the action. They can tell how, when, where, or how much.
Prepositions	Words that show relationships between a noun and the rest of the sentence.
Conjunctions	Words that connect sentences or parts of a sentence.
Interjections	Words that express feelings.

In Part 1 of this book, you will learn about the different parts of speech. You will learn how to recognize the parts of speech in sentences. You will also learn how to use the different parts of speech effectively and correctly in sentences of your own.

Introducing Part 1

Ask students to recall the experience of learning to do something, such as learning to ride a bike. Elicit the different actions of the activity that have to be mastered. Then ask students if they ever think about those rules once they have mastered the activity. Most students will probably respond that they do not. Point out that they still have to do all those things correctly, it's just that now they can focus on the whole experience rather than the individual actions.

Then ask if anyone sees a similarity between writing and an activity they have learned, such as riding a bike. If necessary, explain that before people can use words effectively, they have to master the rules of grammar. Just as to ride a bike they have to know where to place their hands and feet, to write they have to know where to place each word in a sentence. Explain that by the end of Part 1 of this book, they will have mastered these rules. Then they can focus on their ideas and the whole experience of writing.

Chapter 1

Planning Guide

The Noun

	Student Text Lesson			
	Student Pages	Vocabulary	Practice Exercises	Lesson Review
Lesson 1 Finding Nouns in Sentences	4-14	✔	✔	14
Lesson 2 Singular and Plural Nouns	15-19	✔	✔	19
Lesson 3 Nouns That Are Possessive	20-23	✔	✔	23

Chapter Activities

Teacher's Resource Library

Community Connection 1: Nouns in Your Neighborhood

Assessment Options

Student Text

Chapter 1 Review

Teacher's Resource Library

Chapter 1 Mastery Tests A and B

Teaching Strategies							Language Skills			Learning Styles						Teacher's Resource Library		
Reviewing Skills	Teacher Alert	Follow-up Activity	Career Application	Home Application	Global Connection	Community Application	Identification Skills	Writing Skills	Punctuation Skills	Visual/Spatial	Auditory/Verbal	Body/Kinesthetic	Logical/Mathematical	Group Learning	LEP/ESL	Activities	Workbook Activities	Self-Study Guide
4	6	14	9		8		✔	✔	✔		5					1-2	1-2	✔
15	19	19		17			✔	✔	✔						17	3	3	✔
20	23			25			✔	✔	✔	21							4-5	✔

Chapter at a Glance

(Answer Keys for the Teacher's Resource Library begin on page 330 of this Teacher's Edition.)

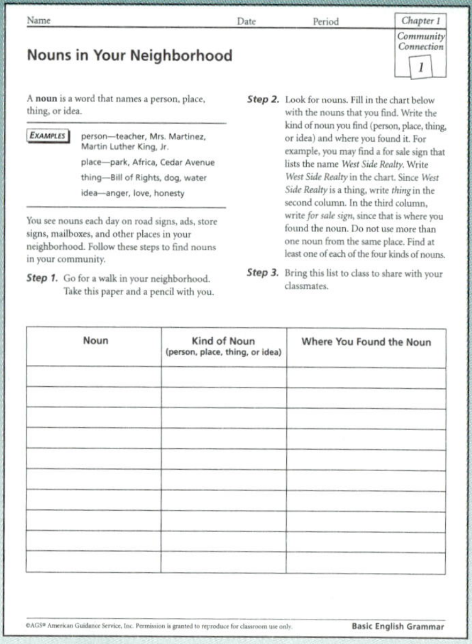

Name Date Period — *Chapter 1* *Community Connection* *1*

Nouns in Your Neighborhood

A **noun** is a word that names a person, place, thing, or idea.

EXAMPLES
- person—teacher, Mrs. Martinez, Martin Luther King, Jr.
- place—park, Africa, Cedar Avenue
- thing—Bill of Rights, dog, water
- idea—anger, love, honesty

You see nouns each day on road signs, ads, store signs, mailboxes, and other places in your neighborhood. Follow these steps to find nouns in your community.

Step 1. Go for a walk in your neighborhood. Take this paper and a pencil with you.

Step 2. Look for nouns. Fill in the chart below with the nouns that you find. Write the kind of noun you find (person, place, thing, or idea) and where you found it. For example, you may find a for sale sign that lists the name *West Side Realty.* Write *West Side Realty* in the chart. Since *West Side Realty* is a thing, write *thing* in the second column. In the third column, write *for sale sign,* since that is where you found the noun. Do not use more than one noun from the same place. Find at least one of each of the four kinds of nouns.

Step 3. Bring this list to class to share with your classmates.

Noun	Kind of Noun (person, place, thing, or idea)	Where You Found the Noun

 Basic English Grammar

Community Connection 1

Chapter 1 The Noun

Stores advertise the names of products to buy. Newspapers include the names of people, places, things, and ideas. No matter where you are, you find that everything and everyone in the world has a name. Things and people need names so that everyone can talk about them more easily.

A noun is a word that names a person, place, thing, or idea.

In Chapter 1, you will learn about nouns. Each lesson is about the different types of nouns used in everyday speech and writing.

Goals for Learning

- To identify nouns in sentences
- To identify proper nouns in sentences
- To write the plural form of nouns
- To write the possessive form of nouns

3

Reading Vocabulary

advertise (6)	include (5)
identify (6)	product (5)

Introducing the Chapter

Use the photograph to introduce the idea that everything and everyone in the world has a name. Ask students to name everything that they see in the picture. Elicit both common nouns and proper nouns and list these on the board as students name them. Then ask students to make up sentences about what is happening in the photograph using words listed on the board. Ask students if they think it would be possible to discuss the picture without using any of these words. Then point out that the words on the board are nouns. Nouns name people and things. Explain that by the end of Chapter 1, students will understand how nouns make it possible to discuss people, places, things, events, and ideas.

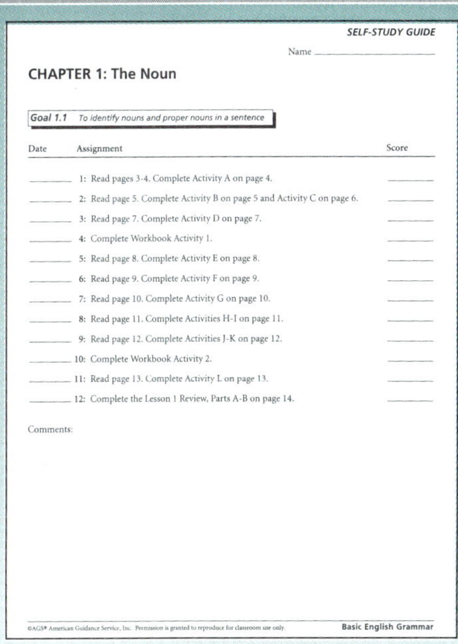
SELF-STUDY GUIDE

Name ____________

CHAPTER 1: The Noun

Goal 1.1 To identify nouns and proper nouns in a sentence

Date	Assignment	Score
______	1: Read pages 3-4. Complete Activity A on page 4.	______
______	2: Read page 5. Complete Activity B on page 5 and Activity C on page 6.	______
______	3: Read page 7. Complete Activity D on page 7.	______
______	4: Complete Workbook Activity 1.	______
______	5: Read page 8. Complete Activity E on page 8.	______
______	6: Read page 9. Complete Activity F on page 9.	______
______	7: Read page 10. Complete Activity G on page 10.	______
______	8: Read page 11. Complete Activities H-I on page 11.	______
______	9: Read page 12. Complete Activities J-K on page 12.	______
______	10: Complete Workbook Activity 2.	______
______	11: Read page 13. Complete Activity L on page 13.	______
______	12: Complete the Lesson 1 Review, Parts A-B on page 14.	______

Comments:

©AGS® American Guidance Service, Inc. Permission is granted to reproduce for classroom use only. Basic English Grammar

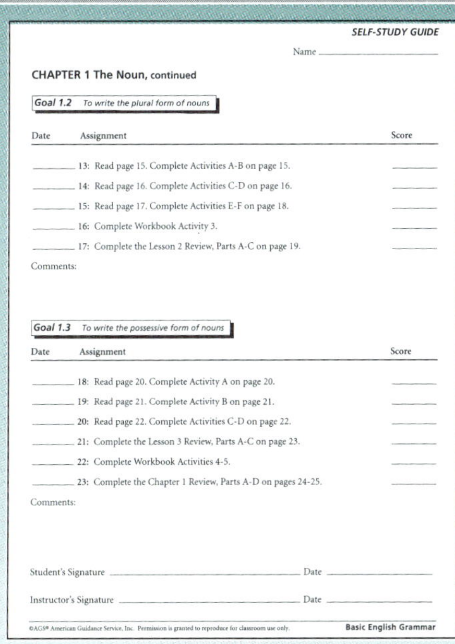
SELF-STUDY GUIDE

Name ____________

CHAPTER 1 The Noun, continued

Goal 1.2 To write the plural form of nouns

Date	Assignment	Score
______	13: Read page 15. Complete Activities A-B on page 15.	______
______	14: Read page 16. Complete Activities C-D on page 16.	______
______	15: Read page 17. Complete Activities E-F on page 18.	______
______	16: Complete Workbook Activity 3.	______
______	17: Complete the Lesson 2 Review, Parts A-C on page 19.	______

Comments:

Goal 1.3 To write the possessive form of nouns

Date	Assignment	Score
______	18: Read page 20. Complete Activity A on page 20.	______
______	19: Read page 21. Complete Activity B on page 21.	______
______	20: Read page 22. Complete Activities C-D on page 22.	______
______	21: Complete the Lesson 3 Review, Parts A-C on page 23.	______
______	22: Complete Workbook Activities 4-5.	______
______	23: Complete the Chapter 1 Review, Parts A-D on pages 24-25.	______

Comments:

Student's Signature ____________ Date ____________

Instructor's Signature ____________ Date ____________

©AGS® American Guidance Service, Inc. Permission is granted to reproduce for classroom use only. Basic English Grammar

Chapter 1 Self-Study Guide

Lesson at a Glance

Chapter 1 Lesson 1

Overview This lesson introduces nouns, including common and proper nouns, collective nouns, compound nouns, and concrete and abstract nouns.

Objectives

- To identify nouns in sentences.
- To distinguish between common and proper nouns.
- To capitalize proper nouns.
- To distinguish between concrete and abstract nouns.

Student Pages 4–14

Teacher's Resource Library

Activities 1–2

Workbook Activities 1–2

Reading Vocabulary

agent (5)
capitalize (9)
concert (5)
decision (5)
insurance (7)
liter
noun
parentheses
policy (7)
quality (5)
require (6)

Teaching Suggestions

Introducing the Lesson

Point to people, places, and things in the classroom and ask students to name what you point to. Explain that each of these words is a noun. Then explain that names for ideas are also nouns. Help students arrive at a definition for the word *ideas.* Use nouns from their definition to write heads on the board, such as *Thoughts* and *Emotions.* Ask students to suggest nouns that could fit in each category. Write students suggestions on the board.

Reviewing Skills

Remind students that every word in a sentence has a purpose. Then review the names of the different parts of speech and their purposes.

Lesson 1 Finding Nouns in Sentences

Noun
Names a person, place, thing, or idea.

A **noun** is a word that names a person, place, thing, or idea.

EXAMPLES

Person:	The insurance **agent** sold Alex a policy.
Place:	Most **states** require car owners to have insurance.
Thing:	Alex saved his **money** and bought a **car**.
	The **door** was squeaky, but Alex fixed it.
Idea:	Alex had to make a **decision**.
	It took **time** to decide.

Activity A Write ten nouns on your paper to go with each group of nouns listed below. Two examples are given in parentheses.

1) time (day, second)
2) places (garage, city)
3) things (book, coat)
4) amounts (size, liter)
5) events (concert, party)
6) persons (student, man)
7) actions (race, trip)
8) qualities (honesty, trust)

Common noun
Names a general type of person, place, thing, or idea.

Proper noun
Names a particular person, place, thing, or idea.

A **common noun** is the name of a general type of person, place, thing, or idea.

A **proper noun** is the name of a particular person, place, thing, or idea.

A common noun is capitalized only if it is the first word of a sentence or part of a title. A proper noun is always capitalized.

Presenting Activity A

Help students identify all the other nouns in the example sentences and whether the noun names a person, place, thing, or idea.

Activity A Answers

Answers will vary.

EXAMPLES

Common Nouns	Proper Nouns
president	George Washington
athlete	Roberto Clemente
team	Chicago Bulls
book	*Robinson Crusoe*
director	Steven Spielberg
place	Alaska
day	Tuesday
document	the Constitution
movie	*Jurassic Park*

Activity B Write these nouns on your paper. Write a proper noun beside each common noun. Write a common noun beside each proper noun.

Examples president — John F. Kennedy
Canada — country

1) teacher

2) city

3) holiday

4) dog

5) river

6) player

7) team

8) newspaper

9) neighbor

10) singer

11) street

12) band

13) month

14) Ireland

15) Bugs Bunny

16) World Series

17) French

18) Atlantic Ocean

19) Ohio

20) *Star Wars*

Reading Vocabulary

athlete (6) director (7) **common noun** document (6) constitution (6) **proper noun**

■ Presenting Activity B

Before having students complete Activity B on their own, have partners work together to write their own list of proper nouns to go with each common noun listed in the chart at the top of the page. Then have students take turns reading the proper noun they wrote to go with each common noun.

Activity B Answers

Answers will vary.

Learning Styles

Auditory/Verbal

Divide the class into two equal teams. Have them stand facing one another. Invite the first student in Team 1 to look at the objects around the classroom and to call out the name of a common noun. Invite the first student in Team 2 to name a proper noun for that common noun. Continue until all the students on both teams have named a common or a proper noun. Then have the two teams trade places and repeat the activity.

The Noun Chapter 1 **5**

Presenting Activity C

Ask students to write the answers to the following questions on their papers: Who is someone you admire? Do you live in a city or town? What is the name of your school? What state would you like to visit? What sport or leisure activity do you enjoy? Reread each question and invite students to share their answers. Have them tell whether they capitalized an answer and explain why or why not. After students complete Activity C, have class members compare and discuss answers.

Activity C Answers

3) Florida **5)** Michael J. Fox **6)** Brazil **8)** July **9)** Mars **10)** England **11)** James **13)** America **15)** Katharine Hepburn **16)** Christmas **17)** Mr. Wong **19)** California **20)** Wednesday **23)** Michael Jordan **25)** Cal Ripken **26)** Colorado River **28)** Miami **30)** Rocky Mountains

Teacher Alert

You may wish to take this opportunity to point out that when a proper noun is made up of more than one word (*Rocky Mountains, Michael Jordan*), each word is capitalized, with the exception of some short words such as *a, an, the,* and *of* (*Statue of Liberty*).

Activity C Write these nouns on your paper. Capitalize the proper nouns. A proper noun names a particular person, place, thing, or idea.

1) school
2) actor
3) florida
4) ocean
5) michael j. fox
6) brazil
7) lake
8) july
9) mars
10) england
11) james
12) road
13) america
14) paper
15) katharine hepburn
16) christmas
17) mr. wong
18) carpenter
19) california
20) wednesday
21) planet
22) movie
23) michael jordan
24) high school
25) cal ripken
26) colorado river
27) book
28) miami
29) singer
30) rocky mountains

The name of a particular place is a proper noun. The name of a country, state, city, street, or building is a proper noun.

EXAMPLES Common Nouns	Proper Nouns
city	New York City, Los Angeles
river	the Mississippi River
street	Main Street
apartment	Apartment 103
route	Route 96
high school	Montgomery High School
park	Rock Creek Park

Activity D Write these sentences on your paper. Capitalize the proper nouns. Every sentence will have at least one proper noun.

1) Roberto mailed a package to houston, texas.

2) His friend lives at 602 river drive, apartment 119.

3) Last year roberto went to a new high school.

4) He liked northview senior high very much.

5) Roberto and sue went swimming in the lake.

6) The lake was at the end of south shore drive.

7) I met Josie at the corner of schoolhouse road and high street.

8) Our plane was supposed to land in atlanta, georgia.

9) Because of the storm, the pilot announced that we would land in memphis, tennessee.

10) Mayor Johnson invited the band from the james middle school to march in the parade.

Reading Vocabulary

senior (6)

■ Presenting Activity D

Before having students complete Activity D on their own, have them write their own list of proper nouns to go with each common noun listed in the chart at the top of the page. Then have students take turns reading the proper noun they wrote to go with each common noun. As students do Activity D, emphasize that some sentences may have more than one proper noun and that each part of a proper noun made up of more than one word should be capitalized.

Activity D Answers

1) Houston, Texas **2)** River Drive, Apartment **3)** Roberto **4)** Northview Senior High **5)** Sue **6)** South Shore Drive **7)** Schoolhouse Road, High Street **8)** Atlanta, Georgia **9)** Memphis, Tennessee **10)** James Middle School

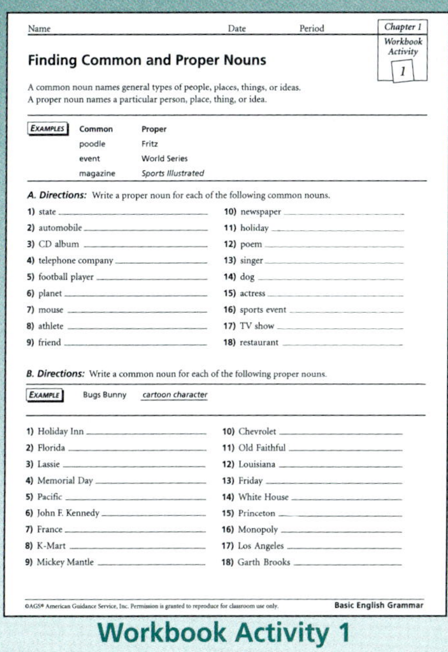

Name ______ Date ______ Period ______ *Chapter 1* *Workbook Activity* *1*

Finding Common and Proper Nouns

A common noun names general types of people, places, things, or ideas.
A proper noun names a particular person, place, thing, or idea.

EXAMPLES Common	Proper
poodle	Fritz
event	World Series
magazine	*Sports Illustrated*

A. Directions: Write a proper noun for each of the following common nouns.

1) state ______	**10)** newspaper ______
2) automobile ______	**11)** holiday ______
3) CD album ______	**12)** poem ______
4) telephone company ______	**13)** singer ______
5) football player ______	**14)** dog ______
6) planet ______	**15)** actress ______
7) mouse ______	**16)** sports event ______
8) athlete ______	**17)** TV show ______
9) friend ______	**18)** restaurant ______

B. Directions: Write a common noun for each of the following proper nouns.

EXAMPLE Bugs Bunny *cartoon character*

1) Holiday Inn ______	**10)** Chevrolet ______
2) Florida ______	**11)** Old Faithful ______
3) Lassie ______	**12)** Louisiana ______
4) Memorial Day ______	**13)** Friday ______
5) Pacific ______	**14)** White House ______
6) John F. Kennedy ______	**15)** Princeton ______
7) France ______	**16)** Monopoly ______
8) K-Mart ______	**17)** Los Angeles ______
9) Mickey Mantle ______	**18)** Garth Brooks ______

 Basic English Grammar

Workbook Activity 1

Reading Vocabulary

abbreviate (8) abbreviation (8)

■ Presenting Activity E

Draw the outline of an envelope on the board. Invite volunteers to write their name and address in the top left corner of the envelope and the name and address of a friend or relative in the middle of the envelope. Have the class check to see that the student has capitalized the addresses properly and used abbreviations where appropriate.

Activity E Answers

1) Mr. Joe Keller
Route 2, Box 206
Marshall, IA 50152

2) Mrs. Karen Blackhorse
99 Norris Ave.
Waterloo, NY 13165

3) Mr. C. J. Diaz
1580 Eaton Way
Burke, VA 22015

4) Ms. Dionne Williams
41 Maple Lane
Lyon, CA 94104

5) Ms. Holli Rezek
3189 Regent St.
Ocean Springs, MS 39564

6) Mr. Sumio Nishimura
143 Stonesboro Dr.
Apartment 8B
Louisville, KY 40229

Global Connection

Encourage students with relatives and friends in various parts of the world to write the addresses of these people during Presenting the Activity. Have students note the differences in the way foreign addresses are written.

An abbreviation is a short form of a word. If the whole word is a proper noun, the abbreviation is capitalized.

Examples	Proper Noun	Abbreviation
	Maryland	MD
	Doctor Smith	Dr. Smith
	Main Street	Main St.

Activity E Most of the words in an address are proper nouns. Write these addresses on your paper. Capitalize all of the proper nouns. Abbreviate the names of streets and states when possible.

1) mr. joe keller
route 2, box 206
marshall, iowa 50152

2) mrs. karen blackhorse
99 norris avenue
waterloo, new york 13165

3) mr. c. j. diaz
1580 eaton way
burke, virginia 22015

4) ms. dionne williams
41 maple lane
lyon, california 94104

5) ms. holli rezek
3189 regent street
ocean springs, mississippi 39564

6) mr. sumio nishimura
143 stonesboro drive
apartment 8B
louisville, kentucky 40229

8 *Chapter 1 The Noun*

Parts of the country are proper nouns. Directions are common nouns.

EXAMPLES

Part of the country:	I visited the **South** last spring.
Direction:	I am going **south** next spring.

Activity F Write these sentences on your paper. Capitalize the proper nouns. Not every sentence will have a proper noun.

1) When alex graduated from high school, he took a trip to the south.

2) On the first day, he drove 300 miles southwest.

3) He started in baltimore and spent the first night in north carolina.

4) On the second day, alex drove west to visit some friends in tennessee.

5) The next day alex headed southeast to florida.

6) I've never been west of the mississippi river.

7) Next year, we plan to take a trip to the west.

8) We'll fly to california and then rent a car.

9) After we visit local sights, we'll drive north to san francisco.

10) My cousins from the northern part of the state will join us on a tour of the southwest.

11) I met hector's uncle who lives in the northeast.

12) Their house is located in the northeastern part of vermont.

Reading Vocabulary

graduate (6) tour (5)

■ Presenting Activity F

Have students use the following words in sentences, first as a part of the country and then as a direction: *north, west, northwest, northeast, south, southwest, east, southeast.* Write the sentences on the board as students say them, having them tell you when to capitalize the above words.

Activity F Answers

1) Alex, South **2)** none **3)** Baltimore, North Carolina **4)** Alex, Tennessee **5)** Alex, Florida **6)** Mississippi River **7)** West **8)** California **9)** San Francisco **10)** Southwest **11)** Hector's, Northeast **12)** Vermont

APPLICATION

Career Connection Have students find a few company names in the Yellow Pages of the telephone directory and write each company address as they would for the address on an envelope. Have them make up names and titles of people at the companies to use in the addresses. Remind them that when writing job application letters, they should find out the correct spelling of the full name and title of the person to whom the letter will be sent. It is equally important to write the name and address correctly on the envelope. This will ensure that the letter is delivered to the proper person and place.

The Noun Chapter 1 **9**

Reading Vocabulary

biology (10) physical (5)
credit (5) social (5)
education (5) subject (5)
introduction (6)

■ Presenting Activity G

Work with students to create a chart of subjects and courses they are taking. Write subject names across the top of the chart and student names down the left side of the chart. Under the subject names, have students fill in the specific courses and languages they are taking.

	Language	Math
Rico	English Spanish I	Algebra I
Ruby	English Composition Italian II	Geometry
Lily	English Spanish II	Algebra II
Zach	French I	Introduction to Calculus

Activity G Answers

1) English **2)** math and social studies **3)** Math I **4)** physical education **5)** Earth Science II **6)** science **7)** Drama II **8)** Introduction to Music **9)** Japanese, Chinese, and French **10)** geography or history **11)** American History I or World History II **12)** Italian, English

The name of a language and a particular course are proper nouns. The name of a subject is a common noun.

Examples	**Proper Nouns**	**Common Nouns**
	English, Spanish	language
	History I	social studies
	Introduction to Biology	science

Activity G Write the word or words that should appear in each sentence to make it correct.

1) Karl got an A in (English, english).

2) Next year Alex is taking (math and social studies, Math and Social Studies).

3) Jennifer signed up for (math I, Math I).

4) Ima enjoys (physical education, Physical Education).

5) Danny is going on a field trip in (earth science II, Earth Science II).

6) Who teaches your (science, Science) class this year?

7) The students in (drama II, Drama II) will put on a play for their class project.

8) Miguel decided to take (introduction to music, Introduction to Music) for extra credit.

9) Kuri speaks (japanese, chinese, and french; Japanese, Chinese, and French).

10) Did you do better in (geography or history, Geography or History)?

11) Joanie had to choose between (american history I or world history II, American History I or World History II).

12) Our (italian, Italian) teacher does not let us speak (english, English) during class.

10 *Chapter 1 The Noun*

A title is a proper noun. Books, songs, movies, and people are some of the things that can have a title. The first word and all main words in a title are capitalized.

EXAMPLES

Reverend Frank Garcia	*Lord of the Rings*
"The Star-Spangled Banner"	*The Red Pony*

Activity H Write these titles on your paper. Capitalize the first word and all main words.

1) *the red badge of courage*

2) *the sound of music*

3) *the tonight show*

4) *the world almanac*

5) president andrew jackson

Activity I Write these sentences on your paper. Capitalize the proper nouns.

1) On wednesday alex came home from florida.

2) His sister jennifer was watching television.

3) "Hello, alex," jennifer said. "Welcome home from the south."

4) "Your boss, mr. wilson, called you yesterday," Jennifer told him.

5) "He wants you to report to the office on millstream drive tomorrow."

6) "Thanks," alex said. "Why are you home? I thought you were taking a french class."

7) "The class meets in the morning. How about taking me for a ride in your new car? I'd like to go south myself."

8) "OK," alex agreed. "Let's go."

Reading Vocabulary

almanac (7) title (5)
spangle (6)

Presenting Activity H

Point out that words such as *a, an, the,* and *of* are usually not capitalized in titles unless they are the first word. Then ask for volunteers to write the following on the board: favorite book; favorite movie; favorite television show; favorite song; a United States president, including the word *president.* Help students find and correct any mistakes in capitalization in the titles. Then have students complete Activity H independently.

Activity H Answers

1) *The Red Badge of Courage* **2)** *The Sound of Music* **3)** *The Tonight Show* **4)** *The World Almanac* **5)** President Andrew Jackson

Presenting Activity I

You may wish to review what students have learned about proper nouns and capitalization before having them complete this activity. Some students may also benefit from working with a partner or in a small group.

Activity I Answers

1) Wednesday, Alex, Florida **2)** Jennifer **3)** Alex, Jennifer, South **4)** Mr. Wilson **5)** Millstream Drive **6)** Alex, French **7)** none **8)** Alex

Reading Vocabulary

audience (5)
collective noun
compound noun
hyphen (6)
innocent (5)
jeans (6)
jury (6)
secretary (5)
separately
sweatshirt

■ Presenting Activity J

Read the examples with students and ask them to name at least two more words that name a group of people and two more words that name a group of things.

Activity J Answers

1) team 2) club
3) neighborhood 4) navy
5) jury

■ Presenting Activity K

Write these sentences on the board: *Leon parked the car in front of Town Hall. The band played as the team ran onto the field.* Ask students to read the sentences to themselves and raise their hands when they have found all the nouns. When everyone has raised his or her hand, ask for a volunteer to come and circle all the nouns. Then have students complete Activity K on their own.

Activity K Answers

1) forget-me-not, flower
2) vice president, graduation
3) Denali National Park, Alaska
4) Anita, maid-of-honor, wedding 5) Kim, jeans, sweatshirt, backpack

---

Collective noun
Names a group of people or things.

A **collective noun** is the name of a group of people or things.

EXAMPLES

Groups of people:	group, audience, crowd
Groups of things:	herd, flock, collection

Activity J Find five nouns that name a group of things or people in these sentences. Write them on your paper.

1) The baseball team practiced every day.
2) Alex's club had a meeting every Thursday.
3) The whole neighborhood went to the picnic.
4) Carla decided to join the navy.
5) The jury found the man innocent.

Compound noun
A noun that is more than one word.

The names of people or things may be compound. **Compound nouns** may be written as two or more words. Sometimes the words are written separately. Sometimes hyphens are used.

EXAMPLES

White House	son-in-law	high school
Dr. An Chin	Maple Street	Secretary of State

Activity K Write all the nouns in these sentences on your paper.

1) A forget-me-not is a lovely blue flower.
2) The vice president spoke at our graduation.
3) Denali National Park is in Alaska.
4) Anita was the maid-of-honor at the wedding.
5) Kim stuffed jeans and a sweatshirt in her backpack.

Name Date Period

Chapter 1
Workbook Activity
2

Find the Nouns

A noun is a word that names a person, place, thing, or idea.

EXAMPLES
Person — Mr. Jones, farmer
Group — team, family
Place — California, school
Thing — horse, book
Idea — courage, peace

Directions: Circle all of the nouns in these sentences.

EXAMPLES
(Jerry) took the (trail) down to (Blue Lake.)
Your (visit) gave us (happiness.)

1) Mrs. Parham thanked George for his politeness.
2) Cindy and her family are moving to Kansas.
3) José found his book under the couch.
4) The audience cheered the violinist
5) The soldier was given a medal for bravery.
6) The big horse easily jumped the fence.
7) The crowd watched the game with pleasure.
8) Yoshi and her mother fixed the car.
9) Many hikers have climbed Blueberry Mountain.
10) Henry found the newspaper on the porch.
11) I think the price of that coat is too high.
12) Walter has a good knowledge of baseball.
13) The waters of Long Pond shone in the sunlight.
14) Mr. Wilson had a new idea about the party.
15) Alice took the dictionary off the shelf.
16) The Doors are my favorite singing group.
17) Was John Adams the third president?
18) Cora had a dream about her cat.
19) Peter found a ring with a blue stone.
20) His speed will help Tom win the race.

 Basic English Grammar

Workbook Activity 2

Concrete noun
Something you can see or touch.

Abstract noun
An idea that you cannot see or touch.

A noun may be abstract or concrete.

A **concrete noun** is a word that names something you can see or touch.

An **abstract noun** is a word that names something you can think about or talk about. You cannot see it or touch it. An abstract noun is an idea.

EXAMPLES	Concrete Nouns	Abstract Nouns
	money	cost
	clock	time
	school	education
	steel	strength

Activity L Write the abstract noun in each pair of words on your paper.

1)	fever	thermometer
2)	law	judge
3)	price	price tag
4)	pizza	hunger
5)	year	calendar
6)	earthquake	disaster
7)	kindness	friend
8)	telephone	communication
9)	tears	disappointment
10)	fame	actor

Reading Vocabulary

abstract noun
communication (6)
concrete noun
disaster (5)
fame (5)
thermometer (6)

■ Presenting Activity L

To be sure students grasp the concept of abstract and concrete nouns, you may wish to do the first two or three items orally as a class. After students complete the activity, encourage them to make up their own related pairs of abstract and concrete nouns. Invite students to read their word pairs aloud and have the class identify the abstract noun in each pair.

Activity L Answers

1) fever **2)** law **3)** price **4)** hunger **5)** year **6)** disaster **7)** kindness **8)** communication **9)** disappointment **10)** fame

Name Date Period — *Chapter 1 Activity 1*

Concrete Nouns

Nouns can be concrete or abstract. Concrete nouns are names of real things—things you can see or feel.

EXAMPLES car, typewriter, smile, mountain, book

Directions: Write five concrete nouns that belong in each group below. Study the examples in parentheses.

1) Vehicle (bicycle, airplane) a. ___ b. ___ c. ___ d. ___ e. ___

2) Thing to read (book, cereal box) a. ___ b. ___ c. ___ d. ___ e. ___

3) Flower (marigold, petunia) a. ___ b. ___ c. ___ d. ___ e. ___

4) Building (office, school) a. ___ b. ___ c. ___ d. ___ e. ___

5) Person (doctor, athlete) a. ___ b. ___ c. ___ d. ___ e. ___

6) Furniture (chair, stool) a. ___ b. ___ c. ___ d. ___ e. ___

 Basic English Grammar

Activity 1

Name Date Period — *Chapter 1 Activity 2*

Abstract Nouns

Nouns can be concrete or abstract. Abstract nouns are names of ideas, qualities, characteristics, acts, and quantities.

EXAMPLES decision, size, love

Directions: Write five abstract nouns that belong in each group below. Study the examples in parentheses.

1) Feeling (fear, pain) a. ___ b. ___ c. ___ d. ___ e. ___

2) Quantity (size, pound) a. ___ b. ___ c. ___ d. ___ e. ___

3) Time (minute, June) a. ___ b. ___ c. ___ d. ___ e. ___

4) Action (race, decision) a. ___ b. ___ c. ___ d. ___ e. ___

5) Quality (honesty, courage) a. ___ b. ___ c. ___ d. ___ e. ___

6) Event (game, Super Bowl) a. ___ b. ___ c. ___ d. ___ e. ___

 Basic English Grammar

Activity 2

Reading Vocabulary

appointment (6) mileage (7) coverage

Part A Answers

1) Alex Jones (proper noun—concrete), car (common noun—concrete) **2)** week (common noun—abstract), amount (common noun—abstract), money (common noun—concrete—collective) **3)** money (common noun—concrete—collective), bank (common noun—concrete), interest (common noun—abstract—collective) **4)** decision (common noun—abstract), car (common noun—concrete) **5)** car (common noun—concrete), mileage (common noun—abstract—collective) **6)** Alex (proper noun—concrete), ad (common noun—concrete), newspaper (common noun—concrete) **7)** phone number (common noun—concrete), appointment (common noun—abstract) **8)** Alex (proper noun—concrete), automobiles (common noun—concrete), weeks (common noun—abstract) **9)** car (common noun—concrete), price (common noun—abstract) **10)** Alex (proper noun—concrete), feeling (common noun—abstract), seller (common noun—concrete)

Part B Answers

1) month, Alex, job **2)** money, car, road **3)** state, owners, insurance **4)** Alex, plans **5)** cost, Alex, coverage

Follow-up Activity

Select a brief passage from a literature book, newspaper, or magazine or have students select a passage of their own choice. Have students find and list all the nouns in the passage under two headings: *Common Nouns* and *Proper Nouns.*

Lesson 1 Review

Part A Write all the nouns in these sentences on your paper. Write whether each noun is *common, proper, concrete, abstract,* or *collective.*

1) Alex Jones wanted a car very much.
2) Every week he saved a certain amount of money.
3) He put his money in a bank and received interest.
4) A decision about a car would not be easy.
5) He wanted a small car that would get good mileage.
6) Alex saw an ad in the newspaper.
7) He called the phone number and made an appointment.
8) Alex looked at automobiles for weeks.
9) Then he found the perfect car. The price was right.
10) Alex had a good feeling. He trusted the seller.

Part B Write the nouns in these sentences on your paper.

1) Last month Alex got another part-time job.
2) He needed the money to keep his car on the road.
3) His state requires car owners to buy insurance.
4) Alex had to choose among several different plans.
5) The cost was high, but Alex got full coverage.

Lesson 2 Singular and Plural Nouns

Singular noun
Names one person, place, thing, or idea.

Plural noun
Names more than one person, place, thing, or idea.

A **singular noun** is the name of one person, place, thing, or idea.

A **plural noun** is the name of more than one person, place, thing, or idea.

Most plural nouns end in *-s* or *-es.* When the plural noun ends in *-es,* the plural has an extra syllable. You can hear the difference if you say the words aloud.

Examples

Singular Nouns		Plural Nouns	
ship	group	ships	groups
quiz	church	quizzes	churches
dish	six	dishes	sixes

Activity A Write the plural of each singular noun on your paper. Add either an *-s* or *-es.* Say the plural aloud. You will hear the extra syllable when the plural noun ends in *-es.*

Examples town — towns guess — guesses

1) bunch	**5)** school	**9)** wish	**13)** patch
2) address	**6)** ladder	**10)** bush	**14)** icicle
3) car	**7)** mountain	**11)** idea	**15)** sled
4) fox	**8)** ax	**12)** tax	**16)** quiz

Activity B Number your paper 1–16. Next to each number, write whether the word is *singular* or *plural.*

1) action	**5)** reports	**9)** crowds	**13)** circus
2) bosses	**6)** address	**10)** doctor	**14)** committee
3) team	**7)** majority	**11)** Alex	**15)** women
4) nations	**8)** agents	**12)** monsters	**16)** Elm Street

Lesson at a Glance

Chapter 1 Lesson 2

Overview This lesson presents singular and plural nouns and explains how they are formed.

Objectives

- To write the plural form of regular and irregular nouns.
- To distinguish between singular and plural nouns.
- To locate and correct misspelled plural nouns in sentences.

Student Pages 15–19

Teacher's Resource Library

Activity 3

Workbook Activity 3

Reading Vocabulary

aloud
icicle (6)
majority (6)
plural noun
quiz (6)
singular noun

Teaching Suggestions

■ Introducing the Lesson Discuss the definitions of *singular noun* and *plural noun* and provide additional examples.

■ Reviewing Skills Ask students to identify the common and proper nouns in sentences you read aloud.

■ Presenting Activity A Have the class say the singular and plural forms of each activity item, paying attention to the end sounds.

Activity A Answers
1) bunches 2) addresses 3) cars 4) foxes 5) schools 6) ladders 7) mountains 8) axes 9) wishes 10) bushes 11) ideas 12) taxes 13) patches 14) icicles 15) sleds 16) quizzes

■ Presenting Activity B Suggest that students put the words *a* or *an* before each noun. If it sounds correct, the word is probably singular.

Activity B Answers
1) singular 2) plural 3) singular 4) plural 5) plural 6) singular 7) singular 8) plural 9) plural 10) singular 11) singular 12) plural 13) singular 14) singular 15) plural 16) singular

Reading Vocabulary

alley (5)
consonant
county (5)
injury (6)
vowel (6)

■ Presenting Activity C

Have students complete Activity C as a group activity. Draw a chart on the board, similar to the one shown on the page, with the main headings *Nouns That Change* and *Nouns That Do Not Change.* Under each main heading, create two columns with the subheads *singular* and *plural.* Write the two activity examples (turkey and county) in the appropriate spaces in the chart and discuss their plural spellings. Then discuss the plural spelling of each activity item and invite students to write the singular and plural forms of each noun given in the chart.

Activity C Answers

1) monkeys **2)** chimneys **3)** countries **4)** bodies **5)** journeys **6)** injuries **7)** armies **8)** navies **9)** bays **10)** days

■ Presenting Activity D

Write this sentence on the board: *The boys and their familys went on many journies together.* Help students apply the spelling rules on the page to find and correct the spelling mistakes in the sentence. Then have them complete Activity D independently.

Activity D Answers

1) countries, spies, armies **2)** cities **3)** injuries

Nouns that end in *-y* and have a consonant before the *-y* become plural by changing the *-y* to *-i* and adding *-es.*

Nouns that end in *-y* and have a vowel before the *-y* become plural by simply adding an *-s.*

EXAMPLES

Nouns That Change		Nouns That Do Not Change	
city	cities	key	keys
lady	ladies	alley	alleys
spy	spies	boy	boys

Activity C Write these nouns on your paper. Beside each noun, write its plural.

Examples turkey — turkeys county — counties

1) monkey
2) chimney
3) country
4) body
5) journey
6) injury
7) army
8) navy
9) bay
10) day

Activity D Find the spelling mistakes in these sentences. Write the sentences correctly on your paper.

1) Both countrys had spys in their armys.
2) He received keys to two of the citys he visited on his journey.
3) The doctor said their injurys were not serious.

The plural of most nouns that end in *-f* or *-fe* is made by adding *-s*.

EXAMPLES	roof	roofs	chief	chiefs

Some nouns that end in *-f* or *-fe* change the *-f* to *-v* and add *-s* or *-es*.

EXAMPLES	leaf	leaves	calf	calves
	knife	knives	wolf	wolves

The plural of some nouns ending with a consonant and an *-o* is formed by adding *-es*. Others add only the *-s*.

EXAMPLES	hero	heroes	photo	photos
	tomato	tomatoes	hairdo	hairdos

The plural of nouns ending with a vowel and an *-o* is formed by adding *-s*.

EXAMPLES	radio	radios	rodeo	rodeos

A few nouns become plural by changing letters within the word.

EXAMPLES	man	men	foot	feet
	mouse	mice	woman	women
	tooth	teeth	goose	geese

Some singular and plural nouns are spelled the same.

EXAMPLES	deer	sheep
	trout	series

Reading Vocabulary

hairdo photo

APPLICATION

At Home

Irregular plurals present a constant challenge, especially to students acquiring English. Encourage students to create their own personal dictionaries of irregular spellings. They can copy each rule presented on page 17, along with the examples, onto a separate notebook page. Whenever they come across another noun that fits one of these rules, they can add it to the page. Students can use their personal dictionaries to check spelling when completing homework assignments or when writing personal or business letters and correspondence.

LEARNING STYLES

LEP/ESL

Invite students for whom English is a second language to explain to the class how they form plurals in their primary language. Encourage them to print examples on the board.

Reading Vocabulary

loaf (5) rancher

■ Presenting Activity E Do the first activity item orally with the class. Encourage students to refer back to page 17 as they complete the remaining items in Activity E on their own.

Activity E Answers

1) deer, men **2)** sheep **3)** trout **4)** World Series **5)** loaves, potatoes

■ Presenting Activity F

Suggest that students use a dictionary as they complete Activity F. If necessary, put a sample dictionary entry for both a regular and irregular noun on the board to show students how plural spellings are indicated in a dictionary entry. After students complete Activity F, invite them to share their sentences with the class.

Activity F Answers

Sentences will vary. Plurals are given.

1) calves **2)** beliefs **3)** feet **4)** men **5)** teeth **6)** children **7)** teams **8)** knives **9)** ladies **10)** monkeys **11)** tomatoes **12)** potatoes **13)** mice **14)** heroes **15)** deer **16)** chiefs **17)** buses **18)** moose **19)** women **20)** elves

Activity E Find the spelling mistakes in these sentences. Write the sentences correctly on your paper.

1) Two deers surprised the mans in the woods.

2) The rancher bought eighty sheeps.

3) We went fishing and caught seven trouts.

4) The Reds won two World Serieses in a row.

5) They ate two loafs of bread and ten potatos.

Activity F Write the plural of each singular noun on your paper. Then write a sentence using each plural noun.

Example goose — geese The geese honked as they flew.

1) calf
2) belief
3) foot
4) man
5) tooth
6) child
7) team
8) knife
9) lady
10) monkey
11) tomato
12) potato
13) mouse
14) hero
15) deer
16) chief
17) bus
18) moose
19) woman
20) elf

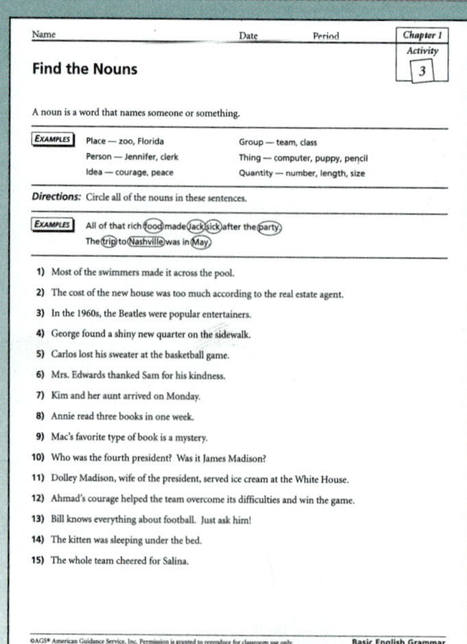

Name Date Period — *Chapter 1 Activity 3*

Find the Nouns

A noun is a word that names someone or something.

EXAMPLES Place — zoo, Florida; Person — Jennifer, clerk; Idea — courage, peace; Group — team, class; Thing — computer, puppy, pencil; Quantity — number, length, size

Directions: Circle all of the nouns in these sentences.

EXAMPLES All of that rich food made Jack sick after the party.
The trip to Nashville was in May.

1) Most of the swimmers made it across the pool.
2) The cost of the new house was too much according to the real estate agent.
3) In the 1960s, the Beatles were popular entertainers.
4) George found a shiny new quarter on the sidewalk.
5) Carlos lost his sweater at the basketball game.
6) Mrs. Edwards thanked Sam for his kindness.
7) Kim and her aunt arrived on Monday.
8) Annie read three books in one week.
9) Mac's favorite type of book is a mystery.
10) Who was the fourth president? Was it James Madison?
11) Dolley Madison, wife of the president, served ice cream at the White House.
12) Ahmad's courage helped the team overcome its difficulties and win the game.
13) Bill knows everything about football. Just ask him!
14) The kitten was sleeping under the bed.
15) The whole team cheered for Salina.

 Basic English Grammar

Activity 3

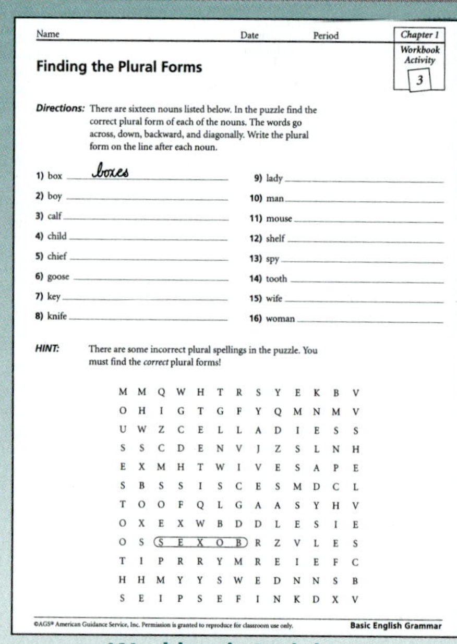

Name Date Period — *Chapter 1 Workbook Activity 3*

Finding the Plural Forms

Directions: There are sixteen nouns listed below. In the puzzle find the correct plural form of each of the nouns. The words go across, down, backward, and diagonally. Write the plural form on the line after each noun.

1) box boxes
2) boy
3) calf
4) child
5) chief
6) goose
7) key
8) knife
9) lady
10) man
11) mouse
12) shelf
13) spy
14) tooth
15) wife
16) woman

HINT: There are some incorrect plural spellings in the puzzle. You must find the *correct* plural forms!

M M Q W H T R S Y E K B V
O H I G T G F Y Q M N M V
U W Z C E L L A D I E S S
S S C D E N V J Z S L N H
E X M H T W I V E S A P E
S B S S I S C E S M D C L
T O O F Q L G A A S Y H V
O X E X W B D D L E S I E
O S S E X O B R Z V L E S
T I P R R Y M R E I E F C
H H M Y Y S W E D N N S B
S E I P S E F I N K D X V

 Basic English Grammar

Workbook Activity 3

Lesson 2 Review

Part A Find six plural nouns in this paragraph. Write them in order on your paper.

> The traffic in front of the house was heavy for about two hours. About twenty people came to the party. Everyone seemed to be wearing new clothes. The guests stood in small groups around the snacks and around the stereo. They talked about their summer fun and the year to come.

Part B Write the plural of each noun on your paper.

1) woman
2) sheep
3) goose
4) tomato
5) life
6) hero
7) key
8) spy
9) child
10) city
11) tax
12) policy
13) dish
14) potato
15) address
16) deer
17) path
18) agent
19) party
20) knife
21) trout
22) mouse
23) stereo
24) business

Part C Write the word that should appear in each sentence to make it correct.

1) In six months, Hector grew two (inchs, inches).
2) There are many large (citys, cities) along the east coast of the United States.
3) Tom's (feet, feets) were sore after the five-mile hike.
4) These (tomatoes, tomatos) will make the salad taste better.
5) My brother had two (cavitys, cavities) filled at the dentist.

Reading Vocabulary

dentist (5) stereo
snack (6)

Part A Answers

hours, people, clothes, guests, groups, snacks

Part B Answers

1) women **2)** sheep **3)** geese **4)** tomatoes **5)** lives **6)** heroes **7)** keys **8)** spies **9)** children **10)** cities **11)** taxes **12)** policies **13)** dishes **14)** potatoes **15)** addresses **16)** deer **17)** paths **18)** agents **19)** parties **20)** knives **21)** trout **22)** mice **23)** stereos **24)** businesses

Part C Answers

1) inches **2)** cities **3)** feet **4)** tomatoes **5)** cavities

Teacher Alert

Some students may be confused by the word *people,* which at one time was considered a collective noun. In modern usage, however, *people* is considered a plural noun with no singular form.

Follow-up Activity

Challenge small groups of students to write a story using as many of the singular and plural forms of the nouns in Part B as possible. Invite students to share their stories with the class.

The Noun Chapter 1 **19**

Lesson at a Glance

Chapter 1 Lesson 3

Overview This lesson explains possessive nouns and how they are formed.

Objectives

- To distinguish between plurals and possessives.
- To identify possessive nouns in sentences.
- To write the singular and plural possessive form of nouns.

Student Pages 20–23

Teacher's Resource Library

Workbook Activities 4–5

Reading Vocabulary

apostrophe
author (6)
autograph (5)
inspect
ownership (7)
possessive noun

Teaching Suggestions

Introducing the Lesson

Discuss the definition of a possessive noun and the examples given. Be sure students understand the concept of possessives and how they are formed before having them do the activities in the lesson.

Reviewing Skills

Have students form the plurals of regular and irregular nouns.

Presenting Activity A

Before having students complete the activity on their own, ask them to find the words in bold that have an apostrophe. Remind students that possessives are formed with an apostrophe; plurals are not.

Activity A Answers

1) Alex's—possessive
2) pages—plural
3) friends—plural
4) friend's—possessive
5) car's—possessive
6) tires—plural

Lesson 3 Nouns That Are Possessive

Possessive noun
Shows ownership or relationship.

A **possessive noun** is one that shows ownership or a relationship. A possessive noun ends in *-s* and has an apostrophe.

EXAMPLES

Ownership:	That car belongs to Alex. That is **Alex's** car.
Relationship:	Jennifer is the sister of Alex. Jennifer is **Alex's** sister.

Remember that most plural nouns end in *-s* or *-es*. A noun that is possessive also ends in *-s*. Plurals and possessive nouns sound the same when they are said aloud. Many people get plurals and possessives mixed up when they write them. A written possessive noun looks different from a plural noun. The possessive noun uses an apostrophe. Look at the examples below. Notice the difference in the meaning.

EXAMPLES

Plural Noun	Possessive Noun
We bought two **tapes**.	He can't find the **tape's** case.
I read three interesting **books**.	The **book's** author autographed it.
The **planes** had engine trouble.	The **plane's** engine failed.

Activity A Write the word in bold in these sentences on your paper. Beside each word, write whether it is *plural* or *possessive*.

Example Chicago has some of the **world's** tallest buildings.
world's — possessive

1) **Alex's** insurance policy came in the mail.
2) The policy had several **pages**.
3) A few of Alex's **friends** stopped by the house.
4) They came to see their **friend's** new car.
5) They went out to inspect the **car's** tires.
6) The **tires** were brand new.

A possessive noun can be singular or plural. Study the examples below.

EXAMPLES Make a singular noun possessive by adding *-'s.*

Singular	Singular Possessive
teacher	teacher's desk
child	child's bike

Make a plural noun that ends in *-s* possessive by adding only an apostrophe.

Plural	Plural Possessive
teachers	teachers' meeting
trees	trees' leaves

When a plural noun does not end in *-s,* make it possessive by adding *-'s.*

Plural	Plural Possessive
men	men's department
children	children's room

Activity B Write the possessive nouns in these sentences on your paper. Beside each possessive noun, write whether it is *singular* or *plural.*

Example The **ladies'** department had a sale. **ladies'**—plural

1) The monkeys' fur was black.

2) The cat slept on the sofa's cushion.

3) Alex had to replace the camera's batteries.

4) The mice's tracks led under the baseboard.

5) Last week the children's room was painted.

Reading Vocabulary

baseboard
cushion (6)
replace (6)
sofa (5)

■ Presenting Activity B

Create four columns on the board with the heads *Singular, Singular Possessive, Plural,* and *Plural Possessive.* Under *Singular,* write *girl, boat, spy, woman;* under *Plural* write *girls, boats, spies, women.* Then have students suggest phrases that show possession to go with each singular noun and each plural noun. Give oral examples, such as *girl's pen, spies' secrets.* Write these examples and students' suggestions on the board. Elicit from students the correct spelling and where to place the apostrophe for each phrase.

Activity B Answers

1) monkeys'—plural
2) sofa's—singular
3) camera's—singular
4) mice's—plural
5) children's—plural

LEARNING STYLES

Visual/Spatial

Divide the class into pairs. Give each pair a colorful magazine picture. On the board, print the following categories: 1) sentence with a singular noun; 2) sentence with a plural noun; 3) sentence with a singular possessive; 4) sentence with a plural possessive. Encourage the partners to use their magazine picture to create a sentence for each of the four categories. Afterward, ask each set of partners to read one sentence aloud. Have the class name the sentence category. Note: Keep the magazine pictures for use with the Learning Styles activity on page 47.

Reading Vocabulary

chapter (5) refer (6)
expression (5) sunflower

Presenting Activity C

Before students complete Activity C, ask volunteers to say and spell the singular and plural form of each activity item. After students have reviewed and corrected their answers for Activity C, encourage them to use the singular and possessive forms of each noun in sentences.

Activity C Answers

1) chapter's, chapters' 2) agent's, agents' 3) person's, persons' 4) state's, states' 5) fox's, foxes' 6) president's, presidents' 7) child's, children's 8) church's, churches' 9) crowd's, crowds' 10) navy's, navies' 11) job's, jobs' 12) thing's, things' 13) noun's, nouns' 14) goose's, geese's 15) wife's, wives' 16) audience's, audiences' 17) man's, men's 18) foot's, feet's 19) sunflower's, sunflowers' 20) county's, counties'

Presenting Activity D

Before students do the activity on their own, read through each item with them and help them determine which answer choice in each item is singular possessive and which is plural possessive.

Activity D Answers

1) cents' 2) weeks' 3) minute's 4) dollars' 5) week's

Activity C Write the singular possessive form and the plural possessive form for these words on your paper.

Examples club club's clubs' lady lady's ladies'

1) chapter	**11)** job
2) agent	**12)** thing
3) person	**13)** noun
4) state	**14)** goose
5) fox	**15)** wife
6) president	**16)** audience
7) child	**17)** man
8) church	**18)** foot
9) crowd	**19)** sunflower
10) navy	**20)** county

A number of common expressions contain possessive forms. Many refer to time or to price.

EXAMPLES ten dollars' worth one day's trip
three days' vacation

Activity D Write the word that should appear in each sentence to make it correct.

1) Mark likes to put in his two (cents', cent's) worth.
2) Alex gets two (weeks', week's) vacation every year.
3) You will only have a (minutes', minute's) wait.
4) I'd like five (dollar's, dollars') worth of stamps.
5) We hoped for a rest at the (week's, weeks') end.

22 Chapter 1 The Noun

Lesson 3 Review

Part A Write the possessive nouns in these sentences on your paper. Add apostrophes where they are needed.

1) Alexs job is very important to him.
2) He has worked in Mr. Wilsons store for one year.
3) Mr. Wilson sells mens sports clothes.
4) Every week at the salespersons meeting, they talk about their work.
5) Mr. Wilsons plan is to make Alex a manager some day.

Part B Some nouns in these sentences are in bold. Write them on your paper. Beside each noun, write whether it is a *plural noun* or a *possessive noun.* Add an apostrophe if it is needed.

Example Several **years** ago, Jennifer and Alex went to New York.
years—plural noun (no apostrophe is needed)

1) Jennifer and Alex went to New York City with their **parents**.
2) They wanted to see some of the **worlds** tallest buildings.
3) **Alexs** favorite place was the Statue of Liberty.
4) One of the **familys** most enjoyable places was Lincoln Center.
5) On their way to lunch, they saw a **womens** street band.
6) A street juggler and a mime had them in **stitches**.
7) The **crowds** of people and the subways were exciting.
8) At the **trips** end, they were sorry to leave the city.

Part C Write the word that should appear in each sentence to make it correct.

1) He got ten (dollars, dollars') worth of gas.
2) My (sisters, sister's) boyfriend is coming for dinner.
3) The (monkeys, monkey's) chattering made everyone laugh.
4) We drove to work in (Alexs, Alex's) new car.

Reading Vocabulary

juggler
liberty (5)
manager (6)
mime
salesperson
stitch (5)

Part A Answers

1) Alex's 2) Wilson's 3) men's 4) salespersons' 5) Wilson's

Part B Answers

1) parents—plural 2) world's—possessive 3) Alex's—possessive 4) family's—possessive 5) women's—possessive 6) stitches—plural 7) crowds—plural 8) trip's—possessive

Part C Answers

1) dollars' 2) sister's 3) monkey's 4) Alex's

Teacher Alert

Monitor students as they complete the Review activities. Note who is struggling with the concepts presented in this lesson. Try to provide one-on-one or small group support for these individuals.

Name Date Period *Chapter 1 Workbook Activity* 4

Selecting the Correct Possessive Form

A noun that is possessive shows ownership or relationship. You make a singular noun possessive by adding *-'s*. You make a plural noun that ends in *-s* possessive by adding an apostrophe ('). You make a plural noun that does not end in *-s* possessive by adding *-'s*.

EXAMPLES dog — the dog's bowl
horses — the horses' saddles
people — the people's meeting

Directions: Circle the correct form of the words in parentheses.

EXAMPLE Don found (Marcia, Marcia's) hat.

1) Many (trees, tree's) branches waved in the wind.
2) One (team's, teams') score was the best.
3) That (fires', fire's) heat warms the room.
4) A small dinosaur munched the (plant's, plants) stem.
5) Paula said that one (band's, bands') music was best.
6) The (childrens', children's) books are at school.
7) John put the (cats', cat's) bowls in the sink.
8) Lilly found a (mouse's, mouses) nest in the grass.
9) Many (hikers', hiker's) feet were sore.
10) These (books, books') prices are high.
11) Have you seen the (men's, mens') baseball uniforms?
12) This (snakes, snake's) skin is striped.
13) My (friends, friend's) house is very comfortable.
14) Have you seen (Jean's, Jeans') scarf?
15) The (coach's, coaches') whistle is loud.

 Basic English Grammar

Workbook Activity 4

Name Date Period *Chapter 1 Workbook Activity* 5

Using Nouns Correctly

Directions: Circle the mistake in each sentence. Then write the sentence correctly on the lines below.

EXAMPLE Nancy and her sister liked to watch Television.
Nancy and her sister liked to watch television.

1) New york city is one of the most exciting places in the world.
2) Janet, her Brother Andy, and her parents visited the city.
3) They stayed in one of the citys finest hotels.
4) They visited the Empire State building and the Statue of Liberty.
5) The family bought ticket's for Madison Square Garden.
6) Radio city music hall was one of their favorite places.
7) Central Park was fun. They fed the monkeys at the Zoo.
8) Shopping for mens clothes was especially interesting for Mr. Jones.
9) Janets last day was spent looking for a souvenir to take home to her friend Darleen.
10) She bought a picture showing Central Park in fall with all its tree's leaves turned to red and gold.

 Basic English Grammar

Workbook Activity 5

Chapter 1 Review

The Teacher's Resource Library includes two parallel forms of the Chapter 1 Mastery Test. The difficulty level of the two forms is equivalent. You may wish to use one form as a pretest and the other form as a posttest.

Reading Vocabulary

college (5) composition (5)
community (5) topic (5)

Part A Answers

1) party 2) Alex, Jennifer, parents, room 3) Mrs. Jones, living room 4) Glasses, bowls, dishes 5) Alex, Jennifer, friends', mess

Part B Answers

1) August, Jennifer, Alex
2) Jennifer, Jackson High School
3) Alex, Hanover Community College 4) Mr. Wilson's
5) Jennifer, French 6) Alex, English
7) Alex, South 8) English
9) "My First Trip to Florida"
10) Alex, Ms. Romero

Part C Answers

1) wolves 2) cities 3) quizzes 4) teachers 5) students 6) monkeys 7) houses 8) parties 9) children 10) teeth

Chapter 1 Review

Part A Write the nouns in these sentences on your paper. Be sure to include possessive nouns.

1) The party was over.
2) Alex and Jennifer let their parents go into the room.
3) Mrs. Jones looked at the living room.
4) Glasses, empty bowls, and dishes were everywhere.
5) Alex and Jennifer cleaned up their friends' mess.

Part B Write all of the proper nouns in these sentences. Capitalize any proper nouns that are not capitalized.

1) The summer was almost over. In august, Jennifer and Alex would both return to school.
2) Jennifer was going to be a senior at jackson high school.
3) Alex was going to hanover community college.
4) He also planned to work part-time at mr. wilson's store.
5) Jennifer was taking french, math, and science.
6) Alex was taking english and business subjects.
7) Alex remembered his trip to the south.
8) When his english teacher asked him to write a composition, he had a good topic.
9) He decided to title his paper, "my first trip to florida."
10) Alex was proud when ms. romero chose to read his paper aloud to the class.

Part C Write the plural form of each of these singular nouns.

1) wolf	5) student	9) child
2) city	6) monkey	10) tooth
3) quiz	7) house	
4) teacher	8) party	

Name ____ Date ____ Period ____ *Chapter 1 Mastery Test A page 1*

Chapter 1 Mastery Test A

Part A Circle all of the nouns in these sentences.

1) Cy Young won more games than any other pitcher in baseball.
2) His record of 511 wins is far ahead of any other person.
3) I bet you never heard of Old Hoss Radbourn.
4) Old Hoss won 308 games in his pitching career.
5) Each year the best pitcher in baseball wins a special award.
6) It is called the Cy Young Award.
7) The first person to win the Cy Young Award was Don Newcombe.
8) Jim Palmer was a pitcher with the Baltimore Orioles.
9) Palmer won the Cy Young Award three times.
10) Every year one player from each league wins this prize.

Part B Rewrite these sentences. Capitalize all of the proper nouns.

1) We saw cal ripken play baseball at camden yards in baltimore.
2) Next year henry plans to take spanish and algebra I.
3) Jackie visited the midwest last august.
4) In june robert has an appointment with dr. welsey.
5) For many years "60 minutes" has been a popular news program.

 Basic English Grammar

Name ____ Date ____ Period ____ *Chapter 1 Mastery Test A page 2*

Chapter 1 Mastery Test A, continued

Part C Write the plural form of each of these singular nouns.

1) bunch ____	11) knife ____
2) city ____	12) report ____
3) fox ____	13) foot ____
4) spy ____	14) woman ____
5) key ____	15) mouse ____
6) radio ____	16) church ____
7) deer ____	17) chief ____
8) roof ____	18) tomato ____
9) country ____	19) tooth ____
10) photo ____	20) injury ____

Part D Write the possessive form that should appear in each sentence to make it correct.

1) The ____ cover was torn. (book's, books')
2) Jerry bought ten ____ worth of gas. (dollar's, dollars')
3) His ____ room is sunny. (children's, childrens')
4) Three ____ gifts helped the food shelf. (church's, churches')
5) I could hardly see the ____ crack. (dish's, dishes')
6) The teacher read two ____ papers aloud. (student's, students')
7) ____ sister goes to our school. (Sharon's, Sharons')
8) My ____ screen was dim. (computer's, computers')
9) The ____ flavor was sweet. (bread's, breads')
10) Four ____ anchors were dropped. (ship's, ships')

 Basic English Grammar

Chapter 1 Mastery Test A

Part D Write the word that should appear in each sentence to make it correct.

1) Alex and his friend (miguel, Miguel) went to the movies.
2) They were seeing (*star wars, Star Wars*) for the fifth time.
3) The theater had special prices on (wednesday, Wednesday).
4) They were going to the (Early Show, early show).
5) Alex had to study for an (english, English) test.
6) Miguel also went to (hanover community college, Hanover Community College).
7) Miguel was taking (Basic Computers I, basic computers I).
8) He planned to become a (computer operator, Computer Operator).
9) On the way home there was a lot of (traffic, traffics).
10) Alex and Miguel talked about their (colleges, college's) team.
11) They wondered about the (teams', team's) chances.
12) When they got home, (Alexs, Alex's) sister was waiting.
13) Miguel had been one of (Jennifer's, Jennifers) friends for years.
14) "Did you get your (money's, moneys) worth?" Jennifer asked.
15) "Yes. It is the (worlds, world's) best movie!" he said.

Test Taking Tip Do not wait until the night before a test to study. Plan your study time so that you can get a good night's sleep the night before a test.

Reading Vocabulary

basic (7) operator (5)
computer theater (5)

Part D Answers

1) Miguel 2) *Star Wars* 3) Wednesday 4) early show 5) English 6) Hanover Community College 7) Basic Computers I 8) computer operator 9) traffic 10) college's 11) team's 12) Alex's 13) Jennifer's 14) money's 15) world's

Application

At Home

Students who have trouble mastering the concepts of forming plurals and possessives can make flash cards to use at home. Suggest that students write the singular form of a noun on one side of the card. On the other side, they can write the plural form, singular possessive, and plural possessive form of the noun. Students can use the cards themselves or they can work with a family member.

Name Date Period | *Chapter 1 Mastery Test B page 1*

Chapter 1 Mastery Test B

Part A Circle all of the nouns in these sentences.

1) The clock on the wall ticked loudly.
2) I often use my computer to do my homework.
3) The radio sat on the table beside the sofa.
4) Roger gave his mother a CD for her birthday.
5) My brother put fresh flowers on the dining room table.
6) Mickey and George played golf this afternoon.
7) We always have a turkey for Thanksgiving dinner.
8) People driving along the road stopped to watch the deer.
9) Kirby Puckett is among the best hitters in baseball.
10) Tom opened a checking account at the bank.

Part B Rewrite these sentences. Capitalize all of the proper nouns.

1) In june we went to disney world in florida.
2) This fall sally plans to take computer basics I and english.
3) One of my favorite books is *robinson crusoe.*
4) My aunt marie lives in the south.
5) On wednesday we visited the empire state building in new york.

 Basic English Grammar

Name Date Period | *Chapter 1 Mastery Test B page 2*

Chapter 1 Mastery Test B, continued

Part C Write the plural form of each of these singular nouns.

1) guess ______	11) man ______
2) ladder ______	12) potato ______
3) county ______	13) calf ______
4) wolf ______	14) party ______
5) path ______	15) mouse ______
6) goose ______	16) navy ______
7) dish ______	17) rodeo ______
8) sheep ______	18) leaf ______
9) body ______	19) series ______
10) moose ______	20) hero ______

Part D Write the possessive form that should appear in each sentence to make it correct.

1) Jack gets one ______ vacation every year. (month's, months')
2) Please give me two ______ worth of stamps. (dollar's, dollars')
3) The ______ desk is full of papers. (teacher's, teachers')
4) "What about the ______ chances?" they asked the coach. (team's, teams')
5) There is the ______ best restaurant. (town's, towns')
6) The ______ grazing stripped the field bare. (sheep's, sheeps')
7) Three ______ lodging is all I need. (night's, nights')
8) ______ Spanish test is tomorrow. (Jane's, Janes')
9) The bookstore offered readings of two ______ works. (writer's, writers')
10) Four ______ petals had opened. (flower's, flowers')

 Basic English Grammar

Chapter 1 Mastery Test B

Chapter 2

Planning Guide

The Pronoun

	Student Text Lesson: Student Pages	Vocabulary	Practice Exercises	Lesson Review
Lesson 1 Personal Pronouns	28-34	✔	✔	34
Lesson 2 Relative Pronouns	35-38	✔	✔	38
Lesson 3 Pronouns That Ask Questions	39-42	✔	✔	42
Lesson 4 Demonstrative Pronouns	43-45	✔	✔	45
Lesson 5 Indefinite Pronouns	46-49	✔	✔	49

Chapter Activities

Teacher's Resource Library

Community Connection 2: Listening for Pronouns

Assessment Options

Student Text

Chapter 2 Review

Teacher's Resource Library

Chapter 2 Mastery Tests A and B

Teaching Strategies							Language Skills			Learning Styles						Teacher's Resource Library		
Reviewing Skills	Teacher Alert	Follow-up Activity	Career Application	Home Application	Global Connection	Community Application	Identification Skills	Writing Skills	Punctuation Skills	Visual/Spatial	Auditory/Verbal	Body/Kinesthetic	Logical/Mathematical	Group Learning	LEP/ESL	Activities	Workbook Activities	Self-Study Guide
28	29-30	34	29		29		✔	✔	✔						30	4-5	6-8	✔
35	36	38					✔	✔	✔				38					✔
39	40	42					✔	✔	✔			41						✔
43		45					✔	✔	✔					44				✔
46	46	51		49		47	✔	✔	✔	47						6	9-10	✔

Chapter at a Glance

(Answer Keys for the Teacher's Resource Library begin on page 330 of this Teacher's Edition.)

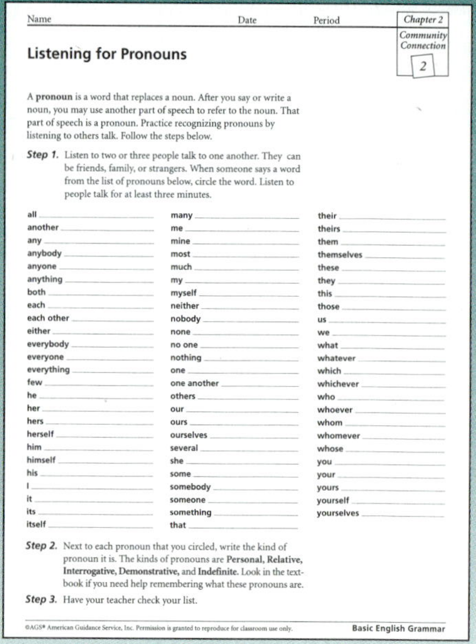

Name Date Period

Chapter 2
Community Connection
2

Listening for Pronouns

A **pronoun** is a word that replaces a noun. After you say or write a noun, you may use another part of speech to refer to the noun. That part of speech is a pronoun. Practice recognizing pronouns by listening to others talk. Follow the steps below.

Step 1. Listen to two or three people talk to one another. They can be friends, family, or strangers. When someone says a word from the list of pronouns below, circle the word. Listen to people talk for at least three minutes.

all ______	many ______	their ______
another ______	me ______	theirs ______
any ______	mine ______	them ______
anybody ______	most ______	themselves ______
anyone ______	much ______	these ______
anything ______	my ______	they ______
both ______	myself ______	this ______
each ______	neither ______	those ______
each other ______	nobody ______	us ______
either ______	none ______	we ______
everybody ______	no one ______	what ______
everyone ______	nothing ______	whatever ______
everything ______	one ______	which ______
few ______	one another ______	whichever ______
he ______	others ______	who ______
her ______	our ______	whoever ______
hers ______	ours ______	whom ______
herself ______	ourselves ______	whomever ______
him ______	several ______	whose ______
himself ______	she ______	you ______
his ______	some ______	your ______
I ______	somebody ______	yours ______
it ______	someone ______	yourself ______
its ______	something ______	yourselves ______
itself ______	that ______	

Step 2. Next to each pronoun that you circled, write the kind of pronoun it is. The kinds of pronouns are **Personal, Relative, Interrogative, Demonstrative,** and **Indefinite.** Look in the textbook if you need help remembering what these pronouns are.

Step 3. Have your teacher check your list.

 Basic English Grammar

Community Connection 2

Chapter 2 The Pronoun

You talk with people every day in school, at work, in the community, and at home. When you do, you often use the person's name. You talk about the things you do and the thoughts you have.

Whenever you speak or write, you use nouns to name the person or thing you are telling about. When you want to refer to that person or thing again, you can repeat the noun, or you can use a pronoun. A pronoun is a word used in place of a noun.

In Chapter 2, you will learn how to recognize and use pronouns. Each lesson in the chapter focuses on different types of pronouns and their correct use in writing and speaking.

Goals for Learning

- To identify pronouns in sentences
- To identify the type of pronoun such as personal, indefinite, relative, and demonstrative
- To identify correct usage of pronouns in sentences

27

Reading Vocabulary

community (5) identify (6)
focus (7) refer (6)

Introducing the Chapter

Ask students to listen very carefully as you pretend to leave a message on the answering machine of your friend Anita. Use the message below or make up one of your own in which you repeat nouns rather than use pronouns.

Hi Anita,

It's Helena [or insert your first name]. How is Anita? What has Anita been doing lately? How is Anita's mother? Helena called to tell you that Helena has two tickets to Saturday's baseball game. The game starts at 2. Does Anita want to go with Helena? Jeff and Chris are coming, too. Jeff and Chris hope Anita can come.

Ask students what was odd about the message, repeating it if necessary. Elicit that the speech was unnatural; that in natural speech, we use pronouns to refer back to people and things mentioned earlier. Then read the message again, using pronouns where appropriate. Explain to students that as they do the activities in Chapter 2, they will learn how pronouns can make speech and writing sound smooth and natural.

SELF-STUDY GUIDE

Name __________

CHAPTER 2: The Pronoun

Goal 2.1 To identify pronouns and personal pronouns in a sentence

Date	Assignment	Score
____	1: Read pages 27-30. Complete Activity A on page 30	____
____	2: Complete Workbook Activities 6-7.	____
____	3: Complete Activities B-C on page 31 and Activity D on page 32.	____
____	4: Complete Workbook Activity 8.	____
____	5: Read page 33. Complete Activity E on page 33.	____
____	6: Complete the Lesson 1 Review, Parts A-B on page 34.	____

Comments:

Goal 2.2 To identify the correct usage of relative pronouns

Date	Assignment	Score
____	7: Read page 35. Complete Activity A on page 35.	____
____	8: Complete Activities B-C on page 36.	____
____	9: Complete Activities D-F on page 37.	____
____	10: Complete the Lesson 2 Review, Parts A-B on page 38.	____

Comments:

Goal 2.3 To identify the correct usage of interrogative pronouns

Date	Assignment	Score
____	11: Read page 39. Complete Activity A on page 39.	____
____	12: Read page 40. Complete Activity B on page 40 and Activity C on page 41.	____
____	13: Complete the Lesson 3 Review, Parts A-B on page 42.	____

Comments:

 Basic English Grammar

SELF-STUDY GUIDE

Name __________

CHAPTER 2 The Pronoun, continued

Goal 2.4 To identify the correct usage of demonstrative pronouns

Date	Assignment	Score
____	14: Read page 43. Complete Activity A on page 43.	____
____	15: Complete Activities B-C on page 44.	____
____	16: Complete the Lesson 4 Review, Parts A-B on page 45.	____

Comments:

Goal 2.5 To identify the correct usage of indefinite pronouns

Date	Assignment	Score
____	17: Read pages 46-47. Complete Activities A-B on page 48.	____
____	18: Complete Workbook Activities 9-10	____
____	19: Complete the Lesson 5 Review, Parts A-B on page 49.	____
____	20: Complete the Chapter 2 Review, Parts A-C on pages 50-51.	____

Comments:

Student's Signature __________ Date ______

Instructor's Signature __________ Date ______

 Basic English Grammar

Chapter 2 Self-Study Guide

Lesson at a Glance

Chapter 2 Lesson 1

Overview This lesson presents personal pronouns, including *-self* pronouns, and explains antecedents.

Objective

- To identify personal pronouns and their antecedents in sentences.

Student Pages 28–34

Teacher's Resource Library

Activities 4–5

Workbook Activities 6–8

Reading Vocabulary

antecedent
distinguish (6)
gender (10)
personal pronoun
pronoun
replace (6)

Teaching Suggestions

Introducing the Lesson

Write this sentence on the board, underlining as shown: *Paula drove Mike and Joe to the mall.* Ask students to say the same sentence using different words in place of the underlined words. The words should not change the meaning of the sentence. Help students replace the underlined words with pronouns. Write students' sentences on the board, underlining the pronouns. Point out that the underlined words in the new sentences take the place of the underlined words—*Paula* and *Mike and Joe*—in the original sentence.

Reviewing Skills

As a review, ask students to provide a definition of a noun and to give examples.

Lesson 1 Personal Pronouns

Pronoun
A part of speech that takes the place of a noun.

A **pronoun** is a word that replaces a noun. Without pronouns, you would have to repeat the same nouns over and over again.

EXAMPLE Susan said that Susan was going to call Susan's mother.
Susan said that **she** was going to call **her** mother.

Antecedent
The noun that a pronoun replaces.

Every pronoun has an **antecedent**. The antecedent is the noun to which the pronoun refers. The pronoun must agree with the antecedent in number and gender.

EXAMPLE **Ellis** is a senior.
He is on the track team.
(**Ellis** is the antecedent for the pronoun **he**.)

Personal pronoun
A pronoun that takes the place of a noun and that refers to a person or object.

Personal pronouns distinguish among the speaker, the person spoken to, and the person or thing spoken about.

A first person pronoun refers to the speaker.

EXAMPLE **I** am late.

A second person pronoun refers to the person spoken to.

EXAMPLE **You** are late.

A third person pronoun refers to the person or thing spoken about.

EXAMPLE **He** is late.

Personal pronouns express number. They can be singular or plural.

EXAMPLES

Singular (one)	Plural (more than one)
I am late.	**We** are late.
She is leaving.	**They** are leaving.

Personal pronouns express gender. The three genders are *masculine* (male), *feminine* (female), and *neuter* (those that are neither masculine nor feminine).

EXAMPLES

Masculine:	**He** is tall.
Feminine:	**She** is my friend.
Neuter:	**It** is a notebook.

Nominative pronoun
A pronoun used as the subject of a sentence.

Objective pronoun
A pronoun used as the object of a sentence.

Possessive pronoun
A pronoun that shows ownership or relationship.

Personal pronouns express case. The case reflects the way the pronoun is used in a sentence.

A pronoun may be used in the **nominative** case as the subject of the sentence, in the **objective** case as an object in the sentence, or in the **possessive** case to show ownership.

EXAMPLES

Nominative:	**He** is in my Spanish class. (subject)
Objective:	I gave it to **him**. (object of the preposition *to*)
Possessive:	That book is **hers**.

Reading Vocabulary

feminine (7)
masculine (7)
neuter (11)
nominative pronoun
object (4)
objective pronoun
ownership (7)
plural (6)
possessive pronoun
singular (8)
subject (5)

Teacher Alert

Be sure students understand the nominative, objective, and possessive cases before moving on in the lesson.

Global Connection

In some languages, nouns are either masculine or feminine. The gender of the word is often indicated by the word's ending or by the form of the article or adjective that describes it. Pronouns used to replace these nouns are either masculine or feminine. Invite students who speak a second language to share pronouns in that language and give examples of their use in sentences.

Application

Career Connection
Point out to students that in the past some English words that named people in the work force were masculine even when they referred to women; for example, *fireman* and *mailman*. Today these words have been replaced by genderless terms, such as *firefighter* and *letter carrier*.

Reading Vocabulary

chart (5) item (6)

Teacher Alert

Before you introduce the activity, review the elements of a chart and how to read a chart. Point out the chart title and column headings and explain their purpose. Demonstrate how to find information in a chart by pointing to an item in the first column and tracing your finger across the row.

Presenting Activity A

After reading the directions together, invite volunteers to demonstrate how to find the activity example answers in the chart.

Activity A Answers

1) they **2)** it **3)** our/ours **4)** you **5)** their/theirs **6)** me **7)** your/yours **8)** you

Learning Styles

LEP/ESL

Ask students for whom English is a second language to duplicate on the board the boxed set of words on page 30. Ask them to print the personal pronouns from their primary language next to the English ones. One by one, have the students say aloud a simple sentence using an English personal pronoun. Then have them repeat the sentence using the non-English personal pronoun.

Personal Pronouns

	Nominative	Objective	Possessive
Singular			
First person	I	me	my, mine
Second person	you	you	your, yours
Third person	he, she it	him, her it	his, her, hers its
Plural			
First person	we	us	our, ours
Second person	you	you	your, yours
Third person	they	them	their, theirs

Activity A Write a pronoun for each numbered item on your paper. Use the chart above for help.

Examples first person, singular, nominative — **I**
second person, plural, possessive — **your, yours**
third person, singular, objective, masculine — **him**

1) third person, plural, nominative

2) third person, singular, objective, neuter

3) first person, plural, possessive

4) second person, singular, objective

5) third person, plural, possessive

6) first person, singular, objective

7) second person, singular, possessive

8) second person, plural, nominative

Name Date Period *Chapter 2 Activity 4*

Singular and Plural Pronouns

A pronoun replaces a noun. It takes a plural pronoun to replace a plural noun. The word *you* can be singular or plural.

Singular pronouns — I, he, she, it, me, you, him, her
Plural pronouns — we, they, them, you, our, their

Directions: Find all the pronouns. Label them *S* for singular and *P* for plural. If a pronoun can be either singular or plural, write both labels.

Examples
She (S) was going to the party with her (S) friends.
They (P) promised to pick her (S) up at eight o'clock.
Where did you (S,P) put your (S,P) shoes?

1) Our family went to Tennessee last spring.
2) Amy's friends took her to the airport to say good-bye
3) We traveled by plane to Nashville.
4) There we saw the Grand Ole Opry.
5) The singers and musicians tried their best to entertain us.
6) We sat in the upper balcony.
7) Although we couldn't see their faces, we could hear them singing.
8) Many of them played fiddles and guitars.
9) Their instruments are very valuable.
10) The audience sat quietly in their seats.
11) They applauded loudly when the songs were over.
12) They all loved country music. You might like it, too.
13) After the show, we all left our seats and went back to our bus.
14) The bus took us back to the hotel at the end of the day.

 Basic English Grammar

Activity 4

Name Date Period *Chapter 2 Activity 5*

Personal Pronouns

	Nominative	Objective	Possessive
Singular			
First person	I	me	my, mine
Second person	you	you	your, yours
Third person	he, she, it	him, her, it	his, her, hers, its
Plural			
First person	we	us	our, ours
Second person	you	you	your, yours
Third person	they	them	their, theirs

Directions: Rewrite each sentence below. Replace the words in bold print with the correct pronouns from the personal pronoun chart above.

1) "Would **Jennifer** pass the butter?" asked Mickey.
2) Ray and Alicia celebrated **Ray and Alicia's** fiftieth wedding anniversary.
3) The puppy buried **the puppy's** bone in the backyard.
4) Tracy couldn't find her coat. "Have you seen **the coat**?" **Tracy** asked.
5) **Samantha and her sister** worked together for years.
6) "**Mike and I** live in that house," said Kevin.
7) **Bill and Brenda** visited **Beth and Jeffrey** in Tennessee last month.
8) "Where on earth is **the newspaper**?" asked Mary.

 Basic English Grammar

Activity 5

Activity B Rewrite each of these sentences on your paper. Replace the words in bold with a pronoun.

Example I saw **Mary** yesterday.
I saw **her** yesterday.

1) I have **a hammer and a saw.**

2) **The gloves** are lost.

3) **An airplane** is flying overhead.

4) I wrote a letter to **George**.

5) **Anita's** house is in the country.

6) "That book is **mine**," Katie said.

7) "That is **our** room," Katie said.

8) "**Katie** is late," Laura said.

9) **Lian and I** are going to the dance.

Activity C Rewrite each of these sentences on your paper. Replace the words in bold with a pronoun.

Example At the end of the first day of school, **Gina** was tired.
At the end of the first day of school, **she** was tired.

1) **Gina and Karen** waited for the school bus.

2) "The teacher gave **Gina** homework," Gina said.

3) Gina decided to do **homework** as soon as she got home.

4) **Gina's** homework was not difficult.

5) The teacher told **Gina** to write a paragraph in Spanish.

6) "What is the paragraph about?" **Karen** asked.

7) "What I did on **Gina**'s vacation, of course!" Gina laughed.

■ Presenting Activity B

Ask a volunteer to explain why *her* was used to replace *Mary* in the activity example. Then do the first two items orally with the class before having students complete the activity independently.

Activity B Answers

1) them 2) They 3) It
4) him 5) Her 6) hers
7) their 8) She 9) We

■ Presenting Activity C

Have a volunteer explain why *she* was used to replace *Gina* in the activity example. Then do the first two items orally with the class before having students complete the activity independently.

Activity C Answers

1) They 2) me 3) it 4) Her
5) her 6) she 7) my

Name Date Period *Chapter 2 Workbook Activity 6*

Singular and Plural Pronouns

Directions: Find all the pronouns. Label them **S** for singular or **P** for plural. If a pronoun can be either singular of plural, write both labels.

Examples
P P
We are going to get our grades.
S,P S,P
Where did you put your socks?

1) They took a bus to the circus.
2) Our classroom is much too hot.
3) Those are not my favorite pictures.
4) My cousin has his own horse.
5) We shall soon arrive.
6) Do you know how to find your way?
7) Does he know where we can find them?
8) Our team won an important game today.
9) David knows where the bikes are because he saw them.
10) They go to a different school from ours.
11) Is this one of your hats?
12) "That is my classroom," he said.
13) Somebody told her where to go.
14) Lisa saw us at the picnic.
15) He told the secret to nobody.
16) All of the trucks were noisy.
17) Nancy helped herself to some pizza.
18) My teacher told us the answer when we had finished the test.
19) We mended the fence ourselves.
20) Carlos told her where to find the kitchen.

 Basic English Grammar

Workbook Activity 6

Name Date Period *Chapter 2 Workbook Activity 7*

Selecting the Correct Pronoun

Directions: Rewrite each sentence below. Replace the underlined words with the correct pronouns from the personal pronoun chart.

PERSONAL PRONOUNS

	Nominative	Objective	Possessive
Singular			
First person	I	me	my, mine
Second person	you	you	your, yours
Third person	he, she, it	him, her, it	his, her, hers, its
Plural			
First person	we	us	our, ours
Second person	you	you	your, yours
Third person	they	them	their, theirs

1) "May Fred have a sandwich?" Fred asked.
2) "Here are Janet's books," said Janet. "Where are Ted's?" Janet said to Ted.
3) "I want Ted to help," Janet said to Ted.
4) I put my papers right here. Have you seen my papers?
5) "Ted invited Fred for dinner," Ted said to Janet.
6) "Fred and I are hungry," said Ted.
7) "This is Ted's chair; that one is Janet's," said Ted.
8) "Ted and Janet are happy that you could have dinner with Ted and Janet," said Janet.

 Basic English Grammar

Workbook Activity 7

Reading Vocabulary

emphasis (8) | *-self* pronoun
indicate (6)

■ Presenting Activity D

Help students recall the definition of *antecedent.* Have them refer back to page 28 if necessary. Then invite a volunteer to explain the example and tell why *their* was used to refer back to *Corey and Beth* instead of *his* or *her.*

Activity D Answers

1) her—Jennifer
2) She—Jennifer
3) They—Jennifer and Michelle
   them—Jennifer and Michelle
4) they—kids
5) he—Luís
6) I—Jennifer
7) You—Jennifer
   my—Michelle
   We—Jennifer and Michelle
8) me—Jennifer
9) I—Jennifer
   your—Michelle
   you—Michelle
10) it—note
11) She—mother
   you—Michelle
   your—Michelle
12) We—Jennifer and Michelle
   I—Michelle
   him—brother

Activity D Write the pronoun or pronouns in each of these sentences on your paper. Beside each pronoun, write its antecedent.

Example Finally **Corey and Beth** got on **their** bus.
their *(personal pronoun)* **Corey and Beth** *(antecedent)*

1) Jennifer had her Spanish book.
2) She and Michelle talked all the way home.
3) They laughed about a joke Luís had told them.
4) "The kids at school took a vote. They decided Luís tells the best jokes," Jennifer said.
5) "He is a funny person!" Michelle agreed.
6) "I am hungry," Jennifer said.
7) "You can stop by my house," Michelle said. "We can fix a hamburger."
8) "A hamburger sounds very good to me," Jennifer said.
9) "I think your mother left you a note," Jennifer said.
10) Michelle asked, "What does it say?"
11) "She wants you to pick up your brother from day care," Jennifer replied.
12) "We can eat our hamburgers first. Then I will go get him," Michelle said.

-Self pronoun
A pronoun that ends with -self *and indicates action done to or by another pronoun or a noun in the sentence.* -Self *pronouns are also used to show emphasis.*

*-**Self*** **pronouns** refer to another pronoun or a noun. They always come after the noun or pronoun to which they refer. Sometimes *-self* pronouns are used to show emphasis.

EXAMPLES

I hurt **myself**. (indicates action done to the pronoun *I*)

The child played by **herself.** (indicates action done by the noun *child*)

Luis ate the whole pie **himself**. (shows emphasis)

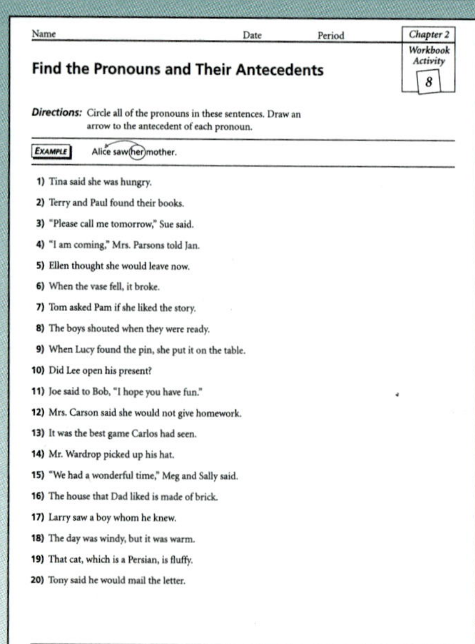

Name Date Period | *Chapter 2* *Workbook Activity* 8

Find the Pronouns and Their Antecedents

Directions: Circle all of the pronouns in these sentences. Draw an arrow to the antecedent of each pronoun.

EXAMPLE Alice saw her mother.

1) Tina said she was hungry.
2) Terry and Paul found their books.
3) "Please call me tomorrow," Sue said.
4) "I am coming," Mrs. Parsons told Jan.
5) Ellen thought she would leave now.
6) When the vase fell, it broke.
7) Tom asked Pam if she liked the story.
8) The boys shouted when they were ready.
9) When Lucy found the pin, she put it on the table.
10) Did Lee open his present?
11) Joe said to Bob, "I hope you have fun."
12) Mrs. Carson said she would not give homework.
13) It was the best game Carlos had seen.
14) Mr. Wardrop picked up his hat.
15) "We had a wonderful time," Meg and Sally said.
16) The house that Dad liked is made of brick.
17) Larry saw a boy whom he knew.
18) The day was windy, but it was warm.
19) That cat, which is a Persian, is fluffy.
20) Tony said he would mail the letter.

 Basic English Grammar

Workbook Activity 8

32 *Chapter 2 The Pronoun*

-Self Pronouns		
	Singular	**Plural**
First person	myself	ourselves
Second person	yourself	yourselves
Third person	himself, herself, itself	themselves

Activity E Write the *-self* pronouns in these sentences on your paper. Beside each *-self* pronoun, write *singular* or *plural.*

Example Janet studied her math by herself.
herself—singular

1) The glass fell off the shelf by itself.

2) Ema and Janet cleaned the kitchen themselves.

3) I myself prefer spicy food.

4) We cooked dinner by ourselves.

5) Try to answer the question by yourself.

6) The baby sat up by himself.

7) Clean up this mess by yourselves.

8) He went to the movies by himself.

9) She whispered something to herself.

Reading Vocabulary

prefer (6) spicy (5)

■ Presenting Activity E

Before students begin this activity, have them study the *-self* pronouns in the chart. Then have partners test each other by asking questions such as, "What are the third person, singular *-self* pronouns?"

Activity E Answers

1) itself—singular
2) themselves—plural
3) myself—singular
4) ourselves—plural
5) yourself—singular
6) himself—singular
7) yourselves—plural
8) himself—singular
9) herself—singular

Reading Vocabulary

principal (5) senior (6)
science (5)

Part A Answers

1) It—day
2) his—principal
3) her—Katie
4) himself—Pete
5) their—students
6) They—Lilly and Pete
7) herself—Rosa

Part B Answers

1) They—Laura and Katie
2) She—Ms. Turner
3) him—James Melcher
4) it—phone number
5) me—Katie
6) he—James

Follow-up Activity

Have students select a short passage from a literature text or a magazine article. Have the students identify all the personal pronouns and their antecedents in the passage.

Lesson 1 Review

Part A Write the personal pronouns in these sentences on your paper. Beside each personal pronoun, write its antecedent.

1) The first day of school was over. It had been very pleasant.
2) The principal gave his usual welcome-back speech.
3) Katie enjoyed her new classes.
4) Pete was humming to himself in the halls.
5) The students enjoyed seeing their old friends.
6) Lilly and Pete are in the same math class. They plan to study together.
7) Rosa walked home by herself after school.

Part B Some of the pronouns in these sentences are in bold. Write the bold pronoun on your paper. Beside each pronoun, write the noun or nouns that the pronoun has replaced.

1) Laura and Katie are both seniors. **They** are old friends.
2) Ms. Turner is the homeroom teacher. **She** also teaches science.
3) James Melcher is in the class. Katie has known **him** for years.
4) "Can I have your phone number?" James asked Katie. "Here **it** is," Katie said.
5) "Please call **me** this evening," Katie said.
6) She wondered if **he** would call.

34 *Chapter 2 The Pronoun*

Lesson 2 Relative Pronouns

Relative pronouns
The pronouns who, whom, whose, which, that, what, whoever, whomever, whichever, *and* whatever.

The **relative pronouns** are *who, whom, whose, which, that,* and *what.* Like personal pronouns, relative pronouns must agree with their antecedents.

Who, whom, and *whose* refer to people.

Which and *what* refer to things.

That refers to people or things.

The compound relative pronouns are *whoever, whomever, whichever,* and *whatever.* The antecedent of a compound relative pronoun may be understood by the listener or reader.

EXAMPLES

Black shoes and brown shoes are on sale. I'll choose **whichever** is the best price. (The antecedent of *whichever* is *black shoes* or *brown shoes.*)

Whoever wants to go swimming should come now. (The antecedent of **whoever** is understood.)

Activity A Write these sentences on your paper. Circle the relative pronouns.

1) The car that Alex bought is blue and white.

2) Alex wanted a car that had four doors.

3) Alex's friend, who is a mechanic, inspected the car.

4) The mechanic gave him a written report, which Alex appreciated.

5) Alex also had a friend whose father owned a garage.

Lesson at a Glance

Chapter 2 Lesson 2

Overview This lesson presents relative pronouns, including compound relative pronouns.

Objective

- To identify relative pronouns and their antecedents in sentences.

Student Pages 35–38

Reading Vocabulary

appreciate (5)
compound (6)
inspect (5)
mechanic (6)
relative pronoun

Teaching Suggestions

Introducing the Lesson
Discuss the definition of relative pronouns. Be sure students understand the distinction between relative pronouns that refer to people and those that refer to things. Emphasize that *that* can refer to people or things.

Reviewing Skills Ask students to tell what they have learned about pronouns so far. Elicit a definition of a *pronoun.* Then discuss the purpose of pronouns in writing and speaking and how they are used to make ideas sound more natural.

Presenting Activity A
Before having students complete this activity, have them work together to make a chart of relative pronouns similar to the charts on pages 30 and 33. Help students create appropriate heads for their chart. Invite a volunteer to write the chart on the board.

Activity A Answers
1) that 2) that 3) who 4) which 5) whose

Reading Vocabulary

actress (6) screwdriver (5)
antique (6)

■ Presenting Activity B

Before having students complete the activity independently, review the definition of *antecedent.* Then have a volunteer read the activity example and explain the answers given.

Activity B Answers

1) who—man 2) whom—man
3) that—cars 4) that—car
5) that—screwdriver

■ Presenting Activity C

Before students complete this activity, ask them to name the relative pronouns and tell which ones refer to people, which ones refer to things, and which one can be used to refer to both people and things.

Activity C Answers

1) whatever 2) who 3) which
4) whatever 5) that 6) whose
7) Whoever 8) what 9) who
10) that

Teacher Alert

Writers often use *that* instead of *which* to introduce an essential clause, or a clause that is necessary to the meaning of the sentence. However, students should be aware that *which* is still correct.

Activity B The relative pronouns in these sentences are in bold. Write each relative pronoun on your paper. Beside each relative pronoun, write its antecedent.

Example The car **that** Alex bought is blue and white.
that (*relative pronoun*) **car** (*antecedent*)

1) The man **who** owned the garage sold Alex new tires.

2) He is the man **whom** I met last week.

3) Andy likes cars **that** have four-wheel drive.

4) The mechanic has a car **that** is an antique.

5) Did you see the screwdriver **that** I was using?

Activity C Find the relative pronouns in these sentences. Write them on your paper.

1) Do whatever you think should be done.

2) My sister, who wants to be an actress, tried out for the school play.

3) My dog, which is a hound, barks at everyone.

4) You may have whatever you want for dinner.

5) Here are the shoes that I bought.

6) Andy has a friend whose cousin caught a forty-pound fish.

7) Whoever wants to go first should come upstairs now.

8) I found what I wanted.

9) I know the man who won the lottery.

10) Eleni rented the video that you wanted to see.

Activity D Write the pronouns in the list below on your paper.

1) himself	**8)** bus	**15)** friend
2) whoever	**9)** lady	**16)** you
3) car	**10)** Ms. Woo	**17)** whatever
4) Andy	**11)** I	**18)** themselves
5) which	**12)** what	**19)** its
6) that	**13)** whom	**20)** happiness
7) he	**14)** school	**21)** she

Activity E Make two columns on your paper. Write *Personal Pronouns* at the top of the first column. Write *Relative Pronouns* at the top of the second column. Then write the pronouns below in the correct column.

1) we	**8)** you	**15)** whom
2) that	**9)** who	**16)** whichever
3) which	**10)** ours	**17)** that
4) what	**11)** them	**18)** themselves
5) mine	**12)** whose	**19)** whoever
6) its	**13)** us	**20)** whatever
7) I	**14)** itself	**21)** he

Activity F Write the pronoun that should appear in each sentence to make it correct.

1) There are the shoes (who, that) I want.

2) My dog, (who, which) is still a puppy, eats anything.

3) There is the lady (whom, what) I met last week.

4) I like a house (who, that) has a big yard.

Reading Vocabulary

column (5)

■ Presenting Activity D

Ask students to name the types of pronouns they have learned and to give two examples of each type.

Activity D Answers

Only pronouns listed
1) himself **2)** whoever **5)** which **6)** that **7)** he **11)** I **12)** what **13)** whom **16)** you **17)** whatever **18)** themselves **19)** its **21)** she

■ Presenting Activity E

Remind students of the difference between personal and possessive pronouns. Before students begin Active E, be sure they understand that they are to create two columns on their paper. Suggest that students work with a partner to complete the activity.

Activity E Answers

Personal Pronouns	Relative Pronouns
1) we	**2)** that
5) mine	**3)** which
6) its	**4)** what
7) I	**9)** who
8) you	**12)** whose
10) ours	**15)** whom
11) them	**16)** whichever
13) us	**17)** that
14) itself	**19)** whoever
18) themselves	**20)** whatever
21) he	

■ Presenting Activity F

Suggest that students try each pronoun in parentheses in the sentence to see which one sounds most correct before they write their answers.

Activity F Answers

1) that **2)** which **3)** whom **4)** that

Reading Vocabulary

include (5) secretary (5)
jeans (6) steak (5)

Part A Answers

1) who—mechanic
2) Whoever—Andy or Frank
3) whatever—video
4) whom—man
5) whichever—steak or chicken
6) whose—friend
7) that—jeans
8) that—ring
9) that—the gift
10) who—Theo

Part B Answers

1) Who 2) that 3) that
4) who 5) that

Follow-up Activity

Have students use the list of words in Lesson 2, Activities D and E in original sentences.

Learning Styles

Logical/Mathematical
Challenge the class to create a set of icons for the six relative pronouns *who, whom, whose, which, what,* and *that.* First, invite a student to print them in alphabetical order on the board. Then divide the class into six groups. Assign a relative pronoun to each group. Encourage each group to create an icon or symbol that will help the class remember the pronoun. Afterward, have a volunteer make a poster of the six icons and post it in the classroom for ready reference.

Lesson 2 Review

Part A Write the relative pronouns in these sentences on your paper. Include the compound relative pronouns. Beside the pronoun, write its antecedent.

Example I like food that is very spicy.
that *(relative pronoun)* **food** *(antecedent)*

1) The mechanic who checked Alex's car did a good job.
2) Alex said to Andy and Frank, "Whoever wants to go for a ride should come now."
3) At the video store, choose whatever you would like to see.
4) There is the man whom I met in Florida.
5) We have steak and chicken. You may have whichever you prefer.
6) Will had a friend whose sister was in the play.
7) Did you see the jeans that I was wearing?
8) Deena has a ring that belonged to her grandmother.
9) I got the gift that I wanted for my birthday.
10) Theo, who is my cousin, works at the mall.

Part B Write the pronoun that should appear in each sentence to make it correct.

1) (Who, What) is that man?
2) The skateboard (who, that) Hank bought was expensive.
3) I need a chair (who, that) has a high back.
4) My sister, (who, that) is a secretary, just got a raise.
5) Did you see the pen (who, that) I was using?

38 *Chapter 2 The Pronoun*

Lesson 3 Pronouns That Ask Questions

Interrogative pronouns

Pronouns that introduce questions: who, whom, which, what, *and* whose.

An **interrogative pronoun** introduces a question. These pronouns are *who, whom, which, what,* and *whose.*

EXAMPLES

Who is planning the dance?
Whom did you ask to the dance?
Which shoes did Katie buy?
What pages are we to read for homework?
Whose book is on the table?

Who, whom, which, what, and *whose* are interrogative pronouns only when they ask a question.

EXAMPLES

Interrogative:	**Who** is going with Andy to the dance?
Relative:	Andy asked a girl **who** is in his class.

Activity A Some pronouns in these sentences are in bold. Write them on your paper. Beside each pronoun, write whether it is *interrogative* or *relative.*

1) **Which** season of the year do you like best?
2) **What** is the name of your book?
3) Tell me the people **who** are going to the dance.
4) Do you know **what** the answer is?
5) **Who** is your favorite singer?
6) **Whom** do you like the most?
7) He is the man **whose** billfold I found.

Lesson at a Glance

Chapter 2 Lesson 3

Overview This lesson presents interrogative pronouns and explains the difference between the use of interrogative and relative pronouns.

Objective

- To identify interrogative pronouns in sentences.

Student Pages 39–42

Reading Vocabulary

interrogative pronouns

Teaching Suggestions

- **Introducing the Lesson** Discuss the meaning of *interrogative.* Explain that an interrogative sentence asks a question and ends in a question mark. Ask students for examples of interrogative sentences.

- **Reviewing Skills** Remind students of the relative pronouns *who, whom, which, what, whose,* and *that.* Ask students to use each of these relative pronouns in a sentence and identify its antecedent.

- **Presenting Activity A** Before students begin the activity, have them point out the sentences that ask questions.

Activity A Answers

1) Which—interrogative
2) What—interrogative
3) who—relative
4) what—relative
5) Who—interrogative
6) Whom—interrogative
7) whose—relative

Reading Vocabulary

definite (6)   series (5)

■ **Presenting Activity B** Read aloud the first item and discuss the answer choices. Ask students which pronoun belongs in the sentence and why. Students can then complete the activity on their own.

Activity B Answers

1) Which 2) What 3) Who
4) Whose 5) Whom 6) Who
7) What

Teacher Alert

People often confuse the use of *who* and *whom*. You may wish to point out that if students are unsure of whether to use *who* or *whom*, they can change the question to a statement. If the sentence already has a subject, *whom* should be used; for example, "(Who, Whom) did you see on the bus?" could be changed to "You did see whom on the bus."

Interrogative pronouns must agree with their antecedents. The antecedents are the answers to the questions that the interrogative pronouns ask.

Use *who, whom,* or *whose* when the answer to the question is a person or people.

Examples
Who is your English teacher?
Whom did you see on the bus?
Whose idea was that?

Use *what* when the answer to the question is a thing, place, or idea.

Examples
What is the name of your street?
What are your answers to the first three questions?

Use *which* when the answer to the question is a choice between two or more definite people or things.

Examples
Which boy will win the race?
Which newspaper do you read?

Activity B Write the pronoun that should appear in each sentence to make it correct.

1) (Which, What) of these fish is larger?
2) (Which, What) do you want for dinner?
3) (Who, What) will win the World Series?
4) (Who, Whose) mother teaches at our school?
5) (Whom, Whose) did Kevin ask to the dance?
6) (Who, Which) plays third base for the team?
7) (Who, What) is the world's tallest building?

Activity C Make two columns on your paper. Write *Interrogative Pronouns* at the top of the first column. Write *Relative Pronouns* at the top of the second column. Then find the interrogative and relative pronouns in the sentences below. Write them in the correct column.

Example Which of the teams that you played on was the best?

Interrogative Pronouns	*Relative Pronouns*
Which	**that**

1) Alex has a friend whose uncle lives in Canada.
2) Name all of the states that you have visited.
3) What is the name of your book?
4) Choose the book that you want.
5) Tell me which book you like best.
6) Who is the coach of your baseball team?
7) Which tree is taller?
8) What is your favorite subject in school?
9) Do whatever you think is right.
10) Which of the books is the one that the author signed?

Reading Vocabulary

author (6)

■ Presenting Activity C

You may wish to have students do this activity as a group. Ask for a volunteer to make the columns and write the answers on the board.

Activity C Answers

Interrogative Pronouns	Relative Pronouns
3) What	1) whose
6) Who	2) that
7) Which	4) that
8) What	5) which
10) Which	9) whatever
	10) that

Learning Styles

Body/Kinesthetic

Invite partners to use their bodies to present a "snapshot" of something. (For example, two students might pose silently in front of the room as if they are riding a bike together. Or they might stand silently as if one is singing into a microphone and the other is playing a guitar.) After each set of partners "poses," have the class use the five interrogative pronouns—*who, whom, which, what,* and *whose*—to ask the partners questions about their snapshot. Challenge the class to use all five pronouns to ask questions of each set of partners.

Reading Vocabulary

Atlantic	Pacific
mall	theater (5)

Part A Answers

1) Which **2)** Who **3)** What
4) Whose **5)** Whom

Part B Answers

1) It—personal
what—relative
they—personal
2) What—interrogative
3) Whatever—relative
me—personal
4) Which—interrogative
we—personal
5) that—relative
6) Who—interrogative
us—personal
7) I—personal
that—relative
I—personal
8) which—relative
he—personal
9) What—interrogative
it—personal
I—personal
that—relative
I—personal
her—personal
10) Whomever—relative
you—personal
it—personal

Follow-up Activity

Have students write sentences using the interrogative pronouns *who, which,* or *what.* Invite students to read their sentences aloud. Ask the class to identify the interrogative pronoun in each sentence.

Lesson 3 Review

Part A Write the interrogative pronouns in these sentences on your paper.

1) Which ocean do you live closest to, Atlantic or Pacific?
2) Who wrote that book?
3) What country does Queen Elizabeth rule?
4) Whose jacket is on the chair?
5) Whom did you see at the mall?

Part B Write the pronouns in these sentences on your paper. Beside each pronoun, write whether it is *personal, relative,* or *interrogative.*

Example What is the movie that you saw yesterday?

What — interrogative
that — relative
you — personal

1) It was Friday night. Alex and Andy talked about what they would like to do.
2) "What is playing at the movies?" Alex asked.
3) "Whatever is playing is okay with me," Andy said.
4) "Which theater should we go to?" Alex asked.
5) "The theater that has the best prices," Andy joked.
6) "Who else might like to go with us?" Alex asked.
7) "I think that I will ask Katie," Andy answered.
8) Alex thought for a moment about which girl he could ask.
9) "What is the name of Katie's friend? Is it Laura? I think that I will ask her," Alex decided.
10) "Whomever you decide to ask, make it quick. The movie starts soon," Andy said.

Lesson 4 Demonstrative Pronouns

Demonstrative pronouns
Pronouns that point to nouns: this, these, that, *and* those.

Demonstrative pronouns refer to nouns. *This* and *that* are used with singular nouns. *These* and *those* are used with plural nouns.

EXAMPLES

Singular:	**This** is my book.
Plural:	**These** are my books.
Singular:	**That** is an expensive house.
Plural:	**Those** are expensive houses.

This and *these* point out persons and things that are close. *That* and *those* point out persons and things that are farther away.

EXAMPLES **This** is my house. **That** is my house.

Activity A Write these sentences on your paper. Circle the demonstrative pronouns.

1) Is that the movie you saw?

2) Those are new socks.

3) These are the pictures from my vacation.

4) Hang that up in the closet, please.

5) This is my neighbor, Mrs. Loomis.

6) Those are beautiful flowers.

7) Are these your favorite colors?

8) This is our neighbor's new puppy.

9) That is my uncle's new car.

10) Is this the book you wanted?

Lesson at a Glance

Chapter 2 Lesson 4

Overview This lesson presents demonstrative pronouns.

Objectives

- To have students identify demonstrative pronouns in sentences.
- To distinguish between personal, relative, interrogative, or demonstrative pronouns.

Student Pages 43–45

Reading Vocabulary

demonstrative pronouns

Teaching Suggestions

Introducing the Lesson

Explain that the word *demonstrative* comes from *demonstrate* which means "to explain" or "to make clear." Explain that demonstrative pronouns make ideas clear by pointing out exactly which person or object is being discussed.

Reviewing Skills

Invite students to recall what they have learned about the different kinds of pronouns. Have them use the different kinds of pronouns (personal, relative, interrogative) in sentences.

Presenting Activity A

Before having students complete the activity on their own, write the first item on the board. Ask students to read the sentence aloud and identify the demonstrative pronoun. Invite a volunteer to come to the board and circle the demonstrative pronoun. After students complete the activity, ask them to read their answers and tell which nouns in the sentences the demonstrative pronouns are explaining or pointing out.

Activity A Answers

1) that **2)** Those **3)** These **4)** that **5)** This **6)** Those **7)** these **8)** This **9)** That **10)** this

■ Presenting Activity B

Suggest that students try each pronoun in parentheses in the sentence to see which one sounds most correct before they write their answers. After the activity, invite students to read the sentences with the answers in place. Have them explain how they made their choice.

Activity B Answers

1) that **2)** This **3)** Those **4)** those **5)** This **6)** That **7)** These **8)** that **9)** that **10)** These

■ Presenting Activity C

Before having students complete the activity independently, invite volunteers to give an oral example sentence for each pronoun. You might challenge students to use the pronouns in a four-sentence paragraph.

Activity C Answers

Sentences will vary. Check that *that* is used as a demonstrative pronoun and not as a relative pronoun.

Learning Styles

Interpersonal/ Group Learning

Divide the class into groups of four. Invite each group to create a short story using the four demonstrative pronouns—*this, that, these,* and *those.* Then ask each group to read its story to the class. As each group reads, have the rest of the students raise their hands when they hear one of the demonstrative pronouns.

Activity B Write the pronoun that should appear in each sentence to make it correct.

1) Was (this, that) a shooting star I saw?

2) (This, These) is my house.

3) Look across the street. (These, Those) are new houses.

4) Are (that, those) the people who just moved in?

5) "(This, Those) just came for you," Mrs. Thomas said as she handed Kate a big package.

6) (That, Those) is my best friend.

7) Tom bought two new CDs. "(These, That) are really great!" he said to Jamal.

8) A car went speeding down the street. "Did you see (this, that)?" asked Amanda.

9) "I made fruit salad for dessert," said Aunt Tina. "Do you like (that, those)?"

10) "(These, That) are my favorite jeans," Zach said to Marco.

Activity C Write a sentence using each of the demonstrative pronouns.

1) this

2) that

3) these

4) those

44 *Chapter 2 The Pronoun*

Lesson 4 Review

Part A Write the demonstrative pronouns in these sentences on your paper.

1) Do you think Nicole would like these?
2) Those are exactly alike.
3) Pick that up, please.
4) These are very beautiful poems.
5) Is this yours?
6) Did you see that?
7) Tim gave me this.
8) Does that belong to Anna?
9) This is Sal's house.
10) Those are friends of Tyrone.

Part B Write the pronouns in these sentences on your paper. Beside each pronoun, write whether it is *personal, relative, interrogative,* or *demonstrative.*

Example "Who said that?" Michael asked.
Who — interrogative **that — demonstrative**

1) Alex works at a store that sells men's clothes.
2) "Which evenings am I working?" he asked.
3) "Whichever you want," said his boss, Mr. Jackson.
4) Alex decided on the hours that he wanted.
5) "What department am I in tonight?" Alex asked.
6) "Go to the stockroom and help them with inventory."
7) Alex asked the people who were in the stockroom what he should do first.
8) "You can start by counting those," said the woman who was in charge.

Reading Vocabulary

inventory (8) stockroom
poem (5)

Part A Answers

1) these 2) Those 3) that
4) These 5) this 6) that
7) this 8) that 9) This
10) Those

Part B Answers

1) that—relative
2) Which—interrogative
I—personal
he—personal
3) Whichever—relative
you—personal
his—personal
4) that—relative
he—personal
5) What—interrogative
I—personal
6) them—personal
7) who—relative
what—relative
he—personal
8) You—personal
those—demonstrative
who—relative

Follow-up Activity

Have students work cooperatively to create a bulletin board display of the different types of pronouns.

Lesson at a Glance

Chapter 2 Lesson 5

Overview This lesson presents indefinite pronouns and explains agreement of verbs and indefinite pronouns in sentences.

Objective

- To identify and use indefinite pronouns correctly in sentences.

Student Pages 46–49

Teacher's Resource Library

Activity 6

Workbook Activities 9–10

Reading Vocabulary

confuse (5)
indefinite pronoun (8)

Teaching Suggestions

Introducing the Lesson

Discuss the meaning of *indefinite.* Have students read aloud the lists of singular and plural indefinite pronouns and those that can be both. Be sure students understand the concept of subject-verb agreement and pronoun-pronoun agreement before going on to any of the activities in the lesson.

Reviewing Skills

As a review of the concept of singular and plural, have students make a list of five singular and five plural nouns. Then have them use the words as subjects in sentences, noting the subject-verb agreement in each sentence.

Teacher Alert

Subject-verb agreement and pronoun-pronoun agreement with indefinite pronouns may be a difficult concept for even the best students to grasp. If necessary, provide additional examples of correct and incorrect usage.

Lesson 5 Indefinite Pronouns

Indefinite pronoun
A pronoun that refers to a noun that is not named.

Indefinite pronouns replace nouns that are understood by the listener or reader. Some indefinite pronouns are always singular. Some indefinite pronouns are always plural.

These indefinite pronouns are always singular:

another	everybody	nothing
anybody	everyone	one
anyone	everything	one another
anything	much	somebody
each	neither	someone
each other	nobody	something
either	no one	

A singular indefinite pronoun takes a singular verb. Do not get confused by words that come between the subject and verb.

EXAMPLES
Correct: **Everyone has** a ticket.
Neither of us **wants** to miss the beach.
Incorrect: **Neither** of us **want** to miss the beach.

The following indefinite pronouns are always plural:

both	many	several
few	others	

A plural indefinite pronoun takes a plural verb.

EXAMPLES
Several of the guests **have** arrived.
The **others are** on their way.

Some indefinite pronouns may be singular or plural, depending on their use. These indefinite pronouns may be singular or plural:

all	most	several
any	none	

When an indefinite pronoun refers to a singular word, the indefinite pronoun is singular. It takes a singular verb.

EXAMPLES

None of the test **was** hard. (*None* refers to *test*, a singular noun.)

All of the garden **looks** beautiful. (*All* refers to *garden*, a singular noun.)

When an indefinite pronoun refers to a plural word, the indefinite pronoun is plural. It takes a plural verb.

EXAMPLES

None of the questions **were** hard. (*None* refers to *questions*, a plural noun.)

All of the flowers **look** beautiful. (*All* refers to *flowers*, a plural noun.)

When an indefinite pronoun is the antecedent of another pronoun, be sure that both pronouns agree in number.

EXAMPLES

All of the boys took **their** seats. (*All* is plural and is the antecedent of *their*.)

Every **one** of the girls has **her** ticket. (*One* is singular and is the antecedent of *her*.)

If the gender of the indefinite pronoun is not clear, you may use both the masculine and feminine pronouns.

EXAMPLE **Everyone** brought **his** or **her** ticket.

APPLICATION

In the Community

Remind students that whenever they have an opportunity to speak before their peers, coworkers, or any group of people, they should write down what they will say and then review it to be sure that they have used pronouns correctly. They should check that the antecedents are obvious and that subject-verb agreement is correct. Point out that a clear presentation makes ideas easier to follow and understand.

LEARNING STYLES

Visual/Spatial

Divide the class into pairs. Give each pair a colorful magazine picture. Challenge each pair to use its picture to create five sentences that contain an indefinite pronoun. Afterward, have volunteer pairs read their sentences. Ask the students to raise their hands when they hear an indefinite pronoun. As this happens, have a student print the indefinite pronoun on the board. Challenge the class to provide examples for all the indefinite pronouns contained in the boxes on pages 46 and 47. Note: Keep these pictures for use in the Learning Styles activity on page 82.

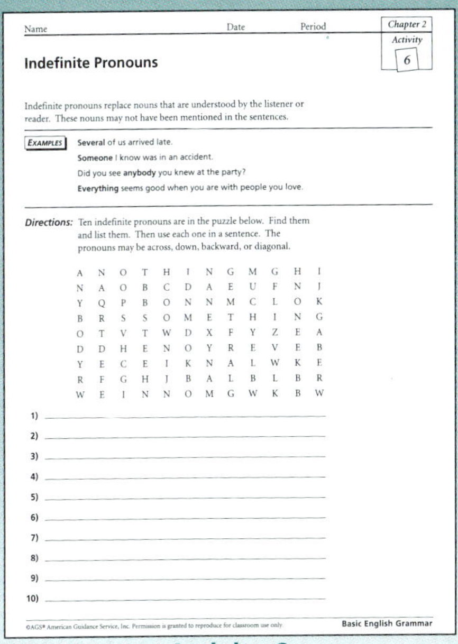

Name Date Period

Chapter 2 *Activity* 6

Indefinite Pronouns

Indefinite pronouns replace nouns that are understood by the listener or reader. These nouns may not have been mentioned in the sentences.

EXAMPLES

Several of us arrived late.

Someone I know was in an accident.

Did you see **anybody** you knew at the party?

Everything seems good when you are with people you love.

Directions: Ten indefinite pronouns are in the puzzle below. Find them and list them. Then use each one in a sentence. The pronouns may be across, down, backward, or diagonal.

A	N	O	T	H	I	N	G	M	G	H	I
N	A	O	B	C	D	A	E	U	F	N	J
Y	Q	P	B	O	N	N	M	C	L	O	K
B	R	S	S	O	M	E	T	H	I	N	G
O	T	V	T	W	D	X	F	Y	Z	E	A
D	D	H	E	N	O	Y	R	E	V	E	B
Y	E	C	E	I	K	N	A	L	W	K	E
R	F	G	H	J	B	A	L	B	L	B	R
W	E	I	N	N	O	M	G	W	K	B	W

1) __________

2) __________

3) __________

4) __________

5) __________

6) __________

7) __________

8) __________

9) __________

10) __________

 Basic English Grammar

Activity 6

Reading Vocabulary

bride (5) wedding (5)

■ Presenting Activity A

Have students work with a partner to complete this activity. Afterward, have partners share their answers with the class. Have students explain the subject-verb agreement in sentences in which the indefinite pronoun is the subject of the sentence.

Activity A Answers

1) Everyone **2)** anyone **3)** None **4)** one another **5)** Few **6)** Everyone **7)** Each **8)** no one **9)** some **10)** Everything **11)** each other **12)** Some **13)** nothing **14)** someone **15)** Other, anyone

■ Presenting Activity B

Have students complete this activity as a group. Invite volunteers to read each sentence and the answer choices aloud. Then have students discuss and choose the correct answer. Be sure students understand why an answer is correct before going on to the next item.

Activity B Answers

1) is **2)** is **3)** are **4)** is **5)** has **6)** his or her **7)** were **8)** his **9)** their **10)** its

Activity A Write the indefinite pronouns in these sentences on your paper.

1) Everyone brought food to the picnic.

2) Jack did not know anyone at the party.

3) None of the boys were late.

4) Try to be nice to one another.

5) Few of the students enjoyed the bus ride.

6) Everyone talked to the bride at the wedding.

7) Each of the guests brought a present.

8) Sam saw no one that he knew.

9) Li knew some of the people in the class.

10) Everything is ready for the party.

11) Try to help each other.

12) Some of the food was too spicy.

13) Karl knew nothing about the Red River.

14) Julia knows someone in that neighborhood.

15) Other than Sara, I do not know anyone here.

Activity B Write the word that should appear in each sentence to make it correct.

1) Everybody (is, are) coming to the party.

2) Everything in the closet (is, are) Katie's.

3) Some of those people (is, are) going home now.

4) Someone (is, are) reading that book.

5) Somebody (has, have) my pencil.

6) Everyone must leave (his or her, their) coat on.

7) Several of the guests (was, were) late.

8) Each of the men brought (his, their) wife.

9) None of the children remembered (his or her, their) lunch.

10) One of those coats is missing (its, their) buttons.

Lesson 5 Review

Part A Write a sentence on your paper for each of these indefinite pronouns.

1) someone

2) everyone

3) no one

4) anybody

5) nothing

6) none

7) everything

8) something

9) all

10) nobody

Part B Find ten indefinite pronouns in these sentences. Write them on your paper.

1) Everyone in Mr. Jackson's store was getting ready for the fall sale.

2) All of the salespeople came to work early that day.

3) Everybody was quiet as he or she worked.

4) Nobody said anything.

5) Suddenly someone laughed.

6) "Why are we all so quiet?" one of the women asked.

7) They all looked at each other.

8) "Some of us remember last year's sale," Alex said.

9) "I think many of you will need a vacation after today," he said.

Part A Answers

Answers will vary. Be sure to check for correct subject-verb agreement and pronoun-pronoun agreement in students' sentences.

Part B Answers

1) Everyone **2)** All **3)** Everybody **4)** Nobody, anything **5)** someone **6)** one **7)** each other **8)** Some **9)** many

Application

At Home

Encourage students to make a list of the different types of pronouns to keep at home. They might also like to jot down any ideas in the chapter that they had difficulty with, for example, subject-verb agreement with indefinite pronouns. Suggest that students use the list and notes when writing personal letters and for completing writing assignments in other classes.

Name ____ Date ____ Period ____ *Chapter 2 Workbook Activity 9*

Finding Pronouns

There are five kinds of pronouns. They are: personal, relative, interrogative, demonstrative, and indefinite.

Directions: Find the pronouns in these sentences. Underline each pronoun. Label it as either *personal, relative, interrogative, demonstrative,* or *indefinite.*

EXAMPLES
What (*interrogative*) is our (*personal*) shortest way home?
We (*personal*) saw those (*demonstrative*) flowers yesterday.
Does anyone (*indefinite*) have a camera?
John met the man who (*relative*) owned the truck.

1) I dislike having nothing to do.

2) Who is your favorite singer?

3) This is the prettiest lake.

4) There is the dog that barks at night.

5) Mrs. Wolfe is the teacher whom I had for science.

6) A few finished early.

7) Which television shows do you like?

8) George saw a deer, but Jim saw none.

9) Those are not my favorite foods.

10) The Jacket that Josh likes is red.

11) Carla brought some of the cake to the picnic.

12) What is the name of your dog?

13) Connie gave the message to him.

14) Who will bring the salad?

15) Several of the group said hello to us.

16) Sandy is the person who is the best cook.

 Basic English Grammar

Workbook Activity 9

Name ____ Date ____ Period ____ *Chapter 2 Workbook Activity 10*

Using Pronouns Correctly

Directions: Circle the mistake in each sentence. Then write the sentence correctly on the line.

EXAMPLE
We made that cake (ourself!)
We made that cake ourselves!

1) My aunt, which is a famous actress, visits us each year.

2) She brings hers dog that likes to bark at all of us.

3) Last year Aunt Faye took the pup to obedience school herself.

4) The pup, who's name is Bully, learned to sit up and beg.

5) "What kind of dog food do you buy?" I asked Aunt Faye.

6) "I buy a dry food," she said. "Its better for Bully's teeth."

7) Nobody is as smart about dogs as mine Aunt Faye.

8) Us kids always ask her advice about pets.

9) We have a pair of goldfish who we named Fred and Ethel.

10) Aunt Faye likes us to teach them fish some tricks.

11) Almost any fish can be trained to beg for it's food.

 Basic English Grammar

Workbook Activity 10

Chapter 2 Review

The Teacher's Resource Library includes two parallel forms of the Chapter 2 Mastery Test. The difficulty level of the two forms is equivalent. You may wish to use one form as a pretest and the other form as a posttest.

Reading Vocabulary

odd (5)

Part A Answers

1) her **2)** She **3)** They **4)** This **5)** us

Part B Answers

1) It—personal
2) Everyone—indefinite
his—personal
her—personal
3) No one—indefinite
4) Everybody—indefinite
5) What—interrogative
we—personal
one—indefinite
6) We—personal
our—personal
someone—indefinite
7) that—relative
I—personal
each—indefinite
us—personal
8) That—demonstrative
all—indefinite
9) she—personal
10) Those—demonstrative
who—relative

Chapter 2 Review

Part A Write the pronouns in these sentences on your paper.

1) Katie looked for her new homeroom.

2) She walked up the stairs to the third floor.

3) Katie found an old friend. They were in the same homeroom.

4) "This must be the place," said Katie.

5) "Lucky us!" laughed Laura.

Part B The pronouns in these sentences are in bold. Write the pronouns on your paper. Beside each pronoun, write whether it is *personal, relative, interrogative, demonstrative,* or *indefinite.*

Example **That** is the **one that I** like best.

That—demonstrative **that—relative**
one—indefinite **I—personal**

1) **It** was the dry season of the year.

2) **Everyone** was watering **his** or **her** yard.

3) **No one** was expecting rain for a while.

4) "**Everybody** must try to save water," Mr. Jones announced.

5) "**What** should **we** do?" **one** of the neighbors asked.

6) "**We** could stop watering **our** lawns," **someone** said.

7) "**I** suggest **that each** of **us** water only once a week," Mrs. Mendez said.

8) "**That** is a good idea," Katie said, and **all** of the neighbors agreed.

9) "The people on the even side of the street should water on weekdays," **she** said.

10) **Those who** live on the odd side will water on weekends.

50 *Chapter 2 The Pronoun*

Name Date Period | *Chapter 2 Mastery Test A page 1*

Chapter 2 Mastery Test A

Part A Write the pronoun that correctly completes each sentence.

1) Fred bought ____________ a new coat. (hisself, himself)
2) ____________ prefer to play golf. (We, Us)
3) ____________ of these computers should I buy? (Which, What)
4) Everyone served ____________ at dinner. (themselves, theirselves)
5) Nobody knows ____________ wrote that music. (who, whom)
6) Each girl brought ____________ own pen. (their, her)
7) Katie and ____________ are trying out for track. (me, I)
8) All of the boys are hoping to see ____________ favorite movie. (his, their)
9) Jim was late for ____________ class. (his, him)
10) Those are the shoes ____________ Tanya wanted. (what, that)

Part B Write the antecedent for each bold pronoun in these sentences.

1) Howard and Mike waited for **their** ride. ____________
2) The fellow **who** plays guitar is on stage. ____________
3) Joellen ate **her** lunch outside. ____________
4) "Where is **my** book?" asked Sara. ____________
5) Mac has a friend **whose** computer is for sale. ____________
6) Fred and Gail painted the house **themselves**. ____________
7) "Carol and I did **our** homework," said Jane. ____________
8) Ron sold the car to Jerry and **his** wife. ____________
9) Lora went to the art fair by **herself**. ____________
10) That is the woman **whom** I saw. ____________

 Basic English Grammar

Name Date Period | *Chapter 2 Mastery Test A page 2*

Chapter 2 Mastery Test A, continued

Part C Circle all of the pronouns in these sentences.

1) They knew someone who might like a pet bird.
2) She wanted her hair cut short.
3) We wondered whose dog dug that hole.
4) What school do they play next?
5) Does anybody want those tickets?
6) Whatever you like is what we will eat.
7) Who is your math teacher?
8) This is the day we see that movie.
9) Did you see the book that I was reading?
10) We helped ourselves to this good food.

Part D Identify the kind of pronoun that is in bold in each sentence. Write *Demonstrative, Relative, Indefinite, Personal,* or *Interrogative.*

1) **It** was spring at last. ____________
2) **Everyone** was tired of bad weather. ____________
3) Look at **that** sky! ____________
4) Have **you** ever seen anything so blue? ____________
5) They wanted a car **that** had four doors. ____________
6) **What** is that? ____________
7) **Nobody** thought it would rain. ____________
8) **Whoever** wants to ride should get in. ____________
9) She invited **those** friends to the party. ____________
10) **Who** would like a soda? ____________

 Basic English Grammar

Chapter 2 Mastery Test A

Part C Write the word that should appear in each sentence to make it correct.

1) Chris was a person (who, which) liked to be active.
2) "I think I need more exercise," he told (hisself, himself).
3) "(Whose, What) type of exercise would I enjoy the most?"
4) "Biking is an exercise (whom, that) I would enjoy."
5) He heard of a new bike trail in the next town. "(This, That) would be a good place to go," he said.
6) "(Which, Who) of my friends might like to join me?"
7) "Rico is someone (whom, which) I could ask."
8) "Nobody (enjoy, enjoys) the outdoors as much as Rico."
9) "We must wear helmets to protect (ourself, ourselves)," Rico said.
10) "Is (this, that) the safest helmet in the store?" Chris asked, pointing to the helmet on the top shelf.
11) "(Whose, Which) do you think I should buy?" he asked Rico.
12) "Either of those (is, are) fine."
13) "I think my bike is missing one of (its, it's) parts," Rico said.
14) "Do (whatever, whichever) needs to be done to get ready for our ride," Chris said.
15) "This is going to be great," both of the boys agreed as they began (his, their) ride.

Test Taking Tip Be sure you understand what the test question is asking. Reread it if you have to.

Reading Vocabulary

active (6) helmet (5)

Part C Answers

1) who 2) himself 3) What 4) that 5) That 6) Which 7) whom 8) enjoys 9) ourselves 10) that 11) Which 12) is 13) its 14) whatever 15) their

Follow-up Activity

Ask students to bring newspaper articles to class on a topic of their choice. Have students work in groups to evaluate the use of pronouns in the articles. Provide them with questions that they can use as an evaluation checklist. Some sample questions are:

- Were pronouns used to make ideas flow more naturally?
- Were pronoun antecedents always clear?
- Did pronouns and verbs agree in number and gender?

At the end of the activity, volunteers may want to read aloud the articles that each group gave the best evaluation.

Name Date Period | *Chapter 2 Mastery Test B page 1*

Chapter 2 Mastery Test B

Part A Write the pronoun that correctly completes each sentence.

1) Arnold found ________ a puppy. (hisself, himself)
2) Those are the shoes ________ I want. (who, that)
3) They built that house ________. (themselves, theirselves)
4) No one knew ________ baked that cake. (who, what)
5) Each boy brought ________ own baseball glove. (their, his)
6) Amber and ________ would like to have pancakes. (I, me)
7) Tyrone wondered ________ was going to the game. (who, whom)
8) Yolanda sang ________ favorite song. (hers, her)
9) ________ statue is the world's largest? (Which, What)
10) Did you see ________ new houses? (that, those)

Part B Write the antecedent for each bold pronoun in these sentences.

1) Gary has a friend **who** lives in Montana. ________
2) Gary went there by **himself**. ________
3) "My friend Karl and **I** camped," said Gary. ________
4) Karl has a friend **whose** hobby is fly casting. ________
5) The boys did some fly casting **themselves**. ________
6) Karl and Gary cooked **their** fish. ________
7) "**That** is a meadowlark." said Karl. ________
8) "**What** is the name of this tree?" Gary asked. ________
9) "Where is **my** backpack?" asked Karl. ________
10) Karl found it under **his** sleeping bag. ________

 Basic English Grammar

Name Date Period | *Chapter 2 Mastery Test B page 2*

Chapter 2 Mastery Test B, continued

Part C Circle all of the pronouns in these sentences.

1) What state did they visit on their trip?
2) He himself knew nothing about it.
3) Everyone who is going should be on that bus by now.
4) No one thought anything could stop this flood.
5) They kept it from those three towns on the river.
6) Our dog chews its bone on that step.
7) Which kind of books does this person write—fiction or nonfiction?
8) They each came from towns in that part of Ohio.
9) Whose corn will be up to our knees by July 4?
10) Choose whichever music you like.

Part D Identify the kind of pronoun that is in bold in each sentence. Write *Demonstrative, Relative, Indefinite, Personal,* or *Interrogative.*

1) Montana is **one** of the largest states. ________
2) **Its** population is less than a million. ________
3) **Everyone** knows about Glacier National Park. ________
4) **That** is a scenic wonderland. ________
5) Have **you** ever been to a powwow? ________
6) Montana has 200 lakes **that** you can visit. ________
7) Explorers Lewis and Clark visited **this** state. ________
8) The state fair, **which** is in Great Falls, happens in July. ________
9) **What** state would you like to visit? ________
10) **Which** mountain is your favorite? ________

 Basic English Grammar

Chapter 2 Mastery Test B

Chapter 3

Planning Guide

The Adjective

	Student Text Lesson			
	Student Pages	Vocabulary	Practice Exercises	Lesson Review
Lesson 1 What Is an Adjective?	54-56	✔	✔	56
Lesson 2 The Articles—*A, An, The*	57-59		✔	59
Lesson 3 Adjectives That Are Capitalized	60-62		✔	62
Lesson 4 Nouns Used as Adjectives	63-64		✔	64
Lesson 5 Possessives Used as Adjectives	65-66		✔	66
Lesson 6 Numbers Used as Adjectives	67-69		✔	69
Lesson 7 Demonstratives Used as Adjectives	70-71		✔	71
Lesson 8 Using Adjectives to Makes Comparisons	72-75	✔	✔	75

Chapter Activities

Teacher's Resource Library

Community Connection 3: Adjectives in Literature

Assessment Options

Student Text

Chapter 3 Review

Teacher's Resource Library

Chapter 3 Mastery Tests A and B

Teaching Strategies							Language Skills			Learning Styles						Teacher's Resource Library		
Reviewing Skills	Teacher Alert	Follow-up Activity	Career Application	Home Application	Global Connection	Community Application	Identification Skills	Writing Skills	Punctuation Skills	Visual/Spatial	Auditory/Verbal	Body/Kinesthetic	Logical/Mathematical	Group Learning	LEP/ESL	Activities	Workbook Activities	Self-Study Guide
54	55	56			55		✔	✔	✔				56			7-8	11	✔
57		59	59	58	57		✔	✔	✔									✔
60	61-62						✔	✔	✔								12	✔
63		64					✔	✔	✔		64							✔
65	65-66						✔	✔	✔									✔
67		69			68		✔	✔	✔					69				✔
70	71						✔	✔	✔			71					13	✔
72	73	75				77	✔	✔	✔					74		9	14-15	✔

Chapter at a Glance

Chapter 3: The Adjective

pages 52–77

(Answer Keys for the Teacher's Resource Library begin on page 330 of this Teacher's Edition.)

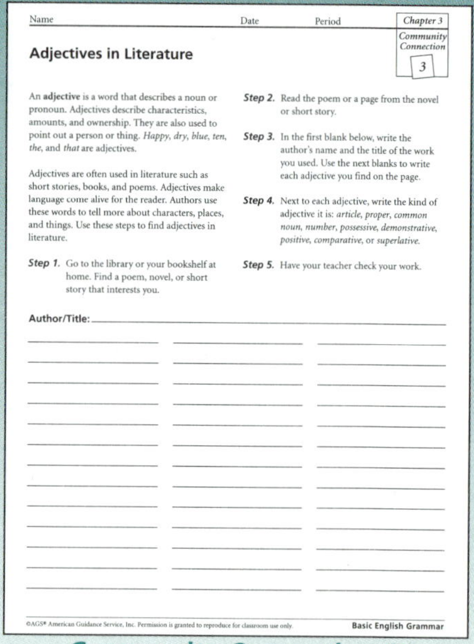

Name Date Period | Chapter 3 Community Connection 3

Adjectives in Literature

An **adjective** is a word that describes a noun or pronoun. Adjectives describe characteristics, amounts, and ownership. They are also used to point out a person or thing. *Happy, dry, blue, ten, the*, and *that* are adjectives.

Adjectives are often used in literature such as short stories, books, and poems. Adjectives make language come alive for the reader. Authors use these words to tell more about characters, places, and things. Use these steps to find adjectives in literature.

Step 1. Go to the library or your bookshelf at home. Find a poem, novel, or short story that interests you.

Step 2. Read the poem or a page from the novel or short story.

Step 3. In the first blank below, write the author's name and the title of the work you used. Use the next blanks to write each adjective you find on the page.

Step 4. Next to each adjective, write the kind of adjective it is: *article, proper, common noun, number, possessive, demonstrative, positive, comparative*, or *superlative.*

Step 5. Have your teacher check your work.

Author/Title: ______________________

 Basic English Grammar

Community Connection 3

Chapter 3 The Adjective

When you tell someone about something you have seen, you use words to help the person picture what you saw. When you tell someone about something you have heard, you use words to help the person imagine the sounds you heard.

An adjective is a word that describes a noun or a pronoun. You make your ideas clearer and more interesting by using adjectives.

In Chapter 3, you will learn about adjectives. Each lesson in the chapter focuses on a different type of adjective and its use in writing and speaking.

Goals for Learning

- To recognize adjectives in sentences and to identify the nouns that the adjectives describe
- To recognize articles and numbers used as adjectives in sentences
- To recognize and capitalize proper adjectives
- To recognize demonstrative pronouns and possessive nouns used as adjectives
- To use adjectives correctly to make comparisons

53

Reading Vocabulary

capitalize (9)
comparison (6)
demonstrative
describe (5)
focus (7)
identify (6)
possessive
proper (5)

Introducing the Chapter

Invite two or three volunteers to take turns describing a painting, a song, a place, or an event that made a great impression on them. Before each student begins to speak, ask what he or she will be describing. Write the subject of the description in the center of a cluster diagram. As each student speaks, record the more descriptive adjectives that the student uses in the diagram. Then, focus students' attention on the words in the diagrams. Ask students why these words were important to the descriptions. What would the descriptions have been like without them? Elicit through discussion, that these words made each student's ideas clearer and more interesting. Then ask if anyone knows what part of speech these words are. If necessary, explain that they are adjectives. By the end of Chapter 3, students will understand how to use adjectives effectively to make their writing clearer, more lively, and more interesting.

SELF-STUDY GUIDE

Name

CHAPTER 3: The Adjective

Goal 3.1 *To recognize adjectives in sentences and to identify the nouns that the adjectives describe*

Date	Assignment	Score
	1: Read pages 53-54. Complete Activities A-B on page 54.	
	2: Read page 55. Complete Activity C on page 55.	
	3: Complete Workbook Activity 11.	
	4: Complete the Lesson 1 Review, Parts A-B on page 56.	

Comments:

Goal 3.2 *To recognize articles used as adjectives in sentences*

Date	Assignment	Score
	5: Read page 57. Complete Activities A-B on page 58.	
	6: Complete the Lesson 2 Review on page 59.	

Comments:

Goal 3.3 *To recognize and capitalize proper adjectives*

Date	Assignment	Score
	7: Read page 60. Complete Activities A-B on page 60.	
	8: Complete Activities C-D on page 61.	
	9: Complete Workbook Activity 12.	
	10: Complete the Lesson 3 Review, Parts A-B on page 62.	

Comments:

Goal 3.4 *To recognize possessive nouns used as adjectives*

Date	Assignment	Score
	11: Read page 63. Complete Activity A on page 63.	
	12: Complete the Lesson 4 Review, Parts A-B on page 64.	
	13: Read page 65. Complete Activities A-B on page 65.	
	14: Complete the Lesson 5 Review on page 66.	

Comments:

 Basic English Grammar

SELF-STUDY GUIDE

Name

CHAPTER 3 The Adjective, continued

Goal 3.5 *To recognize numbers used as adjectives in sentences*

Date	Assignment	Score
	15: Read page 67. Complete Activities A-B on page 67.	
	16: Complete Activity C on page 68.	
	17: Complete the Lesson 6 Review, Parts A-B on page 69.	

Comments:

Goal 3.6 *To recognize demonstrative pronouns used as adjectives*

Date	Assignment	Score
	18: Read page 70. Complete Activities A-B on page 70.	
	19: Complete Workbook Activity 13.	
	20: Complete the Lesson 7 Review on page 71.	

Comments:

Goal 3.7 *To use adjectives correctly to make comparisons*

Date	Assignment	Score
	21: Read page 72. Complete Activity A on page 72.	
	22: Read page 73. Complete Activity B on page 73.	
	23: Complete Workbook Activity 14.	
	24: Read page 74. Complete Activities C-D on page 74.	
	25: Complete Workbook Activity 15.	
	26: Complete the Lesson 8 Review, Parts A-C on page 75.	
	27: Complete the Chapter 3 Review, Parts A-D on pages 76-77.	

Comments:

Student's Signature ______ Date ______

Instructor's Signature ______ Date ______

 Basic English Grammar

Chapter 3 Self-Study Guide

Lesson at a Glance

Chapter 3 Lesson 1

Overview This lesson explains what an adjective is and the ways adjectives can be used to describe nouns and pronouns.

Objectives

- To identify adjectives and the words they describe.
- To add adjectives to sentences.

Student Pages 54–56

Teacher's Resource Library

Activities 7–8

Workbook Activity 11

Reading Vocabulary

adjective	fantastic (7)
cucumbers	reel (5)

Teaching Suggestions

Introducing the Lesson

Discuss the definition of an adjective and the different ways adjectives can be used. Invite students to replace the adjective in each example sentence with other adjectives that answer the same question.

Reviewing Skills

Review the definitions of *noun* and *pronoun*. Write sample sentences on the board and have students identify the nouns and pronouns in them.

Presenting Activity A

Have students do this activity orally.

Activity A Answers

1) fantastic—vacation, summer—vacation 2) enough—time 3) first—day, huge—fish 4) next—day, three—trout 5) big—bear, black—bear, our—camp

Presenting Activity B

Do the first item with students before having them complete the activity independently.

Activity B Answers

Answers will vary.

Lesson 1 What Is an Adjective?

Adjective
A word that tells about a noun or a pronoun. An adjective tells what kind, which one, how many, *or* how much.

An **adjective** is a word that describes a noun or pronoun. An adjective answers the question *What kind? Which one? How many?* or *How much?* about a noun or a pronoun. More than one adjective may be used to describe a noun or a pronoun.

EXAMPLES

What kind?	We stayed in a **small beach** house.
Which one?	I live in **that** house.
How many?	We have lived in **five** states.
How much?	He had **some** money.

Activity A Some of the adjectives in these sentences are in bold. Write the adjectives on your paper. Next to the adjective, write the noun that the adjective describes.

Example David bought an **expensive new** reel.
expensive new—reel

1) What a **fantastic summer** vacation they had at the lake!
2) We did not have **enough** time to do everything.
3) On the **first** day we were there, Vince caught a **huge** fish.
4) The **next** day, David hooked **three** trout.
5) At night, a **big black** bear came into **our** camp.

Activity B Rewrite these sentences on your paper. Add one or more adjectives before each noun in bold.

1) Students brought **books** to **class**.
2) **People** brought **food**.
3) **School** started early.
4) I saw **mountains** and **rivers**.
5) Diana planted **tomatoes** and **cucumbers**.

Name Date Period *Chapter 3 Activity 7*

Locating Adjectives in Sentences

Adjectives are words that describe nouns or pronouns in sentences. They can limit or change the meaning of a noun or pronoun.

EXAMPLES The **bright red** flowers cheered up the patient.
She is **very tired**.
The athlete, **tall** and **powerful**, stood ready to begin the game.

Directions: Find the adjectives in each sentence and circle them. Draw an arrow from the adjective to the word it describes. *The, a,* and *an* are always adjectives. Do not circle them for this exercise.

EXAMPLE My new car was expensive.

1) Alex is smart, loyal, and fun.
2) James Melcher is tall and handsome.
3) Katie adores her sweet puppy named Jetson.
4) Because the weather was warm, everyone decided to go on a hike.
5) The lemonade, tart and cold, hit the spot after the walk.
6) Laura, lovely and sweet-tempered as always, is a popular girl at school.
7) "Where is that big, heavy book that I was reading?" asked Alex.
8) After the walk, Dina was tired and thirsty.
9) "Where did that loud noise come from?" someone asked.
10) It was a bright, red cardinal that was singing in the tall oak tree.
11) Cardinals like to live in thick woods.
12) Young children love to feed wild birds during the cold winter months.

 Basic English Grammar

Activity 7

Most adjectives come before the noun that they are describing. Adjectives may, however, follow the noun for emphasis. Then, they are set off from the rest of the sentence with commas.

EXAMPLES The **sleepy** child was crying.

The child, **sleepy** and **hungry**, was crying.

Predicate adjective

An adjective that follows a linking verb and tells about the subject.

A **predicate adjective** comes after the noun or pronoun it describes.

EXAMPLES He was **sleepy** and **hungry**.

They seem **happy**.

Activity C Find the adjectives in these sentences. Write them on your paper. Beside each adjective, write the noun or pronoun that the adjective describes.

1) The lake was beautiful on that morning.

2) The water was clear and cool.

3) David saw a large fish jump out of the sparkling water.

4) Vince used a trusty old rod.

5) The boys fished for eight hours.

6) For a long time, nothing happened.

7) They remained hopeful.

8) By late afternoon, they had caught many fish.

9) They were tired but happy with themselves.

10) Vince told funny stories as they rode home.

Reading Vocabulary

comma
rod (5)
emphasis (8)
predicate adjective

Presenting Activity C

Be sure students understand how to use commas to set off adjectives used for emphasis. Students should also understand the definition of predicate adjective. If necessary, write several more examples of each use of adjectives on the board. You might wish to have students help you place the commas in new example sentences with adjectives that follow the noun for emphasis.

Activity C Answers

1) beautiful—lake **2)** clear—water, cool—water
3) large—fish, sparkling—water
4) trusty—rod, old—rod
5) eight—hours **6)** long—time
7) hopeful—They **8)** late—afternoon, many—fish
9) tired—They, happy—They
10) funny—stories

TEACHER ALERT

Be sure students understand that a predicate adjective follows a linking, or state-of-being, verb. You may wish to provide students with a list of linking verbs.

Name Date Period — Chapter 3 Activity 8

Adjectives Are Words of Power

Directions: Each word in the box below is an adjective. Use a dictionary to find the meaning of the word if necessary. Choose one word from the box that fits the meaning of each sentence. Then write that word in the blank.

Word Box

chilly	dull	unbelievable
shining	one-of-a-kind	energetic
undependable	favorite	
round	praiseworthy	

1) Alex has an ______________ disposition.

2) In the winter, the weather in Brownsville can be ______________ .

3) The ______________ lake glistened in the early morning light.

4) Katie's tomatoes grew ______________ and red in her garden.

5) Alex's ______________ class is math.

6) Many of Alex's friends thought the math teacher's lectures were ______________ .

7) "Alex's high grades in math were ______________ ," thought his teacher.

8) Some people think that James is ______________ .

9) "Brandy, the brown Labrador retriever, is ______________ ," thought Ines.

10) "What an ______________ movie!" agreed Katie and Laura.

 Basic English Grammar

Activity 8

Name Date Period — Chapter 3 Workbook Activity 11

Words of Power

Directions: Find all of the adjectives in these sentences. Write the adjectives on the line.

1) "You are impossible," Aunt Mary said to Roger after he lost his eighth pair of gloves.

2) "Please don't be thoughtless of the family," pleaded Ken.

3) The knife with sawlike edges was used to carve the roast.

4) The movie showed a grim and horrible accident.

5) Anne, my sister, has shiny blonde hair.

6) The puppy had a curious look that made everyone laugh.

7) We stood on the porch and enjoyed the bright sky.

8) Mother described her wedding ring as priceless.

9) Everyone thought the army was unconquerable.

10) People sometimes criticize the complicated system of government.

 Basic English Grammar

Workbook Activity 11

GLOBAL CONNECTION

Invite students who speak another language to explain the placement of adjectives in sentences in their primary language. You may also have students translate the adjectives in the activity into their primary language.

The Adjective *Chapter 3* **55**

Part A Answers

1) chilly—weather **2)** heavy—coat **3)** several—classes **4)** favorite—class **5)** easy—Math **6)** his—car

Part B Answers

Answers will vary. Check that all adjectives are circled.

Follow-up Activity

Have students select one or two passages from a literature selection or from a magazine or newspaper article. Ask students to identify all the adjectives and the noun or pronoun each adjective describes in the selection.

Learning Styles

Logical/Mathematical
On the board, print the following pattern—adjective/noun. Ask the students to call out the persons, places, and things they see in the classroom. Print their suggestions in a vertical list under the word *noun* on the board. Then challenge them to describe each noun by calling out an adjective. Print these under the word *adjective.* Print a second pattern—adjective/adjective/noun. Continue the activity, but this time, challenge the class to come up with two adjectives to describe each noun. Print their responses on the board under the second pattern.

Lesson 1 Review

Part A Some of the adjectives in these sentences are in bold. Write them on your paper. Beside each one, write the noun or pronoun that the adjective describes.

1) In October, the weather can be **chilly**.

2) David decided to wear a **heavy** coat.

3) He had **several** classes on Wednesdays.

4) David's **favorite** class was math.

5) Math was **easy** for him.

6) He drove to the college in **his** car.

Part B Rewrite these sentences on your paper. Add as many adjectives as you can to each sentence. Circle all the adjectives in your sentences.

1) Diana has a dog.

2) David bought a coat.

3) The fisher cast a line into the lake.

4) It was morning.

5) The store had a sale.

6) I have a job.

7) Ray plays piano.

8) Annie's jacket has a hole in it.

Lesson 2 The Articles—*A, An, The*

The articles *a, an,* and *the* are always used as adjectives. They are placed before nouns in sentences. The definite article is *the.* Use *the* when you are talking about a particular person or thing. The indefinite articles are *a* and *an.* Use *a* or *an* when you are talking about a general group of people or things.

EXAMPLES

Sharon wanted to go to **a** movie.
(Sharon does not have a particular movie in mind.)

Vince would like to see **an** adventure movie.
(Vince wants to see any adventure movie.)

Eli saw **the** movie yesterday.
(Eli saw a particular movie.)

Use the article *a* before a word that begins with a consonant sound.

Use the article *an* before a word that begins with a vowel sound.

EXAMPLES

a large apple	**an** apple
a hard assignment	**an** assignment
a mistake	**an** honest mistake

The article *a* is used with singular nouns. The article *the* can be used with singular and plural nouns.

EXAMPLES

I bought **a** book.
(*Book* is singular.)

David bought **the** book.
(*Book* is singular.)

He bought **the** books.
(*Books* is plural.)

Lesson at a Glance

Chapter 3 Lesson 2

Overview This lesson presents the articles *a, an,* and *the* and explains their use as adjectives.

Objectives

- To identify articles in sentences.
- To determine when to use *the, a,* or *an.*

Student Pages 57–59

Reading Vocabulary

consonant	singular (8)
plural (6)	vowel (5)

Teaching Suggestions

■ Introducing the Lesson
To prepare students for the information presented in this lesson, discuss the meanings of *definite* and *indefinite* and *general* and *particular.* Be sure students understand how the examples illustrate the concepts presented.

■ Reviewing Skills Help students recall the definition of *adjective* and ask them to give sample sentences with adjectives.

GLOBAL CONNECTION

Invite students who speak another language to explain the masculine and feminine forms of articles and the masculine and feminine endings of adjectives in their primary language. Encourage students who are comfortable writing in their primary language to write sample sentences on the board. Ask them to point out the articles and other adjectives and the noun or pronoun each adjective describes.

Reading Vocabulary

assignment (6) projector (8)
index (5) topic (5)

Presenting Activity A

Have partners work together to write six sentences that use *a, an,* or *the.* Suggest that they try to use each article at least twice. Invite each pair to read their sentences aloud and explain why they used *a, an,* or *the* in each sentence.

Activity A Answers

1) The, the, the **2)** The, a **3)** The, the **4)** The, the, the **5)** a, the **6)** The, the **7)** an **8)** a

Presenting Activity B

Invite a volunteer to read sentence 1 aloud twice—first with *a,* and then with *an.* Ask students which article belongs in the sentence and why. Then have students complete the activity on their own. When they have finished, invite students to read the sentences aloud with the answers in place. Ask students to explain how they knew when to use *a* or *an.*

Activity B Answers

1) an **2)** an **3)** a **4)** an **5)** an **6)** a **7)** an **8)** a **9)** a **10)** an

Application

At Home

Suggest that students look over letters and other correspondence they have written at home to check for the correct use of articles.

Activity A Write these sentences on your paper. Circle all of the articles.

1) The math class was the first class of the day.

2) The students had a homework assignment.

3) The first part of the class was easy.

4) The class discussed the answers to the problems.

5) "I got a different answer to the problem," Jamal said.

6) The teacher explained the problem.

7) She used an overhead projector.

8) Later she handed out a new assignment.

Activity B Write the article that should appear in each sentence to make it correct.

1) Suki packed (a, an) apple for her lunch.

2) They waited for (a, an) hour.

3) The teacher spoke in (a, an) soft voice.

4) They had (a, an) English lesson.

5) I read (a, an) article about elephants.

6) He had (a, an) message for his boss.

7) Look up the topic in (a, an) index.

8) They saw (a, an) horror movie.

9) Not (a, an) cloud was in sight.

10) Jack is (a, an) honest man.

58 *Chapter 3 The Adjective*

Lesson 2 Review

Lesson Review Write the article that should appear in each sentence to make it correct.

1) Look at (a, the) blue coat in the window.
2) Did you enjoy eating (a, the) peaches?
3) Mrs. Jones put (a, the) groceries on the table.
4) We went to New York City to see (a, an) play.
5) Chicago is (a, an) American city.
6) They did (a, the) activity in class.
7) A hammer is (a, an) useful tool.
8) Did you see (a, the) pencils I left here?
9) Where is (a, an) envelope?
10) I was in (a, an) earthquake in California.
11) We have (a, an) eight-foot tree in our yard.
12) Have you ever seen (a, an) bald eagle?
13) (A, The) snakes crawled on a rock to sun themselves.
14) They did (a, an) math activity.
15) "What (a, an) awful day this has been!" she said.
16) What happened to (a, the) flower vase?

Reading Vocabulary

bald (6)

Lesson Review Answers

1) the **2)** the **3)** the **4)** a
5) an **6)** the **7)** a **8)** the
9) an **10)** an **11)** an **12)** a
13) The **14)** a **15)** an **16)** the

Follow-up Activity

Divide students into teams or partners. Have each team of students write ten sentences in which *a, an,* and *the* are used correctly and incorrectly ten times each. Have teams exchange sentences and find all the mistakes.

Application

Career Connection

Job applicants are often asked to explain orally or in writing why they would like a certain job. Discuss with students how using articles correctly with job titles (for example, *a* secretary, *an* assistant manager) demonstrates a command of the English language that can help their chances of being hired. Incorrect usage, on the other hand, could have a negative effect.

The Adjective Chapter 3 **59**

Lesson at a Glance

Chapter 3 Lesson 3

Overview This lesson presents proper adjectives and explains how they are formed.

Objectives

- To identify and use proper adjectives in sentences.
- To distinguish proper adjectives from proper nouns.

Student Pages 60–62

Teacher's Resource Library

Workbook Activity 12

Reading Vocabulary

capital (5)
culture (7)
democratic (6)
literature (6)
native (5)
social (5)
woven (5)

Teaching Suggestions

Introducing the Lesson

Use the examples given to explain that proper adjectives, like all other kinds of adjectives, are used to describe nouns and pronouns.

Reviewing Skills

Provide a review of proper nouns and ask students for examples.

Presenting Activity A

Provide examples of proper adjectives that are separated by other words from the noun or pronoun they describe, as in item 6. Ask students to suggest other sentences that follow the same pattern.

Activity A Answers

1) none **2)** Spanish—book
3) English—class, Shakespearean—literature
4) American—literature
5) Native American—cultures
6) Native American—blanket
7) Thai—food

Presenting Activity B

Invite volunteers to provide sample sentences orally before having students write their sentences in Activity B.

Lesson 3 Adjectives That Are Capitalized

Proper adjectives are made from proper nouns. A proper adjective always begins with a capital letter.

EXAMPLES		
	Proper noun:	He is an **American**.
	Proper adjective:	He is an **American** soldier.
	Proper noun:	I visited **Mexico**.
	Proper adjective:	I love **Mexican** food.

Activity A Write the proper adjectives in these sentences on your paper. Beside each proper adjective, write the noun or pronoun it describes. Read carefully. Some capitalized words are proper nouns.

1) Bess studied Spanish first period.

2) She almost forgot her Spanish book.

3) In her English class, Bess was studying Shakespearean literature.

4) She liked American literature better.

5) This year in social studies, we learned about Native American cultures.

6) This beautiful woven blanket is Native American.

7) Bess had never tasted Thai food.

Activity B Use these proper adjectives in sentences. Write the sentences on your paper. Be sure to use these words as adjectives that describe nouns or pronouns.

1) Spanish
2) German
3) Chinese
4) Democratic
5) African
6) Brazilian
7) American
8) Olympic

Activity B Answers

Answers will vary. Sentences should be complete, and proper adjectives should be used correctly.

Activity C Complete each sentence with a proper adjective. Write the complete sentence on your paper.

1) We ordered ______ dressing for our salad.

2) Mr. Cruz likes ______ cheese.

3) Lori studied the ______ language last year.

4) They live in Germany, but they are ______ citizens.

5) He belongs to the ______ political party.

6) Is ______ cooking easier than it looks?

7) We saw examples of ______ art.

8) Both his grandparents are ______.

Activity D Write the words in bold on your paper. Beside each word, write whether it is used as a proper noun or a proper adjective. Beside each proper adjective, write the noun or pronoun it describes.

1) I like **French** onion soup.

2) Mark lives in **Philadelphia**.

3) He is a **Philadelphia** boy.

4) Kareem watched the **Russian** jugglers.

5) He practiced saying "hello" and "good-bye" in **Russian**.

6) Amy Tan is an **Asian American** writer.

7) Next summer I want to travel along the **Spanish** coast.

8) I'd like to study **Spanish** first.

9) The exchange student who stayed with us last year was **Spanish**.

10) The instructions for the VCR were in **Japanese**.

11) The high school band will march in the **Thanksgiving Day** parade.

12) That is an **African** elephant.

Reading Vocabulary

instruction (5) Philadelphia
juggler political (6)

Presenting Activity C

Write three sentences on the board with blanks in place of proper adjectives. Invite students to fill in each blank with a proper adjective. To stress that there is no one correct answer for the activity items, accept several responses for each of the sample sentences.

Activity C Answers

Answers will vary. Each sentence should contain a proper adjective.

Presenting Activity D

Write the words *America, Japan, Spain, Mexico,* and *China* on the board. Work with students to form other proper nouns and proper adjectives from these words. Encourage students to use these words in sentences as proper nouns and proper adjectives.

Activity D Answers

1) proper adj.—onion soup **2)** proper noun **3)** proper adj.—boy **4)** proper adj.—jugglers **5)** proper noun **6)** proper adj.—writer **7)** proper adj.—coast **8)** proper noun **9)** proper adj.—student **10)** proper noun **11)** proper adj.—parade **12)** proper adj.—elephant

Name ______ Date ______ Period ______ *Chapter 3 Workbook Activity 12*

Proper Adjectives

A. Directions: Circle the proper adjectives in these sentences. Then copy the sentence and capitalize all of the proper adjectives.

EXAMPLE Did you see my (french) book?
Did you see my French book?

1) Michael ordered a swiss cheese and ham sandwich on rye.

2) He was eating in a small palm beach restaurant.

3) Slowly he got out his german dictionary.

4) Later he would read about spanish culture.

5) He planned a european vacation after graduation.

B. Directions: Circle the proper adjectives. Write a sentence using each proper adjective.

1) Switzerland, Swiss

2) France, French

3) Democrat, Democratic

4) Shakespeare, Shakespearean

5) Spain, Spanish

 Basic English Grammar

Workbook Activity 12

Teacher Alert

Because a word may be spelled the same whether it is a proper adjective or a proper noun, emphasize how important it is for students to read all the words in a sentence before they write an answer for each item.

Reading Vocabulary

Canadian	Italian
Democrat (7)	memorial (5)

Part A Answers

1) Ford—truck **2)** Swiss—cheese **3)** Spanish—folktales, Italian—folktales **4)** Maine—coast **5)** American—father, Canadian—mother **6)** Memorial Day—picnic

Part B Answers

Sentences will vary. Proper adjectives are given.

1) German **2)** Fourth of July **3)** Spanish **4)** United States **5)** Democratic **6)** South American **7)** Chinese

Teacher Alert

Students should be reminded that *Democratic* is usually a proper adjective only when used to describe one of the political parties of the United States. (*the Democratic party*) When used to describe other nouns (for example, *a democratic idea* or *a democratic policy*) it is considered an adjective and is not capitalized.

Lesson 3 Review

Part A Write these sentences on your paper. Capitalize all of the proper adjectives. Then draw an arrow from the proper adjective to the noun it describes.

Example Jon likes the beat of Latin music.

1) My older sister fixed up that old ford truck.

2) He likes swiss cheese.

3) We read several spanish and italian folktales.

4) They spent the summer camping along the maine coast.

5) Melissa's father is american and her mother is canadian.

6) You are invited to our memorial day picnic.

Part B Make each proper noun a proper adjective and use it in a sentence. Write the sentences on your paper. Draw an arrow from each proper adjective to the noun or pronoun it describes.

1) Germany

2) Fourth of July

3) Spain

4) United States

5) Democrat

6) South America

7) China

62 Chapter 3 The Adjective

Lesson 4 Nouns Used as Adjectives

Common nouns can be used as adjectives. To figure out if a word is a noun or an adjective, look at how it is used in the sentence.

EXAMPLES

Noun:	Paul ordered a large **salad**.
Adjective:	What kind of **salad** dressing would you like? (*Salad* describes the noun *dressing.*)
Noun:	Vera plays **basketball**.
Adjective:	Vera plays on the **basketball** team. (*Basketball* describes the noun *team.*)

Activity A Write the words in bold on your paper. Beside each word, write whether it is a *noun* or an *adjective.* If a word is an adjective, write the noun that the adjective describes.

1) I'm looking for a **summer** job.

2) My sister found a great job for the **summer**.

3) She was hired by the **city**.

4) It sponsors a **jobs** program for teens.

5) Vera will be working as a **park** leader.

6) She will probably work at the **park** near our house.

7) The pay is good for a **city** job.

8) She gets to be outside all day playing **basketball** with little kids.

9) Wasn't Vera one of the best **basketball** players on the girls' team?

10) In fact, three different **college** coaches have called her.

11) They have offered her a **scholarship** to play at their school.

12) Vera has not decided which **college** she will go to yet.

Lesson at a Glance

Chapter 3 Lesson 4

Overview This lesson presents common nouns used as adjectives.

Objectives

- To identify common nouns used as adjectives in sentences.
- To use common nouns as adjectives in sentences.

Student Pages 63–64

Reading Vocabulary

college (5) sponsor (8)
scholarship

Teaching Suggestions

Introducing the Lesson

After discussing the examples given, ask students to use *salad* and *basketball* as adjectives in other sentences. Write the sentences on the board and ask students to identify the noun that *salad* or *basketball* describes in each sentence.

Reviewing Skills

Review the definitions of *noun* and *adjective* with students.

Presenting Activity A

Write the first item in the activity on the board and ask students to find a noun and an adjective that is not an article in the sentence. Then have students work with a partner to complete the activity. Afterward, ask partners to share their answers with the class and to provide two additional sentences in which common nouns are used as adjectives.

Activity A Answers

1) adjective—job **2)** noun
3) noun **4)** adjective—program
5) adjective—leader **6)** noun
7) adjective—job **8)** noun
9) adjective—players
10) adjective—coaches
11) noun **12)** noun

Reading Vocabulary

athlete (6) interview (6)
computer (8) spaghetti (5)

Part A Answers

1) lunch—bag **2)** newspaper—meeting **3)** school—paper **4)** sports—reporter **5)** team—members **6)** track—event **7)** spaghetti—dinner **8)** bus—ride **9)** interview—notes **10)** computer—room

Part B Answers

Answers will vary. Check that words have been used as adjectives.

Follow-up Activity

Encourage students to look for nouns used as adjectives in newspaper and magazine advertisements and in book, movie, and restaurant reviews. Have students list the adjectives with the nouns they describe. Then invite them to share their list with the class.

Learning Styles

Auditory/Verbal

Ask a volunteer to begin naming aloud all the nouns—persons, places, things—in the classroom. Encourage the other students to listen carefully to the volunteer and to raise their hands when they hear a noun that they can turn into an adjective. Have someone make a list of these nouns. Ask a volunteer to create a sentence that uses the noun as an adjective. Have someone make a list of these sentences. Post both lists and encourage the students to add to the lists in the upcoming days.

Lesson 4 Review

Part A Write the common nouns used as adjectives in these sentences on your paper. Beside each adjective, write the noun it describes.

1) Bill grabbed his lunch bag and ran out the door.

2) He was going to be late for the newspaper meeting.

3) Bill enjoyed working on the school paper.

4) As the sports reporter, he went to all the games.

5) Talking to team members before and after the games was fun.

6) Last week, he covered a big track event.

7) The night before, he joined the team for a spaghetti dinner.

8) On the bus ride the next day, he spoke to the coaches and athletes.

9) He jotted down his interview notes in a notebook.

10) After the game, he went to the computer room at school to write his article.

Part B Write a sentence on your paper using each of these common nouns as an adjective. Draw an arrow from the adjective to the noun it describes.

1) baseball

2) fruit

3) winter

4) tomato

5) school

64 *Chapter 3 The Adjective*

Lesson 5 Possessives Used as Adjectives

Possessive pronouns are sometimes called possessive adjectives. They tell something about the nouns they describe. A possessive adjective describes a noun by telling which one or whose.

EXAMPLES His house is on the corner. (Which house? *his* house)
Is that **their** room? (Whose room? *their* room)

A possessive adjective can be used with a possessive noun.

EXAMPLE That is **my sister's** book.
(The possessive adjective *my* describes *sister*.
Whose sister? *my* sister)
(The possessive noun *sister's* shows ownership.
Whose book? *sister's* book)

Activity A The possessive adjectives in these sentences are in bold. Write them on your paper. Beside each possessive adjective, write the noun it describes.

Example He left **his** hat on the bus.
his — hat

1) I always like to get **my** money's worth.
2) **Our** family has always shopped in **their** store.
3) **Your** dog has a guilty look on **its** face.
4) We are having **her** birthday party next Saturday.
5) **His** picture was in the newspaper yesterday.

Activity B Find the possessive adjectives in these sentences. Write them on your paper. Beside each possessive adjective, write the noun it describes.

1) His bike is missing.
2) Your coat was in the living room.
3) I helped my mother's friend look for her ring.
4) There was a rabbit in my garden.
5) Their dog likes to hide its bones under our porch.

Lesson at a Glance

Chapter 3 Lesson 5

Overview This lesson presents possessive adjectives.

Objective

- To identify possessive adjectives and the nouns they describe in sentences.

Student Pages 65–66

Reading Vocabulary

guilty (6) ownership (7)

Teaching Suggestions

Introducing the Lesson

Work with students to create a chart with the title *Possessive Adjectives.* Have students list the appropriate words under the headings *Singular* (*my, your, his, her, its*) and *Plural* (*our, your, their*).

Reviewing Skills

Provide a review of possessive nouns and how they are formed.

Presenting Activity A

Do the example and the first item orally with the class. After students have completed the activity, have them share their answers with the class.

Activity A Answers

1) my—money 2) our—family, their—store 3) Your—dog, its—face 4) her—party 5) His—picture

Presenting Activity B

Before having students complete the activity on their own, invite them to use the possessive adjectives in the chart created in Introducing the Lesson in written sentences on the board. Have the class identify the noun each possessive adjective describes.

Activity B Answers

1) His—bike 2) Your—coat 3) my—mother, her—ring 4) my—garden 5) Their—dog, its—bones, our—porch

TEACHER ALERT

Be sure students understand that the words *my, your, his, her, its, our, your,* and *their* can be called either possessive pronouns or possessive adjectives when they are used before a noun. Emphasize that neither term is more or less correct than the other.

Reading Vocabulary

calculator compare (5)

Teacher Alert

You may wish to point out that a possessive adjective is often separated from the noun it describes by another adjective. You can use the first item in the Lesson Review as an example.

Lesson Review Answers

1) their—homework **2)** Your—answer **3)** my—answer **4)** his—answer **5)** our—answers **6)** their—problems **7)** our—math **8)** my—calculator **9)** its—battery **10)** his—desk

Lesson 5 Review

Lesson Review Find the possessive adjectives in these sentences. List them on your paper in order. Beside each one, write the noun that the adjective describes.

1) Dave and Vince did their math homework together.

2) "Your second answer is wrong," Dave said.

3) "Here is my answer."

4) Dave tried to explain his answer.

5) "I think both of our answers are wrong," Vince said.

6) They compared their problems.

7) "We should check our math," Vince suggested.

8) "Use my calculator to check."

9) The calculator did not work because its battery was dead.

10) Vince found some new batteries in his desk.

Lesson 6 Numbers Used as Adjectives

A number can be used as an adjective to describe a noun. Numbers describe by telling how many.

EXAMPLES Mrs. Jones canned **twenty** jars of pears. (How many jars? *twenty*)

Twelve people came to the party. (How many people? *twelve*)

An indefinite pronoun also can be used as an adjective to describe a noun. When indefinite pronouns are used as adjectives, they describe by telling how many. However, the amount is not exact.

EXAMPLES

Pronoun: **Several** of the guests arrived late.

Adjective: **Several** years went by before I saw her again. (How many years? *several*)

Activity A Write a sentence on your paper for each number word listed below. Use the word as an adjective. Circle the noun or pronoun that the adjective describes.

1) few	**4)** some	**7)** four
2) thirty-three	**5)** most	**8)** several
3) one	**6)** eighty	**9)** all

Activity B The number words used as adjectives in the following sentences are in bold. Write them on your paper. Beside each adjective, write the noun that the adjective describes.

Example **Many** people read that book.
Many — people

1) **Twenty-five** people signed up for the class.
2) **One** student dropped out.
3) After a **few** weeks, the teacher gave a test.
4) **Several** members of the class got a perfect grade.
5) **Most** students enjoyed the class.

Activity B Answers

1) Twenty-five—people
2) One—student 3) few—weeks
4) Several—members
5) Most—students

Lesson at a Glance

Chapter 3 Lesson 6

Overview This lesson presents numbers and indefinite pronouns used as adjectives. It also explains how to distinguish between a number used as a pronoun and an adjective.

Objectives

- To identify and use numbers as adjectives in sentences.
- To distinguish between numbers used as pronouns and adjectives.

Student Pages 67–69

Reading Vocabulary

exact (6) member (5)
indefinite (8)

Teaching Suggestions

Introducing the Lesson

Use these sentences to point out the difference between numbers used as nouns and numbers used as adjectives: *He wrote a nine on his paper.* (noun) *He drew nine cats.* (adjective) Encourage students to ask questions about anything they do not understand in the text.

Reviewing Skills

Review the definition of indefinite pronouns and ask students for examples.

Presenting Activity A

Have volunteers give sample sentences aloud for each item listed before having students do the activity on their own.

Activity A Answers

Answers will vary. Check that adjectives have been used correctly.

Presenting Activity B

Invite a volunteer to explain the directions and the example. Then have students do the activity.

Reading Vocabulary

barbecue (7)

Presenting Activity C

Write the following words on the board: *several, some, many, all, five, sixteen, thirty-three.* Then divide students into pairs and have each of the partners write a sentence for each word. Explain that they should try to use at least two of the words as pronouns and the rest as adjectives. Have partners exchange papers and identify the number words and whether each is used as a pronoun or an adjective. Encourage students to discuss any words they are not sure of with their partners.

Activity C Answers

1) eighty—adjective **2)** several—adjective **3)** Everyone—pronoun **4)** Many—adjective **5)** few—adjective **6)** Most—adjective **7)** six—adjective **8)** No one—pronoun **9)** Some—adjective **10)** Others—pronoun

Global Connection

Invite students who speak another language to translate the number words in activities *A, B,* and *C* into their primary language. Students may wish to make a chart to compare the spelling and pronunciation of the same number word in several different languages, including English.

Activity C The number words in these sentences are in bold. Write them on your paper. Beside each one, write whether it is used as a *pronoun* or an *adjective.*

Example **All** of the students signed up for **six** classes.
All—pronoun
six—adjective

1) The hurricane winds were **eighty** miles an hour.

2) The storm lasted for **several** hours.

3) **Everyone** on the block watched the storm.

4) **Many** trees blew down in the neighborhood.

5) We watched as a **few** cars drove through the storm.

6) **Most** people stayed inside.

7) The electricity was out for **six** hours.

8) **No one** could cook dinner or watch television.

9) **Some** families went out for dinner.

10) **Others** tried to barbecue in their yards.

Lesson 6 Review

Part A Write the number words used as adjectives in these sentences on your paper. Beside each adjective, write the noun it describes.

1) One Sunday, several friends and I visited the City Animal Park.
2) Each animal was in a natural setting.
3) We watched three chimpanzees swing from trees.
4) Eight lions and six tigers climbed over a rocky ledge.
5) There were many birds flying around the park.
6) For lunch, Willy ate two tacos and drank some lemonade.
7) We walked around for several hours.
8) Few people wanted to go home.
9) I took twenty-four photographs of the alligators and crocodiles.
10) Most children and adults would enjoy a visit to the City Animal Park.

Part B Complete these sentences by adding a number used as an adjective. Write the complete sentences on your paper.

1) During the hurricane, winds were blowing at ______ miles an hour.
2) ______ friends on our block are going on a picnic today.
3) Derek is taking ______ classes this year.
4) The movie lasted for ______ minutes.
5) ______ people were unhappy about the decision.

Reading Vocabulary

adult (6) photograph (6)
decision (5) taco

Part A Answers

1) One—Sunday, several—friends **2)** Each—animal **3)** three—chimpanzees **4)** Eight—lions, six—tigers **5)** many—birds **6)** two—tacos, some—lemonade **7)** several—hours **8)** Few—people **9)** twenty-four—photographs **10)** Most—children and adults

Part B Answers

Answers will vary. Responses should be complete sentences.

Follow-up Activity

Ask volunteers to write their sentences from Activity A, page 67, on the board or use an overhead projector and a transparency. Have students identify the number words in each sentence and the noun or pronoun each number word describes.

Learning Styles

Interpersonal/ Group Learning

Recall the song "She'll Be Coming Round the Mountain" and the nursery rhyme "Pease Porridge Hot." Encourage volunteers to find the number used as an adjective—"She'll be driving *six* white horses" and "pease porridge in the pot *nine*-days old." Divide the class into groups of three. Challenge each group to think of a song or nursery rhyme that uses a number as an adjective. Make a list of the songs and rhymes and post it. Encourage the students to add to it as they think of more songs and rhymes in the upcoming days.

Lesson at a Glance

Chapter 3 Lesson 7

Overview This lesson explains how demonstrative pronouns can be used as adjectives.

Objectives

- To distinguish between demonstrative pronouns and adjectives.
- To identify demonstrative adjectives and the nouns they describe.

Student Pages 70–71

Teacher's Resource Library

Workbook Activity 13

Reading Vocabulary

cabinet (5)

Teaching Suggestions

Introducing the Lesson

Discuss the difference between demonstrative pronouns and demonstrative adjectives. Ask students for two more examples of each. Write them on the board for students to use as reference.

Reviewing Skills Review the definition of a demonstrative pronoun.

Presenting Activity A

Write *this, that, these,* and *those* on four cards. Distribute the cards to students and have them use the word on their card in sentences as a pronoun and as an adjective. Repeat this activity so that every student has a chance to participate. If you have a large class, make more than four cards.

Activity A Answers

1) This—adj. 2) these—adj. 3) that—adj., this—adj. 4) those—adj. 5) that—adj. 6) This—pronoun 7) That—pronoun

Lesson 7 Demonstratives Used as Adjectives

The demonstrative pronouns—*this, that, these,* and *those*—can be used as adjectives to describe a noun. They answer the question *Which one or ones?*

EXAMPLES

Pronoun:	**That** is a mistake.
Adjective:	**That** mistake was Cal's. (Which mistake? *that* one)

Activity A The demonstratives in these sentences are in bold. Write them on your paper. Beside each one, write whether it is an *adjective* or a *pronoun.*

1) "**This** Sunday, let's go to the football game together," Leslie said.
2) My brother gave me **these** tickets.
3) "Do you think **that** team will win a game **this** year?" Elvin asked.
4) "Some of **those** new players are great," Leslie answered.
5) "I like **that** new fullback."
6) "**This** should be a good season," Elvin said.
7) "**That** will have to be proved," said Leslie.

Activity B Write these sentences on your paper. Underline five demonstrative adjectives. Then draw an arrow to the noun each demonstrative adjective describes.

Example Those players are on our team.

1) The football game that day was exciting.
2) "Where are those snacks you promised?"
3) "Look in that cabinet over the refrigerator."
4) "That is where my mother keeps those things."
5) "These sandwiches look good enough to eat."

Presenting Activity B

Have students explain the directions in their own words before they begin the activity.

Activity B Answers

1) that—day 2) those—snacks 3) that—cabinet 4) those—things 5) These—sandwiches

Name Date Period

Chapter 3 Workbook Activity 13

Finding Adjectives

Adjectives describe nouns and pronouns. They also limit the noun by giving it a number or quantity. Articles such as *a, an,* and *the* are adjectives, too. So are possessive nouns and pronouns. Demonstratives such as *this* and *that* also may be adjectives.

Directions: The paragraphs below contain 38 adjectives. Find each one and circle it. The number in parentheses indicates the number of adjectives in that paragraph.

Community Television

Janet and Darleen signed up for television training. They have cable television in their town. The cable company gives free training. Janet and Darleen learned to use the company's cameras. (8)

They decided to produce a television program. It was the most exciting activity of the summer. They would be television producers. (7)

That first day, they checked out the cameras. Next they drove to the county fair. Janet operated the heavy camera. Darleen worked the tape recorder. Producing a show was not difficult. (11)

What a good time they both had! (2)

After they finished their show, Janet and Darleen gave the finished tape to the cable company. The company showed their program on the free access channel. (10)

 Basic English Grammar

Workbook Activity 13

Lesson 7 Review

Lesson Review Find the demonstratives used as adjectives in the following sentences. Write them on your paper. Beside each one, write the noun it describes.

1) On that day, we went to a baseball game.

2) Those people behind us yelled through the whole game.

3) I would have liked to see that last play again.

4) We could have watched this game on television at home.

5) That would not have been as much fun as this day has been.

6) I felt bad for those umpires when the fans booed them.

7) Would you like to keep these ticket stubs to remember the fun we had?

8) Do you think that friend of yours could get us tickets to the next home game?

9) I want to keep these plastic cups from our soft drinks.

10) My sister has a set of those cups.

Reading Vocabulary

booed stub (5)

■ **Lesson Review** If students are unsure of any answers in these activities, have them review the material in the lesson to find the correct answers.

Lesson Review Answers

1) that—day **2)** Those—people **3)** that—play **4)** this—game **5)** this—day **6)** those—umpires **7)** these—stubs **8)** that—friend **9)** these—cups **10)** those—cups

Teacher Alert

Caution students against confusing the demonstrative *that* with the relative pronoun *that*. Review the use of *that* as a relative pronoun. Provide students with several examples of each. Then ask students to give examples of their own.

Learning Styles

Body/Kinesthetic
Ask volunteers to work in pairs. Assign each set a sentence in the review on page 71. Ask one partner in each set to be the demonstrative adjective in the sentence. Ask the other partner to be the noun the demonstrative adjective describes. Have the partners stand and read their sentence. Then, ask each set of partners to read its sentence again. This time, ask the "demonstrative adjective" and the "noun" to step forward and give one another a "high five" when they read the adjective and the noun.

Lesson at a Glance

Chapter 3 Lesson 8

Overview This lesson presents the degrees of comparison.

Objectives

- To compare with adjectives.
- To identify and use different degrees of comparison with adjectives in sentences.

Student Pages 72–75

Teacher's Resource Library

Activity 9

Workbook Activities 14–15

Reading Vocabulary

comparative adjective
positive adjective
strict (6)
superlative adjective

Teaching Suggestions

Introducing the Lesson

Discuss the degrees of comparison and the examples given. When you are sure students understand the information in the text, ask them to use the adjectives in the first Example box in sentences. Help students recognize and correct any errors in usage in their sentences.

Reviewing Skills Review what students have learned about adjectives so far.

Presenting Activity A

Suggest that students create a chart on their papers with the headings, *Positive, Comparative,* and *Superlative.* Then have students write the activity answers in their charts.

Activity A Answers

1) younger, youngest 2) older, oldest 3) kinder, kindest 4) shorter, shortest 5) greener, greenest 6) slower, slowest 7) later, latest 8) stricter, strictest 9) brighter, brightest

Lesson 8 Using Adjectives to Make Comparisons

Positive adjective
An adjective that describes one noun.

Comparative adjective
An adjective that compares one noun with another.

Superlative adjective
An adjective that compares one noun with two or more other nouns.

Adjectives can be used to compare people or things. There are three degrees of comparison: **positive**, **comparative**, and **superlative**.

EXAMPLES

Positive	Comparative	Superlative
strong	stronger	strongest
easy	easier	easiest
big	bigger	biggest
careful	more careful	most careful
popular	less popular	least popular
good	better	best
bad	worse	worst

Use the positive degree to describe one thing.
Use the comparative degree to compare two things.
Use the superlative degree to compare more than two things.

EXAMPLES

Incorrect: Luke is Darlene's brother. Luke is **oldest**.
Correct: Luke is Darlene's brother. Luke is **older**. (Two people are being compared.)
Correct: Of the three children, Matt is **oldest**. (More than two people are being compared.)

Most one-syllable adjectives form their comparative and superlative degrees by adding *-er* and *-est.*

Activity A Write the adjectives on your paper. Write their comparative and superlative degrees beside each one.

Example tall — **taller, tallest**

1) young	**4)** short	**7)** late
2) old	**5)** green	**8)** strict
3) kind	**6)** slow	**9)** bright

Some two-syllable adjectives form their comparative and superlative degrees by adding *-er* and *-est*. Others form their comparative and superlative degrees by using *more* and *most*.

Examples

Positive	Comparative	Superlative
happy	happier	happiest
careful	more careful	most careful

Adjectives of more than two syllables form their comparative and superlative degrees by using *more* and *most*. Adjectives can also be compared with *less* and *least*.

Examples

Positive	Comparative	Superlative
wonderful	more wonderful	most wonderful
successful	more successful	most successful
excited	less excited	least excited
generous	less generous	least generous

Activity B The adjectives in the following sentences are in bold. Write them on your paper. Beside each one, write whether it is *positive*, *comparative*, or *superlative*.

Example Danny is the **most helpful** person I know.
most helpful—superlative

1) That is the **least comfortable** chair.

2) Chris thought the movie was **terrible**.

3) The young girl was the **most talented** actress in the play.

4) I have never seen a **sadder** face.

5) This coat is **less expensive** than the other one.

Reading Vocabulary

generous (5) talent (5) successful (5)

Presenting Activity B

Create a chart on the board with the headings *Positive, Comparative,* and *Superlative.* List the following adjectives in the *Positive* column: *silly, hopeful, frightened, horrible, courageous.* Then help students fill in the chart by comparing each of these adjectives. Elicit from students when to use *-er* and *-est, more* and *most,* and *less* and *least.* After students complete Activity B, ask a volunteer to add the adjectives in bold to the appropriate columns in the chart. Then help students compare these adjectives to fill in the chart.

Activity B Answers

1) least comfortable—superlative 2) terrible—positive 3) most talented—superlative 4) sadder—comparative 5) less expensive—comparative

Teacher Alert

This may be a good opportunity to remind students of some common spelling rules, such as changing *y* to *i* before adding *-er* and *-est* to two-syllable words that end in *y* and doubling the final consonant of one-syllable CVC words. Use the words *happier* and *happiest* at the top of the page and *sadder* in item 4 of the activity as examples.

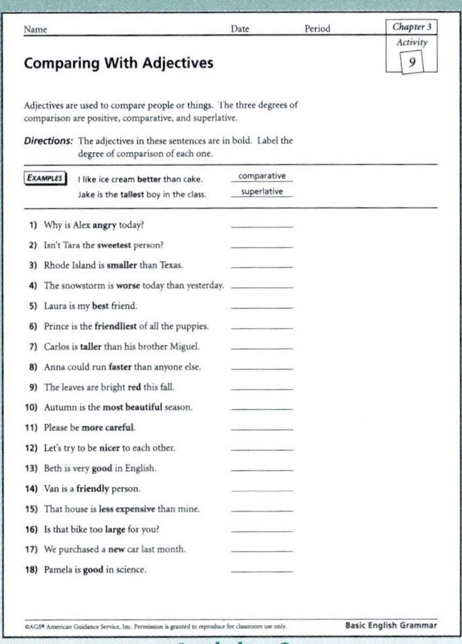

Name Date Period — Chapter 3 Activity 9

Comparing With Adjectives

Adjectives are used to compare people or things. The three degrees of comparison are positive, comparative, and superlative.

Directions: The adjectives in these sentences are in bold. Label the degree of comparison of each one.

Examples I like ice cream **better** than cake. comparative
Jake is the **tallest** boy in the class. superlative

1) Why is Alex **angry** today? ______
2) Isn't Tara the **sweetest** person? ______
3) Rhode Island is **smaller** than Texas. ______
4) The snowstorm is **worse** today than yesterday. ______
5) Laura is my **best** friend. ______
6) Prince is the **friendliest** of all the puppies. ______
7) Carlos is **taller** than his brother Miguel. ______
8) Anna could run **faster** than anyone else. ______
9) The leaves are bright **red** this fall. ______
10) Autumn is the **most beautiful** season. ______
11) Please be **more careful**. ______
12) Let's try to be **nicer** to each other. ______
13) Beth is very **good** in English. ______
14) Van is a **friendly** person. ______
15) That house is **less expensive** than mine. ______
16) Is that bike too **large** for you? ______
17) We purchased a **new** car last month. ______
18) Pamela is **good** in science. ______

 Basic English Grammar

Activity 9

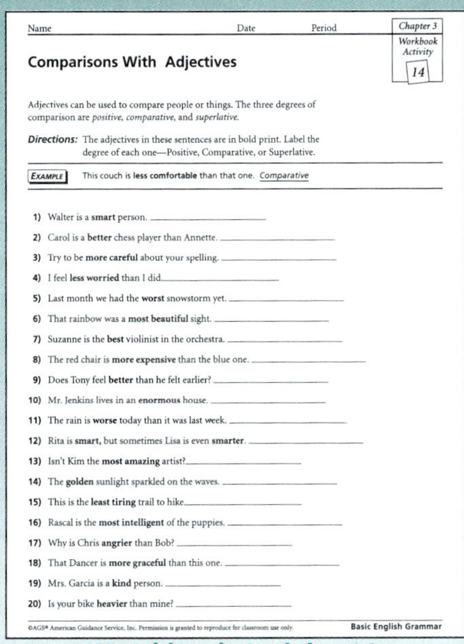

Name Date Period — Chapter 3 Workbook Activity 14

Comparisons With Adjectives

Adjectives can be used to compare people or things. The three degrees of comparison are *positive, comparative,* and *superlative.*

Directions: The adjectives in these sentences are in bold print. Label the degree of each one—Positive, Comparative, or Superlative.

Example This couch is **less comfortable** than that one. *Comparative*

1) Walter is a **smart** person. ______
2) Carol is a **better** chess player than Annette. ______
3) Try to be **more careful** about your spelling. ______
4) I feel **less worried** than I did. ______
5) Last month we had the **worst** snowstorm yet. ______
6) That rainbow was a **most beautiful** sight. ______
7) Suzanne is the **best** violinist in the orchestra. ______
8) The red chair is **more expensive** than the blue one. ______
9) Does Tony feel **better** than he felt earlier? ______
10) Mr. Jenkins lives in an **enormous** house. ______
11) The rain is **worse** today than it was last week. ______
12) Rita is **smart,** but sometimes Lisa is even **smarter**. ______
13) Isn't Kim the **most amazing** artist? ______
14) The **golden** sunlight sparkled on the waves. ______
15) This is the **least tiring** trail to hike. ______
16) Rascal is the **most intelligent** of the puppies. ______
17) Why is Chris **angrier** than Bob? ______
18) That Dancer is **more graceful** than this one. ______
19) Mrs. Garcia is a **kind** person. ______
20) Is your bike **heavier** than mine? ______

 Basic English Grammar

Workbook Activity 14

Reading Vocabulary

graceful (5) St. Augustine
irregular (7)

■ Presenting Activity C

Have students take turns using *good, better, best* and *bad, worse, worst* in oral sentences. Praise students who are able to use these words correctly the first time. Help students who have difficulty to recognize and correct their errors.

Activity C Answers

Answers will vary. Check that adjectives have been used correctly.

■ Presenting Activity D

Divide the class into small groups. Have group members take turns being the "group reader." Explain that the reader will read an activity item aloud two times with a different answer in place each time. Other members of the group should write down the correct answer. Students can then compare and explain their answers.

Activity D Answers

1) reddest **2)** taller **3)** oldest **4)** more comfortable **5)** best **6)** easier **7)** least **8)** more graceful

Learning Styles

Interpersonal/ Group Learning

Prepare a set of cards that contains the positive form of the adjectives in the boxes on pages 72–74. Place these cards in a box. Divide the class into groups of three. Ask each group to draw a card from the box. Challenge each group to compose three sentences that show the use of the positive, comparative, and superlative forms of the adjective the students drew from the box. Ask the group members to stand in the correct order as they say their sentence aloud.

Some adjectives form their comparative and superlative degrees in an irregular way.

Examples

Positive	Comparative	Superlative
good	better	best
bad	worse	worst

Activity C Use these adjectives correctly in a sentence. Write the sentences on your paper.

1) least useful
2) smaller
3) most successful
4) more wonderful
5) less careful
6) better
7) worst
8) heaviest
9) lighter
10) best

Activity D Write the form of the adjective that should appear in each sentence to make it correct.

1) That is the (redder, reddest) sunset I have ever seen.

2) Which of those two buildings is (taller, tallest)?

3) St. Augustine is the (oldest, older) city in Florida.

4) This chair is the (more comfortable, most comfortable) of the two.

5) That movie was the (goodest, best) I have ever seen.

6) Yesterday's homework was (easier, easiest) than today's.

7) Roger is the (least, less) selfish person I know.

8) Kerry is (gracefuller, more graceful) than I could ever be.

Lesson 8 Review

Part A Make three columns on your paper as shown in the example. Write the adjectives below in the correct column.

Example	*Positive*	*Comparative*	*Superlative*
	pretty	**friendlier**	**best**

1) bad
2) prettier
3) less difficult
4) worse
5) more careful
6) easiest
7) less comfortable
8) most generous
9) least horrible
10) worst
11) popular
12) good

Part B Some of the adjectives in these sentences are in bold. Write them on your paper. Beside each one, write whether it is *positive, comparative,* or *superlative.*

1) Emma is **older** than Britt.
2) This cloth feels **nice**, but that one feels **nicer**.
3) Of the two athletes, Lewis is the **faster** runner.
4) That comic is **funny**.
5) Hector plays tennis **better** than his twin brother Paco.
6) Of all the photographs, this one is the **best**.
7) I thought that her voice was soft, but yours is even **softer**.

Part C Write these adjectives on your paper. Beside each one, write its comparative and superlative forms.

1) small
2) useful
3) fast
4) famous
5) stern
6) soft
7) comfortable
8) smart
9) angry
10) horrible

The Adjective Chapter 3 75

Reading Vocabulary

column (5) horrible (5)
comic (6) tennis (5)

Part A Answers

1) Positive 2) Comparative 3) Comparative 4) Comparative 5) Comparative 6) Superlative 7) Comparative 8) Superlative 9) Superlative 10) Superlative 11) Positive 12) Positive

Part B Answers

1) older—comparative 2) nice—positive, nicer—comparative 3) faster—comparative 4) funny—positive 5) better—comparative 6) best—superlative 7) softer—comparative

Part C Answers

1) smaller, smallest 2) more useful, most useful 3) faster, fastest 4) more famous, most famous 5) sterner, sternest 6) softer, softest 7) more comfortable, most comfortable 8) smarter, smartest 9) angrier, angriest 10) more horrible, most horrible

Follow-up Activity

Prepare a list of adjectives used in this lesson. Divide the class into two teams. Read the positive, comparative, or superlative form of one of the adjectives on your list. The team whose turn it is has to identify the degree of comparison and supply the two missing forms.

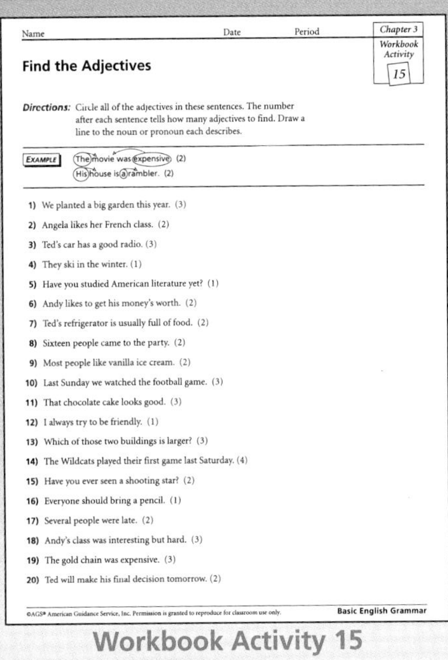

Name Date Period

Chapter 3 Workbook Activity 15

Find the Adjectives

Directions: Circle all of the adjectives in these sentences. The number after each sentence tells how many adjectives to find. Draw a line to the noun or pronoun each describes.

EXAMPLE The movie was expensive. (2)
His house is a rambler. (2)

1) We planted a big garden this year. (3)
2) Angela likes her French class. (2)
3) Ted's car has a good radio. (3)
4) They ski in the winter. (1)
5) Have you studied American literature yet? (1)
6) Andy likes to get his money's worth. (2)
7) Ted's refrigerator is usually full of food. (2)
8) Sixteen people came to the party. (2)
9) Most people like vanilla ice cream. (2)
10) Last Sunday we watched the football game. (3)
11) That chocolate cake looks good. (3)
12) I always try to be friendly. (1)
13) Which of those two buildings is larger? (3)
14) The Wildcats played their first game last Saturday. (4)
15) Have you ever seen a shooting star? (2)
16) Everyone should bring a pencil. (1)
17) Several people were late. (2)
18) Andy's class was interesting but hard. (3)
19) The gold chain was expensive. (3)
20) Ted will make his final decision tomorrow. (2)

 Basic English Grammar

Workbook Activity 15

Chapter 3 Review

The Teacher's Resource Library includes two parallel forms of the Chapter 3 Mastery Test. The difficulty level of the two forms is equivalent. You may wish to use one form as a pretest and the other form as a posttest.

Reading Vocabulary

elect (5)
include (5)
election (5)

Part A Answers

1) The, cool, clear **2)** happy, the, beautiful, autumn **3)** a, long **4)** The, sunny, warm, delightful **5)** A, young, noisy, cheerful, the

Part B Answers

1) my—homeroom **2)** new—officers, school—year **3)** smart—Li, loyal—Li, fun—Li **4)** good—president **5)** close—election

Chapter 3 Review

Part A Write all the adjectives in these sentences on your paper. Be sure to include articles.

1) The day was cool and clear.

2) Everyone was happy about the beautiful autumn weather.

3) After school, Rita and Pat went for a long walk.

4) The weather, sunny and warm, was delightful.

5) A group of young children, noisy but cheerful, got on the bus.

Part B Write the bold adjectives in these sentences on your paper. Beside each adjective, write the noun or pronoun that the adjective describes.

Example The **new** car was **expensive.**
new—car **expensive—car**

1) The students in **my** homeroom had a meeting.

2) They elected **new** officers for the **school** year.

3) "Li is **smart**, **loyal**, and **fun**," said Sue Ann.

4) "She will be a **good** president."

5) The election was **close**, but Li won.

Name ______ Date ______ Period ______

Chapter 3 Mastery Test A page 1

Chapter 3 Mastery Test A

Part A Circle each of the adjectives in these sentences. Underline the nouns that the adjectives describe.

1) Clare planned a large breakfast.

2) Clare's mother enjoys a big breakfast.

3) She served her mother a tall glass of cold orange juice.

4) Clare made six fluffy waffles and four pieces of French toast.

5) Those waffles and that French toast looked very tasty.

6) The Vermont maple syrup soaked into their waffles.

7) "That was an enormous breakfast!" her mother declared.

8) The spring day was bright and cheerful.

9) "It looks like a good day for a brisk walk," said Clare.

10) "That exercise is perfect after our huge breakfast," agreed Clare's mother.

Part B Rewrite these sentences. Capitalize the proper adjectives.

1) My spanish class comes before my english class.

______

2) The parade on thanksgiving day is always fun.

______

3) My friend Lek was born in Thailand.

______

4) We went to New York City to hear latin music.

______

5) Is Kenya an african country?

______

 Basic English Grammar

Name ______ Date ______ Period ______

Chapter 3 Mastery Test A page 2

Chapter 3 Mastery Test A, continued

Part C Read each of these sentences. Write in the correct degree of comparison for the word shown in parentheses.

1) My brother is ______ than I am. (short)

2) Of all my friends, I got the ______ seats for the concert. (good)

3) Because I was ______ than before, I made the free throw. (careful)

4) Joetta feels quite ______ today. (strong)

5) Sammy got the ______ news that he'd heard all week. (wonderful)

6) That is the ______ door in the building. (heavy)

7) This test is very ______. (easy)

8) St. Paul is the ______ of the two cities. (large)

9) Of all her attempts, her third try was ______. (successful)

10) No one runs the bases ______ than Ozzie. (fast)

Part D Identify the kind of adjective each word is. Write *Article, Number, Proper, Demonstrative,* or *Possessive.*

1) American ______ **6)** an ______

2) their ______ **7)** eighty ______

3) those ______ **8)** Mexican ______

4) the ______ **9)** this ______

5) several ______ **10)** player's ______

 Basic English Grammar

Chapter 3 Mastery Test A

Part C Write all the adjectives in these sentences on your paper. Be sure to include articles.

1) Joel and Paula decided to have an autumn party.
2) The party was on a Saturday evening.
3) Their parents gave them permission.
4) Paula found some old party decorations in the attic.
5) They bought fifty red apples and ten gallons of cider.
6) Joel carved an enormous pumpkin.
7) Some guests said they should all dunk for the apples.
8) "What an old-fashioned idea!" Paula said.
9) Several people brought more food.
10) Later everyone agreed that the party was the best one yet.

Part D Write the words in bold in these sentences on your paper. Beside each word, write whether it is a *noun* or an *adjective.*

1) That **history** book belongs to James Melcher.
2) They all went to the **meeting** room.
3) The **meeting** began at three o'clock.
4) The **south** wind was warm.
5) The wind came from the **South.**

Test Taking Tip Before you begin a test, look it over quickly. Try to set aside enough time to complete each section.

Reading Vocabulary

cider (6)
decoration (6)
old-fashioned (5)

Part C Answers

1) an, autumn **2)** The, a, Saturday **3)** Their **4)** some, old, party, the **5)** fifty, red, ten **6)** an, enormous **7)** Some, the **8)** an, old-fashioned **9)** Several, more **10)** the, the, best

Part D Answers

1) history—adjective **2)** meeting—adjective **3)** meeting—noun **4)** south—adjective **5)** South—noun

Application

In the Community

At some time in their lives, students may have the opportunity to write opinion letters to newspapers, letters of complaint to businesses, and letters to request information from groups and associations. Point out that their readers will be more inclined to pay attention to these letters if the ideas are presented in grammatically correct language. Suggest that students take the time to read their letters aloud before sending them. Hearing what they have written can help students catch mistakes. Students should pay special attention to the use of comparative and superlative forms of adjectives.

Name Date Period *Chapter 3 Mastery Test B page 1*

Chapter 3 Mastery Test B

Part A Circle each of the adjectives in these sentences. Underline the nouns that the adjectives describe.

1) Dale and his brother liked the nature park near their home.
2) Ken, Dale's brother, spotted two red squirrels in the park.
3) He held out a fresh peanut to an approaching squirrel.
4) The lively squirrel had a large, bushy tail.
5) "That squirrel looks hungry," Dale said to Ken.
6) The nearby oak tree was the squirrel's home.
7) "Those two birds on that branch are English sparrows," said Ken.
8) "Is that tree on the hill a Chinese elm?" asked Ken.
9) The brothers captured a toad by the small pond.
10) The slippery toad looked contented when they let it go.

Part B Rewrite these sentences. Capitalize the proper adjectives.

1) His father came from San José, the costa rican capital.
2) It was cold and rainy over the memorial day weekend.
3) Tom likes his german class better than his english class.
4) Does Panama touch the south american continent?
5) Earthquakes are common but frightening for california citizens.

 Basic English Grammar

Name Date Period *Chapter 3 Mastery Test B page 2*

Chapter 3 Mastery Test B, continued

Part C Read each of these sentences. Write in the correct degree of comparison for the word shown in parentheses.

1) The grass looked ______ this week than last week. (green)
2) My mother is ______ than I am. (tall)
3) I got the ______ cold of anyone in the family. (bad)
4) Hong Kong is the ______ of the two cities. (large)
5) Kip was ______ than I was about the play. (excited)
6) Of all her friends, Tamra gave the ______ gift. (generous)
7) Delaware is the ______ state in the country. (old)
8) The stars are very ______ tonight. (bright)
9) The tickets were the ______ of the three choices. (expensive)
10) Everyone slept ______ this morning. (late)

Part D Identify the kind of adjective each word is. Write *Article, Number, Proper, Demonstrative,* or *Possessive.*

1) African ______ 6) the ______
2) those ______ 7) a ______
3) Arnold's ______ 8) her ______
4) these ______ 9) many ______
5) thirty ______ 10) French ______

 Basic English Grammar

Chapter 3 Mastery Test B

Chapter 4

Planning Guide

The Action Verb

	Student Text Lesson: Student Pages	Vocabulary	Practice Exercises	Lesson Review
Lesson 1 Finding the Verb in a Sentence	80-83	✔	✔	83
Lesson 2 Verbs Express Tense	84-92	✔	✔	92
Lesson 3 The Progressive Forms	93-97	✔	✔	97
Lesson 4 Uses of the Verb *Do*	98-100		✔	100
Lesson 5 The Conditional Forms	101-104	✔	✔	104
Lesson 6 Active and Passive Forms	105-107	✔	✔	107

Chapter Activities

Teacher's Resource Library

Community Connection 4: Using Action Verbs

Assessment Options

Student Text

Chapter 4 Review

Teacher's Resource Library

Chapter 4 Mastery Tests A and B

Teaching Strategies							Language Skills			Learning Styles						Teacher's Resource Library		
Reviewing Skills	Teacher Alert	Follow-up Activity	Career Application	Home Application	Global Connection	Community Application	Identification Skills	Writing Skills	Punctuation Skills	Visual/Spatial	Auditory/Verbal	Body/Kinesthetic	Logical/Mathematical	Group Learning	LEP/ESL	Activities	Workbook Activities	Self-Study Guide
80	81	83	83			82	✔	✔	✔	82								✔
84	85, 90			89	86		✔	✔	✔						92	10-11	16	✔
93					94		✔	✔	✔		94						17-18	✔
98	98	100			99		✔	✔	✔								19	✔
101	101						✔	✔	✔			104				12		✔
105		109	107				✔	✔	✔				107				20	✔

Chapter at a Glance

(Answer Keys for the Teacher's Resource Library begin on page 330 of this Teacher's Edition.)

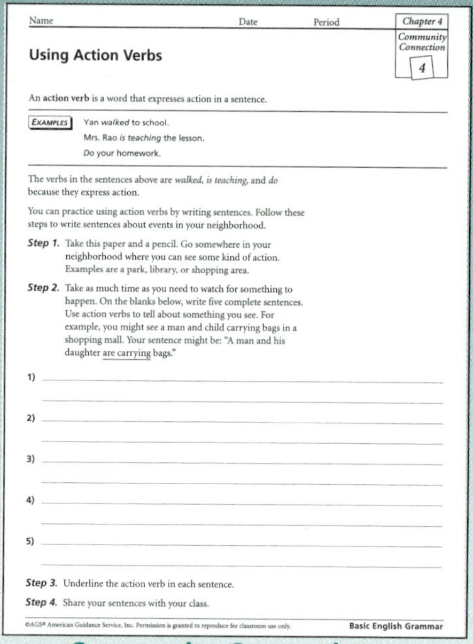

Name ____ Date ____ Period ____ *Chapter 4 Community Connection 4*

Using Action Verbs

An **action verb** is a word that expresses action in a sentence.

EXAMPLES Yan *walked* to school.
Mrs. Rao *is teaching* the lesson.
Do your homework.

The verbs in the sentences above are *walked*, *is teaching*, and *do* because they express action.

You can practice using action verbs by writing sentences. Follow these steps to write sentences about events in your neighborhood.

Step 1. Take this paper and a pencil. Go somewhere in your neighborhood where you can see some kind of action. Examples are a park, library, or shopping area.

Step 2. Take as much time as you need to watch for something to happen. On the blanks below, write five complete sentences. Use action verbs to tell about something you see. For example, you might see a man and child carrying bags in a shopping mall. Your sentence might be: "A man and his daughter are carrying bags."

1) ____________________

2) ____________________

3) ____________________

4) ____________________

5) ____________________

Step 3. Underline the action verb in each sentence.

Step 4. Share your sentences with your class.

 Basic English Grammar

Community Connection 4

Chapter 4 The Action Verb

At home, in the workplace, and in the community, you are often busy moving about and doing things. Exercising, working, eating, and thinking are just a few examples of the actions you do every day. When you talk or write about what you have done or seen, you use words that show action.

A verb is a word that expresses action or a state of being. An action verb is a word that expresses either physical or mental action.

In Chapter 4, you will learn about action verbs. Each lesson in the chapter focuses on the correct use and form of action verbs in sentences.

Goals for Learning

- To identify verbs and verb phrases in sentences
- To identify the correct form of verbs in sentences
- To recognize active and passive verbs

Reading Vocabulary

active (6)	mental (6)
community (5)	passive (10)
focus (7)	phrase (6)
identify (6)	physical (5)

Introducing the Chapter

Engage students in a discussion about the many different actions they perform during a single day. Then ask students to look at the photograph. How many different words can they think of to describe what the person is doing. Lead students to suggest action verbs such as *driving, operating, steering, working, thinking, concentrating, farming,* and so on. Write the words on the board as students suggest them. Accept any reasonable responses. Point out that all of these words are verbs that express action. Explain to students that in Chapter 4, they will have an opportunity to use action verbs in sentences to describe a variety of events.

SELF-STUDY GUIDE

Name ____________

CHAPTER 4: The Action Verb

Goal 4.1 *To identify verbs and verb phrases in sentences*

Date	Assignment	Score
______	1: Read pages 79-80. Complete Activity A on page 80.	______
______	2: Complete Activities B-C on page 81.	______
______	3: Read page 82. Complete Activities D-E on page 82.	______
______	4: Complete the Lesson 1 Review, Parts A-B on page 83.	______

Comments:

Goal 4.2 *To identify the correct form of verbs in sentences*

Date	Assignment	Score
______	5: Read page 84. Complete Activity A on page 84. Read page 85. Complete Activity B on page 85.	______
______	6: Read pages 86-87. Complete Activities C-D on page 87.	______
______	7: Complete Activities E-F on page 88.	______
______	8: Read page 89. Complete Activity G on page 89. Read page 90. Complete Activity H on page 90.	______
______	9: Complete Workbook Activity 16.	______
______	10: Read page 91. Complete Activities I-J on page 91.	______
______	11: Complete the Lesson 2 Review on page 92.	______
______	12: Read page 93. Complete Activity A on page 93.	______
______	13: Read page 94. Complete Activities B-C on page 95.	______
______	14: Complete Workbook Activity 17.	______
______	15: Complete Activities D-E on page 95. Complete Activity F on page 96.	______

 Basic English Grammar

SELF-STUDY GUIDE

Name ____________

CHAPTER 4 The Action Verb, continued

Goal 4.2 continued *To identify the correct form of verbs in sentences*

Date	Assignment	Score
______	16: Complete Workbook Activity 18.	______
______	17: Complete the Lesson 3 Review, Parts A-B on page 97.	______
______	18: Read page 98. Complete Activities A-B on page 99.	______
______	19: Complete Workbook Activity 19.	______
______	20: Complete the Lesson 4 Review, Parts A-B on page 100.	______
______	21: Read pages 101-102. Complete Activity A on page 102.	______
______	22: Complete Activities B-C on page 103.	______
______	23: Complete the Lesson 5 Review, Parts A-B on page 104.	______

Comments:

Goal 4.3 *To recognize active and passive verbs*

Date	Assignment	Score
______	24: Read page 105. Complete Activity A on page 105.	______
______	25: Complete Activities B-C on page 106.	______
______	26: Complete Workbook Activity 20.	______
______	27: Complete the Lesson 6 Review, Parts A-B on page 107.	______
______	28: Complete the Chapter 4 Review, Parts A-B on pages 108-109.	______

Comments:

Student's Signature ____________ Date ______

Instructor's Signature ____________ Date ______

 Basic English Grammar

Chapter 4 Self-Study Guide

Lesson at a Glance

Chapter 4 Lesson 1

Overview This lesson presents the concept of verbs as words that express action; it also shows the relationship of the subject and verb in a sentence and introduces verb phrases.

Objective

- To identify verbs, verb phrases, and subjects in sentences.

Student Pages 80–83

Reading Vocabulary

action verb subject (5)

Teaching Suggestions

Introducing the Lesson

After reading the text and reviewing the first three examples, encourage students to ask questions about anything that seems unclear. Then make two columns on the board with the heads: *Physical action* and *Mental action*. Ask volunteers for examples of verbs that express either physical or mental action and have students write their responses in the appropriate columns. Leave the list on the board for future reference.

Reviewing Skills

Provide a review of the parts of speech students have studied so far, including nouns, pronouns, and adjectives.

Presenting Activity A

Write sentences on the board with these verbs: *work, believe, dance, laugh, hope.* Ask students to read each sentence aloud and identify the verb. Help students determine which verbs express physical action and which express mental action.

Activity A Answers

1) parked 2) waved 3) likes 4) called 5) reminded

Lesson 1 Finding the Verb in a Sentence

Action verb
A word that expresses physical or mental action in the past, present, or future.

An **action verb** is a word that expresses the action in a sentence. The verb tells what someone or something does, did, or will do. Find the verb in a sentence by asking yourself two questions:

1. Who or what is doing something? (subject)
2. What are they doing? (verb)

EXAMPLE Every morning, Mr. Okada **reads** the newspaper.
Who is doing something? *Mr. Okada* (subject)
What does he do? *reads* (verb)

A sentence can have more than one verb.

EXAMPLE Donna **washed** and **wiped** the dishes after breakfast.
She **opened** her book and **began** her homework.

Some verbs express mental action, which cannot be seen.

EXAMPLE Mr. Okada **likes** his job.
Donna **thinks** about her test.

Activity A Write the verbs in these sentences on your paper.

1) Mr. Okada parked his car.

2) Several of his friends waved to him.

3) He likes all the people at the office.

4) Pam called her boss.

5) She reminded him about the meeting.

Activity B List the subjects and verbs in these sentences. Write *S* beside the subject and *V* beside the verb.

Example The secretary answers the telephone.

secretary—S answers—V

1) In the office everyone works hard.

2) Some people sort mail.

3) Others load it on trucks.

4) The trucks haul the mail to other places.

5) Letter carriers deliver mail to homes and offices.

6) Mrs. Davis works in an office.

7) She prepares the payroll.

8) Her assistant enters the information into a computer.

9) The computer prints the checks.

Activity C Find the verb or verbs in each sentence. List them on your own paper.

Examples The employees went to their desks and worked.

went, worked

1) Mr. Torres rode his bike to work on Tuesday.

2) He drank some juice and ate a bagel.

3) The telephone rang three times and then stopped.

4) His boss called back a few minutes later.

5) Mr. Torres wondered about the new client, Ms. Peters.

6) He sat in the meeting room and waited for everyone.

7) Ms. Peters and her assistant arrived on time.

8) They all shook hands and said, "Hello."

Reading Vocabulary

assistant (6)	employee (6)
bagel	haul (5)
client (8)	payroll
computer (8)	secretary (5)

■ Presenting Activity B

Ask students to use the verbs that were listed on the board in the introduction in oral sentences. Ask students to identify the subject and the verb in each sentence.

Activity B Answers

1) everyone—S, works—V
2) people—S, sort—V
3) Others—S, load—V
4) trucks—S, haul—V
5) Letter carriers—S, deliver—V
6) Mrs. Davis—S, works—V
7) She—S, prepares—V
8) assistant—S, enters—V
9) computer—S, prints—V

■ Presenting Activity C

Write these pairs of verbs on the board: *eat/drink, skipped/hopped, ran/hid, sing/dance.* Invite volunteers to create a sentence for each pair of verbs. Students can use the example sentence as a model.

Activity C Answers

1) rode **2)** drank, ate
3) rang, stopped **4)** called
5) wondered **6)** sat, waited
7) arrived **8)** shook, said

Teacher Alert

You may wish to provide additional instruction on simple subjects. Emphasize that for the activities in this lesson, the subject refers to the noun or pronoun that answers the question *Who or what is doing something?* Point out that they are not to include any words or phrases that describe the subject or tell more about the verb.

Reading Vocabulary

policy (7)
supervisor (7)
underline
verb phrase

Presenting Activity D

Work with students to create a list of helping verbs on the board or on poster paper. Suggest that students look at activities D and E for ideas. The list should include the following: *have, has, had, should, could, will,* and *may.* Students can refer to the list as they complete the activity.

Activity D Answers

1) had spoken **2)** thought **3)** should have known **4)** could have helped **5)** has announced **6)** will meet **7)** support

Presenting Activity E

Encourage students to create their own list of five verbs, including at least two verb phrases. Have partners exchange lists and practice making up sentences for each verb or verb phrase.

Activity E Answers

Sentences will vary.

Application

In the Community

To help raise public awareness of an organization's needs, volunteers in these organizations may be asked to write copy (text) for radio and television announcements, newspaper articles, posters, and flyers. The use of strong action verbs in any public service announcement can help grab people's attention and will, therefore, be more effective in getting the message to the community at large. Have students listen for public service announcements on the radio and television. Ask them to note the strong action verbs. Then have them recall some examples of public service announcements for the class.

Verb phrase
A main verb and one or more helping verbs.

A **verb phrase** is made up of more than one verb. A verb phrase contains a main verb and one or more helping verbs. The helping verbs *help* the main verb to show action.

Examples

Mr. Torres **has poured** his juice.
poured—main verb *has*—helping verb

Annie **should have come** with us.
come—main verb *should have*—helping verbs

Activity D Write the verb or verb phrase in each of these sentences on your paper.

1) Mrs. Stamos had spoken to Mr. Franklin.

2) Later, he thought about their talk.

3) He should have known about the problem sooner.

4) They could have helped each other.

5) Mr. Franklin has announced a new policy.

6) From now on, workers will meet with their supervisors once a week.

7) All of the employees support the new policy.

Activity E Use each verb or verb phrase below in a sentence. Write the sentences on your paper. Underline each subject once and each verb or verb phrase twice.

1) accept
2) balance
3) will comfort
4) contain
5) lift
6) could have been
7) examine
8) write
9) should remember
10) may think

Learning Styles

Visual/Spatial

Divide the class into pairs. Give each pair a magazine picture. Challenge the pairs to find five nouns in their picture. Then ask them to write five verbs to show the action of the nouns. Have students combine the nouns and verbs to make sentences. (For example, depending on the picture, students might write subject/verb combinations like the following: The curtains blow in the breeze. People are driving a car. Fruit grows on trees. Athletes are playing soccer.) Afterward, invite volunteer pairs to share their pictures and sentences with the class. Note: Keep the pictures for use with the Learning Styles activity on page 136.

82 *Chapter 4 The Action Verb*

Lesson 1 Review

Part A Write the verbs in these sentences on your paper.

1) Many different people work at the post office.
2) The public appreciates their efforts.
3) Letters and packages stream into the post office all day and night.
4) Letter carriers load the mail into sacks and deliver it.
5) Mail comes to the post office on trucks.
6) Airplanes also carry mail across the country and the world.
7) Millions of pieces of mail travel from place to place.
8) At the post office, mail handlers unload mail.
9) In smaller post offices, the workers sort the mail.
10) Machines perform this job in big cities.

Part B Write the verb or verb phrase in each of these sentences on your paper.

Example Don has gone to the store.
has gone

1) The newspaper arrived at six o'clock every day.
2) Mrs. Turner heard a thud at the front door.
3) She opened the door.
4) Then she got the paper.
5) She carried it into the kitchen.
6) Mr. Turner scrambled the eggs and put bread into the toaster.
7) He smiled at his wife.
8) She had set the table and had poured their juice.
9) They sat and read the paper.
10) Mr. and Mrs. Turner started every day the same way.
11) By six-thirty, they had eaten and had washed the dishes.
12) Then they both left for work.
13) He took the bus to his job downtown.
14) She drove the car to her office.
15) Each of them looks forward to the weekend.

Reading Vocabulary

appreciate (5) public (5)
handler thud (5)

Part A Answers

1) work **2)** appreciates **3)** stream **4)** load, deliver **5)** comes **6)** carry **7)** travel **8)** unload **9)** sort **10)** perform

Part B Answers

1) arrived **2)** heard **3)** opened **4)** got **5)** carried **6)** scrambled, put **7)** smiled **8)** had set, had poured **9)** sat, read **10)** started **11)** had eaten, had washed **12)** left **13)** took **14)** drove **15)** looks

Follow-up Activity

Encourage students to write several sentences about a recent school, local, or national event. Each sentence must express a complete thought with a subject and a verb. Invite students to share their sentences with the class. Ask students to identify the verbs, verb phrases and subjects in each sentence.

Application

Career Connection
Every job requires different skills and responsibilities. Have students research a career of their choice. Then have them create a poster about the career that describes those skills and responsibilities through a combination of text (action verbs) and pictures. Include some of the following in the poster:

- pictures of people working at the job
- some requirements of the job
- some benefits and rewards of the job
- a short history of the job

Lesson at a Glance

Chapter 4 Lesson 2

Overview This lesson presents the three simple tenses (present, past, future) and three perfect tenses (present perfect, past perfect, future perfect). It explains how regular and irregular verbs form their different tenses.

Objectives

- To find verbs and verb phrases in sentences.
- To identify the tense of verbs and verb phrases in sentences.

Student Pages 84–92

Teacher's Resource Library

Activities 10–11

Workbook Activity 16

Reading Vocabulary

guy (6)	opponent (7)
infinitive	**tense**

Teaching Suggestions

Introducing the Lesson

Write these three sentence starters on the board: *Today, I . . . , Yesterday, I . . . , Tomorrow, I . . . .* Have students take turns saying sentences using each sentence starter and the same verb. As students say the sentences, have them note how the form of the verb changes in each sentence.

Reviewing Skills

Review the meaning of singular and plural, collective nouns, and indefinite pronouns.

Presenting Activity A

Write the first activity item on the board but replace the verb with a blank. Invite students to fill in the blank with a verb in the present, past, or future tense. Elicit as many answers as necessary to cover all of the tenses.

Activity A Answers

1) future 2) present 3) past 4) past 5) past 6) present 7) present 8) present 9) future

Lesson 2 Verbs Express Tense

Tense
The time that the verb expresses in a sentence.

The verb in a sentence expresses **tense**, or time. Verbs use endings, helping verbs, or both to express tense.

Every verb has an infinitive form which is *to* plus the present tense of the verb. Verbs can express present, past, and future tense. Form the past tense by adding *-ed* to the present tense. Form the future tense by using the helping verb *will* or *shall.*

EXAMPLES

Infinitive:	**to fish**
Present tense:	I **fish** in that lake all summer. (Shows an action done in the present time.)
Past tense:	I **fished** in that lake last summer. (Shows an action done in the past.)
Future tense:	I **will fish** in that lake next summer. (Shows an action that will be done in the future.)

Activity A The verb in each of these sentences is in bold. Write the tense of the verb on your paper.

1) The Wilson Wildcats **will play** their first football game on Saturday.

2) The team **practices** every day.

3) They **wondered** about their opponents.

4) The coach **called** the team together.

5) He **talked** to them about the game plan.

6) "I **believe** in you guys."

7) The team **knows** the plan.

8) They **want** a victory on Saturday.

9) They **will do** their very best.

Add *-s* or *-es* to the present tense of the verb if the subject is singular.

EXAMPLES

Singular subject:	James **practices** every day.
Plural subject:	The players **practice** every day.

Remember: collective nouns (names of groups acting as one) are singular. Some indefinite pronouns, such as *everyone,* are also singular.

EXAMPLES

Singular subject:	The team **practices** after school.
Plural subject:	Both teams **practice** after school.
Singular subject:	Everyone **wants** a victory.

Activity B Write the verb that should appear in each sentence to make it correct.

1) James (hope, hopes) for a victory.

2) He (play, plays) tackle on the team.

3) Greg and Lorenzo both (play, plays) quarterback.

4) The coach (choose, chooses) the quarterback for each game.

5) Adam (catch, catches) every pass during practice.

6) All of them (go, goes) to practice every day.

7) Everyone (look, looks) forward to the games.

8) The whole team (work, works) hard.

Reading Vocabulary

collective (11)	quarterback
indefinite (8)	singular (8)
plural (6)	tackle (6)

■ Presenting Activity B

Invite a volunteer to read item 1 aloud twice—first with *hope,* and then with *hopes.* Ask students which form of the verb belongs in the sentence and why. Then have students complete the activity on their own. When they have finished, invite students to read the sentences aloud with the answers in place. Ask students to explain how they knew which form of the verb to use.

Activity B Answers

1) hopes **2)** plays **3)** play **4)** chooses **5)** catches **6)** go **7)** looks **8)** works

TEACHER ALERT

Subject-verb agreement can be confusing for many students. Some students may think that a plural subject with an *-s* ending should take a verb with an *-s* ending. Point out that it is actually the opposite; if one (either subject or verb) has an *-s* ending the other usually doesn't. Use the items in the activity and additional examples, if necessary, to stress this rule.

The Action Verb Chapter 4 **85**

Reading Vocabulary

future perfect
irregular (7)
past perfect
present perfect

Global Connection

Tell students that speakers of all languages have ways to express relationships in time. Write the following sentences on the board:

I have a book.

I had a book.

I will have a book.

Have students who speak languages other than English translate each sentence into their own language. Discuss the varied ways in which distinctions in tense can be made—not always with a change in verb form.

Present perfect
The verb tense that shows an action started in the past and continuing up to the present.

Past perfect
The verb tense that shows one action completed before another past action.

Future perfect
The verb tense that shows an action that will be completed before a certain time in the future.

The three perfect tenses are **present perfect**, **past perfect**, and **future perfect**. They are formed by using the helping verb *have*.

Examples

Present perfect:	James **has tackled** his opponent many times. (Shows an action that started in the past and continues up to the present. This action is likely to happen again.)
Past perfect:	James **had tackled** him before the whistle blew. (Shows that one action was completed before another past action began.)
Future perfect:	In a few minutes, our team **will have won** the game. (Shows an action that will be completed before a certain time in the future.)

Regular verbs form their past tense by adding *-ed* to the present tense. Irregular verbs form their past tense in different ways. *Have* is an irregular verb.

You need to know the different forms of *have* to form the perfect tenses of verbs.

(To) Have

Present tense	(singular)	James **has** the football now.
	(plural)	They **have** nine points.
Past tense		The team **had** the lead.
Future tense		The team **will have** a victory.
Present perfect	(singular)	He **has had** the ball three times.
	(plural)	They **have had** the ball most of the game.
Past perfect		When the quarter ended, they **had had** enough.
Future perfect		In one week, we **shall have had** a winning season.

86 *Chapter 4 The Action Verb*

The verb *have* can be a main verb or a helping verb.

EXAMPLES

Have as a main verb:	I **have** a good team. (*have* used alone)
Have as a helping verb:	I **have scored** a touchdown. (*have* used with the verb *scored*)

Activity C Write the verb that should appear in each sentence to make it correct.

1) The Wilson Wildcats (has, have) the football.

2) The team (has, have) scored a touchdown.

3) The Wildcats have (have, had) the ball for most of the quarter.

4) They will (has, have) given the other team few chances.

5) We soon will (have, had) earned the victory.

Activity D Decide whether *have* is the main verb or the helping verb in each sentence. Write your answers on your paper.

1) The quarterback has worked hard today.

2) He has thrown several good passes.

3) Hector has a good record so far.

4) We have one win and no losses.

5) The coach has expressed high hopes for the rest of the season.

Presenting Activity C

Invite volunteers to read each item aloud and tell whether the subject is singular or plural. Suggest that students refer to the chart on the bottom of page 86 as they complete the activity.

Activity C Answers

1) have **2)** has **3)** had **4)** have **5)** have

Presenting Activity D

Have students explain in their own words the difference between a helping verb and a main verb. Then have partners test each other with sentences in which *have* is a helping verb or a main verb. Students can model their sentences on those in the activity. You may wish to monitor the activity to determine which students are having difficulty with this concept. Provide extra help for those students who need it.

Activity D Answers

1) helping verb **2)** helping verb **3)** main verb **4)** main verb **5)** helping verb

Reading Vocabulary
discuss (5)

Presenting Activity E
Suggest that students create a chart for the activity items with the heads *present perfect, past perfect,* and *future perfect.* They can then refer to the filled-in chart as they write their sentences.

Activity E Answers
Sentences will vary. The present perfect, past perfect, and future perfect of each verb should be used in separate sentences and underlined for each item given.

Presenting Activity F
Write these verbs on the board: *call, wash,* and *wonder.* Divide the class into three teams. Ask for a volunteer from each team to come and write sentences for each of the six verb tenses, using *he* or *she* and one of the verbs. Students can ask teammates for help if they get stuck. Repeat this activity several times, replacing the verbs each time with three new regular verbs.

Activity F Answers
Students may use *he, she,* or *it* as the subject of their sentences.

1) She walks. She walked. She will walk. She has walked. She had walked. She will have walked. **2)** She works. She worked. She will work. She has worked. She had worked. She will have worked. **3)** She fishes. She fished. She will fish. She has fished. She had fished. She will have fished. **4)** She listens. She listened. She will listen. She has listened. She had listened. She will have listened. **5)** It roars. It roared. It will roar. It has roared. It had roared. It will have roared.

Activity E Write the present perfect, past perfect, and future perfect tenses of the verbs below in sentences on your paper. Underline the verb in each sentence.

Example jump

He has jumped. He had jumped. He will have jumped.

1) act	**6)** offer
2) discuss	**7)** open
3) improve	**8)** pass
4) lock	**9)** yell
5) move	**10)** shout

Activity F Write all six tenses of the verbs below in sentences on your paper. Use the third person singular (he, she, or it). Underline the verb in each sentence.

Example	whisper
present:	She whispers.
past:	She whispered.
future:	She will whisper.
present perfect:	She has whispered.
past perfect:	She had whispered.
future perfect:	She will have whispered.

1) walk

2) work

3) fish

4) listen

5) roar

Remember: Most verbs in the English language are regular. They form their past and perfect tenses by adding *-d* or *-ed* to their present form.

When a verb ends in *-y* and the letter before the *-y* is a consonant, change the *-y* to *-i*. Then add the ending for the tense.

EXAMPLES

I **worry** sometimes.

She never **worries.**

He **worried** all day.

Activity G Write the correct tense of the verb in the parentheses to complete each sentence.

1) Yesterday Kim (play) tennis.

2) Andy (apply) for a job last week.

3) Melissa (buy) a new outfit once a month.

4) Last year James (work) on the school newspaper.

5) Eric (enjoy) last week's football game.

6) This morning they (hurry) to school.

7) Sandra (reply) to Aunt Emily's letter.

8) Yesterday he (stay) home from school.

9) That loud thunder (terrify) me.

10) The witness (testify) for two days during the trial.

Reading Vocabulary

apply (6)	testify (7)
consonant	trial (5)
parentheses	witness (5)

■ Presenting Activity G

To help students understand when the *y* to *i* spelling rule applies, write the words *play* and *apply* on the board. Ask students to help you add endings to each word. Elicit from students that you should just add *-s* and *-ed* to *play* with no other spelling changes; you should change the *y* to *i* before adding *-es* or *-ed* to *apply.* Repeat this process, using all of the other verbs in the activity except *buy.*

Activity G Answers

1) played **2)** applied **3)** buys **4)** worked **5)** enjoyed **6)** hurried **7)** replied **8)** stayed **9)** terrified/terrifies **10)** testified

APPLICATION

At Home

Encourage students to review their homework assignments and personal correspondence to be sure that they have applied the *y* to *i* spelling change rule correctly. They may wish to make a bookmark with the spelling rule as it is given on page 89 written on one side and the names of the six verb tenses and examples of each written on the other side.

The Action Verb Chapter 4 **89**

Reading Vocabulary

assignment (6)
fielder
participle

■ Presenting Activity H

Give students an opportunity to practice using the past and past participle forms of the irregular verbs in the chart on page 90. Begin by writing sample sentences for *begin* and *catch* on the board; have students identify the past tense and past participle tense of each verb. Then encourage volunteers to write or say sentences using the past and past participle forms of the other verbs in the chart.

Activity H Answers

1) taught 2) gave 3) saw 4) eaten 5) seen 6) begun 7) knew 8) caught 9) came 10) gone 11) went 12) chosen

Teacher Alert

Some irregular verbs, such as see and go, are misused by many English-speaking people. Hearing these words used incorrectly on a regular basis can create a problem for students, especially those students acquiring English. Suggest that all students practice saying and writing sentences with these verbs used correctly whenever they get a chance.

The past participle is the third part of the verb. It is used with *have, has,* or *had* to form the perfect tenses of irregular verbs. Look at these commonly used irregular verbs.

Examples

Present	Past	Past Participle
begin	began	(have) begun
catch	caught	(have) caught
choose	chose	(have) chosen
come	came	(have) come
eat	ate	(have) eaten
give	gave	(have) given
go	went	(have) gone
know	knew	(have) known
see	saw	(have) seen
teach	taught	(have) taught

Activity H Write the past or past participle form of the verb in parentheses to complete each sentence.

1) Ms. Lee has (teach) math for many years.
2) Carol (give) her old bike to her sister.
3) Leon (see) an old friend at the movies.
4) They have already (eat) their dinner.
5) Have you ever (see) that movie?
6) Phillip had (begin) his homework already.
7) Jackie (know) the answer to the question.
8) The fielder (catch) the deep fly ball.
9) The news (come) on TV at six o'clock.
10) Where has Monica (go)?
11) Saturday everyone (go) to the game.
12) I have (choose) a partner for the assignment.

Name ____ Date ____ Period ____ *Chapter 4 Activity 10*

Irregular Verb Forms

A verb has four main forms. These forms are called the principal parts.

Present	Past	Past Participle	Present Participle
begin	began	(have) begun	(is) beginning
break	broke	(have) broken	(is) breaking
buy	bought	(have) bought	(is) buying
do	did	(have) done	(is) doing
choose	chose	(have) chosen	(is) choosing
eat	ate	(have) eaten	(is) eating
give	gave	(have) given	(is) giving
go	went	(have) gone	(is) going
know	knew	(have) known	(is) knowing
see	saw	(have) seen	(is) seeing
take	took	(have) taken	(is) taking

Directions: Write the correct form of the verb in parentheses in the blank.

Examples Jack __bought__ his sweater at the department store. (buy)
Sally __has seen__ that movie seven times. (see)

1) Barak has ____ the show already. (see)
2) Heather is ____ her old bike away. (give)
3) Mark ____ Julia to go to the dance with him. (choose)
4) Will you ____ to the skating rink with me? (go)
5) Jamie has ____ a lot of ice cream today! (eat)
6) Which band have you ____ for the prom? (choose)
7) Taunya ____ her mother's antique vase. (break)
8) Matt is ____ his homework. (do)
9) Mr. Tran has ____ French for years. (teach)
10) Yesterday, Shira ____ a new book. (begin)
11) What have you ____ with my pen? (do)
12) We ____ our old television to friends. (give)

 Basic English Grammar

Activity 10

Name ____ Date ____ Period ____ *Chapter 4 Workbook Activity 16*

Irregular Verb Forms

A verb has four main forms. These forms are called the *principal parts.*

Present	Past	Past Participle	Present Participle
break	broke	(have, has, had) broken	(is, are) breaking
buy	bought	(have, has, had) bought	(is, are) buying
do	did	(have, has, had) done	(is, are) doing
find	found	(have, has, had) found	(is, are) finding
grow	grew	(have, has, had) grown	(is, are) growing
have	had	(have, has, had) had	(is, are) having
make	made	(have, has, had) made	(is, are) making
ride	rode	(have, has, had) ridden	(is, are) riding
speak	spoke	(have, has, had) spoken	(is, are) speaking
take	took	(have, has, had) taken	(is, are) taking
write	wrote	(have, has, had) written	(is, are) writing

Directions: Fill in the blank with the correct form of the word in parentheses.

Examples Karen __buys__ her clothes at that store. (buy)
Mark has __grown__ three inches this year. (grow)

1) Carol is ____ a letter. (write)
2) Have you ____ your shoes yet? (find)
3) Have you ever ____ on a train? (ride)
4) I have ____ a nice time today. (have)
5) The garden vegetables have ____ six inches overnight. (grew)
6) Janet ____ her aunt a letter last week. (write)
7) The new lamp has ____. (break)
8) Ted ____ a sandwich for lunch. (make)
9) Now he is ____ a sandwich for Janet. (make)
10) Have you ____ your homework yet? (do)
11) The people ____ about the city's problems. (speak)
12) Everyone ____ a suggestion. (make)
13) Have you ____ your clothes to the cleaners? (take)
14) Lee went to the store and ____ the groceries. (buy)
15) The student has ____ many sentences. (wrote)
16) They have ____ the information that they needed. (find)
17) Andy ____ the bus to work every day. (ride)
18) That kind of dish ____ easily. (break)

 Basic English Grammar

Workbook Activity 16

The words in a verb phrase are usually written together. However, they may be separated by another word or words in the sentence.

EXAMPLES

She **has** finally **written** the letter.

Has Donna really **gone** to the library?

Michael **will** probably **finish** his homework after the game.

Activity I Write the verb phrase in each of these sentences on your paper. Ignore any words that come between the helping verb and the main verb.

1) James has always given his best.

2) Have you ever heard that song before?

3) Victor has often seen him at the field.

4) I had not met her before today.

5) Have you ever studied Spanish?

6) Carl will probably bring his lunch.

7) Jane and Sam have never gone to an art museum.

8) Connie had seldom enjoyed a book so much.

Activity J Write the tense of each bold verb or verb phrase on your paper.

1) **Will** you **drive** me to the store?

2) Yesterday Beth **lost** her gloves.

3) Ms. Potter **teaches** my math class.

4) The coach finally **chose** all of the players.

5) Melissa **had known** most of the players for years.

6) A reporter **has written** about many of our games.

7) His latest story **will appear** in tomorrow's paper.

8) By noon everyone in town **will have read** it.

Reading Vocabulary

ignore (5) seldom (5)
reporter separate (5)

■ Presenting Activity I

Have students identify the words that separate the verb phrase in each of the examples. Point out that the second sentence is a question. Explain that the first word of a question is often the first part of a verb phrase. Provide two or three more examples of questions that demonstrate this fact.

Activity I Answers

1) has given **2)** Have heard **3)** has seen **4)** had met **5)** have studied **6)** will bring **7)** have gone **8)** had enjoyed

■ Presenting Activity J

Before having students complete the activity on their own, review the six tenses of verbs and ask students for examples of each in sentences.

Activity J Answers

1) future **2)** past **3)** present **4)** past **5)** past perfect **6)** present perfect **7)** future **8)** future perfect

Name Date Period *Chapter 4 Activity 11*

Verb Tense

A verb can have six regular tenses. They are: present, past, future, present perfect, past perfect, and future perfect. Use the helping verb *have* to form the perfect tense. Use the helping verb *will* to form the future tense.

EXAMPLE cook

Present:	She cooks. (or) They cook.
Past:	She cooked.
Future:	She will cook.
Present perfect:	She has cooked. (or) They have cooked.
Past perfect:	She had cooked.
Future perfect:	She will have cooked.

Directions: In the following sentences, name the tense of the verb in bold print.

EXAMPLE Alex **cooked** dinner for the family ____past____

1) Sally **wrote** a letter to Aunt Marie. ______________

2) The loud thunderstorm **terrified** the cat. ______________

3) Rita **has run** the mile in five minutes. ______________

4) **Give** me your name, please. ______________

5) Some people **eat** whatever they want. ______________

6) Nikki **has gone** to Canada on a fishing trip. ______________

7) The quarterback **had thrown** a long pass. ______________

8) Yesterday we **returned** home from Nashville. ______________

9) Maya **writes** very well. ______________

10) We **will have completed** this assignment on time. ______________

11) Everyone **will have helped** with dinner. ______________

12) Jamal **has written** his term paper. ______________

13) The trial **lasted** for three weeks. ______________

14) Paul **will travel** to China next summer. ______________

15) Last year Karen **visited** Montana. ______________

 Basic English Grammar

Activity 11

The Action Verb *Chapter 4* **91**

Reading Vocabulary

championship
congratulations
cougar (6)
county (5)
extend (5)
fumble (6)
recover (6)

Lesson Review

Verbs are listed in the order they appear in the story.

enjoyed—past
threw—past
ended—past
came—past
made—past
tackled—past
fumbled—past
recovered—past
marched—past
scored—past
will have extended—future perfect
offer—present
will face—future
hopes—present
have looked—past perfect

Learning Styles

LEP/ESL

Ask ESL students to recreate the information in the box on page 90 in their primary language. Ask them to write the tenses for the boxed verbs in both English and their primary language. Have them write their lists on the board. Then use the board lists as a review. Ask the students for whom English is a primary language to work with the ESL students to make up sentences—in English and in a non-English language—for a verb in the list.

Lesson 2 Review

Lesson Review Write the all the verbs and verb phrases in the story below on your paper. Beside each verb or verb phrase, write its tense.

Wildcats devour Lincoln Lions

On Saturday, September 30, the Wilson Wildcat fans enjoyed a 21-3 victory over the Lincoln Lions.

Quarterback George Benetez threw two touchdown passes in the first half. The half ended at 14-0. The Lions' only score came in the third quarter with a field goal.

James Melcher made a big play late in the final quarter. He tackled the Lions' running back. The running back fumbled the ball. The Wildcats recovered on their 48-yard line. Wilson marched down the field and scored the final goal. Many fans will have already extended congratulations to Melcher. We offer ours now for a fine play.

Next week the Wildcats will face the Crofton Cougers. The team hopes for a winning season. They have looked forward to the county championship years.

Lesson 3 The Progressive Forms

Progressive form
The form of a verb that ends in -ing and uses a form of the verb be as a helping verb to show continuing action.

The **progressive forms** of verbs express continuing action. Compare the two sentences below.

Present	Melissa **practices** the trumpet twice a week. (Shows an action that is done frequently.)
Present progressive	Melissa **is practicing** the trumpet. (Shows an action that is being done now.)

The fourth part of the verb has the ending *-ing* and is called the present participle.

EXAMPLES

Present	Present Participle
work	working
see	seeing
be	being

A progressive form is a verb phrase. It is made from a form of the verb *be* plus the present participle.

EXAMPLES

Present progressive:	He **is working**.
Past progressive:	He **was working**.
Future progressive:	He **will be working**.
Present perfect progressive:	He **has been working**.
Past perfect progressive:	He **had been working**.
Future perfect progressive:	He **will have been working**.

Activity A Write the verb phrase in each of these sentences on your paper.

1) Hai Sin was practicing her flute when the phone rang.
2) Soon Tom will be practicing the drums.
3) Sam has been practicing for thirty minutes.
4) Cathy had been practicing the trumpet when I interrupted her.
5) In five minutes, the band will have been practicing for an hour.

Lesson at a Glance

Chapter 4 Lesson 3

Overview This lesson presents the progressive forms of verbs and the different forms of the verb *be.*

Objectives

- To locate verbs in sentences.
- To use the verb *be* correctly in sentences.
- To identify and use the twelve forms of regular verbs in sentences.

Student Pages 93–97

Teacher's Resource Library

Workbook Activities 17–18

Reading Vocabulary

compare (5)
frequently
progressive form

Teaching Suggestions

■ Introducing the Lesson
As you present the information, be sure students understand that continuing action means action that continues, or goes on, for an extended time.

■ Reviewing Skills Review the verb tenses along with the forms of the verb *be.*

■ Presenting Activity A
Before having students complete the activity, have them use the six progressive forms of these verbs in sentences: *paint, sing, play, think,* and *speak.* First help students form the present participle of each verb. Then have them say sentences like those shown in the example for the verb *work.*

Activity A Answers
1) was practicing **2)** will be practicing **3)** has been practicing **4)** had been practicing **5)** will have been practicing

Global Connection

Students might be interested to learn the pronunciation and spelling of the verb *be* in several languages. Write the verb *be* in the center of a web and ask students for other English forms of the verb *be.* Add these to the outside of the web. Then invite students who speak other languages to say forms of the verb *be* in their primary language. Have them write these forms of *be* in the web. Encourage students to explain when each of the forms shown in the web is used.

■ Presenting Activity B

Have students complete these sentences with a form of the verb *be:*

He has ________ very sick.

My aunt ________ visiting next week.

I will ________ leaving soon.

Activity B Answers

1) been 2) be 3) been 4) been 5) is

Learning Styles

Auditory/Verbal

Divide the class into groups of three. Assign each group one line of the "to be" list in the box on page 94. (Note that the box contains 12 lines that show the progressive form of the verb *to be.*) Ask each group to read its line aloud. Then challenge each group to create three sentences that show the progression of the verb. Record these sentences on an audio tape. Encourage the students to use this tape in the days that follow to learn the "to be" progression.

Verbs form their progressive form by adding *-ing* to the present tense and using the helping verb *be.*

Be is an irregular verb.

You need to know the different forms of *be* to form the progressive tense of verbs.

(To) Be

Simple Tenses

Present	Past	Future
I am	I was	I shall be
you are	you were	you will be
he is	he was	he will be
we are	we were	we shall be
you are	you were	you will be
they are	they were	they will be

Perfect Tenses

Present Perfect	Past Perfect	Future Perfect
I have been	I had been	I shall have been
you have been	you had been	you will have been
he has been	he had been	he will have been
we have been	we had been	we shall have been
you have been	you had been	you will have been
they have been	they had been	they will have been

Activity B Write on your paper the correct form of the verb *be* to complete each sentence.

1) I have ________ on an airplane six times.

2) Jack will ________ going to Seattle next week.

3) Doris has ________ in my class every year.

4) By noon, Mac will have ________ working for four hours.

5) Sara ________ leaving for Florida on Friday.

Activity C Write a sentence for each of these verbs on your paper.

1) will have been going

2) has been working

3) had been eating

4) is beginning

5) were whispering

6) am opening

Activity D Write the tense of each bold verb phrase on your paper.

1) Mario **had** never **gone** to Texas before this year.

2) He **is flying** there for a vacation.

3) He **will be leaving** at noon.

4) Mario **has been packing** all morning.

5) They **are going** to the airport now.

Activity E Write a sentence for each verb, using the tense given in parentheses. Underline the verb or verb phrase in your sentence.

Example pass (present progressive)
Ted is passing the salad to Bill.

1) drive (future progressive)

2) have (past progressive)

3) fish (present progressive)

4) see (future perfect progressive)

5) pour (past perfect progressive)

6) go (simple past)

7) wonder (present perfect progressive)

8) jump (present perfect)

■ Presenting Activity C

Invite volunteers to use each verb phrase listed in an oral sentence before having students write sentences on their own.

Activity C Answers

Answers will vary.

■ Presenting Activity D

Have partners work together to write examples of verbs in the three perfect and six progressive tenses. Then invite them to share their verbs with the class. Suggest that students refer back to the examples on page 93 as they do Activity D.

Activity D Answers

1) past perfect **2)** present progressive **3)** future progressive **4)** present perfect progressive **5)** present progressive

■ Presenting Activity E

Create two sets of six cards. On one set of cards, write each of the six progressive forms. On the other set, write each of these verbs: *go, fly, leave, pack, whisper, jump.* Place the cards face down in two separate piles. Have students take turns selecting a card from each pile and then using the verb selected in the tense selected in a sentence. Shuffle the cards after two or three students take their turns.

Activity E Answers

Answers will vary.

Name Date Period

Chapter 4 *Workbook Activity* *17*

Verb Phrases

When the verb has more than one word, it is called a verb phrase. We use helping verbs to express *tense.* We always place the helping verb in front of the main verb.

EXAMPLES
run — Present
will run — The helping verb *will* is added to express future tense.
is running — The helping verb *is* expresses progressive tense.
has been running — Past perfect progressive tense requires two helping verbs.

Directions: Read each sentence carefully. Find the verb or verb phrase and draw a circle around it.

EXAMPLE George Washington (was born) in Wakefield, Virginia.

1) George Washington's early childhood was spent on a farm.

2) His father died when he was eleven years old.

3) George had studied mathematics and surveying.

4) Then he lived with his brother Lawrence.

5) Lawrence would later build Mount Vernon.

6) George was surveying the Shenandoah Valley.

7) He began a diary at that time.

8) George went with Lawrence to Barbados in the West Indies.

9) There he caught smallpox.

10) He had many scars from that disease.

11) George's brother Lawrence died.

12) Lawrence had willed George all of his land, including Mount Vernon.

13) Washington's military career started in 1753.

14) Governor Dinwiddie had sent him on missions to the Ohio region.

15) He was engaged in battles with the French for several years.

16) George married Martha Custis in 1759.

 Basic English Grammar

Workbook Activity 17

Reading Vocabulary

accompany (5) items (6)
include (5)

Presenting Activity F

Review the rules presented in the examples and encourage students to ask questions about anything they do not understand. Suggest that as students do the activity, they read the sentence to themselves twice, with a different answer in place each time. They should choose the answer that sounds most correct to them.

Activity F Answers

1) playing **2)** played
3) going **4)** accompanying
5) raising **6)** raised **7)** selling
8) sold **9)** bought **10)** giving

Activity F Write the verb that should appear in each sentence to make it correct.

Examples Use the present participle (verb + *-ing*) with any forms of the helping verb *be*.
Sheila **is fixing** her bike.

Use the past participle form (verb + *-ed*) with any forms of the helping verb *have*.
Sheila **has fixed** her bike.

If the verb phrase includes both *have* and *be*, use the present participle (verb + *-ing*).
Sheila **has been fixing** her bike.

1) Rosa has been (playing, played) the trumpet for several years.

2) She has (playing, played) in the Wilson band for two years.

3) This year the band is (going, gone) to Florida for a national contest.

4) Some of the parents will be (accompanying, accompanied) the band.

5) The band members have been (raising, raised) money all year.

6) So far they have (raising, raised) more than one thousand dollars.

7) Everyone is (selling, sold) school t-shirts.

8) So far, they have (selling, sold) a thousand items.

9) Rosa herself has (buying, bought) t-shirts for her mom and her two sisters.

10) She will be (giving, gave) them as birthday presents.

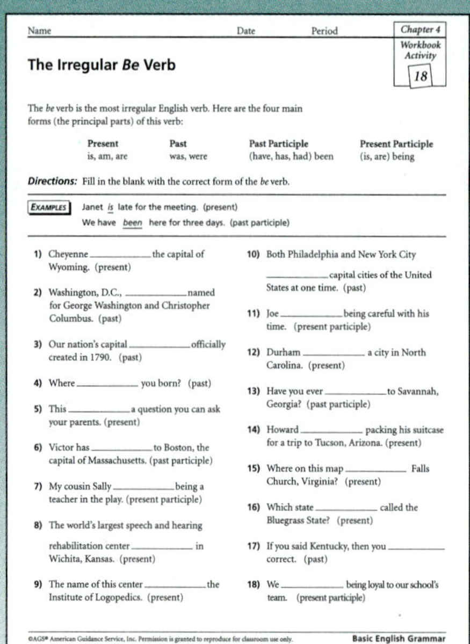

Name Date Period *Chapter 4 Workbook Activity 18*

The Irregular *Be* Verb

The *be* verb is the most irregular English verb. Here are the four main forms (the principal parts) of this verb:

Present	Past	Past Participle	Present Participle
is, am, are	was, were	(have, has, had) been	(is, are) being

Directions: Fill in the blank with the correct form of the *be* verb.

EXAMPLES Janet *is* late for the meeting. (present)
We have *been* here for three days. (past participle)

1) Cheyenne ______ the capital of Wyoming. (present)

2) Washington, D.C., ______ named for George Washington and Christopher Columbus. (past)

3) Our nation's capital ______ officially created in 1790. (past)

4) Where ______ you born? (past)

5) This ______ a question you can ask your parents. (present)

6) Victor has ______ to Boston, the capital of Massachusetts. (past participle)

7) My cousin Sally ______ being a teacher in the play. (present participle)

8) The world's largest speech and hearing rehabilitation center ______ in Wichita, Kansas. (present)

9) The name of this center ______ the Institute of Logopedics. (present)

10) Both Philadelphia and New York City ______ capital cities of the United States at one time. (past)

11) Joe ______ being careful with his time. (present participle)

12) Durham ______ a city in North Carolina. (present)

13) Have you ever ______ to Savannah, Georgia? (past participle)

14) Howard ______ packing his suitcase for a trip to Tucson, Arizona. (present)

15) Where on this map ______ Falls Church, Virginia? (present)

16) Which state ______ called the Bluegrass State? (present)

17) If you said Kentucky, then you ______ correct. (past)

18) We ______ being loyal to our school's team. (present participle)

 Basic English Grammar

Workbook Activity 18

Lesson 3 Review

Part A Write sentences on your paper using the verb *sharpen* in each of the six regular tenses and the six progressive forms. *Sharpen* is a regular verb. The first one has been done for you.

1) present—Phillip **sharpens** his pencil before class.
2) past
3) future
4) present perfect
5) past perfect
6) future perfect
7) present progressive
8) past progressive
9) future progressive
10) present perfect progressive
11) past perfect progressive
12) future perfect progressive

Part B Write the verbs or verb phrases in this paragraph on your paper. Beside each verb or verb phrase, write its tense.

> Louis Armstrong played the trumpet. He earned a special place in American history. As a child, he lived in an orphanage in New Orleans. There he first studied the cornet. In 1922, he played on a Mississippi riverboat. He joined a band in Chicago. Then in 1924, Armstrong moved to New York City. Soon he was playing the trumpet. He invented a completely new style. By 1925, he was recording his music. Later he formed his own band. People also loved his husky voice. In the 1930s, Armstrong starred in movies. His popularity continued for the rest of his life. One of his records, "Hello, Dolly!" sold two million copies in 1964. Armstrong died in 1971. People will remember this man and his music for a long time.

Reading Vocabulary

cornet	popularity
orphanage (6)	style (5)

Part A Answers

Sentences will vary. Verb forms are given.

1) sharpens **2)** sharpened **3)** will sharpen **4)** has (have) sharpened **5)** had sharpened **6)** will have sharpened **7)** is (am, are) sharpening **8)** was (were) sharpening **9)** will be sharpening **10)** have (has) been sharpening **11)** had been sharpening **12)** will have been sharpening

Part B Answers

Verbs are given in the order they appear in the paragraph.

played—past, earned—past, lived—past, studied—past, played—past, joined—past, moved—past, was playing—past progressive, invented—past, was recording—past progressive, formed—past, loved—past, starred—past, continued—past, sold—past, died—past, will remember—future

Lesson at a Glance

Chapter 4 Lesson 4

Overview This lesson presents the verb *do* as a helping verb and as a main verb.

Objectives

- To identify verb phrases with the helping verb *do* in sentences.
- To distinguish between the verb *do* used as a helping verb or main verb in sentences.

Student Pages 98–100

Teacher's Resource Library

Workbook Activity 19

Reading Vocabulary

negative (8)

Teaching Suggestions

Introducing the Lesson

After reading the text and reviewing the examples, ask students to demonstrate their understanding of the information presented by providing additional examples modeled after each example given.

Reviewing Skills

Have students identify and give examples of each of the tenses.

Teacher Alert

Remind students that the verb *do* is an irregular verb; its past and past participle forms (*did, have done*) are *not* formed by adding *-d* or *-ed* to the infinitive.

Lesson 4 Uses of the Verb *Do*

The helping verbs *do* and *did* are used with a negative word, such as *not.*

Examples

Many stores **do** *not* **close** on holidays. (present)

Dan **did** *not* **find** his book. (past)

The helping verbs *do* and *did* also are used to form questions.

Examples

Do you **like** strawberries? (present)

Did you **finish** that book? (past)

The helping verbs *do* and *did* are used only with the present form of the main verb.

Example

Did you **go** home? (The verb *go* is present.)

The verb *do* can also be used as a main verb. The main verb *do* means "to perform an action." It can be used in all tenses.

Examples

Present:	Brigette **does** her chores early.
Past:	Victor **did** his work well.
Future:	Everyone **will do** his part.
Present perfect:	The family **has done** its work well.
Past perfect:	We **had done** the yard work by dinnertime.
Future perfect:	Soon he **will have done** his lessons.

Activity A Write all the verbs and their helpers in these sentences on your paper.

1) Did you see Anita at lunch?

2) Jack never did find his gloves.

3) The family is doing the dishes.

4) Do you read the newspaper?

5) Where do you do your homework?

Activity B Write the bold verb in these sentences on your paper. Beside it, write whether *do* is a helping verb, a main verb, or both.

Example Soon he **will have done** his report.
will have done—main verb

1) After dinner Eric and Melissa **did** the dishes.

2) Finally they **had done** all their chores.

3) Melissa **had** already **done** her homework.

4) "**Did** you **see** my math book?" Eric asked.

5) "What **did** you **do** with it this time?" she asked.

6) "I **did** not **see** it today," he said.

7) **Did** Eric ever **find** his book?

8) Soon he **was doing** his math.

■ Presenting Activity A

Before having students complete the activity, have partners take turns asking each other questions with *do* and *did*. The listening partner should identify the main verb and helping verb in each question.

Activity A Answers

1) did see **2)** did find **3)** is doing **4)** do read **5)** do do

■ Presenting Activity B

Write these sentences on the board and have students identify the main verb and helping verb or verbs in each sentence.

I should not have done that.

She does not want any help.

Activity B Answers

1) did—main verb **2)** had done—main verb **3)** had done—main verb **4)** Did see—helping verb **5)** did do, main verb and helping verb **6)** did see—helping verb **7)** did find—helping verb **8)** was doing—main verb

Global Connection

An idiom is an expression whose meaning goes beyond the actual meaning of the words in the idiom. The verb *do* is part of several English idioms, including: *to do without; to do in; that will do; to do away with; how do you do?* Write these and other idioms with *do* on the board and discuss their meanings. Invite students who speak other languages to provide expressions with similar meanings in their primary language.

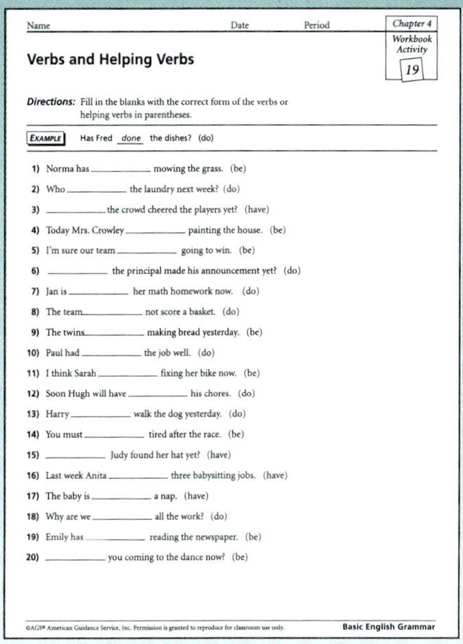

Name Date Period

Chapter 4 *Workbook Activity* *19*

Verbs and Helping Verbs

Directions: Fill in the blanks with the correct form of the verbs or helping verbs in parentheses.

EXAMPLE Has Fred _done_ the dishes? (do)

1) Norma has ______ mowing the grass. (be)

2) Who ______ the laundry next week? (do)

3) ______ the crowd cheered the players yet? (have)

4) Today Mrs. Crowley ______ painting the house. (be)

5) I'm sure our team ______ going to win. (be)

6) ______ the principal made his announcement yet? (do)

7) Jan is ______ her math homework now. (do)

8) The team ______ not score a basket. (do)

9) The twins ______ making bread yesterday. (be)

10) Paul had ______ the job well. (do)

11) I think Sarah ______ fixing her bike now. (be)

12) Soon Hugh will have ______ his chores. (do)

13) Harry ______ walk the dog yesterday. (do)

14) You must ______ tired after the race. (be)

15) ______ Judy found her hat yet? (have)

16) Last week Anita ______ three babysitting jobs. (have)

17) The baby is ______ a nap. (have)

18) Why are we ______ all the work? (do)

19) Emily has ______ reading the newspaper. (be)

20) ______ you coming to the dance now? (be)

 Basic English Grammar

Workbook Activity 19

Reading Vocabulary

prune (6) task (5)

Part A Answers

1) did **2)** was doing **3)** will have done **4)** had done **5)** did complete **6)** does

Part B Answers

1) do—present **2)** did rake—past **3)** have raked—present perfect **4)** Does plant—present **5)** will have done—future perfect **6)** have done—present perfect **7)** Did do—past **8)** are doing—present perfect **9)** did trim—past **10)** does look—present

Follow-up Activity

Have students write ten original sentences, using *do* as a main verb in five sentences and as a helping verb in five sentences. Sentences should include the use of *do* in questions. Invite students to read several of their sentences to the class. Ask listeners to identify the verb and any helpers in each sentence and tell whether *do* is used as a helping verb or main verb.

Lesson 4 Review

Part A Write the verb or verb phrase in each of these sentences on your paper.

1) Yesterday, Tanya did her yard work.

2) She was doing yard work all afternoon.

3) Soon she will have done the entire yard.

4) She had done all of the weeding, too.

5) Did Tanya complete her tasks?

6) Who does the yard work at your house?

Part B Write the verb or verb phrase in each of these sentences on your paper. Beside each verb or verb phrase, write its tense.

1) In the fall, people do extra yard work.

2) Did you rake your leaves yet?

3) They have already raked their yard.

4) Does your family plant grass seed in the fall?

5) Soon they will have done the whole yard.

6) I have already done my part.

7) Did Dad do the front yard?

8) The boys are doing the pruning.

9) They did not trim the fruit trees this year.

10) How does the yard look?

Activity B Write the verb that should appear in each sentence to make it correct.

1) Every day Andy (exercise, exercises) at the gym.

2) They (exercise, exercises) on a regular basis.

3) Julian (might, mights) exercise today.

4) He would (goes, go) every day if he had the time.

Activity C Write the verb phrase in each of these sentences on your paper.

1) Cam's purse will hold many things.

2) She should clean it up.

3) In fact, she must clean it up.

4) She cannot find anything in it.

5) Cam should have bought a new purse.

6) She might be buying a new one.

7) Should she buy a new purse?

8) Yes, she should.

Reading Vocabulary

basis (7) purse (5)
gym (5)

Presenting Activity B

Have volunteers read each item aloud twice, each time with a different answer in place. Students should write the answer they think sounds most correct. After, students can compare and explain their answer choices. Then encourage students to use the other answer choice in each item correctly in sentences.

Activity B Answers

1) exercises **2)** exercise **3)** might **4)** go

Presenting Activity C

Write these sentences on the board:

Would you have known the answer?

May I come with you to the mall?

Yes, you may.

Have students raise their hands when they have identified the verb phrase in each sentence. When all hands are raised, invite volunteers to point out the verb phrase in each sentence.

Activity C Answers

1) will hold **2)** should clean **3)** must clean **4)** can find **5)** should have bought **6)** might be buying **7)** Should buy **8)** should (*buy* is understood)

Reading Vocabulary

error (6)

Part A Answers

1) might be going **2)** could have gone **3)** must go **4)** would leave **5)** should pack **6)** must take **7)** can go **8)** may take **9)** Should take **10)** might rain

Part B Answers

Answers may vary. Possible answers are given.

1) will **2)** may **3)** should **4)** could **5)** can **6)** might **7)** will **8)** would

Learning Styles

Body/Kinesthetic

Create a set of cards that contains the conditional verb forms *may, might, can, could, shall, should, will, would,* and *must.* Give the set of cards to one student. Have the student shuffle the cards and then deal one to another student. Ask that student to use the conditional verb form on the card to create a sentence. Have the first student print the sentence on the board and underline the verb form. Continue with this process until all the students have created a sentence and printed it on the board.

Lesson 5 Review

Part A Write the verb or verb phrase in each of these sentences on your paper.

1) Next week, I might be going to Indiana.

2) I could have gone last year.

3) This year I must go.

4) I would leave on Monday if possible.

5) I should pack my bags.

6) I must take my winter coat.

7) I can go by plane.

8) I may take only one bag.

9) Should I take an umbrella?

10) It might rain.

Part B Write a conditional helping verb on your paper to complete each sentence.

1) Suke ______ go to the movies with Danny.

2) Danny ______ ask her to go.

3) Al ______ finish his work by noon.

4) He ______ finish sooner if he hurries.

5) Lily said that Erin ______ use the school computer.

6) With a computer, Erin ______ write a better paper.

7) That computer program ______ catch grammar and spelling errors.

8) Gerry ______ like that program.

Name ______ Date ______ Period ______ *Chapter 4 Activity 12*

Conditional and Emphatic Verbs

We often form verb phrases using conditional and emphatic helping verbs.
We often use these helping verbs to ask questions.

Conditional verbs: can, could, will, would, must, shall, should, may, might
Jonas **can build** a cabinet with his tools.
Nicole **must** do her homework before dinner.
Would you **help** me now?

Emphatic verbs: do, did, done
Did you **lose** this ring?
I **did** not **lose** that ring.

Directions: Read each sentence carefully. Circle the verb phrase.

EXAMPLES I (would like) that dessert.
(Did) you (make) that quilt yourself?

1) I must have gone to nearly every country in the world.

2) Lisa might have gone home by now.

3) They should have exercised already.

4) Did you know about Aza?

5) He might win a Nobel Peace prize.

6) They must leave soon for Philadelphia.

7) William can sing very loud.

8) Holly and her sister Gina might come for dinner next week.

9) Do you like carrots?

10) We must rake the front yard this afternoon.

11) Did John do the backyard yet?

12) They did not trim the trees last year.

13) We must do them this year.

14) "Do you like strawberries?" Ray asked.

 Basic English Grammar

Activity 12

Lesson 6 Active and Passive Verbs

Active verb
A verb that is used if the subject does the action.

Use an **active verb** if the subject is doing the action. The sentence tells who did what.

EXAMPLE Carlos **wrote** a story.

Passive verb
A verb that is used when the action happens to the subject.

Use a **passive verb** if the action happens to the subject. The sentence tells what was done by whom.

EXAMPLE The story **was written** by Carlos.

To form the passive verb, use the helping verb *be* with the past participle (the third part of the verb).

EXAMPLE

Correct:	The story **was written** by Carlos.
Incorrect:	The story **was wrote** by Carlos.

In some sentences that use passive voice, the person doing the action is not named. The person is "understood."

EXAMPLES

Today the bank **was robbed**.	(by someone)
The pass **was thrown** well.	(by someone)

Activity A Write the verbs and their helpers in these sentences on your paper.

1) The note was discovered by Mary.
2) We were disturbed by a loud noise.
3) The telephone was finally answered.
4) The ball was hit to left field.
5) The car was greased last month.

Lesson at a Glance

Chapter 4 Lesson 6

Overview This lesson presents active and passive voice.

Objectives

- To identify verbs in the active and passive voice.
- To use verbs in the active voice and passive voice in sentences.

Student Pages 105–107

Teacher's Resource Library

Workbook Activity 20

Reading Vocabulary

active verb passive verb

Teaching Suggestions

Introducing the Lesson

Write these two sentences beside each other on the board: *Anita threw the ball. The ball was thrown by Anita.* Help students apply the definitions of *active verb* and *passive verb* to each sentence to determine which sentence is in the active voice and which is in the passive voice. Be sure students understand how the passive verb is formed before having them complete the activities in this lesson.

Reviewing Skills

Provide a review of the principal parts of verbs (*present, past, past participle*).

Presenting Activity A

Have students complete these sentences with passive verbs: *The winning photograph ________ by a young child. Those wooden toys ________ by my grandfather. The movie ________ in Africa .*

Activity A Answers

1) was discovered 2) were disturbed 3) was answered 4) was hit 5) was greased

Reading Vocabulary

raven (5)

Presenting Activity B

Students will have an easier time completing the activity if they follow this procedure for each item: 1) read the sentence; 2) identify the subject and the verb ; 3) decide if the subject is doing the action or if the action is happening to the subject. Remind students that if the subject is performing the action the verb is active; if the action is happening to the subject, the verb is passive.

Activity B Answers

1) wrote—active 2) was written—passive 3) wrote—active 4) was written—passive 5) was baked—passive 6) baked—active

Presenting Activity C

Do the first item in the activity to provide examples of ways to vary the sentence content and verb tense. (Active: He should cover his book. I will cover the paper with paint./Passive: The pot of soup was covered by the chef. The pool will be covered for the winter.)

Activity C Answers

Answers will vary.

Activity B Write the verbs in these sentences on your paper. Beside each verb, write whether it is *active* or *passive.*

1) John Steinbeck wrote many stories.
2) *The Red Pony* was written by John Steinbeck.
3) Edgar Allan Poe wrote many poems.
4) "The Raven" was written by Poe.
5) That cake was baked by my aunt.
6) My aunt baked that cake.

Activity C Write two sentences for each of these verbs on your paper. In the first sentence, use the word as an active verb. In the second sentence, use the word as a passive verb.

1) cover
2) direct
3) discover
4) disturb
5) teach
6) hit
7) invent
8) cook
9) answer
10) pack

Name Date Period

Chapter 4 Workbook Activity 20

Active and Passive Verbs

A verb is active if the subject is doing the action.

EXAMPLE Marcia **ripped** her jeans.

A verb is passive if something happens to the subject.

EXAMPLE Marcia's jeans **were ripped**.

Directions: The verb in each sentence is in bold print. Decide whether it is active or passive. Circle your answer.

EXAMPLES That picture **was painted** by my mother. (Active, (Passive))
My mother **painted** that picture. ((Active), Passive)

1) Those flowers **were dug** up by the dog. (Active, Passive)
2) We **packed** our bags for the trip. (Active, Passive)
3) Tom's best coat **was lost**. (Active, Passive)
4) Alison's glasses **were found** in the gym. (Active, Passive)
5) My cat **had been chased** by a dog. (Active, Passive)
6) I **met** my new neighbors today. (Active, Passive)
7) The treasure **was found** in a cave. (Active, Passive)
8) We **played** the album twice. (Active, Passive)
9) The windows **were washed** this week. (Active, Passive)
10) A wasp **flew** into the classroom. (Active, Passive)
11) The tigers **snarled** at each other. (Active, Passive)
12) The ball of string **was** hopelessly **snarled**. (Active, Passive)
13) The melody **was played** by the clarinets. (Active, Passive)
14) The statue **was made** of bronze. (Active, Passive)
15) Beth **painted** a portrait of her sister. (Active, Passive)
16) Mary **hit** the ball for a triple. (Active, Passive)
17) Jim **kicked** the extra point. (Active, Passive)
18) The barn **was struck** by lightning (Active, Passive)
19) Larry **was chased** by a lion. (Active, Passive)
20) Mr. Tibbetts **drove** the van. (Active, Passive)

 Basic English Grammar

Workbook Activity 20

Lesson 6 Review

Part A Write the verb and any helper in these sentences on your paper.

1) The cotton gin was invented by Eli Whitney.

2) Cotton seeds are removed from the cotton.

3) In 1842, the Oregon Trail was explored by John Fremont.

4) Fremont was later elected as one of California's first senators.

5) *Gone With the Wind* was written by Margaret Mitchell.

6) Her book was made into a successful movie.

7) Indiana was settled in 1808 by Tecumseh, a Shawnee leader.

8) Tecumseh was killed at the battle of the Thames in Canada during the War of 1812.

9) In 1848, Lewis Cass was defeated by Zachary Taylor.

10) Taylor was elected as President of the United States.

Part B Rewrite each of these sentences on your paper. Change the verb in bold from passive to active.

Example Passive: The cotton gin **was invented** by Eli Whitney.

Active: Eli Whitney **invented** the cotton gin.

1) The batter **was hit** by the wild pitch.

2) John's bag **was packed** by his mother.

3) The telephone **was answered** by the receptionist.

4) The neighbors **were disturbed** by the barking dog.

5) The oil **was changed** last month by the mechanic.

Reading Vocabulary

receptionist senator (6)

Lesson Review

Because of the difficult vocabulary in both activities, read through all the items once with students before having them work on their own.

Part A Answers

1) was invented **2)** are removed **3)** was explored **4)** was elected **5)** was written **6)** was made **7)** was settled **8)** was killed **9)** was defeated **10)** was elected

Part B Answers

1) The wild pitch hit the batter. **2)** John's mother packed his bag. **3)** The receptionist answered the telephone. **4)** The barking dog disturbed the neighbors. **5)** The mechanic changed the oil last month.

Application

Career Connection

Secretaries, office managers, teachers, lawyers, and so many other workers depend on good communication skills to do their job effectively. One sign of a good communicator is his or her careful and sparing use of the passive voice. Although the use of passive voice is not grammatically incorrect, active voice is more emphatic and direct. Writers and speakers should use passive voice only when to do otherwise would produce an awkward and unclear sentence.

Learning Styles

Logical/Mathematical

Divide the class into groups of three. Ask each group to examine the sentences in Activity B on page 106 and in Part A and Part B on page 107. Challenge the groups to find the passive pattern in these sentences. (Note: The students may find the following two patterns: 1. In the sentences with a passive verb, the actor follows the verb and the word *by* introduces the actor. 2. The sentences with a passive verb always use a helping verb, such as *was* and *are.*) Ask a volunteer to print these patterns on a poster for the classroom.

Chapter 4 Review

The Teacher's Resource Library includes two parallel forms of the Chapter 4 Mastery Test. The difficulty level of the two forms is equivalent. You may wish to use one form as a pretest and the other form as a posttest.

Reading Vocabulary

career (6) minor (6)
contract (6) nickname (5)

Part A Answers

1) began **2)** gave **3)** played **4)** sold **5)** pitched, batted **6)** broke **7)** had been looking **8)** was sent **9)** would play **10)** led **11)** was hitting **12)** set **13)** had hit **14)** hit **15)** was elected

Part B Answers

1) went **2)** play **3)** practices **4)** want **5)** likes

Chapter 4 Review

Part A Write the verb or verb phrase in each of these sentences on your paper.

1) George Herman Ruth began his baseball career in 1914.
2) His teammates gave him the nickname "Babe."
3) He first played with the minor league Baltimore Orioles.
4) Baltimore sold his contract to the Boston Red Sox.
5) Babe pitched and batted left-handed.
6) In 1919, he broke all of the records for home runs in a season.
7) The New York Yankees had been looking at Ruth for some time.
8) In 1920, he was sent to the Yankees.
9) He would play in games in the outfield.
10) He led the league in home runs for many years.
11) He was hitting more home runs every year.
12) In 1927, he set a new world record.
13) He had hit sixty home runs in a single year.
14) In his last game, Babe Ruth hit three home runs in a row.
15) He was elected to the Baseball Hall of Fame in 1936.

Part B Number your paper from 1 to 25. Write the verb that should appear in each sentence to make it correct.

1) Mr. Torres (went, gone) to work.
2) The Wildcats will (play, played) their first game on Saturday.
3) The team (practice, practices) every day.
4) They (want, wants) a victory.
5) Everyone (like, likes) to win.

Name ______ Date ______ Period ______ *Chapter 4 Mastery Test A page 1*

Chapter 4 Mastery Test A

Part A Complete each sentence. Write the correct form of the verb in parentheses.

1) Juana usually __________ her bike to school. (ride)
2) Would you __________ me the spoon? (pass)
3) What are you __________ tomorrow? (do)
4) We could have __________ the floors last week. (sand)
5) Anna and Kurt have __________ Spanish for two years. (study)
6) Mike __________ his favorite pencil. (break)
7) Gerry has __________ a new car. (price)
8) Claudia had __________ her homework. (finish)
9) Jamal was __________ an apple. (eat)
10) Will you have __________ to the cleaners by then? (be)

Part B Circle the verb or verb phrase in each sentence.

1) I would like a second piece of bread.
2) Janice and Randy may come to dinner next week.
3) We must plant a garden this year.
4) Do you know the cost of a CD?
5) Bill plays tennis very well.
6) Willis and Cara will be trimming the bushes this Saturday.
7) Do you like blackberry cobbler?
8) Larry might have finished by now.
9) Did you hear about Sophie?
10) Would you have gone anyway?

 Basic English Grammar

Name ______ Date ______ Period ______ *Chapter 4 Mastery Test A page 2*

Chapter 4 Mastery Test A, continued

Part C Write each verb in the tense that is shown.

	Verb	Tense	
1)	clear	past	__________
2)	finish	future perfect	__________
3)	go	present perfect	__________
4)	call	past perfect	__________
5)	plan	present progressive plural	__________
6)	close	future	__________
7)	practice	past progressive singular	__________
8)	last	future perfect progressive	__________
9)	sell	future progressive	__________
10)	rake	present	__________

Part D Write whether the verb in these sentences is *active* or *passive.*

1) The book was written by Toni Morrison. __________
2) Rhonda put the cover on the jar. __________
3) The lawn mower was tuned up in April. __________
4) Pedro drew a sad face on the clown. __________
5) Hak was disturbed by the noise. __________
6) Dinner was burned when we got home. __________
7) Rae listens to CDs every evening. __________
8) The carrots were peeled. __________
9) Cheri usually is given a ride to work. __________
10) The wild pitch hit the batter. __________

 Basic English Grammar

Chapter 4 Mastery Test A

6) He (have, has) never had an injury.

7) They have (score, scored) two touchdowns.

8) Monday they (hurryed, hurried) to work.

9) Last week the man (testifies, testified) at the trial.

10) I have (beginned, begun) my work.

11) He (bring, brings) his lunch every day.

12) Yvonne (knowed, knew) the answer.

13) Sara always (do, does) her work well.

14) The band (is, are) practicing now.

15) The children (is, are) riding their bikes.

16) He (be, is) flying to Florida.

17) Did you (finish, finished) that book?

18) Did Juan (go, went) home yet?

19) He (must, musts) go home now.

20) Janine (is, could) be finished by noon.

21) The book was (wrote, written) by Jack London.

22) That cake was (bake, baked) by Bob.

23) The electric lightbulb was (inventing, invented) by Thomas Edison.

24) We (was, were) disturbed by the bell.

25) The barking dog (make, made) everyone angry.

Test Taking Tip Before you answer any question on an exam, skim through the whole test to find out what is expected of you.

Reading Vocabulary

injury (6)

(Part B Answers, continued)

6) has 7) scored 8) hurried 9) testified 10) begun 11) brings 12) knew 13) does 14) is 15) are 16) is 17) finish 18) go 19) must 20) could 21) written 22) baked 23) invented 24) were 25) made

Follow-up Activity

Encourage students to write a paragraph about a person they admire. Tell them to describe the person's accomplishments and explain why they admire that person. Emphasize that students should try to use a variety of action verbs in their sentences. Invite students to share their paragraphs with the class. Then have them go back and identify the verb used in each sentence and its tense.

Name Date Period | *Chapter 4 Mastery Test B page 1*

Chapter 4 Mastery Test B

Part A Complete each sentence. Write the correct form of the verb in parentheses.

1) The family ______ to California last Thanksgiving. (fly)
2) Where did you ______ for lunch today? (go)
3) Mr. Beck will have been ______ for three years. (teach)
4) We might have ______ a new puppy. (find)
5) Asia has ______ Latin for three years. (take)
6) Are you ______ your money for something special? (save)
7) Owen will ______ the gate early today. (lock)
8) Hai had ______ in that lake before. (fish)
9) Bobbi often ______ volleyball for fun. (play)
10) Will you ______ to the grocery store for me? (walk)

Part B Circle the verb or verb phrase in each sentence.

1) Ahmad has gone to the mall.
2) Betty and Sam may visit us next summer.
3) Lila had purchased a new computer.
4) Do you know the price of milk?
5) Twyla has been acting for three years.
6) Bob will be making money this winter with his snow shoveling.
7) Do you like black beans and rice?
8) Edna and I may have eaten there before.
9) Did you read about Pearl?
10) Would you have made plans differently?

 Basic English Grammar

Name Date Period | *Chapter 4 Mastery Test B page 2*

Chapter 4 Mastery Test B, continued

Part C Write each verb in the tense that is shown.

Verb	Tense	
1) warn	past	______
2) rise	future	______
3) use	present progressive plural	______
4) write	past progressive singular	______
5) worry	future perfect	______
6) work	future progressive	______
7) like	present perfect	______
8) continue	future perfect progressive	______
9) end	past perfect	______
10) dream	present	______

Part D Write whether the verb in these sentences is *active* or *passive*.

1) Harsha flew an airplane four times. ______
2) The airport was closed during the storm. ______
3) They ate lunch in the park. ______
4) That class is held every year. ______
5) The poem was written by Langston Hughes. ______
6) She greased the car. ______
7) The shades were pulled down. ______
8) The grass was mowed too short. ______
9) Ketta walked ten miles. ______
10) The windshield wipers were stuck. ______

 Basic English Grammar

Chapter 4 Mastery Test B

Chapter 5

Planning Guide

The State-of-Being Verb

	Student Text Lesson			
	Student Pages	Vocabulary	Practice Exercises	Lesson Review
Lesson 1 What Is a State-of-Being Verb?	112-116	✔	✔	116
Lesson 2 Action or State of Being?	117-121		✔	121
Lesson 3 Using State-of-Being Verbs	122-125		✔	125

Chapter Activities

Teacher's Resource Library

Community Connection 5: State-of-Being Verbs in the Media

Assessment Options

Student Text

Chapter 5 Review

Teacher's Resource Library

Chapter 5 Mastery Tests A and B

Teaching Strategies							Language Skills			Learning Styles						Teacher's Resource Library		
Reviewing Skills	Teacher Alert	Follow-up Activity	Career Application	Home Application	Global Connection	Community Application	Identification Skills	Writing Skills	Punctuation Skills	Visual/Spatial	Auditory/Verbal	Body/Kinesthetic	Logical/Mathematical	Group Learning	LEP/ESL	Activities	Workbook Activities	Self-Study Guide
112	112	116					✔	✔	✔				114			13-14	21-22	✔
117	117	121			118		✔	✔	✔						119		23-24	✔
122		125	127	124			✔	✔	✔		125					15		✔

Chapter at a Glance

Chapter 5: The State-of-Being Verb pages 110–127

(Answer Keys for the Teacher's Resource Library begin on page 330 of this Teacher's Edition.)

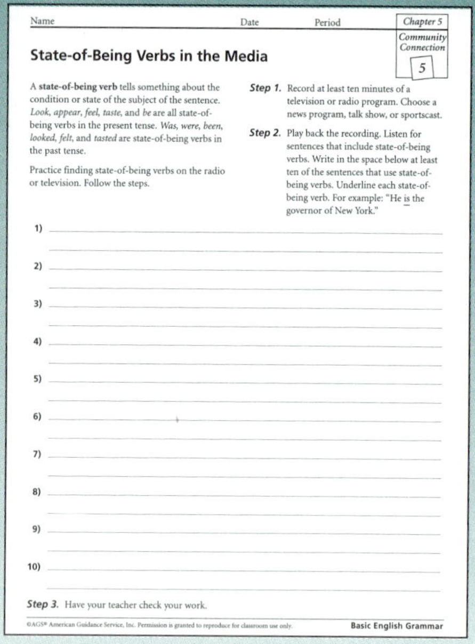

Name ______ Date ______ Period ______ *Chapter 5* *Community Connection* 5

State-of-Being Verbs in the Media

A **state-of-being verb** tells something about the condition or state of the subject of the sentence. *Look, appear, feel, taste,* and *be* are all state-of-being verbs in the present tense. *Was, were, been, looked, felt,* and *tasted* are state-of-being verbs in the past tense.

Practice finding state-of-being verbs on the radio or television. Follow the steps.

Step 1. Record at least ten minutes of a television or radio program. Choose a news program, talk show, or sportscast.

Step 2. Play back the recording. Listen for sentences that include state-of-being verbs. Write in the space below at least ten of the sentences that use state-of-being verbs. Underline each state-of-being verb. For example: "He is the governor of New York."

1) ______

2) ______

3) ______

4) ______

5) ______

6) ______

7) ______

8) ______

9) ______

10) ______

Step 3. Have your teacher check your work.

 Basic English Grammar

Community Connection 5

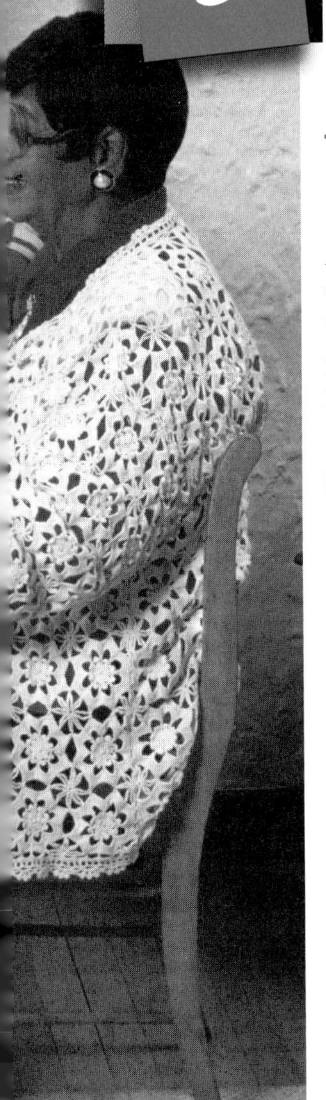

Chapter 5

The State-of-Being Verb

When you discuss relationships and feelings, you may say sentences such as these: I *am* their son. The food *tastes* wonderful.

A verb is a word that expresses action or a state of being. A state-of-being verb tells something about the condition or state of the subject of the sentence.

In Chapter 5, you will learn about state-of-being verbs. Each lesson in the chapter focuses on the correct use and form of state-of-being verbs in sentences.

Goals for Learning

- To identify state-of-being verbs and verb phrases in sentences
- To distinguish between active and state-of-being verbs and verb phrases in sentences
- To identify the correct form of state-of-being verbs in sentences

Reading Vocabulary

discuss (5)
distinguish (6)
focus (7)
identify (6)
phrase (6)
relationship (6)
subject (5)

Introducing the Chapter

Ask students to describe what is happening in the photograph. Encourage students to say sentences that explain who each person in the picture is and how the person is feeling. Lead students to use state-of-being verbs in their sentences, providing model sentences such as *The woman in the sweater is their Grandma. She seems happy. Grandma felt chilly without her sweater.* Write these and other sentences students suggest on the board. Circle the state-of-being verbs in each sentence. Explain that verbs that tell who someone is or how they are feeling are called state-of-being verbs. The lessons and practice activities in Chapter 5 are designed to help them understand how to use state-of-being verbs correctly.

SELF-STUDY GUIDE

Name ______

CHAPTER 5: The State-of-Being Verb

Goal 5.1 *To identify being verbs and verb phrases in sentences*

Date	Assignment	Score
______	1: Read pages 111-112. Complete Activity A on page 112.	______
______	2: Complete Workbook Activity 21.	______
______	3: Read page 113. Complete Activities B-C on page 113.	______
______	4: Read page 114. Complete Activity D on page 114.	______
______	5: Read page 115. Complete Activities E-F on page 115.	______
______	6: Complete Workbook Activity 22.	______
______	7: Complete the Lesson 1 Review, Parts A-B on page 116.	______

Comments:

Goal 5.2 *To distinguish between active and being verbs and verb phrases in sentences*

Date	Assignment	Score
______	8: Read pages 117-118. Complete Activity A on page 119.	______
______	9: Read page 119. Complete Activity B on page 119.	______
______	10: Complete Activities C-D on page 120.	______
______	11: Complete Workbook Activities 23-24.	______
______	12: Complete the Lesson 2 Review, Parts A-B on page 121.	______

Comments:

 Basic English Grammar

SELF-STUDY GUIDE

Name ______

CHAPTER 5 The State-of-Being Verb, continued

Goal 5.3 *To identify the correct form of being verbs in sentences*

Date	Assignment	Score
______	13: Read page 122. Complete Activity A on page 122.	______
______	14: Read page 123. Complete Activities B-C on page 123.	______
______	15: Read page 124. Complete Activity D on page 124.	______
______	16: Complete the Lesson 3 Review on page 125.	______
______	17: Complete the Chapter 5 Review, Parts A-D on pages 126-127.	______

Comments:

Student's Signature ______ Date ______

Instructor's Signature ______ Date ______

 Basic English Grammar

Chapter 5 Self-Study Guide

Lesson at a Glance

Chapter 5 Lesson 1

Overview This lesson introduces state-of-being verbs.

Objectives

- To use state-of-being verbs in sentences.
- To find verbs and verb phrases in sentences and identify their tense.
- To distinguish between action verbs and state-of-being verbs.

Student Pages 112–116

Teacher's Resource Library

Activities 13–14

Workbook Activities 21–22

Reading Vocabulary

describe (5)
exist (6)
linking verb
state-of-being verb
tackle (6)

Teaching Suggestions

Introducing the Lesson

Discuss the purpose of a state-of-being verb in a sentence and the distinction between a state-of-being verb and an action verb.

Reviewing Skills

Review the definition of an action verb.

Presenting Activity A

Invite volunteers to read each of the example sentences with a different adjective or noun after the state-of-being verb. Encourage students to use a variety of verbs from the list as they complete Activity A.

Activity A Answers

Sentences should reflect correct use of linking verbs.

Teacher Alert

Students should understand that the terms *state-of-being verb* and *linking verb* are interchangeable.

Lesson 1 What Is a State-of-Being Verb?

State-of-being verb
A verb that explains or describes the subject of a sentence. A state-of-being verb is also called a linking verb.

A **state-of-being verb** tells something about the condition or state of the subject of the sentence. A state-of-being verb does not tell what the subject is doing. State-of-being verbs are also called linking verbs.

EXAMPLES

State-of-being verb:	Roberto **is** a tackle on the football team.
Action verb:	Roberto **plays** on the football team.

In the first sentence, the verb *is* helps to make a statement about Roberto. In the second sentence, the verb *plays* tells the action that Roberto does.

The most common state-of-being verb is *be* and all its forms: *am, is, are, was, were, be, being, been. To be* means "to exist, to live, or to happen."

Here are some other commonly used state-of-being, or linking, verbs:

appear	grow	seem
become	keep	smell
feel	look	stay
get	remain	taste

Activity A Read the examples. Then write five more sentences about Roberto on your paper. Use state-of-being verbs. Underline the verb in each sentence.

Examples
Roberto **seems** nice.
Roberto **is** a student.
Roberto **grew** tall.
Roberto **gets** taller every year.
Roberto **looks** friendly.

Name Date Period *Chapter 5 Activity 13*

Finding State-of-Being Verbs

Every sentence has a verb. A state-of-being verb tells something about the condition of the subject of the sentence. It does not tell what the subject is doing. The most commonly used state-of-being verb is *be.*

Directions: Each of the sentences below has a state-of-being verb or verb phrase as its main verb. Circle the verb or verb phrase.

1) Alex and his friend Dave are in Wisconsin.
2) The cheese in Wisconsin is very fine.
3) It tastes better than most cheese.
4) Wisconsin cheese smells especially inviting.
5) The cheese tasted terrific to Alex.
6) He had become a cheese expert.
7) Dave seemed happy with the trip.
8) He appeared especially joyful to Alex.
9) "Have you become a fan of Wisconsin cheese also?" asked Alex.
10) "I have grown fonder of it recently," laughed Dave.
11) Alex and Dave felt tired from their trip.
12) "We should look our best tomorrow," said Alex.
13) Our meeting with the governor is at noon.
14) "We could easily be there at noon," said Dave.
15) Alex and Dave remained at the cheese factory for a while.
16) The cheese tasted too good to leave.
17) "It gets better every year," said Alex.
18) "It looks better, too," said Dave.

 Basic English Grammar

Activity 13

The verb *be* can also be a helping verb. It can be used with a main verb to express progressive tenses.

EXAMPLES Jamie **is cooking** dinner.
Eric **was talking** softly.

In addition, *be* is used to form passive verbs. *Be* is a helping verb in those verb phrases, too.

EXAMPLE The picture **was painted** by Norman Rockwell.

Activity B Write the verb or verb phrase in each of these sentences on your paper. Beside each verb or verb phrase, write whether the verb *be* is a main verb or a helping verb.

1) Dawn was feeling fine yesterday.
2) Today she is sick.
3) She is going to the doctor.
4) Dawn will be absent from school.
5) She will probably be better tomorrow.

Be is almost always a state-of-being verb when it is the main verb of the sentence. Some other state-of-being verbs can also express an action. If you can substitute a form of *be* for these verbs, they are state-of-being verbs. If not, they are action verbs.

EXAMPLES

State-of-being verb:	The stew **tasted** good. (You could say: The stew *was* good.)
Action verb:	Michael **tasted** the stew. (You cannot say: Michael *was* the stew.)

Activity C Write the verb or verb phrase in each of these sentences on your paper. Beside each verb or verb phrase, write whether it is an *action verb* or a *state-of-being verb.*

1) The old house smelled musty and stale.
2) The children were smelling the flowers.
3) The boys grew beans, squash, and corn in their garden.
4) Your body will grow stronger with exercise.
5) He feels sick.

Reading Vocabulary

musty (8) stale (6)
passive (10) substitute (6)
progressive (7) tense (6)
squash (5)

■ Presenting Activity B

Remind students that a verb phrase is made up of a main verb and one or more helping verbs. Then write these sentences on the board: *Dawn was given some medicine by the doctor. She has not been well.* Help students identify the verb phrase in each sentence and determine whether *be* is a main verb or a helping verb.

Activity B Answers

1) was feeling—helping verb **2)** is—main **3)** is going—helping **4)** will be—main **5)** will be—main

■ Presenting Activity C

You may wish to do this activity as a group. Have students read the first sentence aloud and identify the verb or verb phrase in the sentence. Then ask students to read the sentence again, substituting a form of *be* for the verb. Have students raise their hands if they think the sentence makes sense and the verb or verb phrase is a state-of-being verb. Have them keep their hands down if they think the verb or verb phrase is an action verb.

Activity C Answers

1) smelled—state-of-being **2)** were smelling—action **3)** grew—action **4)** will grow—state-of-being **5)** feels—state-of-being

The State-of-Being Verb *Chapter 5* **113**

■ Presenting Activity D

Write the six tenses on the board. Then ask partners to work together to write a sentence with a state-of-being verb for each tense. Students can use the example sentences as models. When students have finished, point to a tense and invite volunteers to read their sentences for that tense. Ask the class to identify the verb or verb phrase in each sentence. Then have students work independently to complete Activity D.

Activity D Answers

1) is—present **2)** will be—future **3)** has been—present perfect **4)** was—past **5)** had been—past perfect **6)** will have become—future perfect **7)** had felt—past perfect **8)** have been—present perfect **9)** grows—present **10)** did seem—past

Learning Styles

Logical/Mathematical
Challenge volunteers to turn the state-of-being verbs in Activity D on page 114 into action verbs. (For example, Sentence #1 could become "'The Tell-Tale Heart' tells an interesting story." Sentence #2 could become "Playing football makes Sam happy.") If the students have difficulty with this activity, encourage them to picture the subject in each sentence doing something. Note: Sentence #9 does not include a state-of-being verb and should not be used for this activity.

State-of-being verbs also express tense.

Examples		
	Present:	The water **feels** warm.
	Past:	He **looked** good yesterday.
	Future:	Mary **will be** fifteen next week.
	Present perfect:	I **have been** hungry all day.
	Past perfect:	Jack **had seemed** tired by dinnertime.
	Future perfect:	Carol **will have been** sick for a week tomorrow.

Activity D Write the verb or verb phrase in each of these sentences on your paper. Beside each verb or verb phrase, write its tense.

1) "The Tell-Tale Heart" is an interesting story.

2) Sam will not be happy about that.

3) Mrs. Franco has been our neighbor for two years.

4) She was a Spanish teacher.

5) We had been the winners twice.

6) We will have become tired by then.

7) The cloth had felt smooth and soft.

8) They have been asleep all morning.

9) This plant grows best in the shade.

10) Did Mr. Lee seem upset to you?

Name Date Period | *Chapter 5 Activity 14*

State-of-Being Verbs Express Tense

State-of-being verbs express tense.

Examples		
	Present:	The air **seems** cool.
	Past:	The pie **tasted** better yesterday.
	Future:	The band **will appear** soon.
	Present perfect:	Jody **has been tired** all week.
	Past perfect:	Rob **has become** president of the company.
	Future perfect:	Maria **will have been** a teacher for ten years in June.

Directions: Circle the verb or verb phrase in these sentences. Write the tense in the space provided.

1) Diana felt fine yesterday ______
2) *The Red Pony* is a short novel by John Steinbeck. ______
3) Patty has been nice today. ______
4) Lauren will be twelve on her next birthday. ______
5) Barbara looks beautiful in her new dress. ______
6) Michael became a doctor like his father. ______
7) Cheese keeps fresh in the refrigerator. ______
8) Fire safety was the topic at the assembly today. ______
9) Stephanie will not be here today. ______
10) The food had looked better in the past. ______
11) Tomorrow Carla will be on a trip. ______
12) Bruce felt better after his vacation. ______
13) Have you looked this happy before? ______
14) Is dinner ready? ______
15) I will be there at three o'clock. ______
16) Tom grew two inches this year. ______
17) Our neighbors have been in that house for years. ______

 Basic English Grammar

Activity 14

Name Date Period | *Chapter 5 Workbook Activity 21*

Find the Linking Verb

Directions: Circle the linking verb in each sentence.

1) The U.S. Senate is in Washington, D.C.
2) The Chesapeake Bay Bridge is more than five miles long.
3) Every spring people are able to walk across the bridge.
4) We were so tired after we walked across the bridge.
5) "Have you ever felt this tired before?" asked Franklin.
6) Wool blankets are soft and warm.
7) They feel warm in winter.
8) The breakfast bacon smells inviting early in the morning.
9) Have you ever felt frightened during a thunderstorm?
10) Lightning and thunder appear dangerous to many people.
11) I feel safe inside the house.
12) The chipmunk in our woodpile appeared friendly.
13) Our puppy seemed pleased with his new home.
14) We felt rested after our long nap.
15) After the party, everyone felt too tired to sleep.
16) The puppy smelled bad after he played in the rain.
17) After his bath, he looked clean again.
18) My dog and I remained best friends for many years.
19) That long book looks like a challenge!
20) Short stories seem easier to me.

 Basic English Grammar

Workbook Activity 21

State-of-being verbs may be used in the progressive form. Use the verb *be* as a helping verb. Then use the present participle form (*-ing*) of the verb.

EXAMPLES It **is staying** warm today.
I **will be feeling** fine soon.

Activity E Write the present participle for each state-of-being verb below on your paper. Then write a sentence for each verb.

Example grow—growing I **am growing** taller this year.

1) be
2) seem
3) appear
4) look
5) feel
6) become

Conditional helping verbs may be used with state-of-being verbs.

EXAMPLES Karl **must be** in love.
The dog **could become** angry.

Activity F Write the state-of-being verb or verb phrase in each of these sentences on your paper.

1) Ron and Jamie were ready for Thanksgiving.
2) The roast turkey would taste good.
3) The pumpkin pies in the oven smelled delicious.
4) Everything looked wonderful.
5) "Is dinner ready yet?"
6) The whole family was hungry.
7) "I have been very hungry all day!"
8) Dinner was great!
9) The conversation around the table sounded happy.

Reading Vocabulary

conditional (8) participle
conversation (5)

■ Presenting Activity E

If necessary, remind students that the progressive forms of verbs express continuing action. You may also wish to write the six progressive forms on the board with examples. Alternatively, you can have students turn back to page 93 in Chapter 4 to review the progressive forms. As students do Activity E, point out that they can use any of the progressive forms in their sentences.

Activity E Answers

Sentences will vary. Present participle forms are given.

1) being **2)** seeming
3) appearing **4)** looking
5) feeling **6)** becoming

■ Presenting Activity F

Before students complete Activity F, review the list of conditional helping verbs presented on page 101. Ask volunteers to use each of these conditional forms with a state-of-being verb in a sentence. After students complete Activity F, have them share their answers with the class.

Activity F Answers

1) were **2)** would taste
3) smelled **4)** looked **5)** Is
6) was **7)** have been **8)** was
9) sounded

Reading Vocabulary

active (6)

Part A Answers

1) is **2)** is looking **3)** has felt **4)** is **5)** has been keeping

Part B Answers

1) was served—action **2)** looked—state-of-being **3)** smells—state-of-being **4)** is—state-of-being **5)** tasted—state-of-being **6)** may have—action **7)** looks—state-of-being **8)** feel—state-of-being **9)** seem—state-of-being **10)** must be—state-of-being

Follow-up Activity

Have students locate all the verbs and verb phrases in a short passage from a literature book or magazine article. Have them tell when the verb *be* is used as a helping verb and when it is used as a main verb.

Lesson 1 Review

Part A Write the verb or verb phrase in each of these sentences on your paper.

1) My aunt is eighty years old.

2) She is looking well.

3) She always has felt healthy.

4) Aunt Marie is a good cook.

5) She has been keeping very active.

Part B Write the verb or verb phrase in each of these sentences on your paper. Beside each verb or verb phrase, write whether it is an *action verb* or a *state-of-being verb.*

Example Debbie tasted the turkey. **tasted—action**
Dinner will be ready soon. **will be—state-of-being**

1) Dinner was served at three o'clock.

2) The food looked wonderful.

3) That turkey smells delicious.

4) The drumstick is my favorite part.

5) The sweet potatoes tasted quite fine.

6) May I have more corn?

7) My grandmother looks pleased.

8) I feel full.

9) My parents seem extra quiet.

10) They must be tired from all the cooking.

Name Date Period

Chapter 5 *Workbook Activity* 22

Rename the Subject

State-of-being verbs are called linking verbs. They link the subject with a noun in the predicate. The predicate noun renames the subject.

A. Directions: Find the subject of each sentence and label it *SUBJ.* Circle the linking verb of each sentence. Find the predicate noun of each sentence and label it *P.N.*

EXAMPLE Jack (is) a friend of mine from school. (SUBJ. = Jack; P.N. = friend)

1) Dawn was my best friend last year.

2) Adverbs and adjectives are parts of speech.

3) My friend Pat is a good athlete.

4) C-SPAN is a cable television station.

5) Princeton is a university in New Jersey.

6) The marigold is a lovely flower.

7) My birthday is always a special event.

8) Our new car is a four-door Ford.

9) My favorite dessert is strawberries.

10) An apple is a healthful snack.

B. Directions: Fill in each blank with a noun that renames the subject.

1) NBC is a television ______________ .

2) Sacramento is the ______________ of California.

3) *Star Wars* was a popular ______________ about space.

4) Louis Armstrong was a famous ______________ .

5) Abraham Lincoln was our sixteenth ______________ .

6) Oranges and pears are both ______________ .

7) Lettuce and cucumbers are good ______________ for salads.

8) American and Swiss are both ______________ of cheese.

9) *Gone With the Wind* was a popular ______________ and also a famous ______________ .

10) Democratic and Republican are two political ______________ in the United States.

 Basic English Grammar

Workbook Activity 22

Lesson 2 Action or State of Being?

The verb *be* is almost always a state-of-being verb when it is the main verb in a sentence.

EXAMPLES

The turkey **is** golden brown.

The turkey **is** delicious.

Many other state-of-being verbs can be used as action verbs.

EXAMPLES

Jamie **tasted** the cranberry sauce. (action verb)

The cranberry sauce **tasted** sweet. (state-of-being verb)

In the first sentence, *tasted* expresses action. Jamie did something. In the second sentence, *tasted* expresses a state of being. The condition of the cranberry sauce was sweet.

Here are examples of the different uses of several state-of-being verbs.

EXAMPLES

APPEAR

action: to come into view; to become visible

Jack **appeared** suddenly.
The actor **appeared** on the stage.

being: to seem; to look

They **appear** friendly.
Fred **appears** taller than Mike.

Lesson at a Glance

Chapter 5 Lesson 2

Overview This lesson focuses on state-of-being verbs that can also function as action verbs.

Objectives

- To locate verbs and verb phrases in sentences.
- To determine whether a verb expresses a state-of-being or an action.

Student Pages 117–121

Teacher's Resource Library

Workbook Activities 23–24

Reading Vocabulary

cranberry (5) visible (5)

Teaching Suggestions

Introducing the Lesson

Discuss the difference between action verbs and state-of-being verbs. Invite students to provide sentences with examples of each. Then have students explain how they can determine whether a verb or verb phrase is a state-of-being verb or an action verb. Remind students that if they can substitute a form of *be* or *seem* in the sentence, the verb is a state-of-being verb.

Reviewing Skills

Review the definition of a state-of-being verb.

TEACHER ALERT

You may wish to point out that the verb be is always a state-of-being, or linking, verb *except* when it is followed by certain adverbs and adverb phrases. Examples are: *Alice is here. They have been away. We were at the party.* The verb be is never an action verb.

Reading Vocabulary

cultivate (6) odor (6)
existence (6) physical (7)
mental (6) sensation (6)

Presenting Activity A Do the first two items as a class to be sure students understand when a verb expresses action and when it expresses a state-of-being. Then have students complete the activity on their own.

Activity A Answers

1) action **2)** state of being **3)** state of being **4)** action **5)** action **6)** state of being **7)** state of being **8)** action **9)** state of being **10)** action

Global Connection

Invite students who speak a language other than English to give the words for the verbs *appear, feel, grow, smell,* and *taste* in their primary languages. You might wish to have students write these words in a chart or other graphic organizer.

EXAMPLES

FEEL

action: to touch; to think or believe

She **felt** the soft blanket.
I **feel** that you are right.

being: to be aware of a physical or mental sensation

I **feel** cold.
Denny **feels** happy.

GROW

action: to cause to grow; to cultivate

I **grew** tomatoes in my garden.
The farmer **grows** corn.

being: to come into existence; to spring up

Don **grew** two inches this year.
The day **grew** cold.

SMELL

action: to catch the scent or odor of something

I could **smell** the fresh mountain air.
I **smell** popcorn.

being: to have a certain scent or odor

The bread **smells** delicious.
The skunk **smells** awful.

Activity A Write whether the verb in bold in each of these sentences expresses *action* or a *state of being.*

1) She could **smell** the smoke in the air.

2) The warm cake **smelled** inviting.

3) The oven **felt** too hot.

118 *Chapter 5 The State-of-Being Verb*

4) Mary **felt** a hole in her pocket.

5) Joe **grows** orange trees in Arizona.

6) She **appeared** to have a good time.

7) She **has grown** as tall as I.

8) Our cat **smells** his food before he tastes it.

9) Brad **felt** wonderful about his perfect score.

10) Nora suddenly **appeared** at the party.

If you are not sure whether a verb is a state-of-being verb, remember to try this test. Substitute a form of the verb *be* or *seem* for the verb. If the meaning of the sentence is almost the same, the verb is a state-of-being verb. You cannot substitute a form of *be* for an action verb.

EXAMPLES		
	State-of-being verb:	They **remained** friends. They **were** friends.
	Action verb:	He **got** a new job. He **was** a new job. (not possible)

Activity B Write two sentences for each of these verbs on your paper. In the first sentence, use the verb as an action verb. In the second sentence, use the verb as a state-of-being verb.

appear	feel	grow	look
taste	get	keep	smell

■ Presenting Activity B

Suggest that as students do Activity B, they apply the test described in the text to their own sentences. This will help them check that they have used each verb first as an action verb and then as a state-of-being verb.

Activity B Answers

Sentences will vary.

Learning Styles

LEP/ESL

Ask students for whom English is a second language to look at the boxed words on page 119. Encourage them to use their primary language to say each of the eight boxed words. Ask if the same word in their language can express both state of being and action. Ask them to give examples of the use of both types in their language and to explain how they know the difference.

The State-of-Being Verb Chapter 5 **119**

Reading Vocabulary

shrivel (7) sofa (5)
snack (6)

■ Presenting Activity C

Have students identify the subject in the first two items. Suggest that students picture each sentence as you read it aloud. Ask students which sentence describes the subject doing something that requires movement or action. (#2) What is the person doing? (reading) Remind students that a state-of-being verb does not express action.

Activity C Answers

1) state of being **2)** action **3)** state of being **4)** state of being **5)** state of being **6)** action **7)** action **8)** state of being **9)** action **10)** state of being

■ Presenting Activity D

Discuss the activity examples. Invite students to explain in their own words why *tasted* is an action verb in the first example sentence. Then ask students to use *tasted* as a state-of-being verb in a sentence.

Activity D Answers

1) smell—action **2)** seems—state of being **3)** tastes—state of being **4)** is watching—action **5)** has been—state of being **6)** became—state of being **7)** am saving—action **8)** will be hiking—action **9)** did taste—action **10)** were feeling—state of being

Activity C Remember that a state-of-being verb does not tell what the subject is doing. It does not express action. Write on your paper whether each verb in bold in these sentences expresses *action* or a *state of being.*

1) Their whole family **is** healthy.
2) Mrs. Jones **is reading** a book.
3) Ron **is** asleep on the sofa.
4) He **seems** tired this evening!
5) Mr. Jones **stays** awake.
6) He **is eating** an apple.
7) He **likes** a snack in the evening.
8) Jamie **appears** very busy.
9) She **must be doing** homework.
10) The television **is** loud.

Activity D Write the verb or verb phrase in each of these sentences on your paper. Beside each verb or verb phrase, write whether it expresses *action* or a *state of being.*

Examples	She tasted the soup.	**tasted—action**
	Dinner will be ready soon.	**will be—state of being**

1) Smell these beautiful flowers.
2) The grass seems greener this time of year.
3) Food always tastes better at the beach.
4) That cute little puppy in the window is watching us.
5) This has been a very dry summer.
6) The plants in our garden became yellow and shriveled.
7) I am saving for a new CD player.
8) At this time tomorrow, we will be hiking up a mountain.
9) Did you taste the vegetable pizza?
10) How were you feeling yesterday?

Name Date Period | Chapter 5 | Workbook Activity 23

Describe the Subject

State-of-being verbs do not express action. We use them when we want to describe our subjects.

A. Directions: Complete each sentence with an adjective. Use a different adjective for each sentence.

1) The puppy seems ______ .
2) The pumpkin pie tastes ______ .
3) The kitchen smells ______ .
4) I feel ______ today.
5) The house looks ______ .
6) Vern is ______ and ______ .
7) Since she went on a vacation, Mary looks very ______ .
8) The golden delicious apple is very ______ .
9) Cheese stays ______ in the refrigerator.
10) Our tomato crop this year seems ______ than ever.

B. Directions: Circle the state-of-being verb or verb phrase in each of the following sentences.

1) Harriet will be sixteen in May.
2) Yesterday I felt tired all day.
3) Colleen will have been on her exercise program for a year tomorrow.
4) Tommy has been the leading hitter on the team this year.
5) In the fall the trees turn golden.
6) The stars appeared brighter that night.
7) In the winter the weather gets colder.
8) Legumes are good sources of protein.
9) The peppermint tasted refreshing.
10) We all were happy about the victory.

 Basic English Grammar

Workbook Activity 23

Name Date Period | Chapter 5 | Workbook Activity 24

Action or Being?

Some verbs can be used either to express action or to express a state of being.

EXAMPLE **smell**
Action — She **smelled** the flowers
Being — The flowers **smell** good.

Directions: Read each sentence. The verb is in bold print. Decide whether the verb expresses action or a state of being. Circle the correct answer.

1) You **look** tired today.	ACTION	BEING
2) Did you really **look** for your shoes?	ACTION	BEING
3) I **tasted** everything at the party.	ACTION	BEING
4) Everything **tasted** good to me.	ACTION	BEING
5) The bacon **smelled** inviting.	ACTION	BEING
6) Carol's perfume **smelled** nice.	ACTION	BEING
7) Can you **smell** her perfume?	ACTION	BEING
8) Gail **felt** energetic.	ACTION	BEING
9) The children **felt** the first drops of rain.	ACTION	BEING
10) Sam **keeps** his comb in his pocket.	ACTION	BEING
11) This cheese **keeps** fresh for a month.	ACTION	BEING
12) The Donners **grow** tomatoes every year.	ACTION	BEING
13) Jack **grew** three inches this year.	ACTION	BEING
14) Marcy just **got** a new car.	ACTION	BEING
15) The weather suddenly **got** colder.	ACTION	BEING
16) Howard just **became** the owner of a puppy.	ACTION	BEING
17) Donna suddenly **appeared** in the room.	ACTION	BEING
18) Fred **appears** tired today.	ACTION	BEING
19) Jack **remained** after the others had left.	ACTION	BEING
20) Jim and Randy **remained** friends for years.	ACTION	BEING

 Basic English Grammar

Workbook Activity 24

Lesson 2 Review

Part A Write whether the bold verb in these sentences expresses *action* or a *state of being.*

1) Howard finally **appeared**.
2) He **appears** strong and healthy.
3) I **felt** the soft cloth.
4) The cloth **felt** soft to me.
5) She **looked** everywhere for her cat.
6) Her cat **looked** frightened.
7) The oak tree **grew** eight feet tall.
8) I **grow** radishes in my garden every year.

Part B Write the verb or verb phrase in each of these sentences on your paper. Beside each verb or verb phrase, write whether it expresses *action* or a *state of being.*

1) Mr. Klein was looking for the newspaper.
2) He usually keeps it on the coffee table.
3) That paper gets harder to find every day.
4) Suddenly the newspaper appeared!
5) The newspaper appeared wrinkled.
6) It also looked torn.
7) "Who got this paper before me?"
8) Mr. Klein grew thoughtful for a moment.
9) He spotted the dog under the table.
10) "Some dogs are frisky."
11) Then he smiled.
12) The newspaper was not damaged that much.
13) He remained in his chair with his newspaper for a while.
14) He got the news of the day.

Reading Vocabulary

frisky (6) thoughtful
radish (6)

Part A Answers

1) action 2) state of being 3) action 4) state of being 5) action 6) state of being 7) state of being 8) action

Part B Answers

1) was looking—action 2) keeps—action 3) gets—state of being 4) appeared—action 5) appeared—state of being 6) looked—state of being 7) got—action 8) grew—state of being 9) spotted—action 10) are—state of being 11) smiled—action 12) was damaged—action 13) remained—action 14) got—action

Follow-up Activity

Divide students into pairs and assign each pair a different state-of-being verb. Have them write several sentences using the verb as an action verb and a state-of-being verb. Then invite students to share their sentences with the class. Have the class identify the verb as an action or state-of-being verb.

Lesson at a Glance

Chapter 5 Lesson 3

Overview This lesson focuses on the correct usage of the forms of the irregular verb *be.*

Objectives

- To identify the forms of the verb *be.*
- To use the correct form of the verb *be* in sentences.

Student Pages 122–125

Teacher's Resource Library

Activity 15

Reading Vocabulary

award (5) plural (6)
irregular (7) singular (8)

Teaching Suggestions

Introducing the Lesson

Engage students in a discussion about subject-verb agreement. To be sure students understand the basic terms and rules presented in the lesson, ask students to offer additional examples modeled on those provided in the text.

Reviewing Skills

Review how the different tenses are formed.

Presenting Activity A

Ask students to use each of the forms of the verb *be* in oral sentences. Have the class identify the verb and its form in each sentence.

Activity A Answers

1) am—first person, singular, present **2)** were—third person, plural, past **3)** are—third person, plural, present **4)** is—third person, singular, present **5)** was—third person, singular, past **6)** were—first person, plural, past

Lesson 3 Using State-of-Being Verbs

A state-of-being verb must agree with its subject. Regular verbs and most irregular verbs add an *-s* or *-es* to the present form when the subject is singular.

EXAMPLE	Singular Subject	Plural Subject
	Jack **looks** happy.	They **look** happy.

The past form of the verb stays the same for singular and plural subjects.

EXAMPLE	Singular Subject	Plural Subject
	Donna **looked** nice.	Both girls **looked** nice.

The verb *be* is an irregular verb.

Singular	**Present**	**Past**
First person	I **am**	I **was**
Second person	you **are**	you **were**
Third person	he **is**	he **was**
Plural		
First person	we **are**	we **were**
Second person	you **are**	you **were**
Third person	they **are**	they **were**

Activity A Each of these sentences contains a form of the verb *be.* Write the verb and its form on your paper.

Example He is Michelle's brother.
is—third person, singular, present

1) I am busy today.
2) They were happy to get the award.
3) They are friends of mine.
4) She is a careful driver.
5) The crowd was anxious for the game to be over.
6) We were excited about our trip.

The past participle of *be* is *been*. Use *been* with *have, has,* and *had* to form the perfect tenses.

EXAMPLES Fred **has been** sick.
They **have been** busy all day.
Mike **had been** their helper.

The present participle of *be* is *being*. Use *being* with the helping verb *be* to show the progressive form.

EXAMPLES Donna **is being** nice.
Jack **was being** friendly.

Activity B Write the correct form of the verb *be* in each sentence on your paper.

1) Megan's report ______ due yesterday.
2) They ______ unhappy about my decision.
3) Has he ever ______ a teacher?
4) Yellowstone Park in Wyoming ______ a national park.
5) The children were ______ silly.
6) "You ______ our next patient," the nurse said.
7) I had never ______ a guest in their house before.

Use the verb *be* to show future tense and to show simple conditional forms.

EXAMPLES		
	Future:	He **will be** home soon.
	Conditional:	Jamie **must be** late.

Activity C Write the correct form of the verb *be* in each sentence on your paper.

1) Will you ______ my project partner?
2) I should ______ more careful.
3) Must I always ______ the first one?
4) Can I ______ the last one?
5) Howard will ______ disappointed about the game.

Reading Vocabulary

decision (5) due (5)

■ Presenting Activity B

Write the first activity item on the board and have students tell you what to write in the blank. Ask students to explain why *was* is correct. Then erase the verb and replace the word *yesterday* with *today.* Ask a volunteer to write the correct form of the verb *be* in the sentence. Repeat this procedure, replacing the word *today* with *tomorrow.* After students complete Activity B on their own, invite them to read aloud each sentence with the verb in place.

Activity B Answers

1) was **2)** are/were/will be **3)** been **4)** is **5)** being **6)** are/will be **7)** been

■ Presenting Activity C

Have students provide additional examples of sentences with the verb *be* that show future tense and simple conditional forms.

Activity C Answers

1) be **2)** be **3)** be **4)** be **5)** be

Name ______ Date ______ Period ______ *Chapter 5 Activity 15*

Using the *Be* Verb

EXAMPLES		
	Present:	I am, you are, he (she, it) is, we (you, they) are
	Past:	I was, you were, he (she, it) was, we (you, they) were
	Future:	I (you, he, she, it, we, you, they) will be
	Present perfect:	I (you) have been, he (she, it) has been, we (you, they) have been
	Past perfect:	I (you, he, she, it, we, you, they) had been
	Future perfect:	I (you, he, she, it, we, you, they) will have been

Directions: Write the correct form of the verb *to be* in each space provided.

1) In the fall, there will ______ a horse show.
2) Susan ______ entering her horse named Beauty.
3) She wants Beauty to ______ a blue ribbon winner.
4) Beauty's talent ______ high stepping.
5) Beauty has ______ in many horse shows.
6) On the day of the show, Susan's parents will ______ there.
7) Her friend Nicholas will ______ in the first row.
8) Beauty will have ______ in twelve shows after this one.
9) All of Susan's friends have ______ cheering for Beauty's victory.
10) Susan has ______ nervous before each show.
11) Sometimes she ______ not nervous at all.
12) "Where have you ______?" asked Jim.
13) " I have ______ to shows all over the United States," said Susan.
14) When Beauty pranced into the show ring, Susan ______ calm.
15) Beauty ______ such a beautiful horse.
16) If Beauty wins a blue ribbon, Susan and her horse will have ______ winners again.

 Basic English Grammar

Activity 15

The State-of-Being Verb Chapter 5 123

Reading Vocabulary

mall quarterback

■ Presenting Activity D

Students may hear the kinds of mistakes discussed on this page more readily than they see them. Suggest that students read each item in Activity D aloud and listen for the mistake before they write their answers.

Activity D Answers

1) "Where is Roberto?" Stacy asked. **2)** "They will be practicing late today," she said./"They are practicing late today," she said. **3)** "He is a good quarterback," Sam said. **4)** "We will be going to the mall after school."/"We are going to the mall after school." **5)** "Roberto will be tired after practice," Sam told her.

Application

At Home

Encourage students to use the correct form of the verb *be* whenever they speak or write at home or in the community-at-large. Remind students that all people, especially young children, tend to imitate those people that they admire most. The students' correct use of verb forms can serve as an example for younger siblings and friends who look up to them.

Here are some common mistakes to avoid:

1. Sometimes people leave out the *be* verb or part of the verb phrase in a sentence.

EXAMPLES		
	Incorrect:	The quarterback fast!
	Correct:	The quarterback **is** fast!
	Incorrect:	I be ready soon.
	Correct:	I **will be** ready soon.

2. Sometimes people use *be* instead of the correct present form.

EXAMPLES		
	Incorrect:	They be good friends.
	Correct:	They **are** good friends.
	Incorrect:	Roberto be my brother.
	Correct:	Roberto **is** my brother.

Activity D Each of these sentences contains a mistake with the use of the verb *be*. Write each sentence correctly on your paper.

1) "Where Roberto?" Stacy asked.

2) "They be practicing late today," she said.

3) "He be a good quarterback," Sam said.

4) "We be going to the mall after school."

5) "Roberto be tired after practice," Sam told her.

124 *Chapter 5 The State-of-Being Verb*

Lesson 3 Review

Lesson Review Write the correct form of the verb *be* in each of these sentences on your paper.

1) In November there ______ a contest at Wilson High School.
2) Jun ______ entering the contest.
3) She wanted to ______ the winner of the band scholarship.
4) Her talent ______ playing the tuba.
5) Sixty other students ______ part of the contest.
6) On the night of the contest, Jun's parents ______ excited.
7) Before the contest, Jun had ______ nervous.
8) When she came on stage to play her tuba, she ______ calm.
9) Later, she ______ asked about her future plans.
10) She had ______ thinking about this a lot.
11) "Who will ______ the winner?"
12) Finally, the winners ______ announced.
13) "Jun Tan has ______ chosen as the winner of the Wilson High Band scholarship."
14) Mr. and Mrs. Tan ______ very proud.
15) So ______ her brother Adam.
16) Jun must ______ the happiest of all!

Reading Vocabulary

scholarship tuba
talent (5)

Lesson Review Answers

1) was/will be **2)** is/will be **3)** be **4)** is/was **5)** will be/are/were **6)** were/will be **7)** been **8)** was **9)** was/will be **10)** been **11)** be **12)** were/will be **13)** been **14)** are/were/will be **15)** was/is/will be **16)** be/have been

Follow-up Activity

Encourage students to work together to create a classroom chart of the different forms of the verb *be*, with example sentences for each form. Students should try to work from memory, but can look through the lesson if they have difficulty recalling a particular form.

Learning Styles

Auditory/Verbal
Call on volunteers to read aloud the completed sentences in the review on page 125. As each volunteer completes a sentence, invite the class to call out the tense the volunteer used.

Chapter 5 Review

The Teacher's Resource Library includes two parallel forms of the Chapter 5 Mastery Test. The difficulty level of the two forms is equivalent. You may wish to use one form as a pretest and the other form as a posttest.

Reading Vocabulary

chilly (5)
energy (6)
snowflake

Part A Answers

1) grew **2)** felt **3)** were growing **4)** became **5)** smelled **6)** was **7)** was **8)** would come **9)** was feeling **10)** was

Part B Answers

1) stayed—state of being **2)** got—action **3)** gets—state of being **4)** looked—state of being **5)** smell—action **6)** feels—state of being **7)** felt—action **8)** looked—action **9)** grew—state of being **10)** was getting—state of being

Chapter 5 Review

Part A Write the verb or verb phrase in each of these sentences on your paper.

1) The last days of November grew cold.

2) Winter winds felt chilly.

3) The days were growing shorter.

4) The sky became dark early in the evening.

5) The cool air smelled fresh and clean.

6) On most days the sky was clear.

7) There was little rain that autumn.

8) Soon the first snowfall would come.

9) Everyone was feeling full of energy.

10) It was a pleasant time of the year.

Part B Write the verb or verb phrase in each of these sentences on your paper. Beside each verb or verb phrase, write whether it expresses *action* or a *state of being.*

1) The weather in December stayed cold.

2) People got out their winter coats.

3) "It gets cold earlier every year," Dave complained.

4) One day the sky looked gray.

5) "I can smell snow in the air," said Eli.

6) "It feels too cold for it to snow," Dave said.

7) "Hey! I felt a snowflake," said Eli.

8) They looked in Dave's garage for his sled.

9) The sky grew darker.

10) The snow was getting heavier.

Name ____ Date ____ Period ____ *Chapter 5 Mastery Test A page 1*

Chapter 5 Mastery Test A

Part A Circle the verb or verb phrase in each sentence. Write the tense on the line.

1) Jessica had felt fine all week. ____

2) *The Joy Luck Club* is a novel by Amy Tan. ____

3) Sam appeared happy today. ____

4) Ruby will have been a teacher ten years. ____

5) Andrea has become a nurse. ____

6) Raoul is an actor in California. ____

7) We keep food outside for the birds. ____

8) Keith will not be here tomorrow. ____

9) Pia felt rested after her vacation. ____

10) The flowers grew tall this spring. ____

11) Are you ready? ____

12) Drug education was the topic. ____

13) The air seems colder today. ____

14) The stew will taste better tomorrow. ____

15) Tyrone had become class president. ____

Part B Write the form of the verb *be* that makes each sentence correct.

1) In the spring, there will ____ a flower show.

2) Binh Pham ____ our family dentist.

3) He ____ born in Vietnam.

4) Mr. and Ms. Pettus ____ looking for a new apartment.

5) Mom ____ watching television tonight.

 Basic English Grammar

Name ____ Date ____ Period ____ *Chapter 5 Mastery Test A page 2*

Chapter 5 Mastery Test A, continued

6) I ____ reading a book tonight.

7) Jeremiah is ____ generous with his time.

8) That program will ____ over soon.

9) No one had ____ ready for this winter.

10) They ____ not eager for all the snow shoveling they did.

Part C Write whether the bold verb is an *action* verb or a *state-of-being* verb.

1) Everyone in the park **appears** friendly. ____

2) The cat **appeared** at our door. ____

3) Latasha **tasted** the juice. ____

4) The juice **tastes** sweet. ____

5) Velvet **feels** very soft. ____

6) The lady **felt** the soft cloth. ____

7) April **grows** tomatoes in her window box. ____

8) Tomatoes **grow** best in summer. ____

9) That popcorn **smells** too good to pass up. ____

10) Everyone **smells** the popcorn at the movies. ____

11) She **keeps** cats in her home for people on vacation. ____

12) The lake **became** choppy. ____

13) Hank **seems** upset today. ____

14) The sky **looks** gloomy. ____

15) Lyle **stays** here during summer. ____

 Basic English Grammar

Chapter 5 Mastery Test A

Part C Write the correct form of the verb *be* in each of these sentences on your paper.

1) "It definitely ______ snowing," Eli said.
2) "I ______ ready to go sledding," Dave said.
3) Soon the snow ______ deep enough.
4) They had ______ sledding for an hour.
5) They should ______ going home for dinner.

Part D Write the word that should appear in each sentence to make it correct.

1) Will Carol (be, been) at the meeting tomorrow?
2) She (be, is) almost always on time.
3) They (is, are) old friends of Jason's.
4) The puppy is (been, being) quiet today.
5) I (was, were) thinking about tomorrow's math test.
6) Everyone (was, were) happy about the news.
7) You have always (be, been) my best friend.
8) Al (seem, seems) glad about the new car.
9) Both of the pies (smell, smells) very good.
10) (Is, Are) your last name Miller?

Test Taking Tip

Spend time studying new material for several days or weeks before a test. Don't try to learn new material the night before a test.

Reading Vocabulary

definite (6)

Part C Answers

1) is/was/will be 2) am/was/will be 3) is/was/will be 4) been 5) be

Part D Answers

1) be 2) is 3) are 4) being 5) was 6) was 7) been 8) seems 9) smell 10) Is

APPLICATION

Career Connection

Help students conduct mock job interviews. Have one student take the role of the employer while the other takes the role of the job candidate. Beforehand, students should work together to write a list of questions for the interviewer to ask. Stress that students should use the correct form of the verb *be* in their questions and responses. Point out that using correct grammar during a real job interview can create a favorable impression on their potential employer.

Name Date Period | *Chapter 5 Mastery Test B page 1*

Chapter 5 Mastery Test B

Part A Circle the verb or verb phrase in each sentence. Write the tense on the line.

1) They will remain friends forever. ____________
2) Payne Stewart is a well-known golfer. ____________
3) Mickey felt good after exercising. ____________
4) The turkey turned golden brown. ____________
5) These sweet potatoes taste delicious. ____________
6) Sylvia had seemed unhappy all day. ____________
7) Mom will have been in college two years. ____________
8) Ahmad became an engineer in Detroit. ____________
9) Will you be late? ____________
10) Felisa felt peaceful in the park. ____________
11) The dessert looks good. ____________
12) Juan has gotten well after some rest. ____________
13) The music seems soft and calming. ____________
14) The lake had stayed quiet at sunrise. ____________
15) The bread smells fresh. ____________

Part B Write the form of the verb *be* that makes each sentence correct.

1) In the summer, there will ________ a water ski show.
2) Lok Tan ________ our new neighbor.
3) Ray and Roy ________ twins.
4) Helen will have ________ checking the job ads for two weeks.
5) Vince ________ cooking dinner for the family tonight.

 Basic English Grammar

Name Date Period | *Chapter 5 Mastery Test B page 2*

Chapter 5 Mastery Test B, continued

6) Raina is ________ helpful with the plans.
7) Chantal and Linn ________ here last week.
8) The mail will ________ here soon.
9) ________ the train running on time yesterday?
10) I ________ always early.

Part C Write whether the bold verb is an *action* verb or a *state-of-being* verb.

1) Everyone in the park **appears** friendly. ____________
2) The family **appeared** happy at the ball game. ____________
3) Everyone **tasted** the banana bread. ____________
4) Hot dogs **taste** especially good at the ball park. ____________
5) The air **feels** chilly in March. ____________
6) The boy **felt** the bench to see if it was wet. ____________
7) June **stays** after school for soccer practice. ____________
8) Vegetables **stay** fresh in the refrigerator. ____________
9) The air **gets** warm during the day. ____________
10) They **get** fresh eggs from that farmer. ____________
11) We **keep** warm by the campfire. ____________
12) Dad **keeps** wood for the campfire. ____________
13) Paola **seemed** cheerful. ____________
14) Donna **remained** at the store until it closed. ____________
15) Lana **looked** for a shelter from the storm. ____________

 Basic English Grammar

Chapter 5 Mastery Test B

Chapter 6

Planning Guide

The Adverb

	Student Text Lesson			
	Student Pages	Vocabulary	Practice Exercises	Lesson Review
Lesson 1 Adverbs That Answer Questions About Verbs	130-133	✔	✔	133
Lesson 2 Adverbs of Degree	134-137		✔	137
Lesson 3 Adverbs of Negation	138-139		✔	139
Lesson 4 Recognizing Adverbs	140-143		✔	143
Lesson 5 Comparing With Adverbs	144-146		✔	146
Lesson 6 Using Adverbs Correctly	147-149		✔	149

Chapter Activities

Teacher's Resource Library

Community Connection 6: Finding Adverbs on Labels

Assessment Options

Student Text

Chapter 6 Review

Teacher's Resource Library

Chapter 6 Mastery Tests A and B

Teaching Strategies							Language Skills			Learning Styles						Teacher's Resource Library		
Reviewing Skills	Teacher Alert	Follow-up Activity	Career Application	Home Application	Global Connection	Community Application	Identification Skills	Writing Skills	Punctuation Skills	Visual/Spatial	Auditory/Verbal	Body/Kinesthetic	Logical/Mathematical	Group Learning	LEP/ESL	Activities	Workbook Activities	Self-Study Guide
130	131-132	133			131		✔	✔	✔			133				16	25-26	✔
134		137		136		137	✔	✔	✔				136			17	27	✔
138	138						✔	✔	✔									✔
140		143					✔	✔	✔			143					28	✔
144		146					✔	✔	✔					145		18		✔
147	148	149	150				✔	✔	✔		149						29	✔

Chapter at a Glance

(Answer Keys for the Teacher's Resource Library begin on page 330 of this Teacher's Edition.)

Name ______ Date ______ Period ______ *Chapter 6* *Community Connection* 6

Finding Adverbs on Labels

An **adverb** is a word that modifies or answers questions about a verb, an adjective, or another adverb. Adverbs answer the questions *How? When? Where? How much? How often?* or *To what degree?*

EXAMPLES Jerome sang *loudly*.
(*Loudly* tells *how* Jerome sang.)

Usually he is late.
(*Usually* tells *when* he is late.)

Amy's house is *there*.
(*There* tells *where* Amy's house is.)

One place where you often find adverbs is on product labels. On these labels are directions for how to use the product. They tell how, when, where, how much, how often, and to what degree to use the product. Follow the steps below to find adverbs on product labels.

Step 1. Find at least five different household products that have labels. Examples are window cleaner, cleanser, dish soap, laundry detergent, air freshener, and carpet cleaner.

Step 2. Read the labels. Find ten complete sentences on them that use adverbs.

Step 3. Fill in the chart below. For each of the ten sentences, list the adverb. Tell what question the adverb answers about the verb, adjective, or adverb it modifies. Write *comparative, superlative,* or *positive* to tell which form the adverb is.

Adverb	Question	Comparative/Superlative/ Positive
1)		
2)		
3)		
4)		
5)		
6)		
7)		
8)		
9)		
10)		

Step 4. Share your chart with the class.

 Basic English Grammar

Community Connection 6

Chapter 6

The Adverb

When you are describing people, places, and events, you often use adjectives. You may also want to add descriptive details about *how, when,* or *how often* the event happened. Then you need to use different kinds of describing words.

An adverb is a word that answers questions about a verb, an adjective, or another adverb.

In Chapter 6, you will learn about adverbs. Each lesson in the chapter focuses on recognizing and using adverbs correctly in sentences.

Goals for Learning

- To identify adverbs in sentences
- To identify the word that the adverb answers questions about
- To use adverbs correctly to make comparisons

Reading Vocabulary

adjective
comparison (6)
descriptive
identify (6)

Introducing the Chapter

Focus students' attention on the photograph. Write the following sentences on the board. Ask students to help you complete the following sentences about the photograph by supplying one word to answer the question in each sentence. Lead students to replace the question words with adverbs.

- The folk festival was (*when?*).
- The women smiled *(how?).*
- One woman spoke *(how?)* into the microphone.
- The women waved the flags *(how often?).*

Point out to students that the words they added to the sentences are adverbs. In Chapter 6, they will learn how to use adverbs to make their writing more effective.

SELF-STUDY GUIDE

Name ______________

CHAPTER 6: The Adverb

Goal 6.1 *To identify the word that the adverb answers questions about*

Date	Assignment	Score
______	1: Read pages 129-130. Complete Activities A-B on page 130.	______
______	2: Read page 131. Complete Activity C on page 131.	______
______	3: Complete Activities D-E on page 132.	______
______	4: Complete the Lesson 1 Review, Parts A-B on page 133.	______
______	5: Complete Workbook Activity 25.	______
______	6: Complete Workbook Activity 26.	______

Comments:

Goal 6.2 *To identify adverbs in sentences*

Date	Assignment	Score
______	7: Read page 134. Complete Activity A on page 134.	______
______	8: Complete Activities B-C on page 135.	______
______	9: Complete Activities D-E on page 136.	______
______	10: Complete the Lesson 2 Review, Parts A-B on page 137.	______
______	11: Complete Workbook Activity 27.	______
______	12: Read page 138. Complete Activity A on page 138.	______
______	13: Complete the Lesson 3 Review, Parts A-B on page 139.	______
______	14: Read page 140. Complete Activity A on page 140.	______
______	15: Read page 141. Complete Activities B-C on page 141.	______
______	16: Read page 142. Complete Activity D on page 142.	______
______	17: Complete Workbook Activity 28.	______
______	18: Complete the Lesson 4 Review, Parts A-B on page 143.	______

Comments:

 Basic English Grammar

SELF-STUDY GUIDE

Name ______________

CHAPTER 6 The Adverb, continued

Goal 6.3 *To use adverbs correctly to make comparisons*

Date	Assignment	Score
______	19: Read page 144. Complete Activity A on page 144.	______
______	20: Complete Activities B-C on page 145.	______
______	21: Complete the Lesson 5 Review, Parts A-B on page 146.	______
______	22: Read page 147. Complete Activities A-B on page 147.	______
______	23: Complete Workbook Activity 29.	______
______	24: Read page 148. Complete Activity C on page 148.	______
______	25: Complete the Lesson 6 Review, Parts A-B on page 149.	______
______	26: Complete the Chapter 6 Review, Parts A-C on pages 150-151.	______

Comments:

Student's Signature ______________ Date ______

Instructor's Signature ______________ Date ______

 Basic English Grammar

Chapter 6 Self-Study Guide

Lesson at a Glance

Chapter 6 Lesson 1

Overview This lesson introduces adverbs as words that answer questions about verbs, adjectives, or adverbs.

Objectives

- To identify adverbs in sentences.
- To use adverbs in sentences.

Student Pages 130–133

Teacher's Resource Library

Activity 16

Workbook Activities 25–26

Reading Vocabulary

adverb
assignment (6)
ballerina
gracefully (6)
hem (6)

Teaching Suggestions

Introducing the Lesson

Discuss the information presented in the text. Have students take turns replacing the adverbs in the examples with other adverbs that answer the question *How?*

Reviewing Skills

Review the definition of an action verb.

Presenting Activity A

Do the first item with the class. Give several students a chance to respond to emphasize that there are many possible answers for each item.

Activity A Answers

Answers should answer the question *How was the action done?*

Presenting Activity B

Before students do the activity, help them identify the action verb in each sentence.

Activity B Answers

1) gracefully 2) quickly 3) gladly 4) Slowly 5) hard 6) well 7) fast 8) straight

Lesson 1 Adverbs That Answer Questions About Verbs

Adverb
A word that answers questions about a verb, an adjective, or another adverb. It tells How? When? Where? How often? How long? *or* How many times?

An **adverb** is a word that answers questions about a verb, an adjective, or another adverb. An adverb tells *how, when, where,* or *how much.*

Adverbs that answer the question *How?* are usually used with action verbs. They tell something about the way the action was done.

EXAMPLES

The dog barked **loudly**.
They did the assignment **correctly**.
Jack guessed **right**.
Carla works **quickly**.

Activity A Write these sentences on your paper. Add an adverb that answers the question *How was the action done?* about the verb in bold.

1) The family **ate** their dinner ______.
2) Willis **drives** his car ______.
3) May **sews** ______.
4) Mrs. Barrett **sang** ______.
5) We **cleaned** the house ______.

Activity B Write on your paper the adverb that answers the question *How?* in each of these sentences.

1) The ballerina danced gracefully.
2) The acrobat climbed the ladder quickly.
3) Gail helped us gladly.
4) Slowly Ella found the answers.
5) Juan played the game hard.
6) Anna plays the piano well.
7) I got home fast.
8) She sewed the hem straight.

130 Chapter 6 The Adverb

Name ______ Date ______ Period ______ | Chapter 6 Activity 16

Adverbs Answer Questions About Verbs

Adverbs that answer the question *How?* are usually used with action verbs. They tell us something about the way the action was done.

EXAMPLE

The wind howled **loudly**.
Tom did his homework **carefully**.
Mark guessed **correctly**.
Susan works **fast**.

Directions: Add an adverb to each of these sentences that answers the question *How was the action done?* The verb is in bold.

1) Matt **drives** his car ______.
2) Jennifer **dances** ______.
3) Katie always **helps** us ______.
4) Laura **sings** ______.
5) That band **plays** ______.
6) In the summer, the grass **grows** ______.
7) Jill and I **walk** around the block each morning ______.
8) Carol **sewed** the seam ______.
9) Mrs. Roderick **sang** ______.
10) **Read** these sentences ______.
11) The firefighter **climbed** the ladder ______.
12) ______ the class **completed** their test.
13) The puppy **barked** ______ at the mailman.
14) The children **ate** their snacks ______.
15) The brook **babbled** ______.
16) Usually Jessie **works** ______.
17) Dad likes us to **trim** the lawn ______.
18) Steve **plays** baseball ______.

 Basic English Grammar

Activity 16

Adverbs also answer these questions: *When? How often? How long?* or *How many times?*

They tell something about the time of the action or state of being.

EXAMPLES

I am leaving town **today**.

Sarah will be home **soon**.

I would like to go to the beach **again**.

John will speak **next**.

Carol is **usually** happy.

Adverbs also answer the questions *Where?* or *In what direction?* They tell something about the place of the action or state of being.

EXAMPLES

Lloyd lives **here**.

Leave your coat **downstairs**.

You should turn **left**.

Activity C Write each adverb below in a sentence on your paper. Underline the adverb in each sentence.

1) often

2) tomorrow

3) never

4) still

5) yesterday

6) today

7) now

8) always

9) later

10) twice

11) already

12) again

■ Presenting Activity C

Invite volunteers to replace the adverbs in bold in the first set of examples with other adverbs that answer the questions *When? How often? or How many times?* Repeat this process with the second set of examples, having students supply adverbs that answer the questions *Where?* or *In what direction?* Then have students complete Activity C on their own or with a partner. When students have finished, invite them to share their sentences with the class.

Activity C Answers

Sentences should include the listed words used as adverbs.

TEACHER ALERT

You may wish to point out that the words *tomorrow, yesterday,* and *today* can also be nouns, as in the sentence, "Tomorrow is another day." Students should check their sentences to be sure that they have used *tomorrow, yesterday,* and *today* as adverbs and not as nouns.

GLOBAL CONNECTION

Every language has equivalent terms for such directions as *turn left, make a right, go straight,* and so on. Invite students who speak another language to give these terms in their primary language. Then encourage students to create universal signs for these directions, using pictures and symbols. Beneath each sign, students can write its meaning in English and other languages.

Reading Vocabulary

advance (5)
occasionally
daily (5)
relative (5)

■ Presenting Activity D

Suggest that students follow these steps to help identify the adverbs in each sentence: 1) find the verb; 2) ask *When?* or *How often?* about the verb. As an example, do item 1 with students. Help them identify the verb *begin.* Then ask the question *Begin when?* Begin *immediately.*

Activity D Answers

1) immediately **2)** first
3) instantly **4)** seldom
5) before **6)** lately
7) Sometimes
8) Occasionally **9)** daily
10) yearly

■ Presenting Activity E

Write these sentences on the board: *Put your books there. Go straight for one mile.* Help students find the verb in each sentence. Have them ask *Where?* about the verb in the first sentence and *In what direction?* about the verb in the second sentence. Then have students complete Activity E on their own.

Activity E Answers

1) forward **2)** away
3) right **4)** here **5)** upstairs
6) above **7)** near

Teacher Alert

Use items from Activity D as examples to demonstrate that adverbs may come at the beginning (items 7 & 8), in the middle (4), and at the end of a sentence (1 & 2).

Activity D Write the adverbs in each of these sentences on your paper. The adverbs answer the questions *When?* or *How often?*

1) Please begin immediately!

2) I will go first.

3) They jumped up instantly.

4) Our parents seldom go to the movies.

5) I saw the movie before.

6) The weather has been nice lately.

7) Sometimes I enjoy golf.

8) Occasionally we visit our relatives in Texas.

9) The newspaper is delivered daily.

10) We trim our trees yearly.

Activity E Write the adverbs in each of these sentences on your paper. The adverbs answer the questions *Where?* or *In what direction?*

1) The team advanced the ball forward.

2) Please go away.

3) Turn right at the corner.

4) Hang your coats here.

5) The bedrooms are upstairs.

6) They looked at the stars above.

7) The storm was near.

132 *Chapter 6 The Adverb*

Lesson 1 Review

Part A Write all the adverbs in these sentences on your paper. A sentence may have more than one adverb.

1) Yesterday, the dog happily buried his bone.
2) Today, he looked for it.
3) He barked loudly for Carla.
4) "I bet you lost your bone again," Carla scolded gently.
5) The dog jumped up and down constantly.
6) Jokingly she said, "Sometimes you are a silly dog."
7) Finally, Carla found the bone.
8) She gave it to the dog quickly.
9) Immediately, he ran away with it.
10) "Be careful with it now!" she reminded him.

Part B Complete each sentence by writing an adverb that answers the question in parentheses about the verb in bold.

1) The students **rushed** to their desks (How?).
2) (How often?), their teacher **gave** them a surprise quiz.
3) Otis **came** in late (How often?).
4) Mr. Wang **walked** (Where?).
5) The silence seemed to **last** (How long?).

Reading Vocabulary

constantly
gently (6)
jokingly
parentheses

Part A Answers

1) Yesterday, happily **2)** Today **3)** loudly **4)** again, gently **5)** up, down, constantly **6)** Jokingly, Sometimes **7)** Finally **8)** quickly **9)** Immediately, away **10)** now

Part B Answers

Answers should answer the question in parentheses.

Follow-up Activity

Have students find pictures in magazines that illustrate the following adverbs: *gracefully, smoothly, slowly, happily, loudly, fast, quickly, cautiously.* Invite students to display a picture and make up a sentence about it, using the adverb the picture illustrates.

Learning Styles

Body/Kinesthetic

Give each student a note card. Ask each student to print an action verb on the card. Collect the cards. Give the set of cards to a volunteer to shuffle. Afterward, have the volunteer draw one card and give it to another student. Ask this student to read the verb on the card and to make up a sentence that uses the verb and an adverb that modifies the verb. Continue this procedure as long as time permits. Challenge volunteers to use their bodies to demonstrate the action of the verb, and the adverb.

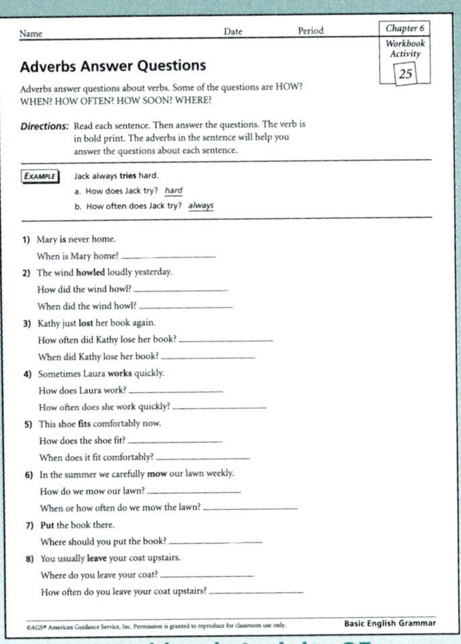

Name ____ Date ____ Period ____

Chapter 6 Workbook Activity 25

Adverbs Answer Questions

Adverbs answer questions about verbs. Some of the questions are HOW? WHEN? HOW OFTEN? HOW SOON? WHERE?

Directions: Read each sentence. Then answer the questions. The verb is in bold print. The adverbs in the sentence will help you answer the questions about each sentence.

EXAMPLE Jack always **tries** hard.
a. How does Jack try? *hard*
b. How often does Jack try? *always*

1) Mary **is** never home.
When is Mary home? ____
2) The wind **howled** loudly yesterday.
How did the wind howl? ____
When did the wind howl? ____
3) Kathy just **lost** her book again.
How often did Kathy lose her book? ____
When did Kathy lose her book? ____
4) Sometimes Laura **works** quickly.
How does Laura work? ____
How often does she work quickly? ____
5) This shoe **fits** comfortably now.
How does the shoe fit? ____
When does it fit comfortably? ____
6) In the summer we carefully **mow** our lawn weekly.
How do we mow our lawn? ____
When or how often do we mow the lawn? ____
7) **Put** the book there.
Where should you put the book? ____
8) You usually **leave** your coat upstairs.
Where do you leave your coat? ____
How often do you leave your coat upstairs? ____

 Basic English Grammar

Workbook Activity 25

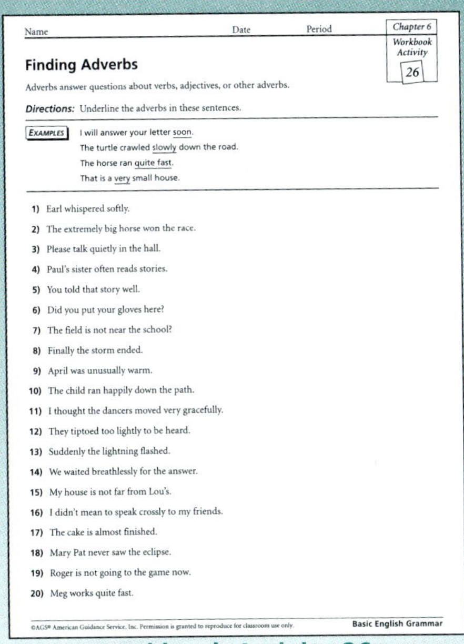

Name ____ Date ____ Period ____

Chapter 6 Workbook Activity 26

Finding Adverbs

Adverbs answer questions about verbs, adjectives, or other adverbs.

Directions: Underline the adverbs in these sentences.

EXAMPLES I will answer your letter soon.
The turtle crawled slowly down the road.
The horse ran quite fast.
That is a very small house.

1) Earl whispered softly.
2) The extremely big horse won the race.
3) Please talk quietly in the hall.
4) Paul's sister often reads stories.
5) You told that story well.
6) Did you put your gloves here?
7) The field is not near the school?
8) Finally the storm ended.
9) April was unusually warm.
10) The child ran happily down the path.
11) I thought the dancers moved very gracefully.
12) They tiptoed too lightly to be heard.
13) Suddenly the lightning flashed.
14) We waited breathlessly for the answer.
15) My house is not far from Lou's.
16) I didn't mean to speak crossly to my friends.
17) The cake is almost finished.
18) Mary Pat never saw the eclipse.
19) Roger is not going to the game now.
20) Meg works quite fast.

 Basic English Grammar

Workbook Activity 26

The Adverb Chapter 6 **133**

Lesson at a Glance

Chapter 6 Lesson 2

Overview This lesson presents adverbs of degree.

Objectives

- To identify adverbs of degree in sentences.
- To use adverbs of degree in sentences.

Student Pages 134–137

Teacher's Resource Library

Activity 17

Workbook Activity 27

Reading Vocabulary

extremely (6) headache

Teaching Suggestions

Introducing the Lesson

Be sure students understand the term *adverbs of degree* before having them do the activities.

Reviewing Skills Remind students that adjectives are words that describe nouns and pronouns.

Presenting Activity A

Write the first three items in Activity A on the board. Do the first item for students. Draw an arrow from *so* to *noisy* and explain that *so* answers the question *How noisy?* Then have the class identify the adverbs of degree and the words they tell about in the next two items. Have students complete the rest of Activity A on their own.

Activity A Answers

1) so 2) quite 3) unusually 4) very 5) extremely 6) especially 7) rather 8) very 9) amazingly 10) certainly

Lesson 2 Adverbs of Degree

Adverbs that answer questions about adjectives and other adverbs are called adverbs of degree. They answer these questions: *How much? How little? How often?* and *To what degree?*

Examples

It is **very** cold here.

The adverb *very* tells about the adjective *cold*.

How cold is it?

It is **very** cold!

I work **extremely** fast.

The adverb *extremely* tells about the adverb *fast*.

How fast?

Extremely fast!

The adverb of degree is usually placed before the adjective or adverb.

Activity A Write these sentences on your paper. Circle the adverbs of degree.

1) His old truck is so noisy.
2) Your puppy is quite friendly.
3) That is an unusually large pumpkin.
4) What a very funny movie that was!
5) He has an extremely bad headache.
6) I am especially tired this morning.
7) Mark has a rather interesting idea for the project.
8) The child spoke in a very soft voice.
9) What an amazingly simple test that was!
10) Your plan is certainly clever.

Activity B Write on your paper the adverb that tells about the adjective in bold.

1) I am almost **ready** to go.
2) Fernando was rather **happy** today.
3) That coat is too **small** for you.
4) Ms. Edwards was quite **pleased** with the class.
5) They were completely **satisfied** with their new stove.
6) An extremely **strong** wind blew down the old oak tree.
7) That was a very **odd** thing for him to do.
8) She spoke in an unusually **soft** voice.
9) I'm not entirely **sure** of my plans.
10) Your puppy has so **much** energy!

Activity C Write on your paper the adverb that tells about the adverb in bold.

1) Do your homework very **carefully**.
2) Alissa works too **quickly**.
3) The band played unusually **well**.
4) I am leaving sometime **today**.
5) He went far **away**.
6) Rita left much **later** than Donya.
7) Carlo swims rather **often**.
8) The children walked quite **slowly**.
9) Ellie gets up so **early** for work.
10) She tried awfully **hard** to win the race.

Reading Vocabulary

energy (6) odd (5)

■ Presenting Activity B

Read through all the sentences in Activity B with students. Ask students to read aloud the adjective in bold in each sentence and to find the noun or pronoun the adjective describes. Then have students complete Activity B on their own. When they have finished, invite students to share their answers with the class.

Activity B Answers

1) almost 2) rather 3) too 4) quite 5) completely 6) extremely 7) very 8) unusually 9) entirely 10) so

■ Presenting Activity C

Before having students complete Activity C on their own, have them read aloud the adverb in bold in each sentence and tell what question it answers about the verb.

Activity C Answers

1) very 2) too 3) unusually 4) sometime 5) far 6) much 7) rather 8) quite 9) so 10) awfully

Name Date Period | *Chapter 6* *Activity* *17*

Adverbs of Degree

Adverbs that answer questions about adjectives and other adverbs are called adverbs of degree. They answer the question *How much? How little? How often?* and *To what degree?*

EXAMPLE It is **very** cold.
Very is the adverb of degree. It modifies the adjective *cold*.

That dog barks **too** much.
Too is the adverb of degree. It modifies the adverb *much*.

A. ***Directions:*** In these sentences the word in bold is an adjective. Circle the adverb of degree—the word that tells about the adjective.

EXAMPLE I am (nearly) **ready** to leave.

1) Anna was very **pleased** with the book.
2) These shoes are too **small** for me.
3) The weather today is so **beautiful**.
4) Matthew was rather **sad** today.
5) The very **strong** wind blew down the TV antenna.

B. ***Directions:*** In these sentences the word in bold is an adverb. Circle the adverb of degree—the word that tells about the adverb.

EXAMPLE The band at the prom played (unusually) **well**.

1) I am leaving sometime **tomorrow**.
2) Lorie works very **quickly**.
3) Todd left for the beach much **sooner** than Ron.
4) Jimmy hits the ball very **hard**.
5) Donna plays tennis quite **often**.

 Basic English Grammar

Activity 17

Reading Vocabulary

tennis (5)

■ Presenting Activity D

Before students do the activity, have them tell whether the word in bold in each sentence is an adjective or adverb. Then ask for volunteers to give sample answers for the first two items in the activity.

Activity D Answers

Each answer should include a different adverb of degree.

■ Presenting Activity E

Remind students that adverbs of degree answer questions about adjectives and other adverbs. Then invite volunteers to write sentences for the first two or three items in Activity E on the board; have them underline the adverb of degree in each sentence. Then ask the class to identify the adjective or adverb each underlined adverb tells about in the sentences on the board. After students have completed Activity E, invite them to share their sentences with the class.

Activity E Answers

Sentences should include an adverb of degree.

Application

At Home

The word *very* may be one of the most over-used words in the English language. Encourage students to note how many times they use or hear the word *very* in a single conversation. Suggest that students avoid the use of *very* by using more precise language when they speak and write. For example, instead of saying, "He is very angry," they might say, "He was furious." Suggest that students take a survey of how many times they hear the word *very* in one day.

Activity D Write these sentences on your own paper. Add an adverb of degree before the adjective or adverb in bold. Use a different adverb in each sentence.

1) The **strong** man lifted five hundred pounds.
2) Pedro is **ready**.
3) Your new sweater is **pretty**.
4) Rhoda does her work **well**.
5) Anne plays tennis **often**.
6) Lin works **quickly**.
7) Dana is **late**.
8) The bus arrived **early**.
9) We watched the **small** bug crawl across the table.
10) Mom is **happy** about her new job.

Activity E Use each adverb of degree below in a sentence. Write the sentences on your paper.

1) very
2) too
3) quite
4) rather
5) somewhat
6) extremely
7) unusually
8) completely
9) so
10) almost

Learning Styles

Logical/Mathematical

Divide the class into groups of four. Give each group a colorful magazine picture. Encourage the groups to use their pictures to create five sentences that represent the following pattern: adjective/noun/verb/adverb of degree/adverb that answers a question about the verb. (For example, a group might create the following: "The best runner ran extremely fast.") Afterward, invite the groups to share their pictures and sentences. Ask the class to call out the adverbs of degree they hear in each sentence. Note: Keep the pictures for use with the Learning Styles activity on page 156.

Lesson 2 Review

Part A Write the adverbs of degree in these sentences on your paper.

1) Lou enjoyed his job at the bookstore very much.

2) Saturday was an unusually busy day.

3) Lou worked extremely hard.

4) Mrs. Marshall was completely satisfied with Lou's work.

5) "You are an exceptionally good worker," she told him.

6) "You can expect a very nice raise next month."

7) Lou was quite pleased to hear that!

8) The extra money would be so nice.

Part B Write each of these sentences on your paper. Add an adverb of degree to tell about the adjective or adverb in bold in the sentence. Try to use a different adverb in each sentence.

1) December is a **cold** month.

2) People must dress **warmly**.

3) Many of the trees are **bare**.

4) The skies may be **cloudy**.

5) **Soon** we will have snow.

6) I will be ready to go shopping **tomorrow**.

7) The wind was **noisy** all night.

8) Reggie was **proud** of his accomplishment.

Reading Vocabulary

accomplishment (6)
exceptionally

Part A Answers

1) very 2) unusually
3) extremely 4) completely
5) exceptionally 6) very
7) quite 8) so

Part B Answers

Each sentence should include a different adverb of degree.

Follow-up Activity

Invite students to use each of the adverbs in the review activities in sentences of their own.

Application

In the Community
Point out to students that people who participate in community programs are often asked their opinions of these programs. Whenever students are asked to evaluate community programs in which they participate, they can use adverbs of degree to effectively describe the positive and negative aspects of a program. Have students brainstorm a list of adverbs of degree that could be used.

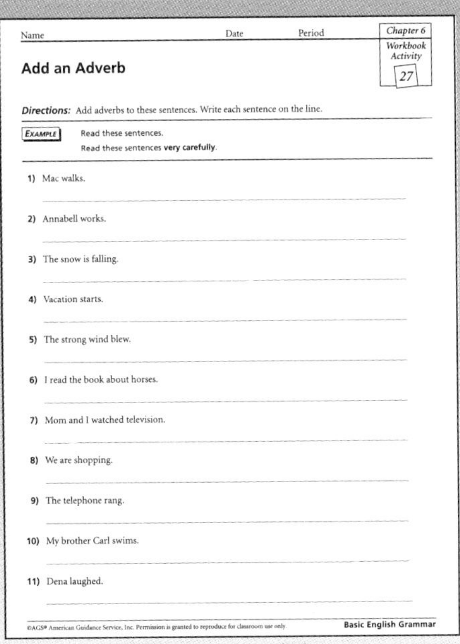

Name Date Period *Chapter 6 Workbook Activity 27*

Add an Adverb

Directions: Add adverbs to these sentences. Write each sentence on the line.

EXAMPLE Read these sentences.
Read these sentences **very carefully**.

1) Mac walks.

2) Annabell works.

3) The snow is falling.

4) Vacation starts.

5) The strong wind blew.

6) I read the book about horses.

7) Mom and I watched television.

8) We are shopping.

9) The telephone rang.

10) My brother Carl swims.

11) Dena laughed.

 Basic English Grammar

Workbook Activity 27

Lesson at a Glance

Chapter 6 Lesson 3

Overview This lesson presents adverbs of negation.

Objective

- To identify adverbs of negation.

Student Pages 138–139

Reading Vocabulary

contraction (9) negative (8)
negation

Teaching Suggestions

Introducing the Lesson

Invite a volunteer to look up the words *negation* and *negative* in the classroom dictionary. Have the student share the meanings of these words with the class. Then discuss the information and examples presented in the text.

Reviewing Skills

Ask students to provide examples of adverbs that tell about verbs, adjectives, and other adverbs.

Presenting Activity A

Do the first two items on the board, having students circle just the *n't* in *couldn't.* Then have students work on their own.

Activity A Answers

1) not 2) n't 3) not
4) never 5) never 6) n't
7) never 8) never 9) n't
10) never

Teacher Alert

If necessary, point out that a contraction is formed when two words are joined to make one shorter word. The apostrophe takes the place of letters that are dropped when the two words are joined, for example: *did* + *not* − *o* = *didn't.* Point out that *won't* is an exception to how contractions are usually formed.

Lesson 3 Adverbs of Negation

Never and *not* are adverbs of negation. A negative adverb means that the action will not happen or that the state of being is not present. The adverb *not* is often hidden in a contraction.

Examples

She is **never** home.
Carol is **not** at school today.
My brother **won't** eat his dinner. (will not)
They **didn't** find the book. (did not)

Remember that adverbs tell something about a verb, an adjective, or another adverb.

Activity A Write these sentences on your paper. Circle the adverbs of negation.

1) There is not enough snow to ski.
2) Fernando couldn't find his pencil.
3) It was not his fault.
4) I have never met him.
5) They had never been there before.
6) Isn't that a beautiful painting?
7) She never answers the phone during dinner.
8) Susan would never quit her job.
9) The play didn't start on time.
10) Lynn has never been on an airplane.

Lesson 3 Review

Part A Write the adverbs of negation in these sentences on your paper.

1) Nick won't be at play practice tonight.

2) He does not think he's good enough.

3) The director never praised Nick.

4) I can't think of anyone who would be better in that part.

5) He should never quit acting.

6) We mustn't let him quit.

Part B Rewrite these sentences on your paper. Add an adverb of negation to each sentence.

Example The weather is warm enough for swimming.
The weather is **not** warm enough for swimming.

1) Greg could swim across the pool.

2) I have seen Ruby.

3) Virgil goes to the beach.

4) I have time for lunch.

5) Our neighbors have been here before.

6) Yoko did find her book.

Reading Vocabulary

director (7)

Part A Answers

1) n't **2)** not **3)** never
4) n't **5)** never **6)** n't

Part B Answers

Answers may vary. Possible responses are given.

1) Greg could never swim across the pool. **2)** I haven't seen Ruby. **3)** Virgil never goes to the beach. **4)** I never have time for lunch. **5)** Our neighbors have never been here before. **6)** Yoko did not find her book.

Lesson at a Glance

Chapter 6 Lesson 4

Overview This lesson explains how some adverbs are formed. It also provides practice in distinguishing adverbs from adjectives.

Objective

- To distinguish between adjectives and adverbs in sentences.

Student Pages 140–143

Teacher's Resource Library

Workbook Activity 28

Reading Vocabulary

definition (6) describe (5)

Teaching Suggestions

Introducing the Lesson

Discuss the information in the text. Emphasize that when students are in doubt about whether a word is an adverb, they should ask themselves the questions adverbs answer. If the word answers one of those questions, it is an adverb.

Reviewing Skills

Review the questions that adverbs and adjectives answer about the words they describe.

Presenting Activity A

Do this activity orally with the class. If students have difficulty with an item, help them figure out which word the bold word tells about.

Activity A Answers

1) adjective 2) adverb
3) adjective 4) adverb
5) adjective 6) adverb
7) adverb 8) adverb
9) adverb 10) adverb
11) adverb 12) adjective
13) adjective 14) adjective
15) adverb 16) adverb
17) adjective 18) adverb
19) adjective 20) adverb

Lesson 4 Recognizing Adverbs

Sometimes people are not sure whether a word is an adjective or an adverb. Review the definitions of those two parts of speech.

An adjective describes a noun or pronoun.

EXAMPLES

Nancy is **tall**.

The word *tall* describes *Nancy*.

Nancy is a noun; therefore, *tall* is an adjective.

An adverb answers a question about a verb, an adjective, or another adverb in a sentence.

EXAMPLES

Nancy walked **outside**.

The word *outside* tells where Nancy walked.

Walked is a verb; therefore, *outside* is an adverb.

Activity A Write the words in bold on your paper. Beside each word, write whether it is an *adjective* or an *adverb*.

1) Larry is **late**.
2) He is **here**.
3) That house is **large**.
4) She works **hard**.
5) He is a **hard** worker.
6) Jack lives **here**.
7) **Today** we ran.
8) We arrived **late**.
9) They arrived **later**.
10) We looked **up**.
11) He runs **fast**.
12) He's a **fast** runner.
13) He is **fast**.
14) The answer is **clear**.
15) Speak **clearly**!
16) We practice **daily**.
17) Do **daily** exercises.
18) Let's leave **early**.
19) Is this the **early** show?
20) We **usually** eat at noon.

Many adverbs are made from adjectives by adding the ending *-ly*.

EXAMPLES

Adjectives	Adverbs
The cloth is **soft**.	He sang **softly**.
The candy is **sweet**.	She smiled **sweetly**.
Carol looks **happy**.	Fernando laughed **happily**.

Activity B Write the words in bold on your paper. Beside each word, write whether it is an adjective or an adverb.

1) The sea was very **calm** today.

2) Donna walked **calmly** out of the room.

3) Between classes the halls were **quiet**.

4) The boy **quietly** watched the movie.

5) "This is an **extremely** difficult case," the lawyer said.

6) "This is an **extreme** case," the lawyer said.

7) My new puppy is always **hungry**.

8) The hikers ate lunch **hungrily**.

Sometimes an adverb is made from a noun by adding *-ly*.

EXAMPLES

Noun	Adverb
May I have **part** of that?	He is **partly** finished.

Activity C Write the words in bold on your paper. Beside each word, write whether it is a noun or an adverb.

1) The books were in alphabetical **order**.

2) Please do things **orderly**.

3) We went to the store every **week**.

4) The family shops **weekly**.

5) The bills arrive every **month**.

6) We pay our bills **monthly**.

Reading Vocabulary

alphabetical (6) lawyer (5)
extreme (5)

Presenting Activity B

Write these adjectives on the board: *bad, sad, calm, brave, quick,* and *lucky.* Ask students to use each of these adjectives in a sentence. Then ask volunteers to make each of these adjectives an adverb by adding *-ly.* If necessary, remind students to change *-y* to *-i* before adding *-ly* to words that end in *y.* Ask students to use the adverbs in sentences. Students can then complete Activity B on their own.

Activity B Answers

1) adjective 2) adverb
3) adjective 4) adverb
5) adverb 6) adjective
7) adjective 8) adverb

Presenting Activity C

Before students complete Activity C, have them explain the difference between a noun and an adverb in their own words.

Activity C Answers

1) noun 2) adverb
3) noun 4) adverb
5) noun 6) adverb

Reading Vocabulary

advice (5) timely (10)
costly (6)

■ Presenting Activity D

Write these words on the board: *jolly, silly, hourly, unfriendly, nightly.* Help students to identify the words that are just adjectives (*jolly, silly, unfriendly*) and those that can be used as adjectives and adverbs (*hourly, nightly*). Have students use these two words in sentences as adjectives and then as adverbs.

Activity D Answers

1) adjective **2)** adjective
3) adjective **4)** adverb
5) adjective **6)** adjective
7) adjective **8)** adverb
9) adverb **10)** adjective

Not all words ending in *-ly* are adverbs. Many common adjectives end in *-ly*, too.

EXAMPLES

Dwayne received some **fatherly** advice from Mr. Belindo.

Fatherly is an adjective that describes the noun *advice.*

Janell is a **friendly** person.

Friendly is an adjective that describes the noun *person.*

Other words that end in *-ly* may be used as adjectives or adverbs.

EXAMPLES

Adjectives	Adverbs
He did the **daily** report.	He reported **daily**.
We left in the **early** morning.	We left **early**.

Activity D Write the words in bold on your paper. Beside each word, write whether it is an adjective or an adverb.

1) New cars are very **costly**.

2) **Only** Vanessa arrived on time.

3) That is an **ugly** cut.

4) They sat **quietly** and waited.

5) Donna's report was **timely**.

6) That is a **lovely** song.

7) Mr. Santos missed his **early** class.

8) They **easily** won first prize.

9) The car skidded **dangerously** close to us.

10) The music has a **lively** beat.

Name ______ Date ______ Period ______

Chapter 6 Workbook Activity 28

Adverbs and Adjectives

Some adjectives, as well as adverbs, end in *-ly.*

Directions: Decide whether the word in bold print in each sentence is an adjective or an adverb. Label it correctly.

EXAMPLES We take a **weekly** magazine. *Adjective*
The child giggled **happily**. *Adverb*

1) Andy looked up **hopefully**. ______
2) We took the **early** bus to the city. ______
3) The wind blew **wildly** all night. ______
4) Our family has **partly** finished eating the soup. ______
5) The **daily** newspaper was late. ______
6) I **hastily** scribbled a note. ______
7) Speak **calmly** to the frightened dog. ______
8) Certain plants contain **deadly** poisons. ______
9) Maura found a **wriggly** earthworm in the garden. ______
10) People have to pay certain taxes **yearly**. ______
11) We told Nick to treat the pony **gently**. ______
12) The wrecked car was a **ghastly** sight. ______
13) Lucy bought some **crinkly** paper to wrap the gift. ______
14) The speaker gave his speech too **rapidly**. ______
15) The music the band played was **lively**. ______
16) I think the brown sandals are too **costly**. ______
17) That was a **silly** remark! ______
18) Mr. Bacon chuckled **cheerfully**. ______
19) The story I heard was most **unlikely**. ______
20) Try not to speak **crossly** to your sister. ______
21) Mrs. Peterson is a very **friendly** neighbor. ______

 Basic English Grammar

Workbook Activity 28

142 *Chapter 6 The Adverb*

Lesson 4 Review

Part A Write the words in bold on your paper. Beside each word, write whether it is an adverb or an adjective.

1) This **deadly** poison will get rid of all kinds of bugs.
2) Mr. Ozawa prepared his **yearly** report.
3) We receive a newspaper **daily**.
4) Please try to come to class **early**.
5) Carla smiled **happily**.
6) Where have you been **lately**?
7) I am **partly** finished with my report.
8) They went to Chicago on the **early** train.
9) We listened to the **daily** weather report.
10) The drought left the land bare and **ugly**.

Part B Write two sentences for each of the words below on your paper. In the first sentence, use the word as an adjective. In the second sentence, use the word as an adverb.

1) fast
2) early
3) late
4) weekly
5) hard
6) inside
7) best

Reading Vocabulary

drought (5)

Part A Answers

1) adjective **2)** adjective
3) adverb **4)** adverb
5) adverb **6)** adverb
7) adverb **8)** adjective
9) adjective **10)** adjective

Part B Answers

The first sentence in each pair should include the listed word as an adjective. The second sentence should include the listed word as an adverb.

Follow-up Activity

List the following words randomly on the board: *active, actively, brave, bravely, cautious, cautiously exact, exactly, kind, kindly, selfish, selfishly, warm, warmly.* Have volunteers circle the adverbs and underline the adjectives in the list. Then invite students to make up oral sentences for each word.

Learning Styles

Body/Kinesthetic

On separate note cards, print each adverb and adjective printed in bold on pages 140–143. Have a volunteer choose one card and say the word aloud. Challenge other volunteers to create a sentence that uses the card word as an adjective or an adverb. Ask the volunteer to print each word of the created sentence on a sheet of paper and to stand before the class and hold the sheets in order. Have the class read the sentence aloud and announce whether the volunteer used the word as an adjective or an adverb.

Lesson at a Glance

Chapter 6 Lesson 5

Overview This lesson presents the positive, comparative, and superlative forms of adverbs.

Objectives

- To identify adverbs in sentences.
- To write the three degrees of comparison of adverbs.
- To use adverbs correctly to make comparisons.

Student Pages 144–146

Teacher's Resource Library

Activity 18

Reading Vocabulary

comparative (10) positive (6)
irregular (7) superlative (10)

Teaching Suggestions

Introducing the Lesson

After discussing the degrees of comparisons and how they are formed, have students practice forming the comparative and superlative forms of the following adverbs: *hard, high, swiftly, quietly.*

Reviewing Skills

Discuss the three degrees of comparison of adjectives.

Presenting Activity A

Help students compose sentences using the positive, comparative, and superlative form of each adverb in the chart at the top of the page. Put the following sentences on the board as models: *Otis runs fast. His friend Joey runs faster. Of the three friends, Paco runs fastest.* Then have students complete Activity A on their own.

Activity A Answers

1) comfortably **2)** more comfortably **3)** most comfortably **4)** calmly **5)** more calmly **6)** most calmly **7)** well **8)** better **9)** best

Lesson 5 Comparing With Adverbs

Many adverbs are used to make comparisons. The three degrees of comparison are positive, comparative, and superlative.

Examples

Positive	Comparative	Superlative
fast	faster	fastest
slowly	more slowly	most slowly
happily	less happily	least happily
well	better	best

One-syllable adverbs form their comparative and superlative forms by adding *-er* and *-est.* Adverbs of more than one syllable usually form their comparative and superlative forms by using *more* and *most.* Adverbs can also be compared with *less* and *least.* A few adverbs are irregular, such as *well, better,* and *best.*

Remember to use the comparative form to compare two things. Use the superlative form to compare more than two things.

Examples

Kim finished **more quickly** than Ben.

Tom worked **most quickly** of them all.

Activity A Write the adverbs in each of these sentences on your paper.

1) This shoe fits comfortably.

2) This shoe fits more comfortably than that one.

3) Of the three, that shoe fits most comfortably.

4) Victor is speaking calmly.

5) He is speaking more calmly than Hector.

6) He speaks most calmly when he has practiced his speech.

7) Jack writes well.

8) He writes better this year than last year.

9) He writes best about football.

Activity B Write each adverb below on your paper. Beside each adverb, write its comparative and superlative forms.

Example softly—**more softly, most softly**

1) loudly

2) brightly

3) fast

4) hard

5) gladly

6) clearly

7) softly

8) angrily

Activity C Write the correct form of the adverb in parentheses to complete each sentence.

1) The lights shone (brightly) tonight than any night this week.

2) Liz sings (well) than Fernando.

3) Dan works (hard) when he is interested.

4) Of all the students, Kim worked (quickly).

5) Zeke played the trumpet (loudly) than his brother.

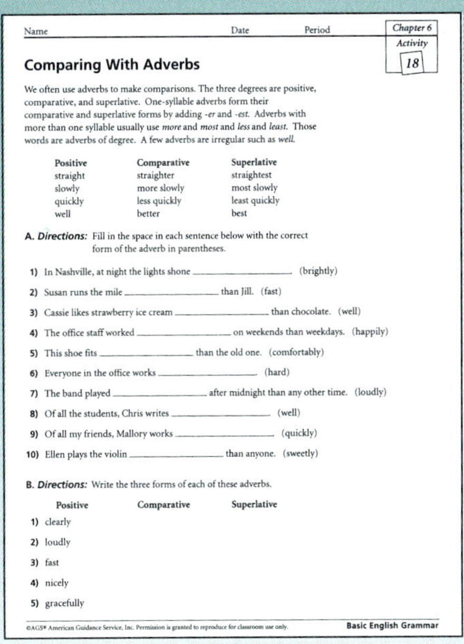

Name Date Period

Chapter 6 *Activity* *18*

Comparing With Adverbs

We often use adverbs to make comparisons. The three degrees are positive, comparative, and superlative. One-syllable adverbs form their comparative and superlative forms by adding *-er* and *-est.* Adverbs with more than one syllable usually use *more* and *most* and *less* and *least.* Those words are adverbs of degree. A few adverbs are irregular such as *well.*

Positive	Comparative	Superlative
straight	straighter	straightest
slowly	more slowly	most slowly
quickly	less quickly	least quickly
well	better	best

A. *Directions:* Fill in the space in each sentence below with the correct form of the adverb in parentheses.

1) In Nashville, at night the lights shone ______________. (brightly)

2) Susan runs the mile ______________ than Jill. (fast)

3) Cassie likes strawberry ice cream ______________ than chocolate. (well)

4) The office staff worked ______________ on weekends than weekdays. (happily)

5) This shoe fits ______________ than the old one. (comfortably)

6) Everyone in the office works ______________. (hard)

7) The band played ______________ after midnight than any other time. (loudly)

8) Of all the students, Chris writes ______________. (well)

9) Of all my friends, Mallory works ______________. (quickly)

10) Ellen plays the violin ______________ than anyone. (sweetly)

B. *Directions:* Write the three forms of each of these adverbs.

	Positive	Comparative	Superlative
1)	clearly		
2)	loudly		
3)	fast		
4)	nicely		
5)	gracefully		

 Basic English Grammar

Activity 18

Reading Vocabulary

angrily

■ Presenting Activity B

You may wish to have students write their responses for Activity B in a chart similar to the one shown below.

Positive	Comparative	Superlative
softly	more softly	most softly

Activity B Answers

1) loudly, more loudly, most loudly **2)** brightly, more brightly, most brightly **3)** fast, faster, fastest **4)** hard, harder, hardest **5)** gladly, more gladly, most gladly **6)** clearly, more clearly, most clearly **7)** softly, more softly, most softly **8)** angrily, more angrily, most angrily

■ Presenting Activity C

Do the first item in Activity C orally with the class. Then have students complete the activity on their own.

Activity C Answers

1) more brightly **2)** better **3)** hard, harder, hardest **4)** most quickly **5)** more loudly

Learning Styles

Interpersonal/Group Learning

Divide the class into groups of five. Ask each group to choose one adverb from the list in Activity B on page 145. Invite each group to write a story or play—with setting, characters, and plot—and to use the positive, comparative, and superlative form of the chosen adverb in the story or play. Afterward, have each group read its story or play. Encourage the other students to raise their hands as they hear the three uses of the adverb.

Reading Vocabulary

briskly chorus (5)

Part A Answers

1) faster—comparative **2)** hard—positive **3)** best—superlative **4)** less quickly—comparative **5)** more loudly—comparative **6)** least happily—superlative **7)** better—comparative **8)** most loudly—superlative **9)** more quietly—comparative **10)** well—positive

Part B Answers

1) more happily, most happily **2)** more quickly, most quickly **3)** better, best **4)** more loudly, most loudly **5)** more politely, most politely **6)** more sweetly, most sweetly **7)** more noisily, most noisily **8)** more briskly, most briskly **9)** more sadly, most sadly **10)** more kindly, most kindly

Follow-up Activity

Divide the class into teams and have each team write a list of twenty adverbs. Have teams exchange lists. Each team must then write the comparative and superlative form of each adverb on the list.

Lesson 5 Review

Part A Write the adverbs in each of these sentences on your paper. Beside each adverb, write the degree of comparison.

Example Sarah dances most unusually.
most unusually—superlative

1) Paul runs the mile faster than Sam.
2) Everyone in class worked hard.
3) I work best when I am rested.
4) Carl reads less quickly than Mike.
5) The choir sang the chorus more loudly than the verses.
6) Everyone worked least happily at the end of the day.
7) I like apples better than pears.
8) The winds howled most loudly at midnight.
9) The children played more quietly after lunch.
10) Irene plays the drums well.

Part B Write each adverb below on your paper. Beside each adverb, write its comparative and superlative forms.

Example quietly—**more quietly, most quietly**

1) happily
2) quickly
3) well
4) loudly
5) politely
6) sweetly
7) noisily
8) briskly
9) sadly
10) kindly

146 *Chapter 6 The Adverb*

Lesson 6 Using Adverbs Correctly

Adverbs often tell when the action in a sentence is taking place. *Ago* indicates past time. *Later* indicates future time. In a statement, the tense of the verb and the adverb of time usually must agree.

EXAMPLES

Maria **sang** long **ago**.

Jack **will sing later**.

Tom **will sing next**.

(The adverb *next* suggests that the action will happen in the future. The verb should be in future tense.)

Tomorrow we **will go** to work.

(The adverb *tomorrow* is future time. The verb should be in future tense.)

Activity A In the sentences below, the adverbs of time are in bold. Write the correct tense of the verb in parentheses to complete each sentence.

1) We (go) there a year **ago**.
2) **Yesterday** we (be) late to class.
3) Sally (arrive) **soon**.
4) Tiny (eat) his dinner **now**.

Always use an adverb in a sentence when answering a question about a verb.

EXAMPLES

Correct: She sighed **softly**. (How did she sigh? *softly*)

Incorrect: She sighed **soft**. (*Soft* is an adjective.)

Activity B Choose the correct word in parentheses. Write it on your own paper.

1) Fernando laughed (happy, happily).
2) The winds howled (loud, loudly).
3) She left home (quick, quickly)!
4) Sit there (quiet, quietly)!

Name Date Period — Chapter 6 Workbook Activity 29

Choosing the Correct Adverb

We know that verbs express time.

EXAMPLES We **will sing**. (future) We **sang**. (past)

Adverbs also express time.

EXAMPLES We sang **yesterday**. (past) We will sing **tomorrow**. (future)

RULE: In a sentence, the tense of the verb and the adverb of time must agree.

Directions: In the following sentences, the adverbs of time are in bold. The verbs are in parentheses at the end of each sentence. Complete each sentence with the correct form of the verb.

EXAMPLE We lived there **last year**. (live)
We are eating dinner **now**. (eat)

1) **Last week** we ______ a party. (give)
2) **Tomorrow** the puppy ______ . (arrive)
3) Aunt Mary ______ us **later** in the day. (visit)
4) Please ______ dinner **immediately**. (fix)
5) **Sometimes** I ______ reading. (enjoy)
6) **Daily** the mail ______ . (come)
7) Yolanda ______ **next**. (sing)
8) In the winter it ______ **always** cold. (be)
9) **Now** ______ the time for all good men to come to the aid of their country. (be)
10) We **already** ______ our application to the bank. (send)
11) Fred ______ here **soon**. (be)
12) **Yesterday** Michael ______ to be president of the class. (agree)
13) **Today** I ______ to a swimming meet. (go)
14) **Lately** the weather ______ cool. (be)
15) We ______ the bushes in the front yard **yearly**. (trim)

 Basic English Grammar

Workbook Activity 29

Lesson at a Glance

Chapter 6 Lesson 6

Overview This lesson focuses on using adverbs correctly.

Objectives

- To use the correct verb tense with adverbs of time.
- To use an adverb to tell about a verb.
- To use *good* and *well* correctly.

Student Pages 147–149

Teacher's Resource Library

Workbook Activity 29

Reading Vocabulary

indicate (6) tense (6)

Teaching Suggestions

Introducing the Lesson

Discuss the usage rules presented in the lesson, encouraging students to ask questions about anything that is unclear.

Reviewing Skills

Review verb tenses with students.

Presenting Activity A

Help students identify the time that the adverb in bold indicates in each item. Suggest that as students do Activity A, they read each sentence to themselves with the answer in place to see if it makes sense.

Activity A Answers

1) went **2)** were **3)** will arrive **4)** is eating/will eat

Presenting Activity B

Do the first item with students. Elicit through discussion why *happily* is the correct response. After students complete Activity B, have them explain their answers.

Activity B Answers

1) happily **2)** loudly **3)** quickly **4)** quietly

Reading Vocabulary

state-of-being

■ **Presenting Activity C** Be sure students have a clear understanding of when to use *good* and *well*. Then do the first two items in Activity C with the class. Elicit from students why *good* is the correct answer for item 1 and why *well* is the correct answer for item 2. Then have students complete Activity C on their own. Some students may benefit from working with a partner. Encourage partners to discuss each item before writing their responses.

Activity C Answers

1) good 2) well 3) good
4) well 5) well/good
6) well 7) well 8) good
9) well 10) good/well

Teacher Alert

The use of *good* and *well* causes problems for many students. Check students' responses to Activity C to get an indication of which students need additional support with this skill. Offer one-on-one instruction or suggest that students work in small groups with students who have mastered the usage of *good* and *well.*

Use *good* and *well* correctly. *Good* is always an adjective and describes a noun. Never use *good* to answer questions about a verb.

EXAMPLE

Correct: We had a **good** day. (What kind of day? a *good* day)

Incorrect: They worked **good** together. (The adjective *good* should not be used to answer the question *How did they work?*)

Well is usually an adverb. *Well* means to do something correctly.

EXAMPLE

Correct: She speaks **well**. (How does she speak? *well*)

Incorrect: She speaks **good**. (The adjective *good* should not be used to answer the question *How does she speak?*)

Good and *well* can both be used after state-of-being verbs. In both sentences below, *good* and *well* are adjectives.

EXAMPLE

Correct: I feel **good** today. (describes emotions)

Correct: I feel **well** today. (describes health)

Activity C Write either *good* or *well* on your paper to complete each sentence correctly.

1) Carol is ______ at arithmetic.
2) Dan dances very ______.
3) She did her ______ deed for the day.
4) Mike always does his work ______.
5) Paco isn't feeling ______ today.
6) Billy does everything ______.
7) Ellie paints very ______.
8) Michael had a ______ game yesterday.
9) Lulu sings very ______.
10) Do you feel ______ enough to go to the movies.

Lesson 6 Review

Part A Rewrite each of these sentences correctly on your paper.

1) Yesterday we are late to class.

2) Please finish that work quick.

3) Louis Armstrong played the trumpet very good.

4) Owen and I work good as partners.

5) "Julio spoke now," the teacher reminded the class.

6) Annie always talks very soft.

7) The phone works poor.

8) The children are playing so quiet.

9) Jonas dances good for a five-year-old.

10) The bus arrived soon.

Part B The word in bold in each of these sentences is an adverb. Write the form of the verb that should appear in each sentence to make it correct. Beside each verb, write its tense.

Example I (sit) at that desk **yesterday**.
sat—past tense

1) **Tomorrow** we (go) to work.

2) We (eat) at that restaurant a long time **ago**.

3) Our friends (arrive) **soon**.

4) The men (clean) our rug **yesterday**.

5) I (wash) the car **earlier today**.

Reading Vocabulary

restaurant (5)

Part A Answers

Answers may vary. Possible responses are given.

1) Yesterday, we were late to class. **2)** Please finish that work quickly. **3)** Louis Armstrong played the trumpet very well. **4)** Owen and I work well as partners. **5)** "Julio is speaking now," the teacher reminded the class. **6)** Annie always talks very softly. **7)** The phone works poorly. **8)** The children are playing so quietly. **9)** Jonas dances well for a five-year-old. **10)** The bus will arrive soon.

Part B Answers

1) will go **2)** ate **3)** will arrive **4)** cleaned **5)** washed

Follow-up Activity

Have students write ten sentences using the adjective *good* in five sentences and the adverb *well* in the other five sentences.

Learning Styles

Auditory/Verbal

Call on volunteers to read aloud the sentences as they appear in Part A of the review on page 149. Invite other volunteers to repeat the sentence aloud, but to improve it by using the correct verb form or adverb.

The Adverb Chapter 6 **149**

Chapter 6 Review

The Teacher's Resource Library includes two parallel forms of the Chapter 6 Mastery Test. The difficulty level of the two forms is equivalent. You may wish to use one form as a pretest and the other form as a posttest.

Reading Vocabulary

announcement   dismiss (5)
cashier (7)

Part A Answers

1) early **2)** very **3)** somewhat, patiently **4)** early **5)** so **6)** anyway **7)** extremely **8)** never **9)** probably, very **10)** unusually **11)** more, slowly **12)** Finally **13)** carefully **14)** almost **15)** excitedly **16)** quickly **17)** Soon **18)** still **19)** already, outside **20)** here

Application

Career Connection

Engage students in a discussion of the kinds of things people can do to help themselves get a job. Then divide the class into small groups and have each group of students create a poster with a list of guidelines or tips for successful job hunting. Tell students to try to use at least one adverb in each tip or guideline. Offer the following as examples: *Dress neatly. Speak confidently. Arrive early for your interview.*

Chapter 6 Review

Part A Write all the adverbs in these sentences on your paper. A sentence may have more than one adverb.

1) A heavy snowfall arrived early in December.

2) Most of the people at Wilson High School were very happy.

3) The teachers and students waited somewhat patiently.

4) They were expecting an announcement that school would be dismissed early.

5) At home Joe was not so pleased.

6) He had to go to work anyway.

7) He knew the roads would be extremely slippery.

8) The grocery store never closed for snow.

9) Business at the store would probably be very slow.

10) Yesterday had been unusually busy for a Tuesday.

11) Joe drove more slowly that day.

12) Finally, he arrived at work.

13) He walked across the parking lot carefully.

14) The store was almost empty.

15) The other cashiers were talking excitedly about the snow.

16) The day passed quickly.

17) Soon it was time for Joe to leave.

18) "I still have time to go sledding," he thought to himself.

19) He found Tina already outside.

20) "Hey! I'm here!" he called to her.

Name ______ Date ______ Period ______ *Chapter 6 Mastery Test A page 1*

Chapter 6 Mastery Test A

Part A Write the word that each bold adverb answers questions about.

1) The ballerina dances **gracefully**. ______

2) The carpenter climbed the ladder **carefully**. ______

3) The moon shone **brightly** on the rippling water. ______

4) We picked things up **quickly** and left. ______

5) She is **very** easy to please. ______

6) I can't keep up with you when you run **so** fast. ______

7) Ben was **completely** finished by day's end. ______

8) We will go to the movies **tomorrow**. ______

9) Abby walked **upstairs**. ______

10) The team flew to Chicago **later** than they planned. ______

11) He left work **early** on Monday. ______

12) Cal Ripken, Jr. plays shortstop **very** well. ______

13) I am **nearly** ready to leave. ______

14) Everyone here works **rather** quickly. ______

15) The sunset this evening is **unusually** beautiful. ______

Part B Write the correct form of the adverb in parentheses to complete each sentence.

1) Which of you two serves the ball ______? (well)

2) Who finished ______ of all the team members? (quickly)

3) He dribbled the ball somewhat ______. (slowly)

4) She sings the ______ when she has practiced. (well)

5) This star shines ______ than that one. (brightly)

 Basic English Grammar

Name ______ Date ______ Period ______ *Chapter 6 Mastery Test A page 2*

Chapter 6 Mastery Test A, continued

6) Because it is the shortest, February goes by ______ of all the months. (swiftly)

7) Chan fed the group quite ______. (gladly)

8) Teresa writes ______ than her brother. (clearly)

9) Of all the crew, Mark husked corn ______. (rapidly)

10) Jonell eats her soup very ______. (noisily)

Part C Circle all of the adverbs in these sentences.

1) "I will never buy a thing at that store again," said Joe angrily.

2) My dog barks loudly when she wants a bone.

3) He started his homework immediately.

4) Please do it now.

5) The child jumped up and down almost constantly.

6) I never get too much of the beach.

7) Some people find skiing very exciting.

8) The team advanced forward quickly.

9) Michael Jordan can jump higher than nearly anyone.

10) "Hang your coats here," said the hostess cheerfully.

11) He does not walk alone around the lake.

12) The gate swings squeakily when the wind blows strongly.

13) Zoe boldly walked ahead of the other scouts.

14) Quietly the cat now approached the mouse.

15) Abel eagerly went twice for a second helping.

 Basic English Grammar

Chapter 6 Mastery Test A

Part B Write the adverbs in these sentences on your paper.

1) You should follow the directions carefully.
2) Clues to the puzzle are hidden everywhere.
3) The weather was very cold yesterday.
4) You are making too much noise.
5) I was almost asleep.
6) Julie threw her dog's old collar away today.
7) Is it true that it hardly rains in southern California?
8) The basement is quite damp this time of year.
9) He made a rather strange request.
10) She almost always arrives late.

Part C Write the form of the adverb that should appear in each sentence to make it correct.

1) Of all the girls, Donna runs (fast).
2) Charlie works (slowly) than Jim.
3) Beth sings well, but Dan sings (well).
4) When I am tired, I work (quickly) than when I am rested.
5) The cardinal sings (sweetly) than the blue jay.

Test Taking Tip Review your corrected tests. You can learn from previous mistakes.

Reading Vocabulary

cardinal
clue (5)
request (6)

Part B Answers

1) carefully 2) everywhere
3) very, yesterday 4) too
5) almost 6) away, today
7) hardly 8) quite 9) rather
10) almost, always, late

Part C Answers

1) fastest 2) more slowly
3) better 4) more quickly
5) more sweetly

Name Date Period

Chapter 6 Mastery Test B page 1

Chapter 6 Mastery Test B

Part A Write the word that each bold adverb answers questions about.

1) Jessye Norman sings **beautifully**. ________
2) The plumber turned the wrench **slowly**. ________
3) The stars glistened **brilliantly** in the dark sky. ________
4) We retreated **hastily** from the bear's path. ________
5) Using a computer is **extremely** easy. ________
6) Toby walks **too** slowly for the dog. ________
7) Bea was **totally** exhausted by day's end. ________
8) We went on a five-mile hike **yesterday**. ________
9) Sondra ran **downstairs**. ________
10) **Later** we will talk about the book. ________
11) I exercise **early**. ________
12) Wayne Gretzky plays hockey **very** well. ________
13) We can **almost** see through the fog. ________
14) Everyone here works **fairly** well together. ________
15) The lakes were frozen **solid**. ________

Part B Write the correct form of the adverb in parentheses to complete each sentence.

1) Manuel writes quite ________. (clearly)
2) They greeted all of the guests very ________. (warmly)
3) This shoe fits ________ than that one. (comfortably)
4) Which of the two team members swam ________? (fast)
5) Of the three kittens, this one takes to strangers ________. (easily)

 Basic English Grammar

Name Date Period

Chapter 6 Mastery Test B page 2

Chapter 6 Mastery Test B, continued

6) Bonnie treats her friends rather ________. (well)
7) Gabe paddles the canoe ________ of the foursome. (skillfully)
8) Nelly speaks ________ than Nick does. (calmly)
9) Of all the days, I get my work done ________ on Fridays. (quickly)
10) Harry hits the ball ________ of anyone on the team. (hard)

Part C Circle all of the adverbs in these sentences.

1) Yesterday two students were early for biology lab.
2) My cat purrs softly when he wants catnip.
3) Kim and Lee work well together.
4) Please clean your room today.
5) We are expecting company soon.
6) For more fun time, always do your chores immediately.
7) During a storm, the roads can be extremely slippery.
8) People drive more slowly when the weather is very bad.
9) Most people do not like very cold weather.
10) The store had an unusually good sale on basketball shoes.
11) I probably will not be very late.
12) Sherry never runs alone later than sunset.
13) The door bangs noisily when the wind blows forcefully.
14) Tom proudly showed his awards today.
15) Peacefully the bear now sleeps.

 Basic English Grammar

Chapter 6 Mastery Test B

Chapter 7

Planning Guide

The Preposition

	Student Text Lesson			
	Student Pages	Vocabulary	Practice Exercises	Lesson Review
Lesson 1 Understanding Prepositions	154-157	✔	✔	157
Lesson 2 The Prepositional Phrase Used as an Adjective	158-160		✔	160
Lesson 3 The Prepositional Phrase Used as an Adverb	161-163		✔	163
Lesson 4 The Object of the Preposition	164-167		✔	167
Lesson 5 Preposition or Adverb?	168-169		✔	169

Chapter Activities

Teacher's Resource Library

Community Connection 7: Using Prepositions to Give Directions

Assessment Options

Student Text

Chapter 7 Review

Teacher's Resource Library

Chapter 7 Mastery Tests A and B

Midterm Mastery Test

Teaching Strategies							Language Skills			Learning Styles						Teacher's Resource Library		
Reviewing Skills	Teacher Alert	Follow-up Activity	Career Application	Home Application	Global Connection	Community Application	Identification Skills	Writing Skills	Punctuation Skills	Visual/Spatial	Auditory/Verbal	Body/Kinesthetic	Logical/Mathematical	Group Learning	LEP/ESL	Activities	Workbook Activities	Self-Study Guide
154		157			155		✔	✔	✔	156						19-20		✔
158	159	160					✔	✔	✔						160		30	✔
161				163			✔	✔	✔					162		21	31-32	✔
164	165-166	167					✔	✔	✔	167							33	✔
168			171			169	✔	✔	✔		169						34	✔

Chapter at a Glance

Chapter 7: The Preposition pages 152–171

Teacher's Resource Library

- Activities 19–21
- Workbook Activities 30–34
- Community Connection 7
- Chapter 7 Self-Study Guide
- Chapter 7 Mastery Tests A and B
- Midterm Mastery Test

(Answer Keys for the Teacher's Resource Library begin on page 330 of this Teacher's Edition.)

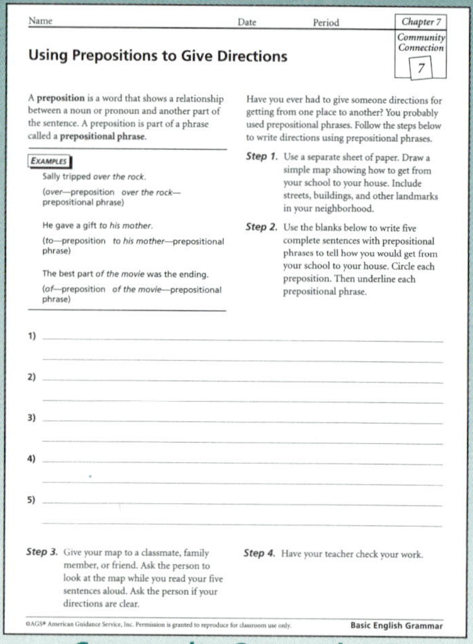

Name Date Period | *Chapter 7* *Community Connection* 7

Using Prepositions to Give Directions

A **preposition** is a word that shows a relationship between a noun or pronoun and another part of the sentence. A preposition is part of a phrase called a **prepositional phrase**.

EXAMPLES

Sally tripped *over the rock*.
(*over*—preposition *over the rock*—prepositional phrase)

He gave a gift *to his mother*.
(*to*—preposition *to his mother*—prepositional phrase)

The best part *of the movie* was the ending.
(*of*—preposition *of the movie*—prepositional phrase)

Have you ever had to give someone directions for getting from one place to another? You probably used prepositional phrases. Follow the steps below to write directions using prepositional phrases.

Step 1. Use a separate sheet of paper. Draw a simple map showing how to get from your school to your house. Include streets, buildings, and other landmarks in your neighborhood.

Step 2. Use the blanks below to write five complete sentences with prepositional phrases to tell how you would get from your school to your house. Circle each preposition. Then underline each prepositional phrase.

1) ______________________________

2) ______________________________

3) ______________________________

4) ______________________________

5) ______________________________

Step 3. Give your map to a classmate, family member, or friend. Ask the person to look at the map while you read your five sentences aloud. Ask the person if your directions are clear.

Step 4. Have your teacher check your work.

 Basic English Grammar

Community Connection 7

Chapter 7

The Preposition

Suppose you are telling someone how you will be spending the evening. You might say, "I am going *to* the movies. A friend is coming *with* me." Words such as *to* and *with* show connection among words.

A preposition is a word that shows a relationship between a noun or pronoun and another word in the sentence. A preposition is the first word of a prepositional phrase. Prepositional phrases give information about ideas in sentences.

In Chapter 7, you will learn about prepositions, prepositional phrases, and their purposes. Each lesson in the chapter focuses on recognizing prepositions and their purpose in sentences. Knowing how prepositions work in a sentence will help you better understand relationships among ideas.

Goals for Learning

- To identify prepositions in sentences
- To identify prepositional phrases in sentences
- To distinguish between adjective and adverb phrases
- To distinguish between prepositions and adverbs
- To identify the correct form of pronouns used as objects of prepositions

153

Reading Vocabulary

connection (6) identify (6)
distinguish (6) relationship (6)

Introducing the Chapter

Invite volunteers to describe what they do after school and on weekends for work and fun. As students offer ideas, lead them to add prepositional phrases to their sentences that add information and expand their ideas. For example, if a student were to say, "I play soccer," you might ask "when and where do you play and with whom?" The student might then say something such as "I play soccer on Sunday afternoons at the park with my brother and our friends." Write the expanded sentence on the board, underlining the prepositional phrases. Then explain that each of these groups of words is a prepositional phrase. Tell students that by the end of Chapter 7, they will understand how they can use prepositional phrases to add information to their sentences to make their ideas more complete and precise.

SELF-STUDY GUIDE

Name ____________

CHAPTER 7: The Preposition

Goal 7.1 *To identify prepositions and prepositional phrases in sentences*

Date	Assignment	Score
______	1: Read pages 153-154. Complete Activity A on page 154.	______
______	2: Read page 155. Complete Activity B on page 155.	______
______	3: Read page 156. Complete Activities C-D on page 156.	______
______	4: Complete the Lesson 1 Review, Parts A-B on page 157.	______

Comments:

Goal 7.2 *To distinguish between adjective and adverb phrases*

Date	Assignment	Score
______	5: Read page 158. Complete Activities A-B on page 158.	______
______	6: Complete Workbook Activity 30.	______
______	7: Read page 159. Complete Activities C-D on page 159.	______
______	8: Complete the Lesson 2 Review on page 160.	______
______	9: Read page 161. Complete Activities A-B on page 161.	______
______	10: Read page 162. Complete Activities C-D on page 162.	______
______	11: Complete Workbook Activity 31.	______
______	12: Complete the Lesson 3 Review, Parts A-B on page 163.	______
______	13: Complete Workbook Activity 32.	______

Comments:

 Basic English Grammar

SELF-STUDY GUIDE

Name ____________

CHAPTER 7 The Preposition, continued

Goal 7.3 *To identify the correct form of pronouns used as objects of prepositions*

Date	Assignment	Score
______	14: Read page 164. Complete Activities A-B on page 164.	______
______	15: Read page 165. Complete Activities C-D on page 165.	______
______	16: Complete Workbook Activity 33.	______
______	17: Read page 166. Complete Activities E-F on page 166.	______
______	18: Complete the Lesson 4 Review on page 167.	______

Comments:

Goal 7.4 *To distinguish between prepositions and adverbs*

Date	Assignment	Score
______	19: Read page 168. Complete Activities A-B on page 168.	______
______	20: Complete Workbook Activity 34.	______
______	21: Complete the Lesson 5 Review, Parts A-B on page 169.	______
______	22: Complete the Chapter 7 Review, Parts A-D on pages 170-171.	______

Comments:

Student's Signature ____________ Date ____________

Instructor's Signature ____________ Date ____________

 Basic English Grammar

Chapter 7 Self-Study Guide

Lesson at a Glance

Chapter 7 Lesson 1

Overview This lesson introduces the preposition and prepositional phrase.

Objectives

- To use prepositions in sentences.
- To identify prepositional phrases in sentences.

Student Pages 154–157

Teacher's Resource Library

Activities 19–20

Reading Vocabulary

preposition
prepositional phrase
relate (6)

Teaching Suggestions

Introducing the Lesson

After discussing the information in the text, have students take turns completing the sentence *Joseph spoke* ________ *Ben.* with a different preposition each time. Students should select prepositions from the list that make sense in the sentence. Be sure students note how each preposition changes the meaning of the sentence.

Reviewing Skills

Review nouns and pronouns, especially the objective case of personal pronouns.

Presenting Activity A

Do Activity A orally with the students. Then ask students to do the activity on their own, using different prepositions from the ones you used the first time.

Activity A Answers

Answers will vary. Possible answers are given.

1) on/under 2) by/about 3) in/beside 4) under/on 5) with/near

Lesson 1 Understanding Prepositions

> **Preposition**
> *A word that shows how a noun or pronoun is related to another word in the sentence.*

> **Prepositional phrase**
> *A phrase that begins with a preposition and ends with a noun or a pronoun.*

A **preposition** shows a relationship between a noun or a pronoun and another word in the sentence. The noun or pronoun that follows the preposition is called the object of the preposition.

The preposition, the object of the preposition, and any words in between make up a **prepositional phrase**.

EXAMPLES

Danzel gave his ticket **to Angie**. (The preposition *to* shows the relationship of *Angie*, the object of the preposition, to *gave*.)

Jan read the letter **from Mary**. (The preposition *from* shows the relationship of *Mary*, the object of the preposition, to *letter*.)

When the preposition changes, the relationship between the words in the sentence changes. Notice how the relationship between *spoke* and *Ben* changes in the following sentences.

EXAMPLES

Joseph spoke **to** Ben.
Joseph spoke **about** Ben.
Joseph spoke **for** Ben.

Here is a list of commonly used prepositions.

about	around	beneath	for	near	out	to
above	at	beside	from	of	over	under
across	before	down	in	off	past	until
after	behind	during	into	on	through	with

Activity A Complete each of these sentences with a preposition. Write the complete sentence on your paper. More than one preposition may make sense in the sentence. Choose just one.

1) The apples ______ the tree are ripe.
2) The story ______ Edgar Allan Poe was written in 1838.
3) The girl ______ the picture is my sister.
4) The boots ______ the chair are mine.
5) The girl ______ Ken is a good dancer.

Name ______ Date ______ Period ______ *Chapter 7 Activity 19*

Understanding Prepositions

A preposition expresses a relationship between one part of a sentence and another word. That word is called the object of the preposition. The object of a preposition is a noun or a pronoun. A preposition and its object form a prepositional phrase.

EXAMPLES across the street / in the morning / on the radio / before winter / for her / in my class

Word List

about	behind	in	over
above	beneath	into	past
across	beside	near	through
after	down	of	to
around	during	off	under
at	for	on	until
before	from	out	with

Directions: Write a preposition in the space that correctly completes the thought. You may use words from the Word List above.

EXAMPLES The bird **in** the tree is singing.
Tree is the object of the preposition *in*.

1) The star ______ the movie was Denzel Washington.
2) The man ______ the picture is my father.
3) The boy ______ Susan is handsome.
4) Ice cream ______ chocolate syrup is my favorite dessert.
5) The apples ______ the tree are called red delicious apples.
6) The book ______ the table is mine.
7) My friend ______ Boston just moved in across the street.
8) The fans ______ the bleachers cheered for their team.
9) The picture ______ the wall was painted by Georgia O'Keeffe.
10) The pie ______ the table won first prize.
11) The house ______ the lake is for sale.
12) A letter ______ Kitty arrived today.

 Basic English Grammar

Activity 19

In a prepositional phrase, the preposition may have more than one object.

EXAMPLE Conchetta is friends with **Luke** and **Theo**. (*Luke* and *Theo* is the compound object of the preposition *with*.)

In a prepositional phrase, the object of a preposition may have adjectives in front of it.

EXAMPLE across **the muddy** field

Because adverbs can answer questions about adjectives, a prepositional phrase may also contain an adverb.

EXAMPLE after the **very** long meeting

Usually when the object of the preposition is a pronoun, no other words are between the preposition and its object or objects.

EXAMPLES to him beside it between you and me

A sentence may have more than one prepositional phrase.

EXAMPLE We bought groceries **for supper at the store.**

Activity B Write the prepositional phrases in these sentences on your paper. Underline the preposition once and its object or objects twice. A sentence may have more than one prepositional phrase.

1) Write your name in the left-hand corner.
2) They live near a very busy highway.
3) Would you please sit on the bench with Sal and me?
4) Give this book about Mexico to him.
5) Early in the morning, the sun shines through the front window.

Reading Vocabulary

adverb
compound (6)
adjective

Presenting Activity B

Write this sentence on the board: *Your coat is on the shelf in the closet.* Ask students to identify the prepositional phrases in the sentence. Then invite volunteers to underline the prepositions once and their objects twice. After students complete Activity B on their own, ask them to share their answers with the class.

Activity B Answers

1) in the left-hand corner
2) near a very busy highway
3) on the bench, with Sal and me
4) about Mexico, to him
5) in the morning, through the front window

GLOBAL CONNECTION

Mime is a universal language. Students who are learning English may benefit from seeing and acting out how different prepositions can change the meaning of a sentence. Write this sentence on the board: *She walked ________ him.* Then have pairs of students think of a preposition to complete the sentence and mime the sentence. Have the class guess the preposition that completes the sentence being mimed. Students who speak another language can first say the prepositional phrase in their primary language and then in English.

Reading Vocabulary

addition (5) spite (5)

■ Presenting Activity C

Have students take turns making up sentences for item 1. Ask the class to identify the prepositional phrase and the object or objects of the preposition in each sentence. Then have students complete Activity C on their own.

Activity C Answers

Sentences will vary.

■ Presenting Activity D

Before having students do Activity D on their own, invite them to use the compound prepositions listed in the example box. Ask students to write their sentences on the board and have the class identify the prepositional phrase in each sentence.

Activity D Answers

1) According to Jorge **2)** instead of Tim **3)** in place of Judy **4)** In spite of the heavy rain **5)** in front of Karl **6)** Because of his bad cold

Learning Styles

Visual/Spatial

Divide the class into pairs. Give each pair a colorful magazine picture. Point out the list of ten compound prepositions in the box on page 156. Challenge each set of partners to compose ten sentences about its picture and to use one of the compound prepositions in each sentence. Afterward, have each pair read its sentences aloud. Ask the other students to raise their hands when they hear a compound preposition. Note: Keep the pictures for use with the Learning Styles activity on page 207.

Activity C Write sentences for each of these prepositions on your paper.

Example around—Her house is **around the corner**.

1) about	**4)** during	**7)** under	**10)** through
2) through	**5)** beside	**8)** in	**11)** behind
3) with	**6)** down	**9)** across	**12)** after

Compound prepositions are made up of more than one word.

Examples		
	according to	in spite of
	because of	instead of
	in addition to	out of
	in front of	as far as
	in place of	along with

Activity D Write the prepositional phrase in these sentences on your paper. Underline the compound preposition in each phrase.

Example John stood in front of Maria.—in front of Maria

1) According to Jorge, the party was fun.

2) I am going instead of Tim.

3) Tranh will speak in place of Judy.

4) In spite of the heavy rain, they played the soccer game.

5) Donna sat in front of Karl.

6) Because of his bad cold, Abdul stayed home.

156 *Chapter 7 The Preposition*

Lesson 1 Review

Part A Write the prepositional phrases in these sentences on your paper. Underline the preposition once. Underline its object twice. A sentence may have more than one prepositional phrase.

1) My dog Honey was sleeping in the shade under a tree.
2) Suddenly, a loud noise in the street frightened her.
3) Honey ran around the yard wildly.
4) From the porch, I called her inside the house.
5) She dashed up the stairs instantly.
6) I almost fell onto my back when she jumped into my arms.
7) The noise had come from my neighbor's old car.
8) In spite of its age, the car still ran.
9) Mr. Kostas did have trouble starting the car during a rainstorm.
10) After a few tries, he could usually get it going.

Part B Write all the prepositional phrases in these sentences on your paper. A sentence may have more than one prepositional phrase.

1) Emilio was studying for his final exams.
2) He stayed in his room and studied for several hours.
3) Cal called him on the telephone.
4) "I need some help from you with my math," he said.
5) Cal lived around the corner.
6) After a few minutes, he arrived in a panic.
7) He burst into Emilio's room.
8) "Please help me with these problems," Cal begged.
9) In addition to a math test, Cal had an English test the next day.
10) In spite of his worries, Cal passed both tests.

Reading Vocabulary

exam panic (5)

Part A Answers

1) in the shade, under a tree
2) in the street 3) around the yard
4) From the porch, inside the house
5) up the stairs 6) onto my back, into my arms 7) from my neighbor's old car 8) In spite of its age
9) during a rainstorm 10) After a few tries

Part B Answers

1) for his final exams 2) in his room, for several hours 3) on the telephone 4) from you, with my math 5) around the corner
6) After a few minutes, in a panic
7) into Emilio's room 8) with these problems 9) In addition to a math test 10) In spite of his worries

Follow-up Activity

Create a set of preposition cards, with a preposition printed on each card. Divide the class into two teams. Have team members take turns selecting a card from the pile and saying a sentence with a prepositional phrase that begins with the preposition on the card. The other team gets a point if it can identify the prepositional phrase and its object. The team with the most points wins.

Name ____ Date ____ Period ____ *Chapter 7 Activity* 20

Prepositional Phrases as Modifiers

A. *Directions:* Underline the prepositional phrases in the following sentences. Circle the word each phrase modifies.

EXAMPLE Jack (went) to the picnic.

1) Katie went to a class.
2) She looked through her notebook.
3) Open the textbook to page 72.
4) Katie began reading from the chapter.
5) She asked a question about the material.
6) She went to her room.
7) Katie went to the children's playroom.
8) She talked with the children happily.
9) The children talked to Katie.
10) She decided to become a teacher of young children.

B. *Directions:* Write five sentences of your own using the preposition *to*.

1) ____
2) ____
3) ____
4) ____
5) ____

 Basic English Grammar

Activity 20

The Preposition Chapter 7 **157**

Lesson at a Glance

Chapter 7 Lesson 2

Overview This lesson presents adjective phrases.

Objectives

- To identify adjective phrases and the words they describe.
- To add adjective phrases to sentences.

Student Pages 158–160

Teacher's Resource Library

Workbook Activity 30

Reading Vocabulary

define (7) poem (5)
describe (5)

Teaching Suggestions

■ Introducing the Lesson

Discuss the text and examples with students. Provide additional examples by replacing the phrase in bold in each example sentence with another adjective phrase.

■ Reviewing Skills

Have students identify adjectives and the nouns or pronouns they modify in several sample sentences.

■ Presenting Activity A

Do the activity orally with the class. Then encourage students to replace the adjective phrase in each sentence with a different adjective phrase.

Activity A Answers

1) boy 2) flowers 3) house 4) None 5) poem

■ Presenting Activity B

Do the first item orally with the class before having students complete Activity B independently. Write the sentence on the board and have students take turns adding an adjective phrase to it.

Activity B Answers

Each sentence should include an adjective phrase to describe the noun in bold.

Lesson 2 The Prepositional Phrase Used as an Adjective

A prepositional phrase begins with a preposition and ends with a noun or a pronoun. A prepositional phrase may be used as an adjective phrase or as an adverb phrase.

An adjective is a word that describes or defines a noun or pronoun. A prepositional phrase used as an adjective does the same thing as an adjective. The phrase tells *which one, what kind,* or *how many.*

EXAMPLES The house **across the street** was sold. (*Which house?* The one *across the street.*)

This book **by Judy Blume** is popular. (*Which book?* The one *by Judy Blume.*)

An adjective usually comes before the noun it describes. An adjective phrase always follows the noun it describes.

EXAMPLES		
	Adjective:	The **Wilson High** team won.
	Prepositional phrase:	The team **from Wilson High** won.

Activity A Write the adjective phrase in bold on your paper. Beside each phrase, write the noun or pronoun it describes.

Example A friend **of mine** called. **of mine—friend**

1) The boy **with me** is my cousin.
2) The flowers **on the table** are beautiful.
3) We built a house **of bricks and stone**.
4) None **of the girls** left early.
5) The poem **by Maya Angelou** was beautiful.

Activity B Rewrite these sentences on your paper. Add an adjective phrase to describe the noun in bold. Be sure each phrase begins with a preposition.

1) The **story** was exciting to read.
2) Sue bought **tickets**.
3) Mom studied the **map**.
4) The **lamp** needed a new bulb.
5) The **house** looked empty.

Name Date Period *Chapter 7 Workbook Activity 30*

Prepositional Phrases as Adjectives

A prepositional phrase can change a noun or pronoun just like an adjective. Sometimes you will find them after the noun or pronoun. In the first example, ***on the corner*** answers the question, ***Which house?***

EXAMPLE The house on the corner is for sale.

In the example below, the prepositional phrase ***of my friends*** gives us more information about the pronoun ***All.***

EXAMPLE All of my friends arrived early.

Directions: Underline the prepositional phrases in these sentences. Draw an arrow from each prepositional phrase to the noun or pronoun it changes. Do your work like the examples above.

1) Wimbledon is a tennis tournament in England.
2) Most of the world's best players participate.
3) A man from West Germany, Boris Becker, is the youngest man to win the tournament.
4) What kind of racket did he use?
5) All of his matches in the tournament were exciting.
6) The play by Boris Becker was wonderful to watch.
7) Many of his points made the audience applaud.
8) Wimbledon tennis courts with their grass surfaces are different.
9) Kevin Curran, a man with a powerful serve, was Becker's final opponent.
10) The boy with the smile on his face is how some remember him.
11) The player with red hair also describes Boris Becker.
12) Millions watch the finals on center court at Wimbledon, England.

 Basic English Grammar

Workbook Activity 30

An adjective phrase can describe the object of another preposition.

> **EXAMPLE** The man **at the end of the line** is Mr. Jones.
>
> The adjective phrase *at the end* describes the noun *man*; the adjective phrase *of the line* describes the noun *end*.

Activity C Write the adjective phrases in these sentences on your own paper. Beside each phrase, write the noun or pronoun it describes.

1) The woods beside the lake near our house are dark.

2) Elvin's dad owns a shoe store in the mall beside Jones River.

3) The woman with the baby in her arms is my aunt.

4) The lamp on the table beside your bed needs a new lightbulb.

5) All of the people in the auditorium cheered.

Activity D Rewrite these sentences on your paper. Add an adjective phrase after each noun or pronoun in bold.

1) **Everyone** enjoys the football **games**.

2) Several **friends** are coming to the **party**.

3) The **dish** fell from the **counter**.

4) The **man** bought a new **car**.

5) The **teacher** liked that **book**.

6) The **library** closed at **noon**.

Reading Vocabulary

auditorium (5) mall

■ Presenting Activity C

Do Activity C as a whole class activity. Write each item on the board. Have students identify the prepositional phrases for you to underline. Then invite volunteers to draw an arrow from each prepositional phrase in a sentence to the noun or pronoun it describes.

Activity C Answers

	Adjective Phrase	Word Described
1)	beside the lake	woods
	near our house	lake
2)	in the mall	store
	beside Jones River	mall
3)	with the baby	woman
	in her arms	baby
4)	on the table	lamp
	beside your bed	table
5)	of the people	All
	in the auditorium	people

■ Presenting Activity D

Do the first item on the board, having students supply adjective phrases to describe the words in bold. Help students check that the phrase tells *which one, what kind,* or *how many* about the word in bold.

Activity D Answers

Each sentence should include an adjective phrase after each noun or pronoun in bold.

TEACHER ALERT

You may wish to point out that when one adjective phrase follows another adjective phrase, both phrases may be describing the same noun or pronoun, as in *Read this poem about city life by my sister.*

The Preposition Chapter 7 **159**

Reading Vocabulary

cruise (6) massive (7)
glacier (5) population (5)

Lesson Review Answers

1) in Alaska, temperatures **2)** throughout the state, pines **3)** of Alaska, history **4)** of Alaska, explorer **5)** from Russia, People **6)** on the southeast coast, Juneau **7)** in the United States, state **8)** of Alaska, population **9)** of our last frontiers, one **10)** from Washington State, aunt **11)** through Alaska's icy waters, cruise **12)** on the postcard, picture **13)** near Juneau, Mendenhall Glacier **14)** before her, glacier **15)** about her cruise, stories

Follow-up Activity

Write the following nouns and pronouns on the board: *car, coat, magazine, monkey, teacher, someone, everyone, all.* Have students select one noun and one pronoun from the list and write five prepositional phrases about each word.

Learning Styles

LEP/ESL

Ask ESL volunteers to create an adjectival phrase for an object you will give them. Present each volunteer with an object such as a book, desk, student's name, plant, poster, chalk, or eraser. Ask the volunteers to create an adjectival phrase in their primary language about the noun. Afterward, ask each volunteer to say the phrase in English and to explain whether it tells *which one, what kind,* or *how many* about the noun.

Lesson 2 Review

Lesson Review Write the adjective phrases in these sentences on your paper. Beside each phrase, write the noun or pronoun it describes.

Example The pen on Frank's desk has no ink.
on Frank's desk—pen

1) January temperatures in Alaska are very cold.

2) The beautiful pines throughout the state are snow-covered.

3) Maria studied the history of Alaska.

4) Vitus Bering was the first explorer of Alaska.

5) People from Russia also explored Alaska.

6) Juneau, on the southeast coast, became Alaska's capital city.

7) Alaska became the largest state in the United States.

8) The population of Alaska is very small.

9) Alaska is one of our last frontiers.

10) My aunt from Washington State visited Alaska.

11) Her vacation cruise through Alaska's icy waters lasted fourteen days.

12) The picture on the postcard she sent us showed a glacier.

13) Aunt Rita visited Mendenhall Glacier near Juneau.

14) The massive glacier before her covered an entire valley.

15) Her stories about her cruise are exciting.

Lesson 3 The Prepositional Phrase Used as an Adverb

An adverb is a word that answers questions about a verb. A prepositional phrase used as an adverb does the same thing as an adverb. It answers the questions *How? When? Where?* and *How much?* or *How long?*

EXAMPLES		
	Adverb:	We shopped **rapidly**.
	Adverb phrases:	We shopped **in a hurry**. (*How did we shop? in a hurry*)

An adverb phrase may come anywhere in a sentence.

EXAMPLES
After supper, we napped.
We napped **after supper**.

Activity A Write the adverb phrase in bold in these sentences on your paper. Beside each phrase, write the question that the adverb phrase answers about the verb. Write *How? When? Where? How Much?* or *How long?*

1) **For three hours**, the band played.
2) Maria ironed her dress **with great care**.
3) Dad slid the roast **into the oven**.
4) **Before midnight**, the report was written.
5) Write your paragraph **in ink**.
6) They stayed **about an hour**.

An adverb phrase can also answer the question *Why?* about a verb.

EXAMPLE They were crying **because of the sad ending**. (*Why were they crying? because of the sad ending*)

Activity B Write the adverb phrase that answers the question *Why?* in each of these sentences on your paper.

1) I ran inside because of the rain.
2) She shopped for dinner.
3) Will you sing for me?
4) Because of his fever, Jeff stayed home.

Lesson at a Glance

Chapter 7 Lesson 3

Overview This lesson presents adverb phrases.

Objectives

- To identify adverb phrases in sentences.
- To add adverb phrases to sentences.

Student Pages 161–163

Teacher's Resource Library

Activity 21

Workbook Activities 31–32

Reading Vocabulary

fever (5)

Teaching Suggestions

Introducing the Lesson

After discussing the text, ask students to explain the difference between an adverb and an adjective phrase.

Reviewing Skills

Review the definition of adverbs.

Presenting Activity A

Ask students to find the verb in the first item. Then have students apply each question to the verb to figure out which one the phrase answers. (*How long?*) Students can follow this process as they do Activity A.

Activity A Answers

1) How long? **2)** How? **3)** Where? **4)** When? **5)** How? **6)** How long?

Presenting Activity B

Before students do Activity B, write on the board: *The car skidded because of the ice.* Ask students to find the verb (*skidded*) and the adverb phrase that answers *Why?* about the verb. (*because of the ice*)

Activity B Answers

1) because of the rain **2)** for dinner **3)** for me **4)** Because of his fever

Reading Vocabulary

firefighter trash (6)
official (5)

Presenting Activity C

Do the activity orally with the class. Then encourage students to replace the adverb phrase or phrases in each sentence with different adverb phrases.

Activity C Answers

1) in the trash can 2) on the third floor, in that tall building 3) with her mother, at the store 4) for the school newspaper 5) from the fire 6) Because of the weather 7) by five minutes

Presenting Activity D

Write the first item on the board and have students take turns adding an adverb phrase. Encourage students to try to answer a different question each time. Then have students complete Activity D on their own.

Activity D Answers

Each sentence should include an adverb phrase that answers the question *How? When? Where?* or *How much?* about the word in bold.

Learning Styles

Interpersonal/ Group Learning

Divide the class into groups of three. Ask each group to think of an action to do in the classroom, create a sentence with the action and an adverbial phrase, and demonstrate the sentence. (For example, a group could demonstrate the sentence "We picked up a paper off the floor.") As each group silently demonstrates its sentence, have the class decide what action and adverbial phrase is being demonstrated and which question the phrase answers: *How? When? Where? How much?* or *How long?* (In the example, the phrase "off the floor" answers the question "From *where* did we pick it up?")

An adverb can describe an adjective or another adverb. An adverb phrase can do the same.

Examples

Fred is now taller **by three inches.** (*Taller* is an adjective. The adverb phrase *by three inches* tells how much taller Fred is.)

In the race, Dan ran faster than Jack **by eight seconds.** (*Faster* is an adverb. The adverb phrase *by eight seconds* tells how much faster Dan ran.)

Activity C Write the adverb phrases in these sentences on your paper. A sentence may have more than one adverb phrase.

1) Put the paper in the trash can.
2) His office is on the third floor in that tall building.
3) She shopped with her mother at the store.
4) Carol wrote for the school newspaper.
5) The firefighters saved the family from the fire.
6) Because of the weather, officials ended the game.
7) Tina is older than her sister by five minutes.

Activity D Rewrite these sentences on your paper. Add an adverb phrase that answers *How? When? Where?* or *How much?* about the word in bold.

1) Zack **walks** every day.
2) They **arrived**.
3) Luisa **took** her coat.
4) Bob got the **highest** grade on the test.
5) The winds **blew** very hard.
6) Please **answer**.

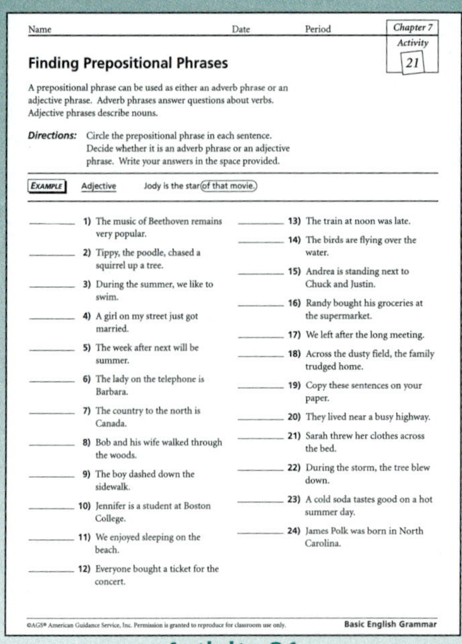
Name Date Period Chapter 7 Activity 21

Finding Prepositional Phrases

A prepositional phrase can be used as either an adverb phrase or an adjective phrase. Adverb phrases answer questions about verbs. Adjective phrases describe nouns.

Directions: Circle the prepositional phrase in each sentence. Decide whether it is an adverb phrase or an adjective phrase. Write your answers in the space provided.

Example Adjective Jody is the star (of that movie.)

_____ 1) The music of Beethoven remains very popular.
_____ 2) Tippy, the poodle, chased a squirrel up a tree.
_____ 3) During the summer, we like to swim.
_____ 4) A girl on my street just got married.
_____ 5) The week after next will be summer.
_____ 6) The lady on the telephone is Barbara.
_____ 7) The country to the north is Canada.
_____ 8) Bob and his wife walked through the woods.
_____ 9) The boy dashed down the sidewalk.
_____ 10) Jennifer is a student at Boston College.
_____ 11) We enjoyed sleeping on the beach.
_____ 12) Everyone bought a ticket for the concert.
_____ 13) The train at noon was late.
_____ 14) The birds are flying over the water.
_____ 15) Andrea is standing next to Chuck and Justin.
_____ 16) Randy bought his groceries at the supermarket.
_____ 17) We left after the long meeting.
_____ 18) Across the dusty field, the family trudged home.
_____ 19) Copy these sentences on your paper.
_____ 20) They lived near a busy highway.
_____ 21) Sarah threw her clothes across the bed.
_____ 22) During the storm, the tree blew down.
_____ 23) A cold soda tastes good on a hot summer day.
_____ 24) James Polk was born in North Carolina.

 Basic English Grammar

Activity 21

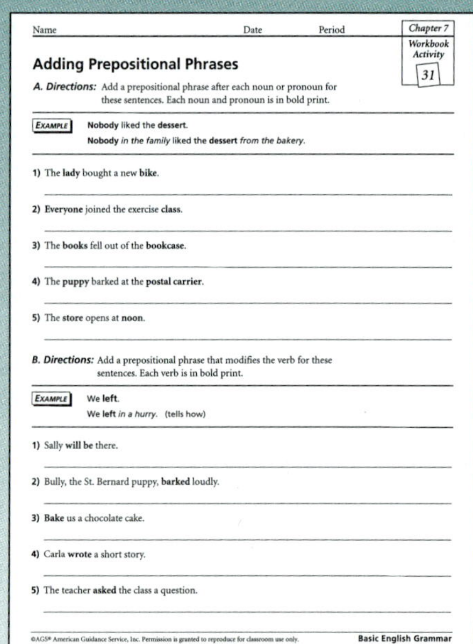
Name Date Period Chapter 7 Workbook Activity 31

Adding Prepositional Phrases

A. Directions: Add a prepositional phrase after each noun or pronoun for these sentences. Each noun and pronoun is in bold print.

Example **Nobody** liked the **dessert.**
Nobody *in the family* liked the **dessert** *from the bakery.*

1) The **lady** bought a new **bike**.
2) **Everyone** joined the exercise **class**.
3) The **books** fell out of the **bookcase**.
4) The **puppy** barked at the **postal carrier**.
5) The **store** opens at **noon**.

B. Directions: Add a prepositional phrase that modifies the verb for these sentences. Each verb is in bold print.

Example We **left**.
We **left** *in a hurry.* (tells how)

1) Sally **will be** there.
2) Bully, the St. Bernard puppy, **barked** loudly.
3) **Bake** us a chocolate cake.
4) Carla **wrote** a short story.
5) The teacher **asked** the class a question.

 Basic English Grammar

Workbook Activity 31

162 Chapter 7 The Preposition

Lesson 3 Review

Part A Write the adverb phrases in these sentences on your paper. A sentence may have more than one adverb phrase.

1) Marcus studies computer technology at Hanover Community College.
2) He will study there for two years.
3) Someday Marcus might work on computers in a bank.
4) During the early 1950s, the first computers were installed in business firms.
5) Now computers sit on office desks everywhere.
6) At school, Marcus learns about computer languages.
7) A computer programmer works with computer languages.
8) Because of the programmer's directions, the computer performs its job without a problem.

Part B Write whether the prepositional phrase in bold is an adjective or adverb phrase. Write your answers on your paper.

1) The letter **from Mary** arrived yesterday.
2) **At the concert**, the orchestra played the music **of Brahms.**
3) Both boys go **to Hanover Community College.**
4) Bess plays **for the Wilson High School soccer team.**
5) The gift **from my aunt** arrived **before my birthday.**
6) **During the winter** we enjoy skiing.
7) Honey chased a cat **up a tree.**
8) A girl **in my class** wrote a short story **about her summer vacation.**
9) She sent the story **to a magazine.**
10) The day **after tomorrow** is my birthday.

Name Date Period

Chapter 7 Workbook Activity 32

Prepositional Phrases

A prepositional phrase can be used as either an adverb or an adjective.

Adverbs answer questions about verbs.
Adjectives describe nouns and pronouns.

EXAMPLES He threw the ball over the house (adverb). (Where?)
Nancy got a letter from Mary (adjective). (Which one?)

Directions: Find all of the prepositional phrases. Label them as adverbs or adjectives. Do your work like the examples above.

1) I want the dessert with chocolate sauce.
2) The pears on the tree are ready to be picked.
3) The girl with Victor is very pretty.
4) Most of the students like football games in the fall.
5) Janet studies history in school.
6) Ted likes mustard on his hamburgers.
7) The girl at the end of the line is an old friend.
8) After the party Andy rode home with Ted.
9) Darleen and Janet went to the game on Saturday.
10) The tomatoes in our garden are ripe.
11) Some people like coffee with cream and sugar.
12) Mrs. Jones shopped with Janet for new shoes.
13) The quiz on Friday was easy.
14) The car disappeared around the corner.
15) The horse with the white markings is very fast.

 Basic English Grammar

Workbook Activity 32

Reading Vocabulary

computer (8) programmer
orchestra (6) technology

Part A Answers

1) at Hanover Community College **2)** for two years **3)** on computers, in a bank **4)** During the early 1950s, in business firms **5)** on office desks **6)** At school, about computer languages **7)** with computer languages **8)** Because of the programmer's directions, without a problem

Part B Answers

1) adjective phrase **2)** adverb phrase, adjective phrase **3)** adverb phrase **4)** adverb phrase **5)** adjective phrase, adverb phrase **6)** adverb phrase **7)** adverb phrase **8)** adjective phrase, adjective phrase **9)** adverb phrase **10)** adjective phrase

APPLICATION

At Home

Encourage students to create a personal dictionary of adjective and adverb phrases. As they read on their own, suggest that they jot down adjective and adverb phrases that they think add interest to the story or article they are reading. They can also include the noun, pronoun, or verb that the phrase describes. Students can refer to their lists for ideas when they write.

Lesson at a Glance

Chapter 7 Lesson 4

Overview This lesson explains the difference between an infinitive and a prepositional phrase that begins with *to.* It also explains how to identify the correct form of pronouns used as objects of prepositions.

Objectives

- To distinguish an infinitive from a prepositional phrase.
- To identify the correct form of pronouns used as objects of prepositions.

Student Pages 164–167

Teacher's Resource Library

Workbook Activity 33

Reading Vocabulary

confuse (5) infinitive

Teaching Suggestions

Introducing the Lesson

Discuss the text and examples with students.

Reviewing Skills

Review the structure of a prepositional phrase.

Presenting Activity A

List these phrases on the board: *to the market, to Spain, to run, to a movie, to cry, to our house.* Ask students whether each phrase is an infinitive or a prepositional phrase. Then have students complete Activity A on their own.

Activity A Answers

1) prepositional phrase 2) infinitive 3) prepositional phrase 4) infinitive 5) infinitive 6) infinitive 7) prepositional phrase 8) infinitive 9) prepositional phrase 10) prepositional phrase

Lesson 4 The Object of the Preposition

The object of the preposition is always a noun or a pronoun. Do not confuse a prepositional phrase with an infinitive, which begins with the word *to.* The word that follows *to* in an infinitive is a verb.

EXAMPLES

Infinitives:	He wants **to leave** early. He hopes **to have** a job.
Prepositional phrases:	Chen went **to the bank**. Fran wrote a letter **to her aunt**.

Activity A Write on your paper whether the phrase in bold in these sentences is an *infinitive* or a *prepositional phrase.*

1) Marcus went **to his class.**
2) He likes **to work** with computers.
3) "Turn **to page 8,**" the teacher said.
4) Marcus began **to read** his lesson.
5) He wanted **to ask** the teacher a question.
6) He went **to practice** on the computer.
7) Bill sent a get-well card **to his friend.**
8) The girl ran **to catch** the bus.
9) People on the bus waved **to her.**
10) Lynda climbed **to the top** of a high hill.

Activity B Write five sentences on your paper using the word *to.* Beside each sentence, write whether *to* introduces a prepositional phrase or an infinitive.

Presenting Activity B

Before having students do Activity B on their own, ask each student to say one infinitive and one prepositional phrase that begins with *to.*

Activity B Answers

Each sentence should include the word *to,* labeled to tell whether *to* introduces a prepositional phrase or an infinitive.

The object of the preposition is always a noun or a pronoun. If the object of a preposition is a pronoun, it must be in the objective case.

EXAMPLE Incorrect: She sat between Hector and **I**.
Correct: She sat between Hector and **me**.

Possessive nouns and pronouns are NOT used as objects of prepositions.

EXAMPLE Incorrect: Roland went home with **his**.
Correct: Roland went home with **him**.
OR
Roland went home with **his friend**.

Activity C Write the prepositional phrases in these sentences on your paper. Underline the object of the preposition in each phrase.

1) Daria wanted to study with her friend.

2) The table was empty, so I put my books on it.

3) Patrick studied by himself.

4) We bought gifts for everyone.

5) They had to choose between them.

6) Marty asked, "May I have a salad with this?"

Activity D Write these sentences on your paper. Correct any mistakes.

1) Please bring a coat for Pete and I.

2) Sam bought a soda for his.

3) Susan passed out papers to theirs.

4) Let's keep this secret between you and I.

Reading Vocabulary

objective (7) possessive

Presenting Activity C

Before students do Activities C and D, you may wish to have them look at the Personal Pronouns chart on page 30 to review the objective case of pronouns. It may also help to write the example sentence *She sat between Hector and me.* on the board and have students replace *me* with other objective pronouns, including *her, him, it, you, us,* and *them.*

Activity C Answers

1) with her friend **2)** on it **3)** by himself **4)** for everyone **5)** between them **6)** with this

Presenting Activity D

Before students complete Activity D on their own, have the class read each sentence aloud, listening for mistakes.

Activity D Answers

1) Please bring a coat for Pete and me. **2)** Sam bought a soda for him. **3)** Susan passed out papers to them. **4)** Let's keep this secret between you and me.

TEACHER ALERT

If students are unclear about which pronoun to use in a compound construction, they should try dropping the other parts of the compound. (*Please bring a coat for Pete and me.*)

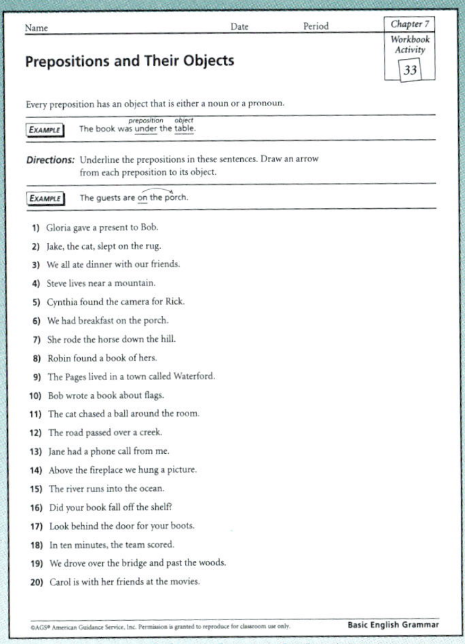
Name Date Period | *Chapter 7 Workbook Activity* 33

Prepositions and Their Objects

Every preposition has an object that is either a noun or a pronoun.

EXAMPLE The book was under (preposition) the table (object).

Directions: Underline the prepositions in these sentences. Draw an arrow from each preposition to its object.

EXAMPLE The guests are on the porch.

1) Gloria gave a present to Bob.
2) Jake, the cat, slept on the rug.
3) We all ate dinner with our friends.
4) Steve lives near a mountain.
5) Cynthia found the camera for Rick.
6) We had breakfast on the porch.
7) She rode the horse down the hill.
8) Robin found a book of hers.
9) The Pages lived in a town called Waterford.
10) Bob wrote a book about flags.
11) The cat chased a ball around the room.
12) The road passed over a creek.
13) Jane had a phone call from me.
14) Above the fireplace we hung a picture.
15) The river runs into the ocean.
16) Did your book fall off the shelf?
17) Look behind the door for your boots.
18) In ten minutes, the team scored.
19) We drove over the bridge and past the woods.
20) Carol is with her friends at the movies.

 Basic English Grammar

Workbook Activity 33

Reading Vocabulary

confidence (5) mathematics (6)
education (5) separate (5)

■ Presenting Activity E

Write this sentence on the board: *What is she staring at?* Help students identify the preposition and its object by asking students to rephrase the sentence as a statement. (*She is staring at what.*) Students can use this strategy as they do Activity E on their own.

Activity E Answers

1) about, Whom **2)** with, Whom **3)** about, What **4)** of, What

■ Presenting Activity F

Read the paragraph with students before having them work independently.

Activity F Answers

1) of Mary Lyon **2)** in the education **3)** of women **4)** in 1797 **5)** in 1849 **6)** in schools **7)** in New Hampshire **8)** in Massachusetts **9)** In those days **10)** for middle-class women **11)** In 1837 **12)** in Massachusetts **13)** of the school **14)** about mathematics, science, and Latin **15)** of everyone **16)** through her work **17)** in themselves

Teacher Alert

Ending a sentence with a preposition was once discouraged in formal grammar. However, this rule has been ignored so often that ending a sentence with a preposition has become acceptable to most writers and speakers. Nevertheless, students can avoid this issue by rewording their sentences or by dropping unnecessary prepositions, as in *What was she thinking of?*

The object of a preposition usually comes after the preposition. However, sometimes the preposition and its object are separated in sentences that ask questions.

Example

Object	Preposition
What did you do that **for**?	

Activity E Write on your paper the prepositions and their objects in these sentences on your paper.

1) Whom are you talking about?

2) Whom are Dionne and Len with?

3) What is that book about?

4) What was she was thinking of?

Activity F Write all the prepositional phrases in this paragraph on your paper. Do **not** include the three infinitives that are in the paragraph.

> Have you ever heard of Mary Lyon? She was a pioneer in the education of women. Mary Lyon was born in 1797. She died in 1849. She taught in schools in New Hampshire and in Massachusetts. In those days, only rich women could get a good education. She raised money to begin a school for middle-class women. In 1837, she opened a school in Massachusetts. The name of the school was Mount Holyoke. There women studied about mathematics, science, and Latin. Mary Lyon's only goal was to teach. She won the love of everyone through her work. Mary Lyon wanted to give women confidence in themselves.

166 *Chapter 7 The Preposition*

Lesson 4 Review

Lesson Review Write the prepositional phrases in these sentences on your paper.

1) Marcus would like to get a job in a bank or an accounting firm.

2) He likes to work with computers.

3) Marcus had to study for a test.

4) He studied with Anita and me.

5) The teacher gave the test to everyone.

6) The students had to concentrate hard on the questions.

7) They had prepared for the test all week.

8) Marcus made a mistake on his paper.

9) "What did I do that for?" he thought.

10) Finally, he was finished with the test.

11) He gave his paper to the teacher and breathed a sigh of relief.

12) Marcus waved good-bye to his friends and ran out the door.

13) The bus came early on Wednesdays, and he didn't want to miss it.

14) The bus driver waited for Marcus to get to the bus stop.

15) During the ride, Marcus took some time to think about the test.

Reading Vocabulary

accounting (5) concentrate (5)

Lesson Review Answers

1) in a bank or an accounting firm **2)** with computers **3)** for a test **4)** with Anita and me **5)** to everyone **6)** on the questions **7)** for the test **8)** on his paper **9)** for What **10)** with the test **11)** to the teacher, of relief **12)** to his friends, out the door **13)** on Wednesdays **14)** for Marcus, to the bus stop **15)** During the ride, about the test

Follow-up Activity

Select a short passage from a piece of literature or newspaper article. Have students work with a partner to identify all the prepositional phrases in the passage and to determine whether each phrase is an adjective phrase or adverb phrase.

Learning Styles

Visual/Spatial

Print a noun, such as the word *team*, on the board. Ask volunteers to use the noun as the object of a preposition and to create a web of prepositional phrases around it. (For example, for the word *team*, the students might write *by* the team, *for* the team, *after* the team, *behind* the team. If students need help remembering prepositions, direct them to the list on page 154.) Continue the activity by printing another noun or pronoun next to the first web. Afterward, ask volunteers to circle all the prepositions and to draw an X through all the nouns on the board.

The Preposition Chapter 7 **167**

Lesson at a Glance

Chapter 7 Lesson 5

Overview This lesson explains the difference between prepositions and adverbs.

Objectives

- To distinguish between adverbs and prepositions in sentences.
- To add prepositional phrases to sentences.

Student Pages 168–169

Teacher's Resource Library

Workbook Activity 34

Reading Vocabulary

principal (5) quarterback

Teaching Suggestions

Introducing the Lesson

Discuss the text and the examples. Be sure students understand the distinction between an adverb and a preposition before having them do the activities.

Reviewing Skills

Review the definition and purpose of adverbs.

Presenting Activity A

Do the first two items with the class. Ask students to explain how they know that *in* is an adverb in item 1 and a preposition in item 2. Then have students do Activity A on their own.

Activity A Answers

1) adverb 2) preposition
3) adverb 4) preposition
5) adverb 6) preposition
7) adverb 8) preposition

Presenting Activity B

Read and discuss the example. Then have students take turns adding different prepositional phrases to the sentence: *The boy arrived.*

Activity B Answers

Each sentence should include at least one prepositional phrase.

Lesson 5 Preposition or Adverb?

Some words can be either a preposition or an adverb. A preposition always has an object. An adverb does not.

EXAMPLES

Adverb:	Gabriel climbed **aboard**. (*Aboard* is not followed by a noun or a pronoun.)
Preposition:	Gabriel climbed **aboard** the boat. (*Aboard* relates its object, the noun *boat*, to the rest of the sentence.)

Activity A Write the word in bold on your paper. Beside it write whether it is an *adverb* or a *preposition.*

1) Please come **in**.
2) Howard walked **in** the woods.
3) Turn the lights **off** when you leave.
4) Jane jumped **off** the stage.
5) I will come **by** later.
6) Sam lives **by** the lake.
7) Last night, Mike came **over**.
8) Honey jumped **over** the fence easily.

Activity B Write these sentences on your paper. Add at least one prepositional phrase to each sentence to make it more interesting. Be sure to add only prepositional phrases.

Example The boy arrived.

The boy **from San Antonio** arrived **in the evening**.

1) My aunt wrote me a letter.
2) The principal spoke.
3) My neighbor bought a new car.
4) The quarterback threw the ball.
5) The crowd cheered.

Name Date Period

Chapter 7 Workbook Activity 34

Preposition or Adverb?

Some words can be used either as prepositions or as adverbs. A preposition has an object, and an adverb does not.

Directions: Read each sentence. Decide whether the word in bold print is a preposition or an adverb. Write your answer on the line.

EXAMPLES Put the cat **out**! *adverb*
Look **out** the window. *preposition*

______ 1) The dog's toy was **underneath** the sofa.
______ 2) Look **underneath**.
______ 3) Throw the ball **up** higher.
______ 4) My house is **up** the street.
______ 5) From the top of the Empire State Building, the cars **below** were tiny.
______ 6) The subway train runs **below** the ground.
______ 7) **Down, down,** the rain poured.
______ 8) The rain rushed **down** the gutters rapidly.
______ 9) Look **outside** and see the lightning.
______ 10) **Outside** the window we saw the lightning.
______ 11) I'd like some honey **in** my tea, please.
______ 12) Bring the dog **in** right now!
______ 13) The dog is **in** his house.
______ 14) Let's throw the ball **around** before the game.
______ 15) The guys threw the ball **around** the bases.

 Basic English Grammar

Workbook Activity 34

Lesson 5 Review

Part A Write the word in bold on your paper. Beside it write whether it is an *adverb* or a *preposition.*

1) The dog sat **outside** and barked all afternoon.

2) Leave the package **outside** the door.

3) Haven't we met **before**?

4) The elephant disappeared **before** our eyes!

5) Quick! Come look **out** the window!

6) There was a crash of thunder and the lights went **out**.

7) Sit **down** and rest awhile.

8) The old car rumbled **down** the highway.

9) The houses **along** the coast were in danger during the storm.

10) I broke my leg and had to hobble **along** on crutches for six weeks.

Part B Write two sentences for each of these words on your paper. In the first sentence, use the word as a preposition. In the second sentence, use the word as an adverb.

1) in	6) up
2) on	7) underneath
3) below	8) inside
4) around	9) near
5) about	10) through

Reading Vocabulary

crutch (6) underneath (5)
hobble (6)

Part A Answers

1) adverb 2) preposition
3) adverb 4) preposition
5) preposition 6) adverb
7) adverb 8) preposition
9) preposition 10) adverb

Part B Answers

Two sentences should be written for each listed word. One sentence should use the word as a preposition and the other should use the word as an adverb.

Application

In the Community

Point out that using prepositions correctly when giving directions can make the difference between someone getting where they are going and someone getting lost. Have small groups of students select two or three specific sites in the community. These may include historical sites, public buildings, parks, theaters, or any well-known places. Students can work together to write directions to these sites from the school. When all the groups are finished, review each set of directions as a class. Then assemble the directions in a booklet to place in the school library.

Learning Styles

Auditory/Verbal

Call on volunteers to read aloud the sentences they wrote for Part B of the review on page 169. Record their sentences on an audio tape and encourage students to listen to the tape in the upcoming days and to note the difference between a word used as an adverb and one used as a preposition.

Chapter 7 Review

The Teacher's Resource Library includes two parallel forms of the Chapter 7 Mastery Test. The difficulty level of the two forms is equivalent. You may wish to use one form as a pretest and the other form as a posttest.

Chapters 1–7 Midterm Mastery Test

The Teacher's Resource Library includes the Midterm Mastery Test. This test is pictured on page 327 of this Teacher's Edition. The Midterm Mastery Test assesses the major learning objectives for Chapters 1–7.

Reading Vocabulary

anniversary (7) mow (6)
assignment (6)

Part A Answers

1) adjective phrase **2)** adjective phrase **3)** adverb phrase **4)** adverb phrase **5)** adverb phrase **6)** adverb phrase, adverb phrase **7)** adjective phrase, adverb phrase **8)** adverb phrase, adjective phrase **9)** adjective phrase **10)** adverb phrase

Part B Answers

1) for a minute **2)** in a yellow sports car **3)** for dinner **4)** with his secret sauce **5)** After supper **6)** On Sunday, up Sugar Drop Mountain, with Connie and me **7)** For a beginner **8)** of the trails **9)** to the top, without a problem **10)** on Channel 6, for outdoor fun

Chapter 7 Review

Part A Write the prepositional phrase in bold in these sentences on your paper. Beside each prepositional phrase, write whether it is an *adjective phrase* or an *adverb phrase.*

1) The dress **in the window** is on sale.
2) The letter **from Aunt Vera** arrived yesterday.
3) Carol waited **for the mail.**
4) **In the spring** we will plant a garden.
5) I mowed the lawn **for my neighbor.**
6) Jiro traveled **across the country** last summer **in a bus.**
7) I put my homework assignment **for English class inside my book.**
8) **During the night**, seventeen inches **of snow** fell.
9) The painting **of your grandparents** is beautiful.
10) I did it **for their fiftieth anniversary party.**

Part B Write all the prepositional phrases in these sentences on your paper.

1) Mike came to see me for a minute.
2) He arrived in a yellow sports car.
3) We invited him to stay for dinner.
4) Dad made pizza with his secret sauce.
5) After supper, we all helped clean up.
6) On Sunday, Mike will hike up Sugar Drop Mountain with Connie and me.
7) For a beginner, that's a good mountain to hike.
8) Some of the trails are steep.
9) Still, Mike should be able to make it to the top without a problem.
10) The weather woman on Channel 6 said Sunday would be a great day for outdoor fun.

170 *Chapter 7 The Preposition*

Name ______ Date ______ Period ______ *Chapter 7 Mastery Test A page 1*

Chapter 7 Mastery Test A

Part A Circle all of the prepositions in these sentences.

1) In the fall we rake leaves into a pile over the flower bed.
2) We take the leaves off the flower beds around mid April.
3) Howie made pizza for his friends from Dallas.
4) Everyone was happy about the score of the game.
5) Gus saw Ronny at the mall behind the school.
6) I put a letter to Suzy through the mail slot near the door.
7) A pail of water spilled across the floor and under the door.
8) Our family likes cake with ice cream on top of it.
9) We rent a cabin beside a lake during the summer.
10) The cat disappeared beneath the sofa after the guests arrived.

Part B Write the correct form of the pronoun in parentheses as the object of the preposition in each sentence.

1) Will you come with ______? (I)
2) Please get tickets for Pete and ______. (he)
3) The cat sat beside ______ on the sofa. (she)
4) Mr. and Ms. Gomez gave presents to ______ children. (they)
5) Between the neighbors and ______, we collected two bags of cans. (we)
6) When I scrub the deck, I also clean under ______. (it)
7) I was behind ______ on the freeway. (you)
8) We got a letter from ______ last week. (they)
9) Gladys put a scarf around ______ neck. (she)
10) We like to play games at ______ house. (we)

 Basic English Grammar

Name ______ Date ______ Period ______ *Chapter 7 Mastery Test A page 2*

Chapter 7 Mastery Test A, continued

Part C Write whether the bold prepositional phrase in each sentence is used as an adjective or an adverb.

1) Springtime **in Texas** is beautiful. ______
2) Wildflowers grow **throughout the state.** ______
3) You see them **along roadsides and fields.** ______
4) Those spots are a glorious spectacle **of color.** ______
5) The state flower **of Texas** is the bluebonnet. ______
6) The bluebonnet is a member **of the lupine family.** ______
7) People **from Texas** go driving to see the bluebonnets. ______
8) Indian paintbrush also grows **in fields.** ______
9) Delicate pink primroses nod **in the breeze.** ______
10) Red phlox blaze **in many fields.** ______
11) Goat-foot morning glories show the five-pointed symbol **of the Lone Star State.** ______
12) **At Enchanted Rock State Natural Area**, claret cup cactus blossoms. ______
13) Texas **in summer** sports different blooms. ______
14) The summer flowers endure **through heat and hard rains.** ______
15) Texas owes thanks **to Lady Bird Johnson** for so many wildflowers. ______
16) She helped to start the project **for the state.** ______
17) It began **during the time** her husband was the American president. ______
18) Millions of seeds were planted **across the state.** ______
19) Texans will enjoy the flowers **for years.** ______
20) Visitors **to Texas** also admire what Lady Bird did. ______

 Basic English Grammar

Chapter 7 Mastery Test A

Part C Write these sentences on your paper. Add at least one prepositional phrase to each one to make the sentence more interesting.

1) Everyone was happy.
2) The weather was good.
3) The family went out.
4) They came home.
5) The family was tired.
6) We rested.
7) Louis did his homework.
8) Laverne called.
9) The sun set and the moon appeared.
10) The sky became dark.

Part D Write these sentences on your paper. Correct any mistakes.

1) Nathan watched television with his.
2) Mario wrote a letter to I.
3) Between you and I there has always been trust.
4) Alex bought a present for.
5) On the bus, Mark sat behind Clay and she.

Test Taking Tip

When taking a true/false test, read each statement carefully. Write *true* only when the statement is totally true. Write *false* if part or all of the statement is false.

Part C Answers

Each sentence should include at least one prepositional phrase.

Part D Answers

1) Nathan watched television with him. **2)** Mario wrote a letter to me. **3)** Between you and me there has always been trust. **4)** Alex bought a present for you. **5)** On the bus, Mark sat behind Clay and her.

APPLICATION

Career Connection

Many jobs require workers to write reports and evaluations. The use of prepositional phrases can make these reports and evaluations precise and informative as well as interesting to read.

Name Date Period | *Chapter 7 Mastery Test B page 1*

Chapter 7 Mastery Test B

Part A Circle all of the prepositions in these sentences.

1) During the summer we go swimming in the pond down the road by the woods.
2) For a snack, Alice made popcorn with butter.
3) Carlos was happy about his golf score on Tuesday.
4) Kim saw her friends at the party before they left.
5) The pile of books beside the desk near the window was huge.
6) A package from the store will arrive for me tomorrow.
7) A firefighter from our town jumped off a roof during a fire.
8) Ty picked up apples under the tree behind the house.
9) The children ran into the house and hid beneath the bed.
10) We took the cans and glass to the recycling center after work.

Part B Write the correct form of the pronoun in parentheses as the object of the preposition in each sentence.

1) What did you do with __________ book? (I)
2) My parents gave that CD to __________. (we)
3) If we want to get past that bridge, we have to get across __________ first. (it)
4) We couldn't get around __________ in line. (they)
5) Gonzo sat beside __________ at the game. (he)
6) Between you and __________, I think this is silly. (I)
7) Do I have to go through __________ to get that done? (you)
8) Please excuse __________ mess while we paint the room. (we)
9) Lucia wanted me to give this drawing to __________. (she)
10) Are we near __________ apartment yet? (they)

 Basic English Grammar

Name Date Period | *Chapter 7 Mastery Test B page 2*

Chapter 7 Mastery Test B, continued

Part C Write whether the bold prepositional phrase in each sentence is used as an adjective or an adverb.

1) Florida **in winter** is warm. __________
2) Palm trees **throughout the state** stay green all year. __________
3) Have you studied the history **of Florida**? __________
4) People **from Spain** explored there. __________
5) Ponce de Leon was an early explorer **in the state**. __________
6) Florida's population is rapidly **on the rise**. __________
7) Many growers **in the state** raise oranges and grapefruit. __________
8) **At the Florida border**, everyone tastes the orange and grapefruit juice. __________
9) The juice **from these fruits** tastes sweet. __________
10) A favorite tourist place is located **in central Florida**. __________
11) Epcot Center and Disney World are **in Orlando**. __________
12) Epcot Center is part **of Disney World**. __________
13) Disneyland has been **in California** for years. __________
14) Everyone looks **for a parade**. __________
15) People stand **in line** to see shows at Epcot. __________
16) People love the beaches **in Miami**. __________
17) **On the gulf coast**, searching for seashells is popular. __________
18) The waters **of the Atlantic Ocean** are a beautiful blue. __________
19) The sands are white **on Florida's east coast**. __________
20) You would enjoy going **to Florida**. __________

 Basic English Grammar

Chapter 7 Mastery Test B

Chapter 8

Planning Guide

The Conjunction

	Student Text Lesson			
	Student Pages	Vocabulary	Practice Exercises	Lesson Review
Lesson 1 Coordinating Conjunctions	174-179	✔	✔	179
Lesson 2 Subordinating Conjunctions	180-184	✔	✔	184
Lesson 3 Correlative Conjunctions	185-187	✔	✔	187

Chapter Activities

Teacher's Resource Library

Community Connection 8: Conjunctions in Newspapers and Magazines

Assessment Options

Student Text

Chapter 8 Review

Teacher's Resource Library

Chapter 8 Mastery Tests A and B

Teaching Strategies							Language Skills			Learning Styles						Teacher's Resource Library		
Reviewing Skills	Teacher Alert	Follow-up Activity	Career Application	Home Application	Global Connection	Community Application	Identification Skills	Writing Skills	Punctuation Skills	Visual/Spatial	Auditory/Verbal	Body/Kinesthetic	Logical/Mathematical	Group Learning	LEP/ESL	Activities	Workbook Activities	Self-Study Guide
174	176-177	179	177				✔	✔	✔						174		35	✔
180	180				181		✔	✔	✔	184						22-23	36	✔
185		187		188		189	✔	✔	✔			185				24	37	✔

Chapter at a Glance

(Answer Keys for the Teacher's Resource Library begin on page 330 of this Teacher's Edition.)

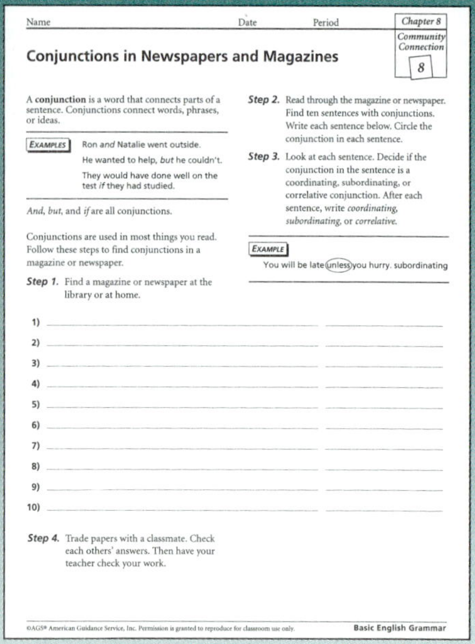

Name ______ Date ______ Period ______

Chapter 8 Community Connection 8

Conjunctions in Newspapers and Magazines

A **conjunction** is a word that connects parts of a sentence. Conjunctions connect words, phrases, or ideas.

EXAMPLES
Ron *and* Natalie went outside.
He wanted to help, *but* he couldn't.
They would have done well on the test *if* they had studied.

And, *but*, and *if* are all conjunctions.

Conjunctions are used in most things you read. Follow these steps to find conjunctions in a magazine or newspaper.

Step 1. Find a magazine or newspaper at the library or at home.

Step 2. Read through the magazine or newspaper. Find ten sentences with conjunctions. Write each sentence below. Circle the conjunction in each sentence.

Step 3. Look at each sentence. Decide if the conjunction in the sentence is a coordinating, subordinating, or correlative conjunction. After each sentence, write *coordinating*, *subordinating*, or *correlative*.

EXAMPLE
You will be late (unless) you hurry. subordinating

1) ______ ______
2) ______ ______
3) ______ ______
4) ______ ______
5) ______ ______
6) ______ ______
7) ______ ______
8) ______ ______
9) ______ ______
10) ______ ______

Step 4. Trade papers with a classmate. Check each others' answers. Then have your teacher check your work.

 Basic English Grammar

Community Connection 8

Chapter 8 The Conjunction

A conjunction is like a bridge between two parts of a sentence. Words like *and, but,* and *for* connect words in a sentence. A conjunction can connect words, phrases, or ideas that do the same job in a sentence. Using conjunctions when you write and speak can help you write sentences that are smooth and easy to understand.

In Chapter 8, you will learn about conjunctions. Each lesson in the chapter focuses on recognizing and using different kinds of conjunctions in sentences.

Goals for Learning

- To identify conjunctions in sentences
- To write compound sentences using coordinating conjunctions
- To write complex sentences using subordinating conjunctions
- To write sentences using correlative conjunctions

Reading Vocabulary

complex (9) phrase (6)
identify (6)

Introducing the Chapter

Focus students' attention on the bridge in the photograph. Invite volunteers to name different bridges they have been on, seen, or read about. Then engage students in a discussion about the main purpose of a bridge. Ask students if a bridge by itself serves any function. Elicit that a bridge is a structure that connects two divided pieces of land. Then draw a simple bridge on the board. Beside it write the word *and.* Ask students if they recognize any similarity between the bridge and the word *and.* Accept any reasonable responses. Point out, if necessary, that the word *and* by itself has no purpose. When it is placed between words in a sentence, however, *and* acts like a bridge to connect ideas. Explain that *and* is a conjunction. By the end of Chapter 8, students will understand how they can use conjunctions to connect their ideas.

SELF-STUDY GUIDE

Name ______________

CHAPTER 8: The Conjunction

Goal 8.1 *To write compound sentences using coordinating conjunctions*

Date	Assignment	Score
______	1: Read pages 173-174. Complete Activity A on page 174.	______
______	2: Read page 175. Complete Activities B-C on page 175.	______
______	3: Complete Workbook Activity 35.	______

Comments:

Goal 8.2 *To identify conjunctions in sentences*

Date	Assignment	Score
______	4: Read page 176. Complete Activities D-E on page 176.	______
______	5: Read page 177-178. Complete Activities F-G on page 178.	______
______	6: Complete the Lesson 1 Review on page 179.	______

Comments:

 Basic English Grammar

SELF-STUDY GUIDE

Name ______________

CHAPTER 8 The Conjunction, continued

Goal 8.3 *To write complex sentences using subordinating conjunctions*

Date	Assignment	Score
______	7: Read pages 180-181. Complete Activities A-B on page 181.	______
______	8: Complete Activities C-D on page 182.	______
______	9: Read page 183. Complete Activities E-F on page 183.	______
______	10: Complete the Lesson 2 Review, Parts A-B on page 184.	______
______	11: Complete Workbook Activity 36.	______

Comments:

Goal 8.4 *To write sentences using correlative conjunctions*

Date	Assignment	Score
______	12: Read page 185. Complete Activity A on page 185.	______
______	13: Read page 186. Complete Activity B on page 186.	______
______	14: Complete the Lesson 3 Review, Parts A-B on page 187.	______
______	15: Complete Workbook Activity 37.	______
______	16: Complete the Chapter 8 Review, Parts A-D on pages 188-189.	______

Comments:

Student's Signature ______________ Date ______

Instructor's Signature ______________ Date ______

 Basic English Grammar

Chapter 8 Self-Study Guide

Lesson at a Glance

Chapter 8 Lesson 1

Overview This lesson introduces the concept of conjunctions, focusing on coordinating conjunctions.

Objectives

- To identify and use coordinating conjunctions in sentences.
- To punctuate sentences with coordinating conjunctions.
- To distinguish between prepositions and conjunctions.

Student Pages 174–179

Teacher's Resource Library

Workbook Activity 35

Reading Vocabulary

conjunction	referee (6)
connect (5)	relate (6)
coordinating conjunction	

Teaching Suggestions

Introducing the Lesson

Use the examples to illustrate the definition of *coordinating conjunction.*

Reviewing Skills

Review the parts of speech students have studied in previous chapters.

Presenting Activity A

Write the following sentence on the board and ask students to find the coordinating conjunction: *The boy and his mother got on the bus.* Help students see that *and* connects *boy* and *mother*—two nouns that are used the same way in the sentence. They both tell who got on the bus. Then have students complete Activity A on their own.

Activity A Answers

1) and 2) and 3) and 4) yet 5) but 6) or 7) so 8) for 9) nor

Lesson 1 Coordinating Conjunctions

Conjunction
A word that connects related words or groups of words.

Coordinating conjunction
A conjunction that connects words or groups of words that do the same job in a sentence.

A **conjunction** is a word that connects parts of a sentence. A conjunction can connect words, phrases, or ideas that are used in the same way.

There are three kinds of conjunctions: the *coordinating conjunction,* the *subordinating conjunction,* and the *correlative conjunction.*

A **coordinating conjunction** connects words, phrases, or sentences that do not depend on each other to make sense. The following are the seven coordinating conjunctions:

and	nor	so
but	or	yet
for		

EXAMPLES

Words:	Rich plays the guitar **and** the trumpet.
Phrases:	He ran around the corner **and** out of sight.
Ideas:	I'd like to help you, **but** I'm busy.

Activity A Write the coordinating conjunction in each of these sentences on your paper.

1) Eight and eight make sixteen.
2) All night the winds blew and the snow fell.
3) The referee blew her whistle and stopped the game.
4) He had little money, yet he walked into the room like a king.
5) The actor sang well, but he could not dance.
6) I will drink juice or milk.
7) There was nothing good on television, so I went for a walk.
8) I could not study, for I had a headache.
9) Lois isn't hungry, nor am I.

Learning Styles

LEP/ESL

Invite ESL students to create a list of the seven coordinating conjunctions in the box on page 174. Have them write the list in their primary language on the board. Ask each ESL student to choose one conjunction from the list. Ask volunteers to create English sentences that use these seven conjunctions and to say the sentences aloud. Then ask each volunteer to repeat the sentence, but to pause by the conjunction. Have the ESL student say aloud the conjunction—in non-English—that goes in the sentence. Then have the volunteer complete the sentence.

Activity B Complete each sentence with a coordinating conjunction. Write the conjunctions on your paper.

1) I will have milk ______ water with my dinner.

2) Paco hits well, ______ he cannot throw a curve ball.

3) Vic tried hard ______ made the team.

4) Louisa studies hard, ______ she always has time for her friends.

5) After school we played CDs ______ relaxed.

6) John Adams ______ Thomas Jefferson were vice-presidents of the United States.

7) President Harry Truman was born in 1884 ______ died in 1972.

A coordinating conjunction may connect two or more complete ideas.

EXAMPLE I will drink juice. I will drink milk.

I will drink juice **or** milk. (The coordinating conjunction *or* connects the two objects *juice* and *milk*. The words that are the same in both sentences are not repeated.)

Activity C Use coordinating conjunctions to connect the related ideas in the following pairs of sentences. Write the new sentences on your paper. You may need to change the verb form.

1) Lena likes tacos. Andy likes tacos.

2) Lloyd plays football. Lloyd plays baseball.

3) Langston Hughes wrote short stories. Langston Hughes wrote poetry.

4) I grew tomatoes in my garden. I grew green beans in my garden.

5) Laura tried out for the basketball team. Her twin sister SueAnn tried out for the basketball team.

Name Date Period

Chapter 8 *Workbook Activity* 35

Using Conjunctions to Connect

Directions: Connect the ideas in the following pairs of sentences using conjunctions. Follow the example below. You may need to change the verb form.

EXAMPLE Jack had cake for dessert. Jack had ice cream.
Jack had cake and ice cream for dessert.

1) My favorite baseball player is Cal Ripken. My other favorite player is Kirby Puckett.

2) John Steinbeck wrote *The Red Pony.* He wrote *The Grapes of Wrath.*

3) My garden has zinnias. It has marigolds. It has weeds.

4) For the picnic, we bought hot dogs. We bought rolls.

5) Betty likes hot dogs. She doesn't like hamburgers.

6) This soda is sugar-free. It is also caffeine-free.

7) My older brother, Casey, plays soccer. My little brother, Jimmy, plays soccer.

8) I have a poodle named Velvet. I have a poodle named Coco.

9) Velvet is black. Coco is champagne.

10) Our telephone is Touch-Tone. Our telephone is yellow.

 Basic English Grammar

Workbook Activity 35

Reading Vocabulary

poetry (6) taco
relax (5) vice-president (5)

Presenting Activity B

Point out that more than one conjunction may make sense in each sentence before doing the first two items orally with students. Then have students complete the activity on their own.

Activity B Answers

1) and/or **2)** but/yet **3)** and **4)** and/but/yet **5)** and **6)** and **7)** and

Presenting Activity C

Write these sentences on the board: *Joe enjoys watching old movies. Edie enjoys watching old movies.* Help students recognize the related ideas in these sentences. Elicit that both Joe and Edie enjoy watching old movies. Then help students combine these sentences, using a conjunction. (*Joe and Edie enjoy watching old movies.*) Be sure students note the verb form change. After students complete Activity B, invite them to share their sentences with the class.

Activity C Answers

1) Lena and Andy like tacos. **2)** Lloyd plays football and baseball. **3)** Langston Hughes wrote short stories and poetry. **4)** I grew tomatoes and green beans in my garden. **5)** Laura and her twin sister SueAnn tried out for the basketball team.

Reading Vocabulary

item (6)
punctuate (7)
miniature (6)
series (5)

■ Presenting Activity D

Write the first item on the board and help students find the three items in a series and the conjunction that connects them in the sentence. Next, elicit from students where to place commas. Have students work with a partner to complete the remaining items in Activity D.

Activity D Answers

1) bushes, trees,/and **2)** tulips, daffodils,/and **3)** washed up, changed our clothes,/and **4)** no commas/and **5)** brother, sister,/and **6)** going to a movie, playing miniature golf,/or

■ Presenting Activity E

Invite volunteers to write sample sentences for items 1 and 2 on the board. Encourage one or two of the volunteers to write a sentence with items in a series, punctuated correctly. Then have students work independently to complete Activity E. Afterwards, invite students to share their sentences and tell where they used commas and why.

Activity E Answers

Each sentence should include a coordinating conjunction and have correct punctuation for items in a series.

Teacher Alert

You may wish to explain that a comma is used in writing to show a pause in thought. Commas separate ideas so that readers do not get confused.

Use a comma to separate words or phrases in a series. A series is three or more words or phrases. Place the comma after each item in the series. Do not put a comma after the last item in the series.

Examples

Lisa and Becky arrived late. (Only two people—do not use commas)

Lisa, Becky, and Sue arrived late. (Three people—use commas)

We planted flowers in the front, in the back, and on the sides of the house. (Three phrases—use commas)

Activity D Write these sentences on your paper. Add commas only where they are needed. Circle the conjunctions.

1) We planted bushes trees and flowers around the house.

2) We planted tulips daffodils and petunias.

3) Later we washed up changed our clothes and went out to dinner.

4) I ordered a salad and milk.

5) My brother sister and mother ordered the soup.

6) After dinner we talked about going to a movie playing miniature golf or taking a walk around the lake.

Activity E Use each of these conjunctions in a sentence. Write your sentences on your paper. Try to write at least two sentences that contain items in a series. Be sure to punctuate any items in a series correctly.

1) and
2) but
3) or
4) nor
5) yet
6) for

176 *Chapter 8 The Conjunction*

Two or more sentences joined with a conjunction usually need a punctuation mark. Use a comma to separate sentences joined with *and, but, nor, or, for, so,* or *yet.*

EXAMPLES Marco dug up the garden, **and** Leslie planted the seeds.

Our family loves spinach, **but** none of us likes beets.

Sentences that are very short often do not need a comma to separate them.

EXAMPLES We went out and then we went home.

She is tall and he is short.

When you join complete sentences with the following words, use a semicolon (;) in front of them and a comma (,) after them.

also	furthermore	nevertheless
accordingly	however	otherwise
besides	instead	therefore
consequently	moreover	

EXAMPLES Lisa likes to play the piano; **however,** she doesn't like to practice.

Lance worked all day; **nevertheless,** he didn't finish.

Reading Vocabulary

consequently (8)
nevertheless
punctuation (7)
spinach

TEACHER ALERT

In addition to the information presented in the text, explain that when each item in a series is connected by *and* or *or,* do not use a comma to separate the items. Write this example on the board to illustrate this point: *We walked and talked and laughed.*

APPLICATION

Career Connection
Students who pursue careers in such fields as the food service industry, construction, and retail sales may find that their job responsibilities include ordering business supplies and merchandise. Although most items would ordinarily be listed individually on an order form, smaller businesses may submit their orders in letter form. Have students practice ordering materials for a business, such as a children's clothing shop, in a letter. Students should try to include conjunctions and items in a series in their letters. For example, they might list the colors or size of an article of clothing in a series. When they have finished, suggest that students exchange letters with a partner who can check for correct punctuation.

The Conjunction *Chapter 8* **177**

Reading Vocabulary

equipment (5) otherwise (5)
manager (6) tennis (5)

■ Presenting Activity F

Because of the level of difficulty involved, you may wish to do Activity F as a class. Write the first item on the board and work through it with students, helping them to identify the conjunction and punctuate the sentence correctly. Follow the same procedure with the remaining items.

Activity F Answers

1) hurry; otherwise, **2)** shopping; instead, **3)** Lisa read a book, Marco did homework, Mr. Martinez watched TV, and **4)** school, but **5)** trees; furthermore, **6)** food, but

■ Presenting Activity G

Before students do Activity G, remind them that a prepositional phrase begins with a preposition and ends with the object of the preposition, which is always a noun or pronoun. Emphasize that a prepositional phrase never has a verb.

Activity G Answers

1) conjunction **2)** conjunction **3)** preposition 4) preposition

The words *but* and *for* can be used either as conjunctions or as prepositions.

EXAMPLES

Conjunction:	Becky feeds her puppy dog food, **but** he prefers steak!
Preposition:	No one was hungry **but** Rob.
Conjunction:	Randy brought the equipment, **for** he was the team manager.
Preposition:	We knew that he would work hard **for** the team.

Activity F Write these sentences on your paper. Punctuate them correctly.

1) Lisa must hurry otherwise she will be late.

2) We wanted to go shopping instead we stayed home.

3) After dinner Lisa read a book Marco did homework Mr. Martinez watched TV and Mrs. Martinez just relaxed.

4) Karl rode the bus to school but he walked home.

5) The storm blew down several trees furthermore it damaged some telephone lines.

6) Roberto was hungry for Italian food but his sister wanted Chinese food.

Activity G Write on your paper whether the word in bold is a *preposition* or a *conjunction.*

1) Paul played tennis well, **for** he practiced every day.

2) The new apartment was beautiful, **but** the rent was high.

3) Everyone liked the story **but** Yolanda.

4) The students cheered loudly **for** their team.

178 *Chapter 8 The Conjunction*

Lesson 1 Review

Lesson Review Write these sentences on your paper. Circle the coordinating conjunctions. Add any missing punctuation.

1) A new girl moved to the town where Lisa and Becky live.
2) Her name is Antoinette but everyone calls her Toni.
3) Toni is hearing impaired but she reads lips and signs.
4) She learned sign language and lip reading at a special school for the hearing impaired.
5) Some people think all hearing-impaired people should learn to read lips and others think sign language is best.
6) Lisa and Becky wanted to learn sign language for they wanted to be able to communicate with Toni.
7) Toni explained that some signs stand for whole words and ideas but that not every word or idea has a sign.
8) Some words have to be spelled out letter by letter therefore they would have to learn the finger alphabet.
9) There are twenty-six hand symbols in the finger alphabet and each symbol stands for a letter of the alphabet.
10) Toni showed the girls how to form each letter with their fingers gave them a booklet that showed all the symbols and told them to practice every day.
11) Becky Lisa and their mom practiced signing together at the dinner table each evening.
12) Toni often came over so she was able to help them.
13) Soon they could use signs or finger spelling easily.
14) "Next, we will start learning signs for whole words and ideas," Toni told them.
15) Sign language helped Toni Becky and Lisa communicate furthermore it was fun to learn something new and useful.

Reading Vocabulary

communicate (6) impaired (8)
furthermore (6) symbol (xx)

Lesson Review Answers

1) and (no punctuation) **2)** Antoinette, but **3)** impaired, but/and **4)** and (no punctuation) **5)** lips, and **6)** and/language, for **7)** and/but/or (no punctuation) **8)** letter; therefore, **9)** alphabet, and **10)** showed . . . fingers, gave . . . symbols, and **11)** Becky, Lisa, and **12)** over, so **13)** or (no punctuation) **14)** and (no punctuation) **15)** Toni, Becky, and/communicate; furthermore, it/and

Follow-up Activity

Have students use the conjunctions listed on pages 174 and 177 in original sentences that tell about an event that recently took place at school or in the community.

The Conjunction Chapter 8 **179**

Lesson at a Glance

Chapter 8 Lesson 2

Overview This lesson presents subordinating conjunctions and independent and dependent clauses.

Objectives

- To identify dependent clauses introduced by subordinating conjunctions.
- To connect independent and dependent clauses with subordinating conjunctions.
- To distinguish between prepositions and conjunctions.

Student Pages 180–184

Teacher's Resource Library

Activities 22–23

Workbook Activity 36

Reading Vocabulary

clause (7)
dependent (7)
independent (6)
subject (5)
subordinating conjunction

Teaching Suggestions

Introducing the Lesson

Discuss the terms introduced in the text. Be sure students understand the difference between an independent, or main, clause, and a dependent clause before having them do the activities.

Reviewing Skills

Review the definition of a conjunction.

Teacher Alert

The concepts presented in this lesson assume that students have a basic understanding of what a subject, predicate, and sentence are. It may be helpful for students if you provide simple definitions of these terms.

Lesson 2 Subordinating Conjunctions

Subordinating conjunction

A conjunction that connects a dependent clause with an independent clause in a sentence.

A **subordinating conjunction** connects an independent clause with a dependent clause. An independent clause expresses a complete idea. A dependent clause is a group of words that has a subject and a verb but does not express a complete idea. Since a dependent clause does not express a complete thought by itself, it cannot stand alone as a sentence. A dependent clause depends on the main, or independent, clause to make sense. Like adverbs, dependent clauses answer the questions *When? Where? Why?* and *How?*

EXAMPLE

Subordinating conjunction:	**If** the rain stops, we can start practice. (The subordinating conjunction *if* connects the incomplete idea *if the rain stops* to the main clause *we can start practice*.)

A dependent clause may be found at the beginning or the end of a sentence. Use a comma after a dependent clause only when it is at the beginning of the sentence.

EXAMPLES

Comma:	**Unless you hurry**, you won't finish. **After the party was over**, we went home.
No comma:	You won't finish **unless you hurry**. We went home **after the party was over**.

Here is a list of some commonly used subordinating conjunctions:

after	in order that	when
although	since	whenever
as	so	where
because	unless	wherever
if	until	while

Activity A Write the dependent clause in each of these sentences on your paper. Circle the subordinating conjunctions.

1) If you want to play the piano better, you have to practice.

2) I plan to study until I finish.

3) Justin saved his money in order that he could go to college.

4) When Lisa gets here, we will leave.

5) They ate popcorn while they watched the movie.

Activity B Add an independent clause (a complete thought) to each of these dependent clauses to make sentences. Write the sentences on your paper.

1) Although we had just eaten breakfast,

2) Until the other team scored,

3) Because my mom is at work,

4) Since I flew on an airplane,

5) When I finish this book,

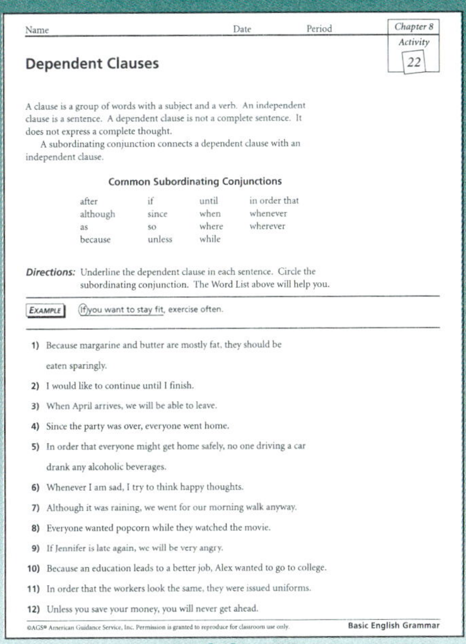
Name Date Period

Chapter 8 *Activity* 22

Dependent Clauses

A clause is a group of words with a subject and a verb. An independent clause is a sentence. A dependent clause is not a complete sentence. It does not express a complete thought.

A subordinating conjunction connects a dependent clause with an independent clause.

Common Subordinating Conjunctions

after	if	until	in order that
although	since	when	whenever
as	so	where	wherever
because	unless	while	

Directions: Underline the dependent clause in each sentence. Circle the subordinating conjunction. The Word List above will help you.

EXAMPLE If you want to stay fit, exercise often.

1) Because margarine and butter are mostly fat, they should be eaten sparingly.

2) I would like to continue until I finish.

3) When April arrives, we will be able to leave.

4) Since the party was over, everyone went home.

5) In order that everyone might get home safely, no one driving a car drank any alcoholic beverages.

6) Whenever I am sad, I try to think happy thoughts.

7) Although it was raining, we went for our morning walk anyway.

8) Everyone wanted popcorn while they watched the movie.

9) If Jennifer is late again, we will be very angry.

10) Because an education leads to a better job, Alex wanted to go to college.

11) In order that the workers look the same, they were issued uniforms.

12) Unless you save your money, you will never get ahead.

 Basic English Grammar

Activity 22

Reading Vocabulary

college (5) wherever

Presenting Activity A

Write this sentence on the board: *While you were out, Amy called twice.* Work with students to identify and label the main, or independent, clause and dependent clause in this sentence. Discuss how students determined which was which. Then invite a volunteer to circle the subordinating conjunction in the dependent clause, *While you were out.* After students complete Activity A on their own, discuss their answers.

Activity A Answers

1) If you want to play the piano better/If **2)** until I finish/until **3)** in order that he could go to college/in order that **4)** When Lisa gets here/When **5)** while they watched the movie/while

Presenting Activity B

Have a volunteer do item 1 on the board. Encourage the class to check that the student has added an independent clause that expresses a complete thought. Then erase the independent clause and invite another volunteer to complete the sentence. Repeat this process until you are sure students can complete Activity B on their own.

Activity B Answers

Each sentence should include an independent clause.

Global Connection

Invite students who speak another language to translate the coordinating conjunctions on pages 174 and 177 and the subordinating conjunctions on this page into their primary languages. Encourage students to explain differences in use and connotation, if any, between the English and non-English words.

The Conjunction *Chapter 8* **181**

Reading Vocabulary

championship   wrestling (5)

Presenting Activity C

Have a volunteer do item 1 on the board. Encourage the class to check that the student has introduced the dependent clause with a subordinating conjunction, and that the sentence has been punctuated correctly. Then have students complete Activity C on their own.

Activity C Answers

Each sentence should include a dependent clause. Subordinating conjunctions should be circled.

Presenting Activity D

Encourage students to use a different subordinating conjunction in each sentence and to try to vary the position of the conjunction. Then do item 1 together as a class before having students complete Activity D on their own.

Activity D Answers

Sentences may vary. Possible answers are given.

1) Zack is lifting weights because he wants to be on the wrestling team. **2)** Pete went to the library whenever he needed a book. **3)** Since Tina moved to town in March, she has been in Becky's English class. **4)** While I was asleep, a storm blew down our tree. **5)** If you will drive today, I will drive tomorrow. **6)** Jan wants to see that play so we will buy tickets ahead of time. **7)** After the baseball team won the championship, the town celebrated. **8)** Tom walked into the room when everyone began to clap. **9)** The sun set as we walked around the lake. **10)** While I am drying the dishes, you can pick out a movie.

Activity C Add a dependent clause to each of these sentences. Write the new complete sentences on your paper. Circle the subordinating conjunctions. Add commas where needed.

1) Dan would like to visit California.

2) Darryl saved twenty-five dollars a week.

3) My neighbors asked me to water their garden.

4) Anne's report was late.

5) Marcus went to the new computer store.

6) The storm forced people to stay home.

7) Cassie watched a nature program about crocodiles.

8) A strange noise woke me up from a deep sleep.

9) Lee left his school books at the library.

10) The front door slammed shut.

Activity D Connect each of these pairs of sentences with a subordinating conjunction. Write the new complete sentences on your paper. Add commas where needed.

1) Zack is lifting weights. He wants to be on the wrestling team.

2) Pete went to the library. He needed a book.

3) Tina moved to town in March. She has been in Becky's English class.

4) I was asleep. A storm blew down our tree.

5) You will drive today. I will drive tomorrow.

6) Jan wants to see that play. We will buy tickets ahead of time.

7) The baseball team won the championship. The town celebrated.

8) Tom walked into the room. Everyone began to clap.

9) The sun set. We walked around the lake.

10) I am drying the dishes. You can pick out a movie.

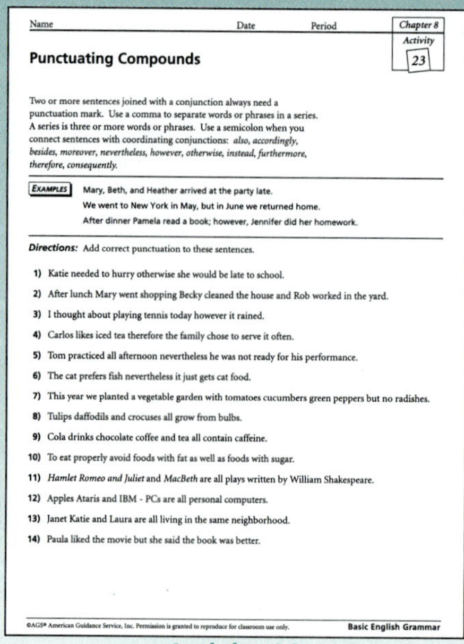

Name Date Period — *Chapter 8* *Activity* 23

Punctuating Compounds

Two or more sentences joined with a conjunction always need a punctuation mark. Use a comma to separate words or phrases in a series. A series is three or more words or phrases. Use a semicolon when you connect sentences with coordinating conjunctions: *also, accordingly, besides, moreover, nevertheless, however, otherwise, instead, furthermore, therefore, consequently.*

EXAMPLES Mary, Beth, and Heather arrived at the party late.
We went to New York in May, but in June we returned home.
After dinner Pamela read a book; however, Jennifer did her homework.

Directions: Add correct punctuation to these sentences.

1) Katie needed to hurry otherwise she would be late to school.

2) After lunch Mary went shopping Becky cleaned the house and Rob worked in the yard.

3) I thought about playing tennis today however it rained.

4) Carlos likes iced tea therefore the family chose to serve it often.

5) Tom practiced all afternoon nevertheless he was not ready for his performance.

6) The cat prefers fish nevertheless it just gets cat food.

7) This year we planted a vegetable garden with tomatoes cucumbers green peppers but no radishes.

8) Tulips daffodils and crocuses all grow from bulbs.

9) Cola drinks chocolate coffee and tea all contain caffeine.

10) To eat properly avoid foods with fat as well as foods with sugar.

11) *Hamlet Romeo and Juliet* and *MacBeth* are all plays written by William Shakespeare.

12) Apples Ataris and IBM - PCs are all personal computers.

13) Janet Katie and Laura are all living in the same neighborhood.

14) Paula liked the movie but she said the book was better.

 Basic English Grammar

Activity 23

Some words can be used either as subordinating conjunctions or as prepositions.

EXAMPLES

Conjunction:	The game was put off **until** the rain stopped. (*Until the rain stopped* is a dependent clause that is connected to the main clause by the subordinating conjunction *until*.)
Preposition:	The game was put off **until** tomorrow. (*Until tomorrow* is a prepositional phrase introduced by the preposition *until*. Remember that prepositional phrases never include verbs.)

Activity E Write on your paper whether the word in bold is a *conjunction* or a *preposition*.

1) Donna went home **after** school.
2) We went home **after** school was over.
3) **Because of** Marco, we won the game.
4) I like that coat **because** it is warm.
5) I haven't heard from her **since** Monday.
6) I'll leave **since** you are here now.
7) **Before** class began, I talked to the teacher.
8) **Before** lunch, I have Spanish class.

Activity F Write the subordinating conjunctions in each of these sentences on your paper.

1) We drove home carefully because it was snowing.
2) We had classes until noon although the weather was bad.
3) If the snow is deep enough, there will be no school tomorrow.
4) School is closed only when the snow is deep.
5) Where Lisa and Marco live, there are usually two deep snows each year.

Reading Vocabulary

include (5) prepositional
preposition

Presenting Activity E

Write these words on the board: *after, before, until, because of,* and *since.* Divide students into pairs. Have each pair select a word from the list and write two sentences for that word, using the word once as a subordinating conjunction and once as a preposition. Invite students to read their sentences aloud. Ask the class to identify the sentence with the preposition and the sentence with the conjunction. Then have students complete Activity E independently.

Activity E Answers

1) preposition 2) conjunction
3) preposition 4) conjunction
5) preposition 6) conjunction
7) conjunction 8) preposition

Presenting Activity F

Before students do Activity F on their own, suggest that they review the list of subordinating conjunctions on page 181.

Activity F Answers

1) because 2) although 3) If
4) when 5) Where

The Conjunction Chapter 8 **183**

Lesson 2 Review

Part A Write these sentences on your paper, adding commas where needed. Circle the subordinating conjunctions in each sentence.

1) Kathy will hold dinner until everyone gets here.

2) If you will help we can finish early.

3) When warm weather arrives Marco and Anthony will go fishing.

4) Until the team scored the fans were quiet.

5) Everyone cheered as the band began playing the school song.

6) I took the bus because I was late.

7) Whenever I hear that song I think about my grandmother.

8) Since we finished our homework early let's watch a movie.

9) We will plant a vegetable garden after the ground thaws.

10) As the clock struck ten I became sleepy.

Part B Connect each of these pairs of sentences with a subordinating conjunction. Write the new sentences on your paper. Add commas where needed. Be sure the sentences make sense.

1) Mai got an excellent grade on her test. She studied hard.

2) I will clean the house. You do the shopping.

3) Jon got hungry about three o'clock. He ate an apple.

4) The weather is too cold. I can't go outside.

5) He lost the election. He didn't have enough help.

6) They waited for the bus. Tommy and Steve went over their notes.

7) The sun was shining. There was a cold, raw wind.

8) Gloria looked all over the house. She found her math book.

9) I get near fresh flowers. I begin to cough.

10) You may not make it to the bank. It closes at three.

Reading Vocabulary

excellent (5) thaw (5)
raw (5)

Part A Answers

1) until (no punctuation) **2)** help, we/If **3)** arrives, Marco/When **4)** scored, the/Until **5)** as (no punctuation) **6)** because (no punctuation) **7)** song, I/Whenever **8)** early, let's/Since **9)** after (no punctuation) **10)** ten, I/As

Part B Answers

Sentences may vary. Possible answers are given.

1) Mai got an excellent grade on her test because she studied hard. **2)** I will clean the house if you do the shopping. **3)** Jon got hungry about three o'clock so he ate an apple. **4)** When the weather is too cold, I can't go outside. **5)** He lost the election because he didn't get enough help. **6)** While they waited for the bus, Tommy and Steve went over their notes.
7) The sun was shining; however, there was a cold, raw wind.
8) Gloria looked all over the house until she found her math book.
9) Whenever I get near fresh flowers, I begin to cough.
10) You may not make it to the bank since it closes at three.

Learning Styles

Visual/Spatial

Divide the class into groups of five. Ask each group to choose five subordinating conjunctions from the box on page 181. Then have the group create ten sentences, two for each conjunction. One of the two sentences should begin with a dependent clause that uses the conjunction; the other should end with a dependent clause that uses the conjunction. Ask each group to create a chart of their conjunctions and sentence examples. Display the charts and encourage the students to read the various charts to look for and memorize the subordinating conjunctions.

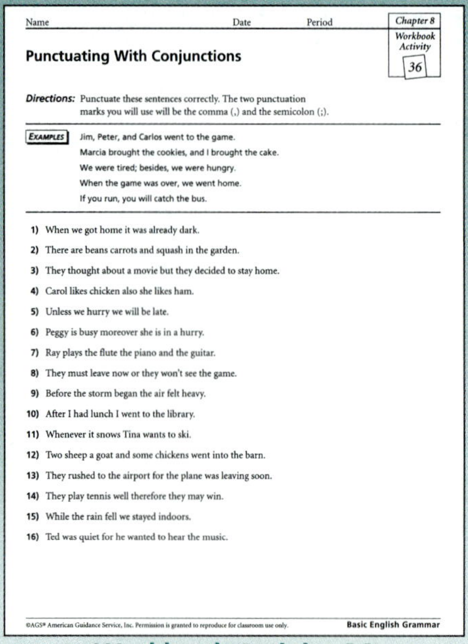

Name Date Period | Chapter 8 Workbook Activity 36

Punctuating With Conjunctions

Directions: Punctuate these sentences correctly. The two punctuation marks you will use will be the comma (,) and the semicolon (;).

EXAMPLES
Jim, Peter, and Carlos went to the game.
Marcia brought the cookies, and I brought the cake.
We were tired; besides, we were hungry.
When the game was over, we went home.
If you run, you will catch the bus.

1) When we got home it was already dark.
2) There are beans carrots and squash in the garden.
3) They thought about a movie but they decided to stay home.
4) Carol likes chicken also she likes ham.
5) Unless we hurry we will be late.
6) Peggy is busy moreover she is in a hurry.
7) Ray plays the flute the piano and the guitar.
8) They must leave now or they won't see the game.
9) Before the storm began the air felt heavy.
10) After I had lunch I went to the library.
11) Whenever it snows Tina wants to ski.
12) Two sheep a goat and some chickens went into the barn.
13) They rushed to the airport for the plane was leaving soon.
14) They play tennis well therefore they may win.
15) While the rain fell we stayed indoors.
16) Ted was quiet for he wanted to hear the music.

 Basic English Grammar

Workbook Activity 36

184 *Chapter 8 The Conjunction*

Lesson 3 Correlative Conjunctions

Correlative conjunctions
A pair of conjunctions that connects words or groups of words that are related.

Correlative conjunctions express a shared relationship and are always used in pairs.

EXAMPLES
Neither Marco **nor** Anthony enjoyed that movie.
Both the actors **and** the story were weak.

Here is a list of the most common pairs of correlative conjunctions:

both	and
either	or
neither	nor
not only	but also
whether	or

Activity A Write the correlative conjunctions in each of these sentences on your paper.

1) Ann Marie will write her report on either James Polk or Benjamin Harrison.
2) Both Polk and Harrison were presidents of the United States.
3) Not only Ann Marie but also Susan must write a report.
4) Neither Polk nor Harrison is very famous.
5) Susan doesn't know whether to write about Chester Arthur or Franklin Pierce.
6) She had heard of neither Arthur nor Pierce before.

Lesson at a Glance

Chapter 8 Lesson 3

Overview This lesson introduces correlative conjunctions.

Objectives
- To identify correlative conjunctions in sentences.
- To use the correct verb form in sentences with correlative conjunctions.

Student Pages 185–187

Teacher's Resource Library
Activity 24
Workbook Activity 37

Reading Vocabulary
relationship (6)
correlative conjunction

Teaching Suggestions

Introducing the Lesson
Discuss the definition of correlative conjunctions. Emphasize that correlative conjunctions are always used in pairs. Then encourage students to use each pair of correlative conjunctions in sentences. Students can use the example sentences as models.

Reviewing Skills Remind students that a verb must agree in number with the subject of a sentence.

Presenting Activity A
Invite students to read all the sentences in Activity A aloud, emphasizing the correlative conjunctions in each sentence. Then ask students to complete the activity on their own.

Activity A Answers
1) either . . . or 2) Both . . . and
3) Not only . . . but also
4) Neither . . . nor
5) whether . . . or
6) neither . . . nor

Learning Styles

Body/Kinesthetic
Write each pair of correlative conjunctions in the box on page 185 on a separate note card. Shuffle the cards and invite a volunteer to choose a card and to use the pair of conjunctions printed on it to create a sentence. Continue with other volunteers. Challenge the volunteers to use their classroom as the context for their sentences. Encourage them to actually pick up or point to objects to demonstrate their sentences and the correlative conjunctions.

Reading Vocabulary

photograph (6) sculpture (7)
plural (6) singular (8)

■ Presenting Activity B

Be sure students understand subject/verb agreement before having them do Activity B independently. If necessary, provide additional examples. As students complete Activity B, encourage them to read each item to themselves twice, with a different answer in place each time. They should choose the answer that sounds most correct to them.

Activity B Answers

1) is **2)** are **3)** is **4)** make **5)** has **6)** love

When subjects are joined with correlative conjunctions, the verb usually agrees with the subject nearer the verb.

EXAMPLES

Incorrect:	**Neither** Justin **nor** Mark are home yet.
Correct:	**Neither** Justin **nor** Mark is home yet. (*Mark* is singular.)
Incorrect:	**Not only** the house **but also** the garage need painting.
Correct:	**Not only** the house **but also** the garage needs painting. (*Garage* is singular.)
Incorrect:	**Either** candy **or** flowers is a nice gift.
Correct:	**Either** candy **or** flowers are a nice gift. (*Flowers* is plural.)

However, when subjects are joined by *and*, the verb always takes the plural form.

EXAMPLE

Incorrect:	**Both** Karla **and** Joe takes piano lessons.
Correct:	**Both** Karla **and** Joe take piano lessons.

Activity B Write the words that should appear in each sentence to make it correct.

1) Either a pencil or a pen (is, are) all right to use.

2) Neither the coat nor the shoes (is, are) on sale.

3) Neither the car nor the truck (is, are) working today.

4) Either perfume or flowers (makes, make) a nice gift for your aunt's birthday.

5) If I'm right, either your photographs or his sculpture (have, has) received an award.

6) Both Yvette and her sister (loves, love) cooking.

Lesson 3 Review

Part A Write the correlative conjunctions in each of these sentences on your paper.

1) The football team scored not only the touchdown but also the extra point.
2) Would you like either milk or juice?
3) Both Chandra and her sister speak three languages.
4) She bought neither the dress nor the suit.
5) Either school will start late or it will be canceled.
6) Carol likes neither ice hockey nor football.
7) Either milk or juice will be fine.
8) For my birthday I got not only skis but also ski poles.
9) Alice didn't know whether to laugh or cry.
10) Kate, Inez, and Dwight are not only in the same homeroom, but they are also in all the same classes.
11) We could not decide whether to eat before the movie or after.
12) The gift was for both Julie and me.
13) Either try harder or don't play.

Part B Complete these sentences with correlative conjunctions. Write the complete sentences on your own paper. There may be more than one correct answer.

1) ______ Mark ______ Justin have part-time jobs.
2) Susan thinks ______ the jeans ______ the shirt fit her right.
3) ______ Estelle ______ her brother is a talented artist.
4) Mr. Morales ______ drives to work ______ takes the bus.
5) Mrs. Brooks must learn ______ the reports ______ just the outlines are due on Monday.

Reading Vocabulary

cancel (7) outline (6)
hockey (5) talented

Part A Answers

1) not only . . . but also
2) either . . . or **3)** Both . . . and
4) neither . . . nor **5)** Either . . . or
6) neither . . . nor **7)** Either . . . or
8) not only . . . but also
9) whether . . . or
10) not only . . . but also
11) whether . . . or
12) both . . . and **13)** Either . . . or

Part B Answers

Some answers may vary. Possible answers are given.

1) Both . . . and **2)** neither . . . nor
3) Not only . . . but also
4) either . . . or **5)** whether . . . or

Follow-up Activity

Assign a topic and suggest that students write a brief paragraph on it, using each type of conjunction they have learned about. Ask them to underline all the conjunctions they use. The following are some possible topics:

- A Person I Admire
- A Skill I Want to Learn and Why
- The Funniest Thing That Happened to Me

Name Date Period *Chapter 8 Activity 24*

Words That Connect

A conjunction is a word that connects two or more parts of a sentence. Conjunctions can connect words, phrases, or sentences. The words, phrases, and sentences connected with conjunctions are called compounds.

EXAMPLES words — Katie **or** Laura
phrases — across the field **and** through the woods
sentences — Katie prefers the beach, **but** Laura likes the mountains.

Directions: Read these sentences. Underline each compound and circle the conjunction.

EXAMPLE The waiter served us our soup and salad.

1) Vanilla or chocolate ice cream is popular at my house.
2) Either milk or cream will be fine in my coffee.
3) No one in our family likes coffee or tea.
4) Jane, Katie, and Laura are waiting in line.
5) On Wednesday it rained, but on Thursday it was sunny.
6) Neither Jackie nor Bobby likes to play tennis.
7) I like to play tennis in the summer and in the winter.
8) The actor took a bow and accepted the applause.
9) Jack is a good hitter, but he cannot field.
10) Hamburgers and hot dogs are traditional food at picnics.
11) My tomatoes are doing well, but the cucumbers have died.
12) All day long the snow fell, and the wind blew.
13) Paula likes to play the piano, but she doesn't care to practice.
14) The restaurant offered raspberry, orange, and lemon sherbet.

 Basic English Grammar

Activity 24

Name Date Period *Chapter 8 Workbook Activity 37*

Finding Conjunctions

There are three main types of conjunctions:

- **Coordinating conjunctions** connect words, phrases, and sentences that are equal.
- **Subordinating conjunctions** connect clauses that are not equal. One is independent, and one is dependent.
- **Correlative conjunctions** are always used in pairs, such as *neither . . . nor.*

Directions: Find the conjunction in each sentence. Underline the word. Identify the type of conjunction.

EXAMPLES *correlative* Both Jefferson and Adams were vice-presidents.
coordinating I like tea, but I don't like coffee.
subordinating Pam always eats popcorn while she watches a movie.

1) Unless you hurry, you won't finish.
2) Either roses or petunias will look pretty there.
3) Dan was hungry; however, he was too tired to eat.
4) We will leave when it is ten o'clock.
5) Darleen has owned Tiny since she was twelve.
6) Candy couldn't decide whether to go swimming or fishing.
7) Poodles, collies, and shepherds are all types of dogs.
8) Both Sue and Darleen came for dinner.
9) Whenever you are ready, we will go.
10) Pat liked the movie, but the book was better.
11) Because the report was due, they worked all evening.
12) I like cookies, but I prefer ice cream.
13) "Darleen and I are leaving now," said Janet.
14) Do you need help, or can you do it yourself?

 Basic English Grammar

Workbook Activity 37

Chapter 8 Review

The Teacher's Resource Library includes two parallel forms of the Chapter 8 Mastery Test. The difficulty level of the two forms is equivalent. You may wish to use one form as a pretest and the other form as a posttest.

Reading Vocabulary

absent (5) festival (5) embarrass (5)

Part A Answers

1) and **2)** whether . . . or **3)** when **4)** but, if **5)** if **6)** After **7)** Either . . . or **8)** but **9)** either . . . or **10)** Although

Part B Answers

Some sentences may vary. Possible answers are given.

1) Paul bought a coat, a scarf, and some gloves. **2)** It rained on Monday and Tuesday. **3)** Dan and Abby were absent. **4)** Anthony asked not only his brother and his cousin Rick but also two other friends. **5)** Lisa would have a good time since she and Anthony have fun together.

APPLICATION

At Home

Encourage students to look through their recent writing assignments as well as personal writing to find places where they can use conjunctions to connect ideas. Students should also check that they have punctuated sentences with conjunctions correctly.

Chapter 8 Review

Part A Write all the conjunctions in these sentences on your paper.

1) Lisa and Tamara were making plans for the Spring Festival dance.

2) Tamara wondered whether Liang or José would ask her.

3) She decided to buy a new dress when she got paid.

4) Lisa wanted to ask Anthony, but she wasn't sure if he would go.

5) She didn't want to embarrass him if he didn't want to go with her.

6) After a few days passed, Lisa decided to ask Anthony.

7) "Either he'll agree to go or he won't," she thought.

8) Anthony did want to go, but first he had to talk to his boss.

9) "I either have to find someone else to work for me, or I'll have to work," he said.

10) Although he had to ask six different people, Anthony finally found someone to work for him.

Part B Rewrite these sentences on your paper. Use a conjunction to connect the ideas.

1) Paul bought a coat. He bought a scarf. He bought some gloves.

2) It rained on Monday. It rained on Tuesday.

3) Dan was absent. Abby was absent.

4) Anthony asked his brother. Anthony asked his cousin Rick. Anthony asked two other friends.

5) Lisa would have a good time. She and Anthony have fun together.

188 *Chapter 8 The Conjunction*

Name Date Period *Chapter 8 Mastery Test A page 1*

Chapter 8 Mastery Test A

Part A Circle all of the conjunctions in these sentences.

1) Fresh strawberries and ice cream were on the dessert menu.

2) We heard thunder and saw lightning in the distance.

3) Alayna was happy, for she received the gift she wanted for her birthday.

4) Both Hal and Kim have part-time jobs.

5) Jackie likes to play the trumpet, yet she doesn't like to practice.

6) The temperature is high today, but tomorrow it should be cooler.

7) Bill would like a big car; however, he wants good gas mileage.

8) Because Carla is athletic, she enjoys many sports.

9) Either chocolate or vanilla will be fine.

10) We like the mountains; nevertheless, we live in the city to be close to work.

Part B Write the correct correlative conjunction in each sentence.

1) Either a banana ________ an apple is a good snack choice.

2) Neither the shoes ________ the boots are on sale.

3) ________ Ray nor Samara is home yet.

4) Not only Mike ________ Sarah is a good friend of theirs.

5) Both flowers ________ perfumed soaps make nice gifts.

6) Whether we stay ________ go depends on the weather.

7) He doesn't care for ________ car racing or wrestling.

8) It makes a difference ________ the mail arrives today or tomorrow.

9) ________ the banks and the post office are closed on Sundays.

10) He applied ________ for that job but also for ten others.

 Basic English Grammar

Name Date Period *Chapter 8 Mastery Test A page 2*

Chapter 8 Mastery Test A, continued

Part C Write a coordinating conjunction from the choices in the box to complete each sentence. Use each conjunction only once.

also	but	furthermore	instead	otherwise
and	consequently	however	nevertheless	so

1) Joyce buried the roses in the fall, ________ she dug them up again in the spring.

2) Sofia and Felix enjoyed their trip to Mexico; ________, they plan to go again in two years.

3) Jonas likes to play tennis; ________, he doesn't like to play soccer.

4) He was finished with his job, ________ he went skating.

5) You need to pass the tests; ________, you may not graduate.

6) Paula missed the first showing; ________, she came late and missed the second showing.

7) Minnesota can be cold in winter; ________, it is a good place to live.

8) Adam worked late three nights last week; ________, he worked on Saturday.

9) Erika was planning to go camping; ________, she went to a friend's home.

10) Dad likes Thai food, ________ Gramp likes Middle Eastern food better.

Part D Connect each pair of sentences with a subordinating conjunction. Write the new complete sentence on the line. Add commas where needed. Be sure each sentence makes sense.

1) My mom is working. I have to watch my little sister.

____

2) Greg flew on an airplane. He lost his fear of flying.

____

3) The sky was cloudy. It was warm and comfortable.

____

4) Sue and Gil will clean this week. We will clean next week.

____

5) Rita went to the store. She needed groceries.

____

 Basic English Grammar

Chapter 8 Mastery Test A

Part C Write these sentences on your paper. Add punctuation where needed.

1) Lisa Anthony Tamara and Liang went to the dance together.
2) Because the night was warm they put the top down on the car.
3) While they were on their way they listened to the radio and talked.
4) "If we don't get there soon we will miss the first dance," Tamara said.
5) "The dance committee wanted a band however they got a disc jockey," Lisa said.
6) When they arrived they hurried to join their friends.
7) "Shall we dance or shall we check out the food," Anthony asked.
8) "Unless you're hungry let's dance," she answered.
9) The music was good and they had a wonderful evening.
10) After the dance they went to a restaurant.

Part D Complete these sentences with conjunctions. Write the completed sentences on your paper. There may be more than one correct answer.

1) They were hungry, ______ they were not tired.
2) ______ Liang ______ Anthony ordered hamburgers.
3) Lisa wanted something healthy ______ she ordered spinach salad.
4) ______ they were eating, the disc jockey from the dance came into the restaurant.
5) They talked about the dance, ______ soon it was time to go home.

Test Taking Tip

Prepare for a test by making a set of flashcards. Write a word on the front of each card. Write the definition on the back. Use the flashcards in a game to test your knowledge.

Reading Vocabulary

disk jockey
hamburger (5)
restaurant (5)
spinach

Part C Answers

1) Lisa, Anthony, Tamara, and
2) warm, they 3) way, they
4) soon, we 5) band; however,
6) arrived, they 7) dance, or
8) hungry, let's 9) good, and
10) dance, they

Part D Answers

Answers may vary. Possible answers are given.

1) but 2) Both . . . and 3) so
4) While 5) but

Application

In the Community

Encourage students to write an article for the school or local newspaper about community organizations and services that need volunteers. Remind students to use conjunctions in their sentences to connect related thoughts and ideas.

Name Date Period | *Chapter 8 Mastery Test B page 1*

Chapter 8 Mastery Test B

Part A Circle all of the conjunctions in these sentences.

1) My friend's name is Rebecca; however, everyone calls her Becca.
2) The apartment is new, so the rent is high.
3) Everyone was cold, yet Chuck was warm.
4) Lila needs to hurry; otherwise, she will be late.
5) Neither Minnie nor Dick enjoy skiing.
6) Pete loves to listen to music, and he plays it loud.
7) Juanita learned to swim, because she wants to be on the swimming team.
8) Although Tony plays the violin, he doesn't have time to be in the school orchestra.
9) I will cancel my cross country skiing date unless it snows more.
10) We wear shorts in the summer, but we wear slacks in the winter.

Part B Write the correlative conjunction to make each sentence correct.

1) Neither Tom ______ Mary has enough time today.
2) Whether we choose a movie ______ a play is OK with me.
3) Not only the fence ______ the house needs painting.
4) ______ radio or television provide entertainment.
5) Both Chris ______ Michelle have mountain bikes.
6) Maggie will be happy ______ we go out or stay home to eat.
7) He ______ read the book but also saw the movie.
8) Mail carriers are stopped by ______ rain nor snow on their appointed rounds.
9) Either the art museum ______ the science museum suits my taste.
10) She ______ cut the grass and washed the car.

 Basic English Grammar

Name Date Period | *Chapter 8 Mastery Test B page 2*

Chapter 8 Mastery Test B, continued

Part C Write a coordinating conjunction from the choices in the box to complete each sentence. Use each conjunction only once.

also	but	furthermore	instead	otherwise
and	consequently	however	nevertheless	so

1) Tonya likes to wash dishes; ______, she doesn't like to dry them.
2) You need to pass your driver's test; ______, you can't get your license.
3) Cy was planning to go fishing; ______, he stayed home.
4) Mom likes baked potatoes, ______ Grandma prefers them mashed.
5) I was bored, ______ I went for a bike ride.
6) Liz planted tulips in the fall, ______ she planted day lilies in the spring.
7) Paul was sick the day of the game; ______, he had to miss it.
8) Jean and Will enjoyed an accounting class; ______, it helped them prepare their tax returns.
9) Jordon made breakfast and lunch all week; ______, he cooked dinner three nights.
10) Kansas City can be quite steamy in summer; ______, it is a wonderful place to live.

Part D Connect each pair of sentences with a subordinating conjunction. Write the new complete sentence on the line. Add commas where needed. Be sure each sentence makes sense.

1) We had just eaten breakfast. We went to the brunch anyway.
______
2) We had been leading. The other team got three baskets.
______
3) I was asleep. The storm blew down a tree.
______
4) Gretta looked everywhere. She found her lens beside the sink.
______
5) Joe waited for the doctor. He reviewed his questions.
______

 Basic English Grammar

Chapter 8 Mastery Test B

Chapter 9

Planning Guide

The Interjection

	Student Text Lesson			
	Student Pages	Vocabulary	Practice Exercises	Lesson Review
Lesson 1 Using Interjections	192-193	✔	✔	

Chapter Activities

Teacher's Resource Library

Community Connection 9: Finding Interjections in a Children's Book

Assessment Options

Student Text

Chapter 9 Review

Teacher's Resource Library

Chapter 9 Mastery Tests A and B

Teaching Strategies							Language Skills			Learning Styles						Teacher's Resource Library		
Reviewing Skills	Teacher Alert	Follow-up Activity	Career Application	Home Application	Global Connection	Community Application	Identification Skills	Writing Skills	Punctuation Skills	Visual/Spatial	Auditory/Verbal	Body/Kinesthetic	Logical/Mathematical	Group Learning	LEP/ESL	Activities	Workbook Activities	Self-Study Guide
192	194			195	194	192, 195	✔	✔	✔				192			25-27	38-39	✔

Chapter at a Glance

Chapter 9: The Interjection pages 190–195

Lesson

1) **Using Interjections** pages 192–193

Chapter 9 Review pages 194–195

Teacher's Resource Library

Activities 25–27

Workbook Activities 38–39

Community Connection 9

Chapter 9 Self-Study Guide

Chapter 9 Mastery Tests A and B

(Answer Keys for the Teacher's Resource Library begin on page 330 of this Teacher's Edition.)

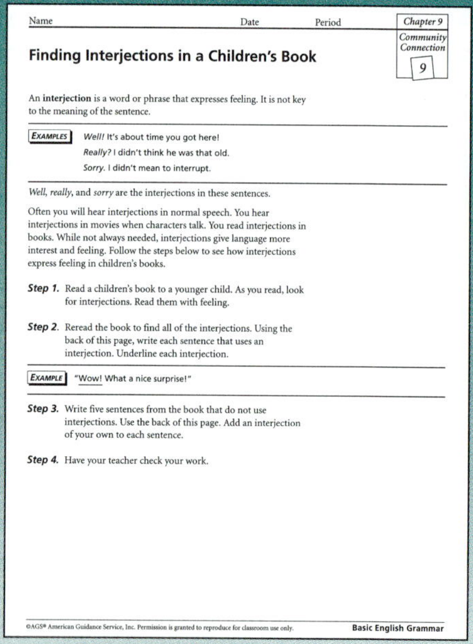

Name Date Period

Chapter 9 *Community Connection* 9

Finding Interjections in a Children's Book

An **interjection** is a word or phrase that expresses feeling. It is not key to the meaning of the sentence.

EXAMPLES *Well!* It's about time you got here!
Really? I didn't think he was that old.
Sorry. I didn't mean to interrupt.

Well, really, and *sorry* are the interjections in these sentences.

Often you will hear interjections in normal speech. You hear interjections in movies when characters talk. You read interjections in books. While not always needed, interjections give language more interest and feeling. Follow the steps below to see how interjections express feeling in children's books.

Step 1. Read a children's book to a younger child. As you read, look for interjections. Read them with feeling.

Step 2. Reread the book to find all of the interjections. Using the back of this page, write each sentence that uses an interjection. Underline each interjection.

EXAMPLE "Wow! What a nice surprise!"

Step 3. Write five sentences from the book that do not use interjections. Use the back of this page. Add an interjection of your own to each sentence.

Step 4. Have your teacher check your work.

 Basic English Grammar

Community Connection 9

Chapter 9 The Interjection

You often use words such as ***Oh no!*** or ***Wow!*** when you are cheering for your favorite team. Words such as *oh no* and *wow* express your excitement.

An interjection is a word or phrase that expresses strong feeling. While an interjection adds interest to a sentence, it is not necessary to the meaning of the sentence.

In Chapter 9, you will learn more about recognizing and using interjections in sentences.

Goals for Learning

- To use interjections in sentences
- To write sentences that contain an interjection
- To punctuate sentences that contain interjections correctly

Reading Vocabulary

phrase (6) punctuate (7)

Introducing the Chapter

Focus students' attention on the facial expressions of the people in the photograph, especially the gentleman in the center. Ask students to tell what they think is happening and what they think the different people are feeling. Then ask them to imagine that there are speech balloons above the heads of the different people. Draw several speech balloons on the board as shown below. Ask students for one or two words that express what each of the people might be feeling. If necessary, stimulate students' ideas by writing "Yeah!" in the first balloon.

Explain to students that words, such as these, that express strong feeling are called interjections. As they complete Chapter 9, they will learn how to use interjections effectively and correctly in sentences.

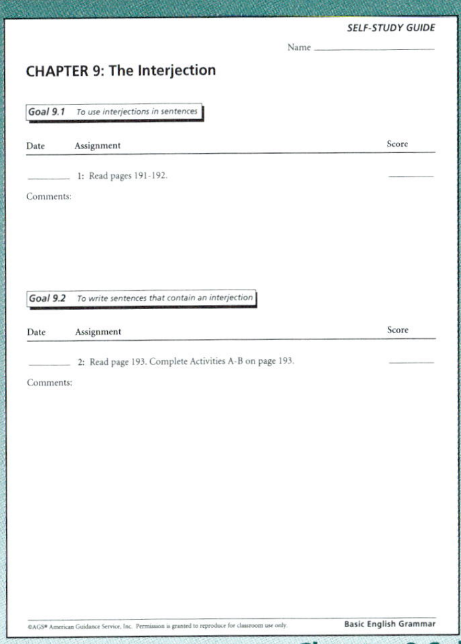

SELF-STUDY GUIDE

Name ______________

CHAPTER 9: The Interjection

Goal 9.1 To use interjections in sentences

Date	Assignment	Score
______	1: Read pages 191-192.	______

Comments:

Goal 9.2 To write sentences that contain an interjection

Date	Assignment	Score
______	2: Read page 193. Complete Activities A-B on page 193.	______

Comments:

 Basic English Grammar

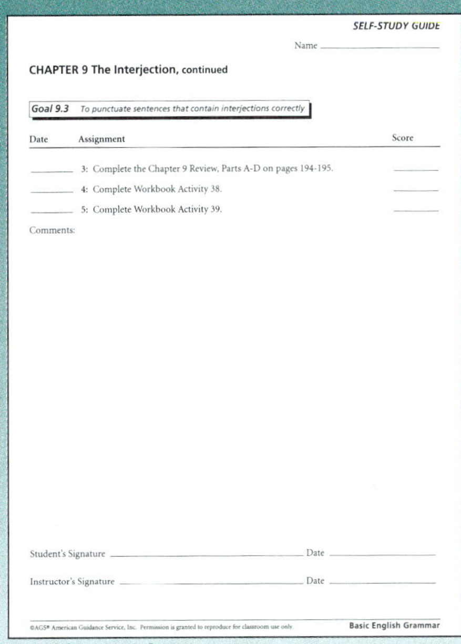

SELF-STUDY GUIDE

Name ______________

CHAPTER 9 The Interjection, continued

Goal 9.3 To punctuate sentences that contain interjections correctly

Date	Assignment	Score
______	3: Complete the Chapter 9 Review, Parts A-D on pages 194-195.	______
______	4: Complete Workbook Activity 38.	______
______	5: Complete Workbook Activity 39.	______

Comments:

Student's Signature ______________ Date ______

Instructor's Signature ______________ Date ______

 Basic English Grammar

Chapter 9 Self-Study Guide

Lesson at a Glance

Chapter 9 Lesson 1

Overview This lesson introduces interjections.

Objectives

- To punctuate sentences with interjections.
- To add interjections to sentences.

Student Pages 192–193

Teacher's Resource Library

Activities 25–27

Workbook Activities 38–39

Reading Vocabulary

exclamation (8) separate (5)
interjection whew
punctuation (7)

Teaching Suggestions

Introducing the Lesson

Discuss the definition of *interjection.* Then encourage students to read each of the example sentences with good oral expression to show the strong feeling conveyed by the interjection in each sentence.

Reviewing Skills

Remind students that every sentence begins with a capital letter and ends with a punctuation mark. Review the different kinds of end punctuation, if necessary.

Learning Styles

Logical/Mathematical

Divide the class into groups of five. Ask each group to choose five interjections from the boxed list on page 192. Encourage each group to create an icon, or symbol, for each of the five interjections. Afterward, have the groups draw their icons on an "Interjection" poster for the classroom.

Lesson 1 Using Interjections

Interjection
A word or phrase that shows strong feeling.

An **interjection** is a word or phrase that expresses a strong feeling. Always separate the interjection from the rest of the sentence with a punctuation mark. Use a comma, a question mark, or an exclamation point. Use an exclamation point after a strong interjection.

EXAMPLES

Hurry! I'll be late again.
Oh? I didn't know you were sick.
Hush! Everyone is working.
Say, could you help me?

Here are some other commonly used interjections:

ah	ouch
alas	quick
gosh	really
ha	sorry
hello	so what
hey	well
hurry	what
my goodness	whew
nonsense	wow
oh, boy	yes

When a period, a question mark, or an exclamation point follows an interjection, capitalize the first word of the sentence.

EXAMPLES

So? Who wants to take a break?
Wow! That is lovely.
Whew! I'm glad I am finished!

192 *Chapter 9 The Interjection*

Name Date Period *Chapter 9 Activity 25*

Recognizing Interjections

Interjections are words that express feelings. We separate an interjection from the rest of the sentence either by a comma or a mark of end punctuation.

Directions: Find and circle the interjections in the sentences below.

1) "Wow, am I exhausted," Sarah said after her travels through the country.
2) Hush, we can't hear the movie.
3) I know you don't like to hear complaining, but my goodness, how can I eat all this food.
4) Hurry! I need your help.
5) Well, maybe I can go camping after all. But, what if I get bit by a snake?
6) Hum, what about Melissa's party? Now, you shouldn't miss that.
7) What a loss! The team was beat in the last three seconds of the game.
8) Ouch! I dropped the book on my foot.
9) Brr, I'm freezing after ice skating all day.
10) Stop! Your arguing is upsetting me.
11) Thanks, I appreciate your efforts.

 Basic English Grammar

Activity 25

Name Date Period *Chapter 9 Activity 26*

Punctuating Interjections

The purpose of an interjection is to express feeling. Many sentences with interjections end in exclamation points.

Capitalize the first word of the sentence after a mark of end punctuation such as a period, a question mark, or an exclamation point. When you use a comma after an interjection, do not capitalize the word that follows.

EXAMPLES

So? Who cares?
Quick! Please help me.
Oh, that is so sweet!

Directions: Punctuate these sentences correctly. Separate the interjection from the rest of the sentence by a mark of end punctuation or a comma. Remember to capitalize the first word of a new sentence.

1) Uh oh that nurse is going to give me a shot
2) Wow what a great car
3) So you finally got here
4) Goodness why are you always late
5) No no I will not take that medicine
6) Whew that tastes awful
7) Alas no one seems to care about me today
8) Really I hadn't heard that before
9) Oh do you really mean that
10) Hush hush don't you cry
11) Say do you know where Carla lives
12) Nonsense that will never work
13) Ouch that hurt
14) Sorry I didn't mean to step on your foot

 Basic English Grammar

Activity 26

Do not capitalize the first word of the sentence that follows the comma after an interjection.

EXAMPLE Ah, that dessert looks great!

Activity A Rewrite these sentences on your paper. Add punctuation after the interjections and at the ends of the sentences. Capitalize the first words of sentences.

1) quick I need help fast

2) wow what a great car that is

3) really I didn't know that

4) well you finally got here

5) whew that was hard

Activity B Write ten sentences that use interjections on your paper. Be sure to punctuate each sentence correctly.

Reading Vocabulary

capitalize (9)

Presenting Activity A

Different students may read each sentence with different feeling. As a result, they may punctuate each sentence differently. It may be helpful to do Activity A together as a class so that you can discuss the different options for punctuating each sentence correctly.

Activity A Answers

End punctuation may vary. Possible answers are given.

1) Quick! I need help fast!
2) Wow! What a great car that is.
3) Really? I didn't know that.
4) Well, you finally got here.
5) Whew! That was hard!

Presenting Activity B

Invite volunteers to provide sample sentences orally before having students complete the activity on their own. When students have finished, have them exchange sentences with a partner who can check for correct punctuation.

Activity B Answers

Each sentence should include an interjection.

Name Date Period — *Chapter 9 Activity 27*

Interjections in Sentences

Interjections express feelings. We use these words most often when we speak rather than when we write. Dialogue is written conversation.

EXAMPLES "Oh, dear," said Mary, "I wonder if Larry is going to be on time for dinner."
"Whew!" said Shelly. "What a hot day!"

Directions: Write 15 sentences in the space below. Use as many interjections as you can.

1) ____
2) ____
3) ____
4) ____
5) ____
6) ____
7) ____
8) ____
9) ____
10) ____
11) ____
12) ____
13) ____
14) ____
15) ____

 Basic English Grammar

Activity 27

Name Date Period — *Chapter 9 Workbook Activity 38*

Using Interjections

Directions: Punctuate these sentences correctly. Remember that an interjection must be separated from the rest of the sentence with a punctuation mark. Capitalize the first word of the sentence.

EXAMPLES *No,* I can't go now.
Whew! I'm glad that's over!
Hey! Stop that.

1) My goodness I am tired.
2) So what who cares if you're mad?
3) Well maybe I can make it to the party.
4) Slow down you are driving too fast.
5) Wow, what a great gift it's just what I wanted.
6) Brr I'm freezing.
7) Ummm that cake looks wonderful.
8) Oh no I forgot my books.
9) Hurry we are going to be late again.
10) Oh that sunset is lovely.
11) Nonsense you don't really think I would believe that.
12) Hello are you there?
13) Hey is anyone home?
14) Alas they are cutting that beautiful tree down.
15) Oh woe is me I am so sad today.
16) Oh boy that new car is fantastic.

 Basic English Grammar

Workbook Activity 38

Name Date Period — *Chapter 9 Workbook Activity 39*

Words of Feeling

A. Directions: Add an interjection to each of these sentences. Also, make sure that you add the correct punctuation. Write each sentence on the line.

EXAMPLE I am tired.
Boy! I am tired.

1) I need help.
2) You are late.
3) I am so happy.
4) I love your new car.
5) Our team won the game.

B. Directions: Capitalize the first word of each of these sentences. Make sure that you add the correct punctuation.

EXAMPLE so who cares
So, who cares?

1) oh boy that was fun
2) whew I am tired
3) hey buddy you're in my way
4) wow what a great hit
5) ha ha that's too funny

 Basic English Grammar

Workbook Activity 39

Chapter 9 Review

The Teacher's Resource Library includes two parallel forms of the Chapter 9 Mastery Test. The difficulty level of the two forms is equivalent. You may wish to use one form as a pretest and the other form as a posttest.

Reading Vocabulary

rip (5)

Part A Answers

Each sentence should include an interjection.

Part B Answers

Punctuation may vary. Possible answers are given.

1) No, I can't help you. **2)** Ouch! That hurts. **3)** Whew! That has a strong smell! **4)** Well, what's new? **5)** Hey! I had better get home. **6)** Alas! She could not make it to the finish line. **7)** Hurry! I hear the train coming! **8)** Honestly, you would think they could behave. **9)** Yikes! A snake just crawled over Pam's foot! **10)** Gosh! This town looks deserted.

Teacher Alert

Some students may mistakenly add a question mark at the end of exclamatory sentences that begin with the word *what*, which frequently begins questions. Caution students to read each sentence carefully and remind them that only sentences that ask a question end in a question mark.

Global Connection

Every country has specific words and phrases that show excitement, anger, and other strong emotions. Select an interjection from the list on page 192, such as "my goodness" or "oh, boy." Then invite bilingual students to teach classmates how to say a similar expression in their primary language.

Chapter 9 Review

Part A Add an interjection to each of these sentences. Write the new sentences on your paper. Be sure to punctuate correctly.

1) Isn't that beautiful?
2) We're having a test.
3) That hurts.
4) I ripped my best shirt.
5) I won!
6) What a sad story that was.
7) We left just in time!
8) You made it!
9) That can't be the right answer.
10) That sure smells great.

Part B Write these sentences on your paper. Punctuate and capitalize each sentence correctly.

1) no I can't help you
2) ouch that hurts
3) whew that has a strong smell
4) well what's new
5) hey I had better get home
6) alas she could not make it to the finish line
7) hurry I hear the train coming
8) honestly you would think they would behave
9) yikes a snake just crawled over Pam's foot
10) gosh this town looks deserted

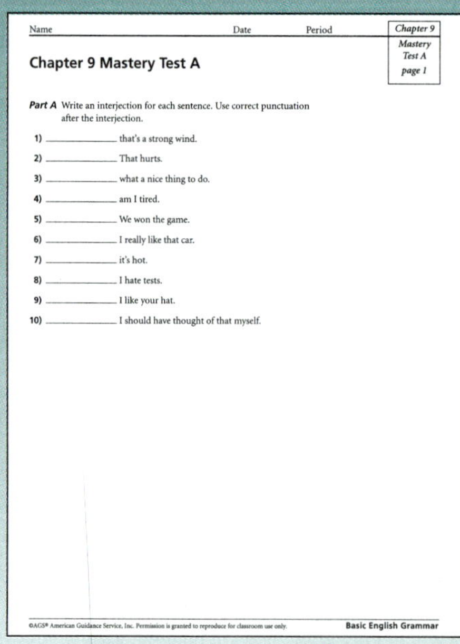

Name Date Period *Chapter 9 Mastery Test A page 1*

Chapter 9 Mastery Test A

Part A Write an interjection for each sentence. Use correct punctuation after the interjection.

1) ________ that's a strong wind.
2) ________ That hurts.
3) ________ what a nice thing to do.
4) ________ am I tired.
5) ________ We won the game.
6) ________ I really like that car.
7) ________ it's hot.
8) ________ I hate tests.
9) ________ I like your hat.
10) ________ I should have thought of that myself.

 Basic English Grammar

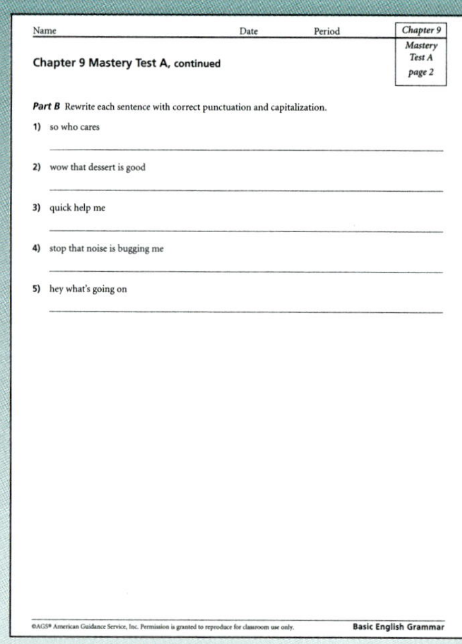

Name Date Period *Chapter 9 Mastery Test A page 2*

Chapter 9 Mastery Test A, continued

Part B Rewrite each sentence with correct punctuation and capitalization.

1) so who cares
2) wow that dessert is good
3) quick help me
4) stop that noise is bugging me
5) hey what's going on

 Basic English Grammar

Chapter 9 Mastery Test A

Part C Complete each sentence with an interjection. Write the sentences on your paper. Punctuate and capitalize each sentence correctly.

1) ______ what a flop that play was
2) ______ you can't be serious
3) ______ that is a wonderful idea
4) ______ I burned my hand on that pot
5) ______ where did you learn to sing like that
6) ______ call the fire department
7) ______ do you mean it
8) ______ no one is going to believe this story
9) ______ was he angry
10) ______ we'll miss the bus

Part D Write 10 sentences using interjections. Be sure to capitalize and punctuate the sentences correctly.

Test Taking Tip When studying for a test, use a marker to highlight important facts and terms in your notes. For a final review, read over highlighted areas.

Name Date Period | *Chapter 9 Mastery Test B page 1*

Chapter 9 Mastery Test B

Part A Write an interjection for each sentence. Use correct punctuation after the interjection.

1) ______ My team finally won.
2) ______ That snow is cold.
3) ______ what a terrific movie that was.
4) ______ I need help.
5) ______ Are you sure about that?
6) ______ Where did you get that idea?
7) ______ I hear you.
8) ______ Where are you going?
9) ______ Is anybody home?
10) ______ but there's no way I can help you with that.

Name Date Period | *Chapter 9 Mastery Test B page 2*

Chapter 9 Mastery Test B, continued

Part B Rewrite each sentence with correct punctuation and capitalization.

1) oh boy what a nice day
2) wow I love that outfit
3) ouch my sunburn is sore
4) hush I am trying to concentrate
5) oh no I lost my contact lens

Chapter 9 Mastery Test B

Reading Vocabulary

flop (5)

Part C Answers

Answers may vary. Possible answers are given.

1) Gosh! What a flop that play was. **2)** No! You can't be serious! **3)** Gee, that is a wonderful idea. **4)** Ouch! I burned my hand on that pot! **5)** Wow! Where did you learn to sing like that? **6)** Quick! Call the fire department! **7)** Really? Do you mean it? **8)** Oh, boy! No one is going to believe this story! **9)** Oh! Was he angry! **10)** Hurry! We'll miss the bus.

Part D Answers

Each sentence should include an interjection.

Application

In the Community

Students might enjoy interviewing their parents, older relatives, friends, and other seniors in the community to find out what kinds of expressions were used in the past to show strong feeling. Students can then create a time-line showing how these expressions have changed over the years.

Application

At Home

Encourage students to list interjections family members and friends use when they speak and write. Students can then compare their lists and perhaps make a master list for the classroom that they can refer to when writing. If necessary, caution students against listing any unacceptable terms.

Part 2

Sentence Construction

You may have noticed that not every sentence has the parts of speech in the same order. A sentence must express a complete thought. It can, however, follow many different patterns to express that thought.

You may also have noticed that not every sentence has the same purpose. Sentences can have different purposes.

Statement	This kind of sentence states a fact or tells about something.
Question	This kind of sentence asks a question.
Command	This kind of sentence gives an order or makes a request.
Strong Feelings	This kind of sentence shows surprise or other strong feelings.

While every sentence must have certain parts to express a complete thought, those parts can be arranged and combined in different ways. There are four basic sentence structures.

Simple	One subject and one predicate
Compound	Two or more ideas joined with a conjunction
Complex	One independent and one dependent clause
Compound-Complex	At least two independent clauses and at least one dependent clause

In Part 2 of this book, you will learn about the different patterns that sentences follow and the different purposes sentences have. You will learn how to capitalize and punctuate sentences so that their purpose is clear. You will learn how to recognize the parts of a sentence. You will also learn how to put these parts together to express a complete thought.

When you know how to construct a sentence, you will be able to speak and write clearly. You will be able to express your ideas and communicate them to others. This is the real purpose of studying grammar.

Introducing Part 2

Ask students to consider what the world would be like if there were only one kind of tree; a single type and color of flower; day after day of the same weather; people who all looked and thought exactly alike; and so on. Help students recognize that variety in nature enriches people's experience of the world. Then point out that, in a similar way, variety in the arrangement of words and phrases in sentences enriches people's experience of the written word. Explain that by the end of Part 2 of this book, students will understand how to construct sentences in a variety of ways for different purposes and effects.

Chapter 10

Planning Guide

Sentences: Subjects and Predicates

	Student Text Lesson			
	Student Pages	Vocabulary	Practice Exercises	Lesson Review
Lesson 1 What Is a Sentence?	200-202	✔	✔	202
Lesson 2 The Subject of the Sentence	203-207	✔	✔	207
Lesson 3 The Predicate	208-211	✔	✔	211
Lesson 4 Kinds of Sentences	212-214		✔	214
Lesson 5 Simple and Compound Sentences	215-217	✔	✔	217

Chapter Activities

Teacher's Resource Library

Community Connection 10: Writing a Letter to the Editor

Assessment Options

Student Text

Chapter 10 Review

Teacher's Resource Library

Chapter 10 Mastery Tests A and B

Teaching Strategies							Language Skills			Learning Styles						Teacher's Resource Library		
Reviewing Skills	Teacher Alert	Follow-up Activity	Career Application	Home Application	Global Connection	Community Application	Identification Skills	Writing Skills	Punctuation Skills	Visual/Spatial	Auditory/Verbal	Body/Kinesthetic	Logical/Mathematical	Group Learning	LEP/ESL	Activities	Workbook Activities	Self-Study Guide
200	200	202	202	201			✔	✔	✔					202			40	✔
203							✔	✔	✔	207						28	41	✔
208							✔	✔	✔	210						29	42	✔
212	212				212	213	✔	✔	✔		214					30	43-44	✔
215							✔	✔	✔				217				45	✔

Chapter at a Glance

Chapter 10: Sentences: Subjects and Predicates pages 198–219

(Answer Keys for the Teacher's Resource Library begin on page 330 of this Teacher's Edition.)

Name ____ Date ____ Period ____ *Chapter 10* *Community Connection* *10*

Writing a Letter to the Editor

Every sentence has two parts: the **subject** and the **predicate**. The subject is what the sentence is talking about. The predicate tells what the subject did or what happened to the subject.

EXAMPLE Lorenzo jumped when he heard the loud noise.

In this sentence, *Lorenzo* is the complete subject. *Jumped when he heard the loud noise* is the complete predicate.

A complete sentence has a subject and a predicate. Some sentences have more than one subject and predicate. Practice finding the subject and predicate in sentences by completing these steps.

Step 1. Think of something in your community that you have a strong opinion about. Examples might be the environment, violence, racism, drugs, or crime. Try to think of something that happened in your community related to this matter. Maybe you felt good about a community cleanup project. Maybe you would like something done about the high crime rate in your city.

Step 2. Look in a newspaper to find the opinion page. Study the letters to the editor. See what people are writing about. Notice how these letters are written.

Step 3. On another sheet of paper, write your own letter to the editor. Make your letter at least 100 words long.

Step 4. Then fill in the chart below with the subject and predicate for five of the sentences in your letter.

Step 5. Have your teacher check your chart and look at your letter. Ask a family member, friend, or classmate to read your letter and tell you if your points are clear.

Step 6. Read the letter to your class.

Step 7. Get the address of your local newspaper. Mail your letter.

Subject	Predicate

 Basic English Grammar

Community Connection 10

Chapter 10

Sentences: Subjects and Predicates

When you tell a story, you express complete ideas so that listeners can picture the characters in the story and what happens to them. You break the ideas in your story into units of meaning called sentences.

A sentence is a group of words that expresses a complete thought. Every sentence has two parts. They are the subject and the predicate. The subject of a sentence is who or what the sentence is about. The predicate tells what the subject did or what happened to the subject.

Each lesson in Chapter 10 focuses on what a sentence is and how subjects and predicates work in different types of sentences.

Goals for Learning

- To identify a sentence
- To identify the subject and predicate in simple sentences
- To identify the noun or pronoun in subjects
- To identify the verb or verb phrase in predicates
- To identify different types of sentences
- To identify the subject and predicate in compound sentences

199

Reading Vocabulary

identify (6)
phrase (5)
predicate
subject (5)

Introducing the Chapter

Call attention to the photograph. Ask students to imagine themselves at this meeting. They expect the gentleman at the head of the table to give a clear business presentation. This is what they hear instead:

- "as president of the company for the last ten years"
- "unless an agreement is reached"
- "struggle for several more months without success"
- "Mr. Akito from our Japanese office"

Ask students what they and probably all of the people at the table would be thinking at the end of such a presentation. Elicit that the gentleman did not express his ideas completely, so none of his ideas make sense. Explain that for a sentence to express a complete thought it must have a subject and predicate. Then point out to students that by the end of Chapter 10, they will be able to recognize a sentence and its two basic parts.

SELF-STUDY GUIDE

Name ______

CHAPTER 10: Sentences: Subjects and Predicates

Goal 10.1 *To identify a sentence*

Date	Assignment	Score
______	1: Read pages 199-200. Complete Activities A-B on page 201.	______
______	2: Complete Workbook Activity 40.	______
______	3: Complete the Lesson 1 Review, Parts A-B on page 202.	______

Comments:

Goal 10.2 *To identify the subject in simple sentences and to identify the noun or pronoun in subjects*

Date	Assignment	Score
______	4: Read page 203. Complete Activity A on page 203.	______
______	5: Read page 204. Complete Activities B-C on page 204.	______
______	6: Complete Workbook Activity 41.	______
______	7: Read page 205. Complete Activities D-E on page 205.	______
______	8: Read page 206. Complete Activities F-G on page 206.	______
______	9: Complete the Lesson 2 Review, Parts A-B on page 207.	______

Comments:

Goal 10.3 *To identify the predicate in simple sentences and to identify the verb or verb phrase in predicates*

Date	Assignment	Score
______	10: Read page 208. Complete Activities A-B on page 208.	______
______	11: Read page 209. Complete Activity C on page 209.	______
______	12: Read page 210. Complete Activities D-E on page 210.	______
______	13: Complete the Lesson 3 Review, Parts A-B on page 211.	______
______	14: Complete Workbook Activity 42.	______

Comments:

 Basic English Grammar

SELF-STUDY GUIDE

Name ______

CHAPTER 10 Sentences: Subjects and Predicates, continued

Goal 10.4 **To identify different types of sentences*

Date	Assignment	Score
______	15: Read pages 212-213. Complete Activity A on page 213.	______
______	16: Complete Workbook Activity 43.	______
______	17: Complete the Lesson 4 Review, Parts A-B on page 214.	______
______	18: Complete Workbook Activity 44.	______

Comments:

Goal 10.5 *To identify the subject and predicate in compound sentences*

Date	Assignment	Score
______	19: Read page 215. Complete Activity A on page 215.	______
______	20: Complete Activities B-C on page 216.	______
______	21: Complete Workbook Activity 45.	______
______	22: Complete the Lesson 5 Review, Parts A-B on page 217.	______
______	23: Complete the Chapter 10 Review, Parts A-D on pages 218-219.	______

Comments:

Student's Signature ______ Date ______

Instructor's Signature ______ Date ______

 Basic English Grammar

Chapter 10 Self-Study Guide

Lesson at a Glance

Chapter 10 Lesson 1

Overview This lesson presents the definition of a sentence.

Objectives

- To distinguish between a sentence and a sentence fragment.
- To write complete sentences from fragments.

Student Pages 200–202

Teacher's Resource Library

Workbook Activity 40

Reading Vocabulary

capital (5) punctuation (7)
exclamation (8) **sentence**

Teaching Suggestions

Introducing the Lesson

Discuss the definition of a sentence and the examples given. If necessary, provide additional examples of incomplete sentences. Write these on the board and help students understand why each is not a sentence, what is missing, and what needs to be added to make each group of words a complete sentence.

Reviewing Skills

Review the difference between capital and lower case letters, and end punctuation.

Teacher Alert

You may wish to point out that some grammar textbooks refer to incomplete sentences as sentence fragments.

Lesson 1 What Is a Sentence?

> **Sentence**
> *A group of words that expresses a complete thought. A sentence always begins with a capital letter and ends with a period, question mark, or exclamation point.*

A **sentence** is a group of words that expresses a complete thought. Every sentence begins with a capital letter and ends with a punctuation mark.

EXAMPLES

Mrs. Johnson sold her old car to Rafael.
What did he pay for the car?
Stop right there!

A group of words may look like a sentence, but if it does not express a complete thought, it is not a sentence.

EXAMPLES

Not a sentence:	The car with the red top. (This group of words does not express a complete thought. What about the car with the red top?)
Sentence:	The car with the red top belongs to her friend.
Not a sentence:	Looked all over town for a car. (This group of words does not express a complete thought. Who looked all over town for a car?)
Sentence:	Rafael looked all over town for a car.
Not a sentence:	Before Rafael bought the car. (This group of words does not express a complete thought. What happened before Rafael bought the car?)
Sentence:	Before Rafael bought the car, his father looked it over.

Activity A For each item below, write *S* on your paper if the group of words is a sentence. Write *NS* if the group of words is not a sentence.

1) Stop for the red light!

2) Before the storm was over.

3) In the house across the street.

4) That's nice.

5) Where does she live?

6) Searching for a new job.

7) She laughed.

8) Jack went fishing.

9) Because of the cold weather.

10) Each day before the sun rises.

11) You can leave now.

12) Everyone at the party had a good time.

13) Chen moved to town in March.

14) On the day of the party for Mrs. Williams.

15) Afterwards, they all helped clean up.

Activity B Copy each group of words from Activity A that you marked *NS* onto your paper. Add words to each item to make it a complete sentence. Check that each sentence begins with a capital letter and ends with a period, question mark, or exclamation point.

Name Date Period

Chapter 10 Workbook Activity 40

Expressing a Complete Idea

A sentence has a subject and a predicate. It expresses a complete idea. Sometimes the subject is understood. A sentence can be long or short.

EXAMPLES Hurry up!
It's pretty.
Harriet went to the prom; later she went to a party.

Directions: Read each group of words below. Write *Yes* on the line if the words form a sentence. Write *No* if the words do not form a sentence.

HINT: Before you choose your answer, ask yourself "Why are the words a sentence?" or "Why aren't they a sentence?"

_______ **1)** After the party.
_______ **2)** Stop it!
_______ **3)** Whew!
_______ **4)** Not my turn.
_______ **5)** Sentences express ideas.
_______ **6)** They are beautiful.
_______ **7)** Carol enjoys playing baseball.
_______ **8)** My little sister.
_______ **9)** Is good at T-Ball.
_______ **10)** Gramps likes that sport called pickleball.
_______ **11)** So do I.
_______ **12)** Leave early.
_______ **13)** One of the girls in my class named Cassie.
_______ **14)** Cassie is a girl in my class.
_______ **15)** She is one of the girls in my class.

 Basic English Grammar

Workbook Activity 40

■ **Presenting Activity A** You may wish to do this activity orally with the class. Invite students to read each item aloud with you, listening to hear if the words express a complete thought. If they decide the item is a sentence, students should raise their hands; if it is not a sentence, students should keep their hands down. Students should be ready to explain why the group of words is or is not a sentence.

Activity A Answers

1) S 2) NS 3) NS 4) S 5) S 6) NS 7) S 8) S 9) NS 10) NS 11) S 12) S 13) S 14) NS 15) S

■ **Presenting Activity B** If you did not do Activity A together as a class, you may wish to check answers for Activity A now. This will ensure that students have correctly identified all of the incomplete sentences. Then ask volunteers to suggest different ways to complete items 2 and 3 in Activity A before having students complete Activity B on their own.

Activity B Answers

Students should write complete sentences for items 2, 3, 6, 9, 10, and 14 from Activity A. Sentences should include correct capitalization and punctuation.

Application

At Home
Encourage students to check recent writing assignments as well as personal writing for incomplete sentences, capitalization errors, and missing end punctuation.

Reading Vocabulary

item (6) professional (6)

Part A Answers

Students should write complete sentences for all items listed here as NS. Sentences will vary.

1) NS 2) S 3) S 4) S
5) NS 6) NS 7) S 8) NS
9) NS 10) S

Part B Answers

Sentences will vary.

Follow-up Activity

Write these groups of words on the board:

- Beside the girl in the red dress
- Across the road watching the parade
- Without a warning, the man with the whistle

Have students add words to one of these items to make it a complete sentence. Then challenge students to write two or three more sentences to go with the first sentence they wrote. Invite students to share their sentences with the class.

Application

Career Connection
The ability to write and recognize a complete sentence is important for many careers. Secretaries and any other employees who must type or edit a supervisor's work as well as compose original letters to clients, suppliers, or fellow employees will not be successful if they cannot write and punctuate a complete sentence correctly.

Lesson 1 Review

Part A For each item below, write *S* on your paper if the group of words is a sentence. If the group of words is not a sentence, copy it onto your paper and add words to make a complete sentence.

1) Our neighbor in the house across the street.
2) They painted the house a light shade of brown.
3) His whole family picked out the color.
4) They needed a two-story ladder.
5) When dark clouds appeared in the sky.
6) The part of the house under the roof.
7) The whole job took them three days.
8) After they were finished.
9) Feeling good about themselves.
10) Professional painters could not have done a better job.

Part B Copy each of the following groups of words onto your paper. Add words to make each one a complete sentence. Be sure to begin each sentence with a capital letter and end with a period, question mark, or exclamation point.

1) the papers on my desk
2) seen in the woods near the lake
3) walking to the game with friends
4) the girl on the bus
5) if anyone calls while I'm out

Learning Styles

Interpersonal/ Group Learning
Divide the class into groups of four. Ask each group to create eight groups of words that do not form a sentence. Have them print these groups on a sheet titled "List 1." On a different sheet of paper titled "List 2," ask them to create sentences out of the eight groups of words. Have each group exchange its List 1 with another group. Have the second group create another List 2 by writing sentences for the list of words it received. Afterward, compare all the List 2 sheets. Discuss how the same group of words can make many different sentences.

202 *Chapter 10 Sentences: Subjects and Predicates*

Lesson 2 The Subject of the Sentence

Subject
Who or what the sentence is about.

Every sentence has two parts: the **subject** and the predicate. The subject is the part of the sentence that tells what is being talked about. The main word in a subject is usually a noun or pronoun. The noun or pronoun and all the words that describe it make up the **complete subject**. The complete subject may be one word or many words.

Complete subject
All the words in the subject. It may be one word or many words.

EXAMPLES

He opened his book. (Who opened the book? *He* opened it.)

The woman who taught us Spanish last year became vice-principal. (Who became vice-principal? *The woman who taught us Spanish last year* did.)

Simple subject
The main noun or pronoun in the subject.

The **simple subject** is the main noun or pronoun in the complete subject.

EXAMPLES

The **quiz** on Friday was easy. (The simple subject is the noun *quiz*. The complete subject is *the quiz on Friday*.)

Mrs. Castillo is our Spanish teacher this year. (The simple subject is the proper noun *Mrs. Castillo*. The complete subject is also *Mrs. Castillo*.)

Activity A Write the complete subject of each of these sentences on your paper. Circle the simple subject. A complete subject may be only one word.

1) Mrs. Castillo comes from Mexico City, Mexico.

2) The entire class speaks in Spanish every day.

3) The teacher asks the students questions in Spanish.

4) They must answer her in Spanish.

5) The students in this class learn quickly.

6) Our book has beautiful photographs of South America.

Lesson at a Glance

Chapter 10 Lesson 2

Overview This lesson introduces the concept of simple subject and complete subject.

Objectives

- To identify the complete subject.
- To identify the simple subject.
- To find the subject in questions and commands.

Student Pages 203–207

Teacher's Resource Library

Activity 28

Workbook Activity 41

Reading Vocabulary

complete subject	**simple subject**
subject	photograph (6)
vice-principal	quiz (6)

Teaching Suggestions

Introducing the Lesson

Discuss the information in the text. Point out to students that they can find the subject by asking themselves, "Who or what is this sentence about?"

Reviewing Skills

Review nouns, pronouns, prepositions, and prepositional phrases.

Presenting Activity A

Write each item in Activity A on the board and help students find the complete and simple subjects.

Activity A Answers

Complete Subject	Simple Subject
1) Mrs. Castillo	Mrs. Castillo
2) The entire class	class
3) The teacher	teacher
4) They	They
5) The students in this class	students
6) Our book	book

Reading Vocabulary

concert (5)
prepositional
preposition
secretary (5)

■ Presenting Activity B

Before having students do Activity B on their own, help them identify the prepositional phrase in each complete subject. Emphasize that the object of a preposition is never the simple subject of the sentence.

Activity B Answers

1) Each **2)** All **3)** Eight
4) secretary **5)** Two

■ Presenting Activity C

Ask students to help you find the complete subjects in these sentences: *The woman in the front row laughed out loud./All of the eggs were cracked.* Then ask students to find the simple subject in each sentence. Elicit through discussion how students knew which noun or pronoun was the simple subject in each sentence. After students complete Activity C on their own, invite them to share their answers with the class.

Activity C Answers

1) I **2)** A friend of Mrs. Castillo
3) Three of our classmates
4) The car with the flat tire
5) Everyone in the band

The simple subject cannot be the object of the preposition.

EXAMPLES

One of the girls was late.

(*One of the girls* is the complete subject. The prepositional phrase *of the girls* describes the simple subject *one*. *Girls* is the object of the preposition *of*; therefore, *girls* cannot be the subject of the sentence.)

The **person** beside Carol is my aunt.

(*The person beside Carol* is the complete subject. The prepositional phrase *beside Carol* describes the simple subject *person*. *Carol* is the object of the preposition *beside*; therefore, *Carol* cannot be the subject of the sentence.)

Activity B The complete subject in each of these sentences is in bold. Write each simple subject on your paper.

1) **Each of the students** wrote the answer on his paper.
2) **All of my friends** like music.
3) **Eight of the students** were absent yesterday.
4) **The secretary in the principal's office** has the flu.
5) **Two of the students** had a fever.

Activity C Write the complete subject in each of these sentences on your paper.

1) I am going to the store.
2) A friend of Mrs. Castillo visited from Spain.
3) Three of our classmates went on the field trip.
4) The car with the flat tire pulled off the road.
5) Everyone in the band practiced for the concert.

The subject of a sentence usually comes before the verb, but it may come after the verb. When a sentence begins with the words *here* or *there*, the subject comes after the verb.

Name Date Period | *Chapter 10 Activity 28*

Finding Subjects

Sometimes when people ask what you are talking about, you probably haven't clearly identified the subject of your sentence.

A subject can be one word or many words. The subject is usually a noun or pronoun, and all the words that describe it.

Directions: Circle the complete subject of each of the following sentences.

EXAMPLES My mother likes to go horseback riding.
I enjoy riding also.
Many horse trails are nearby.

1) People will drive many miles to go to the beach.
2) The beach is a beautiful place.
3) He finally left for work at noon.
4) Several of my friends are athletic.
5) Teachers must have a lot of patience.
6) One of the students yelled across the room.
7) It was on TV last night.
8) The black cat under the table is very hungry.
9) All of us decided to go swimming.
10) This restaurant makes excellent pizza.
11) The principal announced the winners of the contest.
12) Young children enjoy going to the zoo.
13) My sister wants to go to Stanford University.
14) You've probably heard of the song.
15) Finally we were on the airplane.

 Basic English Grammar

Activity 28

Name Date Period | *Chapter 10 Workbook Activity 41*

Finding Subjects

Sometimes when people ask, "What are you talking about?" you probably haven't clearly identified the subject of your sentence.

A subject can be one word or many words. The subject is usually a noun or pronoun and all the words that describe it.

Directions: Underline the complete subject for each of these sentences.

EXAMPLES My sister likes to watch soap operas.
She calls them daytime dramas.
All of these programs are on during the day.

1) Soap operas first became popular on radio.
2) People sat around their radio and listened to the stories.
3) Many of the sponsors were soap companies.
4) Daytime dramas were therefore nicknamed soap operas.
5) One famous soap opera was called "Our Gal Sunday."
6) Your grandmother probably knows about this program.
7) Another popular program in the 1940s was "The Romance of Helen Trent."
8) My grandfather's favorite was "One Man's Family."
9) "One Man's Family" was an evening soap opera.
10) It was on the radio for many years.
11) That program switched to television in the late 1950s.
12) Nowadays people still like soap operas.
13) You've probably heard of "General Hospital."
14) The soap opera stars are very popular.
15) People watch the shows and talk about their favorite characters.

 Basic English Grammar

Workbook Activity 41

EXAMPLES There will be a **bus** at eleven-thirty. (What will be there? A *bus* will be there.)

Here comes **Amy** now. (Who comes now? *Amy* does.)

Activity D Write the simple subject in each of these sentences on your paper.

1) There is a good program on TV tonight.

2) Here is the bus stop.

3) There are no sandwiches left.

In a question, the subject may come between a helping verb and a main verb or the parts of a verb phrase.

EXAMPLES When does **Mary** have math? (The subject *Mary* comes between the helping verb *does* and the main verb *have.)*

Are **you** leaving soon? (The subject *you* comes between the verb phrase *are leaving.)*

When the interrogative pronouns *what, who,* and *which* begin a sentence that asks a question, the interrogative pronoun may be the subject.

EXAMPLES **Who** called?

What is happening?

Which of these books is yours?

Activity E Write the simple subject in each of these sentences on your paper.

1) Will you be going to the meeting?

2) Which of the members will speak?

3) Who will lead the discussion?

4) Has this group ever met before?

Reading Vocabulary

discussion (6) member (5)
interrogative

■ Presenting Activity D

Have students practice finding the simple subject in the following sentences before having them do Activity D on their own. *There are three of my friends in that play./Here is Emilio.* Help students rephrase the sentence before having them look for the subject. (*Three of my friends are in that play./Emilio is here.*) Suggest that students apply this strategy as they do Activity D. If necessary, point out that *bus stop* is a compound word and that a compound word is considered as one word in a sentence.

Activity D Answers

1) program **2)** bus stop **3)** sandwiches

■ Presenting Activity E

Invite students to make up a variety of questions, including some that begin with *what, who,* and *which?* Write students' questions on the board and help them find the simple subject in each sentence. When you feel students are ready, have them do Activity E on their own.

Activity E Answers

1) you **2)** Which **3)** Who **4)** group

Reading Vocabulary

compound (6)

■ Presenting Activity F

Point to a student and say, "Stand up." After the student stands, ask him or her why she stood up. Elicit that the student understood you were talking to him or her. Help students relate this idea to the concept of the understood subject *you* in all commands and requests. Then have them complete Activity F independently.

Activity F Answers

1) you 2) you 3) you 4) you 5) you

■ Presenting Activity G

If necessary, distinguish between a compound noun used as a simple subject and a compound simple subject. Then do the first one or two items orally with students before having them work on their own.

Activity G Answers

1) Freddie, Tricia 2) hat, gloves 3) Spring, summer 4) books, papers 5) sandwiches, juice

In a command or a request, the subject is *you*, even though the word *you* may not appear in the sentence. The subject is understood to be the person spoken to.

EXAMPLES

Please help me set the table.

(You) Please help me set the table.

Jack, come here right now.

Jack, **(you)** come here right now. (Although the person spoken to is named, the subject is still understood to be *you*.)

Activity F Write the simple subject in each of these sentences on your paper.

1) Pedro, help me carry these bags into the house.
2) Open your books to page 45.
3) Denise, please come home right after school.
4) Don't touch that!
5) Please hurry!

The subject of a sentence can be compound (two subjects).

EXAMPLES

Connie and **Brenda** went to class.

The **girl** and her **friend** went shopping.

Activity G Write the compound subject in each of these sentences on your paper.

1) Neither Freddie nor Tricia went to the concert.
2) Both my hat and my gloves were lost.
3) Spring and summer are my favorite seasons.
4) Are my books or my papers in your locker?
5) There are enough sandwiches and juice for everyone.

Lesson 2 Review

Part A Write the simple subject in each of these sentences on your paper. The subject may be understood.

1) Christa wanted a CD player.

2) On Saturday she looked at them in the store.

3) Her birthday was in two weeks.

4) Her mother talked to Christa's brother.

5) "Would Christa like anything special for her birthday?"

6) "Get her a CD player."

7) Who is coming to Christa's party?

Part B Write each of these sentences on your paper. Underline the complete subject. Then circle the simple subject.

1) Baseball season begins soon.

2) Is James on the team?

3) He usually plays first base.

4) There will be a tryout on Friday.

5) Where will tryouts be held?

6) José and Andy play baseball.

7) The state college had a good team last year.

8) Many of their best players have graduated.

9) Here are the names of some players still on the team.

Reading Vocabulary

college (5) tryout
graduate (6)

Part A Answers

1) Christa **2)** she **3)** birthday **4)** mother **5)** Christa **6)** you (understood) **7)** Who

Part B Answers

Complete Subject	Simple Subject
1) Baseball season	season
2) James	James
3) He	He
4) a tryout	tryout
5) tryouts	tryouts
6) José and Andy	José, Andy
7) The state college	college
8) Many of their best players	Many
9) the names of some players	names

Learning Styles

Visual/Spatial

Divide the class into pairs. Give each set of partners a colorful magazine picture. Ask the pairs to write on a sheet of paper all the nouns—people, places, things—they see in the picture. On the board, print the following pattern: adjective/noun/prepositional phrase. Have each create a poster with the pattern heading. Ask the pairs to choose ten nouns and follow the pattern, using their ten nouns to create complete subjects for a possible sentence. Note: Keep the pictures and the posters for use with the Learning Styles activity on page 210.

Sentences: Subjects and Predicates Chapter 10 **207**

Lesson at a Glance

Chapter 10 Lesson 3

Overview This lesson explains predicates.

Objectives

- To identify the complete predicate.
- To identify the main verb or verb phrase.

Student Pages 208–211

Teacher's Resource Library

Activity 29

Workbook Activity 42

Reading Vocabulary

apparently (5)
complete predicate
earring
predicate

Teaching Suggestions

Introducing the Lesson

Emphasize that the subject tells about the doer of the action and the predicate tells about the action.

Reviewing Skills

Review verbs and subjects.

Presenting Activity A

Before having students complete Activity A on their own, have them identify the complete subject in each item.

Activity A Answers

1) lost her earring yesterday 2) found the earring today 3) was missing 4) had apparently stepped on it

Presenting Activity B

Do the first item on the board with students. Then have them complete Activity B independently.

Activity B Answers

1) <u>gave</u> Christa a surprise birthday party 2) <u>baked</u> a carrot cake 3) <u>had decorated</u> the house 4) <u>was arriving</u> home at six-thirty

---

Lesson 3 The Predicate

Predicate
The part of a sentence that tells something about the subject.

Complete predicate
The part of a sentence that contains the main verb and all the words that describe the verb. The main word in the complete predicate is the verb or verb phrase.

The **predicate** of a sentence tells what the subject did or what happened to the subject. The predicate always includes a verb.

The **complete predicate** includes the main verb and all of the words that tell something about the verb. The complete predicate may be one word or many words. Any words in a sentence that are not part of the complete subject are part of the complete predicate.

EXAMPLES

We **studied.**

Andy **will look at new cars this weekend.**

Activity A Write the complete predicate in each of these sentences on your paper.

1) Lena lost her earring yesterday.
2) Denise found the earring today.
3) One of the stones was missing.
4) Someone had apparently stepped on it.

The main part of the complete predicate is the verb or verb phrase. The verb or verb phrase in the complete predicate is sometimes called the simple predicate.

EXAMPLES

James ***helped* his father in the garage.** (The main word in the complete predicate is the verb *helped.*)

Anita ***will meet* us at the library.** (The main words in the complete predicate form the verb phrase *will meet.*)

Activity B Write the complete predicate in each of these sentences on your paper. Underline the verb or verb phrase.

1) Mrs. Barry gave Christa a surprise birthday party.
2) Christa's brother Will baked a carrot cake.
3) Her friends had decorated the house.
4) Christa was arriving home at six-thirty.

Name Date Period | Chapter 10 Activity 29

A Sentence Has Two Parts

Directions: Find the complete subject of each sentence. Underline it once. Then find the complete predicate of each sentence. Underline it twice.

EXAMPLES

<u>Alissa</u> is ready for summer.

(You) Go get the dog.

<u>Many of the students</u> went home after school.

1) The teacher opened the package.
2) Where is my homework?
3) Everyone on the trip was ready for lunch.
4) The mailbox was entirely full of letters.
5) Stop that right now!
6) Both Heather and I were late for class.
7) My exam for English is scheduled to be at 1:00 p.m.
8) The bus driver missed our bus stop today.
9) Two candy bars were left.
10) Ice cream will melt fast in warm weather.
11) The awards committee's final decisions were made.
12) I'm very excited about college.
13) We should go out to dinner tonight.
14) Did any one of you see that movie?
15) They ran off in a hurry.

 Basic English Grammar

Activity 29

Usually the predicate part of the sentence comes after the subject.

EXAMPLE The whole family **enjoyed the party.**

In a question, part of the complete predicate often comes before the subject.

EXAMPLES **Did** you **bring Christa a present?**

Where did you **buy it?**

Are you **having fun?**

Adverbs and prepositional phrases that are part of the complete predicate may be at the beginning of the sentence.

EXAMPLES **At eleven o'clock** everyone **went home.**

Then Will **helped his parents clean up.**

Activity C Write the complete predicate in each of these sentences on your paper. Underline the verb or verb phrase.

1) Did you talk to Christa after the party?

2) Why did Elena leave early?

3) Maybe she was feeling sick.

4) After the party, Christa called Elena.

5) What was wrong?

6) Her mother needed her at home.

7) At the last minute, Mrs. Grasso was called in to work.

8) Elena babysits for her mother.

9) Usually, Mrs. Grasso does not work on weekends.

10) Because of a computer problem, she was needed in the office.

11) Luckily for Elena, the party was almost over.

Reading Vocabulary

computer (8)

Presenting Activity C

Write these sentences on the board: *Will I see you at the party?/What can I do for you?/In the morning, we are leaving for vacation.* Help students find the complete predicate and the verb or verb phrase in each of these sentences. Suggest that students begin by finding the complete subject. Remind students that all the words not in the complete subject are in the complete predicate. Then have students complete Activity C. You may wish to have students who are having difficulty with the material presented in this lesson work with partners who have a good understanding of these concepts.

Activity C Answers

1) Did . . . talk to Christa after the party **2)** Why did . . . leave early **3)** Maybe . . . was feeling sick **4)** After the party . . . called Elena **5)** was wrong **6)** needed her at home **7)** At the last minute . . . was called in to work **8)** babysits for her mother **9)** Usually . . . does not work on weekends **10)** Because of a computer problem . . . was needed in the office **11)** Luckily for Elena . . . was almost over

Reading Vocabulary

advice (5)	mileage (7)
conjunction	rust (5)

■ Presenting Activity D

Write the first item on the board. Help students identify the complete predicate. Then ask them to find the conjunction. Finally, have them find the verbs connected by the conjunction. If necessary, help students eliminate other parts of speech in the predicate to find the compound verb. Then have students complete Activity D.

Activity D Answers

1) looked at new cars but did not buy one **2)** cost too much and used too much gas **3)** got good gas mileage but remained out of his price range **4)** showed rust spots and needed repairs **5)** Should . . . buy that car or look some more **6)** thought about it but could not decide **7)** talked to him and gave him some advice **8)** would save some more money and look again in the spring

■ Presenting Activity E

Invite volunteers to provide sample oral sentences and ask the class to identify the verbs in each sentence. Then have students do Activity E on their own.

Activity E Answers

Each sentence should include compound verbs in the predicate. Each verb or verb phrase should be circled.

Learning Styles

Visual/Spatial

Give each pair that worked together on the Learning Styles activity on page 207 its picture and poster from that activity. On the board, print the following pattern: verb/adverb/prepositional phrase. Ask the pairs to write all the action verbs they see in their picture. Have them use these verbs to create complete predicates. Ask them to add these complete predicates to the list of complete subjects on their posters so as to create ten complete sentences. Note: Save the posters and pictures for use in the Learning Styles activity on page 214.

The verbs in the predicate part of the sentence can be compound. A compound verb is made up of one or more verbs that are joined by a conjunction such as *and, but,* or *or*. Compound verbs share the same subject.

Examples

The sun **moved** behind the cloud and **disappeared**.

The audience **clapped** and **cheered**.

They **looked** calm but **were** very nervous.

Activity D Write the complete predicate in each of these sentences on your paper. Underline the verb or verbs in the predicate.

1) Andy looked at new cars but did not buy one.

2) The big cars cost too much and used too much gas.

3) The small cars got good gas mileage but remained out of his price range.

4) The used cars showed rust spots and needed repairs.

5) Should he buy that car or look some more?

6) He thought about it but could not decide.

7) His parents talked to him and gave him some advice.

8) He would save some more money and look again in the spring.

Activity E Write five sentences with compound verbs in the predicate on your paper. Circle each verb or verb phrase in your sentences.

Lesson 3 Review

Part A Write these sentences on your paper. Underline the complete predicate in each sentence.

Examples Do you like apples?

On Sunday, we will pick apples.

You can pick from the bottom branches or use the ladder.

1) Will you come to our apple picking party this Sunday?
2) When does it start?
3) Around two o'clock, all of my relatives will arrive.
4) Usually, they talk for a while and then climb back into their cars.
5) The apple orchard is not far from our house.
6) We will walk around the orchard and pick apples.
7) Then everyone will return to my house for a huge fall dinner.
8) Can I bring anything?
9) Bring a big appetite!

Part B Write each of these sentences on your paper. Underline the complete predicate. Then circle each main verb or verb phrase.

1) In the spring, people think about outdoor activities.
2) Some of the neighbors are planting flowers.
3) I always know the first day of spring.
4) My neighbor Matt takes his fishing gear out.
5) Usually, he is out in his yard with his fishing rod.
6) He cleans his gear and practices his casting.
7) Every year, he goes on a fishing vacation.
8) He dreams about catching the big one.
9) Last year it got away.
10) Will this year be different?
11) He has already invited us to a fish dinner.

Reading Vocabulary

activity (6) gear (5)
appetite (5) relative (5)

Part A Answers

1) Will . . . come to our apple picking part this Sunday **2)** When does . . . start **3)** Around two o'clock . . . will arrive **4)** Usually . . . talk for a while and then climb back into their cars **5)** is not far from our house **6)** will walk around the orchard and pick apples **7)** Then . . . will return to my house for a huge fall dinner **8)** Can . . . bring anything **9)** Bring a big appetite

Part B Answers

The main verb or verbs are underlined in each answer.

1) In the spring . . . think about outdoor activities **2)** are planting flowers **3)** always know the first day of spring **4)** takes his fishing gear out **5)** Usually . . . is out in his yard with his fishing rod **6)** cleans his gear and practices his casting **7)** Every year . . . goes on a fishing vacation **8)** dreams about catching the big one **9)** Last year . . . got away **10)** Will . . . be different **11)** has already invited us to a fish dinner

Name Date Period

Chapter 10 Workbook Activity 42

A Sentence Has Two Parts

Directions: Find the subject of each sentence. Underline it once. Find the predicate of each sentence. Underline it twice.

EXAMPLES Spring is finally here!
(You) Find the subject and the predicate.
Several teachers and their classes went on a field trip.

HINT: These are simple sentences. All of the words will be either in the subject or the predicate.

1) All of the students enjoyed the trip.
2) Victor, please hurry.
3) Stop that noise!
4) The lady at the end of the line got the last ticket.
5) Everyone jumped out of the bus in a hurry.
6) No one knows the answer to that question.
7) The whole class tried out the new computer.
8) The best hitter on the team couldn't play.
9) Both Sue and Janet got to class on time.
10) Spring and fall are Ted's favorite seasons.
11) Darleen's dog, Tiny, is quite noisy.
12) Twelve dozen chocolate chip cookies were sold.
13) Did any one of you see my coat?
14) Here it is!
15) Now, where are my gloves?

 Basic English Grammar

Workbook Activity 42

Lesson at a Glance

Chapter 10 Lesson 4

Overview This lesson presents different types of sentences and explains their purposes.

Objectives

- To identify types of sentences.
- To write different types of sentences.

Student Pages 212–214

Teacher's Resource Library

Activity 30

Workbook Activities 43–44

Reading Vocabulary

request (6)

Teaching Suggestions

■ Introducing the Lesson Discuss each type of sentence presented in the text. Ask students for additional examples of each type and write them on the board. Have students tell you what end punctuation to use for each sentence.

■ Reviewing Skills Review the definition of a sentence.

Teacher Alert

You may wish to point out that sentences that show strong feeling are often called *exclamatory sentences* or *exclamations.*

Lesson 4 Kinds of Sentences

Every sentence has a purpose. A sentence can make a statement. A sentence can ask a question. A sentence can give a command or make a request. A sentence can show strong feelings.

Examples

Statement:	They went to the concert.
Question:	Are you going to the concert?
Command:	Go to the concert with them.
Strong feeling:	What a great concert that was!

A sentence that makes a statement usually begins with the subject. A statement ends with a period.

Example The **concert** began at eight o'clock.

A sentence that asks a question begins with either a helping verb or an interrogative pronoun or adverb. A question ends with a question mark.

Examples

Are you ready yet?	**Who** is she?
Did you like the music?	**Where** are my shoes?

A sentence that makes a command or request begins with a verb. The subject is understood to be the person spoken to. A command usually ends with a period. A strong command may end with an exclamation mark.

Examples

(You) Please **give** me two tickets.
(You) **Take** your medicine.
(You) **Do** it now!

Global Connection

In Spanish, an inverted question mark comes at the beginning of a question and an inverted exclamation point comes at the beginning of an exclamation. Regular end punctuation appears at the end of each type of sentence. To illustrate, write these sentences on the board or invite a student fluent in Spanish to do so: ¿Qué podemos hacer? (*What can we do?*) / ¡Claro que podrás! (*Of course you can!*)

Name Date Period *Chapter 10 Activity 30*

Interrogative Sentences

Interrogative sentences ask questions. Often questions are formed by putting the verb or part of the verb phrase before the subject. We also use interrogative pronouns and adverbs to form questions.

Examples
Statement — Heather **will be leaving** soon.
Question — **Will** Heather **be leaving** soon?
Interrogative pronoun — **Who** was she?
Interrogative adverb — **Where** are you going?

Directions: Find the subject and the predicate in each of these interrogative sentences. Underline the subject once and underline the predicate twice.

Examples
When are you leaving?
Are you ready?

1) Is this your book?
2) Who can help me?
3) Have you seen that show?
4) Why are you so concerned?
5) Will you be home for dinner?
6) Has anyone finished the project?
7) Do you feel tired?
8) When is the game going to be over?
9) Where did everyone go?
10) Is your car still in the garage?

 Basic English Grammar

Activity 30

A sentence that shows strong feeling or excitement ends with an exclamation mark.

EXAMPLES
I can't believe our team won!
What a great game that was!

Activity A Decide the purpose of each of these sentences. Write *S* on your paper if the sentence makes a statement. Write *Q* if the sentence asks a question. Write *C* if the sentence makes a command or request. Write *SF* if the sentence shows strong feelings or excitement.

1) Are you hungry?

2) I am starved!

3) We can eat at this restaurant.

4) Melissa and her parents had lunch here last week.

5) Do you know what you want?

6) Please order something for both of us.

7) I'm having the soup and sandwich special.

8) That sounds good to me.

9) What kind of sandwich would you like?

10) Decide quickly!

11) I'll have the tuna on dark rye.

12) Here is your check.

13) Has someone made a mistake?

14) This can't be the right amount!

15) Next time, we'll eat at my house.

Reading Vocabulary

restaurant (5) tuna (6)
rye (6)

Presenting Activity A

Before having students do Activity A on their own, invite volunteers to read each item aloud. Encourage readers to think about the words and use good oral expression as they read. Listeners should pay attention to the meaning of the words and the expression. This should help them determine the purpose of each sentence.

Activity A Answers

1) Q 2) SF 3) S 4) S 5) Q 6) C 7) S 8) S 9) Q 10) C/SF 11) S 12) S 13) Q 14) SF 15) S

APPLICATION

In the Community
Students who feel they have a good understanding of sentence structure and sentence purpose may enjoy sharing their knowledge with younger people in the community. Encourage students to volunteer at youth centers, daycare centers, and other organizations where they might work with school-age children to help them write short stories, letters, and simple articles. Students can also help review younger children's school writing assignments to check for complete sentences and correct capitalization and end punctuation.

Name ______ Date ______ Period ______

Chapter 10 Workbook Activity 43

Purposes of Sentences

Every sentence has a purpose.

Directions: Decide whether each sentence is a *request*, a *statement*, a *command*, or a *question*. Write the label on the line. Punctuate each sentence correctly. You may punctuate a command with an exclamation point if you think it expresses strong feeling.

HINT: Requests usually begin with "Please."

EXAMPLES
Where is the bus? *question*
Please shut the door. *request*
Peter ate some pickles. *statement*
Go away quietly. (or !) *command*

1) Does Joel know where we are ______

2) Mr. Nickelson has gone to the dentist ______

3) When do we leave ______

4) Please give Jesse back the book ______

5) Does Ben know you are here ______

6) Be very careful with the vase ______

7) We're having stew for supper ______

8) Did Diane win the math prize ______

9) Please sell lots of tickets ______

10) Run to the window ______

11) Darrell must be sleeping late ______

12) Did Teresa like the play ______

13) Don't forget your glasses ______

14) Please help Mr. Perkins ______

15) Answer my letter at once ______

16) Kathy is mowing the lawn ______

 Basic English Grammar

Workbook Activity 43

Sentences: Subjects and Predicates Chapter 10 **213**

Reading Vocabulary

mall terrific (5)

Part A Answers

Some answers may vary. Possible answers are given.

1) Listen to this new CD.—Request **2)** What a terrific sound that is!—Strong Feeling **3)** Where do you buy your CDs?—Question **4)** The music store at Crosstown Mall has the best prices.—Statement **5)** What is the average price of a tape or CD at the store near school?—Question **6)** Look at the ad in the paper.—Command **7)** That ad lists the prices of the most popular CDs.—Statement **8)** These must be the highest prices in town!—Strong Feeling **9)** Don't ever shop there!—Command/Strong Feeling **10)** I won't!—Strong Feeling

Part B Answers

Sentences will vary.

Learning Styles

Auditory/Verbal

Give each pair that worked together on the Learning Styles activity on page 210 its poster and picture. Have one partner read the complete subject of each of the ten sentences on the poster; have the other partner read the complete predicate. Ask the partners to name the purpose of each sentence—statement, question, command or request, strong feeling. Have the partners change three of their sentences into another purpose and read aloud these new sentences. Have the class state the purpose of each new sentence. Note: Save the posters and pictures for use in the Learning Styles activity on page 294.

Lesson 4 Review

Part A Write the following sentences on your paper. Add correct end marks. Beside each sentence, write its purpose *(Statement, Question, Command or Request, Strong Feeling).*

Example Jump now
Jump now!—Command

1) Listen to this new CD

2) What a terrific sound that is

3) Where do you buy your CDs

4) The music store at Crosstown Mall has the best prices

5) What is the average price of a tape or CD at the store near school

6) Look at the ad in the paper

7) That ad lists the prices of the most popular CDs

8) These must be the highest prices in town

9) Don't ever shop there

10) I won't

Part B Write an example of each kind of sentence listed below on your paper. Be sure to begin each sentence with a capital letter and end it with the correct mark.

1) a statement

2) a question

3) a command

4) a strong command

5) a request

6) a sentence that shows strong feeling or excitement

Name Date Period

Chapter 10 Workbook Activity 44

Interrogative Sentences

Interrogative sentences ask questions. Often questions are formed by putting the verb or part of the verb phrase before the subject.

EXAMPLE Statement — Becky will take French next year.
Question — Will Becky take French next year?

We also use interrogative pronouns and adverbs to form questions.

EXAMPLES Interrogative pronoun — Who was she?
Interrogative adverb — Where are you going?

Directions: Find the subject and the predicate in each of these interrogative sentences. Underline the subject once and underline the predicate twice.

EXAMPLES Where are you going?
Are you leaving soon?

1) Have you seen Billy?

2) Who is that?

3) Isn't that the new puppy's name?

4) Will your friend be staying for lunch?

5) Has anyone in this house seen my other tennis shoe?

6) Do you think the puppy dragged it under the sofa again?

7) Why don't you ask the dog?

8) Can't you ever give me a straight answer?

9) Is this your shoe?

10) How can I ever thank you?

 Basic English Grammar

Workbook Activity 44

Lesson 5 Simple and Compound Sentences

Simple sentence
A sentence that has one subject and one predicate and expresses a complete idea.

Independent clause
A group of words with a subject and a verb. An independent clause expresses a complete thought and can stand alone as a sentence.

Compound sentence
A sentence made up of two independent clauses joined by a conjunction such as and, but, *or* or.

A **simple sentence** has one subject and one predicate. A simple sentence is an **independent clause**, or a sentence that expresses a complete thought.

A **compound sentence** has two or more independent clauses joined together with a conjunction. Each clause has a subject and a predicate and expresses a complete idea. A comma usually comes before the conjunction in a compound sentence.

EXAMPLE

	Subject	Predicate
	Carlo	**took his car to the garage,**
Conj.	Subject	Predicate
and	**the mechanic**	**changed the oil.**

A compound sentence tells about two or more related events.

EXAMPLE

Correct: The car was old, but it still ran well.

Incorrect: The mechanic changed the oil, and gas costs a lot.

Remember that a simple sentence may have a compound subject or a compound verb. A compound sentence has two or more complete ideas, each with its own subject and verb.

Activity A Write these compound sentences on your paper. Circle the complete subject in each independent clause. Underline the complete predicate in each independent clause.

1) They were hungry, but all of the restaurants were closed.

2) Alice has a cat, Mike has a gerbil, and Sandy has a hamster.

3) Mr. Barry likes apples, but Mrs. Barry prefers pears and bananas.

4) Lori plays the piano, and her sister plays the flute.

5) Mrs. Castillo gives a lot of homework, but her tests are easy.

Lesson at a Glance

Chapter 10 Lesson 5

Overview This lesson presents simple and compound sentences.

Objectives

- To find subjects and predicates in compound sentences.
- To distinguish between simple and compound sentences.
- To write compound sentences.

Student Pages 215–217

Teacher's Resource Library

Workbook Activity 45

Reading Vocabulary

clause (7)
compound sentence
independent clause
mechanic (6)
relate (6)
simple sentence

Teaching Suggestions

Introducing the Lesson

After reading the text, write examples of a compound sentence and a simple sentence with a compound subject or compound predicate on the board, and discuss the distinction.

Reviewing Skills

Review complete subjects and predicates.

Presenting Activity A

Do Activity A orally as a class.

Activity A Answers

1) CS: They, all of the restaurants; CP: were hungry, were closed **2)** CS: Alice, Mike, Sandy; CP: has a cat, has a gerbil, has a hamster **3)** CS: Mr. Barry, Mrs. Barry; CP: likes apples, prefers pears and bananas **4)** CS: Lori, her sister; CP: plays the piano, plays the flute **5)** CS: Mrs. Castillo, her tests; CP: gives a lot of homework, are easy

Reading Vocabulary

punctuate (7) stomp
section (5)

■ Presenting Activity B

Before having students do the activity, invite volunteers to give examples of simple sentences with compound subjects, simple sentences with compound verbs, and compound sentences. Write each sentence on the board and have the class identify the complete subjects and complete predicates. Then have students do Activity B on their own.

Activity B Answers

1) S 2) S 3) C 4) C
5) S 6) C 7) C 8) S
9) C 10) S

■ Presenting Activity C

Write these sentences on the board: *The team was tired, but they played well anyway./A new restaurant opened in our neighborhood, and I like Thai food.* Help students identify the independent clauses in each sentence. Then ask students which sentence is correct and which is incorrect. Elicit that the ideas in the first sentence are related; the ideas in the second sentence are not. Then invite students to correct the second sentence by suggesting an independent clause that relates to one of the other clauses.

Activity C Answers

Each sentence should be a compound sentence.

Activity B Number your paper from 1 to 10. Beside each number, write *S* if the sentence is simple. Write *C* if it is compound.

1) Andrea and Michelle signed up for the play.

2) He goes fishing every spring but has never caught the big one.

3) The telephone rang three times, and then it stopped.

4) The girls hurried, but they were late anyway.

5) After school, we came right home and did our homework.

6) The driver stomped hard on the brakes, and the bus skidded.

7) I met Lydia at the corner, and we walked to school together.

8) My brother sold his car and bought a van.

9) Kate and two of her friends signed up for swimming lessons, but the class was full.

10) The Sunday newspaper has a section designed and written completely by teens.

Activity C Write five compound sentences. Be sure the ideas are related. Punctuate each sentence correctly.

216 *Chapter 10 Sentences: Subjects and Predicates*

Lesson 5 Review

Part A Number your paper from 1 to 6. Beside each number, write *S* if the sentence is simple. Write *C* if it is compound.

1) Paul plays on the basketball team and works part time at the grocery store.
2) He is an assistant manager in the deli.
3) The store manager hired him as a bagger, but Paul wanted more responsibility.
4) After two months, Mr. Alvarez and Paul talked.
5) Mr. Alvarez offered Paul the job in the deli, and Paul accepted it.
6) It meant more responsibility, but it also meant a raise in pay.

Part B On your paper, write whether the words in bold in these sentences show a *compound subject, compound verb,* or *independent clauses.*

1) Latisha **called me after school** and **asked for help with her project.**
2) **I met her at the library**, and **we went over the assignment.**
3) **Most of the students in the class were writing research papers**, but **she made a different decision.**
4) Latisha **was designing** and **building a model city.**
5) **One of our teachers** and **several of our classmates** were also at the library.
6) Andrea **spotted us** and **came over to our table.**
7) **Andrea, Latisha,** and **I** are in the same math class.
8) **We walked to the bus stop together**, but **Andrea did not get on the bus with Latisha and me.**
9) **Andrea lives close to the library**, so **she walked home.**
10) We **waved good-bye** and **then got on the bus.**

Reading Vocabulary

assignment (6) manager (6)
assistant (6) responsibility (6)

Part A Answers

1) S 2) S 3) C 4) S 5) C 6) C

Part B Answers

1) compound verb 2) independent clauses 3) independent clauses 4) compound verb 5) compound subject 6) compound verb 7) compound subject 8) independent clauses 9) independent clauses 10) compound verb

LEARNING STYLES

Logical/Mathematical

On the board, print the following headings: 1) compound subject, 2) compound verb, 3) compound sentence/two independent clauses. Invite each student to create three sentences that illustrate these three headings. Ask volunteers to read aloud one or more of their sentences. Call on other volunteers to go to the board and check the heading each sentence represents. Next, call out two subjects or two verbs and ask volunteers to use these to create sentences for the three headings.

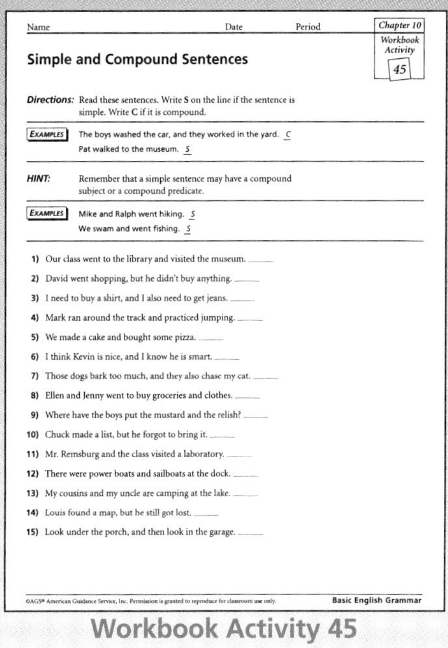

Name Date Period

Chapter 10 Workbook Activity 45

Simple and Compound Sentences

Directions: Read these sentences. Write **S** on the line if the sentence is simple. Write **C** if it is compound.

EXAMPLES The boys washed the car, and they worked in the yard. C
Pat walked to the museum. S

HINT: Remember that a simple sentence may have a compound subject or a compound predicate.

EXAMPLES Mike and Ralph went hiking. S
We swam and went fishing. S

1) Our class went to the library and visited the museum. ____
2) David went shopping, but he didn't buy anything. ____
3) I need to buy a shirt, and I also need to get jeans. ____
4) Mark ran around the track and practiced jumping. ____
5) We made a cake and bought some pizza. ____
6) I think Kevin is nice, and I know he is smart. ____
7) Those dogs bark too much, and they also chase my cat. ____
8) Ellen and Jenny went to buy groceries and clothes. ____
9) Where have the boys put the mustard and the relish? ____
10) Chuck made a list, but he forgot to bring it. ____
11) Mr. Remsburg and the class visited a laboratory. ____
12) There were power boats and sailboats at the dock. ____
13) My cousins and my uncle are camping at the lake. ____
14) Louis found a map, but he still got lost. ____
15) Look under the porch, and then look in the garage. ____

 Basic English Grammar

Workbook Activity 45

Chapter 10 Review

The Teacher's Resource Library includes two parallel forms of the Chapter 10 Mastery Test. The difficulty level of the two forms is equivalent. You may wish to use one form as a pretest and the other form as a posttest.

Reading Vocabulary

comic (6) talent (5)

Part A Answers

Some answers will vary. Possible responses are given.

1) S **2)** As usual, each of the boys on the team showed up early. **3)** Practicing at four instead of three on Monday was an inconvenience. **4)** Because of some changes in the team, everyone was confused during practice. **5)** S

Part B Answers

Some answers may vary. Possible responses are given.

1) Listen to this!—Command/Strong Feeling **2)** She laughed at his joke.—Statement **3)** That was so funny!—Strong Feeling **4)** Please tell that joke to LeeAnn.—Request 5) Are you really hoping to be a stand-up comic?—Question **6)** How exciting that would be!—Strong Feeling **7)** Many people try but don't make it.—Statement **8)** Experience and talent are the key to success.—Statement **9)** Is there a school for stand-up comics?—Question **10)** Find out about it.—Command

Chapter 10 Review

Part A For each item below, write *S* on your paper if the group of words is a sentence. If the group of words is not a sentence, copy it onto your paper and add words to make a complete sentence.

1) The ball landed in the field.
2) As usual, each of the boys on the team.
3) Practicing at four instead of three on Monday.
4) Because of some changes in the team.
5) How does it feel to have a winning record?

Part B Write the following sentences on your paper. Add the correct end marks. Beside each sentence, write its purpose (*Statement, Question, Command or Request, Strong Feeling*).

1) Listen to this
2) She laughed at his joke
3) That was so funny
4) Please tell that joke to LeeAnn
5) Are you really hoping to be a stand-up comic
6) How exciting that would be
7) Many people try but don't make it
8) Experience and talent are the key to success
9) Is there a school for stand-up comics
10) Find out about it

Name Date Period | *Chapter 10 Mastery Test A page 1*

Chapter 10 Mastery Test A

Part A Write *S* if the words are a sentence. Write *NS* if the words are not a sentence.

1) ______ Before you start the test.
2) ______ We stopped at the store.
3) ______ We bought groceries.
4) ______ When Sheelah gets home.
5) ______ On the day of the victory celebration.
6) ______ Mr. Nguyen tilled the field for planting.
7) ______ Although we were tired.
8) ______ Ed and his friend are coming to dinner.
9) ______ The red-berried elder is lovely this year.
10) ______ After the play at the theater.

Part B In each sentence, underline the complete subject. Circle the nouns or pronouns in each subject.

1) Irene and I do not agree about that.
2) Neither the television nor the radio was working.
3) Grandfather and the entire family had to go out for dinner.
4) Our friends Howard and Heidi live in a walk-up.
5) Everything in the freezer thawed out.

Part C In each sentence, underline the complete predicate. Circle the verb or verb phrase in each predicate.

1) The storm had knocked out the electrical power.
2) No one had electricity or telephones for three days.
3) My neighbor fly casts in summer and ice fishes in winter.
4) The highway crews are working day and night to plow the roads.
5) My aunt and he have been married for years.

 Basic English Grammar

Name Date Period | *Chapter 10 Mastery Test A page 2*

Chapter 10 Mastery Test A, continued

Part D Identify the purpose of each sentence. Write *Statement, Question, Command/Request,* or *Feeling.*

1) Who was that masked man? ______
2) Tell me about your vacation. ______
3) We drove to the North Shore last week. ______
4) I am all worn out! ______
5) When do you think you will be back here? ______
6) Please take out the garbage. ______
7) I am so excited! ______
8) Drop this off at the mail box. ______
9) Do you think the gates will be open yet? ______
10) The first day of spring is March 20. ______

Part E Draw a line between the complete subject and the complete predicate in each independent clause.

1) Jo plays the drums, and her mother plays the banjo.
2) A motorcycle is not as expensive as a car, but it is trusty transportation.
3) We stopped at the mall, and we came home after that.
4) Donna has not had any piano lessons, but she plays very well.
5) Deion is coming for dinner, and he is bringing the salad.
6) The roads looked dry and clear, but the black ice fooled us.
7) Talk radio is popular in America, and many people listen.
8) Listeners call the stations, and they express their opinions.
9) I like Elton John's music, but Mike prefers Bobby McFerrin's.
10) English is Andrea's favorite class, but her twin sister's favorite class is math.

 Basic English Grammar

Chapter 10 Mastery Test A

Part C Write each sentence on your paper. Underline the complete subject once and the complete predicate twice. Circle the simple subject and the verb or verb phrase. Remember that the simple subject and the verb can be compound.

1) The car sputtered and came to a stop.
2) What was that strange noise?
3) After a few seconds, the rattling noise stopped, too.
4) His parents and the man at the gas station had warned him about this.
5) Don't buy the car!
6) He did not take their advice and bought the car.
7) Some of his friends did not agree with his decision either.
8) At first, everything was fine.
9) Yesterday, he had driven all the way to Parker City without a problem.
10) Today was a different story.

Part D Write each sentence on your paper. Beside each sentence write whether it is *simple* or *compound*. Then underline the complete subject once and the complete predicate twice in each independent clause.

Example We drove to the lake on Sunday, and Maria's family came on Monday.—compound

1) Each summer, the two families vacation together.
2) All of them look forward to this vacation, and none of them would miss it.
3) The Dawsons live in the city, but the Ortegas live only a short drive from the lake.
4) Mrs. Ortega and Mrs. Dawson met in college, and they have remained friends since then.
5) Their children have known each other all their lives and get along well.

Test Taking Tip

If you know you will be asked to label parts of a sentence on an English test, write sample sentences. Then practice identifying sentence parts.

Reading Vocabulary

decision (5) sputter (5)

Part C Answers

1) CS: The car, SS: car; CP: sputtered and came to a stop, V: sputtered, came **2)** CS: What, SS: What; CP: was that strange noise, V: was **3)** CS: the rattling noise, SS: noise; CP: After a few seconds . . . stopped, too, V: stopped **4)** CS: His parents and the man at the gas station, SS: parents, man; CP: had warned him about this, V: had warned **5)** CS: you (understood), SS: you (understood); CP: Don't buy the car, V: do buy **6)** CS: He, SS: He; CP: did not take their advice and bought the car, V: did take, bought **7)** CS: Some of his friends, SS: Some; CP: did not agree with his decision either, V: did agree **8)** CS: everything, SS: everything; CP: At first...was fine, V: was **9)** CS: he, SS: he; CP: Yesterday . . . had driven all the way to Parker City without a problem, V: had driven **10)** CS: Today, SS: Today; CP: was a different story, V: was

Part D Answers

1) Each summer, the two families vacation together.—simple **2)** All of them look forward to this vacation, and none of them would miss it.—compound **3)** The Dawsons live in the city, but the Ortegas live only a short drive from the lake.—compound **4)** Mrs. Ortega and Mrs. Dawson met in college, and they have remained friends since then.—compound **5)** Their children have known each other all their lives and get along well.—simple

Name Date Period | *Chapter 10 Mastery Test B page 1*

Chapter 10 Mastery Test B

Part A Write *S* if the words are a sentence. Write *NS* if the words are not a sentence.

1) ______ You may begin the test.
2) ______ After the sun sets.
3) ______ When Harvey gets home.
4) ______ The juice bottle was empty.
5) ______ The clock needs to be set.
6) ______ Although the winter has been long.
7) ______ The mountains are clothed in spring colors.
8) ______ Before the rooster crows in the morning.
9) ______ Unless Alicia finds her keys.
10) ______ The dogwood bursts into bloom.

Part B In each sentence, underline the complete subject. Circle the nouns or pronouns in each subject.

1) Mr. Alwin and his English class went to the play.
2) Either the shovel or the hoe can be used.
3) Lucy and all her children are coming.
4) The boys in the scout troop sold magazines.
5) All of the trees were trimmed.

Part C In each sentence, underline the complete predicate. Circle the verb or verb phrase in each predicate.

1) The wind had blown over all of the lawn furniture.
2) We will be planting tomatoes, spinach, and carrots.
3) Steve composes music and writes the words for songs.
4) We are volunteering our time at the food shelf this week.
5) Sarah got together and visited with her friends from France.

 Basic English Grammar

Name Date Period | *Chapter 10 Mastery Test B page 2*

Chapter 10 Mastery Test B, continued

Part D Identify the purpose of each sentence. Write *Statement, Question, Command/Request,* or *Feeling.*

1) Please let me borrow your book. ______
2) Have you taken your dog for a walk? ______
3) That pie tastes wonderful! ______
4) The lake has a dangerous drop-off. ______
5) I'm so hungry. ______
6) Will you join us at the museum? ______
7) Tell me about what you need. ______
8) The assignment is due next week. ______
9) Run over to Aunt Dora's house for me. ______
10) When is the first day of summer? ______

Part E Draw a line between the complete subject and the complete predicate in each independent clause.

1) Kirby plays right field, and Kent plays first base.
2) We were going to the beach, but we got company.
3) Hoa has a computer science degree, and she got a job with a software company.
4) The sky is clear and sunny, but the temperature is below zero.
5) Akin had a cold, and he stayed home.
6) The rent went up, but we didn't hear about it for a month.
7) CDs are popular, and they are better than tapes.
8) Good cooks try new recipes, and their efforts please their guests.
9) Shana likes the beach, but her family likes the mountains.
10) I wanted to go to a movie, but I had to work.

 Basic English Grammar

Chapter 10 Mastery Test B

Chapter 11

Planning Guide

Sentences Patterns

	Student Text Lesson: Student Pages	Vocabulary	Practice Exercises	Lesson Review
Lesson 1 Pattern 1 Sentences	222-230		✔	230
Lesson 2 Pattern 2 Sentences	231-240	✔	✔	240
Lesson 3 Pattern 3 Sentences	241-247	✔	✔	247
Lesson 4 Pattern 4 Sentences	248-251	✔	✔	251

Chapter Activities

Teacher's Resource Library

Community Connection 11: Sentence Patterns in the Newspaper

Diagramming Activities 1-4

Assessment Options

Student Text

Chapter 11 Review

Teacher's Resource Library

Chapter 11 Mastery Tests A and B

Teaching Strategies							Language Skills			Learning Styles						Teacher's Resource Library		
Reviewing Skills	Teacher Alert	Follow-up Activity	Career Application	Home Application	Global Connection	Community Application	Identification Skills	Writing Skills	Punctuation Skills	Visual/Spatial	Auditory/Verbal	Body/Kinesthetic	Logical/Mathematical	Group Learning	LEP/ESL	Activities	Workbook Activities	Self-Study Guide
222	229					228	✔	✔	✔					230				✔
231			238	237			✔	✔	✔			235				31-33	46-47	✔
241	241						✔	✔	✔						242			✔
248					249		✔	✔	✔			248					48	✔

Chapter at a Glance

Chapter 11: Sentence Patterns pages 220–253

Teacher's Resource Library

- **Activities** 31–33
- **Workbook Activities** 46–48
- **Diagramming Activities** 1–4
- **Community Connection** 11
- **Chapter 11 Self-Study Guide**
- **Chapter 11 Mastery Tests A and B**

(Answer Keys for the Teacher's Resource Library begin on page 330 of this Teacher's Edition.)

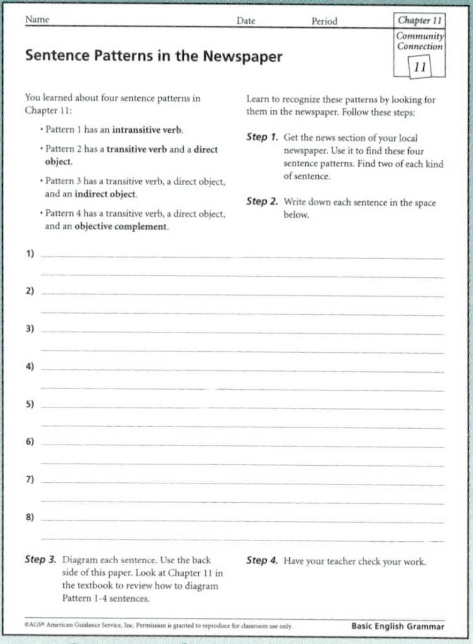

Name Date Period

Chapter 11 Community Connection 11

Sentence Patterns in the Newspaper

You learned about four sentence patterns in Chapter 11:

- Pattern 1 has an **intransitive verb**.
- Pattern 2 has a **transitive verb** and a **direct object**.
- Pattern 3 has a transitive verb, a direct object, and an **indirect object**.
- Pattern 4 has a transitive verb, a direct object, and an **objective complement**.

Learn to recognize these patterns by looking for them in the newspaper. Follow these steps:

Step 1. Get the news section of your local newspaper. Use it to find these four sentence patterns. Find two of each kind of sentence.

Step 2. Write down each sentence in the space below.

1) ____________________

2) ____________________

3) ____________________

4) ____________________

5) ____________________

6) ____________________

7) ____________________

8) ____________________

Step 3. Diagram each sentence. Use the back side of this paper. Look at Chapter 11 in the textbook to review how to diagram Pattern 1-4 sentences.

Step 4. Have your teacher check your work.

 Basic English Grammar

Community Connection 11

Chapter 11

Sentence Patterns

If you do any sewing or woodworking, you know that a pattern often is used as the model for an article you want to make. Languages have patterns, too.

The English language has only a few basic sentence patterns. This chapter focuses on four of those patterns.

Goals for Learning

- To identify transitive and intransitive verbs in sentences
- To identify the parts of sentences with intransitive verbs
- To identify the parts of sentences with direct and indirect objects
- To identify the parts of sentences with subject complements
- To diagram sentences correctly from each of the four sentence patterns
- To diagram sentences with adverbs, adjectives, and prepositional phrases
- To diagram compound sentences

221

Reading Vocabulary

basic (7)
woodworking
identify (6)

Introducing the Chapter

Display the parts of a sewing or woodworking pattern for students to examine. Invite students who sew and do woodworking to explain how patterns are used, or explain yourself. Then ask students why it might be important to use a pattern to make a dress or build a cabinet. Elicit that a pattern determines the way an object turns out. It guarantees, in a way, that the dress and the cabinet will serve their purpose the way the seamstress and the cabinetmaker intended. Then point out that sentences have patterns, too. Writers use different sentence patterns for different purposes to achieve different effects. Explain that by the end of Chapter 11, students will recognize different sentence patterns and learn how to diagram them to show how their parts go together.

SELF-STUDY GUIDE

Name ______________

CHAPTER 11: Sentence Patterns

Goal 11.1 *To diagram sentences with adverbs, adjectives, and prepositional phrases and other Pattern 1 sentences*

Date	Assignment	Score
______	1: Read pages 221-222. Complete Activity A on page 222. Read page 223. Complete Activities B-C on page 223.	______
______	2: Read page 224. Complete Activities D-F on page 224. Read page 225. Complete Activity G on page 225.	______
______	3: Complete Activities H-I on page 226. Read page 227. Complete Activity J on page 227.	______

Comments:

Goal 11.2 *To diagram compound sentences*

Date	Assignment	Score
______	4: Read pages 228-229. Complete Activity K on page 229.	______
______	5: Complete the Lesson 1 Review, Parts A-B on page 230.	______

Comments:

Goal 11.3 *To identify direct objects and transitive and intransitive verbs in sentences*

Date	Assignment	Score
______	6: Read page 231. Complete Activity A on page 231. Read page 232. Complete Activities B-C on page 232.	______
______	7: Complete Workbook Activity 46.	______
______	8: Complete Workbook Activity 47.	______
______	9: Read page 233. Complete Activities D-E on page 233. Read page 234. Complete Activities F-G on page 234.	______
______	10: Read page 235. Complete Activities H-I on page 235. Read page 236. Complete Activity J on page 236.	______

Comments:

Goal 11.4 *To diagram Pattern 2 sentences*

Date	Assignment	Score
______	11: Read pages 237-239. Complete Activity K on page 239.	______
______	12: Complete the Lesson 2 Review, Parts A-B on page 240.	______

Comments:

 Basic English Grammar

SELF-STUDY GUIDE

Name ______________

CHAPTER 11 Sentence Patterns, continued

Goal 11.5 *To identify the parts of sentences with indirect objects*

Date	Assignment	Score
______	13: Read page 241. Complete Activity A on page 241. Read page 242. Complete Activities B-C on page 242.	______
______	14: Read page 243. Complete Activities D-E on page 243. Read page 244. Complete Activity F on page 244.	______
______	15: Read page 245. Complete Activities G-H on page 245.	______

Comments:

Goal 11.6 *To diagram Pattern 3 sentences*

Date	Assignment	Score
______	16: Read page 246. Complete Activity I on page 246.	______
______	17: Complete the Lesson 3 Review, Parts A-B on page 247.	______

Comments:

Goal 11.7 *To identify the parts of sentences with subject complements*

Date	Assignment	Score
______	18: Read page 248. Complete Activity A on page 248.	______
______	19: Complete Activities B-C on page 249.	______

Comments:

Goal 11.8 *To diagram Pattern 4 sentences*

Date	Assignment	Score
______	20: Read page 250. Complete Activity D on page 250.	______
______	21: Complete the Lesson 4 Review, Parts A-B on page 251.	______
______	22: Complete Workbook Activity 48.	______
______	23: Complete the Chapter 11 Review, Parts A-D on pages 252-253.	______

Comments:

Student's Signature ______________ Date ______________

Instructor's Signature ______________ Date ______________

 Basic English Grammar

Chapter 11 Self-Study Guide

Lesson at a Glance

Chapter 11 Lesson 1

Overview This lesson introduces simple Pattern 1 sentences and diagramming.

Objectives

- To identify the subject and verb in Pattern 1 sentences.
- To write Pattern 1 sentences.
- To diagram Pattern 1 sentences.

Student Pages 222–230

Teacher's Resource Library

Diagramming Activity 1

Reading Vocabulary

adjective	phrase (6)
adverb	subject (5)

Teaching Suggestions

Introducing the Lesson

Discuss the definition of Pattern 1 sentences, emphasizing that all the words in a Pattern 1 sentence are either part of the subject or part of the predicate, or verb.

Reviewing Skills

Review the terms simple and complete subject and simple and complete predicate.

Presenting Activity A

Write these sentences on the board: *Marie laughed. / The dog under the chair is sleeping.* Help students identify the complete subject and verb in each sentence and draw a line between the subject and verb. Then review the example provided for Activity A before having students complete Activity A on their own.

Activity A Answers

1) ball / bounced
2) friend / moved
3) Donna / laughed
4) They / were 5) block / are

Lesson 1 Pattern 1 Sentences

Pattern 1 sentences are the simplest kind of sentence pattern. They can express a complete thought with just a subject and verb or verb phrase.

Pattern 1 Sentence: Subject + Verb

EXAMPLES

S V
Sue smiled.

S V
The sun was shining.

Activity A Write each of these Pattern 1 sentences on your paper. Draw a line between the subject and the verb.

Example The dog / was barking.

1) The ball bounced.

2) My best friend moved.

3) Donna laughed.

4) They were singing.

5) The people on our block are meeting.

Pattern 1 sentences may have adjectives and adverbs. An adjective describes a noun or a pronoun. An adverb tells about the verb. In a Pattern 1 sentence, an adverb may come at the beginning of a sentence or between the helping verb and the main verb.

EXAMPLES

Adj. Adj. S V
The newborn kitten purred.

S Adv. V Adv.
Mr. Edmonds often arrives early.

Adv. S V Adv.
Usually, Nina is late.

Activity B Copy these Pattern 1 sentences onto your paper. Write *S* above the subject, *V* above the verb or verb phrase, *Adj.* above any adjectives, and *Adv.* above any adverbs.

Example **Adj. S V Adv.**
The fire was burning brightly.

1) Victor can run fast.
2) That little baby is always smiling.
3) Alison practices often.
4) The old radio works.
5) Yesterday it rained hard.

Activity C Write a Pattern 1 sentence with each of these verbs on your paper. Underline the complete subject once and the complete predicate twice in each sentence.

1) go
2) ask
3) work
4) laugh
5) walk
6) cry
7) fall
8) scream
9) think

A Pattern 1 sentence may have a prepositional phrase. The prepositional phrase may be an adjective phrase that describes the subject. It may be an adverb phrase that tells about the verb.

EXAMPLE

S Adj. Phrase V
The boy behind me coughed.
(Which boy? The one behind me)

S V Adv. Phrase
Sue is walking to the store.
(Where is Sue walking? *to the store*)

Reading Vocabulary
cough (5)
predicate
prepositional
underline

■ Presenting Activity B
After discussing the example, write item 1 on the board. Help students identify and label the sentence parts. Then have students work with partners to complete the remaining items in the activity.

Activity B Answers
1) Victor (S), can run (V), fast (Adv.) **2)** That (Adj.), little (Adj.), baby (S), is smiling (V), always (Adv.) **3)** Alison (S), practices (V), often (Adv.) **4)** The (Adj.), old (Adj.), radio (S), works (V) **5)** Yesterday (Adv.), it (S), rained (V), hard (Adv.)

■ Presenting Activity C
Invite volunteers to write sentences for the first three verbs on the board. Encourage the class to identify the complete subject and complete predicate in each sentence. Then have students complete Activity C independently.

Activity C Answers
Each sentence should include the complete subject underlined once and the complete predicate underlined twice.

Reading Vocabulary
audience (5)

Presenting Activity D
Write these phrases on the board: *in the park, at home, from Mexico.* Have students make up a sentence for each phrase, making sure students have at least one sentence with an adverb phrase and one with an adjective phrase. After discussing the sentences, have students complete Activity D on their own.

Activity D Answers
1) Jaimie / went to school **2)** DeLeo / works at the post office **3)** on the corner / closed **4)** from Ohio / are visiting for two weeks **5)** of flowers / fell from the porch

Presenting Activity E
Discuss the example given for Activity E. Then have students tell whether the word(s) in bold in each of the activity items is the subject or the verb. Have students complete Activity E on their own.

Activity E Answers
Sentences will vary. Students should add the following kinds of words and phrases to each item.

1) adverb **2)** adjective and adverb **3)** adverb **4)** adjective **5)** adverb **6)** adjective and adverb **7)** adverb **8)** adjective

Presenting Activity F
Invite volunteers to give examples of Pattern 1 sentences before having students complete Activity F.

Activity F Answers
Each sentence should be a Pattern 1 sentence.

Activity D Write each of these Pattern 1 sentences on your paper. Draw a line between the complete subject and complete predicate. Underline the prepositional phrase or phrases in each sentence.

Example Everyone in the audience / laughed at the clown.

1) Jaimie went to school.

2) Mr. DeLeo works at the post office.

3) The gas station on the corner closed.

4) Our friends from Ohio are visiting for two weeks.

5) The pot of flowers fell from the porch.

Activity E Write these Pattern 1 sentences on your paper. Add adjectives and adjective phrases if the subject is bold. Add adverbs and adverb phrases if the verb is bold. Add both if the subject and verb are bold.

Example The girl **walked.**
The girl walked **quickly to the store.**

1) The dog **barked.**

2) **A flower grew.**

3) The boys **left.**

4) **The woman** listened.

5) They **ate.**

6) **Snow fell.**

7) We **talked.**

8) **Roberto** is running.

Activity F Write ten Pattern 1 sentences on your paper.

Remember, a Pattern 1 sentence:

- must have a subject and a verb
- may have an adjective, an adverb, or both
- may have a prepositional phrase

224 *Chapter 11 Sentence Patterns*

A Pattern 1 sentence may ask a question. Part of the verb may help to form the question and come at the beginning of the sentence.

EXAMPLES

S V
Who is driving?

V S V
Is the baby crying?

Activity G Write these Pattern 1 sentences on your paper. Circle the subject. Underline the verb or verb phrase.

1) Has Mario written?

2) Which book fell off the shelf?

3) Where does Mr. Davis work?

4) Is Annette still practicing?

5) Are you listening to the radio?

6) Did anyone call?

7) Who whistled?

A Pattern 1 sentence may have a compound subject.

EXAMPLE **Sue** and **Rita** will sing next.

A Pattern 1 sentence may have a compound verb.

EXAMPLE The band **will march** and **play** in a parade.

Two Pattern 1 sentences may be joined with a conjunction to form a compound sentence.

EXAMPLE Mrs. Nelson laughed at the joke, **but** Mr. Nelson only smiled.

Reading Vocabulary

compound (6) conjunction

Presenting Activity G

Before having students complete Activity G on their own, encourage them to work with a partner to write a Pattern 1 sentence that is a question. Invite students to share their sentences and have the class identify the verb or verb phrase in each sentence.

Activity G Answers

1) Mario (S), Has written (V) **2)** book (S), fell (V) **3)** Mr. Davis (S), does work (V) **4)** Annette (S), Is practicing (V) **5)** you (S), Are listening (V) **6)** anyone (S), Did call (V) **7)** Who (S), whistled (V)

Reading Vocabulary

director (7) respond (6)

Presenting Activity H

Depending on the needs of your class, you may wish to do Activity H together, or you may have students work on their own.

Activity H Answers

1) The book and the pencil fell on the floor. book/pencil—simple subjects; fell—verb **2)** Marilyn was laughing one minute and crying the next. Marilyn—simple subject; was laughing/crying—verbs **3)** Lisa and Rico were on time, but Alex wasn't. Lisa/Rico, Alex—simple subjects; were, wasn't—verbs **4)** Clarissa studied for her test, and then she went right to sleep. Clarissa, she—simple subjects; studied, went—verbs **5)** The actors and director came on stage for a final bow, but the writer stayed behind the curtain and listened to the applause. actors, director, writer—simple subjects; came, stayed, listened—verbs

Presenting Activity I

After discussing the example, do the first two or three items together as a class. Then have students complete Activity I on their own.

Activity I Answers

1) band (S), played (V) **2)** Mrs. Draper (S), drove (V) **3)** Everyone (S), laughed (V) **4)** student (S), responded (V) **5)** dog (S), Is barking (V) **6)** Several (S), cried (V) **7)** bike (S), rides (V) **8)** He (S), asked (V) **9)** you (S), Are leaving (V) **10)** band (S), will travel, play (V)

Activity H The following Pattern 1 sentences have a compound subject or a compound verb. Some sentences are compound. Write each sentence on your paper. Then follow these directions for each sentence:

- First, underline the complete subject or subjects once.
- Then, circle the simple subjects.
- Next, underline the complete predicate or predicates twice.
- Then, circle the verbs or verb phrases.

1) The book and the pencil fell on the floor.

2) Marilyn was laughing one minute and crying the next.

3) Lisa and Rico were on time, but Alex wasn't.

4) Clarissa studied for her test, and then she went right to sleep.

5) The actors and director came on stage for a final bow, but the writer stayed behind the curtain.

Activity I Write these Pattern 1 sentences on your paper. Write *S* above the simple subject. Write *V* above the verb or verb phrase.

Example

S V
The Spanish teacher listened closely to her students.

1) The band played loudly at the dance.

2) Mrs. Draper drove off in a hurry.

3) Everyone laughed loudly at the joke.

4) Which student responded to the question?

5) Is your dog barking at my cat again?

6) Several of the people cried during the movie.

7) Emilio's new bike rides smoothly.

8) He asked about the job.

9) Are you leaving for school soon?

10) Our band will travel to Florida and play in front of a large crowd.

226 *Chapter 11 Sentence Patterns*

Diagramming Pattern 1 Sentences

A sentence diagram is a picture of a sentence that helps us see the parts of the sentence more clearly. When you write a sentence, you put different parts of a sentence together. When you diagram, you separate the parts of the sentence to see how they are put together.

To diagram a Pattern 1 sentence, follow steps 1–3.

1. Find the simple subject and the simple predicate (verb or verb phrase) in the sentence.

EXAMPLE The small **kitten** with the black stripe **purred** softly in my arms.

2. Write the simple subject and the simple predicate on a horizontal line.
3. Draw a short vertical line between the subject and predicate.

EXAMPLE

Kitten | purred

Activity J Diagram these simple Pattern 1 sentences.

Example Pedro has been working.

Pedro | has been working.

1) Snow fell.

2) Susan is smiling.

3) Music had been playing.

Reading Vocabulary

diagram (6) separate (5)
horizontal (7) vertical (6)

■ Presenting Activity J

Review the example diagram in the text and the example given for Activity J. Ask students to explain why *Pedro* is to the left of the vertical line and *has been working* is to the right of the line. Be sure students understand that *Pedro* is the simple subject and *has been working* is the simple predicate, or verb. Have students identify the subject and verb in each of the activity items before having them diagram the sentences on their own.

Activity J Answers

1) Snow | fell

2) Susan | is smiling

3) Music | had been playing

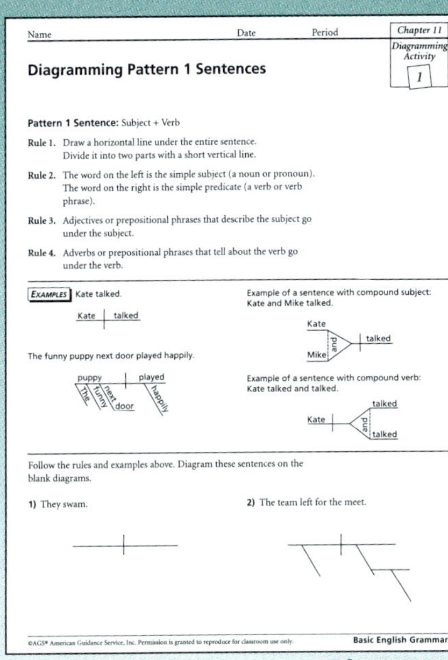

Name Date Period

Chapter 11 *Diagramming Activity* 1

Diagramming Pattern 1 Sentences

Pattern 1 Sentence: Subject + Verb

Rule 1. Draw a horizontal line under the entire sentence. Divide it into two parts with a short vertical line.

Rule 2. The word on the left is the simple subject (a noun or pronoun). The word on the right is the simple predicate (a verb or verb phrase).

Rule 3. Adjectives or prepositional phrases that describe the subject go under the subject.

Rule 4. Adverbs or prepositional phrases that tell about the verb go under the verb.

EXAMPLES Kate talked.

Kate | talked

The funny puppy next door played happily.

puppy | played (The, funny, next door; happily)

Example of a sentence with compound subject: Kate and Mike talked.

Kate and Mike | talked

Example of a sentence with compound verb: Kate talked and talked.

Kate | talked and talked

Follow the rules and examples above. Diagram these sentences on the blank diagrams.

1) They swam.

2) The team left for the meet.

©AGS® American Guidance Service, Inc. Permission is granted to reproduce for classroom use only. **Basic English Grammar**

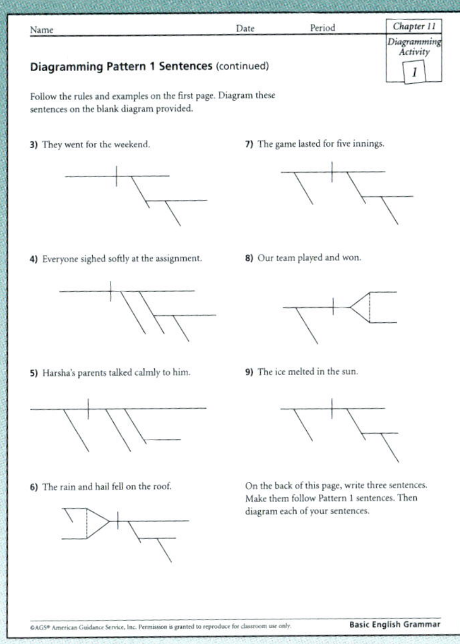

Name Date Period

Chapter 11 *Diagramming Activity* 1

Diagramming Pattern 1 Sentences (continued)

Follow the rules and examples on the first page. Diagram these sentences on the blank diagram provided.

3) They went for the weekend.

4) Everyone sighed softly at the assignment.

5) Harsha's parents talked calmly to him.

6) The rain and hail fell on the roof.

7) The game lasted for five innings.

8) Our team played and won.

9) The ice melted in the sun.

On the back of this page, write three sentences. Make them follow Pattern 1 sentences. Then diagram each of your sentences.

©AGS® American Guidance Service, Inc. Permission is granted to reproduce for classroom use only. **Basic English Grammar**

Diagramming Activity 1

Reading Vocabulary
preposition

Application

In the Community
A diagram provides a graphic explanation of how the parts of a whole are related. Encourage students who volunteer in community service organizations to investigate areas in which a diagram might help volunteers understand and perform their duties more efficiently. Students might also examine how diagrams might be useful to the people that a specific organization serves. For example, a carefully labeled diagram of city hall and other public buildings might be helpful for senior citizens or new members of the community.

To diagram more complex Pattern 1 sentences, follow these steps.

1. Put the adjectives and prepositional phrases that describe the subject below the subject.
2. Place adjectives on slanted lines.
3. Put the preposition on a slanted line and its object on a horizontal line. Put any words that describe the object of the preposition on slanted lines below it.
4. Put the adverbs and prepositional phrases that describe the verb below the verb.
5. Place adverbs on slanted lines.

EXAMPLE

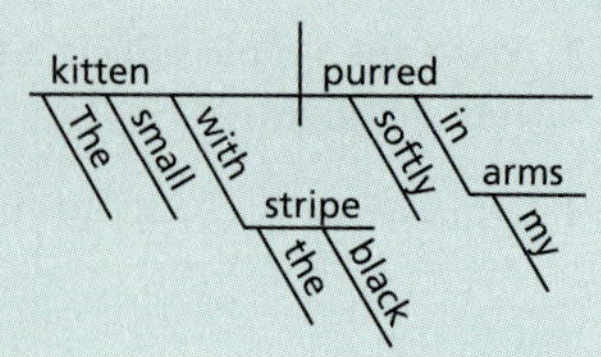

Some Pattern 1 sentences have compound subjects and compound verbs. Some Pattern 1 sentences are compound sentences. These sentences are diagrammed in a special way.

EXAMPLE Compound subject: **Elise** and **Vanessa** sang.

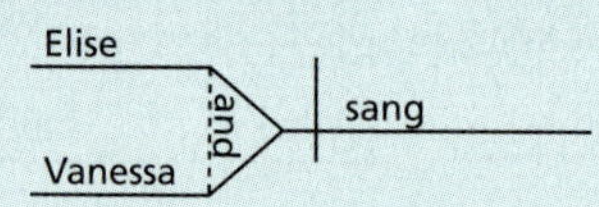

EXAMPLES Compound verb: They **arrived** early and **are sitting** in the den.

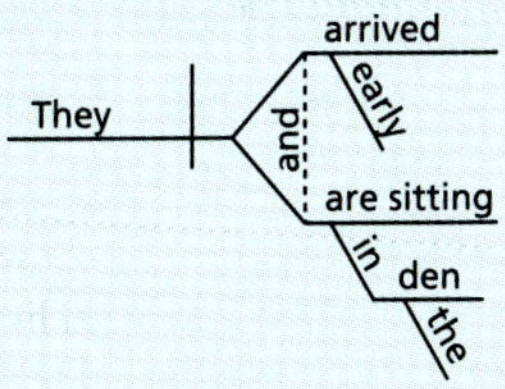

Compound sentence: **Jon walked slowly**, but **we ran ahead.**

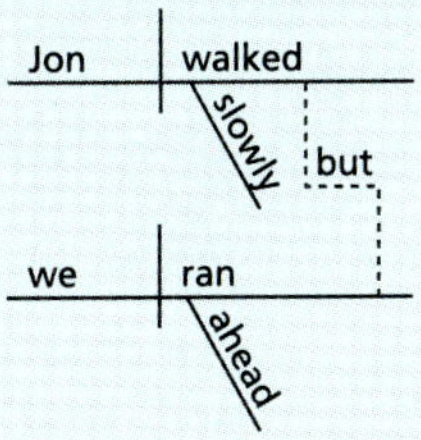

Activity K Diagram these Pattern 1 sentences on your paper. Follow the directions for diagramming that begin on page 227.

1) The school band returned late on Sunday.

2) Everyone on the bus was laughing and singing.

3) Students and parents had been gone for a week.

4) Photographers were everywhere, and reporters wrote quickly.

5) Band members beamed happily into the camera.

6) That group picture was taken after the first event.

TEACHER ALERT

This may be a good opportunity to review coordinating conjunctions. Use the diagram for item 4 to point out that in a compound sentence, the conjunction is a connector and not part of either of the subjects or predicates.

Reading Vocabulary

photograph (6)

Presenting Activity K

Diagram the first item in Activity K as a class. Draw the baseline on the board. Invite volunteers to write in the different parts of the diagram as the class identifies them, beginning with the simple subject and verb. Then suggest that students work with partners to complete Activity K.

Activity K Answers

1)

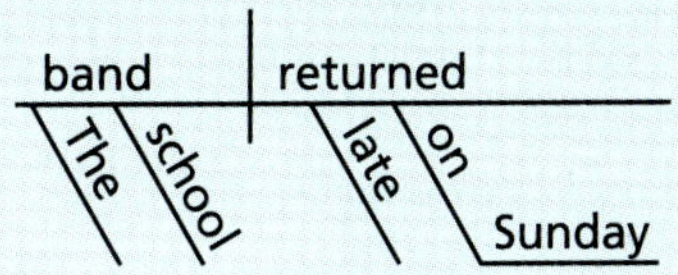

2)

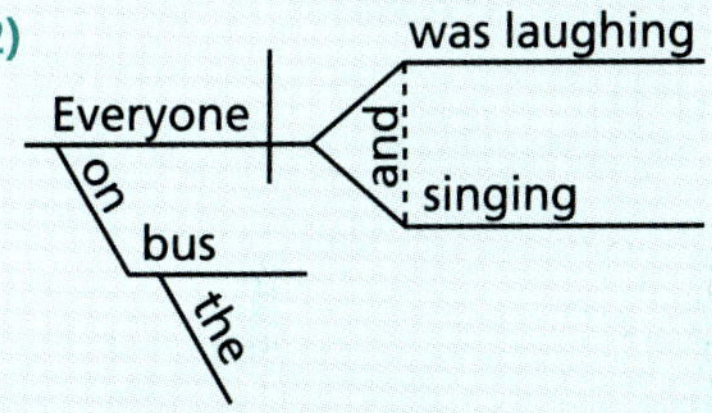

3)

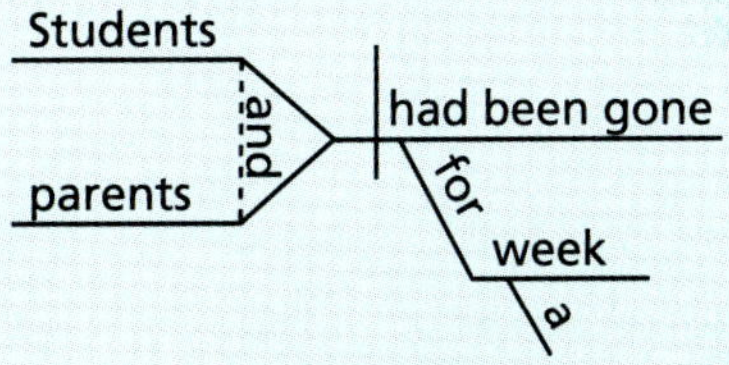

4)

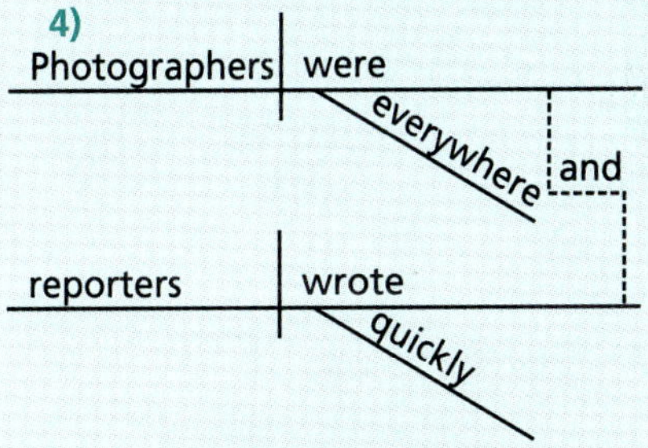

5)

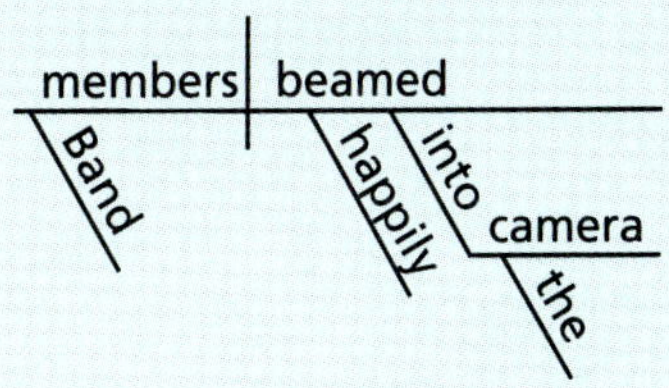

6)

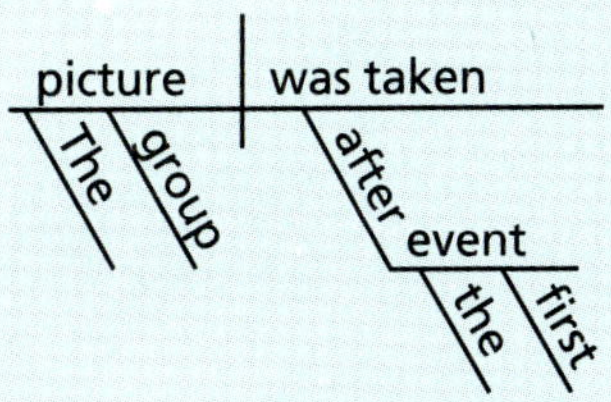

Reading Vocabulary

graduate (6) restaurant (5)
recently (5)

Part A Answers

1) Which students are in the band room? **2)** Everyone in the band will ride on the bus.
3) My trumpet fell on the floor.
4) Luckily, it did not break.
5) Ramon is waiting for you.
6) Is your book under my desk?
7) Liz and her friend from Dallas are eating at my favorite restaurant. **8)** Have you looked for a job recently? **9)** They will stay in school and graduate.
10) We have been practicing and preparing for this trip for a long time.

Part B Answers

1)

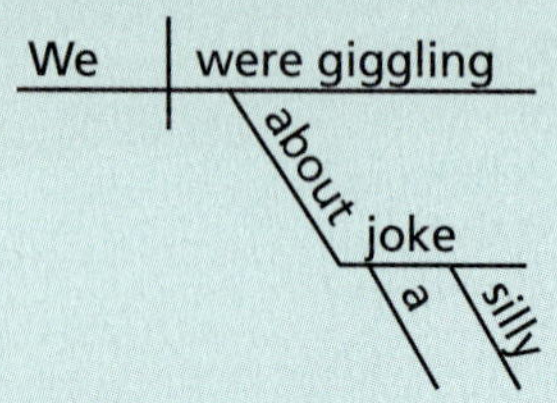

2)

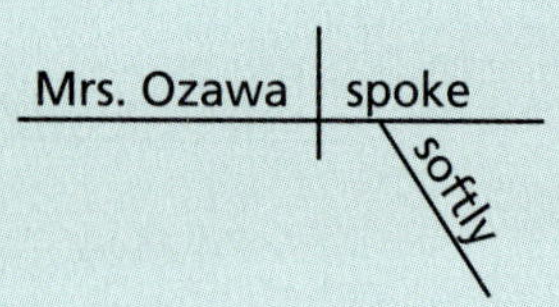

3)

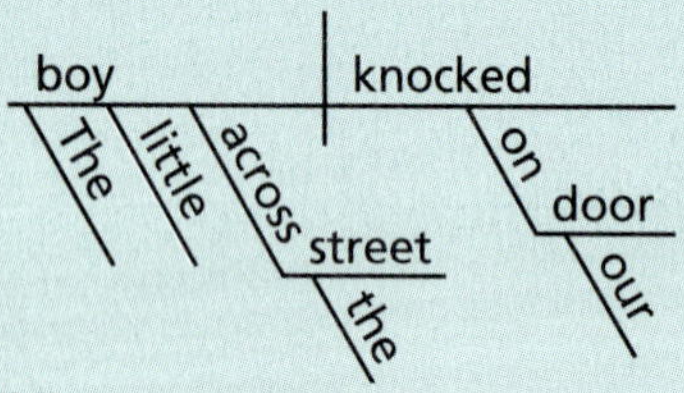

4)

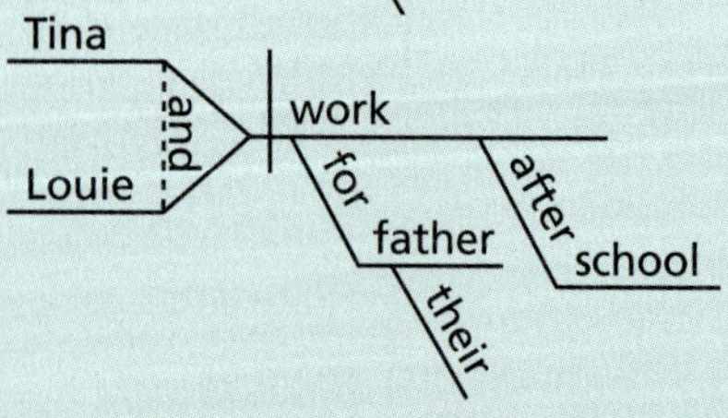

5)

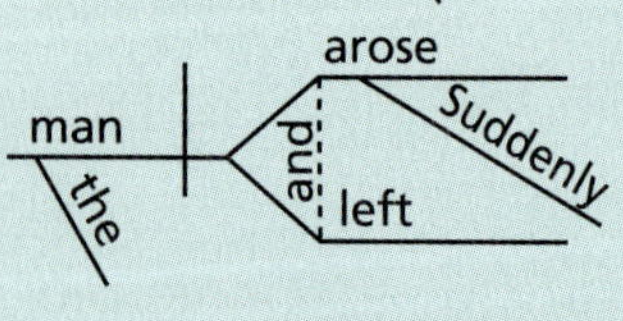

6)

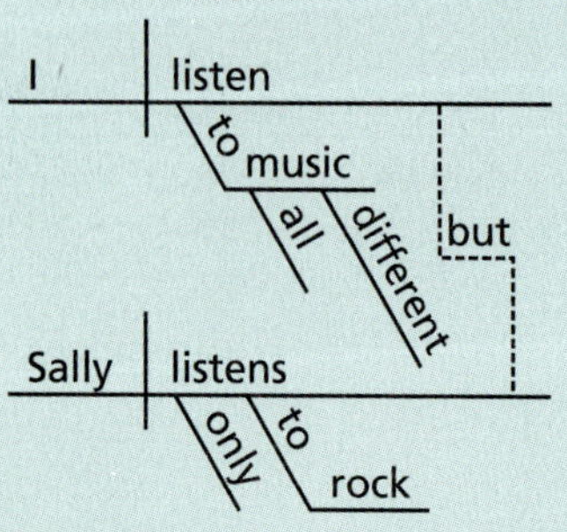

Lesson 1 Review

Part A Write each of these Pattern 1 sentences on your paper. Underline the complete subject once and the complete predicate twice.

1) Which students are in the band room?

2) Everyone in the band will ride on the bus.

3) My trumpet fell on the floor.

4) Luckily, it did not break.

5) Ramon is waiting for you.

6) Is your book under my desk?

7) Liz and her friend from Dallas are eating at my favorite restaurant.

8) Have you looked for a job recently?

9) They will stay in school and graduate.

10) We have been practicing and preparing for this trip for a long time.

Part B Diagram these Pattern 1 sentences.

1) We were giggling about a silly joke.

2) Mrs. Ozawa spoke softly.

3) The little boy across the street knocked on our door.

4) Tina and Louie work for their father after school.

5) Suddenly, the man arose and left.

6) I listen to all different music, but Sally listens only to rock.

230 *Chapter 11 Sentence Patterns*

Learning Styles

Interpersonal/ Group Learning

Determine how many groups of three are in your class. Then create a diagram pattern for each group. (Use the patterns on pages 227–229.) Give each group one pattern and challenge the group to create a sentence that will fit its diagram pattern. Afterward, have each group print its sentence on the board. Challenge the students to diagram each sentence.

Lesson 2 Pattern 2 Sentences

Transitive verb

A verb that shows action passed from the subject of the sentence toward a person or thing.

Intransitive verb

A verb that does not transfer action from the subject to an object.

Direct object

A noun or pronoun that receives the action from a transitive verb.

The two main kinds of verbs are **transitive** and **intransitive.** A transitive verb transfers the action from the subject of a sentence to another person or thing. The person or thing that receives the action is the **direct object.** The direct object is a noun or pronoun.

EXAMPLES John **threw** the **ball.**
(What did John throw? He threw the ball.)

The coach has **changed pitchers** again.
(What has the coach changed? He has changed pitchers.)

An intransitive verb does not have a direct object. The action is not transferred from the subject to another person or thing. A Pattern 1 sentence has an intransitive verb.

EXAMPLES She **is laughing.** The fire **burned.**

A Pattern 2 sentence contains a transitive verb and a direct object. The direct object of the verb is always a noun or pronoun.

Pattern 2 Sentence: Subject + Verb + Direct Object

EXAMPLE

S	V	D.O.
Mr. Allen	made	dinner.

Activity A Write the direct object in each of these sentences on your paper. The verb is in bold.

1) He **found** it.

2) Rosa **took** notes.

3) The teacher **praised** him.

4) The farmer **planted** corn.

Name Date Period | *Chapter 11* *Activity* 31

Direct Objects of Transitive Verbs

A sentence with a transitive verb must have a direct object. The object is a noun or pronoun.

Directions: The transitive verb in each of these sentences is in bold. Circle the direct object.

EXAMPLES Mr. Cooper **opened** the door quickly.
Marty **completed** the exam in one hour.

1) Robin **threw** the softball.
2) Aunt Elizabeth **ate** the entire apple pie!
3) Sam and Susan **watched** the scary movie.
4) The horse **pawed** the ground.
5) Our drama club **will enter** the competition.
6) Jim **wants** spaghetti for dinner.
7) Grandma **sold** her sewing machine.
8) The weatherman **drew** clouds on the map.
9) Carpenters **use** thousands of nails.
10) Mr. Harris **bought** a new car.
11) Mark **writes** articles for the school newspaper.
12) Mrs. Walker **taught** that lesson on Wednesday.
13) Patrick **hit** the ball into center field.
14) The repairman **fixed** the broken heater.
15) Jill **finished** her exercises quickly.

 Basic English Grammar

Activity 31

Name Date Period | *Chapter 11* *Activity* 32

Understanding Intransitive Verbs

An action verb can be either transitive or intransitive. A state-of-being verb is always intransitive.

Directions: The intransitive verb in each sentence is in bold print. Decide whether it is an action verb or a state-of-being verb. Circle the type of verb that is in each sentence.

EXAMPLES		
Cindy **ate** the entire gallon of ice cream.	(Action)	Being
Cindy **is** the treasurer of our club.	Action	(Being)

1) Yesterday **was** beautiful.	Action	Being
2) The stove **is** cool now.	Action	Being
3) The casserole **smells** good.	Action	Being
4) The kitten **cried** all night.	Action	Being
5) **Talk** with us.	Action	Being
6) Everyone **smiled.**	Action	Being
7) Tomorrow **is** our last day.	Action	Being
8) I **walked** to the store.	Action	Being
9) He **is** a big eater.	Action	Being
10) The day **will end** soon.	Action	Being
11) She **was** late for class.	Action	Being
12) The class **laughed** at my funny drawing.	Action	Being
13) My friends **care** very much.	Action	Being
14) This card **is** the best.	Action	Being
15) Only Leslie **appeared** upset.	Action	Being

 Basic English Grammar

Activity 32

Lesson at a Glance

Chapter 11 Lesson 2

Overview This lesson explains transitive and intransitive verbs and introduces Pattern 2 sentences and direct objects.

Objectives

- To identify direct objects in Pattern 2 sentences.
- To write Pattern 2 sentences.
- To diagram Pattern 2 sentences.

Student Pages 231–240

Teacher's Resource Library

Activities 31–33

Workbook Activities 46–47

Diagramming Activity 2

Reading Vocabulary

direct object
intransitive verb
transitive verb

Teaching Suggestions

Introducing the Lesson

Discuss the definitions and the text with students. Provide several more examples of sentences with transitive and intransitive verbs and have students distinguish between the two types. Before proceeding to the activities in the lesson, encourage students to ask questions about the information presented in the text.

Reviewing Skills

Review action verbs, nouns, pronouns, adjectives, and adverbs.

Presenting Activity A

Write these Pattern 2 sentences on the board and work with students to identify the direct object in each sentence: *That artist paints flowers. / Ali will like you. / Lightning struck the house.* Then have students complete Activity A on their own.

Activity A Answers

1) it 2) notes 3) him 4) corn

Reading Vocabulary

describe (5) objective (7)
include (5) wallet (6)

■ Presenting Activity B

Before having students complete Activity B on their own, help them identify the adjectives that describe the direct object in each sentence. If necessary, point out that *mom's* in item 3 is a possessive noun. After students complete Activity B, invite them to share their answers with the class.

Activity B Answers

1) wallet **2)** supper **3)** car **4)** house **5)** song

■ Presenting Activity C

Have students take turns completing each of the following sentences with a pronoun in the objective form: I met ________. / The teacher chose ________. / Maria found ________. Suggest that students refer to the chart on page 232 before responding. Then, have students complete Activity C on their own.

Activity C Answers

1) him **2)** her **3)** them **4)** us **5)** me

Adjectives may be used to describe nouns used as direct objects.

EXAMPLE
S V Adj. Adj. D.O.
Hector sold his old guitar.

Activity B Write the direct object in each of these sentences on your paper. The verb is in bold. Do not include adjectives.

1) Len **lost** his wallet.
2) They **ate** an early supper.
3) He **is washing** his mom's car.
4) The people next door **are painting** their house.
5) She **sang** a beautiful song.

When a pronoun is the direct object, it is always in the objective form.

Forms of Personal Pronouns		
Singular	**Subject**	**Object**
First person	I	me
Second person	you	you
Third person	he	him
	she	her
	it	it
Plural		
First person	we	us
Second person	you	you
Third person	they	them

EXAMPLE
S V D.O.
Marco drove them to school.

Activity C Write the pronoun on your paper that should appear in each sentence to make it correct. Remember that a pronoun used as a direct object is always in the objective form.

1) Did you see (he, him)?
2) Fred saw (she, her) at the library.
3) Before he put on his sneakers, he cleaned (they, them).
4) Tina helped (we, us) with our math homework.
5) He likes (I, me).

Name Date Period *Chapter 11 Activity 33*

Transitive and Intransitive Verbs

A transitive verb has a direct object. An intransitive verb does not have a direct object.

EXAMPLES Transitive — The cat **ate** a gold fish.
Intransitive — She **laughed** happily.

Directions: The verb in each sentence is in bold print. Decide whether it is transitive or intransitive. Underline the objects of the transitive verbs. Circle the type of verb that is in the sentence.

1) The paper **is** on the table. Transitive Intransitive
2) My sister **left** in September. Transitive Intransitive
3) The cheerleaders **will win** the competition. Transitive Intransitive
4) Sue **rode** home with a friend. Transitive Intransitive
5) They **named** the dog Winston. Transitive Intransitive
6) He **is studying** for an exam. Transitive Intransitive
7) She **sold** candy bars at school. Transitive Intransitive
8) The radio **was** too loud. Transitive Intransitive
9) They **painted** the car blue. Transitive Intransitive
10) We **will stay** after work until it's finished. Transitive Intransitive
11) **Take** the letter to the post office. Transitive Intransitive
12) The soccer team **wants** new uniforms. Transitive Intransitive
13) My mom **made** oatmeal raisin cookies. Transitive Intransitive
14) **Stop calling** me that name! Transitive Intransitive
15) We **want** to see that movie. Transitive Intransitive

 Basic English Grammar

Activity 33

Name Date Period *Chapter 11 Workbook Activity 46*

Understanding Intransitive Verbs

An action verb can be either transitive or intransitive. A state-of-being verb is always intransitive.

Directions: The intransitive verb in each sentence is in bold print. Decide whether it is an action verb or a state-of-being verb. Circle the type of verb that is in each sentence.

1) Today **is** lovely. Action Being
2) The sky **darkened**. Action Being
3) **Play** with me please. Action Being
4) The puppy **barked** all night. Action Being
5) It**'s** the sad truth. Action Being
6) Everyone **laughed**. Action Being
7) Wow, that pie **smells** good! Action Being
8) The oven **is** still warm. Action Being
9) Tonight **is** our last softball game of the season. Action Being
10) We **will win** for sure. Action Being
11) Our scorekeeper **was** late. Action Being
12) Oh, well. Who **cares**? Action Being
13) The first batter **walked** to first base. Action Being
14) The second batter **is** a big hitter. Action Being
15) The hard-hit ball **sailed** over the fence. Action Being

 Basic English Grammar

Workbook Activity 46

Activity D Create three columns on your paper with the headings *Subject, Verb,* and *Direct Object.* Then identify the simple subject, the verb, and the direct object in each sentence and write them in the correct column.

Example My Aunt Anita rented a small apartment.

Subject	Verb	Direct Object
Aunt Anita	rented	apartment

1) The cat chased the mouse.

2) I have been studying a new language.

3) The brave firefighters climbed the ladders.

4) Mr. Cha loves that old song!

5) We did not see her.

The complete predicate of a Pattern 2 sentence must have a verb and an object. It may also have an adverb.

EXAMPLES

Adv. S V D.O.
Luckily, Sandy found her notebook.

S V D.O. Adv.
Matt saw a great movie yesterday.

S Adv. V D.O.
I just found it.

Activity E Write the complete predicate in each of these sentences on your paper. (HINT: Find the complete subject first. All of the words left over are in the predicate.)

1) Leon bought his tickets early.

2) You can make dinner now.

3) Kevin ate his dinner quickly.

4) She just woke up.

5) Yesterday Dan lost his favorite baseball cap.

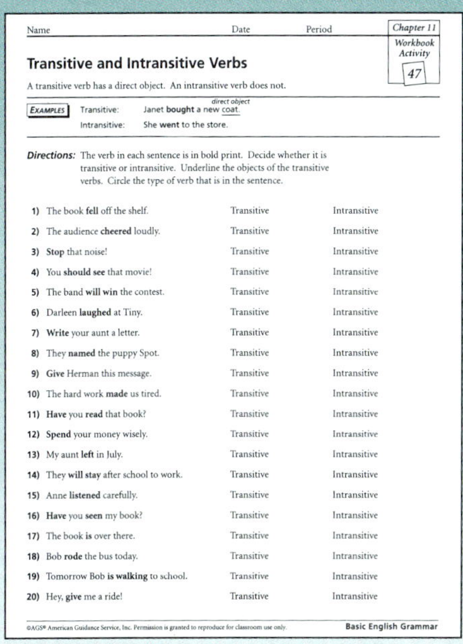

Name Date Period

Chapter 11 *Workbook Activity* 47

Transitive and Intransitive Verbs

A transitive verb has a direct object. An intransitive verb does not.

EXAMPLES Transitive: Janet **bought** a new coat. (direct object)
Intransitive: She **went** to the store.

Directions: The verb in each sentence is in bold print. Decide whether it is transitive or intransitive. Underline the objects of the transitive verbs. Circle the type of verb that is in the sentence.

1) The book **fell** off the shelf.	Transitive	Intransitive
2) The audience **cheered** loudly.	Transitive	Intransitive
3) **Stop** that noise!	Transitive	Intransitive
4) You **should see** that movie!	Transitive	Intransitive
5) The band **will win** the contest.	Transitive	Intransitive
6) Darleen **laughed** at Tiny.	Transitive	Intransitive
7) **Write** your aunt a letter.	Transitive	Intransitive
8) They **named** the puppy Spot.	Transitive	Intransitive
9) **Give** Herman this message.	Transitive	Intransitive
10) The hard work **made** us tired.	Transitive	Intransitive
11) **Have** you **read** that book?	Transitive	Intransitive
12) **Spend** your money wisely.	Transitive	Intransitive
13) My aunt **left** in July.	Transitive	Intransitive
14) They **will stay** after school to work.	Transitive	Intransitive
15) Anne **listened** carefully.	Transitive	Intransitive
16) **Have** you **seen** my book?	Transitive	Intransitive
17) The book **is** over there.	Transitive	Intransitive
18) Bob **rode** the bus today.	Transitive	Intransitive
19) Tomorrow Bob **is walking** to school.	Transitive	Intransitive
20) Hey, **give** me a ride!	Transitive	Intransitive

 Basic English Grammar

Workbook Activity 47

Reading Vocabulary

column (5) firefighters

Presenting Activity D

You may wish to do this activity together as a class. If so, draw a chart on the board with the headings, *Subject, Verb,* and *Direct Object.* Then invite volunteers to fill in the chart as students identify the subject, verb, and direct object in each sentence.

Activity D Answers

1) cat (S), chased (V), mouse (D.O.) **2)** I (S), have been studying (V), language (D.O.) **3)** firefighters (S), climbed (V), ladders (D.O.) **4)** Mr. Cha (S), loves (V), song (D.O.) **5)** We (S), did see (V), her (D.O.)

Presenting Activity E

Remind students that adverbs may come anywhere in a sentence. Then write this sentence on the board: *Tomorrow, Erica is starting a new job.* Ask students to find the complete predicate in the sentence and to identify the different parts of the complete predicate. Then have students complete Activity E on their own.

Activity E Answers

1) bought his tickets early **2)** can make dinner now **3)** ate his dinner quickly **4)** just woke up **5)** Yesterday . . . lost his favorite baseball cap

The predicate part of a Pattern 2 sentence may have a prepositional phrase that tells about the verb, the direct object, or both.

EXAMPLES

S V D.O. Prep. Phrase
Sabrina ate tacos for dinner.
(*For dinner* is an adverb phrase that tells about the verb *ate*. When did Sabrina eat tacos? *for dinner.*)

S V D.O. Prep. Phrase
Sabrina ate both tacos on her dish.
(*On her dish* is an adjective phrase that describes *tacos.* Which tacos? the ones *on her dish.*)

Adv. Phrase S V D.O. Adj. Phrase
After dinner, we played a game of Monopoly.
(When did they play? *after dinner*. What kind of game? *of Monopoly.*)

Activity F Write the complete predicate in each of these sentences on your paper. Then underline the verb once and the direct object twice. Circle each prepositional phrase. Draw an arrow from the prepositional phrase to the word it tells about.

Example Tómas painted the house on the corner on Friday.

painted the house (on the corner) (on Friday.)

1) Carol wrote a letter to her uncle Albert.
2) Sara bought the blue sneakers with the white trim.
3) He carried the two bags of groceries into the house.
4) Before school, we fed the fish in the tank.

Activity G Write Pattern 2 sentences for each verb below on your paper. Each sentence must have a subject, a verb, and an object. You may also add adjectives, adverbs, and prepositional phrases.

1) break	**4)** dig	**7)** catch
2) make	**5)** freeze	**8)** spend
3) bought	**6)** chase	**9)** played

Reading Vocabulary

Monopoly (7) tacos

■ Presenting Activity F

Review the example given for Activity F, making sure that students understand the directions and what they are to do. Students may enjoy completing this activity in small groups on chart paper or on the board. Encourage students to discuss each item before writing their answers.

Activity F Answers

Prepositional phrases are bracketed. Words they modify appear in parentheses.

1) wrote a letter <to her uncle Albert> (letter) **2)** bought the blue sneakers <with the white trim> (sneakers) **3)** carried the two bags <of groceries> (bags) <into the house> (carried) **4)** <Before school> (fed) . . . fed the fish <in the tank> (fish)

■ Presenting Activity G

Invite volunteers to give sample Pattern 2 sentences for the first three items in Activity G before having students complete the activity on their own.

Activity G Answers

Each Pattern 2 sentence should include a subject, a verb, and an object.

234 *Chapter 11 Sentence Patterns*

Pattern 2 sentences may be questions. In some questions that begin with the interrogative pronouns *who, which,* and *what,* the direct object of the verb begins the sentence. Remember, also, that in questions, part of the verb may come before the subject to help form the question.

EXAMPLES

D.O. V S V
What did you see? (You did see what.)

V S V D.O.
Did I see a deer at the window? (I did see a deer.)

Activity H Find the verb or verb phrase and the direct object in each sentence. Write them on your paper. If you are not sure which word is the direct object, try turning the question into a statement.

1) Have you read that article?
2) Whom did she ask to the dance?
3) May I have a piece of pizza?
4) What will he do after graduation?
5) Which of these do you want?

Pattern 2 sentences may also be commands or requests. Remember that the subject of a command or request is always understood to be *you.* The word *you* may or may not appear.

EXAMPLES

V D.O.
Finish your dinner.

V D.O.
Clear the table, please.

Activity I Write each of these sentences on your paper. Circle the verb. Underline the direct object.

1) Take this book to the library.
2) Make vegetable soup for supper, please.
3) Complete your essay at home.
4) Hang your coat in the closet.
5) Have some more soup.

Reading Vocabulary

essay (6) interrogative
graduation (6) request (6)

■ Presenting Activity H

Before having students complete Activity H, work with them to turn each question into a statement. Write the statements on the board or suggest that students write them on their papers.

Activity H Answers

1) Have read (V), article (D.O.)
2) did ask (V), Whom (D.O.)
3) May have (V), piece (D.O.)
4) will do (V), what (D.O.)
5) do want (V), Which (D.O.)

■ Presenting Activity I

Encourage students to provide additional examples of Pattern 2 sentences that are commands or requests. Write the sentences on the board and have the class check that 1) the sentences are commands or requests and 2) they are Pattern 2 sentences with a verb and a direct object. Then have students complete Activity I independently.

Activity I Answers

1) Take (V), book (D.O.)
2) Make (V), soup (D.O.)
3) Complete (V), essay (D.O.)
4) Hang (V), coat (D.O.)
5) Have (V), soup (D.O.)

LEARNING STYLES

Body/Kinesthetic
On the board, print the following pattern: subject/predicate/direct object/prepositional phrase. Ask volunteers to use classroom objects to demonstrate this pattern and to create a sentence that represents the doer of the action, the action, the receiver of the action, and a prepositional phrase that describes the receiver. (For example, a student might pick up a book and say, "Tom picked up a book from the floor." Or a student might open a window and say, "Mary opened the window on the south wall.")

Sentence Patterns Chapter 11 **235**

Reading Vocabulary

clause (7) contents (6)
community (5) independent (6)

■ **Presenting Activity J** Ask students if they have any questions about the information presented in the text. Then discuss the example provided for Activity J. Depending on the needs of your students, you may wish to complete Activity J orally as a class.

Activity J Answers

1) compound object—book, one 2) compound verb—enjoyed, left 3) compound object—wallet, contents 4) compound sentence—LeeAn bought the dress on Monday, she returned it on Tuesday 5) compound verb—saves, uses 6) compound object—piano, violin 7) compound verb—Complete, bring 8) compound sentence—Tim has a part-time job, he also takes classes at the community college

A Pattern 2 sentence may have a compound verb and a compound object. You may join two Pattern 2 sentences together with a conjunction to make a compound sentence.

EXAMPLES		
	Compound verb:	We **cooked** and **served** dinner.
	Compound direct object:	She will play **basketball** or **soccer**.
	Compound sentence:	**I saw Paul**, but **he didn't have my book**.

Each part of the compound verb may have its own direct object.

EXAMPLE

S V D.O. V D.O
We made the pizza and put it in the oven.

Activity J Read each of these Pattern 2 sentences. Write on your paper whether the sentence has a compound verb, has a compound object, or is a compound sentence. Then write the compound verb, compound object, or two independent clauses.

Example We made supper and then cleaned the kitchen.
compound verb—made, cleaned

1) Are you reading that book or this one?
2) We enjoyed the party but left early.
3) They returned the wallet and its contents to the owner.
4) LeeAn bought the dress on Monday, but she returned it on Tuesday.
5) She saves most of her pay for college and uses the rest for spending money.
6) Virginia plays the piano and the violin.
7) Complete the test and bring it to me.
8) Tim has a part-time job; however, he also takes classes at the community college.

Diagramming Pattern 2 Sentences

To diagram a Pattern 2 sentence:

1. Identify the subject, verb, and direct object.
2. Place the object on the baseline with the subject and verb.
3. Draw a short vertical line to separate the verb and the direct object.

EXAMPLE We carefully slid the two loaves of bread into the oven.

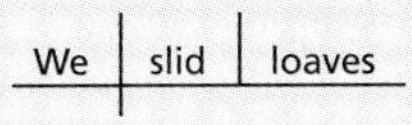

4. Put each adverb, adjective, or prepositional phrase under the word it is describing or telling about.

EXAMPLE

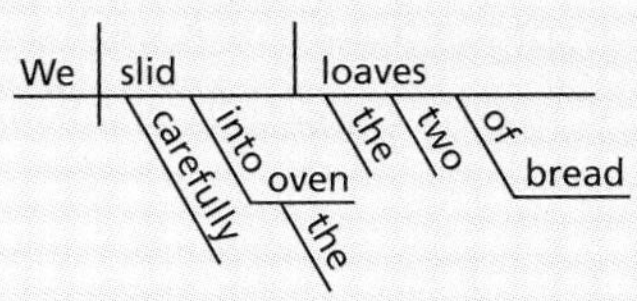

5. Show the understood subject of a command or a request in parentheses.

EXAMPLE Change that flat tire quickly.

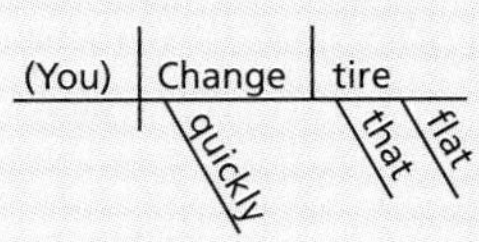

Reading Vocabulary

baseline
parentheses
loaves (5)

Application

At Home

A family tree is a kind of diagram that shows how the parts of a family are related. Encourage students to work with family members to create a family tree. As students work on their family trees, suggest that they keep a journal of the steps they followed. Then invite students to share their personal experiences with the class. Students may wish to combine their experiences to create a list of guidelines for creating a family tree to duplicate and share with others.

Sentence Patterns Chapter 11 **237**

Application

Career Connection
Many different kinds of diagrams are used in the workplace. Being able to read a diagram can be a helpful and even essential skill for some occupations and professions. For example, many construction workers, plumbers, and electricians must be able to read diagrams in order to complete a project; architects must be able to draw and understand diagrams to design houses; car mechanics must be able to read and understand diagrams in automobile manuals in order to make certain repairs; and so on. Engage students in a discussion about different careers they hope to pursue and the types of diagrams they might use in these careers. If possible, provide examples of different diagrams for students to examine and discuss.

6. If the sentence is a question, change it into a statement. Then draw the diagram.

EXAMPLE Did you find your coat? You did find your coat.

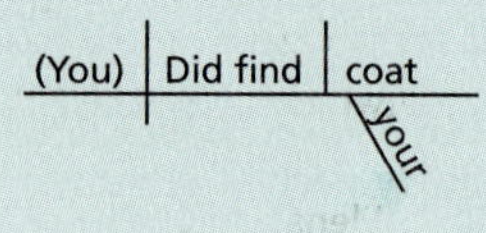

7. Diagram Pattern 2 sentences that have compound verbs or compound objects like this.

EXAMPLES He washed and wiped the dishes.

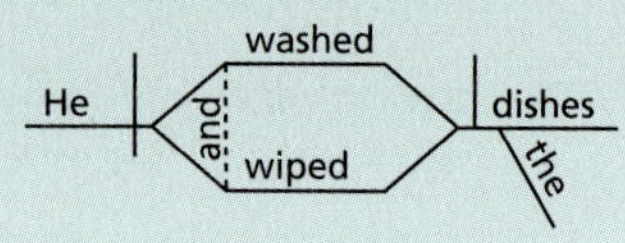

She speaks Spanish and Italian.

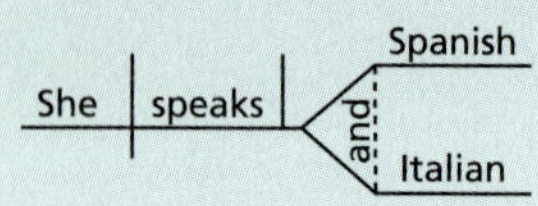

I bought a new sweater and wore it to school.

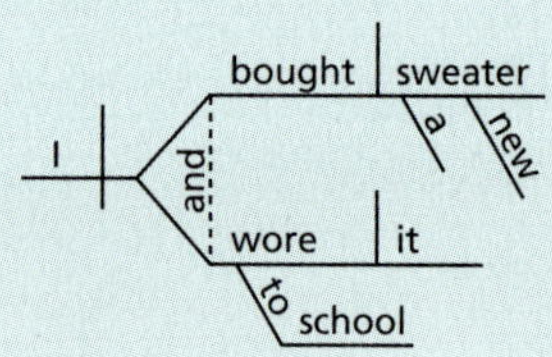

Compound Pattern 2 sentences contain two independent clauses that each express a complete thought.

To diagram a compound sentence:

1. Place each independent clause on its own baseline.
2. Join the two clauses with a dotted line.

EXAMPLE Elena wrote the story, and Jeff drew the pictures.

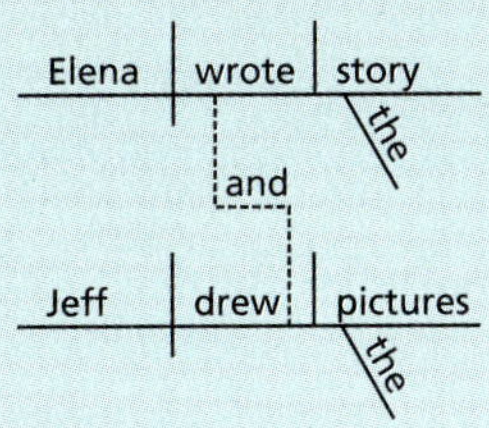

Activity K Diagram these sentences. Look at the examples on pages 237–238.

1) Stop that noise immediately!
2) Jack left his notebook and pen in his locker.
3) Have you seen Sally?
4) Tia likes poetry by Edgar Allan Poe.
5) Mr. Caruso has blue eyes, and his wife has brown eyes.
6) We bought our tickets for the late show and then had dinner.
7) He fixed the car, but it still had a problem.
8) Do you want the soup or the salad with your meal?
9) They scraped and painted the house.

Reading Vocabulary

locker scrape (5)
poetry (6)

Presenting Activity K

Before students complete Activity K on their own, read through the sentences together and ask if there are any questions about any of the sentences.

Activity K Answers

1)
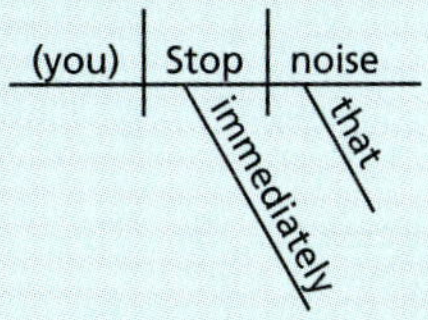

2)
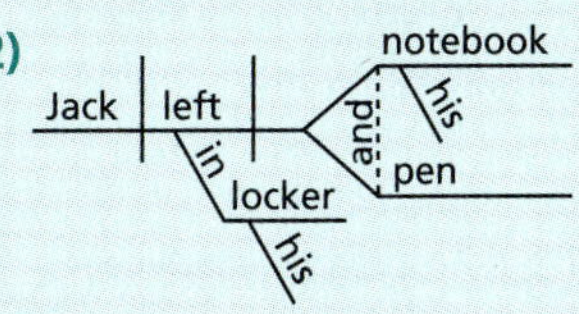

3)
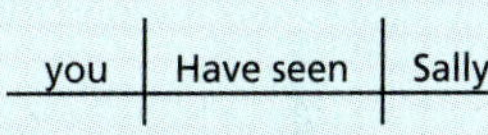

4)
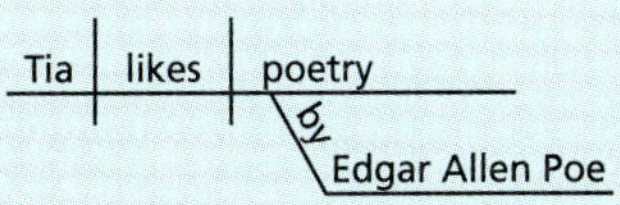

5)
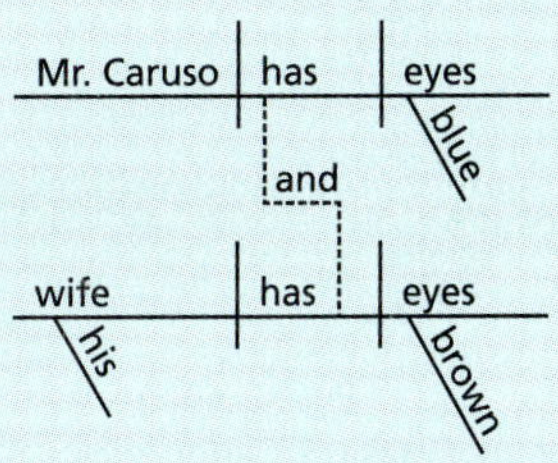

6)
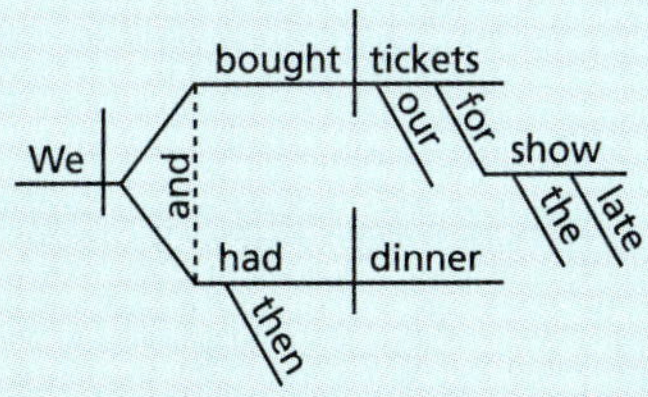

7)
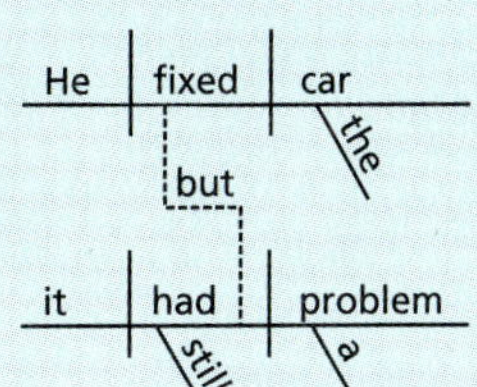

8)
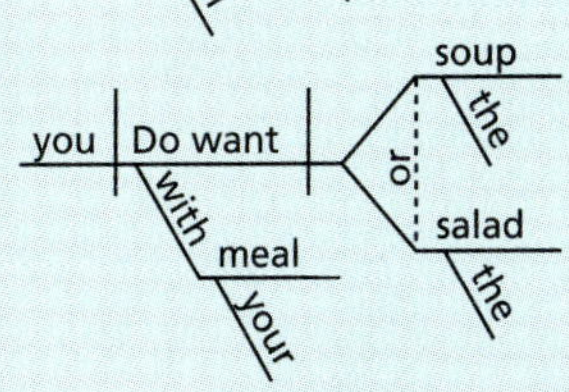

9)
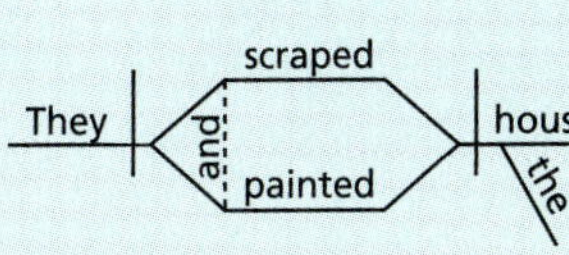

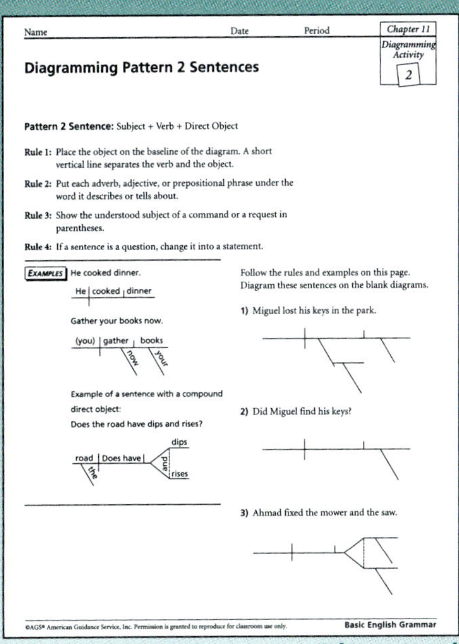
Name Date Period Chapter 11 Diagramming Activity 2

Diagramming Pattern 2 Sentences

Pattern 2 Sentence: Subject + Verb + Direct Object

Rule 1: Place the object on the baseline of the diagram. A short vertical line separates the verb and the object.

Rule 2: Put each adverb, adjective, or prepositional phrase under the word it describes or tells about.

Rule 3: Show the understood subject of a command or a request in parentheses.

Rule 4: If a sentence is a question, change it into a statement.

EXAMPLES He cooked dinner.

Gather your books now.

Example of a sentence with a compound direct object:
Does the road have dips and rises?

Follow the rules and examples on this page. Diagram these sentences on the blank diagrams.

1) Miguel lost his keys in the park.

2) Did Miguel find his keys?

3) Ahmad fixed the mower and the saw.

©AGS® American Guidance Service, Inc. Permission is granted to reproduce for classroom use only. Basic English Grammar

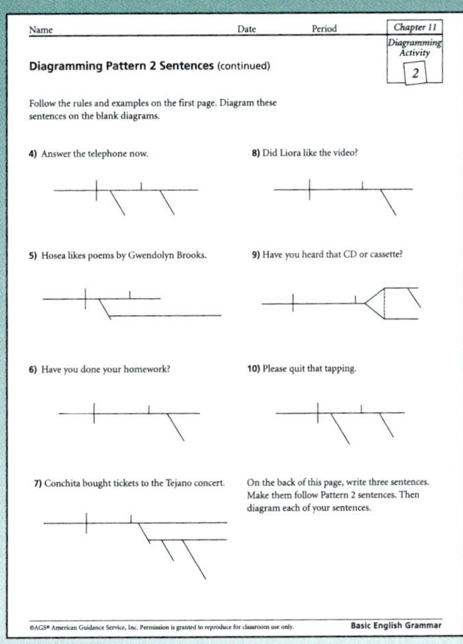
Name Date Period Chapter 11 Diagramming Activity 2

Diagramming Pattern 2 Sentences (continued)

Follow the rules and examples on the first page. Diagram these sentences on the blank diagrams.

4) Answer the telephone now.

5) Hosea likes poems by Gwendolyn Brooks.

6) Have you done your homework?

7) Conchita bought tickets to the Tejano concert.

8) Did Liora like the video?

9) Have you heard that CD or cassette?

10) Please quit that tapping.

On the back of this page, write three sentences. Make them follow Pattern 2 sentences. Then diagram each of your sentences.

©AGS® American Guidance Service, Inc. Permission is granted to reproduce for classroom use only. Basic English Grammar

Diagramming Activity 2

Reading Vocabulary

broccoli
computer (8)
knead (7)
outline (6)

Part A Answers

1) computers **2)** questions **3)** dress **4)** tickets **5)** shrimp and broccoli

Part B Answers

1)

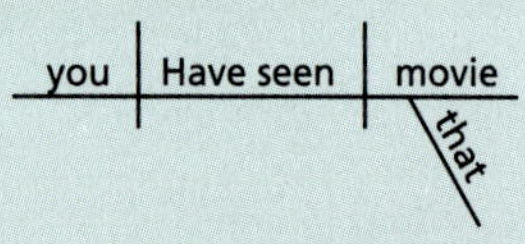

2)

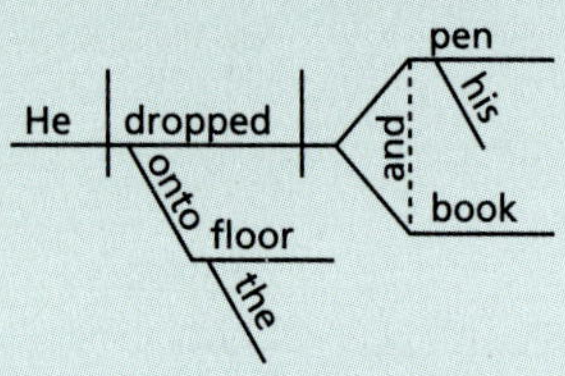

3)

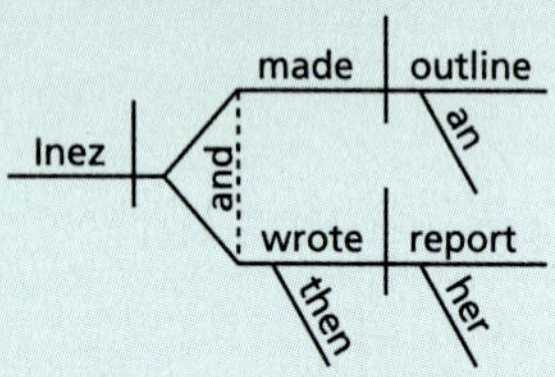

4)

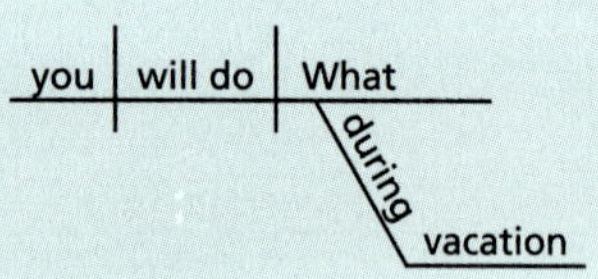

5)

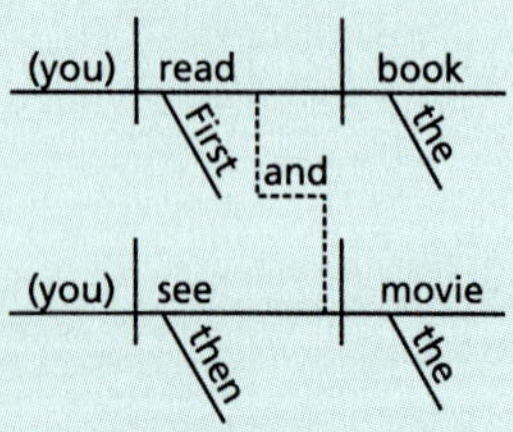

6)

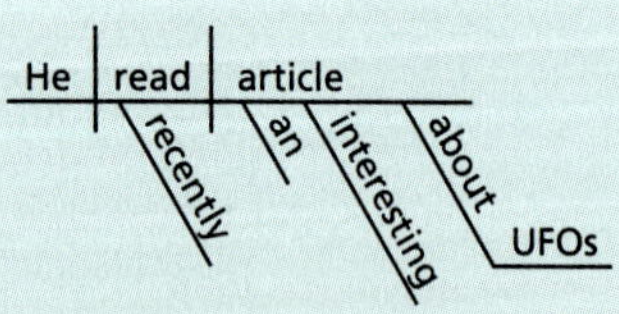

7)

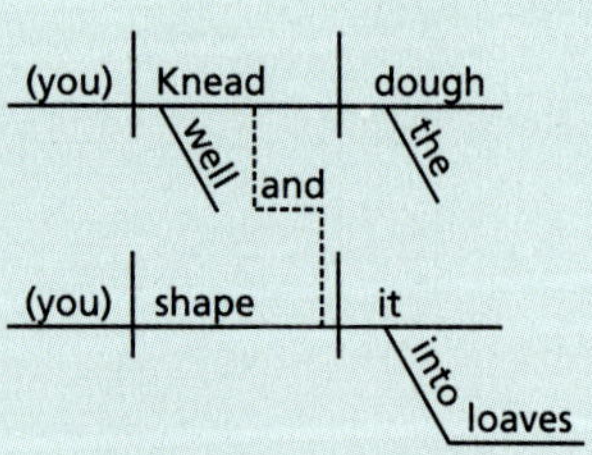

8)

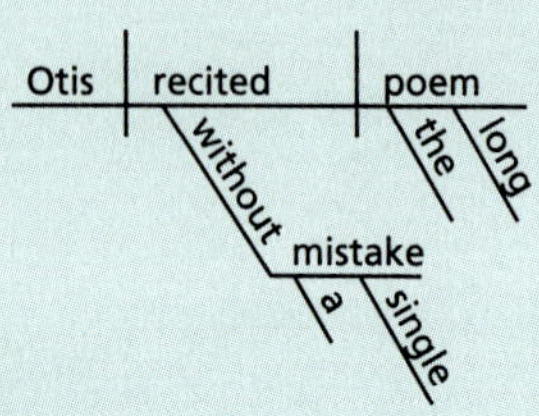

Lesson 2 Review

Part A Write the direct object in each of these sentences on your paper. Some sentences may have more than one direct object.

1) Evan's dad sells computers.

2) The teacher answered the questions.

3) Laura described her new dress to her friends.

4) The museum guard checked our tickets.

5) Loni ordered shrimp and broccoli for lunch.

Part B Diagram these Pattern 2 sentences.

1) Have you seen that movie?

2) He dropped his pen and book onto the floor.

3) Inez made an outline and then wrote her report.

4) What will you do during vacation?

5) First, read the book, and then see the movie.

6) He read an interesting article about UFOs recently.

7) Knead the dough well and shape it into loaves.

8) Otis recited the long poem without a single mistake.

Lesson 3 Pattern 3 Sentences

Indirect object

A noun or pronoun that comes after the verb and before the direct object and usually answers the question to whom, to what, from whom, *or* for what *about the verb.*

A Pattern 3 sentence has a transitive verb, a direct object, and an **indirect object**. The indirect object tells who will receive the direct object. An indirect object is a noun or pronoun that names the person receiving the direct object.

The indirect object comes after the verb and before the direct object in a sentence.

An indirect object answers the question *to whom, to what, for whom,* or *for what* about the verb.

Pattern 3 Sentence:
Subject + Verb + Indirect Object + Direct Object

EXAMPLE

S V Ind. O. D.O.
Karyn wrote Mark a letter.
(Karyn wrote a letter *to whom?* She wrote to Mark.)

Activity A Write the indirect objects in each of these sentences on your paper. (HINT: To find the indirect object, ask the question *to whom, to what, for whom,* or *for what* about the verb.)

1) Joanna gave her mother a gift.

2) I wrote myself a reminder.

3) The school mailed students their final report cards.

4) I offered Chan some pizza.

5) Mrs. López brought me my homework.

6) Marlene showed me her baseball card collection.

7) The bank lent Mr. Nakai money.

8) The salesclerk handed Maya the change.

9) Joseph sold Jon his old bike.

10) The woman bought her twin daughters matching outfits.

Teacher Alert

A sentence may have an indirect object but no direct object, such as "Karyn wrote Mark." and "I told her." In these sentences the direct object is understood.

Lesson at a Glance

Chapter 11 Lesson 3

Overview This lesson introduces Pattern 3 sentences and indirect objects.

Objectives

- To identify indirect objects in Pattern 3 sentences.
- To complete Pattern 3 sentences with indirect objects.
- To diagram Pattern 3 sentences.

Student Pages 241–247

Teacher's Resource Library

Diagramming Activity 3

Reading Vocabulary

indirect object	reminder
outfit (5)	salesclerk

Teaching Suggestions

Introducing the Lesson

Discuss the definitions of indirect object and Pattern 3 sentences. Point out that the words *to* or *for* can usually be inserted before an indirect object.

Reviewing Skills

Review transitive verbs, direct objects, and Pattern 1 and Pattern 2 sentences.

Presenting Activity A

Do the first item with the class before having students complete Activity A. Suggest that students turn each sentence into a question, such as *Joanna gave a gift to whom?*

Activity A Answers

1) mother **2)** myself
3) students **4)** Chan **5)** me
6) me **7)** Mr. Nakai **8)** Maya
9) Jon **10)** daughters

Reading Vocabulary

coupon (6) scholarship
employee (6) secretary (5)

■ Presenting Activity B

Write these sentences on the board: *Judy sang us a song. / Judy sang a song for us.* Help students identify the sentence in which *us* is an indirect object and the sentence in which *us* is an object of a preposition. Then have students complete Activity B independently.

Activity B Answers

1) indirect object **2)** object of a preposition **3)** object of a preposition **4)** indirect object **5)** object of a preposition

■ Presenting Activity C

Discuss the example and do the first item as a class before having students complete Activity C on their own.

Activity C Answers

1) director (S), gave (V), members (I.O.), music (D.O.) **2)** Fred (S), asked (V), Mr. Smith (I.O.), question (D.O.) **3)** company (S), sent (V), school (I.O.) bill (D.O.) **4)** secretary (S), handed (V), boss (I.O.), mail (D.O.) **5)** Mrs. Arloff (S), offered (V), students (I.O.), help (D.O.) **6)** teacher (S), gave (V), class (I.O.), homework (D.O.) **7)** She (S), taught (V), friend (I.O.), sign language (D.O.)
8) Jenny (S), wrote (V), aunt (I.O.), letter (D.O.) **9)** school (S), awarded (V), Tim (I.O.), scholarship (D.O.) **10)** Mr. Jackson (S), gave (V), employee (I.O.), raise (D.O.)

Learning Styles

LEP/ESL
Ask the class to examine the sentences in Activity C on page 242 to discover where the indirect object usually comes in a statement (after the verb and before the direct object). Assign each ESL student a sentence from Activity C to print in English on the board. Then ask the ESL students to print the same sentences in their primary language. Ask them to circle the indirect object and to underline the direct object. Use these sentences to discover if the indirect-object pattern is the same in different languages.

An indirect object is never part of a prepositional phrase.

EXAMPLE		
	Indirect object:	He wrote **me** a letter.
	Object of a preposition:	He wrote a letter to **me**.

Activity B Decide whether the word in bold is an indirect object or the object of a preposition. Write *indirect object* or *object of a preposition* on your paper.

1) Lou gave his **dog** a bone.

2) Helena poured some milk for her **cat**.

3) The store sent coupons to their best **customers**.

4) The server brought **us** lunch.

5) Mrs. Jenkins handed my paycheck to **me**.

Activity C Create four columns on your paper with the headings *Subject, Verb, Indirect Object,* and *Direct Object.* Then identify the simple subject, the verb, the indirect object, and the direct object in each sentence. Write these in the correct column.

Example Mary gave me a birthday present.

Subject	Verb	Indirect Object	Direct Object
Mary	gave	me	present

1) The director gave the band members their music.

2) Fred asked Mr. Smith a question.

3) The music company sent the school a bill.

4) The secretary handed his boss the mail.

5) Mrs. Arloff offered the students her help.

6) The teacher gave the class homework.

7) She taught her friend sign language.

8) Jenny wrote her aunt a letter.

9) The school awarded Tim a scholarship.

10) Mr. Jackson gave every employee a raise.

When the indirect object is a pronoun, the pronoun must be in the objective case. Refer to the chart on page 232.

EXAMPLE

S V Ind. O. D.O.
His boss offered him a promotion.

Activity D Write the pronoun on your paper that should appear in each sentence to make it correct. Remember that a pronoun used as an indirect object is always in the objective form.

1) Tom gave (I, me) the message.

2) Fred sent (he, him) a letter.

3) Martha told (she, her) the answer.

4) That teacher taught (we, us) Spanish.

5) We served (they, them) dinner.

Pattern 3 sentences may have adjectives and prepositional phrases that describe the indirect object.

EXAMPLES

S V Adj. Adj Ind.O. D.O.
Steve wrote his younger sister a letter.

S V Adj. Ind. O. Prep. Phrase D.O.
She gave her friend from Montana a gift.

Activity E Rewrite each of these sentences on your paper. Add an adjective or prepositional phrase to describe the indirect object in bold.

1) Pat sent her **friend** a message.

2) Marcus offered the **woman** his seat.

3) The teacher told the **boy** the answer.

4) We made our **neighbor** an offer.

5) We asked the **mechanic** a question about the car.

Reading Vocabulary

mechanic (6) promotion (6)

■ **Presenting Activity D** Ask students to listen carefully as you read the first item in Activity D aloud twice, each time with a different answer in place. Ask students which sentence is correct, the one with *I* or the one with *me.* Have students explain their choice. Point out that reading each sentence in the activity to themselves twice with each of the answer choices in place will help them "hear" the correct answer.

Activity D Answers

1) me **2)** him **3)** her
4) us **5)** them

■ **Presenting Activity E**
Write the first item in Activity E on the board. Encourage students to take turns adding an adjective or prepositional phrase to the sentence to describe the indirect object *friend.* Then have students complete Activity E on their own. When they have finished, invite them to share their sentences with the class.

Activity E Answers

Each sentence should include an adjective or prepositional phrase that describes the indirect object.

Reading Vocabulary

biscuit (6)

■ Presenting Activity F

Remind students that one way to identify the indirect object in a sentence is to imagine the word *to* or *for* before the noun or pronoun that follows the verb. Additionally, they can reverse the position of the direct object and the indirect object in the sentence. To illustrate this, write the first two items in Activity F on the board as follows: *Tell the answer <to> me. Did you give a biscuit <to> the dog?* Students who are having difficulty recognizing the indirect object may wish to use this method, writing the entire sentence as they complete Activity F.

Activity F Answers

1) me 2) dog 3) me 4) me 5) you 6) yourself 7) Michael 8) me 9) them 10) us

Pattern 3 sentences may be questions. Part of the verb phrase may come before the subject. The question may begin with an interrogative word.

EXAMPLES

V S V Ind.O. D.O.
Will you give Shawn a message?

S V Ind. O. D.O.
Who sent you that letter?

Pattern 3 sentences are often commands or requests.

EXAMPLES

S V Ind.O. D.O.
(You) Show the class your drawing.

S V Ind.O. D.O.
(You) Give me his new address.

Activity F Write the indirect objects in these sentences on your paper.

1) Tell me the answer.

2) Did you give the dog a biscuit?

3) Would you lend me your sweater for the evening?

4) Please teach me Spanish.

5) When did Anna write you that note?

6) Allow yourself enough time for breakfast.

7) Are you giving Michael a present?

8) Who asked me that question?

9) Bring them their coats.

10) Tell us the truth.

244 *Chapter 11 Sentence Patterns*

The indirect object of a Pattern 3 sentence can be compound.

EXAMPLES Fix your **father** and his **friend** some lunch.

Will you give **Tim** and **Simon** a message?

Maria read her younger **brother** and **sister** a bedtime story.

Activity G Complete each of these sentences with a compound indirect object. Write the completed sentences on your paper.

1) Write ______ a letter.

2) Give ______ more time.

3) Please tell ______ the answer.

4) Uncle Fred made ______ model airplanes.

5) Would you lend ______ five dollars?

6) I offered ______ more pizza.

7) Joe asked ______ for help with his project.

8) Kim sent ______ birthday gifts.

Activity H Rearrange each group of words to make a Pattern 3 sentence. Write the sentences on your paper.

1) them served we dinner the

2) gave rose Erica Julio a

3) told team the coach play the the

4) myself snack fixed I a

5) a him he handed dollar

Reading Vocabulary

rearrange snack (6)

■ Presenting Activity G

Write these sentences on the board: *Sing ______ a song./ Jason told ______ his latest joke.* Have students take turns filling in the blanks with compound indirect objects. Then have students work independently to complete Activity G.

Activity G Answers

Sentences will vary but should be completed with compound indirect objects.

■ Presenting Activity H

Write the first item in Activity H on the board. Challenge students to see how fast they can rearrange the words to make a Pattern 3 sentence. Ask students to raise their hands when they finish. When all hands are raised invite a volunteer to read the sentence and identify the indirect object. You can repeat this procedure to complete Activity H, or you can ask students to work on their own.

Activity H Answers

1) We served them the dinner. **2)** Julio gave Erica a rose./Erica gave Julio a rose. **3)** The coach told the team the play. **4)** I fixed myself a snack. **5)** He handed him a dollar.

Sentence Patterns Chapter 11 **245**

Reading Vocabulary
blank (5)

Presenting Activity J

Before having students complete Activity J, review what they have learned about diagramming previously in the chapter. Then discuss the steps and diagram examples presented on page 246. If necessary, have students work together to diagram the first item in Activity J, asking a volunteer to write the diagram on the board. Then have students complete Activity J on their own.

Activity J Answers

1)
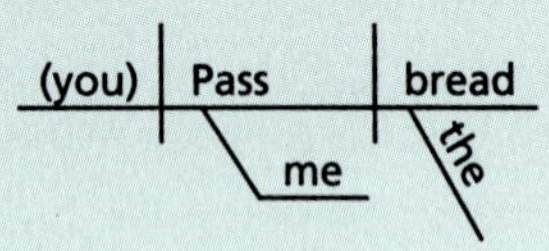

2)
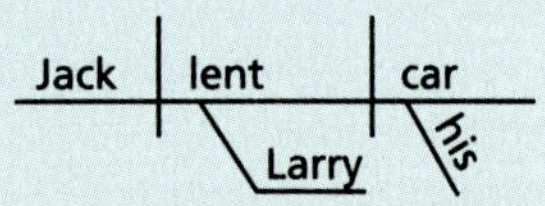

3)
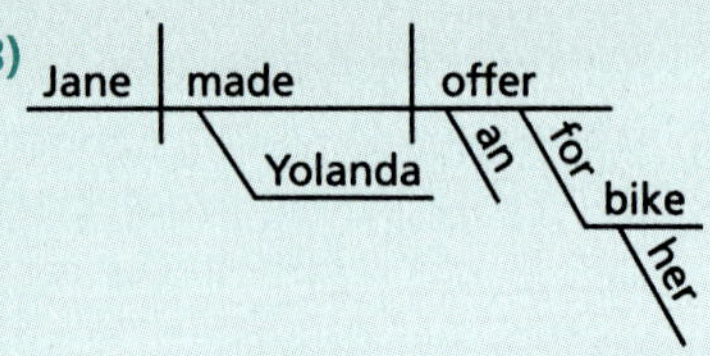

4)
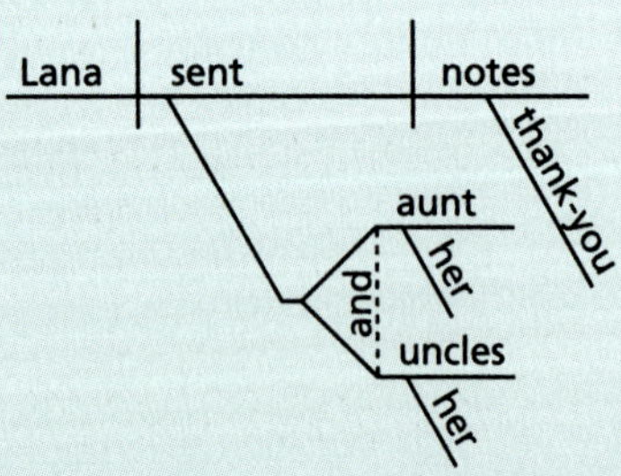

5)
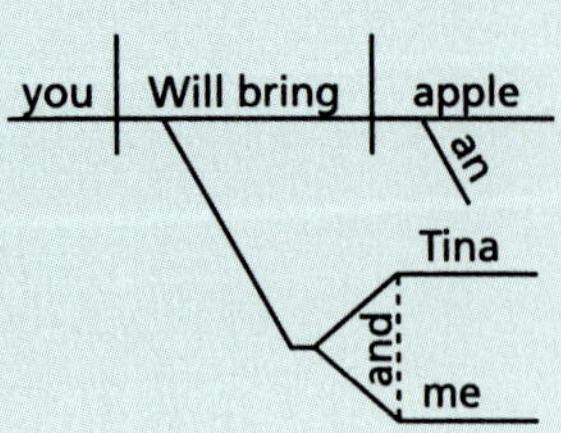

Diagramming Pattern 3 Sentences

To diagram a Pattern 3 sentence:

1. Draw a slanted line and a horizontal line under the verb.
2. Leave the slanted line blank.
3. Write the indirect object on the horizontal line.

EXAMPLE Jack gave him a pencil.

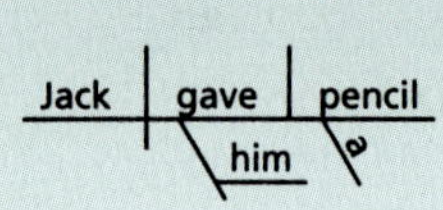

4. Diagram a compound indirect object this way.

EXAMPLE Can you give my sister and me a ride?

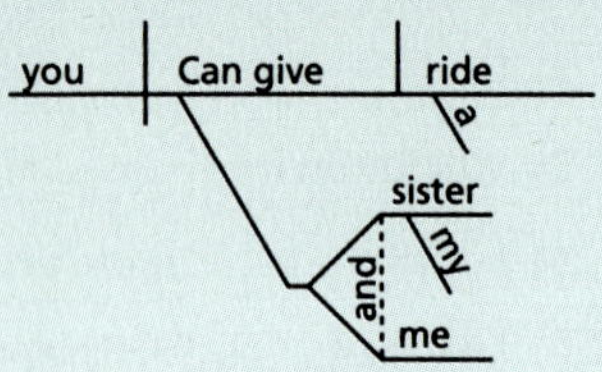

Activity I Diagram these Pattern 3 sentences on your paper. Look at the examples above and on pages 237–238.

1) Pass me the bread.
2) Jack lent Larry his car.
3) Jane made Yolanda an offer for her bike.
4) Lana sent her aunt and her uncles thank-you notes.
5) Will you bring Tina and me an apple?

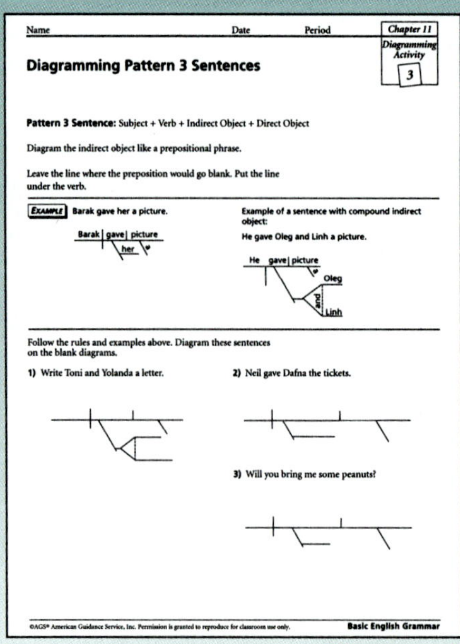

Name Date Period | *Chapter 11* *Diagramming Activity* 3

Diagramming Pattern 3 Sentences

Pattern 3 Sentence: Subject + Verb + Indirect Object + Direct Object

Diagram the indirect object like a prepositional phrase.

Leave the line where the preposition would go blank. Put the line under the verb.

EXAMPLE **Barak gave her a picture.**

Example of a sentence with compound indirect object:

He gave Oleg and Linh a picture.

Follow the rules and examples above. Diagram these sentences on the blank diagrams.

1) Write Toni and Yolanda a letter.

2) Neil gave Dafna the tickets.

3) Will you bring me some peanuts?

 Basic English Grammar

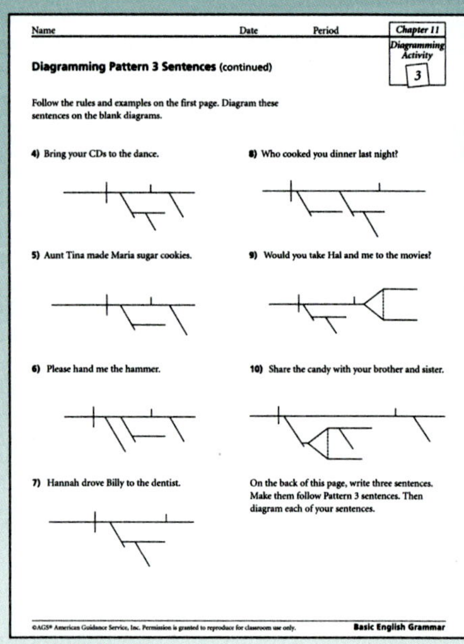

Name Date Period | *Chapter 11* *Diagramming Activity* 3

Diagramming Pattern 3 Sentences (continued)

Follow the rules and examples on the first page. Diagram these sentences on the blank diagrams.

4) Bring your CDs to the dance.

5) Aunt Tina made Maria sugar cookies.

6) Please hand me the hammer.

7) Hannah drove Billy to the dentist.

8) Who cooked you dinner last night?

9) Would you take Hal and me to the movies?

10) Share the candy with your brother and sister.

On the back of this page, write three sentences. Make them follow Pattern 3 sentences. Then diagram each of your sentences.

 Basic English Grammar

Diagramming Activity 3

Lesson 3 Review

Part A Write the indirect objects in these sentences on your paper.

1) Sue brought Rita and Pam some books.
2) After dinner, Grandpa told the family some old stories.
3) Tim asked his grandfather a question.
4) Will you tell me the story about Dad again?
5) Allow yourself several hours for that report.
6) The members of the team gave Kerry an award for her outstanding effort.
7) Give me another chance at the game, please.
8) Chris handed Tómas and Leon their books.
9) Who sold you that bike?
10) Will you make Sam and me some lunch?

Part B Diagram these Pattern 3 sentences on your paper.

1) My uncle offered me a job in his store.
2) She wrote him a long letter.
3) Dan gave Meg and Lian a ride to work.
4) Who gave you that book?
5) Sing me your song, and then I will give you my opinion.
6) Corey brought her mom and dad breakfast in bed.
7) I sent each guest an invitation and directions to my house.

Reading Vocabulary

invitation (5) outstanding (6)

Part A Answers

1) Rita, Pam 2) family 3) grandfather 4) me 5) yourself 6) Kerry 7) me 8) Tómas, Leon 9) you 10) Sam, me

Part B Answers

1)

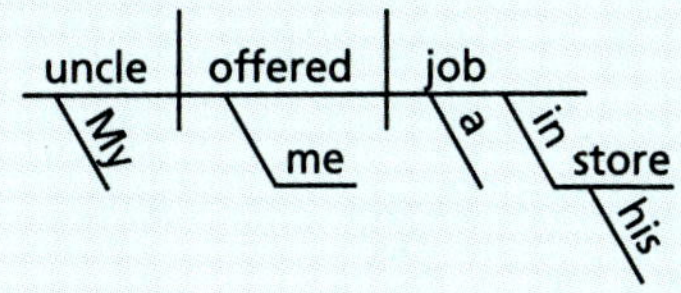

2)

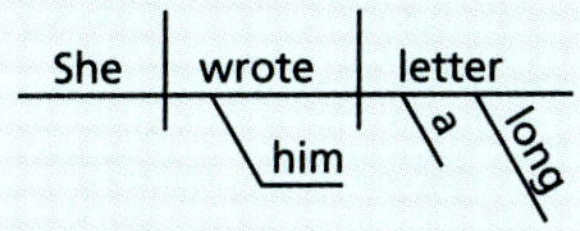

3)

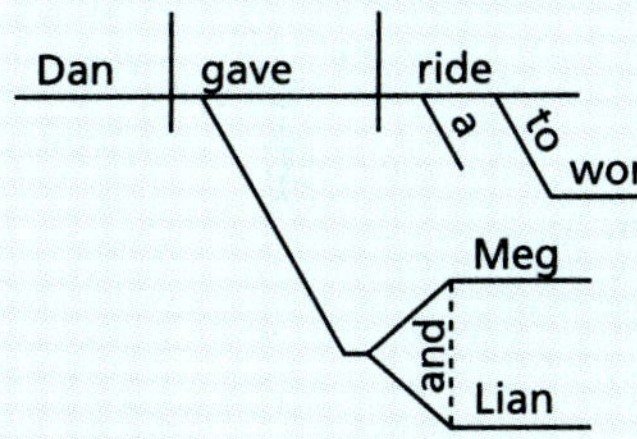

4)

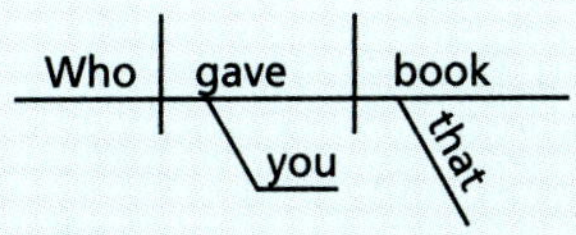

5)

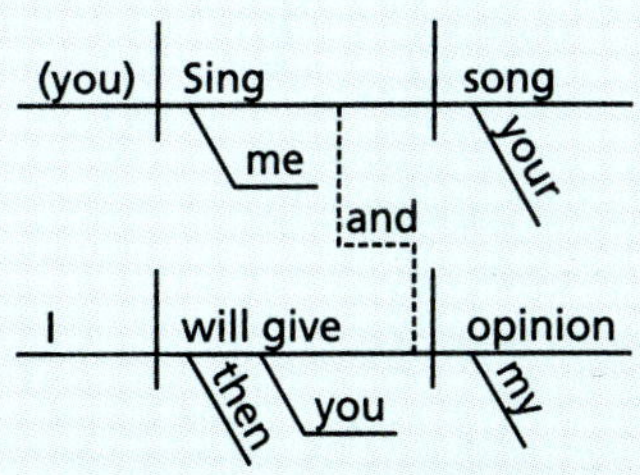

6)

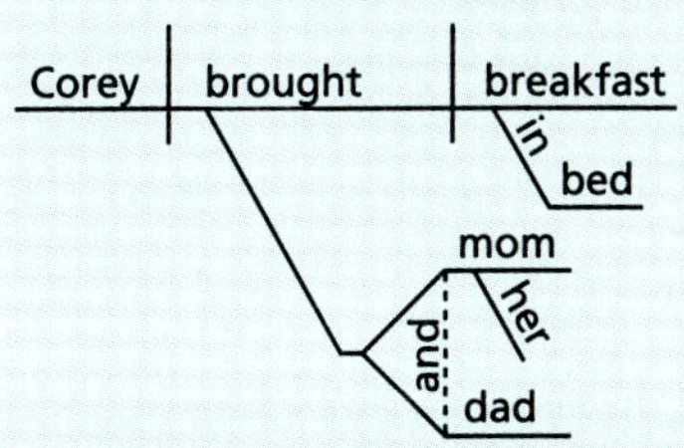

7)

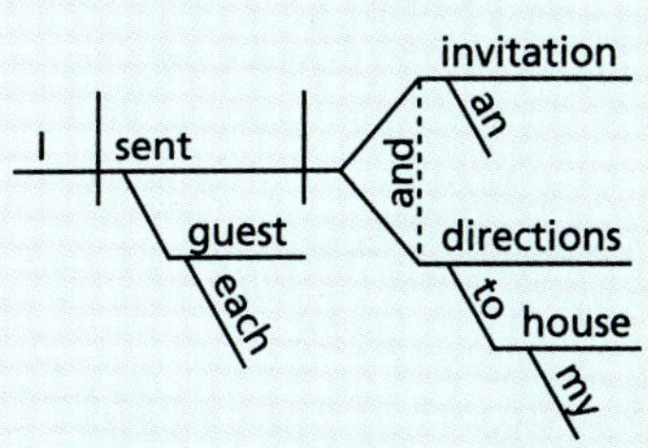

Sentence Patterns *Chapter 11* **247**

Lesson at a Glance

Chapter 11 Lesson 4

Overview This lesson explains objective complements and introduces Pattern 4 sentences.

Objectives

- To identify objective complements in Pattern 4 sentences.
- To write Pattern 4 sentences.
- To diagram Pattern 4 sentences.

Student Pages 248–251

Teacher's Resource Library

Workbook Activity 48

Diagramming Activity 4

Reading Vocabulary

complement (10)
consider (5)
daze (6)
elect (5)
objective complement
spicy (5)

Teaching Suggestions

Introducing the Lesson

Discuss the definitions presented in the text. Ask students to explain in their own words how Pattern 4 sentences differ from Pattern 1, 2, and 3 sentences.

Reviewing Skills

Provide a review of transitive verbs and direct objects.

Presenting Activity A

Do the first item in Activity A as a class, having students identify the objective complement and the direct object that it renames. Then have students complete Activity A on their own or in pairs.

Activity A Answers

1) president 2) colors
3) beautiful 4) dazed
5) sleepy 6) actor
7) president 8) smart
9) spicy 10) brown

Lesson 4 Pattern 4 Sentences

Complement
The part of a sentence that completes the meaning of the verb.

Objective complement
A noun or an adjective that follows a direct object and adds to its meaning.

A Pattern 4 sentence has a transitive verb, a direct object, and an objective complement. A **complement** is a word that completes an idea. An **objective complement** is a noun or an adjective that adds to the meaning of the direct object. The objective complement comes after the direct object in the sentence.

Pattern 4 Sentence:
Subject + Verb + Direct Object + Objective Complement

EXAMPLES

S V D.O. Complement
The Smiths named their baby Christopher.

(*Christopher* is a noun that renames the direct object *baby*.)

S V D.O. Complement
Our neighbors painted their house blue.

(*Blue* is an adjective that adds to the meaning of the direct object *house*.)

Activity A Write the objective complements in these sentences on your paper.

1) The people elected George Washington president in 1788.
2) The frost turned the leaves many colors.
3) Happiness made the girl beautiful.
4) The police found the man dazed.
5) The dark room made us sleepy.
6) Everyone calls Anthony Hopkins a great actor.
7) They made Mrs. Schwartz president of the company.
8) Emilio considers Alison smart.
9) Are you making the tacos spicy?
10) The hot sun turned the grass brown.

Learning Styles

Body/Kinesthetic

Print the words *subject, predicate, direct object,* and *complement* on the board. Ask each student to write these words on separate sheets of paper so that each student has four posters. Ask volunteers to slowly read aloud the sentences in Activity A on page 248. Ask the other students to hold up the correct poster as they hear the subject, predicate, direct object, and the complement in each sentence. Afterward, invite volunteer groups to create sentences that follow the pattern, to stand with their posters in the correct sentence order, and to read the sentence to the group.

Activity B Write these sentences on your paper. Add a noun or an adjective used as an objective complement. Be sure your sentences make sense.

1) He found science class ______.

2) The artist made the pictures ______.

3) We elected Danny ______.

4) Don't make the soup ______.

5) They called him ______.

6) Teenagers often consider adults ______.

7) Most of the students in Mr. Alvarez's math class find his tests ______.

8) The hot oven turned the pizza dough ______.

Activity C Write Pattern 4 sentences on your paper using the verbs below.

1) make or made

2) elect or elected

3) find or found

4) name or named

5) turn or turned

6) call or called

7) consider or considered

8) paint or painted

9) judge or judged

10) declare or declared

Reading Vocabulary

dough (5) science (5)
pizza

■ Presenting Activity B

Write item 1 in Activity B on the board. Invite volunteers to take turns adding an objective complement. When you are sure students understand the concept, have them complete Activity B on their own.

Activity B Answers

Sentences will vary but should be completed with a noun or an adjective used as an objective complement.

■ Presenting Activity C

Remind students that an objective complement is a noun or an adjective that adds to the meaning of the direct object. Then ask students for examples of sentences with objective complements, using any of the verbs provided in Activity C. Write students' sentences on the board and ask the class to identify the objective complement in each sentence. Then have students complete Activity C on their own.

Activity C Answers

Each sentence should be a Pattern 4 sentence.

Global Connection

Some students may receive foreign newspapers in their home. Invite these students to share a newspaper article from one of these papers with the class. You might wish to use an overhead projector or have the student copy sample sentences from the article onto the board. Have students point out different sentence patterns in the article and explain how they compare to sentence patterns in English.

Sentence Patterns Chapter 11 **249**

Reading Vocabulary

chili
dye (5)
excellent (5)
treasurer

■ Presenting Activity D

Discuss the steps for diagramming a Pattern 4 sentence. Then have students work alone or with partners to complete Activity D.

Activity D Answers

1) 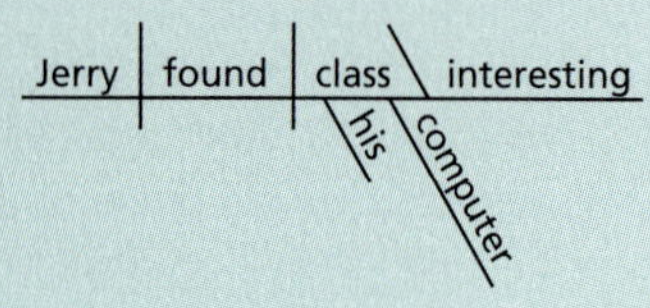

2) 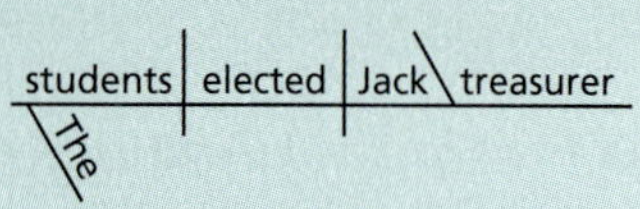

3) 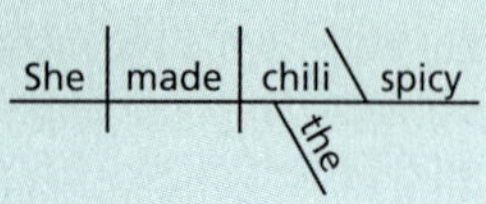

4) 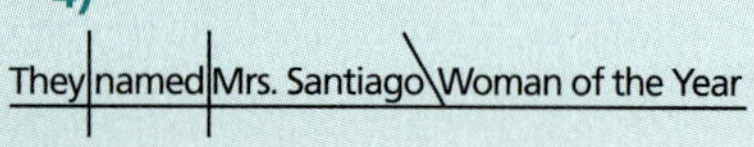

5) 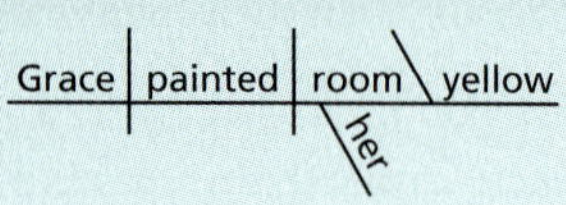

6) 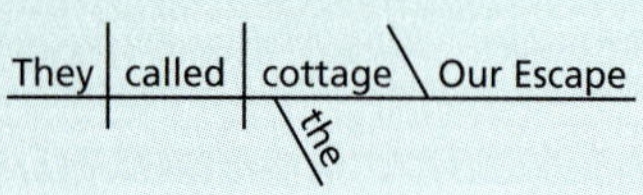

7) 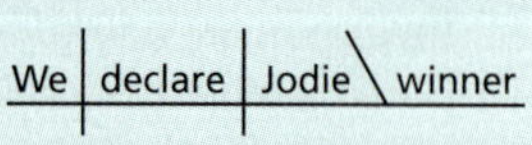

8) 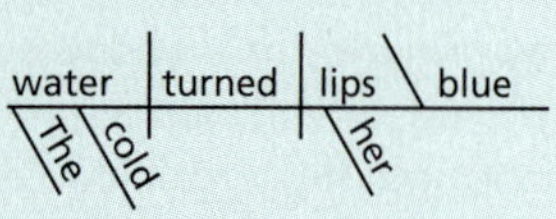

9) 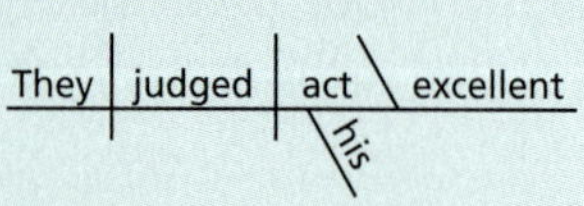

10) 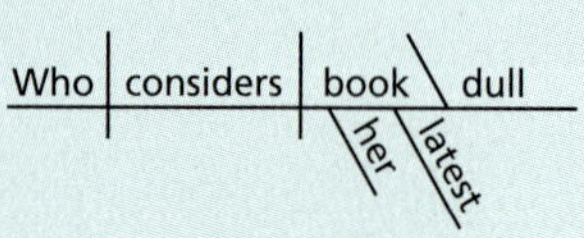

Diagramming Pattern 4 Sentences

To diagram a Pattern 4 sentence:

1. Place the objective complement on the baseline of the diagram next to the direct object.
2. Separate the objective complement from the direct object with a line slanted toward the direct object.

EXAMPLE Alison dyed her blouse red.

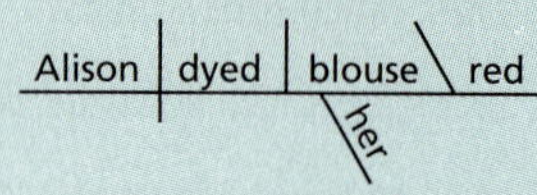

Activity D Diagram the following Pattern 4 sentences on your paper.

1) Jerry found his computer class interesting.
2) The students elected Jack treasurer.
3) She made the chili spicy.
4) They named Mrs. Santiago "Woman of the Year."
5) Grace painted her room yellow.
6) They called the cottage "Our Escape."
7) We declare Jodie winner.
8) The cold water turned her lips blue.
9) They judged his act excellent.
10) Who considers her latest book dull?

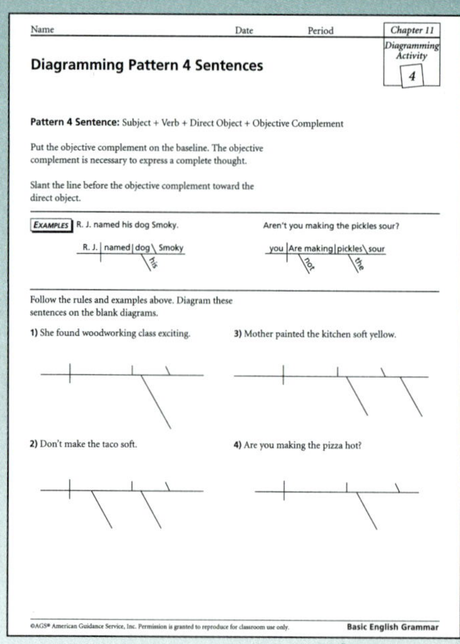

Name Date Period | Chapter 11 Diagramming Activity 4

Diagramming Pattern 4 Sentences

Pattern 4 Sentence: Subject + Verb + Direct Object + Objective Complement

Put the objective complement on the baseline. The objective complement is necessary to express a complete thought.

Slant the line before the objective complement toward the direct object.

EXAMPLES R. J. named his dog Smoky. Aren't you making the pickles sour?

R. J. | named | dog \ Smoky / his

you | Are making | pickles \ sour / not / the

Follow the rules and examples above. Diagram these sentences on the blank diagrams.

1) She found woodworking class exciting.

3) Mother painted the kitchen soft yellow.

2) Don't make the taco soft.

4) Are you making the pizza hot?

 Basic English Grammar

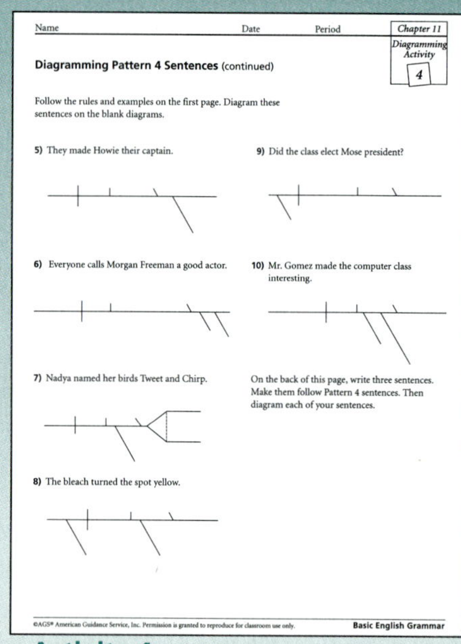

Name Date Period | Chapter 11 Diagramming Activity 4

Diagramming Pattern 4 Sentences (continued)

Follow the rules and examples on the first page. Diagram these sentences on the blank diagrams.

5) They made Howie their captain.

6) Everyone calls Morgan Freeman a good actor.

7) Nadya named her birds Tweet and Chirp.

8) The bleach turned the spot yellow.

9) Did the class elect Mose president?

10) Mr. Gomez made the computer class interesting.

On the back of this page, write three sentences. Make them follow Pattern 4 sentences. Then diagram each of your sentences.

 Basic English Grammar

Diagramming Activity 4

Lesson 4 Review

Part A Write the objective complements in these sentences on your paper.

1) They declared the young boy the winner.
2) We made Joe group leader.
3) They call their hamster Swifty.
4) Old age has turned the dog's hair silver.
5) They dyed the wool many colors.
6) You made that meal delicious!
7) We named the little white kitten Snowball.
8) Did you find that program interesting?
9) What makes him so shy?
10) Do you consider yourself an expert on the subject?

Part B Diagram these Pattern 4 sentences on your paper.

1) The wind turned the day cold.
2) The class will elect Carlotta president.
3) Can we call the puppy Pooch?
4) May and Danzel found the play boring.
5) She painted the inside of her closet purple.

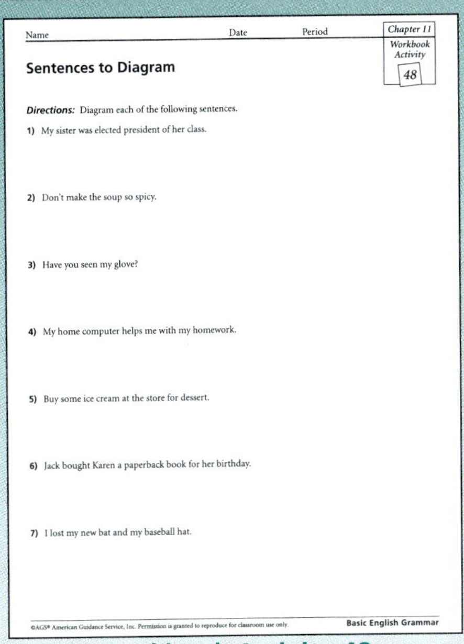
Name Date Period

Chapter 11 *Workbook Activity* 48

Sentences to Diagram

Directions: Diagram each of the following sentences.

1) My sister was elected president of her class.
2) Don't make the soup so spicy.
3) Have you seen my glove?
4) My home computer helps me with my homework.
5) Buy some ice cream at the store for dessert.
6) Jack bought Karen a paperback book for her birthday.
7) I lost my new bat and my baseball hat.

 Basic English Grammar

Workbook Activity 48

Reading Vocabulary

hamster

Part A Answers

1) winner 2) leader 3) Swifty 4) silver 5) colors 6) delicious 7) Snowball 8) interesting 9) shy 10) expert

Part B Answers

1)
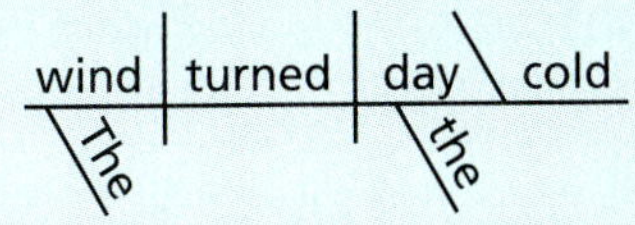

2)
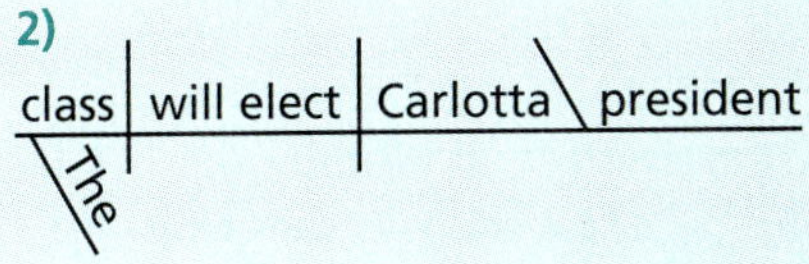

3)
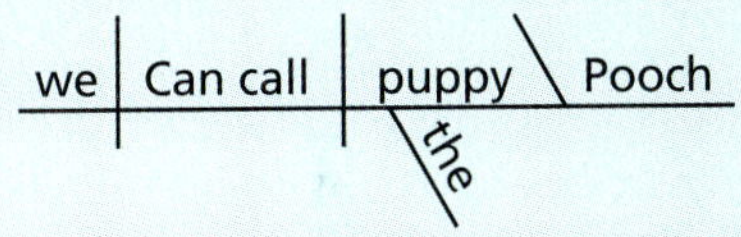

4)
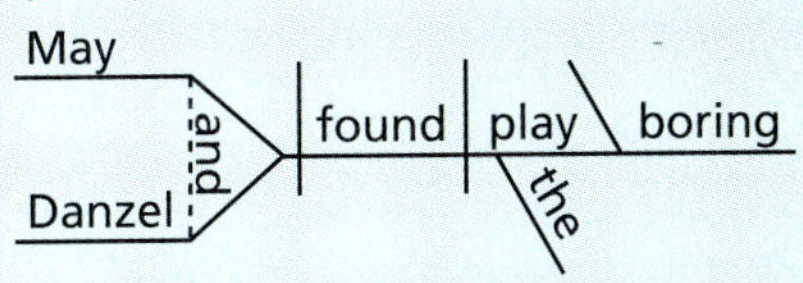

5)
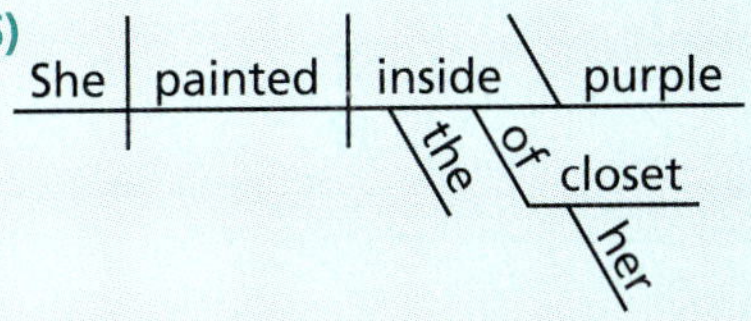

Chapter 11 Review

The Teacher's Resource Library includes two parallel forms of the Chapter 11 Mastery Test. The difficulty level of the two forms is equivalent. You may wish to use one form as a pretest and the other form as a posttest.

Reading Vocabulary

daily (10)
investment (8)
modem
video

Part A Answers

1) transitive 2) transitive 3) intransitive 4) transitive 5) intransitive 6) transitive 7) transitive 8) transitive 9) transitive 10) intransitive

Part B Answers

1) Jiro—indirect object, birthday—object of the preposition 2) Rolling Stones—subject, recorded—verb 3) Some—subject 4) Have read—verb phrase 5) Hand—verb, me—indirect object 6) band—subject, money—direct object 7) John—direct object, president—objective complement 8) you, Jackie—subject 9) Which—direct object, these—object of the preposition 10) you—subject, us—indirect object

Chapter 11 Review

Part A Decide whether the verb in bold in these sentences is transitive or intransitive. Write *transitive* or *intransitive* on your paper.

1) One day Mr. Ellis **bought** a computer.
2) He **called** it an investment in their future.
3) The younger children **clapped** with glee.
4) He **plugged** a modem into the computer.
5) The puppy just **stared** at the computer screen.
6) **Can** we **use** it?
7) They **could play** video games.
8) Mrs. Ellis **keeps** a daily journal on the computer.
9) They **used** it for their tax records.
10) That computer **ran** all evening!

Part B Write the words in bold in these sentences on your paper. Beside each word, write whether it is the *subject, verb* or *verb phrase, direct object, indirect object, object of the preposition,* or *objective complement.*

1) We gave **Jiro** a CD for his **birthday**.
2) The **Rolling Stones recorded** that song.
3) **Some** of us are going to the movies.
4) **Have** you **read** that book?
5) **Hand me** that hammer, please.
6) The **band** raised **money** for the trip.
7) We elected **John president**.
8) Where are **you** and **Jackie** sitting?
9) **Which** of **these** do you want?
10) Will **you** give **us** a ride?

Name Date Period | *Chapter 11 Mastery Test A page 1*

Chapter 11 Mastery Test A

Part A Write *T* if the bold verb is transitive. Write *I* if the bold verb is intransitive.

1) ______ Helen Keller **worked** for better care for people with handicaps.
2) ______ Tulips and daffodils **bloom** in April.
3) ______ Marie Curie **isolated** metallic radium.
4) ______ Martin Luther King, Jr. **won** the 1964 Nobel Peace Prize.
5) ______ Andrew Lloyd Weber **writes** musicals for the theater.
6) ______ Paul Simon **sings** and **composes**.
7) ______ Isak Dinesen **wrote** *Out of Africa.*
8) ______ William Booth **founded** the Salvation Army.
9) ______ Emily and Charlotte Brontë **lived** in England.
10) ______ Chief Crazy Horse **won** the Battle of Little Big Horn.

Part B Identify the simple subject (*S*), the verb (*V*), the direct object (*DO*), the indirect object (*IO*), and the objective complement (*OC*) in each sentence. Not every sentence will have each of these parts.

1) James asked Mr. Cohen a question.
2) Everyone calls Emma Thompson a great actress.
3) Anne named her cat Jemima.
4) Angus wrote his boss a memo.
5) His boss gave everyone a reward.

 Basic English Grammar

Name Date Period | *Chapter 11 Mastery Test A page 2*

Chapter 11 Mastery Test A, continued

Part C Diagram each of these sentences.

1) The little girl ran to the corner.
2) Yesterday I saw bald eagles along the river bluffs.
3) Richard gave Skip a list of items for the sale.
4) The warm spring temperatures turned the grass green.
5) The trees leafed out, and the flowers burst into bloom.

 Basic English Grammar

Chapter 11 Mastery Test A

Part C Write two sentences on your paper for each of the four patterns. Follow the examples.

Pattern 1:	Subject + Verb The frightened girl screamed.
Pattern 2:	Subject + Verb + Direct Object Mary read her report to the class.
Pattern 3:	Subject + Verb + Indirect and Direct Objects Paco gave the puppy a bath.
Pattern 4:	Subject + Verb + Direct Object + Objective Complement Connie considers raw vegetables a healthy snack.

Part D Diagram the following sentences.

1) Which of these do you want?
2) Kevin writes music and lyrics.
3) Kevin's music has variety, and his lyrics have real meaning.
4) He named it "Melody" and sang it for Julia.
5) We can make our own birthday cards on the computer.
6) He has been at the computer for hours.
7) They named their computer "The Whiz."
8) Try it yourself.
9) I can add fast, but the computer adds faster.
10) Walter and Andrea asked their mom a question about the computer.

Test Taking Tip Before you answer any questions on a test, skim through the whole test to find out what is expected of you.

Reading Vocabulary

lyrics (8) variety (6)
melody (5) whiz

Part C Answers

Sentences will vary but should include a sentence for each of the four patterns shown.

Part D Answers

1) 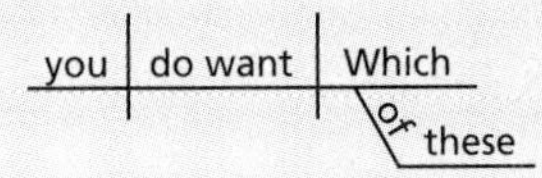

2) 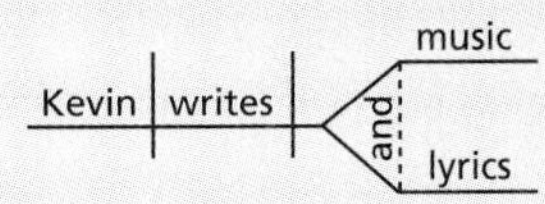

3) 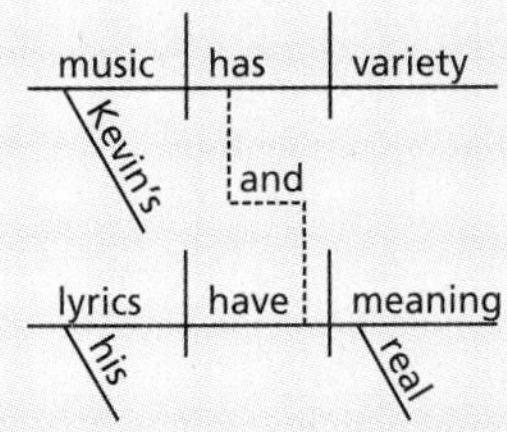

4) 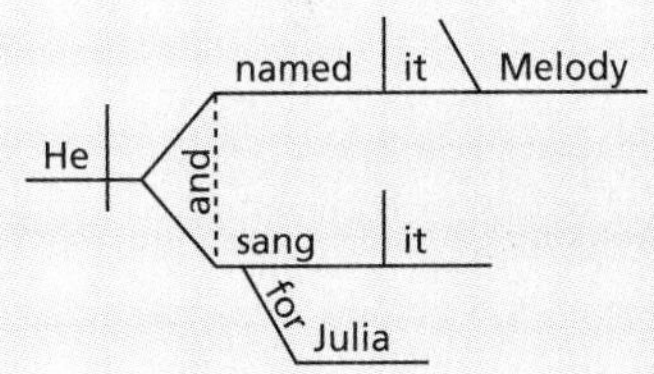

5) 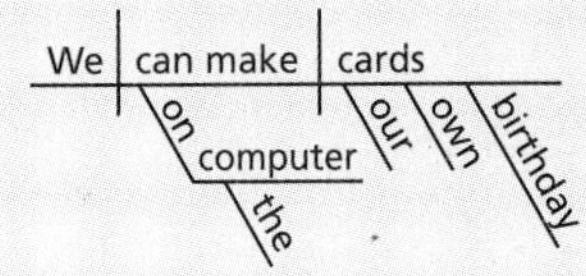

6) 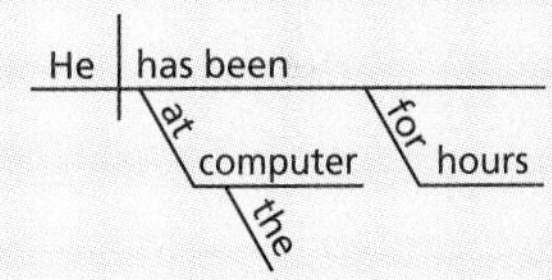

7) 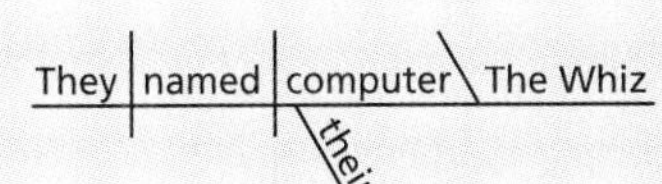

8) 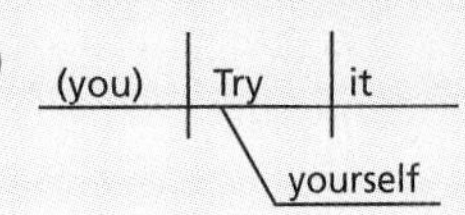

9) 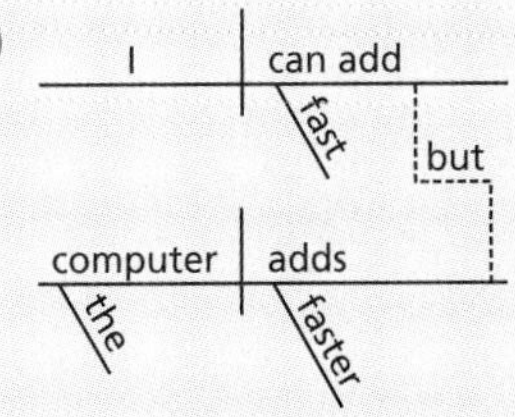

10) 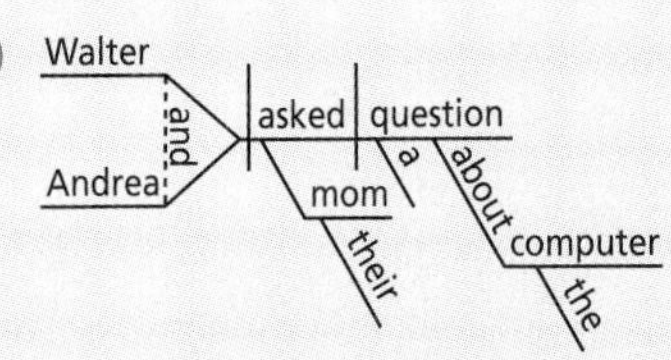

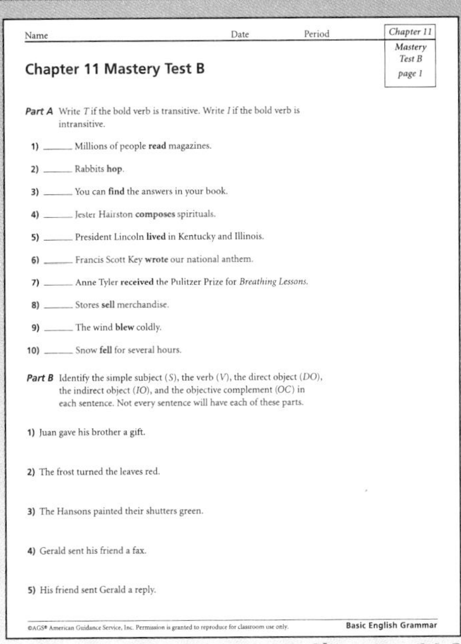

Name Date Period | *Chapter 11 Mastery Test B page 1*

Chapter 11 Mastery Test B

Part A Write *T* if the bold verb is transitive. Write *I* if the bold verb is intransitive.

1) ______ Millions of people **read** magazines.
2) ______ Rabbits **hop**.
3) ______ You can **find** the answers in your book.
4) ______ Jester Hairston **composes** spirituals.
5) ______ President Lincoln **lived** in Kentucky and Illinois.
6) ______ Francis Scott Key **wrote** our national anthem.
7) ______ Anne Tyler **received** the Pulitzer Prize for *Breathing Lessons*.
8) ______ Stores **sell** merchandise.
9) ______ The wind **blew** coldly.
10) ______ Snow **fell** for several hours.

Part B Identify the simple subject (*S*), the verb (*V*), the direct object (*DO*), the indirect object (*IO*), and the objective complement (*OC*) in each sentence. Not every sentence will have each of these parts.

1) Juan gave his brother a gift.
2) The frost turned the leaves red.
3) The Hansons painted their shutters green.
4) Gerald sent his friend a fax.
5) His friend sent Gerald a reply.

 Basic English Grammar

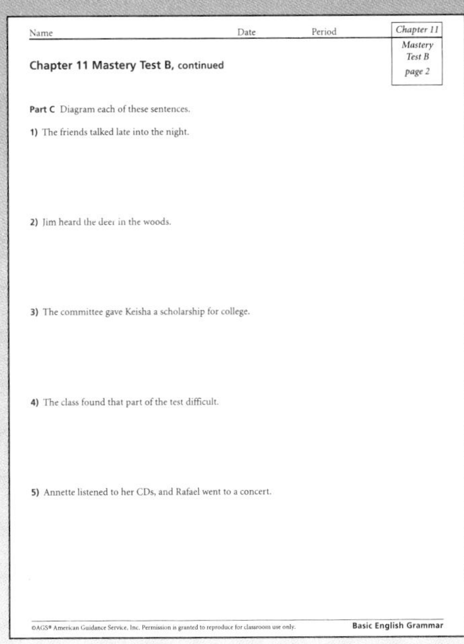

Name Date Period | *Chapter 11 Mastery Test B page 2*

Chapter 11 Mastery Test B, continued

Part C Diagram each of these sentences.

1) The friends talked late into the night.
2) Jim heard the deer in the woods.
3) The committee gave Keisha a scholarship for college.
4) The class found that part of the test difficult.
5) Annette listened to her CDs, and Rafael went to a concert.

 Basic English Grammar

Chapter 11 Mastery Test B

Chapter 12

Planning Guide

Sentences Patterns With a Linking Verb

	Student Text Lesson			
	Student Pages	Vocabulary	Practice Exercises	Lesson Review
Lesson 1 Pattern 5 Sentences	256-264	✔	✔	264
Lesson 2 Pattern 6 Sentences	265-271	✔	✔	271

Chapter Activities

Teacher's Resource Library

Community Connection 12: Finding Linking Verbs in Catalogs

Diagramming Activities 5-6

Assessment Options

Student Text

Chapter 12 Review

Teacher's Resource Library

Chapter 12 Mastery Tests A and B

Teaching Strategies							Language Skills			Learning Styles						Teacher's Resource Library		
Reviewing Skills	Teacher Alert	Follow-up Activity	Career Application	Home Application	Global Connection	Community Application	Identification Skills	Writing Skills	Punctuation Skills	Visual/Spatial	Auditory/Verbal	Body/Kinesthetic	Logical/Mathematical	Group Learning	LEP/ESL	Activities	Workbook Activities	Self-Study Guide
256	260			262			✔	✔	✔			257						✔
265			269		269	272	✔	✔	✔					269		34-36	49-52	✔

Chapter at a Glance

Chapter 12: Sentence Patterns With a Linking Verb

Teacher's Resource Library

- **Activities** 34–36
- **Workbook Activities** 49–52
- **Diagramming Activities** 5–6
- **Community Connection** 12
- **Chapter 12 Self-Study Guide**
- **Chapter 12 Mastery Tests A and B**

(Answer Keys for the Teacher's Resource Library begin on page 330 of this Teacher's Edition.)

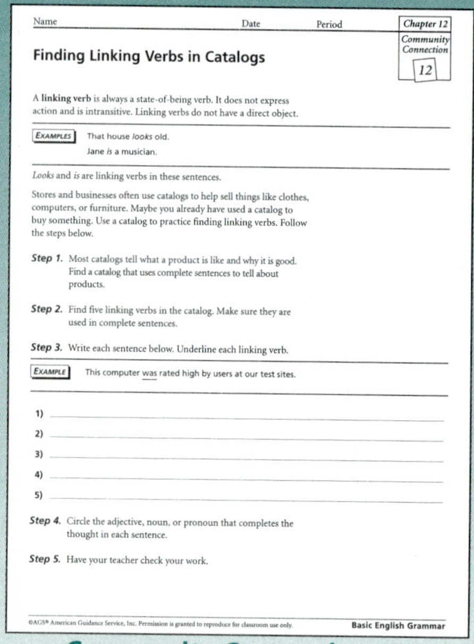

Name ____ Date ____ Period ____ *Chapter 12* *Community Connection* 12

Finding Linking Verbs in Catalogs

A **linking verb** is always a state-of-being verb. It does not express action and is intransitive. Linking verbs do not have a direct object.

EXAMPLES That house *looks* old.
Jane *is* a musician.

Looks and *is* are linking verbs in these sentences.

Stores and businesses often use catalogs to help sell things like clothes, computers, or furniture. Maybe you already have used a catalog to buy something. Use a catalog to practice finding linking verbs. Follow the steps below.

Step 1. Most catalogs tell what a product is like and why it is good. Find a catalog that uses complete sentences to tell about products.

Step 2. Find five linking verbs in the catalog. Make sure they are used in complete sentences.

Step 3. Write each sentence below. Underline each linking verb.

EXAMPLE This computer was rated high by users at our test sites.

1) ____
2) ____
3) ____
4) ____
5) ____

Step 4. Circle the adjective, noun, or pronoun that completes the thought in each sentence.

Step 5. Have your teacher check your work.

 Basic English Grammar

Community Connection 12

Chapter 12

Sentence Patterns With a Linking Verb

Some artists place pieces of glass or stone in a pattern to make a picture. These patterned pictures are called mosaics. In Chapter 11, you learned that sentences have patterns, too. In this chapter, you will learn about sentence patterns that contain linking verbs.

A linking verb, or state-of-being verb, does not express action. Since a linking verb is intransitive, it does not take a direct object.

Each lesson in Chapter 12 focuses on sentences with linking verbs and shows how to diagram these sentences.

Goals for Learning

- To identify the parts of sentences with linking verbs
- To distinguish between predicate adjectives and predicate nouns
- To diagram sentences with linking verbs
- To diagram sentences with adverbs of degree correctly
- To diagram compound sentences with linking verbs correctly

Reading Vocabulary

compound (6)
diagram (6)
distinguish (6)
identify (6)
intransitive
mosaic (7)

Introducing the Chapter

Engage students in a discussion about the mosaic. If necessary, explain that a mosaic is composed of pieces of glass and stone arranged in a pattern. Use these questions to stimulate the discussion:

- What story does this mosaic tell?
- What do you think the artist wanted you to feel?
- Do you find the mosaic pleasing or not? Can you explain why?

Point out that the effect of this mosaic comes from the arrangement, or pattern, of the individual pieces. Had the artist chosen a different pattern, the effect would have been entirely different. Point out that, in a similar way, the effect of a sentence on a reader comes from the writer's arrangement of the individual words. A different arrangement has a totally different effect. Tell students that in Chapter 12 they will have an opportunity to diagram and write sentences with linking verbs.

SELF-STUDY GUIDE

Name ____________

CHAPTER 12: Sentence Patterns With a Linking Verb

Goal 12.1 *To identify the parts of sentences with linking verbs*

Date	Assignment	Score
______	1: Read pages 255-257. Complete Activities A-B on page 257.	______
______	2: Read page 258. Complete Activities C-D on page 258.	______
______	3: Read page 259. Complete Activities E-F on page 259.	______
______	4: Read page 260. Complete Activities G-H on page 260.	______
______	5: Read page 261. Complete Activities I-J on page 261.	______

Comments:

Goal 12.2 *To diagram sentences with linking verbs and adverbs of degree*

Date	Assignment	Score
______	6: Read pages 262-263. Complete Activity K on page 263.	______
______	7: Complete the Lesson 1 Review, Parts A-C on page 264.	______

Comments:

Goal 12.3 *To distinguish between predicate adjectives and predicate nouns*

Date	Assignment	Score
______	8: Read page 265. Complete Activity A on page 265.	______
______	9: Read page 266. Complete Activities B-C on page 266.	______
______	10: Complete Workbook Activity 49.	______
______	11: Read page 267. Complete Activities D-E on page 267.	______
______	12: Read page 268. Complete Activity F on page 268.	______

Comments:

 Basic English Grammar

SELF-STUDY GUIDE

Name ____________

CHAPTER 12 Sentence Patterns With a Linking Verb, continued

Goal 12.4 *To diagram compound sentences with linking verbs correctly*

Date	Assignment	Score
______	13: Read pages 269-270. Complete Activity G on page 270.	______
______	14: Complete the Lesson 2 Review, Parts A-C on page 271.	______
______	15: Complete Workbook Activity 50.	______
______	16: Complete Workbook Activity 51.	______
______	17: Complete Workbook Activity 52.	______
______	18: Complete the Chapter 12 Review, Parts A-E on pages 272-273.	______

Comments:

Student's Signature ____________ Date ______

Instructor's Signature ____________ Date ______

 Basic English Grammar

Chapter 12 Self-Study Guide

Lesson at a Glance

Chapter 12 Lesson 1

Overview This lesson explains linking verbs and predicate adjectives used in Pattern 5 sentences.

Objectives

- To identify linking verbs and predicate adjectives.
- To identify the parts of a Pattern 5 sentence.
- To write Pattern 5 sentences.
- To diagram Pattern 5 sentences.

Student Pages 256–264

Teacher's Resource Library

Diagramming Activity 5

Reading Vocabulary

describe (5)	**predicate**
linking verb	**adjective**
predicate	subject (5)

Teaching Suggestions

Introducing the Lesson

Discuss the information provided in the text. To be sure they understand the concepts presented, encourage students to replace the adjective and noun in the examples *Paul is tall* and *Paul is a student* with other adjectives and nouns.

Reviewing Skills

Provide a review of action verbs and state-of-being verbs.

Teacher Alert

You may wish to point out that words that follow a linking verb and tell about the subject are sometimes called *subject complements.* Be sure students understand the distinction between subject complements and objective complements, which they learned about in Chapter 11.

Lesson 1 Pattern 5 Sentences

Before you learn about Pattern 5 sentences, you need to understand more about verbs.

Linking Verbs

> ***Linking verb***
> *A verb that joins the subject to a noun, pronoun, or adjective in the predicate; it is also called a state-of-being verb.*

An action verb expresses action in a sentence. A **linking verb**, or state-of-being verb, does not express action.

EXAMPLES

Action verb: James **plays** baseball.
Linking verb: James **is** a baseball player.

A linking verb joins the subject to a word in the predicate part of the sentence. That word can be a noun, a pronoun, or an adjective. It helps the sentence express a complete thought.

EXAMPLES

Incomplete sentence: This book is.
Complete sentence: This book is new.

A linking verb is intransitive. It never takes a direct object. Sentences with linking verbs follow two patterns:

> Subject—Linking Verb—Adjective
> Subject—Linking Verb—Noun or Pronoun

EXAMPLES

S L.V. Adj.
Paul is tall.

S L.V. N
Paul is a student.

> ***Predicate adjective***
> *An adjective used after a linking verb. It completes the predicate but describes the subject of the sentence.*

An adjective always describes a noun or pronoun. When an adjective appears after a linking verb, the adjective describes the subject. This adjective is called a **predicate adjective.** It is part of the complete predicate, but it describes the subject of the sentence.

EXAMPLE

	Subject	Complete Predicate
	The weather /	is **sunny** and **mild** today.

(*Sunny* and *mild* are adjectives. What *is sunny and mild?* the *weather is.*)

Activity A Write these sentences on your paper. Circle the linking verb. Underline the predicate adjective or adjectives.

Example My brother (is) funny.

1) New cars can be expensive.
2) That little boy looks tired.
3) My youngest brother grows taller and taller.
4) He was never shy.
5) Tomorrow will be warm and sunny.
6) Cara and Lee Ann were excited.
7) The baby looked hungry and cranky.
8) Joaquim is never angry.

Pattern 5 Sentences

A Pattern 5 sentence has a subject, a linking verb, and a predicate adjective. The predicate adjective describes the subject.

Pattern 5 Sentences:	Subject + Linking Verb + Adjective

EXAMPLE

S L.V. Adj.
This car is expensive.

S L.V. Adj.
It looks great!

Activity B Complete each of these sentences with a predicate adjective. Write the completed sentence on your paper.

1) Today the air feels ______.
2) The sky looks ______.
3) The day has been ______.
4) Everyone seems ______.
5) They appear ______.

■ Presenting Activity A

To prepare students for Activity A, ask them to name some linking verbs. List the verbs on the board as students name them. If necessary, suggest that students refer back to Chapter 5, page 112 in their text. Then discuss the example and have students complete Activity A on their own.

Activity A Answers

1) can be (V), expensive (Adj.) **2)** looks (V), tired (Adj.) **3)** grows (V), taller, taller (Adj.) **4)** was (V), shy (Adj.) **5)** will be (V), warm, sunny (Adj.) **6)** were (V), excited (Adj.) **7)** looked (V), hungry, cranky (Adj.) **8)** is (V), angry (Adj.)

■ Presenting Activity B

Write the first item in Activity B on the board. Invite volunteers to take turns completing the sentence with different predicate adjectives. After students complete Activity B on their own, invite them to share their sentences with the class.

Activity B Answers

Each sentence should be completed with a predicate adjective.

LEARNING STYLES

Body/Kinesthetic

Divide the class into groups of three. Ask each group to choose a sentence from pages 256–264 that shows the following pattern: subject/linking verb/predicate adjective. Point out that the linking verb is like an equal sign. (For example, in the sentence "Mary is athletic," Mary = athletic.) Ask each group to write its subject, equal sign, and predicate adjective on three separate sheets of paper. Have each group stand and demonstrate its sentence with the three placards. Afterward, invite volunteer groups to stand by people, places, and things in the classroom and create sentences using this sentence pattern.

Reading Vocabulary

active (6) create (6)
artistic (5) restless (7)

Presenting Activity C

Do this activity together as a class. Discuss the example. Then draw a chart on the board with the headings: *Subject, Linking Verb,* and *Predicate Adjective.* Invite volunteers to fill in the chart as students identify the subject, linking verb, and predicate adjective in each sentence. As a follow up to this activity, you might invite students to replace the predicate adjective in each sentence with another adjective that changes the meaning of the sentence.

Activity C Answers

	S	*L.V.*	*P. Adj.*
1)	cousin	is	artistic
2)	sauce	tasted	spicy
3)	note	sounds	flat
4)	girl	became	sleepy
5)	weather	turned	cold
6)	actor	appeared	nervous

Presenting Activity D

Before having students complete Activity D on their own, work with them to create a list of adverbs of degree. Suggest that students refer to the list as they complete Activity D and try to use a different adverb in each sentence.

Activity D Answers

Each sentence should include an adverb of degree that tells about the predicate adjective in bold.

Activity C Create three columns on your paper with the titles *Subject, Linking Verb,* and *Predicate Adjective.* Then identify the simple subject, the linking verb, and the predicate adjective in each sentence. Write them in the correct column.

Example Jim's report was interesting.

Subject	Linking Verb	Predicate Adjective
report	was	interesting

1) My cousin is artistic.
2) The sauce tasted spicy.
3) That note sounds flat.
4) The little girl became sleepy.
5) The weather turned cold.
6) The young actor appeared nervous.

A Pattern 5 sentence may have an adverb of degree to tell about the predicate adjective. Adverbs of degree answer questions about adjectives.

EXAMPLE

S L.V. Adv. Pred. Adj.
Her voice sounded **very** loud.

Activity D Write these sentences on your paper. Add an adverb of degree to each sentence to tell about the predicate adjective in bold.

Example I feel **good** today.
I feel **extremely** good today.

1) My grandparents keep **active**.
2) She looks **happy**.
3) He sounds **tired**.
4) The day turned **cold**.
5) They appeared **calm**.
6) You seem **worried**.
7) The children became **restless**.

A Pattern 5 sentence may have adverbs and prepositional phrases that give more information about the predicate adjective.

EXAMPLE

She is always busy after school.

How often? *always*

When? *after school*

Activity E Write these sentences on your paper. Underline the predicate adjectives in each sentence. Then add adverbs or prepositional phrases that tell about each predicate adjective.

1) Jim is tall.

2) That house looks run-down.

3) The sky grew dark.

4) Your painting is colorful.

5) This salad tastes delicious.

6) Your motor sounds odd.

7) Lydia seems quiet.

8) Her notebook is neat.

Activity F Copy these sentences onto your paper. Write *S* above the simple subject, *L.V.* above the linking verb, and *Pred. Adj.* above the predicate adjective.

	S	L.V.	Pred. Adj.
Example The old	house	looked	empty.

1) The month of June is usually pleasant.

2) The days grow longer then.

3) The air feels warmer in June.

4) Maryanne is especially happy about warm weather.

5) The cat becomes friskier, too.

Reading Vocabulary

frisky (6)
phrase (6)
odd (5)
prepositional

Presenting Activity E

Write these sentences on the board: *The children became restless./That girl seems shy.* Ask students to identify the predicate adjective in each sentence. Invite volunteers to add adverbs or prepositional phrases to each sentence to tell about the predicate adjective. Following this, have students complete Activity E on their own.

Activity E Answers

The predicate adjectives are listed below. Each sentence should include an adverb or prepositional phrase that tells about the predicate adjective.

1) tall **2)** run-down **3)** dark **4)** colorful **5)** delicious **6)** odd **7)** quiet **8)** neat

Presenting Activity F

After discussing the example provided for Activity F, invite volunteers to give examples of other sentences with linking verbs and predicate adjectives. Ask the class to identify the linking verbs and predicate adjectives in these sentences. Then ask students to complete Activity F independently.

Activity F Answers

S	*L.V.*	*P. Adj.*
1) month	is	pleasant
2) days	grow	longer
3) air	feels	warmer
4) Maryanne	is	happy
5) cat	becomes	friskier

Sentence Patterns With a Linking Verb *Chapter 12* **259**

Reading Vocabulary

combine (6) infinitive
conjunction request (6)

Presenting Activity G

Remind students that the coordinating conjunctions *and, but,* and *or* connect words that do the same job in a sentence. Then write the first item in Activity G on the board and have volunteers take turns completing the sentence with different compound adjectives. After students complete Activity G on their own, invite them to share their sentences with the class.

Activity G Answers

Each sentence should be completed with compound predicate adjectives.

Presenting Activity H

Before having students complete Activity H on their own, emphasize that the two ideas expressed in a compound sentence must be related. If necessary, illustrate this concept with the following examples:

Incorrect: Their smiles were bright, and the day grew cold.

Correct: Their smiles were bright, and their voices sounded cheerful.

Activity H Answers

Each sentence should be two Pattern 5 sentences combined with a conjunction to form a compound sentence.

TEACHER ALERT

Remind students to put a comma before the conjunction in a compound sentence.

In a Pattern 5 sentence, the predicate adjective may be compound.

EXAMPLE

S L.V. Adj. Adj.
Nina's report was **short** and **funny**.

Activity G Complete each of these sentences with compound predicate adjectives. Write the completed sentences on your paper.

1) The new curtains were ______ and ______.

2) Maryanne's speech will be ______ or ______.

3) Andy's new bike is ______ but not ______.

4) The month of May is ______ and ______.

5) After a big dinner, I am usually ______ and ______.

You may combine two Pattern 5 sentences with a conjunction to form a compound sentence. A compound sentence has two complete thoughts.

EXAMPLE

S L.V. Adj. S L.V. Adj.
Mrs. Davis is usually serious, but Mr. Davis is always funny.

Activity H First, write two related Pattern 5 sentences. Then use one of the following conjunctions to combine the two sentences into a compound sentence.

and for or but

A Pattern 5 sentence may be a command or request. Remember that commands are always in the present tense. Use the infinitive form of linking verbs in commands.

EXAMPLE

L.V. Pred. Adj.
Be quiet.

260 Chapter 12 Sentence Patterns With a Linking Verb

Activity I Copy these commands or requests onto your paper. Underline the linking verb once and the predicate adjective or compound predicate adjective twice.

Example Keep quiet during my report!

1) Look friendly during the job interview.

2) Be nice to your teacher!

3) Stay calm during an emergency.

4) Be ready for your class.

5) Remain loyal and true to your friends.

A Pattern 5 sentence may also be a question. In a Pattern 5 question, the predicate adjective may come right after the subject. The verb or part of a verb phrase may be used to form the question.

EXAMPLES

L.V. S L.V. Pred. Adj.
Did his report seem short?

L.V. S Compound Pred. Adj.
Was April warm and rainy?

Activity J Copy these sentences onto your paper. Circle the subject. Underline the linking verb once and the predicate adjective or compound predicate adjective twice.

Example Is your (brother) upset about something?

1) Are you tired and hungry?

2) Does the school day seem longer to you?

3) Is this bread homemade?

4) Was she excited or nervous about the play?

5) Will these flowers stay fresh until Friday?

Reading Vocabulary

emergency (5) loyal (5)
interview (6)

Presenting Activity I

Discuss the example with students. Point out that in this sentence, the verb *keep* has the same meaning as the linking verbs *remain* or *stay.* Then have students complete Activity I on their own.

Activity I Answers

1) Look friendly 2) Be nice
3) Stay calm 4) Be ready
5) Remain loyal and true

Presenting Activity J

Some students may have trouble identifying the subject or the verb in questions. Suggest that these students change each question into a statement and then try to find the subject, verb, and predicate adjective. Demonstrate this concept by writing the example sentence on the board as a statement: *Your brother is upset about something.*

Activity J Answers

	S	*L.V.*	*P. Adj.*
1)	you	are	tired, hungry
2)	day	does seem	longer
3)	bread	is	homemade
4)	she	was	excited, nervous
5)	flowers	will stay	fresh

Sentence Patterns With a Linking Verb Chapter 12 **261**

Reading Vocabulary
baseline

Application

At Home
Knowing the steps for diagramming a sentence can help students understand sentence structure. Knowing what steps to follow in an emergency, such as a fire, can help prevent injury and perhaps even save someone's life. Encourage students to work with family members to create a list of steps to follow in case of fire. Suggest that they illustrate these steps with helpful diagrams to show, for example, what exits to take and where everyone is to meet outside.

Diagramming Pattern 5 Sentences

To diagram a Pattern 5 sentence:

1. Place the predicate adjective on the baseline of the diagram.
2. Separate the predicate adjective from the verb with a short line slanted toward the verb.

Example The road felt bumpy.

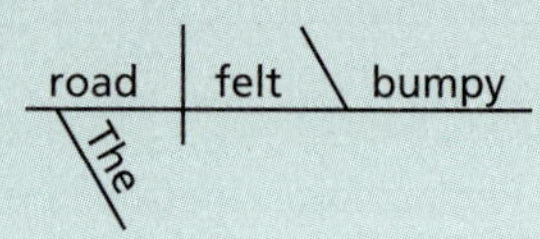

3. Diagram a compound predicate adjective this way.

Example The air was cool and dry.

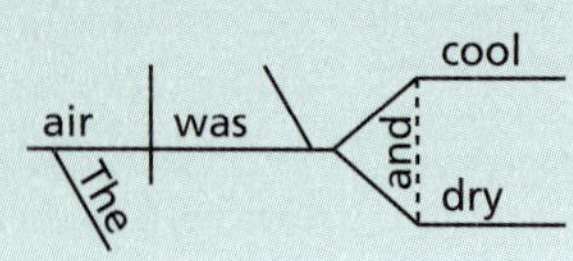

4. Place an adverb of degree under the adjective on a slanted line.

Example The soup was very hot.

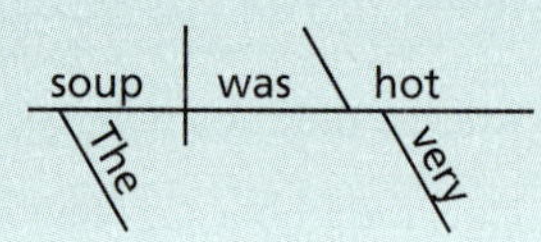

262 Chapter 12 Sentence Patterns With a Linking Verb

5. Show the understood subject of a command or a request in parentheses.

EXAMPLE Be kind.

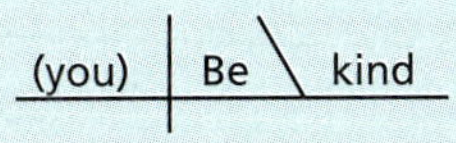

6. If a Pattern 5 sentence is a question, change it into a statement. Then draw the diagram.

EXAMPLE Was your trip fun? Your trip was fun.

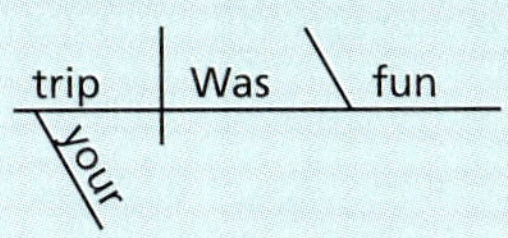

To diagram a compound Pattern 5 sentence:

1. Place each complete thought on its own baseline.
2. Connect each thought with a dotted line.

EXAMPLE Mrs. Davis is usually serious, but Mr. Davis is always funny.

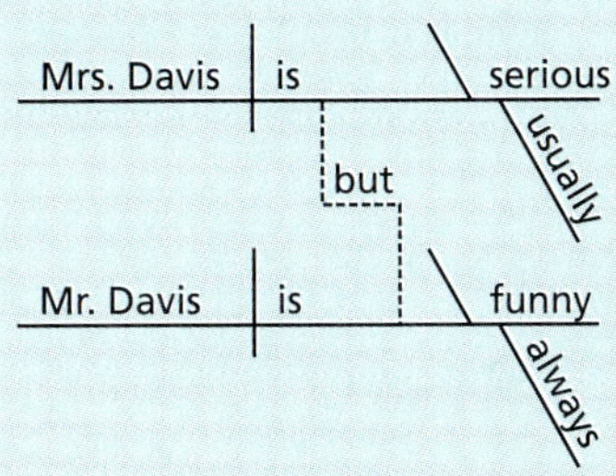

Activity K Diagram these Pattern 5 sentences on your paper. If you need help, look at the rules and examples on page 262 and above.

1) Monday morning was extremely windy, but the air was warm.
2) Stay quiet and absolutely still.
3) Is your puppy afraid of loud noises?

Reading Vocabulary

absolutely (6) extremely (6)
connect (5) parentheses

■ Presenting Activity K

Write these sentences in a row across the top of the board: *She seemed terribly sorry about the accident. / Stay warm and dry. / Is dinner finally ready?* Then ask for pairs of volunteers to come and diagram each sentence on the board. When they have finished, have the class check each diagram and point out any mistakes to be corrected. Then have students complete Activity K on their own.

Activity K Answers

1)

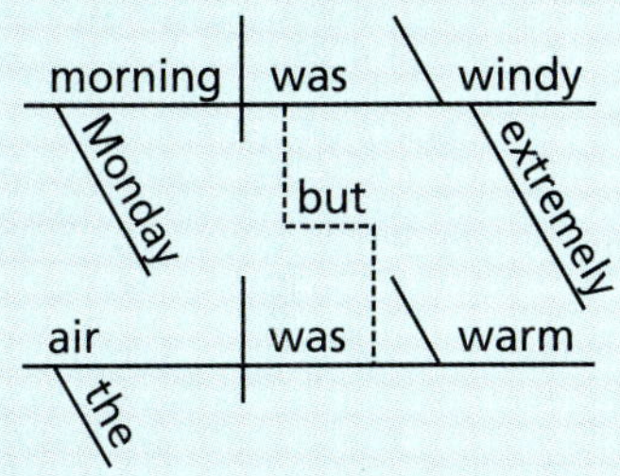

2)

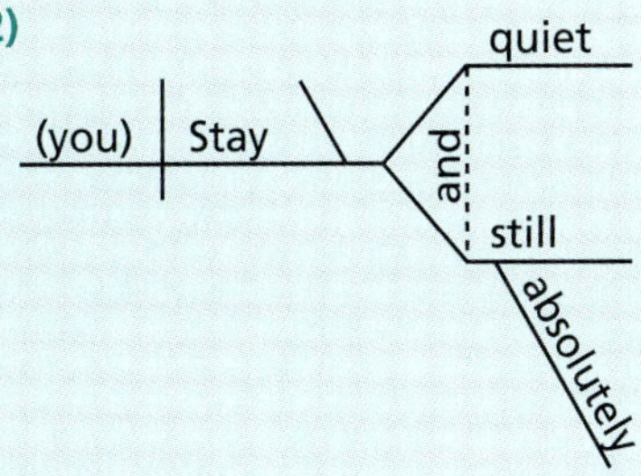

3)

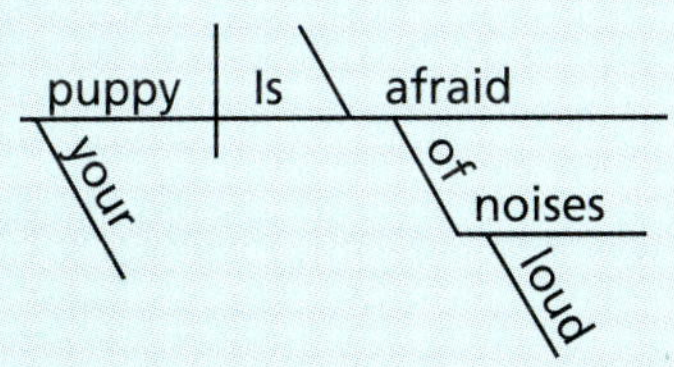

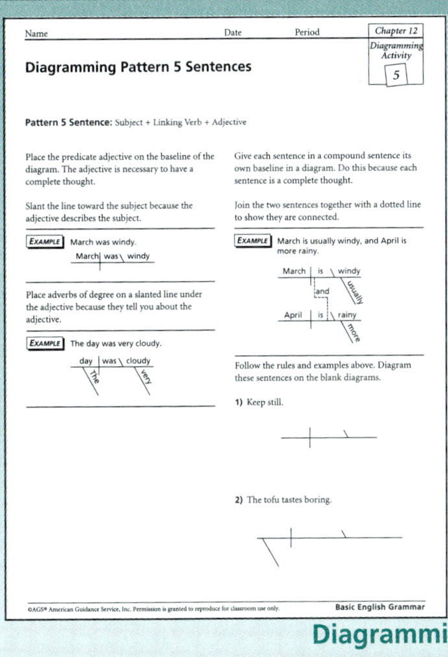

Name Date Period

Chapter 12 *Diagramming Activity* 5

Diagramming Pattern 5 Sentences

Pattern 5 Sentence: Subject + Linking Verb + Adjective

Place the predicate adjective on the baseline of the diagram. The adjective is necessary to have a complete thought.

Slant the line toward the subject because the adjective describes the subject.

EXAMPLE March was windy.

March | was \ windy

Place adverbs of degree on a slanted line under the adjective because they tell you about the adjective.

EXAMPLE The day was very cloudy.

day | was \ cloudy
The
very

Give each sentence in a compound sentence its own baseline in a diagram. Do this because each sentence is a complete thought.

Join the two sentences together with a dotted line to show they are connected.

EXAMPLE March is usually windy, and April is more rainy.

March | is \ windy
usually
and
April | is \ rainy
more

Follow the rules and examples above. Diagram these sentences on the blank diagrams.

1) Keep still.

2) The tofu tastes boring.

 Basic English Grammar

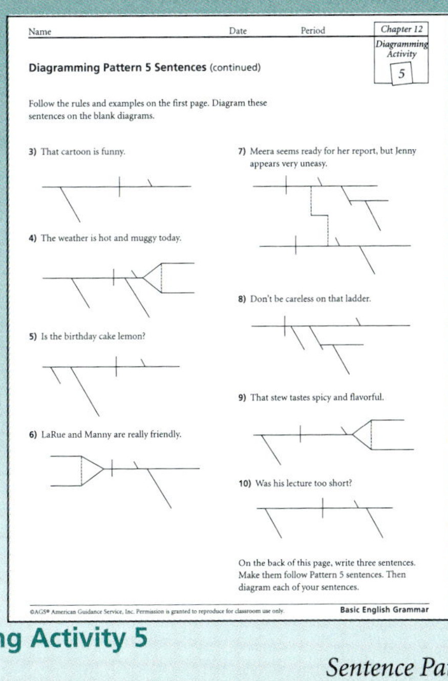

Name Date Period

Chapter 12 *Diagramming Activity* 5

Diagramming Pattern 5 Sentences (continued)

Follow the rules and examples on the first page. Diagram these sentences on the blank diagrams.

3) That cartoon is funny.

4) The weather is hot and muggy today.

5) Is the birthday cake lemon?

6) LaRue and Manny are really friendly.

7) Meera seems ready for her report, but Jenny appears very uneasy.

8) Don't be careless on that ladder.

9) That stew tastes spicy and flavorful.

10) Was his lecture too short?

On the back of this page, write three sentences. Make them follow Pattern 5 sentences. Then diagram each of your sentences.

 Basic English Grammar

Diagramming Activity 5

Sentence Patterns With a Linking Verb Chapter 12 **263**

Reading Vocabulary

athletic (5) computer (8)
chilly (5) powerful (6)

Part A Answers

1) linking verb **2)** action verb
3) action verb **4)** linking verb
5) linking verb

Part B Answers

	L.V.	*P. Adj.*
1)	tasted	sour
2)	appears	friendly
3)	is	athletic
4)	have been	active
5)	is	small, powerful

Part C Answers

1)

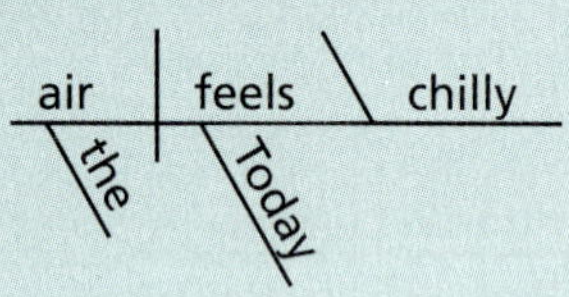

2)

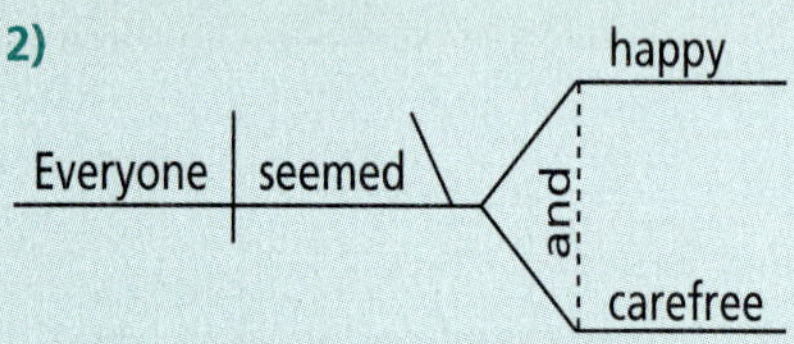

3)

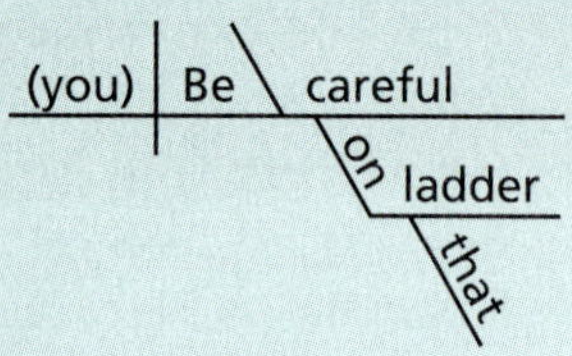

4)

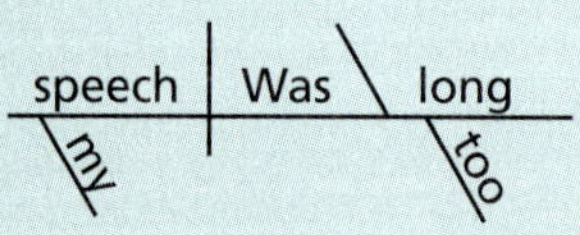

Lesson 1 Review

Part A Write whether the verb in bold in each sentence is a *linking verb* or an *action verb*. Write your answers on your paper. Remember, a linking verb never takes a direct object.

1) **Be** loyal to your friends.

2) Later I **am going** to the movies.

3) **Taste** this stew for me.

4) **Is** it too salty?

5) No, it **tastes** just right!

Part B Write the linking verbs and predicate adjectives in each of these sentences on your paper.

1) The lemon tasted sour.

2) Sue appears friendly.

3) James is very athletic.

4) Have they always been so active?

5) That computer is small but powerful.

Part C Diagram these Pattern 5 sentences on your paper.

1) Today the air feels chilly.

2) Everyone seemed happy and carefree.

3) Be careful on that ladder!

4) Was my speech too long?

264 *Chapter 12 Sentence Patterns With a Linking Verb*

Lesson 2 Pattern 6 Sentences

Predicate nominative

A noun or pronoun that follows a linking verb and renames the subject.

A Pattern 6 sentence has a subject, a linking verb, and a **predicate nominative**. The predicate nominative is a noun or pronoun that renames the subject. Like a predicate adjective, a predicate nominative always follows a linking verb.

Pattern 6 Sentences: Subject + Linking Verb + Noun or Pronoun

EXAMPLE

S L.V. P.N.
That building was once a school.

Activity A Write these sentences on your paper. Write *S* above the subject, *L.V.* above the linking verb, and *P.N.* above the predicate nominative.

S L.V. P.N.
Example Miss Lewis has been our coach.

1) In 1789, George Washington became president.

2) She is my friend.

3) My favorite horror movie is *The Invasion of the Body Snatchers.*

4) The song writer is also a poet.

5) The winner of the race was Emily.

6) They are athletes.

7) The woman in the picture is a neighbor.

8) Charles will be the director.

9) My choice for class president is you.

10) The title of that play is *Raisin in the Sun.*

Lesson at a Glance

Chapter 12 Lesson 2

Overview This lesson introduces predicate nominatives and Pattern 6 sentences.

Objectives

- To identify predicate nominatives.
- To distinguish between predicate adjectives and predicate nominatives.
- To write Pattern 6 sentences.
- To diagram Pattern 6 sentences.

Student Pages 265–271

Teacher's Resource Library

Activities 34–36

Workbook Activities 49–52

Diagramming Activity 6

Reading Vocabulary

athlete (6)
director (7)
invasion (8)
predicate nominative
raisin (6)

Teaching Suggestions

Introducing the Lesson

Discuss the text and the definition of predicate nominatives.

Reviewing Skills

Review predicate adjectives discussed in the previous lesson.

Presenting Activity A

Discuss the example. Then have students complete Activity A on their own.

Activity A Answers

1) George Washington (S), became (L.V.), president (P.N.) **2)** She (S), is (L.V.), friend (P.N.) **3)** movie (S), is (L.V.), *The Invasion of the Body Snatchers* (P.N.) **4)** writer (S), is (L.V.), poet (P.N.) **5)** winner (S), was (L.V.), Emily (P.N.) **6)** They (S), are (L.V.), athletes (P.N.) **7)** woman (S), is (L.V.), neighbor (P.N.) **8)** Charles (S), will be (L.V.), director (P.N.) **9)** choice (S), is (L.V.), you (P.N.) **10)** title (S), is (L.V.), *Raisin in the Sun* (P.N.)

Reading Vocabulary

confuse (5) talent (5)
include (5) transitive

■ **Presenting Activity B** Do the first item orally with the class. Then ask students to complete Activity B on their own. Have students who need extra support work with a partner. Suggest that they first identify the subject and linking verb in each sentence before they try to find the predicate nominative.

Activity B Answers

	P.N.	*Adj.*
1)	president	first
2)	cook	great
3)	person	friendly, helpful
4)	coach	excellent, soccer
5)	teacher	popular

■ **Presenting Activity C** Write the following sentences on the board: *Those boys enjoy baseball. / Baseball is a fun sport.* Help students determine which sentence has the direct object and which has the predicate nominative. Then have students complete Activity C independently.

Activity C Answers

1) direct object **2)** predicate nominative **3)** predicate nominative **4)** direct object **5)** predicate nominative

In a Pattern 6 sentence, adjectives often come before the predicate nominative. The adjective describes the predicate nominative.

EXAMPLE
S L.V. Adj. Adj. P.N.
Fred is a talented baseball player.
(The adjectives *talented* and *baseball* describe the noun *player.*)

Activity B Write these sentences on your paper. Circle the predicate nominative and underline the adjectives that describe it in each sentence. Do not include the articles *the, a,* or *an.*

1) George Washington was the first president.
2) Aunt Marie is a great cook.
3) Carol has always been a friendly, helpful person.
4) Ted has become an excellent soccer coach.
5) Mrs. Marino is a popular teacher.

Do not confuse a noun or pronoun used as a direct object with a predicate nominative. Remember, a direct object receives the action of a transitive verb. A predicate nominative follows an intransitive verb and renames the subject.

EXAMPLE

Direct object:	Ramona introduced the **musician.** (*Musician* receives the action of the transitive verb *introduced.*)
Predicate nominative:	Ramona is a **musician.** (*Musician* renames the subject *Ramona.*)

Activity C Write on your paper whether the word in bold is a *direct object* or a *predicate nominative.*

1) James plays **baseball** in the spring.
2) He is the team **captain.**
3) Tony is the league's best **catcher.**
4) He can also hit the **ball** a mile.
5) He is one of the team's best **hitters.**

Name Date Period *Chapter 12 Activity 34*

Object or Predicate Nominative?

A transitive verb has a direct object. A linking verb can have a predicate nominative. See if you can tell the difference.

Directions: Look at the word in bold print. Decide whether it is a direct object or a predicate nominative. Write your answer in the space provided.

_______ **1)** Paul is the best **player** on the football team.
_______ **2)** My mother makes chewy **cookies.**
_______ **3)** Sky diving is a dangerous **sport.**
_______ **4)** Uncle Tom is the tallest **member** of our family.
_______ **5)** The yearbook staff has many hard **tasks** ahead of them.
_______ **6)** Will our baseball team become the **victors?**
_______ **7)** Our dog bit my best **friend!**
_______ **8)** Spring is my favorite **season.**
_______ **9)** Gerald Ford was a **president** of the United States.
_______ **10)** History is definitely an interesting **subject.**
_______ **11)** Jill is a **member** of the drill team.
_______ **12)** Anne mailed the **letter** on Friday.
_______ **13)** The horse easily jumped over the **fence.**
_______ **14)** Toni was a **cheerleader** last year.

 Basic English Grammar

Activity 34

Name Date Period *Chapter 12 Workbook Activity 49*

Object or Predicate Nominative?

A transitive verb has a direct object. A linking verb can have a predicate nominative. See if you can tell the difference.

EXAMPLES
S V D.O.
John paints pictures.
S L.V. P.N.
John is an artist.

Directions: The noun in each sentence is in bold. Decide whether it is a direct object or a predicate nominative. Write your answer on the line.

_______ **1)** Bill is the **coach** of the softball team.
_______ **2)** Dave plays **shortstop.**
_______ **3)** He hits the **ball** hard!
_______ **4)** Dave is the leading **hitter** on the team.
_______ **5)** This softball team is currently the **leader** in the league.
_______ **6)** Everyone wants the **championship.**
_______ **7)** The championship is the team's **goal** this year.
_______ **8)** John is the **pitcher** for the team.
_______ **9)** He is an excellent **fielder.**
_______ **10)** Big Ed plays **centerfield.**
_______ **11)** He is the tallest **man** on the team.
_______ **12)** Ed can put the **ball** over the fence.
_______ **13)** He is the only **one** in the league.
_______ **14)** Will the team emerge the **victor?**
_______ **15)** That is the burning **question!**

 Basic English Grammar

Workbook Activity 49

A Pattern 6 sentence may have an adverb or a prepositional phrase that answers questions about the linking verb.

EXAMPLES

Larry is **always** a good friend.
(When is Larry a good friend? *always*)

He has been my friend **for years**.
(How long has he been a friend? *for years*)

A Pattern 6 sentence may have a prepositional phrase that describes the predicate nominative.

EXAMPLE

Agatha Christie was the author **of many books**.
(What kind of author? An author *of many books*)

Activity D Write the predicate nominatives in these sentences on your paper. Remember, the predicate nominative is never the object of a preposition.

1) Uruguay is a country in South America.

2) The Nile is one of the world's longest rivers.

3) Mars is the closest planet to the Earth.

4) Pasta has been a popular food in the United States.

5) The most popular movie of 1939 was probably *Gone With the Wind.*

6) *Star Wars* is still Andy's favorite movie.

7) Dana has been Anne's best friend for two years.

Activity E Write five Pattern 6 sentences on your paper. Add as many adverbs, adjectives, and prepositional phrases as you wish. For each sentence, write *S* above the subject, *L.V.* above the linking verb, and *P.N.* above the predicate nominative.

Example Alicia (S) has been (L.V.) Cyndi's best friend (P.N.) since first grade.

Reading Vocabulary

author (6) pasta

■ Presenting Activity D

Read through each item in the activity with students. Work with them to identify the prepositional phrases and objects of the preposition in each sentence. Then have students complete Activity D on their own.

Activity D Answers

1) country **2)** one **3)** planet **4)** food **5)** *Gone With the Wind* **6)** movie **7)** friend

■ Presenting Activity E

Discuss the directions and example given for Activity E. Then invite a volunteer to write another Pattern 6 sentence modeled on the example on the board. Have the class identify the subject, linking verb, and predicate nominative in the sentence for the student to label. Then have students write and label their own sentences to complete Activity E.

Activity E Answers

Each sentence should be a Pattern 6 sentence and should have the subject, linking verb, and predicate nominative labeled.

Reading Vocabulary

architect (6) satisfaction (6)
excellent (5)

■ Presenting Activity F

Before students begin Activity F, help them recall that in commands the subject is always the understood *you*. You might also suggest that students change questions into statements to help them identify the parts more easily. Then, depending on the needs of your students, do Activity F as a class or have students work independently.

Activity F Answers

1) Franklin Pierce (S), Was (L.V.), president (P.N.) **2)** those (S), Are (L.V.), trees, trees (P.N.) **3)** you (understood) (S), Become (L.V.), success (P.N.) **4)** *The Good Earth* (S), is (L.V.), movie, book (P.N.) **5)** Phil, he (S), is, will be (L.V.), student, architect (P.N.)

A Pattern 6 sentence may be a command or a request.

EXAMPLES

L.V. P.N.
Be an honest person.

L.V. P.N.
Always remain a loyal friend.

A Pattern 6 sentence may also be a question.

EXAMPLES

L.V. S L.V. P.N.
Have they always been friends?

L.V. S P.N.
Were you the winner?

A Pattern 6 sentence may have compound parts.

EXAMPLE

S S L.V. P.N. P.N.
Marissa and Sandra are excellent students and super athletes.

You may combine two Pattern 6 sentences with a conjunction to form a compound sentence.

EXAMPLE

S L.V. P.N. S L.V. P.N.
Annie is class president now, and last year she was treasurer.

Activity F Write these sentences on your paper. Write *S* above the subject, *L.V.* above the linking verb, and *P.N.* above the predicate nominative. If a subject is understood, write it in. Some sentences may have compound parts or may be compound sentences.

1) Was Franklin Pierce a U.S. president?
2) Are those oak trees or maple trees?
3) Become a success for your own satisfaction.
4) *The Good Earth* is a movie and a book.
5) Phil is a student now, but he will be an architect some day.

Name Date Period | *Chapter 12 Activity 35*

Complements of Linking Verbs

A linking verb needs a complement. There are two kinds of these complements: a predicate adjective and a predicate noun.

Subject + Linking Verb + Adjective — The adjective describes the subject.
Subject + Linking Verb + Noun — The noun renames the subject.

Directions: Find and circle the complement of the linking verb. Identify it as either an adjective or a noun.

EXAMPLES The oven is hot. ____adjective____
He is the waiter. ____noun____

1) They are excellent skiers. ________
2) We were too tall. ________
3) My dad is the best cook. ________
4) Our dinner was difficult to eat. ________
5) Who was the first person to reach the moon? ________
6) The doctor was especially nice. ________
7) The movie is too long and boring. ________
8) I am ready for a vacation. ________
9) What was the average test score? ________
10) The average score was a 78%. ________
11) She is our favorite actress. ________
12) Pamela is a nursing student. ________

 Basic English Grammar

Activity 35

Name Date Period | *Chapter 12 Activity 36*

Linking Verbs: Yes or No?

Linking verbs express a state of being. They are always intransitive. They link the subject with a noun or an adjective in the predicate. Predicate adjectives describe the subject. Predicate nouns rename the subject.

Directions: Circle the verb in each of these sentences. If it is a linking verb, write *Yes* on the line. If it is not a linking verb, write *No* on the line.

EXAMPLES ____Yes____ She is very excited.
____No____ I threw the football.

________ **1)** Dan and Andy joined the army.
________ **2)** Waterskiing is a popular summer sport.
________ **3)** Suzie's cake looks delicious.
________ **4)** Joanie felt the soft fur coat.
________ **5)** Sam felt very sick.
________ **6)** How many eggs are in a dozen?
________ **7)** Jim's horse bucked him off.
________ **8)** Being happy is all that matters in life.
________ **9)** The movie was a fast-paced adventure.
________ **10)** Our television set is broken.

 Basic English Grammar

Activity 36

Diagramming Pattern 6 Sentences

To diagram a Pattern 6 sentence:

1. Place the predicate nominative on the baseline of the diagram.
2. Separate the predicate nominative from the verb with a line slanted toward the verb.

EXAMPLE Mrs. Castillo is a Spanish teacher.

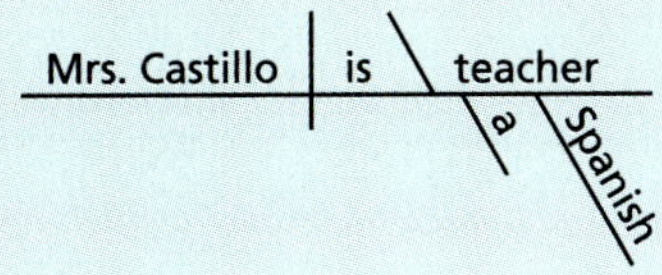

3. Diagram a compound predicate nominative this way.

EXAMPLE Teri is a student and an athlete.

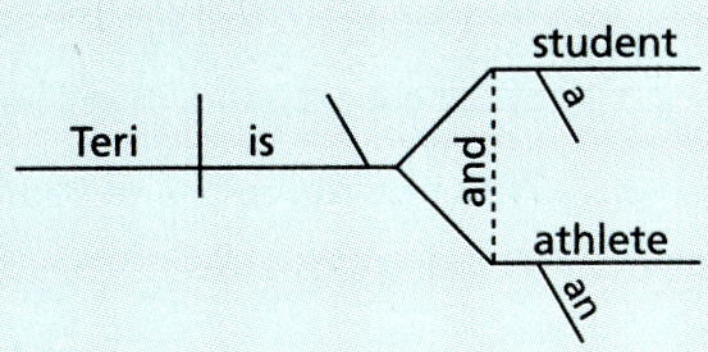

4. If a Pattern 6 sentence is a question, change the question to a statement. Then diagram it.

EXAMPLE

Question		Statement
Is that an oak tree?	→	That is an oak tree.

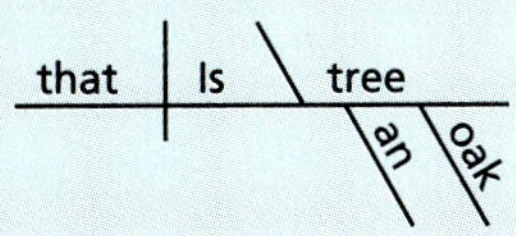

Reading Vocabulary
separate (5)

GLOBAL CONNECTION

Diagrams, maps, charts, and other graphic aids are useful tools for communicating ideas and information to a multilingual audience. Pair English-speaking students with bilingual students. Encourage them to draw a diagram of some concept they are learning about in another class and to label the parts of the diagram in English and the primary language of the bilingual student. Then invite the students to use the diagram and any other graphic aids of their choosing in an oral presentation for the class.

APPLICATION

Career Connection
Point out to students that employers appreciate and reward workers who can think creatively and can present new ideas clearly. Using diagrams, charts, and other graphic aids to present a concept demonstrates that a person has a clear grasp of the subject matter, can organize details, and understands how the details are related. Have students find examples of diagrams, charts, and other graphic aids in newspapers and magazines. Display the examples in the classroom.

LEARNING STYLES

Interpersonal/ Group Learning
Determine how many groups of three are in your class. Then create a diagram pattern for each group. (Use the patterns on page 269.) Give each group one pattern and challenge the group to create a sentence that will fit its diagram pattern. Afterward, have each group print its sentence on the board. Challenge the students to diagram each sentence.

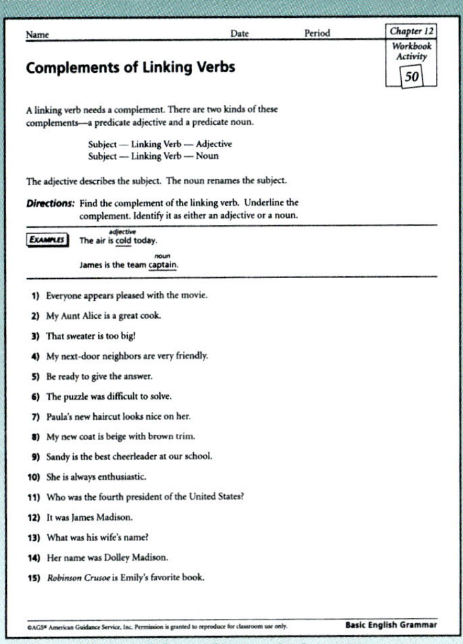

Name Date Period — *Chapter 12* *Workbook Activity* 50

Complements of Linking Verbs

A linking verb needs a complement. There are two kinds of these complements—a predicate adjective and a predicate noun.

Subject — Linking Verb — Adjective
Subject — Linking Verb — Noun

The adjective describes the subject. The noun renames the subject.

Directions: Find the complement of the linking verb. Underline the complement. Identify it as either an adjective or a noun.

EXAMPLES The air is cold (*adjective*) today.
James is the team captain (*noun*).

1) Everyone appears pleased with the movie.
2) My Aunt Alice is a great cook.
3) That sweater is too big!
4) My next-door neighbors are very friendly.
5) Be ready to give the answer.
6) The puzzle was difficult to solve.
7) Paula's new haircut looks nice on her.
8) My new coat is beige with brown trim.
9) Sandy is the best cheerleader at our school.
10) She is always enthusiastic.
11) Who was the fourth president of the United States?
12) It was James Madison.
13) What was his wife's name?
14) Her name was Dolley Madison.
15) *Robinson Crusoe* is Emily's favorite book.

 Basic English Grammar

Workbook Activity 50

Sentence Patterns With a Linking Verb *Chapter 12* **269**

Reading Vocabulary

novelist secretary (5)

■ **Presenting Activity G** Do the first two items on the board with students before having them complete Activity G on their own.

Activity G Answers

1)

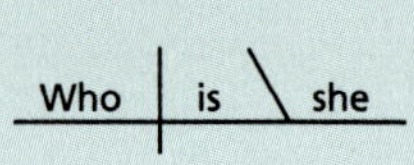

2)

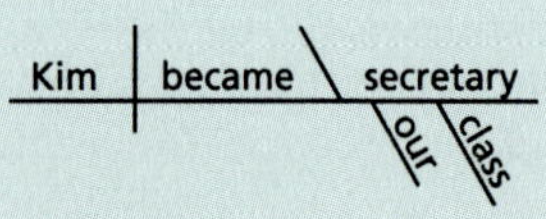

3)

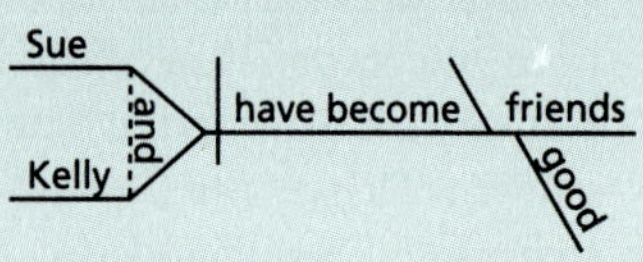

4)

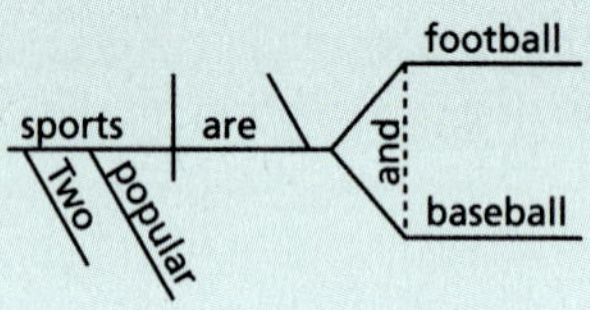

5)

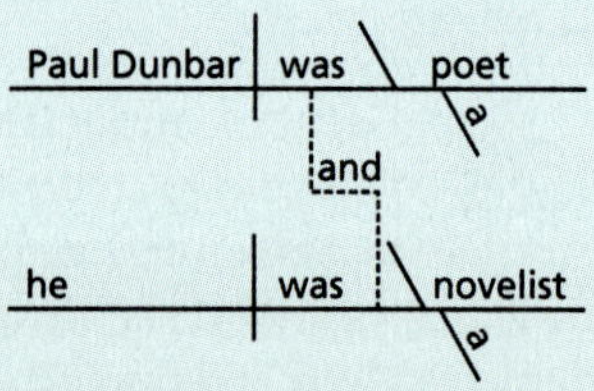

6)

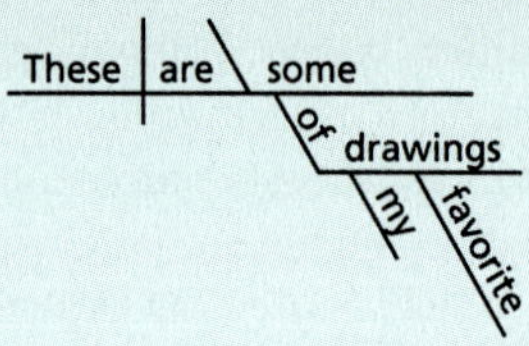

7)

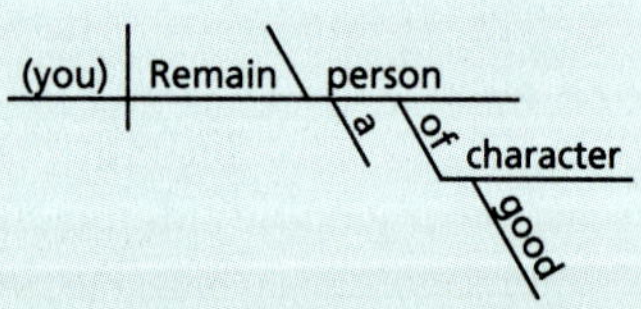

8)

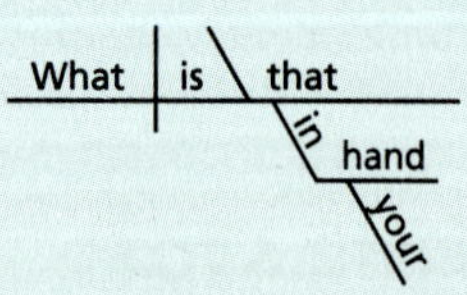

9)

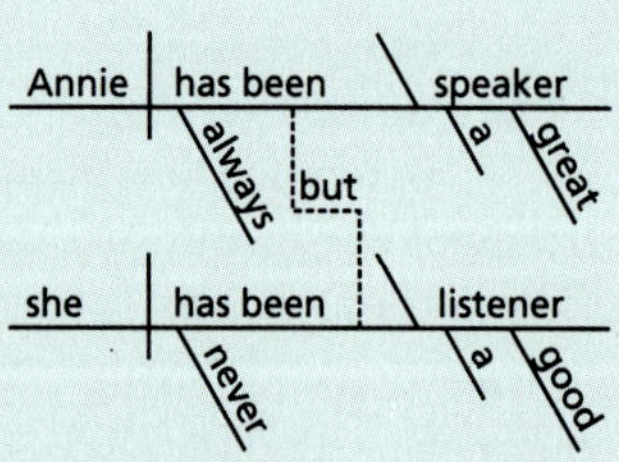

10)

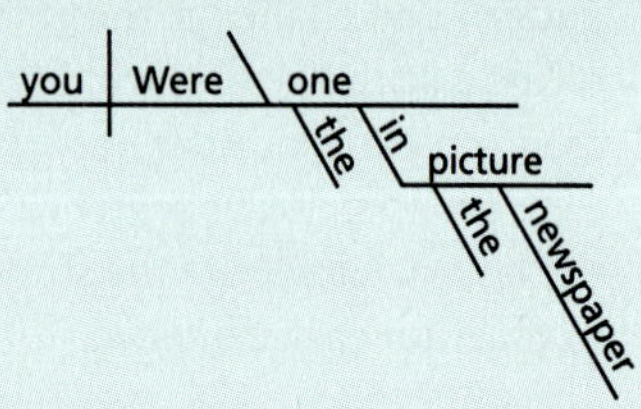

5. Put the understood subject of a command in parentheses.

EXAMPLE Be a good friend.

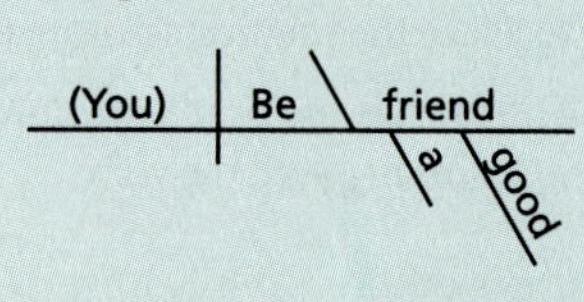

Activity G Diagram these Pattern 6 sentences on your paper.

1) Who is she?
2) Kim became our class secretary.
3) Sue and Kelly have become good friends.
4) Two popular sports are football and baseball.
5) Paul Dunbar was a poet, and he was a novelist.
6) These are some of my favorite drawings.
7) Remain a person of good character.
8) What is that in your hand?
9) Annie has always been a great speaker, but she has never been a good listener.
10) Were you the one in the newspaper picture?

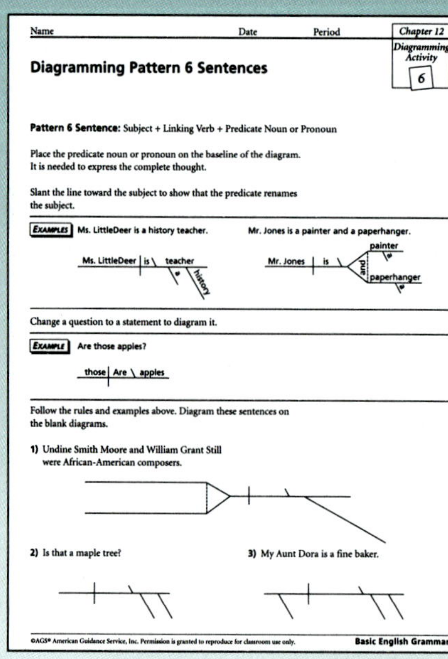

Name Date Period | *Chapter 12* *Diagramming Activity* 6

Diagramming Pattern 6 Sentences

Pattern 6 Sentence: Subject + Linking Verb + Predicate Noun or Pronoun

Place the predicate noun or pronoun on the baseline of the diagram. It is needed to express the complete thought.

Slant the line toward the subject to show that the predicate renames the subject.

EXAMPLES Ms. LittleDeer is a history teacher. Mr. Jones is a painter and a paperhanger.

Change a question to a statement to diagram it.

EXAMPLE Are those apples?

Follow the rules and examples above. Diagram these sentences on the blank diagrams.

1) Undine Smith Moore and William Grant Still were African-American composers.

2) Is that a maple tree?

3) My Aunt Dora is a fine baker.

 Basic English Grammar

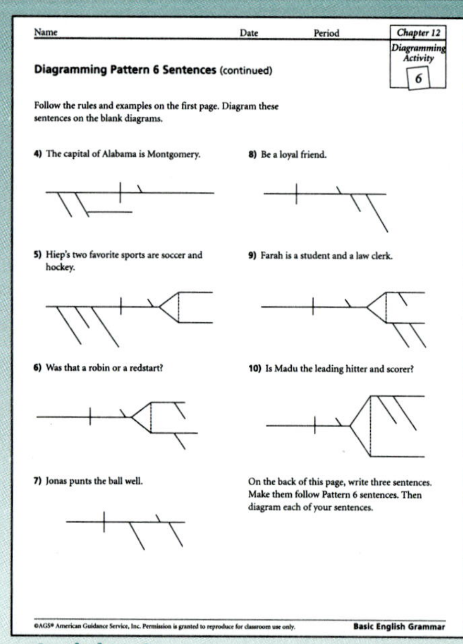

Name Date Period | *Chapter 12* *Diagramming Activity* 6

Diagramming Pattern 6 Sentences (continued)

Follow the rules and examples on the first page. Diagram these sentences on the blank diagrams.

4) The capital of Alabama is Montgomery.

5) Hiep's two favorite sports are soccer and hockey.

6) Was that a robin or a redstart?

7) Jonas punts the ball well.

8) Be a loyal friend.

9) Farah is a student and a law clerk.

10) Is Madu the leading hitter and scorer?

On the back of this page, write three sentences. Make them follow Pattern 6 sentences. Then diagram each of your sentences.

 Basic English Grammar

Diagramming Activity 6

270 *Chapter 12 Sentence Patterns With a Linking Verb*

Lesson 2 Review

Part A Write these Pattern 6 sentences on your paper. For each sentence, write *S* above the subject, *L.V.* above the linking verb, and *P.N.* above the predicate nominative.

S L.V. P.N.
Example Sudan is a country in Africa.

1) Two popular Mexican foods are tacos and burritos.
2) Jupiter is the largest planet in the solar system.
3) Is Dan a friend of yours?
4) Who was that?
5) Lima is the capital of Peru.

Part B Write on your paper whether the word or words in bold in each of these sentences is a *predicate adjective* or *predicate nominative.*

1) *Romeo and Juliet* is a **play** by William Shakespeare.
2) The ending of the play is very **sad**.
3) Edgar Allan Poe was a **poet** and a story **writer**.
4) Warsaw is the **capital** of Poland.
5) Uncle David has always been **artistic**.

Part C Diagram these Pattern 6 sentences on your paper.

1) Janell is a good artist.
2) Be a responsible student and worker.
3) I will play the part of the unemployed singer, and Sal will be the owner of a small theater.
4) Are they the champions?

Reading Vocabulary

burritos	system (5)
solar (6)	unemployed

Part A Answers

	S	L.V.	P.N.
1)	foods	are	tacos, burritos
2)	Jupiter	is	planet
3)	Dan	Is	friend
4)	Who	was	that
5)	Lima	is	capital

Part B Answers

1) predicate nominative
2) predicate adjective
3) predicate nominatives
4) predicate nominative
5) predicate adjective

Part C Answers

1)
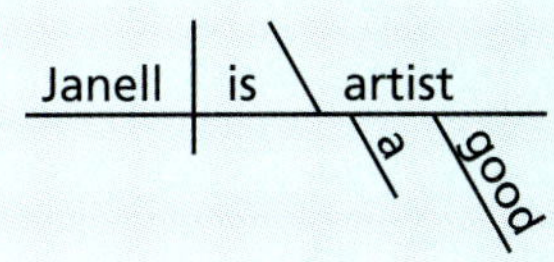

2)
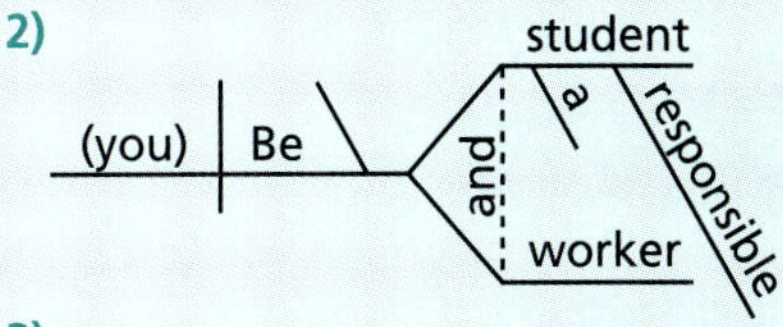

3)
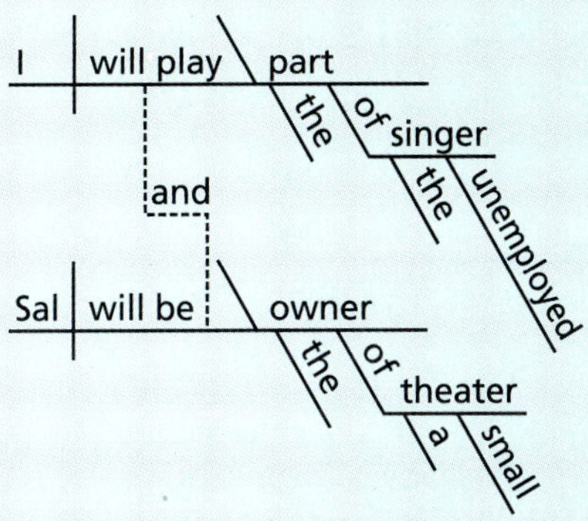

4)
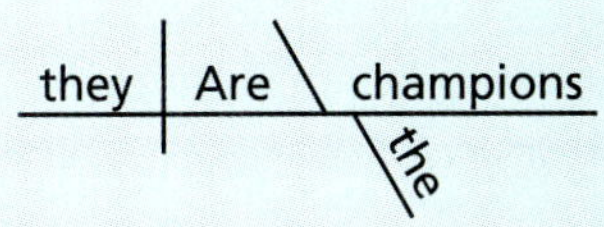

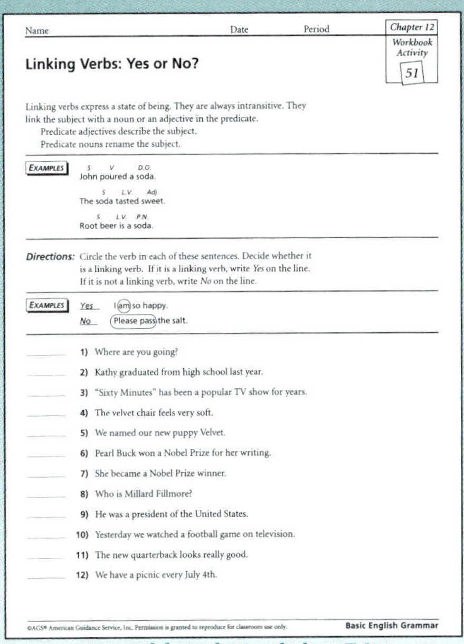

Name Date Period

Chapter 12 Workbook Activity 51

Linking Verbs: Yes or No?

Linking verbs express a state of being. They are always intransitive. They link the subject with a noun or an adjective in the predicate.
Predicate adjectives describe the subject.
Predicate nouns rename the subject.

EXAMPLES
S V D.O.
John poured a soda.
S L.V. Adj.
The soda tasted sweet.
S L.V. P.N.
Root beer is a soda.

Directions: Circle the verb in each of these sentences. Decide whether it is a linking verb. If it is a linking verb, write *Yes* on the line. If it is not a linking verb, write *No* on the line.

EXAMPLES
Yes I (am) so happy.
No (Please pass) the salt.

_____ 1) Where are you going?
_____ 2) Kathy graduated from high school last year.
_____ 3) "Sixty Minutes" has been a popular TV show for years.
_____ 4) The velvet chair feels very soft.
_____ 5) We named our new puppy Velvet.
_____ 6) Pearl Buck won a Nobel Prize for her writing.
_____ 7) She became a Nobel Prize winner.
_____ 8) Who is Millard Fillmore?
_____ 9) He was a president of the United States.
_____ 10) Yesterday we watched a football game on television.
_____ 11) The new quarterback looks really good.
_____ 12) We have a picnic every July 4th.

 Basic English Grammar

Workbook Activity 51

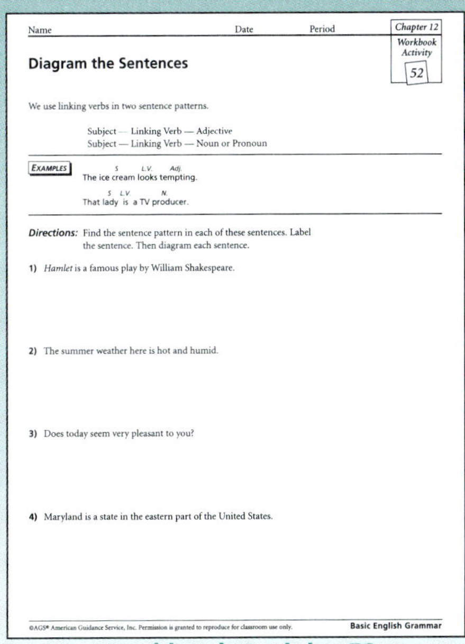

Name Date Period

Chapter 12 Workbook Activity 52

Diagram the Sentences

We use linking verbs in two sentence patterns.

Subject — Linking Verb — Adjective
Subject — Linking Verb — Noun or Pronoun

EXAMPLES
S L.V. Adj.
The ice cream looks tempting.
S L.V. N.
That lady is a TV producer.

Directions: Find the sentence pattern in each of these sentences. Label the sentence. Then diagram each sentence.

1) *Hamlet* is a famous play by William Shakespeare.
2) The summer weather here is hot and humid.
3) Does today seem very pleasant to you?
4) Maryland is a state in the eastern part of the United States.

 Basic English Grammar

Workbook Activity 52

Sentence Patterns With a Linking Verb Chapter 12 **271**

Chapter 12 Review

The Teacher's Resource Library includes two parallel forms of the Chapter 12 Mastery Test. The difficulty level of the two forms is equivalent. You may wish to use one form as a pretest and the other form as a posttest.

Reading Vocabulary

manager (6) messy

Part A Answers

1) action verb **2)** linking verb **3)** linking verb **4)** linking verb **5)** linking verb

Part B Answers

	S	*L.V.*	*P. Adj.*
1)	I	am	sorry
2)	side	is	messy
	side	is	neat
3)	day	was	cool, windy
4)	Aunt Pat	is	happy
5)	she	Was	angry

Part C Answers

1) you (S), Are (L.V.), manager (P.N.)
2) He (S), is (L.V.), boss, uncle (P.N.)
3) she (S), Is (L.V.), one (P.N.)
4) Pablo, family (S), are (L.V.), neighbors (P.N.), Pablo, I (S), have been (L.V.), friends (P.N.)
5) person (S), was (L.V.), Jonas (P.N.)

Application

In the Community

Invite a community service representative to speak to the class about the work his or her organization does to benefit the community. Suggest that the speaker use diagrams and other graphic aids, such as a slide presentation, to create interest for student listeners.

Chapter 12 Review

Part A Write on your paper whether the verb in bold in these sentences is an *action verb* or a *linking verb*. Remember, a linking verb does not take a direct object.

1) Please **taste** the stew.
2) Does it **taste** too spicy?
3) This stew **smells** wonderful.
4) **Be** my pal, and help me clean up.
5) You **seem** upset about something.

Part B Write these sentences on your paper. Write *S* above each subject, *L.V.* above each linking verb, and *Pred. Adj.* above each predicate adjective. Sentences may have compound parts or may be compound.

1) I am sorry.
2) My side of the room is rather messy, but my sister's side is extremely neat.
3) The day was cool and windy.
4) Aunt Pat is always happy.
5) Was she very angry?

Part C Write these sentences on your paper. Write *S* above each subject, *L.V.* above each linking verb, and *P.N.* above each predicate nominative. Sentences may have compound parts or may be compound.

1) Are you the store manager?
2) He is my boss and my uncle.
3) Is she the one in the play?
4) Pablo and his family are our new neighbors, but Pablo and I have been friends for many years.
5) The last person in line was Jonas.

272 *Chapter 12 Sentence Patterns With a Linking Verb*

Name ____ Date ____ Period ____ *Chapter 12 Mastery Test A page 1*

Chapter 12 Mastery Test A

Part A Label the subjects (*S*), linking verbs (*LV*), adverbs (*Adv*), predicate adjectives (*PA*), and predicate nouns (*PN*) in these sentences.

1) Loretta is always friendly.
2) Chip seems distracted today.
3) Marian Anderson was a marvelous singer.
4) Tom and Jane are outstanding athletes.
5) George Burns was a comedian, and he was very lasting.

Part B Write whether the bold word or words is a predicate adjective (*PA*), a predicate noun (*PN*), or a predicate pronoun (*PP*).

1) ______ That girl is my **sister**.
2) ______ Daffodils are **yellow**.
3) ______ Who is **he**?
4) ______ Char will be the **president**.
5) ______ True friends are **they**.
6) ______ Are you **happy** and **excited**?
7) ______ His bedroom is always **neat** and **tidy**.
8) ______ After only three months, he became **director** of the group.
9) ______ Jolene was **president** of the association.
10) ______ Walt felt **nervous** and **shaky** after the accident.

 Basic English Grammar

Name ____ Date ____ Period ____ *Chapter 12 Mastery Test A page 2*

Chapter 12 Mastery Test A, continued

Part C Diagram each of these sentences.

1) The bald eagles were graceful and majestic in flight.
2) Earl seemed happy about his grades.
3) Rhonda becomes a pilot tomorrow.
4) My favorite pastimes are reading and singing.
5) She is a doctor, and she is very caring with her patients.

 Basic English Grammar

Chapter 12 Mastery Test A

Part D Write on your paper whether the word or words in bold in each of these sentences is a *predicate adjective* or *predicate nominative.*

1) Mariana seems **friendly**.
2) Sometimes she is **shy** around strangers.
3) Are you a good **cook**?
4) Leon will be a **senior** next year.
5) Last night, Dena was very **unhappy** about something.
6) She looks awfully **tired** lately.
7) Mr. Franklin is a creative **teacher**.
8) Rebecca and I will be **partners** for the project.
9) The weather has been **warm** and **sunny**.
10) For three months, the top salespeople have been **Santos** and **Ellie**.

Part E Diagram each of the sentences. Beside the diagram, write whether the sentence is Pattern 5 (predicate adjective) or Pattern 6 (predicate noun or pronoun).

1) Her mother is a well-known lawyer.
2) That book will always be one of my favorites.
3) Spring is a nice time of year, but autumn is the best season of all.
4) The message was quite interesting and extremely important.
5) Will they remain friends after graduation?

Test Taking Tip

When studying for a test, learn the most important points. Practice writing or saying the material out loud. Have a partner listen to check if you are right.

Reading Vocabulary

creative (7) lawyer (5)
graduation (6) senior (6)

Part D Answers

1) predicate adjective **2)** predicate adjective **3)** predicate nominative **4)** predicate nominative **5)** predicate adjective **6)** predicate adjective **7)** predicate nominative **8)** predicate nominative **9)** predicate adjective **10)** predicate nominative

Part E Answers

1)
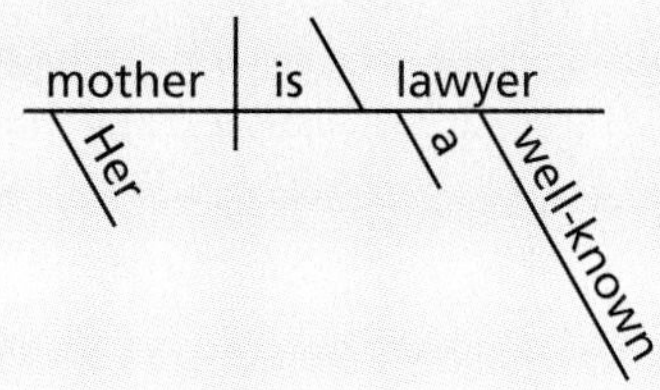

2)
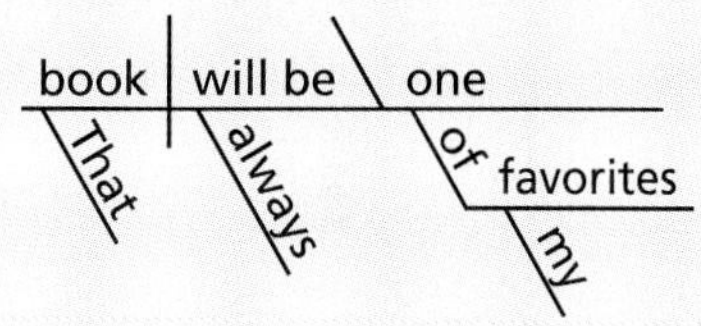

3)
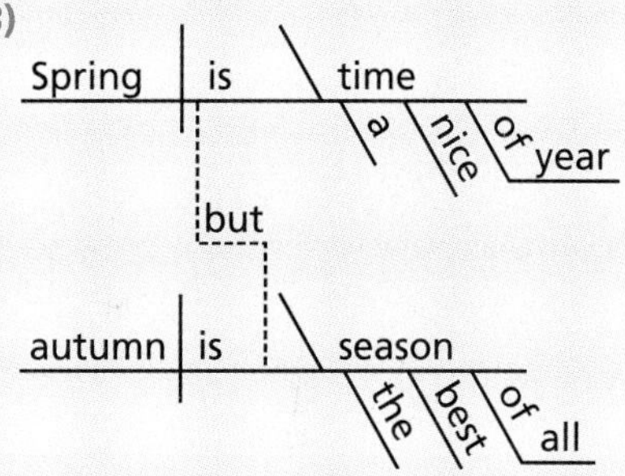

4)
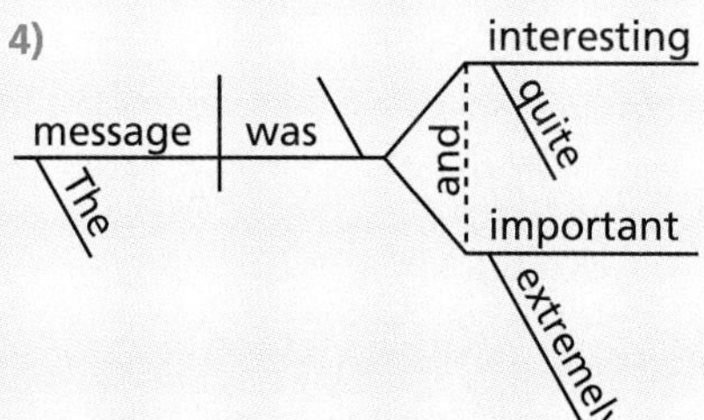

5)
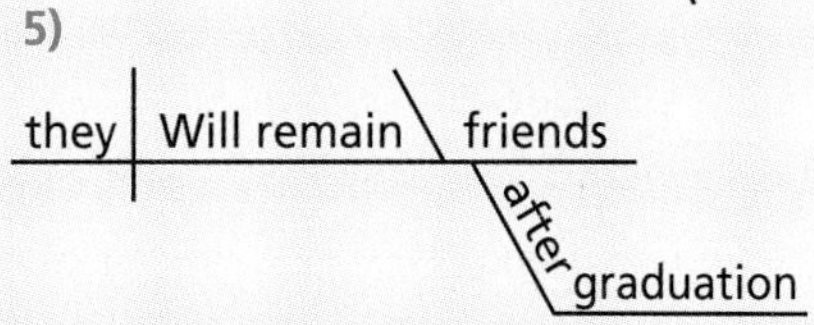

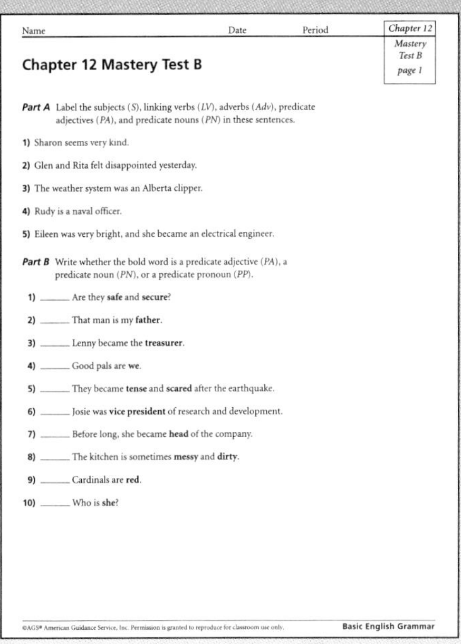

Name Date Period

Chapter 12 Mastery Test B page 1

Chapter 12 Mastery Test B

Part A Label the subjects (*S*), linking verbs (*LV*), adverbs (*Adv*), predicate adjectives (*PA*), and predicate nouns (*PN*) in these sentences.

1) Sharon seems very kind.
2) Glen and Rita felt disappointed yesterday.
3) The weather system was an Alberta clipper.
4) Rudy is a naval officer.
5) Eileen was very bright, and she became an electrical engineer.

Part B Write whether the bold word is a predicate adjective (*PA*), a predicate noun (*PN*), or a predicate pronoun (*PP*).

1) ______ Are they **safe** and **secure**?
2) ______ That man is my **father**.
3) ______ Lenny became the **treasurer**.
4) ______ Good pals are **we**.
5) ______ They became **tense** and **scared** after the earthquake.
6) ______ Josie was **vice president** of research and development.
7) ______ Before long, she became **head** of the company.
8) ______ The kitchen is sometimes **messy** and **dirty**.
9) ______ Cardinals are **red**.
10) ______ Who is **she**?

 Basic English Grammar

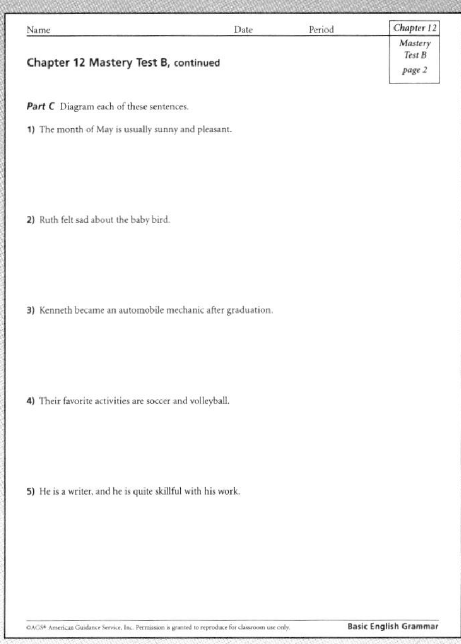

Name Date Period

Chapter 12 Mastery Test B page 2

Chapter 12 Mastery Test B, continued

Part C Diagram each of these sentences.

1) The month of May is usually sunny and pleasant.
2) Ruth felt sad about the baby bird.
3) Kenneth became an automobile mechanic after graduation.
4) Their favorite activities are soccer and volleyball.
5) He is a writer, and he is quite skillful with his work.

 Basic English Grammar

Chapter 12 Mastery Test B

Chapter 13

Planning Guide

Complex Sentences

	Student Text Lesson			
	Student Pages	Vocabulary	Practice Exercises	Lesson Review
Lesson 1 Words, Phrases, and Clauses	276-278	✔	✔	278
Lesson 2 The Adverb Clause	279-281	✔	✔	281
Lesson 3 The Noun Clause	282-286	✔	✔	286
Lesson 4 The Adjective Clause	287-289	✔	✔	289
Lesson 5 Complex and Compound-Complex Sentences	290-295	✔	✔	295

Chapter Activities

Teacher's Resource Library

Community Connection 13: Searching for Complex Sentences in Manuals

Assessment Options

Student Text

Chapter 13 Review

Teacher's Resource Library

Chapter 13 Mastery Tests A and B

Teaching Strategies							Language Skills			Learning Styles						Teacher's Resource Library		
Reviewing Skills	Teacher Alert	Follow-up Activity	Career Application	Home Application	Global Connection	Community Application	Identification Skills	Writing Skills	Punctuation Skills	Visual/Spatial	Auditory/Verbal	Body/Kinesthetic	Logical/Mathematical	Group Learning	LEP/ESL	Activities	Workbook Activities	Self-Study Guide
276					278		✔	✔	✔		278					37-38	53-54	✔
279	280	281					✔	✔	✔				280					✔
282	284-285						✔	✔	✔						285			✔
287		289					✔	✔	✔				288			39	55-56	✔
290			292	296		295	✔	✔	✔	294								✔

Chapter at a Glance

Chapter 13: Complex Sentences pages 274–297

(Answer Keys for the Teacher's Resource Library begin on page 330 of this Teacher's Edition.)

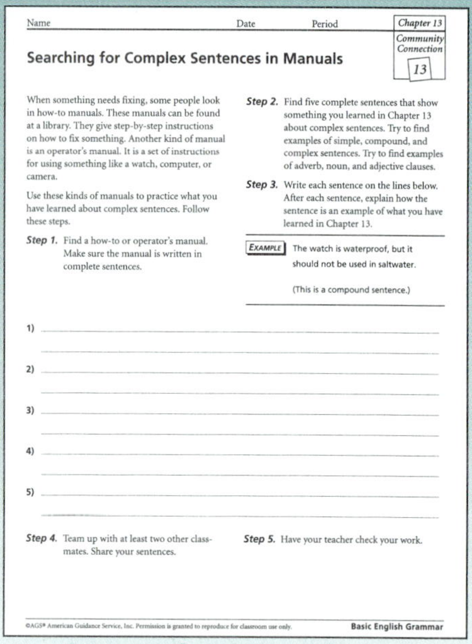

Name ________ Date ________ Period ________ *Chapter 13 Community Connection 13*

Searching for Complex Sentences in Manuals

When something needs fixing, some people look in how-to manuals. These manuals can be found at a library. They give step-by-step instructions on how to fix something. Another kind of manual is an operator's manual. It is a set of instructions for using something like a watch, computer, or camera.

Use these kinds of manuals to practice what you have learned about complex sentences. Follow these steps.

Step 1. Find a how-to or operator's manual. Make sure the manual is written in complete sentences.

Step 2. Find five complete sentences that show something you learned in Chapter 13 about complex sentences. Try to find examples of simple, compound, and complex sentences. Try to find examples of adverb, noun, and adjective clauses.

Step 3. Write each sentence on the lines below. After each sentence, explain how the sentence is an example of what you have learned in Chapter 13.

EXAMPLE The watch is waterproof, but it should not be used in saltwater.

(This is a compound sentence.)

1) ____________

2) ____________

3) ____________

4) ____________

5) ____________

Step 4. Team up with at least two other classmates. Share your sentences.

Step 5. Have your teacher check your work.

 Basic English Grammar

Community Connection 13

Chapter 13

Complex Sentences

When you talk, you use all kinds of sentence structures. You do not even think about them. When you write, you need to be more aware of how you express your thoughts. You need to write sentences that make your meaning clear. This is because your reader cannot ask you to explain your ideas.

You know that a simple sentence is an independent clause. An independent clause expresses one complete thought. You have learned that a compound sentence has two independent clauses joined by a conjunction. You also know that a dependent clause is a group of words with a subject and a verb. A dependent clause does not express a complete idea. A dependent clause cannot stand alone as a sentence.

In this chapter, you will learn more about dependent clauses and sentence structure. This chapter focuses on different kinds of dependent clauses. You will learn how they are used to form complex and compound-complex sentences.

Goals for Learning

- To distinguish among a word, a phrase, and a clause
- To distinguish among simple, compound, complex, and compound-complex sentences
- To distinguish among adverb, noun, and adjective clauses
- To distinguish between a complex and a compound-complex sentence

275

Reading Vocabulary

compound (6)
conjunction
distinguish (6)
independent (6)
structure (6)

Introducing the Chapter

Focus students' attention on the photograph. Then ask students if they have ever used a computer to write such things as letters, essays, or stories. Ask if using a computer helps with the writing process. Do students think that a computer makes it easier to express ideas? Why or why not? Does a computer make it easier to recognize and correct mistakes in sentences? Lead students to understand that although one writer may prefer to use a computer and another may prefer to write longhand, all writers have to understand how to construct interesting, complete sentences if they want readers to enjoy what they write. Explain to students that by the end of Chapter 13, they will know how to form complex and compound-complex sentences to make their writing more lively and interesting.

SELF-STUDY GUIDE

Name ______

CHAPTER 13: Complex Sentences

Goal 13.1 *To distinguish among a word, phrase, and a clause*

Date	Assignment	Score
______	1: Read pages 275-276. Complete Activity A on page 276.	______
______	2: Complete Workbook Activity 53.	______
______	3: Read page 277. Complete Activities B-C on page 277.	______
______	4: Complete Workbook Activity 54.	______
______	5: Complete the Lesson 1 Review, Parts A-B on page 278.	______

Comments:

Goal 13.2 *To distinguish among adverb, noun, and adjective clauses*

Date	Assignment	Score
______	6: Read page 279. Complete Activities A-B on page 279.	______
______	7: Read page 280. Complete Activity C on page 280.	______
______	8: Complete the Lesson 2 Review, Parts A-C on page 281.	______
______	9: Read page 282. Complete Activity A on page 282.	______
______	10: Read page 283. Complete Activity B on page 283.	______
______	11: Read page 284. Complete Activities C-D on page 284.	______
______	12: Read page 285. Complete Activity E on page 285.	______
______	13: Complete the Lesson 3 Review on page 286.	______
______	14: Read page 287. Complete Activities A-B on page 287.	______
______	15: Read page 288. Complete Activities C-D on page 288.	______
______	16: Complete the Lesson 4 Review on page 289.	______
______	17: Complete Workbook Activity 55.	______
______	18: Complete Workbook Activity 56.	______

Comments:

 Basic English Grammar

SELF-STUDY GUIDE

Name ______

CHAPTER 13 Complex Sentences, continued

Goal 13.3 *To distinguish among simple, compound, complex, and compound-complex sentences*

Date	Assignment	Score
______	19: Read page 290. Complete Activity A on page 290.	______
______	20: Read page 291. Complete Activity B on page 291.	______

Comments:

Goal 13.4 *To distinguish between a complex and a compound-complex sentence*

Date	Assignment	Score
______	21: Read pages 292-293. Complete Activities C-D on page 293.	______
______	22: Read page 294. Complete Activities E-F on page 294.	______
______	23: Complete the Lesson 5 Review, Parts A-B on page 295.	______
______	24: Complete the Chapter 13 Review, Parts A-D on pages 296-297.	______

Comments:

Student's Signature ______ Date ______

Instructor's Signature ______ Date ______

 Basic English Grammar

Chapter 13 Self-Study Guide

Lesson at a Glance

Chapter 13 Lesson 1

Overview This lesson explains the difference between phrases and clauses and between dependent and independent clauses.

Objectives

- To distinguish between phrases and clauses.
- To distinguish between dependent and independent clauses.

Student Pages 276–278

Teacher's Resource Library

Activities 37–38

Workbook Activities 53–54

Reading Vocabulary

clause	phrase
dependent clause	prepositional
incomplete (7)	relative (5)
	subordinating

Teaching Suggestions

Introducing the Lesson

Discuss the information presented in the text. Be sure students understand the distinction between phrases and clauses and between dependent and independent clauses. If necessary, provide additional examples modeled on the examples in the text.

Reviewing Skills

Review subjects, verbs, and conjunctions.

Presenting Activity A

Do Activity A orally with the class. Discuss each answer, having students explain how they determined whether the group of words was a phrase or a clause.

Activity A Answers

1) phrase 2) clause 3) phrase 4) phrase 5) clause

Lesson 1 Words, Phrases, and Clauses

Phrase
A group of words without a subject and a verb. A phrase relates to another part of the sentence.

Before you learn about complex sentences, it is important to recall the meanings of three important terms: *word, phrase,* and *clause.*

A word is a set of letters that has meaning.

A **phrase** is a group of words that work together. A phrase does not have a subject and a verb.

EXAMPLES

Prepositional phrase:	across the road
Verb phrase:	has been

Clause
A group of words that has a subject and a predicate. A clause may be independent or dependent.

A **clause** is a group of words with a subject and a verb.

EXAMPLE Clause: **Unless there is a problem**

Activity A Write on your paper whether each group of words is a *phrase* or a *clause.*

1) Over the river.

2) If he leaves.

3) Will have been late.

4) The youngest girl in school.

5) Whoever wants an apple.

There are two kinds of clauses: independent clauses (complete ideas) and dependent clauses (incomplete ideas).

Dependent clause
A dependent clause does not express a complete idea and cannot stand alone as a sentence.

An independent clause is a sentence. It expresses a complete thought.

A **dependent clause** has a subject and a verb, but it is not a sentence. A dependent clause is introduced by either a subordinating conjunction or a relative pronoun.

Name ____ Date ____ Period ____ Chapter 13 Workbook Activity 53

Phrases and Clauses

A phrase is a group of words that are working together. A clause is a group of words with a subject and a predicate. The two kinds of clauses are dependent and independent.

EXAMPLES
Prepositional phrase — under a rock
Dependent clause — since it is raining
Independent clause — the sun was shining

Directions: Look at the underlined groups of words in these sentences. Decide whether they are *prepositional phrases, dependent clauses,* or *independent clauses.* Label each group.

EXAMPLES
dependent clause / *independent clause*: When the bell rang, he went in.
prepositional phrase: We walked quickly through the forest.

1) I saw a fox near the woods.
2) They will not come because the weather is bad.
3) If the store is closed, we will go home.
4) Sam discovered a cave in the hillside.
5) If the team wins, will Kent become captain?
6) Their uncle Walter took the twins to the circus.
7) From the top of the hill, you can see the ocean.
8) Ellen will put up the tent when she arrives.
9) Cliff cooked some eggs, because he was hungry.
10) We all hope that the fair will raise a lot of money.
11) First we climbed up Turtle Hill; then we went down
12) The boy who won first place is a fine artist.
13) When the moon rose, Eric could see the river.
14) They stayed in the park until the sun went down.
15) After the party, we all cleaned the house.

 Basic English Grammar

Workbook Activity 53

Remember that subordinating conjunctions are words like *because, if, when,* and *since.* Relative pronouns are words like *that, which, who, whoever,* and *what.*

EXAMPLE

Independent clause:	Marco walked home.
Dependent clause:	Because he missed the bus

Activity B Write on your paper whether each group of words is a *dependent clause* or an *independent clause.*

1) Whom you asked.

2) That girl is in my class.

3) Until he knows all the answers.

4) The team exercised before practice.

5) Whoever finishes first.

Activity C Write on your paper the word that introduces the dependent clause in each of these sentences.

1) Because Shelly left school late, she missed the bus.

2) I will fix dinner if you are hungry.

3) Joey hoped that the band would win first place.

4) Rick admires the man who coaches his team.

5) What Angela said was not clear to everyone.

6) Since he didn't try out for a part, he won't be in the play.

7) We will start the movie when Tony and Maria arrive.

8) The witness told the police what she had seen.

9) Hank's Restaurant is closed while the owner looks for a new cook.

10) If that coat goes on sale, I will buy it.

Reading Vocabulary

restaurant (5) witness (5)

Presenting Activity B

Write these clauses on the board: *Whenever you are ready/The wind howled during the storm.* Ask the class to identify the dependent clause and the independent clause. Invite volunteers to explain in their own words why the first group of words is a dependent clause and the second group of words is an independent clause. Then have students complete Activity B on their own.

Activity B Answers

1) dependent clause
2) independent clause
3) dependent clause
4) independent clause
5) dependent clause

Presenting Activity C

Before having students work on Activity C, you may wish to have them review the subordinating conjunctions listed on page 181 of their texts. Then do the first two items in Activity C as a class. Point out that as they can see from items 1 and 2, the dependent clause can appear at the beginning or end of the sentence.

Activity C Answers

1) Because 2) if 3) that 4) who 5) What 6) Since 7) when 8) what 9) while 10) If

Name Date Period — Chapter 13 Activity 37

Finding Dependent Clauses

A clause is a group of words with a subject and a predicate. An independent clause is a complete thought or a sentence. A dependent clause has a subject and a predicate, but it does not express a complete thought.

Directions: Read these sentences carefully. Find and circle the dependent clause.

EXAMPLE (Whenever you feel better,) we will leave.

1) After it snows, we like to go sledding.
2) Before Jennifer went to bed, she kissed her father goodnight.
3) Amy said that she couldn't attend.
4) Do you enjoy corn that has just been picked?
5) Because Amy didn't want to leave, she cried for an hour.
6) Sandra feels tired after she plays tennis.
7) The teacher, who just transferred to our school, is very friendly.
8) Do you know the man who drives that car?
9) My best friend, who moved to Texas, sent me a letter.
10) We can go to the concert if you want to go.
11) We all thought that the cookout was nice.
12) The horse that cut his leg still runs fast.
13) Whenever you want to leave, I am ready.
14) Susan will take many classes before she graduates from college.
15) Dogs that bite are very dangerous.

 Basic English Grammar

Activity 37

Name Date Period — Chapter 13 Activity 38

Phrases and Clauses

A phrase is a group of words that work together. A clause is a group of words with a subject and a predicate. The two kinds of clauses are dependent and independent.

EXAMPLES
Prepositional phrase — behind a tree
Dependent clause — because we are late
Independent clause — the rain was falling

Directions: Look at the groups of words in bold in these sentences. Write whether each is a *Prepositional Phrase, Dependent Clause,* or *Independent Clause.* Label each group.

EXAMPLES
After the game was over, (dependent clause) **the team ordered pizza.** (independent clause)
We drove quickly **through the tunnel.** (prepositional phrase)

1) My grandmother decided not to drive **because a storm is coming**.
2) **From the top of the building**, I could see the entire city.
3) When the sun set, **the campers put up their tents**.
4) **Sarah left the party early** because she felt ill.
5) The child **who won first place** is a wonderful musician.
6) **Professor Johnson took the class** on a field trip.
7) I saw a deer **on the edge of the clearing**.
8) **Before we left the football game**, we said good-bye to all of our friends.
9) **What will the coach do** if his team doesn't win the Super Bowl?
10) Sharon found her lost chain **under the sofa**.
11) **If the movie ends before 10:00 p.m.**, can we go for ice cream?
12) **Because she was locked in her stall all day**, my horse Misty was feeling frisky.

 Basic English Grammar

Activity 38

Name Date Period — Chapter 13 Workbook Activity 54

Finding Dependent Clauses

A *clause* is a group of words with a subject and a predicate.
An *independent clause* is a complete thought or a sentence.
A *dependent clause* has a subject and a predicate, but it does not express a complete thought.

Directions: Read these sentences carefully. Find the dependent clause and underline it.

EXAMPLE Whenever you are ready, we will leave.

1) Mr. and Mrs. Jones do not play golf when it rains.
2) Before James arrived, Darleen had waited an hour.
3) Sue said that she would be late.
4) We all thought that the party was nice.
5) Do you like the potato chips that come in a can?
6) Because Janet was graduating from high school, Mrs. Jones planned a party.
7) James feels good after he runs.
8) The girl who visited us last week was my cousin.
9) What I said was not that important.
10) Did you hear what she said?
11) Whoever is hungry should come and eat!
12) We can go out to dinner if you want to.
13) Because it rained, the picnic was called off.
14) My old friend who moved to Cleveland will visit us next week.
15) Do you know the people who live in that house?

 Basic English Grammar

Workbook Activity 54

Complex Sentences Chapter 13 **277**

Reading Vocabulary

advice (5) huddle (5)

Part A Answers

1) clause 2) phrase 3) phrase 4) clause 5) clause

Part B Answers

1) dependent 2) dependent 3) independent 4) independent 5) dependent 6) dependent 7) dependent 8) independent 9) dependent 10) independent

Global Connection

When people are traveling in a country where a different language is spoken, communicating a problem or emergency to authorities can be difficult. Encourage students to create a list of phrases in English that might be helpful for travelers to know in case of a problem or emergency. Divide students into pairs and have them select a country where the people speak a different language from their own. Have them do research to find the translations of the helpful phrases that the class made. Suggest that students look in bilingual dictionaries, talk to language instructors, or interview people in the community who speak the language. Students can then come together to create their own "Traveler's Dictionary of Helpful Phrases."

Learning Styles

Auditory/Verbal

Divide the class into pairs. Assign each pair a sentence from Part B of page 278 or from Activity C on page 277. Have one partner in each pair read the first clause in the sentence. Ask the class to listen carefully to hear whether the clause is complete. (For example, the words *After the party was over* leave one wondering what happened, so this clause is dependent. It depends on other words to be complete.) Have the second partner read the second clause. Ask the class to listen carefully to hear whether that clause is complete.

Lesson 1 Review

Part A Write on your paper whether the word in bold in each of these sentences introduces a *phrase* or a *clause.*

1) We huddled in the cabin **as** the snow fell.
2) She won't be back **until** tomorrow.
3) Everyone has arrived **except** Jody and Bill.
4) I can't leave **until** I finish my report.
5) **When** you know the answer, raise your hand.

Part B Write on your paper whether the clause in bold is an *independent clause* or a *dependent clause.* Remember, an independent clause can stand alone as a sentence.

1) **After the party was over**, we cleaned up and went to bed.
2) Please take this to the woman **who lives next door**.
3) **I am so glad** that you made the team.
4) **This is the last time** that I give advice to anyone.
5) **Because the store went out of business**, many people in town lost their jobs.
6) Everyone stood up and clapped **when Stephanie finished her speech**.
7) Greg and the girl **who gives him a ride to school every day** live on the same street.
8) If you wait just a minute, **I'll walk with you to the bus**.
9) Peter took us for a ride in his new car, **which he bought himself**.
10) **Ask the girl** who is standing at the gate.

Lesson 2 The Adverb Clause

Adverb clause

A dependent clause that works exactly like an adverb in a sentence.

An **adverb clause** is a group of words with a subject and a verb. An adverb clause is a dependent clause that works exactly like an adverb in a sentence. It tells something about the verb.

EXAMPLES

Adverb:	Rick went home **early**.
Adverb phrase:	Rick went home **after practice**.
Adverb clause:	Rick went home **when practice was over**.

Activity A Write on your paper whether the words in bold in each sentence are *adverbs, adverb phrases,* or *adverb clauses.*

1) Amy writes **well** and **often**.

2) Mom always knows exactly **where I put my things**.

3) **Except for you**, I haven't told anyone the news.

4) **Until you find your pen**, you can borrow mine.

5) I can hardly wait **until my birthday**.

Like adverbs, an adverb clause answers questions like *Where? When? Why? How much? How often?* and *How soon?*

EXAMPLES

Where?	Robin smiled **wherever she went**.
When?	**When practice is over**, Rick will go home.
Why?	Paula joined the band **because she likes music**.
How much?	Justin tried **as hard as he could**.
How often?	Mai practices the violin **whenever she has time**.

Activity B Write the adverb clause in each of these sentences.

1) Enrique runs whenever he can.

2) If he gets up early, he runs in the morning.

3) He runs because he enjoys it.

4) Unless it is raining hard, Enrique runs every day.

5) Because I injured my knee, I walk for exercise.

Lesson at a Glance

Chapter 13 Lesson 2

Overview This lesson presents adverb clauses.

Objectives

- To distinguish between adverb phrases and clauses.
- To identify adverb clauses.
- To write sentences with adverb clauses.

Student Pages 279–281

Reading Vocabulary

adverb clause violin (5) injure (6)

Teaching Suggestions

Introducing the Lesson
Discuss the information in the text, focusing on the difference between adverb phrases and clauses.

Reviewing Skills Review adverbs. Have students refer to Chapter 6, Lesson 4 to review how to recognize adverbs.

Presenting Activity A
Before having students complete Activity A on their own, invite volunteers to give examples of sentences with adverbs, adverb phrases, and adverb clauses. Have the class identify the adverb, adverb phrase, or adverb clause in each sentence.

Activity A Answers

1) adverbs **2)** adverb clause **3)** adverb phrase **4)** adverb clause **5)** adverb phrase

Presenting Activity B
Read through all the items in Activity B with students, helping them to identify the two clauses in each sentence. Then have students complete Activity B on their own.

Activity B Answers

1) whenever he can **2)** If he gets up early **3)** because he enjoys it **4)** Unless it is raining hard **5)** Because I injured my knee

An adverb clause may answer questions about another adverb. These clauses act like adverbs of degree. They answer questions such as *How much?* or *How far?*

EXAMPLE

S V D.O. Adv. S V
Roberto hits the ball farther **than anyone else can hit it.**
(How much farther can Roberto hit the ball? farther *than anyone else can*)

An adverb clause may also answer questions about an adjective. These clauses are also adverbs of degree.

EXAMPLE

S V Adj. S V
Sam is taller **than the other boys in the class are.**
(How much taller is Sam? taller *than the other boys in the class are*)

Sometimes part of an adverb clause is missing. The missing part is understood.

EXAMPLES

Roberto hits the ball farther **than anyone else.**
(In the clause *than anyone else*, the words *can hit it* are understood.)

Sam is taller **than the other boys in the class.**
(In the clause *than the other boys*, the verb *are* is understood.)

Activity C Write the adverb clauses in each of these sentences. Add any words that are understood.

1) My dog can bark louder than any other dog on our street can.

2) Irene practices longer than anyone else.

3) Is Vicky taller than Beth?

4) Enrique ran farther than the others ran.

5) Charlotte is as happy as she can be!

Presenting Activity C

Write these sentences on the board: *That girl sings louder than everyone else in the group./She was not as excited as I.* Help students identify the adverb clause in each sentence. Ask them to tell what words are missing from the adverb clause in the second sentence. Then have students complete Activity C on their own.

Activity C Answers

1) than any other dog on our street can (bark) **2)** than anyone else (practices) **3)** than Beth (is tall) **4)** than the others ran **5)** as happy as she can be

TEACHER ALERT

You may wish to point out to students that in comparisons such as *She was not as excited as I*, the words *as . . . as* are correlative conjunctions.

LEARNING STYLES

Logical/Mathematical
Divide the class into groups of three. On the board, print the following patterns: 1) subject/predicate/adverb; 2) subject/predicate/adverbial prepositional phrase; 3) subject/predicate/adverbial dependent clause. Invite each group to create a sentence for each pattern. Ask volunteer groups to read aloud one sentence they have created. Call on other volunteers to go to the board and check the pattern each sentence represents. Next, call out possible predicates—action words—and ask volunteers to use these to create sentences for the three patterns.

Lesson 2 Review

Part A Write on your paper whether the words in bold in the sentences are *adverb phrases* or *adverb clauses.*

1) Toni has been deaf **since birth**.

2) **Because she and Lisa became friends**, Lisa learned sign language.

3) **If you wish to learn**, Toni will help you.

4) Lisa had never signed to anyone **but Toni**.

5) **After she has been signing for a while**, Lisa will be good at it.

Part B Write the adverb clause in each of these sentences on your paper. Add any words that are understood.

1) We will go to the beach when summer arrives.

2) Alexa bought a new bicycle because her old one fell apart.

3) You should get some rest if you are tired.

4) No one can run faster than Enrique.

5) That building is higher than any other city buildings.

Part C Write these sentences on your paper. Add an adverb clause to each sentence.

1) Angie and her brother went to the baseball game.

2) Rain had been falling.

3) The field was wet.

4) The game began.

5) Angie cheered louder.

Reading Vocabulary

deaf (5)

Part A Answers

1) adverb phrase **2)** adverb clause **3)** adverb clause **4)** adverb phrase **5)** adverb clause

Part B Answers

1) when summer arrives **2)** because her old one fell apart **3)** if you are tired **4)** than Enrique (can run) **5)** than any other city buildings (are high)

Part C Answers

Each sentence should include an adverb clause.

Follow-up Activity

Divide students into small groups. Ask each group to select a current topic in the news. Then have the group work together to write a brief paragraph on the topic that they selected. If possible, each sentence in the paragraph should have at least one adverb clause. When students have finished, invite a group representative to read the paragraph to the class. Then have members of the class point out how adverb clauses enhanced the meaning and flow of the paragraph.

Lesson at a Glance

Chapter 13 Lesson 3

Overview This lesson introduces noun clauses and appositives.

Objective

- To identify the function of noun clauses in sentences.

Student Pages 282–286

Reading Vocabulary

indirect
nominative
noun clause
predicate
subject (5)

Teaching Suggestions

■ Introducing the Lesson Discuss the definition of a noun clause and the examples in the text.

■ Reviewing Skills Review nouns and their functions in sentences.

■ Presenting Activity A Do Activity A together as a class. Write each item on the board, underlining the noun clause. Then work with students to identify all the sentence parts except the noun clause. Then help them determine the function of the noun clause. After you complete each item, invite a volunteer to write an original sentence with a noun clause on the board, modeling it on the sentence you just completed.

Activity A Answers

1) direct object 2) subject
3) object of a preposition
4) predicate nominative
5) indirect object

Lesson 3 The Noun Clause

Noun clause
A dependent clause that works exactly like a noun in a sentence.

A **noun clause** is a group of words with a subject and a verb. A noun clause is a dependent clause that works exactly like a noun in a sentence. It may have a predicate nominative or a direct object.

EXAMPLES

Subject:	**What you did** was wonderful. (S: you; L.V.: was; P. Adj.: wonderful)
Predicate nominative:	That book is **what I need**. (S: book; L.V.: is; P.N.: what I need)
Direct object:	I remember **what you said**. (S: I; V: remember; D.O.: what you said)
Indirect object:	I gave **whoever wanted some** a piece of my pizza. (S: I; V: gave; I.O.: whoever wanted some)
Object of preposition:	We made lunch for **whoever was hungry**. (S: We; V: made; D.O.: lunch; O.P.: whoever was hungry)

A noun clause may follow any of the six sentence patterns that you learned about before.

EXAMPLE

Whoever is ready should begin. (S: Whoever; L.V.: is; P. Adj.: ready; V: should begin)
(*Whoever* is the subject of the linking verb *is*. The whole noun clause is the subject of the verb phrase *should begin.*)

Activity A Write on your paper whether the bold noun clause in each sentence is used as the *subject, predicate nominative, direct object, indirect object,* or *object of a preposition.*

1) The teacher said **that my answer was wrong**.
2) **Who will get the lead in the play** has not been decided.
3) They argued about **who should go first**.
4) This is **what I want**.
5) She offered **whoever was still around** a ride home.

A noun clause is introduced in a sentence by a relative pronoun.

Some Common Relative Pronouns	
that	who (subject)
what	whom (object)
whatever	whoever (subject)
whichever	whomever (object)
	whose (possessive)

The pronouns *that* and *what* have only one form. They do not change whether they are subjects or objects. The pronoun *who* does change, however.

- Use *who* when the relative pronoun is the subject of the noun clause.
- Use *whom* when the relative pronoun is the direct object or the object of a preposition in the noun clause.
- Use *who* when the relative pronoun is the predicate nominative in the noun clause.

EXAMPLES

S V D.O.
I remember **who called me.**

D.O. S V
I remember **whom you called.**

P.N. S L.V.
I remember **who you are.**

Activity B Write these sentences with the correct form of the relative pronoun.

1) I know (who, whom) called you.

2) I know (who, whom) you are.

3) I know (who, whom) you saw yesterday.

4) I know (who, whom) you invited to the dance.

5) I know for (who, whom) you bought that gift.

Presenting Activity B

Review with students the common relative pronouns and read with them the bulleted rules for using these pronouns. Then write these sentences on the board: *I saw to (who, whom) you pointed./I saw (who, whom) did that./I saw (who, whom) they met at the mall.* Work with students to label the parts of the noun clause in each sentence to determine whether *who* or *whom* should be used. Then have students complete Activity B on their own.

Activity B Answers

1) who **2)** who **3)** whom **4)** whom **5)** whom

Reading Vocabulary

incorrect salesperson

■ Presenting Activity C

Invite volunteers to write sentences with noun clauses on the board. Have the class identify the noun clause and the word that introduces it. Then have students complete Activity C on their own.

Activity C Answers

Relative pronouns are underlined.

1) who found my book **2)** (that) you lost **3)** What I really need **4)** whoever finds them **5)** (that) Raina found my notes, too

■ Presenting Activity D

Invite volunteers to say sentences in which noun clauses are used in each of the functions listed in the Activity D directions. Then have students complete Activity D independently.

Activity D Answers

1) whoever wants some—object of a preposition **2)** that I would be late—direct object **3)** what I need right now—predicate nominative **4)** What you see—subject **5)** whoever was in the store—indirect object

TEACHER ALERT

Some teachers may disagree about the correctness of omitting *that* at the beginning of a noun clause. Caution students to check with a teacher about his or her policy regarding the omission of *that.* To be safe, students can make it their own policy to never omit *that.*

The relative pronoun *that* often introduces a noun clause. Sometimes it is left out of the sentence and is understood. Either way is correct.

EXAMPLES

Correct:	Do you think **that he is nice**?
Correct:	Do you think **he is nice**?

The other relative pronouns cannot be left out.

EXAMPLES

Correct:	Did you hear **what I said**?
Incorrect:	Did you hear **I said**?

Activity C Write each of these sentences on your paper. Underline the noun clause. Circle the relative pronoun. If the relative pronoun *that* is understood, write it in and circle it.

1) Do you know who found my book?

2) Raina found the book you lost.

3) What I really need are my notes!

4) I am offering a reward to whoever finds them.

5) Do you think Raina found my notes, too?

Activity D Write the noun clauses in each of these sentences on your paper. Beside each noun clause, write whether it is used as the *subject, predicate nominative, direct object, indirect object,* or *object of a preposition.*

Example What I said was not important.
What I said—Subject

1) I made supper for whoever wants some.

2) I knew that I would be late.

3) Some hot soup is what I need right now!

4) What you see is what you get!

5) The salesperson gave whoever was in the store a free CD.

284 *Chapter 13 Complex Sentences*

Appositive
A word or group of words that renames or explains another noun in the same sentence.

An **appositive** renames or explains another noun in the same sentence. An appositive may be a noun, a noun phrase, or a noun clause. Look at each example below. The appositive is in italic. The noun that is renamed or explained by the appositive is in bold.

EXAMPLE

My **friend** *Anna* has a dog.

Meesh, *a toy poodle,* belongs to her.

Meesh's favorite **toy**, *a big rubber bone,* is under the chair.

I have a secret **wish**—*that I will someday be president.*

Activity E Write the appositive in each of these sentences. Beside each appositive, write the noun or nouns the appositive renames or explains.

1) Do you know who wrote this line: "All the world's a stage"?

2) Carlo's big advantage, his powerful leg muscles, kept him going.

3) People laughed at Columbus's idea—the thought that the world was round.

4) The nineteenth constitutional amendment—the amendment that allowed women voting rights—changed history.

5) Herbert Hoover, the thirty-first president, was an engineer.

6) Galileo's invention, the telescope, changed scientific method.

7) The bibliography, a list of books used for reference, appeared at the end of the report.

8) The price was more than I—a student with no regular income—could afford.

9) Kareem, the editor of the school newspaper, is also class president.

10) Friends since kindergarten, Rita and Marianne still enjoy each other's company.

Reading Vocabulary
amendment (7)
appositive
bibliography (9)
constitutional (6)
scientific (6)

Presenting Activity E
Because of the level of difficulty in the vocabulary used in Activity E, you may wish to read through all of the items with students at least once. Then do the first two items together as a class, before asking students to complete Activity E on their own or with partners.

Activity E Answers
1) "All the world's a stage"—line **2)** his powerful leg muscles—advantage **3)** the thought that the world was round—idea **4)** the amendment that allowed women voting rights—amendment **5)** the thirty-first president—Herbert Hoover **6)** the telescope—invention **7)** a list of books used for reference—bibliography **8)** a student with no regular income—I **9)** the editor of the school newspaper—Kareem **10)** Friends since kindergarten—Rita and Marianne

Learning Styles
LEP/ESL
Ask the students for whom English is a second language to choose a sentence from Activity E on page 285 and to print it on the board. Then have the students translate the sentence into their primary language. Ask them to circle the appositive and to underline the noun or nouns the appositive renames or explains. Use these sentences to discover if the pattern and punctuation in non-English languages is similar to the English pattern and punctuation for appositives.

Teacher Alert
Use the examples and the items in Activity E to point out the different ways (*comma, dash, colon*) that appositives may be set off from the rest of the sentence. Use item 10 in Activity E to illustrate the fact that an appositive can sometimes come before the noun that it renames.

Reading Vocabulary

belief (6) lofty
errand (5)

Lesson Review Answers

1) whatever we needed—object of a preposition **2)** that you can guess the answer—direct object **3)** That love conquers all—subject **4)** what I need—predicate nominative **5)** whoever asked for it—indirect object **6)** (that) she's tired—direct object **7)** When the paper is due—subject **8)** Where he was going—subject **9)** where he was going—direct object **10)** what he needs—predicate nominative **11)** whoever asks him—object of a preposition **12)** whoever was struggling in math class—indirect object **13)** that he could win the contest—appositive **14)** what you want—object of a preposition **15)** what the dog brought home—predicate nominative **16)** where he put the book—direct object **17)** who is coming—direct object **18)** How Sue did the job—subject **19)** What she will do next—direct object **20)** whoever wanted a peek—indirect object

Lesson 3 Review

Lesson Review Write these sentences on your paper. Underline the noun clause. Beside each sentence, write whether the noun clause is used as the *subject, predicate nominative, direct object, indirect object, object of a preposition,* or *appositive.*

Examples Did you hear **what she said**?—Direct Object

Sue told **whoever was around** her news. —Indirect Object

1) We went shopping for whatever we needed.
2) I think that you can guess the answer.
3) That love conquers all is a lofty idea.
4) A glass of lemonade is what I need.
5) Mrs. Garret gave whoever asked for it more time for the test.
6) She said she's tired.
7) When the paper is due is not clear.
8) Where he was going was not known.
9) I know where he was going.
10) A good map is what he needs.
11) He will go on an errand for whoever asks him.
12) Adam offered whoever was struggling in math class some help with math.
13) People laughed at Tom's belief—that he could win the contest.
14) Pay for what you want.
15) Is this what the dog brought home?
16) Seth forgot where he put his book.
17) Tell me who is coming.
18) How Sue did the job was important.
19) What she will do next no one knows.
20) She showed whoever wanted a peek her latest painting.

Lesson 4 The Adjective Clause

Adjective clause
A dependent clause that acts like an adjective in a sentence.

An adjective is a word that describes a noun or pronoun. An **adjective clause** is used in a sentence exactly like an adjective.

EXAMPLES

Adjective:	The **middle** girl is my sister.
Adjective phrase:	The girl **in the middle** is my sister.
Adjective clause:	The girl **who is in the middle** is my sister.

Activity A Write on your paper whether the bold words in each sentence are *adjectives, adjective phrases,* or *adjective clauses.*

1) Terry is the player **who scores the most.**
2) The **best** and **most popular** player on our team is Terry.
3) The player **with the most points** on our team is Terry.
4) Ms. Nichols, **who has played soccer all her life,** is the coach.

Like an adjective phrase, an adjective clause follows the noun or pronoun it describes.

EXAMPLES

The book **that I gave him** was expensive. (What book? the book *that I gave him*)

Are you the one **whom I met at the party**? (Which one? the one *whom I met at the party*)

Jim invited Sandy, **who was his partner on the science project**. (Which one is Sandy? the one *who was his partner*)

Activity B Write the adjective clause in each of these sentences. Beside each clause, write the noun it describes.

1) A girl whom I know won first prize in a contest.
2) The present that Gayle gave Susan was for Susan's birthday.
3) The answer that she gave was wrong.
4) The boy who sits in the first seat has been absent all week.
5) We bought a new refrigerator that has its own ice maker.

Activity B Answers

1) whom I know—girl 2) that Gayle gave Susan—present
3) that she gave—answer
4) who sit in the first seat—boy
5) that has its own ice maker—refrigerator

Lesson at a Glance

Chapter 13 Lesson 4

Overview This lesson introduces adjective clauses.

Objective

- To identify adjective clauses and the words they describe.

Student Pages 287–289

Teacher's Resource Library

Activity 39
Workbook Activities 55–56

Reading Vocabulary

absent (5)
adjective clause
describe (5)
project (5)
science (5)

Teaching Suggestions

Introducing the Lesson

Discuss with students the information and examples in the text.

Reviewing Skills

Provide a review of adjectives. Chapter 3, Lesson 1 can be used to remind students what an adjective does in the sentence.

Presenting Activity A

Write on the board: *That is a song.* Ask volunteers to read the sentence aloud, adding an adjective to describe *song.* Repeat this activity, having students add an adjective phrase next and an adjective clause after that. Then have students complete Activity A on their own.

Activity A Answers

1) adjective clause 2) adjectives 3) adjective phrase 4) adjective clause

Presenting Activity B

Do the first item in Activity B with students. Then have them complete Activity B on their own.

Reading Vocabulary

annual (6) organize (6)
director (7)

Presenting Activity C

Write these sentences on the board: *The band member whom I admire most is Karen./This is the room where the band practices.* Help students find the adjective clause in each sentence. Invite a volunteer to come and circle the relative pronoun that introduces each clause. Then have students complete Activity C independently

Activity C Answers

1) where a contest was held **2)** that someone organized for high school bands **3)** whose name is Mr. Smith **4)** which had never been in a contest before **5)** that the band would win first place

Presenting Activity D

Have students take turns adding orally an adjective clause to item 1. Then have students do Activity D independently. After they have completed the activity, suggest that students read their sentences to the class.

Activity D Answers

Each sentence should include an adjective clause that describes the noun or pronoun in bold.

Learning Styles

Logical/Mathematical
Divide the class into groups of three. On the board, print the following patterns: 1) adjective/ subject/predicate; 2) subject/adjectival prepositional phrase/ predicate; 3) subject/adjectival dependent clause/predicate. Invite each group to create a sentence for each pattern. Ask volunteer groups to read aloud one sentence they have created. Call on other volunteers to go to the board and check the pattern each sentence represents. Next, call out possible subjects—people, places, things—and ask volunteers to use these to create sentences for the three patterns.

An adjective clause may be introduced by a relative pronoun. Some common relative pronouns are *who, whom, whose, which, what,* and *that.*

An adjective clause may also be introduced by the words *where* and *when.*

Example The small town **where my dad grew up** is now a large city.

Activity C Write the adjective clause in each of these sentences. Underline the relative pronoun.

1) The band went to Florida, where a contest was held.

2) The contest that someone organized for high school bands is an annual event.

3) The director of the band, whose name is Mr. Smith, was very pleased.

4) The band, which had never been in a contest before, performed well.

5) We all hoped that the band would win first place.

Activity D Write these sentences on your paper. Add an adjective clause that describes the noun or pronoun in bold.

1) The bus took the band to **Florida**.

2) **Pedro** and Chris had a wonderful trip.

3) They stayed in a **hotel**.

4) **Everyone** enjoyed the warm weather.

5) The **contest** was exciting.

Lesson 4 Review

Lesson Review Write these sentences on your paper. Underline the adjective clauses. Beside each clause, write the noun or pronoun it describes.

Example Spring is the season that I like best.—season

1) Please get the bread that is baked at the grocery store.
2) Did you know the people who gave the party?
3) Mike is the one who plays right field.
4) The man whose brother drives our bus is very nice.
5) The outfit that Jenna wore to the party was new.
6) The girl who was in line behind me bought the last tickets.
7) The man who lived next door moved to Florida.
8) Sue's favorite actor is the one whom you liked in that movie.
9) Dwayne read the book, which Joanie suggested, in one night.
10) We rented a new apartment that had three bedrooms.
11) Nori showed me the notes that she had taken for the test.
12) Eduardo's uncle who is an airline pilot arrived in time for the party.
13) She was well-prepared for the test, which she passed with a high grade.
14) The time when you should be thinking about your future is now.
15) I am the person whose book you found.

Reading Vocabulary

airline
well-prepared
outfit (5)

Lesson Review Answers

1) that is baked at the grocery store—bread **2)** who gave the party—people **3)** who plays right field—one **4)** whose brother drives our bus—man **5)** that Jenna wore to the party—outfit **6)** who was in line behind me—girl **7)** who lived next door—man **8)** whom you liked in that movie—one **9)** which Joanie suggested—book **10)** that had three bedrooms—apartment **11)** that she had taken for the test—notes **12)** who is an airplane pilot—uncle **13)** which she passed with a high grade—test **14)** when you should be thinking about your future—time **15)** whose book you found—person

Follow-up Activity

Ask students to select a passage from a short story, newspaper article, or magazine article. Have students work with partners to find all the adjective clauses and the nouns or pronouns they describe in the passage.

Name Date Period | Chapter 13 Activity 39

Dependent Clauses

There are three kinds of dependent clauses: noun clauses, adverb clauses, and adjective clauses.

EXAMPLES
Noun clause — Do you know **what she wants**?
Adverb clause — He jumped **when the alarm sounded**.
Adjective clause — I loved the poem **that the class read**.

Directions: Find and circle the dependent clauses in these sentences. Label each clause. Write *Noun clause, Adverb clause,* or *Adjective clause.*

EXAMPLE Larry studied (before he went to work.)— adverb clause

1) The red dress is exactly what I wanted.
2) We drank some punch because we were thirsty.
3) Whoever wins the lottery will never work again.
4) Chris lost the tennis match that was against her arch rival.
5) We saw a dog that we did not recognize.
6) Did Amanda see what you wrote?
7) Don't use the bike that has a broken seat.
8) Jody dances whenever the radio is on.
9) I want to see the movie that is playing at our theater.
10) He left the restaurant when he was finished eating.
11) Kendra is the horse that no one can ride.
12) Do they know what they are doing?

 Basic English Grammar

Activity 39

Name Date Period | Chapter 13 Workbook Activity 55

Dependent Clauses

There are three kinds of dependent clauses: noun clauses, adverb clauses, and adjective clauses.

EXAMPLES
Noun Clause — Do you know what she will do?
Adverb Clause — He ran when he saw the lion.
Adjective Clause — I like the story that I read.

Directions: Underline the dependent clauses in these sentences. Label each clause as a *Noun Clause, Adverb Clause,* or *Adjective Clause.*

EXAMPLE Stanley studied before he took the test. *(adverb clause)*

1) The plaid shirt is exactly what I need.
2) We ate a snack because we were hungry.
3) Whoever finds the clues may win the game.
4) Adam lost the cap that was his favorite.
5) Jane saw a girl whom she did not know.
6) Did Lee hear what you said?
7) Don't use the pocket that has a hole in it.
8) Paul plays baseball whenever he has time.
9) I think I saw the tiger that escaped from the zoo.
10) Whenever Megan goes, she meets people she likes.
11) Mr. Nesheim is the neighbor whose garden is so beautiful.
12) The motorcycle, which Robert hoped to buy, was expensive.
13) Whenever you have time, tell Gloria the news.
14) Emma is the cat that is gray and white.
15) Had you heard that a hurricane is coming this way?

 Basic English Grammar

Workbook Activity 55

Name Date Period | Chapter 13 Workbook Activity 56

Find the Dependent Clause

A clause is a group of words with a subject and a verb. A dependent clause is not a complete sentence.

Directions: The dependent clause in each sentence is underlined. Decide whether each clause is an adjective clause, an adverb clause, or a noun clause. Label each clause.

EXAMPLE The boy who is on the motorcycle is my brother. *(adjective clause)*

1) Our friend Jack who is an engineer spent a week at our beach cottage which is in Rehoboth, Delaware.
2) After many years had gone by, we saw our old friends whom we had known in high school.
3) Because I was late, I rushed around and forgot my wallet.
4) The picnic will start after the softball game is over.
5) Decide whether the clause is a noun, an adjective, or an adverb clause.
6) Because it is a family favorite, Frances makes potato salad for family picnics.
7) Whoever arrives first will get a special prize.
8) The man who spoke first on the program made everyone laugh because he was so funny.
9) Because Ron and Sandy wanted their St. Bernard puppy to behave, they took her to the obedience school that is on Federal Highway.
10) The girl who lives next door went to London, where she hopes to see the Queen.

 Basic English Grammar

Workbook Activity 56

Lesson at a Glance

Chapter 13 Lesson 5

Overview This lesson explains complex and compound-complex sentences.

Objective

- To distinguish among simple, compound, complex, and compound-complex sentences.

Student Pages 290–295

Reading Vocabulary

complex sentence injury (6)
expression (5) label (6)

Teaching Suggestions

Introducing the Lesson

Discuss the information presented in the text. Focus the discussion on the differences among simple, compound, complex, and compound-complex sentences.

Reviewing Skills

Provide a review of dependent and independent clauses.

Presenting Activity A

Discuss the example given for Activity A. Ask students how they know that this is a complex sentence, and not, for example a simple sentence or a compound sentence. Then have students complete Activity A on their own.

Activity A Answers

1) team (S), practices (V)—simple **2)** practice (S), is (V), players (S), are (V)—complex **3)** team (S), begins (V)—simple **4)** they (S), do warm up (V), injuries (S), are (V)—complex **5)** Baseball (S), is played (V)—simple

Lesson 5 Complex and Compound-Complex Sentences

Sentences may be grouped according to purpose (statement, question, command, or expression of surprise). They may also be grouped according to one of many patterns.

Sentences may also be grouped according to structure. A sentence may be either *simple, compound, complex,* or *compound-complex.*

A simple sentence has one independent clause.

EXAMPLE
S V Prep. Phrase
I will drive to school.

Complex sentence
A sentence that has one main, or independent, clause and at least one dependent clause.

A **complex sentence** has one independent clause and one or more dependent clauses.

EXAMPLE
S V S V Pred. Adj.
I will drive if you are tired.

Activity A Write these sentences on your paper. Label the subject and the verb of each clause as shown. Then write whether the sentence is *simple* or *complex.*

S V S V
Example The team was behind until José hit a home run—**complex**

1) Every afternoon the baseball team practices.

2) When practice is over, the players are tired.

3) The team begins with warm-up exercises.

4) If they don't warm up well, injuries are likely.

5) Baseball is not usually played in the rain.

A complex sentence may have more than one dependent clause.

EXAMPLE

Adjective Clause

Richard Wright, **who was born on a plantation,** worked as a

Adverb Clause

dishwasher **before he became the author of *Native Son*.**

To find an independent clause in a complex sentence:

1. Identify the dependent clause or clauses in the sentence.
2. Read all the words that are not in the dependent clause or clauses. These words make up the independent, or main, clause of the sentence.

Activity B Answer these questions about the sentence shown in the box. Write the answers on your paper.

> Richard Wright, who was born on a plantation, worked as a dishwasher before he became the author of *Native Son.*

1) What is the independent clause in the sentence?

2) What is the subject of the independent clause?

3) What is the verb of the independent clause?

4) Is the verb transitive or intransitive?

5) What are the parts of speech of the words in the phrase *as a dishwasher?*

6) What noun does the adjective clause describe?

7) What question does the adverb clause answer?

8) What are the subject and the verb of the adjective clause?

9) What are the subject and the verb of the adverb clause?

10) There are three verbs (or verb phrases) in the sentence. Which one is a linking verb? What word completes the idea in that clause?

Reading Vocabulary

identify (6) plantation (5)
intransitive transitive

■ Presenting Activity B

Read the directions and the sentence in the box with students. Be sure students understand what they are to do. Then divide students into small groups and have each group complete Activity B. When they have finished, read each activity question aloud and ask a representative from each group to give the group's response to that question. If all responses are the same and are correct, move on to the next item. If responses differ or are incorrect, discuss the answers given and help students identify the correct one.

Activity B Answers

1) Richard Wright worked as a dishwasher **2)** Richard Wright **3)** worked **4)** intransitive **5)** *as*—preposition, *a*—article/adjective, dishwasher—noun **6)** Richard Wright **7)** When did Richard Wright work as a dishwasher? **8)** who—subject, was born—verb **9)** he—subject, became—verb **10)** became—linking verb, author—predicate nominative

Reading Vocabulary

analyze (8)
compound-complex sentence
decision (5)
education (5)
scholarship (5)

APPLICATION

Career Connection

The step-by-step approach of analyzing a compound-complex sentence by breaking it down into smaller parts makes it easier for students to understand the construction and meaning of the sentence. Point out to students that the ability to analyze any complex project by breaking it down into small, simple steps can mean the difference between completing a task and being overwhelmed by it. Workers who can break complicated tasks into manageable steps are an asset to any organization. Suggest that students interview people in different careers and different levels of management about how they deal with difficult or complex problems. Students should ask for examples of times when complicated tasks were made less difficult through a step-by-step approach.

A compound sentence has two independent clauses.

EXAMPLE
S V S V P. Adj.
I would drive, but I am too tired.

Compound-complex sentence
A sentence that has two or more independent clauses and one or more dependent clauses.

A **compound-complex** sentence has at least two independent clauses and one or more dependent clauses.

EXAMPLE
S V S V P. Adj. S V P.N.
I will drive if you are too tired, but it is your decision.

When you want to know how a sentence is constructed, analyze it. To analyze means to break something down into its parts. You can analyze a sentence to find out whether it is compound, complex, or compound-complex.

Here are the steps to analyze sentences.

Nick knows that a college education is important, but if he doesn't get a scholarship, he must wait until he saves some money.

Step 1 The independent clauses are *Nick knows* and *he must wait.* They are joined by the conjunction *but.*

Step 2 The noun clause *that a college education is important* is the direct object of the first independent clause.

Step 3 *If he doesn't get a scholarship* and *until he saves some money* are adverb clauses that tell about the verb *must wait.*

Step 4 This sentence has three independent clauses and two dependent clauses. This is a compound-complex sentence.

Step 5 These are the sentence patterns of each clause:

S V D.O. Conj. S
Nick knows (that a college education is important), but if he
V D.O. S V S V
doesn't get a scholarship, he must wait until he saves some
D.O.
money.

Activity C Write each of these sentences on your paper. Find the independent clauses and the dependent clauses. Beside each sentence, write whether it is *complex* or *compound-complex.*

1) Mr. and Mrs. Johnson play golf when the weather is warm.
2) What I would like is a vacation.
3) Alicia works at the daycare center that is located next to the high school, and her sister works there, too.
4) Because of bad weather, the game was canceled, but it will be played tomorrow.
5) Both of us know that we must study hard, or we will not get into good colleges.

Direct and indirect quotations within sentences are noun clauses.

EXAMPLES

S	V	Direct Object
Mrs. King	said,	**"I enjoyed our golf game."**

S	V	Direct Object
Mrs. King	said	**that she enjoyed the golf game.**

Activity D Change each of these indirect quotations to direct quotations. Punctuate your quotation properly.

1) Mrs. King said that she wants a new putter.
2) I told my boss that I could not come to work today.
3) Anita said that her mother was going back to college.
4) My brother Elvin whispered that he had a surprise for me.
5) Tina told me that she had found my book in her desk.
6) Matthew thought that we should go to a movie.
7) He said his favorite actor was Clint Eastwood.
8) He told his friend Jeffrey that he would stop by and pick him up.
9) Jeffrey said he would be waiting on the front porch.
10) Matthew told him he would be there in fifteen minutes.

Reading Vocabulary

cancel (7) putter
golf (5) quotation (6)

■ Presenting Activity C

Have students do Activity C on their own. Suggest that they follow steps similar to the ones shown on page 292 to tell if a sentence is complex or compound-complex.

Activity C Answers

1) complex 2) complex
3) compound-complex
4) compound-complex
5) compound-complex

■ Presenting Activity D

Review the conventions of punctuating quotations. Then do item 1 on the board, having students tell you how to punctuate the sentence.

Activity D Answers

Some answers may vary. Possible answers are given.

1) Mrs. King said, "I want a new putter." 2) I told my boss, "I cannot come to work today." 3) Anita said, "My mother is going back to college." 4) My brother Elvin whispered, "I have a surprise for you." 5) Tina told me, "I found your book in my desk." 6) Matthew said, "Let's go to a movie." 7) He said, "My favorite actor is Clint Eastwood." 8) He told his friend Jeffrey, "I'll stop by and pick you up." 9) Jeffrey said, "I'll be waiting on the front porch." 10) Matthew told him, "I'll be there in fifteen minutes."

Reading Vocabulary

cashier (7) discourage (6)
college (5) part-time

■ Presenting Activity E

Do Activity E orally as a class. After the questions have been answered correctly, challenge students to make up additional questions about the construction of the sentences. Invite students to ask their questions for the class to answer.

Activity E Answers

1) the compound-complex sentence **2)** Ralph also has a part-time job **3)** adjective clause

■ Presenting Activity F

Before having students complete Activity F on their own, ask them to take turns giving examples of simple, compound, complex, and compound-complex sentences. The class should listen carefully to be sure students have provided accurate examples.

Activity F Answers

1) After school gets out, Tanya hopes that she can find a summer job.—complex **2)** She asked Vic's uncle about a job, but he was not hiring.—compound **3)** She became discouraged about her job search.—simple **4)** Tanya kept on looking because she needed money for college, and she knew there was a job for her somewhere!—compound-complex **5)** A person like Tanya who doesn't give up easily will look until she finds a job.—c omplex

The same idea may be expressed in different kinds of sentences.

EXAMPLES

Simple:	Ralph is a student and a part-time cashier.
Compound:	Ralph is a student, but he also has a part-time job.
Complex:	Ralph, who is a student, also has a part-time job.
Compound-Complex:	Ralph is a student, but he also has a part-time job that he has had since July.

Activity E Answer the following questions about the examples above. Write the answers on your paper.

1) Which sentence provides the most information?

2) What is the independent clause in the third example?

3) What kind of dependent clause is *who is a student* in the third example? Is it a noun, adjective, or adverb clause?

Activity F Write these sentences on your paper. Underline the independent clauses once and the dependent clauses twice. Then write whether the sentence is *simple, compound, complex,* or *compound-complex.*

1) After school gets out, Tanya hopes that she can find a summer job.

2) She asked Vic's uncle about a job, but he was not hiring.

3) She became discouraged about her job search.

4) Tanya kept on looking because she needed money for college, and she knew there was a job for her somewhere!

5) A person like Tanya who doesn't give up easily will look until she finds a job.

LEARNING STYLES

Visual/Spatial

On the board, write the following sentence patterns: 1) simple; 2) compound; 3) complex; 4) compound-complex. Divide the class into pairs. Give each pair a magazine picture to use in creating four sentences that represent the four sentence patterns. Suggest that the partners do the following: a) find the nouns—people, places, things—in the picture; b) consider the actions these nouns could do; c) look for relationships among the nouns and actions; d) write their four sentences. Invite volunteers to read one or more of their sentences. Encourage the class to name the pattern each sentence represents.

Lesson 5 Review

Part A Write on your paper whether each of these sentences is *simple, compound,* or *complex.*

1) I'd like to help you; however, I am very busy today.

2) Do you know what Willie said?

3) I think that I've seen that movie before.

4) The person in the middle of the line is my brother Willie.

5) Cliff said he was hungry.

Part B Analyze each of these sentences. Write on your paper whether a sentence is *simple, compound, complex,* or *compound-complex.*

1) Mrs. Huang planned a party for Kim because she was graduating from high school.

2) She invited Lisa, Elena, Cliff, and Enrique to the party.

3) Mr. Huang thought that Kim's friends should come to the party as their favorite person in history.

4) "It could be fun," Elena told the others.

5) The day of the party arrived, and everyone showed up at the Huang's house in costume.

6) Kim wanted a new watch for a graduation gift.

7) Because she was a swimmer, she wanted one that was waterproof.

8) Almost all good watches are waterproof today.

9) Kim went to the store with her friend Angie, and together they shopped for a waterproof watch that was not too expensive.

10) She found the perfect watch in the first place they looked, and she bought it.

Reading Vocabulary

graduate (6) waterproof

Part A Answers

1) compound 2) complex
3) complex 4) simple
5) complex

Part B Answers

1) complex 2) simple
3) complex 4) complex
5) compound 6) simple
7) complex 8) simple
9) compound-complex
10) compound-complex

Application

In the Community

Engage students in a discussion of how their city or town could be improved. For example, students might believe that more after-school activities for teenagers are needed or that the public transportation system should be improved. Encourage students to choose an issue and write a persuasive speech about what the problem is, why it should be changed, and how this change will benefit the entire community. Remind students that dependent clauses add information to sentences and make ideas more complete. Also, a variety of sentence structures will make their speeches lively and interesting. Then have a "Community Issues Day." Invite government officials, parents, and other members of the community to hear students' speeches.

Complex Sentences Chapter 13 **295**

Chapter 13 Review

The Teacher's Resource Library includes two parallel forms of the Chapter 13 Mastery Test. The difficulty level of the two forms is equivalent. You may wish to use one form as a pretest and the other form as a posttest.

Reading Vocabulary

purchase (5) senior (6)

Part A Answers

1) clause 2) phrase 3) phrase 4) clause 5) clause 6) phrase 7) clause 8) phrase 9) clause 10) phrase

Part B Answers

1) adjective clause 2) adjective clause, adjective clause 3) adverb clause 4) noun clause 5) noun clause 6) adverb clause 7) noun clause 8) adjective clause 9) adverb clause 10) adjective clause

APPLICATION

At Home

Encourage students to review personal letters and other writing projects to check for a variety of sentence structures. Suggest that they add adverb, noun, and adjective clauses to sentences to convey additional information and to make their writing more interesting.

Chapter 13 Review

Part A Write on your paper whether each of these groups of words is a phrase or a clause. Remember, a clause always has a subject and a verb.

1) who planned the party
2) to the party
3) for Kim and her friends
4) that everyone will enjoy
5) because Kim is graduating
6) during her senior year
7) when you leave good friends
8) after so many years
9) after all her friends have gone
10) except for a few

Part B Write on your paper whether each clause in bold is an *adjective clause*, an *adverb clause*, or a *noun clause*.

1) The person **who is planning the party for Kim** is her mother, but we said that we would help.
2) Alex, **who has already graduated**, has gotten Kim a present **that he purchased in Bermuda.**
3) The party will be held **after the graduation exercises are over.**
4) Mrs. Huang has planned a surprise for **whichever guest arrives first.**
5) **Whoever it is** will be surprised.
6) **Because the party is for Kim**, the guests will not expect a gift.
7) Mrs. Huang will prepare plenty of food **for whoever is hungry**.
8) Mr. Huang, **who is a great cook**, is making vegetable egg rolls.
9) **After the party is over**, Kim invited some of her friends for the night.
10) Their house, **which is quite large**, once belonged to a rock star.

Name Date Period

Chapter 13 Mastery Test A page 1

Chapter 13 Mastery Test A

Part A Write whether each group of words is a phrase (*P*), a dependent clause (*DC*), or an independent clause (*IC*).

1) ______ Jackie planned a party.
2) ______ For her mother.
3) ______ Who was having a birthday.
4) ______ The person in the middle.
5) ______ Whoever plans the menu.
6) ______ He is my friend.
7) ______ Unless it rains.
8) ______ Having a picnic is fun.
9) ______ Which her daughter gave her.
10) ______ On top of the world.

Part B Write whether the bold words are an adjective clause (*AC*), an adverb clause (*AVC*), or a noun clause (*NC*).

1) **After school is out,** Janice is going on vacation. ______
2) I travel **wherever I want to go.** ______
3) **Whoever wants to go swimming** can join us. ______
4) The person **who opened the door for me** was very kind. ______
5) The dog **that wandered into our yard** looked lost. ______
6) Ho knew **what his father would say.** ______
7) We got the best seats **because we arrived early.** ______
8) Shelly bought a computer **that has a lot of memory.** ______
9) We disagree about **who should be the next president.** ______
10) They go surfing **whenever they have a chance.** ______

 Basic English Grammar

Name Date Period

Chapter 13 Mastery Test A page 2

Chapter 13 Mastery Test A, continued

Part C Identify each kind of sentence. Write *Simple, Compound, Complex,* or *Compound-Complex.*

1) ______________ Find the independent clause in the sentence.
2) ______________ Most of the sentences that we speak are complex.
3) ______________ The forecast was for snow, and it was correct.
4) ______________ Perry attends junior college, and he has a part-time job, which helps him pay for school.
5) ______________ The fish are biting, so let's go fishing.
6) ______________ The Cubs are in town for a week.
7) ______________ When they went to Oklahoma, Mary drove most of the way.
8) ______________ Mary drove for several miles, and then Josh, who doesn't like driving as well, took over.
9) ______________ Kelly, who is quite tall, hopes to play basketball.
10) ______________ The United States has many national parks.
11) ______________ The Blue Ridge Parkway, which is the longest national park, is in Virginia and North Carolina.
12) ______________ Yosemite National Park is in California, and Big Bend National Park is in Texas.
13) ______________ The Great Smoky Mountain National Park is in Tennessee and North Carolina, and it is the most visited park.
14) ______________ The Voyageurs National Park, which is on the Canadian border, is in northern Minnesota, and canoeing and camping are popular there.
15) ______________ Many of the parks have national forests in them.

 Basic English Grammar

Chapter 13 Mastery Test A

Part C Read the sentence below. Then follow the directions and answer the questions. Write your answers on your paper.

The gift that Mrs. Huang bought for the first guest is a CD.

1) Find the independent clause in the sentence. Write it on your paper.
2) Label the parts of the independent clause.
3) Write the dependent clause on your paper.
4) What are the subject and the verb in the dependent clause?
5) Is the dependent clause an adjective, an adverb, or a noun?
6) Is the sentence simple, compound, complex, or compound-complex?
7) Is the purpose of the sentence a statement, a question, or a command?
8) Write the sentence on your paper. Add an adjective phrase or an adjective clause to describe *CD.*
9) Add an adverb clause.
10) Write a sentence that follows the same pattern as the sentence above.

Part D Write on your paper whether each of these sentences is *simple, compound, complex,* or *compound-complex.*

1) What a wonderful time we had at the party!
2) We all enjoyed the food that Mrs. Huang prepared, and the music was great, too.
3) Who won the CD that Mrs. Huang bought?
4) Carrie and Mark came together, and they arrived first.
5) Mark said that Carrie could have the CD, which was nice of him.

Test Taking Tip When studying for a test, review the topics in the chapter. Then make up a practice test for yourself.

Reading Vocabulary

review (5)

Part C Answers

1) The gift is a CD **2)** gift (subject), is (linking verb), CD (predicate nominative) **3)** that Mrs. Huang bought for the first guest **4)** Mrs. Huang (subject), bought (verb) **5)** adjective clause **6)** complex **7)** statement **8–10)** Sentences will vary.

Part D Answers

1) simple **2)** compound-complex **3)** complex **4)** compound **5)** complex

Name Date Period | *Chapter 13 Mastery Test B page 1*

Chapter 13 Mastery Test B

Part A Write whether each group of words is a phrase (*P*), a dependent clause (*DC*), or an independent clause (*IC*).

1) ______ The telephone was ringing.
2) ______ Unless someone answers it.
3) ______ The middle of the road.
4) ______ Whenever you arrive.
5) ______ The caller left a message.
6) ______ On the way home.
7) ______ After he left the message.
8) ______ To the zoo.
9) ______ Going hiking is a good way to exercise.
10) ______ Which rang a bell with her.

Part B Write whether the bold words are an adjective clause (*AC*), an adverb clause (*AVC*), or a noun clause (*NC*).

1) The firefighter got the cat **that was up in our tree**. ______
2) She sings **whenever she needs a lift**. ______
3) A vacation is **what I need now**. ______
4) The woman **who owns that truck** will come back soon. ______
5) **What you think** makes a difference to me. ______
6) **Because of his age,** he could not get a license. ______
7) Tomas will help you **if you want to learn the program**. ______
8) The school **that they attend** is closing next year. ______
9) The principal said **that it may reopen in two years**. ______
10) **When play practice is over,** we will have pizza. ______

 Basic English Grammar

Name Date Period | *Chapter 13 Mastery Test B page 2*

Chapter 13 Mastery Test B, continued

Part C Identify each kind of sentence. Write *Simple, Compound, Complex,* or *Compound-Complex.*

1) ______________ Manny's favorite band was coming to town.
2) ______________ He had hoped that he could get tickets.
3) ______________ His friends Raven and Frank also wanted to go to the concert.
4) ______________ If the evening is warm and clear, the concert will be outside; however, if it is cold and raining, it will be inside.
5) ______________ The concert hall is huge, and it was filled that night.
6) ______________ Manny had a front-row seat, and his friends sat three rows back.
7) ______________ They waited for an hour for the band to arrive.
8) ______________ Everyone began to think that they would not arrive.
9) ______________ Suddenly the hall grew dark, and when the lights came on again, the band was on stage.
10) ______________ The audience cheered.
11) ______________ The band was great, so it was worth the wait.
12) ______________ Raven thought the band was excellent, and she especially liked their closing number.
13) ______________ When the concert ended, the friends went to the stage door.
14) ______________ After an hour had passed, the band members came out.
15) ______________ The band members were very nice, and although they were tired, they gave autographs to everyone who was there.

 Basic English Grammar

Chapter 13 Mastery Test B

Chapter 14

Planning Guide

The Verbal and the Verbal Phrase

	Student Text Lesson			
	Student Pages	Vocabulary	Practice Exercises	Lesson Review
Lesson 1 Infinitives and Infinitive Phrases	300-305	✔	✔	305
Lesson 2 Gerunds and Gerund Phrases	306-309	✔	✔	309
Lesson 3 Participles and Participial Phrases	310-313	✔	✔	313

Chapter Activities

Teacher's Resource Library
Community Connection 14:
Infinitives, Gerunds, and Participles

Assessment Options

Student Text
Chapter 14 Review

Teacher's Resource Library
Chapter 14 Mastery Tests A and B
Final Mastery Test

Teaching Strategies							Language Skills			Learning Styles						Teacher's Resource Library		
Reviewing Skills	Teacher Alert	Follow-up Activity	Career Application	Home Application	Global Connection	Community Application	Identification Skills	Writing Skills	Punctuation Skills	Visual/Spatial	Auditory/Verbal	Body/Kinesthetic	Logical/Mathematical	Group Learning	LEP/ESL	Activities	Workbook Activities	Self-Study Guide
300	304			305			✔	✔	✔							40-41	57-58	✔
306		309	307				✔	✔	✔									✔
310					314	313	✔	✔	✔							42	59-60	✔

Chapter at a Glance

Chapter 14: The Verbal and the Verbal Phrase

Teacher's Resource Library

Activities 40–42

Workbook Activities 57–60

Community Connection 14

Chapter 14 Self-Study Guide

Chapter 14 Mastery Tests A and B

Final Mastery Test

(Answer Keys for the Teacher's Resource Library begin on page 330 of this Teacher's Edition.)

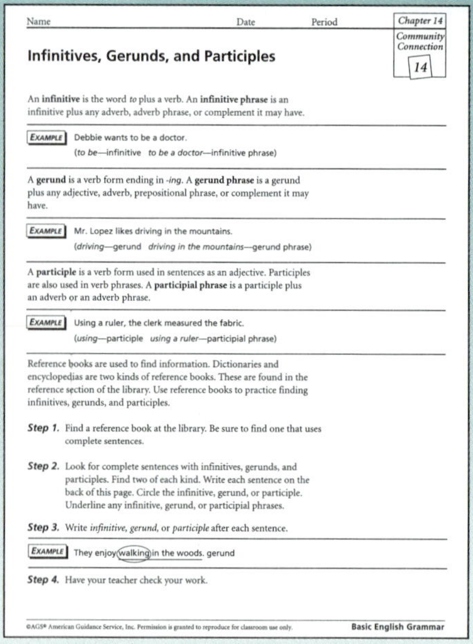

Name Date Period

Chapter 14
Community Connection
14

Infinitives, Gerunds, and Participles

An **infinitive** is the word *to* plus a verb. An **infinitive phrase** is an infinitive plus any adverb, adverb phrase, or complement it may have.

EXAMPLE Debbie wants to be a doctor.
(*to be*—infinitive *to be a doctor*—infinitive phrase)

A **gerund** is a verb form ending in *-ing*. A **gerund phrase** is a gerund plus any adjective, adverb, prepositional phrase, or complement it may have.

EXAMPLE Mr. Lopez likes driving in the mountains.
(*driving*—gerund *driving in the mountains*—gerund phrase)

A **participle** is a verb form used in sentences as an adjective. Participles are also used in verb phrases. A **participial phrase** is a participle plus an adverb or an adverb phrase.

EXAMPLE Using a ruler, the clerk measured the fabric.
(*using*—participle *using a ruler*—participial phrase)

Reference books are used to find information. Dictionaries and encyclopedias are two kinds of reference books. These are found in the reference section of the library. Use reference books to practice finding infinitives, gerunds, and participles.

Step 1. Find a reference book at the library. Be sure to find one that uses complete sentences.

Step 2. Look for complete sentences with infinitives, gerunds, and participles. Find two of each kind. Write each sentence on the back of this page. Circle the infinitive, gerund, or participle. Underline any infinitive, gerund, or participial phrases.

Step 3. Write *infinitive, gerund,* or *participle* after each sentence.

EXAMPLE They enjoy walking in the woods. gerund

Step 4. Have your teacher check your work.

 Basic English Grammar

Community Connection 14

Chapter 14

The Verbal and the Verbal Phrase

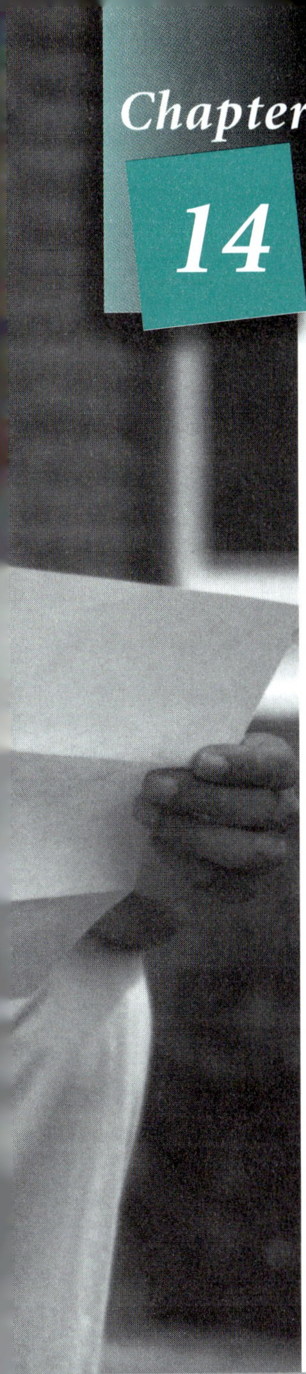

The following sentences include verbals. "Writing a letter is a way *to talk* to a friend. The friend *receiving* your message will be happy *to hear* from you."

A *verbal* is a verb form that is used as a noun or an adjective in a sentence. The three kinds of verbals are *infinitives, gerunds,* and *participles.*

An *infinitive* is a verb form made up of the word *to* plus a verb. It is usually used as a noun, but it may be used as an adjective or adverb. A *gerund* is a verb form that ends in *-ing* and is used as a noun. A *participle* is a verb form that is used as an adjective. It describes a noun or a pronoun. There are present and past participles.

In this chapter, you will learn about verbals and their purpose in sentences.

Goals for Learning

- To identify and use infinitives and infinitive phrases in sentences
- To identify and use gerunds and gerund phrases in sentences
- To identify and use participles and participial phrases in sentences

299

Reading Vocabulary

describe (5) include (5)
identify (6) verbal

Introducing the Chapter

Call attention to the young man reading the letter in the photograph. Then ask students why letters are so much fun to write and to receive. Elicit responses that include verbals and write them on the board. Two examples are:

- Reading a letter from someone far away makes me feel close to that person.
- I like to share the important events in my life with loving friends and relatives.

Underline the verbals in students' responses. Point out to students that each of these words and phrases is a verbal—a verb form used as a noun or an adjective in a sentence. Explain that after completing the activities in Chapter 14, students will be able to recognize verbals and understand how to use them in sentences.

SELF-STUDY GUIDE

Name ______

CHAPTER 14: The Verbal and the Verbal Phrase

Goal 14.1 *To identify and use infinitives and infinitive phrases in sentences*

Date	Assignment	Score
____	1: Read pages 299-300. Complete Activity A on page 300.	____
____	2: Read page 301. Complete Activities B-C on page 301.	____
____	3: Complete Workbook Activity 57.	____
____	4: Read page 302. Complete Activity D on page 302.	____
____	5: Read page 303. Complete Activity E on page 303.	____
____	6: Complete Workbook Activity 58.	____
____	7: Complete Activities F-H on page 304.	____
____	8: Complete the Lesson 1 Review, Parts A-B on page 305.	____

Comments:

Goal 14.2 *To identify and use gerunds and gerund phrases in sentences*

Date	Assignment	Score
____	9: Read page 306. Complete Activity A on page 306.	____
____	10: Read page 307. Complete Activity B on page 307.	____
____	11: Read page 308. Complete Activity C on page 308.	____
____	12: Complete the Lesson 2 Review on page 309.	____

Comments:

 Basic English Grammar

SELF-STUDY GUIDE

Name ______

CHAPTER 14 The Verbal and the Verbal Phrase, continued

Goal 14.3 *To identify and use participles and participial phrases in sentences*

Date	Assignment	Score
____	13: Read page 310. Complete Activity A on page 310.	____
____	14: Read page 311. Complete Activities B-C on page 311.	____
____	15: Complete Activity D on page 312.	____
____	16: Complete the Lesson 3 Review, Parts A-B on page 313.	____
____	17: Complete Workbook Activity 59.	____
____	18: Complete Workbook Activity 60.	____
____	19: Complete the Chapter 14 Review, Parts A-D on pages 314-315.	____

Comments:

Student's Signature ______ Date ______

Instructor's Signature ______ Date ______

 Basic English Grammar

Chapter 14 Self-Study Guide

Lesson at a Glance

Chapter 14 Lesson 1

Overview This lesson introduces infinitives and infinitive phrases.

Objective

- To identify infinitives and infinitive phrases in sentences.

Student Pages 300–305

Teacher's Resource Library

Activities 40–41

Workbook Activities 57–58

Reading Vocabulary

adjective
adverb
infinitive
phrase (5)
predicate

Teaching Suggestions

Introducing the Lesson

Remind students that a verbal is a verb form that is used as a noun or adjective in a sentence. Then discuss the information presented in the text about infinitives.

Reviewing Skills Review the principal parts of a verb.

Presenting Activity A

Write these sentences on the board: *He is learning to drive./I'd like to read your story.* Help students identify the subject and the verb in each sentence. Then ask them to find the infinitive. After this activity, have students complete Activity A on their own.

Activity A Answers

1) to fish **2)** to catch **3)** to clean **4)** to cook **5)** to make

Lesson 1 Infinitives and Infinitive Phrases

Infinitive
A verbal that begins with the word to. *An infinitive can act as a noun, an adjective, or an adverb in a sentence.*

An **infinitive** is a verb form made up of the word *to* plus a verb. It is usually used as a noun, but it may be used as an adjective or adverb.

EXAMPLES

Noun:	I like **to swim**.
Adverb:	He practices **to improve**.
Adjective:	There was plenty of food **to eat**.

An infinitive is usually in the present tense. It can also be in the present perfect tense (*to* + *have* + a verb).

EXAMPLES

Present:	Ella and Julian decided **to go** to the lake.
Present perfect:	They hoped **to have caught** ten fish by noon.

Activity A Write the infinitives in these sentences on your paper.

1) Ella and Julian really like to fish.

2) They hoped to catch enough fish for dinner.

3) Ella agreed to clean the fish.

4) Julian said he would like to cook the fish over an open fire.

5) Ella and Julian were on the lake by seven o'clock, ready to make their first cast.

An infinitive is not a part of the main verb or verb phrase. It may, however, be part of the complete predicate. Remember that the complete predicate is the main verb and all the words that describe that verb.

EXAMPLE

Verb Infinitive Adverb
Claudia / decided to leave early.
Subject Complete Predicate

Activity B Write the complete predicate in each of these sentences. Underline the verb or verb phrase. Circle the infinitive.

1) Donna appeared to be happy.

2) Where do you like to go on vacation?

3) Sam seems to be taller than Fred.

4) Connie hoped to get the lead in the play.

5) Do you want to use the computer?

Do not confuse infinitives with prepositional phrases. An infinitive is *to* + a verb. A prepositional phrase is *to* + a noun or pronoun.

EXAMPLE

Infinitive:	They want **to leave**. (*Leave* is a verb.)
Prepositional phrase:	Let's go **to the lake**. (*Lake* is a noun and the object of the preposition *to*.)

Activity C Write the words in bold in these sentences. Beside each group of words, write whether they are an *infinitive* or a *prepositional phrase.*

Example They wanted **to leave** early.
to leave—infinitive

1) When Ella and Julian got **to the lake**, they saw other people ready **to fish**.

2) They carried their equipment **to the boat**.

3) Soon they were ready **to begin**.

4) Julian always wanted **to be** the one **to catch** the first fish.

5) "Do you hope **to beat** the champion?" Ella said **to Julian**.

6) "I hope **to catch** at least one big one by ten o'clock," said Julian.

7) They said hello **to the other boaters**.

8) "Look!" Ella pointed **to another boat**.

9) "That man just started **to reel** in his line."

10) "He will need a big pan **to cook** that fish!"

Reading Vocabulary

computer (8) equipment (5) confuse (5) prepositional

■ Presenting Activity B

Do the first item in Activity B on the board. Ask volunteers to underline the main verb and circle the infinitive. Do the rest of the activity as a class or ask students to work on their own.

Activity B Answers

1) appeared to be happy **2)** Where do like to go on vacation **3)** seems to be taller than Fred **4)** hoped to get the lead in the play **5)** Do want to use the computer

■ Presenting Activity C

Write these phrases on the board: *to the office, to laugh, to enjoy, to the movie, to school, to play, to Mexico, to vote.* Have students list the infinitives on the left side of their papers and the prepositional phrases on the right. Then have students read their lists aloud to check their answers. Students can complete Activity C independently.

Activity C Answers

1) to the lake—prepositional phrase, to fish—infinitive **2)** to the boat—prepositional phrase **3)** to begin—infinitive **4)** to be, to catch—infinitives **5)** to beat—infinitive, to Julian—prepositional phrase **6)** to catch—infinitive **7)** to the other boaters—prepositional phrase **8)** to another boat—prepositional phrase **9)** to reel—infinitive **10)** to cook—infinitive

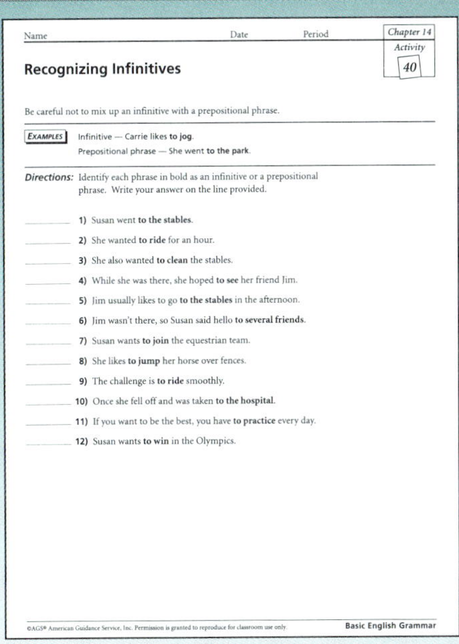

Name Date Period — Chapter 14 Activity 40

Recognizing Infinitives

Be careful not to mix up an infinitive with a prepositional phrase.

EXAMPLES Infinitive — Carrie likes **to jog**.
Prepositional phrase — She went **to the park**.

Directions: Identify each phrase in bold as an infinitive or a prepositional phrase. Write your answer on the line provided.

_____ **1)** Susan went **to the stables**.
_____ **2)** She wanted **to ride** for an hour.
_____ **3)** She also wanted **to clean** the stables.
_____ **4)** While she was there, she hoped **to see** her friend Jim.
_____ **5)** Jim usually likes to go **to the stables** in the afternoon.
_____ **6)** Jim wasn't there, so Susan said hello **to several friends**.
_____ **7)** Susan wants **to join** the equestrian team.
_____ **8)** She likes **to jump** her horse over fences.
_____ **9)** The challenge is **to ride** smoothly.
_____ **10)** Once she fell off and was taken **to the hospital**.
_____ **11)** If you want to be the best, you have **to practice** every day.
_____ **12)** Susan wants **to win** in the Olympics.

 Basic English Grammar

Activity 40

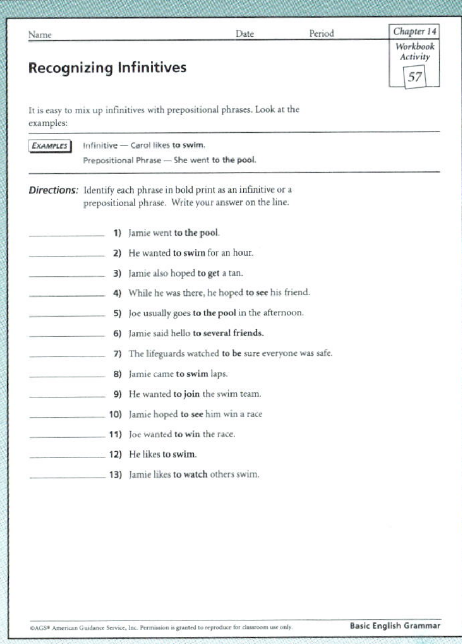

Name Date Period — Chapter 14 Workbook Activity 57

Recognizing Infinitives

It is easy to mix up infinitives with prepositional phrases. Look at the examples:

EXAMPLES Infinitive — Carol likes **to swim**.
Prepositional Phrase — She went **to the pool**.

Directions: Identify each phrase in bold print as an infinitive or a prepositional phrase. Write your answer on the line.

_____ **1)** Jamie went **to the pool**.
_____ **2)** He wanted **to swim** for an hour.
_____ **3)** Jamie also hoped **to get** a tan.
_____ **4)** While he was there, he hoped **to see** his friend.
_____ **5)** Joe usually goes **to the pool** in the afternoon.
_____ **6)** Jamie said hello **to several friends**.
_____ **7)** The lifeguards watched **to be** sure everyone was safe.
_____ **8)** Jamie came **to swim** laps.
_____ **9)** He wanted **to join** the swim team.
_____ **10)** Jamie hoped **to see** him win a race
_____ **11)** Joe wanted **to win** the race.
_____ **12)** He likes **to swim**.
_____ **13)** Jamie likes **to watch** others swim.

 Basic English Grammar

Workbook Activity 57

Reading Vocabulary

ambition (6)
infinitive phrase
nominative subject (5)

■ Presenting Activity D

Before having students complete Activity D, suggest that they work with a partner to make a list of the kinds of questions they ask to identify nouns, adjectives, and adverbs in sentences. If necessary, have students refer back to Chapters 1, 3, and 6 in their text. Then have partners work together to complete Activity D.

Activity D Answers

1) noun 2) noun 3) noun 4) noun 5) noun 6) adverb 7) adverb 8) adjective

Although an infinitive is a verb form, it can be used as a noun, an adverb, or an adjective in a sentence.

Study each sentence pattern to figure out how an infinitive is used in a sentence. Ask yourself the same kinds of questions you ask to identify parts of speech and sentence parts.

EXAMPLES

Noun:	Julian wants **to catch** a big fish. (What thing does Julian want?)
Adverb:	He will need a big pan **to cook** his fish. (Why does he need a big pan?)
Adjective:	Ella had plenty of bait **to use**. (What kind of bait does Ella have?)

Activity D Write the infinitives in bold in these sentences on your paper. Beside each infinitive, write whether it is used as a *noun*, an *adverb*, or an *adjective*. Remember that subjects, predicate nominatives, and direct objects are nouns.

1) **To catch** a big fish was Julian's ambition.
2) His greatest hope was **to reel** in a big one.
3) After an hour, they decided **to move** to another spot.
4) They hoped **to find** a place with some fish.
5) They tried **to stay** cheerful.
6) The fish were hard **to catch**.
7) "Even a little fish would be nice **to see** right now!"
8) "Hey! My time **to pull** in the big one has come!"

Infinitive phrase
A phrase that includes the infinitive plus all the words and phrases that go with the infinitive.

An **infinitive phrase** is an infinitive plus any adverb, adverb phrase, or complement it may have.

An infinitive may have an adverb or an adverb phrase to answer questions about its action.

302 *Chapter 14 The Verbal and the Verbal Phrase*

EXAMPLE

Inf. Adv. Adv. Phrase
To leave early for the lake was the plan.
(The entire infinitive phrase is *to leave early for the lake. Early* is an adverb that answers the question *When? For the lake* is a prepositional phrase that tells about *early*. It answers the question *Where?*)

An infinitive may also have a complement. It may have a direct object, a predicate nominative, or a predicate adjective.

EXAMPLES

Inf. D.O.
He wanted **to find a job**.
(*Job* is the direct object of the infinitive *to find*.)

Inf. P.N.
She wants **to be the president**.
(*President* is the predicate nominative. It follows the linking verb *to be*.)

Inf. Pred. Adj.
They wanted the dinner **to taste good**.
(*Good* is a predicate adjective that follows the linking verb *to taste*. The infinitive *to taste* also acts as an objective complement that tells about the direct object *dinner*.)

Activity E Write the whole infinitive phrase in each of these sentences on your paper.

1) Julian began to reel the fish into the boat.
2) The fish started to fight hard.
3) Julian's fish struggled to win the battle.
4) Ella got a net to help Julian.
5) To land that fish was their goal.

Sometimes the preposition *to* is missing from the infinitive.

EXAMPLES

"Don't make me (to) **laugh**," shouted Ella.
Help me (to) **reel** it in.

Reading Vocabulary

complement (10) objective (7)
goal (5) reel (5)

■ Presenting Activity E

Write these sentence starters on the board: *Lyn offered _______. / Seth hopes _______. / They expected the play _______.* Invite students to take turns completing each sentence with an infinitive phrase. Encourage students to try to vary the kinds of complements in each phrase. Suggest that they use the example sentences that precede Activity E as models. Then have students complete Activity E on their own.

Activity E Answers

1) to reel the fish into the boat **2)** to fight hard **3)** to win the battle **4)** to help Julian **5)** To land that fish

Name Date Period — Chapter 14 Activity 41

Infinitive Phrases

An infinitive is a verb form. It is *to* + a verb. Because an infinitive is a verb, it can have a complement. Adverbs can modify the infinitive. An infinitive plus its complements and modifiers is called an infinitive phrase.

EXAMPLES Lynn wanted **to join the circus**.
John hoped **to win a gold medal in the Olympics**.

Directions: Find and circle the infinitive phrase in each sentence.

1) In the winter, I like to go skiing in the Alps.
2) I don't know whether I want to be an engineer or a scientist.
3) Dan always wants to see the dolphins.
4) To be or not to be, that is the question.
5) Sam never wants to clean his room.
6) Sarah loves to eat steak with corn and potatoes.
7) No one wants to be alone.
8) Everyone's goal in life is to be happy.
9) John likes to fish for catfish.
10) To invest in the company, you must first be employed there.
11) I love to explore spooky buildings.
12) We have to decide on a topic for our report.
13) The baby likes to count his fingers and toes.
14) Elizabeth wants to go to the movies tonight.
15) I want you to be honest with me.

 Basic English Grammar

Activity 41

Name Date Period — Chapter 14 Workbook Activity 58

Infinitive Phrases

An infinitive is a verb form. It is *to* + a verb. Because an infinitive is a verb, it can have a complement. Adverbs can modify the infinitive. An infinitive plus any adverb, adverb phrase, or complement it may have is called an infinitive phrase.

EXAMPLES
INF. D.O.
Jack wanted to join the team.
INF. P.N. Prep. Phrase
Cathy hoped to be the winner of the contest.

Directions: Underline the infinitive phrase in each sentence. Label its parts. Do yours like the examples.

1) In the summer our family likes to sit on the beach.
2) We always hope to see the dolphins.
3) Little Janey likes to count them.
4) While we are there, we also like to walk on the beach.
5) No one wants to get a sunburn.
6) We use a sunscreen to prevent a bad burn.
7) Freddy, the oldest in the family, likes to fish for flounder.
8) Sonny, the youngest, likes to eat flounder!
9) No one wants to clean the fish.
10) That's the biggest problem this family needs to solve today.
11) Oh, to be on the beach again!
12) Oh, to walk barefoot in the sand.
13) I love to feel the ocean breeze.
14) Since Freddy seldom catches fish, we have to decide on a restaurant.
15) The ocean gives us big appetites, so we want dinner to taste good.

 Basic English Grammar

Workbook Activity 58

Reading Vocabulary

gear (5)

■ Presenting Activity F

Write these sentences on the board: *Let's go now. / Will you help me fix my bike?* Help students locate the infinitive in each sentence. Then ask students to complete Activity F on their own.

Activity F Answers

1) help **2)** cheer **3)** see **4)** hold **5)** feel

■ Presenting Activity G

Discuss the example, helping students to recognize that *to catch some fish* follows the linking verb *was* and refers back to *wish.* Then, depending on the ability of your class, do Activity G together or have students work independently.

Activity G Answers

1) to go home—adjective **2)** to pack up their gear—direct object **3)** to set—direct object **4)** to see anything—adverb **5)** To be on the road before dark—subject

■ Presenting Activity H

Before having students do Activity H on their own, have them take turns making up sentences for item 1.

Activity H Answers

Each sentence should contain the infinitive indicated in the activity.

Teacher Alert

Use the examples that precede Activity F to point out that adding the missing *to* to identify an infinitive may make a sentence sound odd. Students shouldn't rely on the sound of the sentence to identify an infinitive.

Activity F Write the infinitive in each of these sentences on your paper.

1) Will you let me help you?

2) They heard the other boaters cheer for Julian.

3) "Let us see the size of that fish," they all said.

4) They watched Julian hold his fish high in the air.

5) Their attention made Julian feel proud.

Activity G Write the infinitive phrase in each of these sentences on your paper. After each one, write how it is used in the sentence.

Example Their wish was to catch some fish.
to catch—predicate nominative

1) It was time to go home.

2) They began to pack up their gear.

3) The sun was beginning to set.

4) Soon, it would be too dark to see anything.

5) To be on the road before dark was their goal.

Activity H Write a sentence for each of these infinitives on your paper. Underline the entire infinitive phrase in each sentence.

1) to laugh

2) to rain

3) to be

4) to watch

304 *Chapter 14 The Verbal and the Verbal Phrase*

Lesson 1 Review

Part A Write the infinitive phrase in each of these sentences on your paper.

Example The hours seemed to fly by.
to fly by

1) Ella and Julian wanted to be home by dark.
2) They decided to stop at six o'clock.
3) Ella began to count the fish.
4) They had hoped to catch many fish.
5) To catch enough fish for dinner had been their goal.
6) "How many fish are big enough to eat?" asked Julian.
7) "We have enough to feed your family and mine," answered Ella.
8) "I'll need a big pan to cook this one," Julian said.
9) "Let's get ready to go home," Ella said.
10) Soon, they were both ready to leave.

Part B Write a sentence for each of these infinitives on your paper. Underline the entire infinitive phrase in each sentence.

1) to be
2) to work
3) to go
4) to find
5) to see

Part A Answers

1) to be home by dark **2)** to stop at six o'clock **3)** to count the fish **4)** to catch many fish **5)** to catch enough fish for dinner **6)** to eat **7)** to feed your family and mine **8)** to cook this one **9)** to go home **10)** to leave

Part B Answers

The infinitive phrase in each sentence should be underlined.

Application

At Home

Suggest that students create a "To Do" list of things they can do at home for themselves and for other members of the family. Students may wish to talk to their parents and other family members to determine what kinds of things they can do to benefit themselves and the family as a whole. Suggest that students use an infinitive to begin every item on their list. Provide the following as a model.

This week I plan:

- To clean my room
- To visit my grandmother
- To help my sister learn to ride a two-wheeler

The Verbal and the Verbal Phrase *Chapter 14* **305**

Lesson at a Glance

Chapter 14 Lesson 2

Overview This lesson presents gerunds and gerund phrases.

Objective

- To identify gerunds and gerund phrases in sentences.

Student Pages 306–309

Reading Vocabulary

appositive	**gerund**
challenge (5)	musical (5)

Teaching Suggestions

Introducing the Lesson

Discuss the definition of *gerund* and the examples of how gerunds function in sentences. Emphasize the fact that gerunds act just like nouns in sentences.

Reviewing Skills

Review the function of nouns and appositives in sentences.

Presenting Activity A

Write these sentences on the board: *Helping you paint is my pleasure./ Sam gets paid for walking his neighbors' dogs.* Help students identify the gerunds in each sentence. As an extra challenge, ask students to tell how the gerund functions in each sentence. Then ask students to complete Activity A on their own or with a partner.

Activity A Answers

1) Riding **2)** running
3) playing **4)** getting
5) Finding **6)** walking
7) catching **8)** Talking
9) fishing **10)** reading, going

Lesson 2 Gerunds and Gerund Phrases

Gerund
A verb form that has an -ing ending. A gerund is always used as a noun.

A **gerund** is a verb form that ends in *-ing*. A gerund is always used as a noun. In sentences, gerunds act like nouns.

EXAMPLES

Subject:	**Drinking** and **driving** do not mix.
Direct object:	The dog began **barking**.
Predicate noun:	My favorite sport is **swimming**.
Object of a preposition:	The student got in trouble for **coming** in late again.
Appositives:	Ella enjoys two things: **fishing** and in-line **skating**.
	You might try the following kinds of exercise: **biking**, **running**, or **rock hiking**.
	Her special talents—**singing** and **dancing**—helped her get the lead in the musical.

Activity A Write the gerunds in each of these sentences on your paper.

1) Riding a bicycle on back roads is great exercise.
2) I like running better.
3) My favorite activity is playing my trumpet.
4) She has trouble getting to school on time.
5) Finding his way through the strange city was a challenge.
6) They were sent to the office for walking in the halls without a pass.
7) His greatest goal was catching a big fish.
8) Talking to my parents can be difficult sometimes.
9) Dolores thinks fishing is dull.
10) She enjoys reading and going to the movies.

Gerund phrase

A phrase that includes the gerund and all the words and phrases that are related to the gerund.

A **gerund phrase** is a gerund plus any adjective, adverb, prepositional phrase, or complement it may have.

Because a gerund acts like a noun in a sentence, it may have an adjective that describes it.

EXAMPLE

Adj. Gerund
I get in trouble for **loud talking.**
(What kind of *talking? loud.* The gerund phrase is the object of the preposition *for.*)

A gerund may also have an adverb or adverb phrase.

EXAMPLE

Gerund Adv. Phrase
Rob likes **running in the morning.**
(When does Rob like *running*? *in the morning. In the morning* is a prepositional phrase used as an adverb. The entire gerund phrase is the direct object of the action verb *like.*)

Because a gerund is a verb form, it may have complements.

EXAMPLE

Gerund D.O.
Riding a bicycle is fun.
(*Bicycle* is the direct object of the gerund *riding.* The gerund phrase is the subject of the verb *is.*)

Activity B Write the gerund phrase in each of these sentences on your paper. Beside it, write whether the gerund phrase acts as a *subject, direct object, predicate nominative, object of a preposition,* or an *appositive* in the sentence.

Example Getting ready for school is the hardest part of my day.
Getting ready for school—subject

1) Yori watched the running of the Boston Marathon on television.
2) One of his dreams was winning that race.
3) When he was very young, he began thinking about entering a marathon some day.
4) Yori enjoys two things: running and winning!

Reading Vocabulary

gerund phrase relate (6)
marathon

■ Presenting Activity B

Discuss the example provided for Activity B. Help students understand that they can tell that the gerund phrase in the example is the subject because it answers the question, "What is the hardest part of my day?" *Getting ready for school* is. You may also wish to review how to identify direct objects, predicate nominatives, objects of prepositions, and appositives in sentences. Then, depending on the needs of your class, do Activity B orally as a class or have students work with a partner to complete the activity.

Activity B Answers

1) the running of the Boston Marathon on television—direct object **2)** winning that race—predicate nominative
3) thinking—direct object
entering a marathon some day—object of a preposition
4) running and winning—appositive

APPLICATION

Career Connection

Job applicants are often asked to explain, in writing, their work experience and their career goals. The use of gerunds and gerund phrases can be especially helpful in accomplishing this task. For example, to explain past work experience, someone might write: *In my last position, I was responsible for answering the telephone, making appointments, and filing patient records.* Encourage students to write a brief paragraph describing their past work experience (at home, as a volunteer, or in a paid position) and a short paragraph describing their career goals. Encourage them to use as many gerunds and gerund phrases as possible in their paragraphs. After they have finished, invite students to share their paragraphs with the class.

Reading Vocabulary

progressive (7)

■ Presenting Activity C

Invite volunteers to take turns providing oral sentences for items 1 and 2 and 6 and 7. Have the class listen carefully to check that students have used the verb phrases and the gerunds correctly. Then ask students to complete Activity C on their own.

Activity C Answers

Sentences will vary. The first five sentences should correctly use the verb phrases listed, and the last five sentences should correctly use gerunds.

Don't confuse progressive verb forms with gerunds.

EXAMPLES		
	Verb phrase:	Yori **has been running** every day.
	Gerund:	Yori likes **running** every day.

Activity C Write sentences on your paper for each of these verb phrases and gerunds. Be sure to use each one correctly.

Verb Phrases	Gerunds
1) will be starting	**6)** being
2) is beginning	**7)** finding
3) were going	**8)** running
4) has been trying	**9)** wishing
5) are planning	**10)** singing

308 *Chapter 14 The Verbal and the Verbal Phrase*

Lesson 2 Review

Lesson Review Write the gerund phrases in each of these sentences on your paper. Underline the gerund or gerunds in each gerund phrase.

Example My hobby is collecting stamps.
collecting stamps

1) Flying an airplane must be a thrill.
2) Reading books is a way to relax.
3) We enjoyed swimming in the lake.
4) An architect earns a salary by designing buildings.
5) My dog always gets in trouble for chasing cats.
6) The singing and dancing were good in that play.
7) I like cooking, but not cleaning up.
8) Finding anything in that messy room must be hard.
9) Locating a needle in a haystack seems impossible.
10) A farmer earns money by growing and selling food.
11) Knowing you has been my pleasure.
12) Some people enjoy weeding their gardens.
13) Planning our vacation was fun.
14) His favorite sport is fishing for trout.
15) Dana's hobby is reading.

Reading Vocabulary

architect (6) pleasure (5)
haystack salary (5)

Lesson Review Answers

1) Flying an airplane **2)** Reading books **3)** swimming in the lake **4)** designing buildings **5)** chasing cats **6)** The singing and dancing **7)** cooking but not cleaning up **8)** Finding anything in that messy room **9)** Locating a needle in a haystack **10)** growing and selling food **11)** Knowing you **12)** weeding their gardens **13)** Planning our vacation **14)** fishing for trout **15)** reading

Follow-up Activity

Have students skim a newspaper or magazine article to find and list as many gerunds as possible. Remind students that a word ending in *-ing* is a gerund if it acts like a noun in a sentence. After, have students compare their lists with partners to see who found the most gerunds.

The Verbal and the Verbal Phrase Chapter 14 **309**

Lesson at a Glance

Chapter 14 Lesson 3

Overview This lesson presents participles and participial phrases.

Objective

- To identify participles and participial phrases in sentences.

Student Pages 310–313

Teacher's Resource Library

Activity 42

Workbook Activities 59–60

Reading Vocabulary

detail (5) **participle**
mushy

Teaching Suggestions

Introducing the Lesson

Discuss the information presented in the text. Be sure students understand the difference between a present participle and a gerund, and the difference between a participle used as an adjective and a participle that is part of a verb phrase.

Reviewing Skills

Review the present and past tense of regular and irregular verbs.

Presenting Activity A

Do the first two items in Activity A with the class. To avoid having students confuse the main verb with the participle in each sentence, help students first identify the main verb or verb phrase in each sentence. Suggest that students follow this same process as they complete Activity A on their own.

Activity A Answers

1) setting 2) cooked
3) reading 4) lost
5) rumbling 6) cracked
7) Steamed 8) fallen
9) frightening 10) bubbling

Lesson 3 Participles and Participial Phrases

Participle
A verb form that is used like an adjective.

A **participle** is another verb form. Participles are used in sentences as adjectives. A participle may be in the present tense or in the past tense.

EXAMPLES

Present tense:	The **running** deer was beautiful.
Past tense:	The house looks larger **painted** white.
	He picked up the pieces of **broken** glass.

Activity A Write the participles in each of these sentences on your paper.

1) The setting sun turned the sky red and purple.
2) Those cooked carrots are mushy.
3) The girl reading that book is my sister.
4) Will you help that lost child find her mother?
5) My rumbling stomach told me I was hungry.
6) The cracked glass hid the details of the painting.
7) Steamed vegetables are good for you.
8) The hikers climbed over the fallen log.
9) What a frightening movie that was!
10) Fish jumped in the bubbling brook.

Do not confuse a participle used as an adjective with a participle that is part of a verb phrase.

EXAMPLES

Participle:	The deer **running** through the woods was beautiful.
Verb phrase:	The deer **was running** through the woods.

Activity B Write on your paper whether the words in bold in these sentences are participles used as *adjectives* or are part of the *verb phrase.*

Example The **barking** dog scared the child. **adjective**
The dog was **barking** at the child. **verb phrase**

1) Your cold is probably **catching**.
2) We will be **catching** the train.
3) The newly **painted** room was bright and cheery.
4) They have **painted** the room a bright yellow.
5) The wind was **howling** all night.
6) The **howling** wind kept us awake all night.

Participial phrase
A phrase that includes the participle and all the words and phrases related to it.

A **participial phrase** is a participle plus any words that complement or describe it. A participle comes right before or right after the noun or pronoun it describes.

EXAMPLE **Running at full speed,** she caught the bus. (The participial phrase *Running at full speed* describes *she*.)

Activity C Write these sentences on your paper. Underline each participial phrase. Draw a line to the noun or pronoun it describes.

1) Howling wildly, the wind frightened the child.
2) Dana lent her book to the girl sitting in the first row.
3) Expecting the worst, Julian was pleasantly surprised with his grade.
4) The keys locked inside the car were of little use.
5) Concentrating on her notes, Mrs. Agnello did not hear Julian enter the room.
6) Mr. Agnello has mailed the letter addressed to the bank.
7) Recommended by his teachers, Chan was given the award.
8) Dinner cooked by her sons was a special treat for Mrs. Agnello.

Reading Vocabulary

concentrate (5)
participial phrase
recommend (6)

■ Presenting Activity B

Write these sentences on the board: *The mirror was broken by the movers./She cut her hand on the broken glass.* Help students identify the past participle in each sentence. Ask students to identify the sentence in which the participle is used as an adjective and the one in which it is used as part of a verb phrase. Then have students do Activity B on their own.

Activity B Answers

1) adjective 2) verb phrase 3) adjective 4) verb phrase 5) verb phrase · 6) adjective

■ Presenting Activity C

Write item 1 in Activity C on the board. Help students locate the participial phrase and the noun it describes. Then invite a volunteer to underline the participial phrase and draw a line to the noun it describes. You may wish to continue this process to complete Activity C as a class, or you can suggest that students work with a partner to complete the activity.

Activity C Answers

1) Howling wildly—wind
2) sitting in the first row—girl
3) Expecting the worst—Julian
4) locked inside the car—keys
5) Concentrating on her notes—Mrs. Agnello 6) addressed to the bank—letter 7) Recommended by his teachers—Chan 8) cooked by her sons—Dinner

Reading Vocabulary

adorable autograph (5)
adore (6) snack (6)

■ Presenting Activity D

Discuss the example given for Activity D with the class. Then do item 1 on the board, having students identify the participial phrase and the word it describes. After having students complete Activity D independently, ask them to share their answers with the class.

Activity D Answers

1) Walking to school—we **2)** Speaking in front of the class—Bobby **3)** missing—items **4)** sleeping—kittens **5)** Swimming at the beach—we **6)** thumping—sound **7)** sunken—treasure **8)** hand-sewn—quilt **9)** scrubbed—face **10)** broken—glass **11)** Trapped in an elevator—girl **12)** adoring—fan **13)** hoping for a victory—team **14)** frozen—lake **15)** chuckling softly to herself—her

Activity D Write the participle used as an adjective or the participial phrase in each of these sentences on your paper. Underline the participle in each participial phrase. Then write the word that the participle or participial phrase describes.

Examples Running at full speed, the girl caught the bus.
Running at full speed—girl

The growling dog frightened the man and his son.
growling—dog

1) Walking to school, we passed a new apartment building.

2) Speaking in front of the class, Bobby got nervous.

3) Snacks are the only missing items in our backpacks.

4) The sleeping kittens looked adorable.

5) Swimming at the beach, we saw a shark.

6) Carol enjoyed the thumping sound of the music.

7) The book told a story about a sunken treasure.

8) Each of the patches on the hand-sewn quilt came from a piece of old clothing.

9) With his freshly scrubbed face, the boy looked younger.

10) Elena swept up the pieces of broken glass from the floor.

11) Trapped in an elevator, the girl cried out for help.

12) An adoring fan asked the rock star for her autograph.

13) The team, hoping for a victory, ran onto the field.

14) The skaters glided across the frozen lake.

15) I heard her chuckling softly to herself.

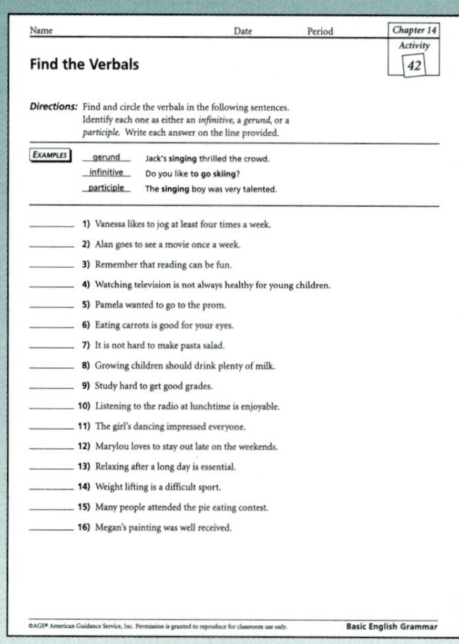

Name Date Period Chapter 14 Activity 42

Find the Verbals

Directions: Find and circle the verbals in the following sentences. Identify each one as either an *infinitive*, a *gerund*, or a *participle*. Write each answer on the line provided.

EXAMPLES
gerund Jack's **singing** thrilled the crowd.
infinitive Do you like **to go skiing**?
participle The **singing** boy was very talented.

______ 1) Vanessa likes to jog at least four times a week.
______ 2) Alan goes to see a movie once a week.
______ 3) Remember that reading can be fun.
______ 4) Watching television is not always healthy for young children.
______ 5) Pamela wanted to go to the prom.
______ 6) Eating carrots is good for your eyes.
______ 7) It is not hard to make pasta salad.
______ 8) Growing children should drink plenty of milk.
______ 9) Study hard to get good grades.
______ 10) Listening to the radio at lunchtime is enjoyable.
______ 11) The girl's dancing impressed everyone.
______ 12) Marylou loves to stay out late on the weekends.
______ 13) Relaxing after a long day is essential.
______ 14) Weight lifting is a difficult sport.
______ 15) Many people attended the pie eating contest.
______ 16) Megan's painting was well received.

©AGS® American Guidance Service, Inc. Permission is granted to reproduce for classroom use only. Basic English Grammar

Activity 42

312 *Chapter 14 The Verbal and the Verbal Phrase*

Lesson 3 Review

Part A Write the participle or the participial phrase in each of these sentences on your paper.

1) We could see the boy running around the track.
2) The man found his lost dog.
3) Rowing rapidly, we soon crossed the river.
4) The broken bike could not be fixed.
5) Standing on the corner, we watched the cars go by.
6) Arriving early, we were first in line for tickets.
7) We waved to the marching soldiers.
8) I wondered who the girl walking by the restaurant was.
9) Totally lost, Dad still would not stop to ask directions.
10) Waving its tail happily, the dog stood and waited for its dinner.

Part B Copy each of these sentences on your paper. Fill in the blank with a participle that makes sense in the sentence.

1) Denise handed out the _____ watermelon.
2) _____ to the hospital, we were almost in an accident.
3) I could not understand what the _____ note meant.
4) The woman _____ on the bench is my mother's friend Lily.
5) We had to throw away the _____ steak.

Reading Vocabulary

restaurant (5) totally

Part A Answers

1) running around the track
2) lost 3) Rowing rapidly
4) broken 5) Standing on the corner 6) Arriving early
7) marching 8) walking by the restaurant 9) Totally lost
10) Waving its tail happily

Part B Answers

Participles will vary.

Application

In the Community

Encourage students to investigate places in the community where signs are needed for the protection and safety of the people or for the preservation of the environment. Then suggest that students design signs for these places. Each sign should have gerund, infinitive, or participle. For example, students might create a sign with the words, *Writing on public property is forbidden* for a place where graffiti often appears. Signs can also have illustrations and graphics. Have students prepare a booklet with their sign designs and suggestions for where to place them. If they wish, they can present a copy of their booklet to city or town officials.

Name Date Period | *Chapter 14 Workbook Activity 59*

Three Kinds of Verbals

A verbal is a verb form that we use as another part of speech.

A. Infinitives and Infinitive Phrases

Directions: Find the infinitive or infinitive phrase and underline it.

EXAMPLE Darleen wanted to go home early.

1) Andy wanted to use the boat.
2) We decided to have steak for dinner.
3) At last we were ready to eat.
4) The squirrel got ready to leap to the next tree.
5) To join the country club was expensive.

B. Gerunds and Gerund Phrases

Directions: Find the gerund or gerund phrase and underline it.

EXAMPLE Janet likes playing her trumpet.

1) Bark gets Tiny into trouble.
2) Finding the right house was difficult.
3) Many people like swimming.
4) Camping is popular in the United States.
5) The most popular sport in the United States is auto racing.

C. Participles and Participial Phrases

Directions: Find the participle or participial phrase and underline it.

EXAMPLES We finally found the lost kitten.
They watched the horse running around the track.
Looking over the side of the tall building, Marlene got frightened.

1) We finally fixed the broken bike.
2) Fixing the bike ourselves, we saved money.
3) Leroy's parents watched him riding the bike.
4) Shouting happily, Leroy enjoyed the ride.
5) Suddenly we heard the bike squeaking loudly again.

 Basic English Grammar

Workbook Activity 59

Name Date Period | *Chapter 14 Workbook Activity 60*

Find the Verbals

Directions: Circle the verbals in these sentences. Identify each one as either an infinitive, a gerund, or a participle. Write each answer on the line.

EXAMPLES
gerund Jack's (singing) thrilled the crowd.
infinitive Do you like (to fish?)
participle The (dancing) contest lasted several hours.

_____ 1) Sammy likes to work out three times a week.
_____ 2) Carol always goes to watch her father play softball.
_____ 3) Hitting a tennis ball is a lot of fun.
_____ 4) Listening to the radio in my car is enjoyable.
_____ 5) Relaxing after a busy day is important.
_____ 6) Weightlifting is a popular activity these days.
_____ 7) The weightlifting contest was attended by many people.
_____ 8) Christy wanted to go to the party with her friends.
_____ 9) Working hard usually brings success.
_____ 10) Frank's band provides the only music needed at the dance.
_____ 11) Snacking on cucumbers helped Roger lose weight.
_____ 12) You can buy stewing tomatoes at a grocery store.
_____ 13) It is not hard to stew tomatoes at home.
_____ 14) Study grammar to improve your compositions.
_____ 15) Remember that writing can be great fun.

 Basic English Grammar

Workbook Activity 60

Chapter 14 Review

The Teacher's Resource Library includes two parallel forms of the Chapter 14 Mastery Test. The difficulty level of the two forms is equivalent. You may wish to use one form as a pretest and the other form as a posttest.

Final Mastery Test

The Teacher's Resource Library includes the Final Mastery Test. This test is pictured on pages 328–329 of this Teacher's Edition. The Final Mastery Test assesses the major learning objectives of this text, with emphasis on Chapters 8–14.

Reading Vocabulary

accomplishment (6)
congratulate (5)
graduate (6)
graduation (6)

Part A Answers

1) to see Elena **2)** to leave good old Wilson High School **3)** to have a party **4)** to meet **5)** to do that after the ceremony **6)** to travel cross country this summer **7)** To see Italy **8)** to work in Spain **9)** to talk about our accomplishments **10)** to graduate from high school first

Part B Answers

1) Planning a party **2)** playing charades at a party **3)** graduating from high school **4)** congratulating each other **5)** laughing and crying at the same time

Global Connection

Every language has familiar sayings that are meant to remind people to be practical, hardworking, moral, and so on. These sayings often include a verbal of some kind, as in the following examples: *Early to bed and early to rise, makes a man healthy, wealthy, and wise. / To err is human, to forgive divine. / Let sleeping dogs lie.* Discuss these examples. Then invite students to share their favorite sayings. Encourage bilingual students to provide non-English sayings and their translations. Have students note the sayings that contain a verbal of some kind.

Chapter 14 Review

Part A Write the infinitive phrases in each of the sentences on your paper.

1) Julian went to the graduation to see Elena.
2) "I am a little bit sorry to leave good old Wilson High School," said Barbara before graduation.
3) "It's a good excuse to have a party," Ella laughed.
4) We should find a place to meet.
5) "Let's plan to do that after the ceremony," Julian said.
6) Did you know that Sam wants to travel cross country this summer?
7) "To see Italy is my dream," Val said.
8) My plan, after I finish college, is to work in Spain.
9) Let's get together in ten years to talk about our accomplishments.
10) That sounds like fun to me, but I think we need to graduate from high school first.

Part B Write the gerund phrase in each of these sentences on your paper.

1) Planning a party is always fun for that group.
2) "I enjoy playing charades at a party," Ella said.
3) For Elena, graduating from high school was a wonderful event.
4) After congratulating each other, Al and Billy looked for their parents.
5) Their actions—laughing and crying at the same time—showed that they had mixed emotions about graduation.

314 *Chapter 14 The Verbal and the Verbal Phrase*

Name ____ Date ____ Period ____ *Chapter 14 Mastery Test A page 1*

Chapter 14 Mastery Test A

Part A Identify the bold word in each sentence as an *Infinitive, Gerund,* or *Participle.*

1) Kathy likes **to** swim. ____
2) The mother tried to calm the **crying** child. ____
3) **Playing** the piano well takes practice. ____
4) Dana wanted **to** be president of the club. ____
5) They like **swimming,** so they go to the pool. ____
6) The outfit was very **becoming** on Tasha. ____
7) **Walking** to the store is good exercise. ____
8) We ran **to** get to our gate in time. ____
9) The **flowing** water looked clear and clean. ____
10) Hugh's greatest pleasure is **skiing.** ____

Part B Write whether each bold phrase is an infinitive phrase (*IP*), a gerund phrase (*GP*), or a participial phrase (*PP*).

1) ____ **Riding a motorcycle** is something Pedro likes to do.
2) ____ Martha agreed **to write the letter**.
3) ____ **The barking dog** kept everyone awake.
4) ____ The plan is **to leave late**.
5) ____ **Working at full speed,** we finished our chores early.
6) ____ **Building houses** is my dad's job.
7) ____ Jamal hoped **to win a scholarship**.
8) ____ **Getting ready for the party** took several hours.
9) ____ **Reeling the fish into the boat** was a struggle.
10) ____ **The chirping bird** awakens me each morning.

 Basic English Grammar

Name ____ Date ____ Period ____ *Chapter 14 Mastery Test A page 2*

Chapter 14 Mastery Test A, continued

Part C Write each group of words as the verbal shown in a complete sentence.

1) to run — *Infinitive as adverb*
2) to watch a sunset — *Infinitive as noun*
3) to paint — *Infinitive as adjective*
4) going home late — *Gerund as object of preposition*
5) driving a car — *Gerund as direct object*
6) knowing how to type — *Gerund as subject*
7) bowling — *Gerund as predicate noun*
8) the howling wind — *Participle*
9) the whining puppy — *Participle*
10) cracked bowl — *Participle*

 Basic English Grammar

Chapter 14 Mastery Test A

Part C Write the participle or participial phrase in each of these sentences on your paper.

1) Smiling from the stage, Sue received her diploma.
2) Roberto, walking across the stage, almost tripped.
3) With trembling voices, the graduates said good-bye to each other.
4) Someone handed a folded piece of paper to Elena.
5) She read the printed note and smiled.

Part D Write the verbal phrases in these sentences on your paper. Beside each one, write whether it is an *infinitive phrase*, a *gerund phrase*, or a *participial phrase.*

1) Standing in front of the school for a last look, the girls had tears in their eyes.
2) "Graduating from high school is something that you will always remember," said Mrs. Castillo.
3) As they drove away, Sue turned to take one last look at her school.
4) Shutting her eyes, Sue knew that she would always remember the good friends that she had made.
5) They all met at Elena's house to celebrate the graduation.
6) Elena had decided to invite all her friends.
7) Opening the door, she welcomed them all inside.
8) Everyone came in carrying food or soft drinks.
9) Barbara wanted everyone to sign her yearbook.
10) Looking around the room, Elena felt happy to see all her friends together.

Test Taking Tip When taking a matching test, match all the items that you know go together for sure. Cross these items out. Then try to match the items that are left.

Reading Vocabulary

diploma (8)

Part C Answers

1) Smiling from the stage
2) walking across the stage
3) trembling 4) folded
5) printed

Part D Answers

1) Standing in front of the school for a last look—participial phrase 2) Graduating from high school—gerund phrase 3) to take one last look at her school—infinitive phrase 4) Shutting her eyes—participial phrase 5) to celebrate the graduation—infinitive phrase 6) to invite all her friends—infinitive phrase 7) Opening the door—participial phrase 8) carrying food or soft drinks—participial phrase 9) to sign her yearbook—infinitive phrase 10) Looking around the room—participial phrase

Name Date Period | Chapter 14 Mastery Test B page 1

Chapter 14 Mastery Test B

Part A Identify the bold word in each sentence as an *Infinitive, Gerund,* or *Participle.*

1) The **broken** glass was dangerous. ______
2) **Going** to the fair is what we look forward to. ______
3) He likes **to** play the trumpet. ______
4) **To** be a musician is his only goal. ______
5) The **laughing** brook babbled beside us. ______
6) We like **going** to movies. ______
7) **Running** before work is how I get my exercise. ______
8) He has very **winning** ways. ______
9) We need **to** be at the train by 10 in the morning. ______
10) **Camping** is the way we like to vacation. ______

Part B Write whether each bold phrase is an infinitive phrase (*IP*), a gerund phrase (*GP*), or a participial phrase (*PP*).

1) ______ **Painting the house** is a major job.
2) ______ This summer we hope **to paint**.
3) ______ Soon we need **to choose the new color.**
4) ______ **Getting color chips** is our next task.
5) ______ **Running to the paint store** takes time.
6) ______ The house would look nice **painted yellow**.
7) ______ The first job will be **scraping the old paint**.
8) ______ Then we have **to prime any bare wood.**
9) ______ **Working in the shade,** we can keep ourselves cool.
10) ______ **The newly painted house** will look so nice.

 Basic English Grammar

Name Date Period | Chapter 14 Mastery Test B page 2

Chapter 14 Mastery Test B, continued

Part C Write each group of words as the verbal shown in a complete sentence.

1) to catch *Infinitive as adverb*
2) to see the sunrise *Infinitive as noun*
3) to climb *Infinitive as adjective*
4) leaving late *Gerund as object of preposition*
5) riding a bike *Gerund as direct object*
6) learning how to ski *Gerund as subject*
7) fishing *Gerund as predicate noun*
8) a whispering breeze *Participle*
9) the laughing child *Participle*
10) chipped tooth *Participle*

 Basic English Grammar

Chapter 14 Mastery Test B

Glossary

A

Abstract noun—(ab strakt´ noun) an idea that you cannot see or touch (p. 13)

Action verb—(ak´ shən vėrb) a word that expresses physical or mental action in the past, present, or future (p. 80)

Active verb—(ak´ tiv vėrb) a verb that is used if the subject does the action (p. 105)

Adjective—(aj´ ik tiv) a word that tells about a noun or pronoun; it tells *what kind, which one, how many,* or *how much* (p. 54)

Adjective clause—(aj´ ik tiv klȯz) a dependent clause that acts like an adjective in a sentence (p. 287)

Adverb—(ad´ vėrb) a word that answers questions about a verb, an adjective, or another adverb; it tells *How? When? Where? How often? How long?* or *How many times?* (p. 130)

Adverb clause—(ad´ vėrb klȯz) a dependent clause that works exactly like an adverb in a sentence (p. 279)

Antecedent—(an tə sēd´ nt) the noun that a pronoun replaces (p. 28)

Appositive—(ə poz´ ə tiv) a word or group of words that renames or explains another noun in the same sentence (p. 285)

C

Clause—(klȯz) a group of words that has a subject and a predicate; a clause may be independent or dependent (p. 276)

Collective noun—(kə lek´ tiv noun) names a group of people or things (p. 12)

Common noun—(kom´ ən noun) names a general type of person, place, thing, or idea (p. 4)

Comparative adjective—(kəm par´ ə tiv aj´ ik tiv) an adjective that compares one noun with another (p. 72)

Complement—(kom´ plə mənt) the part of a sentence that completes an idea (p. 248)

Complete predicate—(kəm plēt´ pred´ ə kit) the part of a sentence that contains the main verb and all the words that describe the verb; the main word in the complete predicate is the verb or verb phrase (p. 208)

Complete subject—(kəm plēt´ sub´ jikt) all the words in the subject; it may be one word or many words (p. 203)

Complex sentence—(kom´ pleks sen´ təns) a sentence with one independent and at least one dependent clause (p. 290)

Compound-complex sentence—(kom´ pound kom´ pleks sen´ təns) a sentence that has two or more independent clauses and one or more dependent clauses (p. 292)

Compound noun—(kom´ pound noun) a noun that is more than one word (p. 12)

Compound sentence—(kom´ pound sen´ təns) a sentence made up of two or more independent clauses joined by a conjunction such as *and, but,* or *or* (p. 215)

Concrete noun—(kon´ krēt noun) something you can see or touch (p. 13)

Conditional form—(kən dish´ ə nəl fôrm) a helping verb that puts a condition, or a requirement, on an action (p. 102)

Conjunction—(kən jungk´ shən) a word that connects related words or groups of words (p. 174)

Coordinating conjunction—(kō ôrd´ n āt ing kən jungk´ shən) a conjunction that connects words or groups of words that do the same job in a sentence (p. 174)

Correlative conjunctions—(kə rel´ ə tiv kən jungk´ shənz) a pair of conjunctions that connects words or groups of words that are related (p. 185)

D

Demonstrative pronouns—(di mon´ strə tiv prō´ nounz) pronouns that point to nouns: *this, these, that,* and *those* (p. 43)

316 *Glossary* *Basic English Grammar*

Dependent clause—(di pen´ dent klȯz) a group of words that does not express a complete idea and cannot stand alone as a sentence (p. 276)

Direct object—(də rekt´ ob´ jikt) a noun or pronoun that receives the action from a transitive verb (p. 231)

F

Future perfect—(fyü´ chər pėr´ fikt) the verb tense that shows an action that will be completed before a certain time in the future (p. 86)

G

Gerund—(jer´ ənd) a verb form that has an *-ing* ending; a gerund is always used as a noun (p. 306)

Gerund phrase—(jer´ ənd frāz) a phrase that includes the gerund and all the words and phrases that are related to the gerund (p. 307)

I

Indefinite pronoun—(in def´ ə nit prō´ noun) a pronoun that refers to a noun that is not named (p. 46)

Independent clause—(in di pen´ dənt klȯz) a group of words with a subject and a verb; an independent clause expresses a complete thought and can stand alone as a sentence (p. 215)

Indirect object—(in də rekt´ ob´ jikt) a noun or pronoun that comes after the verb and before the direct object and usually answers the question *to whom, to what, from whom,* or *for what* about the verb (p. 241)

Infinitive—(in fin´ ə tiv) a verb form made up of the word *to* plus a verb; an infinitive can act as a noun, an adjective, or an adverb in a sentence (p. 300)

Infinitive phrase—(in fin´ ə tiv frāz) a phrase that includes the infinitive plus all the words and phrases that go with the infinitive (p. 302)

Interjection—(in tər jek´ shən) a word or phrase that shows strong feeling (p. 192)

Interrogative pronouns—(in tə rog´ ə tiv prō´ nounz) pronouns that introduce questions; *who, whom, which, what,* and *whose* (p. 39)

Intransitive verb—(in tran´ sə tiv vėrb) a verb that does not transfer action from the subject to an object (p. 231)

L

Linking verb—(lingk´ ing vėrb) a verb that joins the subject to a noun, pronoun, or adjective in the predicate; it is also called a state-of-being verb (p. 256)

N

Nominative pronoun—(nom´ ə nə tiv prō´ noun) a pronoun used as the subject of a sentence (p. 29)

Noun—(noun) names a person, place, thing, or idea (p. 4)

Noun clause—(noun klȯz) a dependent clause that works exactly like a noun in a sentence (p. 282)

O

Objective complement—(əb jek´ tiv kom´ plə mənt) a noun or an adjective that follows a direct object and adds to its meaning (p. 248)

Objective pronoun—(əb jek´ tiv prō´ noun) a pronoun used as the object of a sentence (p. 29)

P

Participial phrase—(pär´ tə sip əl frāz) a phrase that includes the participle and all the words and phrases related to it (p. 311)

Participle—(pär´ tə sip əl) a verb form that is used like an adjective (p. 310)

Passive verb—(pas´ iv vėrb) a verb that is used when the action happens to the subject (p. 105)

Past perfect—(past pėr´ fikt) the verb tense that shows one action completed before another past action (p. 86)

a	hat	e	let	ī	ice	ô	order	ù	put	sh	she	ə { a	in about
ā	age	ē	equal	o	hot	oi	oil	ü	rule	th	thin	e	in taken
ä	far	ėr	term	ō	open	ou	out	ch	child	ŦH	then	i	in pencil
â	care	i	it	ȯ	saw	u	cup	ng	long	zh	measure	o	in lemon
												u	in circus

Basic English Grammar *Glossary* **317**

Personal pronoun—(pėr′ sə nəl prō′ noun) a pronoun that takes the place of a noun and that refers to a person or object (p. 28)

Phrase—(frāz) a group of words without a subject and a verb; a phrase relates to another part of the sentence (p. 276)

Plural noun—(plůr′ əl noun) names more than one person, place, thing, or idea (p. 15)

Positive adjective—(poz′ ə tiv aj′ ik tiv) an adjective that describes one noun (p. 72)

Possessive noun—(pə zes′ iv noun) shows ownership or relationship (p. 20)

Possessive pronoun—(pə zes′ iv prō′ noun) a pronoun that shows ownership or relationship (p. 29)

Predicate—(pred′ ə kit) the part of a sentence that tells something about the subject (p. 208)

Predicate adjective—(pred′ ə kit aj′ ik tiv) an adjective that follows a linking verb and tells about the subject; completes the predicate (pp. 55, 256)

Predicate nominative—(pred′ ə kit nom′ ə nə tiv) a noun or pronoun that follows a linking verb and renames the subject (p. 265)

Preposition—(prep ə zish′ ən) a word that shows how a noun or pronoun is related to another word in the sentence (p. 154)

Prepositional phrase—(prep ə zish′ ə nəl frāz) phrase that begins with a preposition and ends with a noun or a pronoun (p. 154)

Present perfect—(prez′ nt pėr′ fikt) the verb tense that shows an action started in the past and continuing up to the present (p. 86)

Progressive form—(prə gres′ iv fôrm) the form of a verb that ends in *-ing* and uses a form of the verb *be* as a helping verb to show continuing action (p. 93)

Pronoun—(prō′ noun) a part of speech that takes the place of a noun (p. 28)

Proper noun—(prop′ ər noun) names a particular person, place, thing, or idea (p. 4)

R

Relative pronouns—(rel′ ə tiv prō′ nounz) the pronouns *who, whom, whose, which, that, what, whoever, whomever, whichever,* and *whatever* (p. 35)

S

***-Self* pronoun**—(self prō′ noun) a pronoun that ends with *-self* and indicates action done to or by another pronoun or a noun in the sentence; *-self* pronouns are also used to show emphasis (p. 32)

Sentence—(sen′ təns) a group of words that expresses a complete thought; a sentence always begins with a capital letter and ends with a period, question mark, or exclamation point (p. 200)

Simple sentence—(sim′ pəl sen′ təns) a sentence that has one subject and one predicate and expresses a complete idea (p. 215)

Simple subject—(sim′ pəl sub′ jikt) the main noun or pronoun in the subject (p. 203)

Singular noun—(sing′ gyə lər noun) names one person, place, thing, or idea (p. 15)

State-of-being verb—(stāt ov bē′ ing vėrb) a verb that explains or describes the subject of a sentence; a state-of-being verb is also called a *linking verb* (p. 112)

Subject—(sub′ jikt) who or what the sentence is about (p. 203)

Subordinating conjunction—(sə bôrd′ n āt ing kən jungk′ shən) a conjunction that connects a dependent clause with an independent clause in a sentence (p. 180)

Superlative adjective—(sə pėr′ lə tiv aj′ ik tiv) an adjective that compares one noun with two or more other nouns (p. 72)

T

Tense—(tens) the time that the verb expresses in a sentence (p. 84)

Transitive verb—(tran′ sə tiv vėrb) a verb that shows action passed from the subject of the sentence toward a person or thing (p. 231)

V

Verb—(vėrb) a word that expresses action or a state of being in a sentence (p. 1)

Verbal—(vėrb′ əl) a verb form that is used as a noun or an adjective in a sentence (p. 299)

Verb phrase—(vėrb frāz) a main verb and one or more helping verbs (p. 82)

318 *Glossary* *Basic English Grammar*

Index

A

B

Basic English Grammar *Index* **319**

320 *Index Basic English Grammar*

E

F

G

H

I

Basic English Grammar Index **321**

322 *Index Basic English Grammar*

Basic English Grammar Index **323**

Q

R

S

324 *Index Basic English Grammar*

T

Basic English Grammar *Index* **325**

U

V

W

Y

326 *Index Basic English Grammar*

Midterm Mastery Test

Name Date Period

Chapters 1-9 Midterm Mastery Test page 1

Midterm Mastery Test

Part A Identify the part of speech for each bold word. Write *Noun, Pronoun, Adjective, Action Verb, State-of-Being Verb, Adverb, Preposition, Conjunction,* or *Interjection.*

1) ______________ After the cold winter, spring **finally** arrived.
2) ______________ Thurgood Marshall was a justice **on** the Supreme Court.
3) ______________ Labrador retrievers are known to be **friendly** dogs.
4) ______________ Damian and **I** often play cards.
5) ______________ She **dropped** her glasses on the floor.
6) ______________ Angela **and** Benny are at the movies.
7) ______________ Please make me a peanut butter **sandwich.**
8) ______________ **Hurry!** The dog got out again.
9) ______________ The dinner **smells** good.
10) ______________ **Tanya** tried out for the cross country team.
11) ______________ The cat is sleeping **under** the table.
12) ______________ Every state **elects** two senators.
13) ______________ New York and Boston **are** both east coast cities.
14) ______________ Mom votes for Republicans, **but** Dad votes for Democrats.
15) ______________ We are having lunch together **tomorrow.**
16) ______________ **Ouch!** That bee sting hurts.
17) ______________ Choose **whichever** dessert you like.
18) ______________ *Fences* **was written** by August Wilson.
19) ______________ **Neither** Sela **nor** Ahmad had the keys.
20) ______________ Have you answered these questions **correctly**?

 Basic English Grammar

Midterm Mastery Test Page 1

Name Date Period

Chapters 1-9 Midterm Mastery Test page 2

Chapters 1-9 Midterm Mastery Test, continued

Part B Rewrite these sentences on the blank line. Capitalize the proper nouns and adjectives.

1) valerie has a french poodle named mimi.
2) tim likes to eat swiss cheese.
3) We studied the native american tribes of new mexico.
4) My friend hanna is learning spanish with her computer.
5) karl enjoys his english and basic computer II classes.
6) samantha is reading *sense and sensibility.*
7) We plan to see a play on friday, april 21.
8) loren had an african family visit him over summer vacation.
9) I would like italian dressing with my salad.
10) On vacation, tracy went to the rocky mountains in colorado.

 Basic English Grammar

Midterm Mastery Test Page 2

Name Date Period

Chapters 1-9 Midterm Mastery Test page 3

Chapters 1-9 Midterm Mastery Test, continued

Part C Rewrite these sentences on the blank lines. Add the necessary punctuation.

1) Because Tim is Elizas friend he bought her a birthday gift.
2) Sharon bought four dollars worth of stamps but she needs more to mail the package.
3) That coat is Jacks and this one is yours.
4) Ouch That hurt.
5) Peter wanted to be on the wrestling team therefore he lifted weights every day.
6) Kips sister Dionn has three children named Jasper Alf and Evon.
7) Connie wanted to go biking instead she went fishing.
8) Wow I got an A on my test.
9) If at first you don't succeed try try again.
10) Dave shut the closet door however he didn't know the cat was inside.

 Basic English Grammar

Midterm Mastery Test Page 3

Name Date Period

Chapters 1-9 Midterm Mastery Test page 4

Chapters 1-9 Midterm Mastery Test, continued

Part D Write in the blank the word in parentheses that correctly completes each sentence.

1) Either milk or water __________ fine with me. (is, are)
2) Neither Kathy nor her friends __________ in the band. (is, are)
3) James would like to go, __________ he is too busy. (and, but)
4) They planned to go camping; __________, it was too cold. (however, therefore)
5) The __________ tracks led under the woodpile. (mices, mice's)
6) Both of the __________ books were lost. (girl's, girls')
7) The store sold only __________ clothes. (ladies', ladys')
8) Henry XIII had six __________. (wifes, wives)
9) Have you __________ dinner yet? (eaten, ate)
10) Everyone has already __________ home. (gone, went)
11) __________ brother goes to our school. (Moe's, Moes')
12) The girls were early for __________ lesson. (their, them)
13) __________ of these CDs should I buy? (Which, What)
14) Each girl brought __________ own bat and ball. (their, her)
15) My uncle is __________ than my brother. (tall, taller, tallest)
16) This test is very __________. (tricky, trickier, trickiest)
17) Bo got the __________ news of anyone in the class. (good, better, best)
18) Janilynn was __________ her breakfast. (eat, ate, eaten, eating)
19) Quincy has __________ math for four years. (take, took, taken, taking)
20) Which of you two sings __________? (well, better, best)

 Basic English Grammar

Midterm Mastery Test Page 4

Final Mastery Test

Name Date Period

Chapters 1-14 *Final Mastery Test page 1*

Final Mastery Test

Part A Label the parts of each sentence. Use these abbreviations:

S Subject *DO* Direct Object *OC* Objective Complement

V Verb *IO* Indirect Object

1) Amanda went to Howard University.

2) Jimmy won a scholarship.

3) He would play baseball for his school.

4) The college gave Jimmy a uniform.

5) Jimmy is a good athlete.

6) Nadya was excited about her new job.

7) The new baby made the family happy.

8) Only Ed is doing something special tonight.

9) The spring weather was beautiful.

10) The voters arrived at the polls early.

 Basic English Grammar

Final Mastery Test Page 1

Name Date Period

Chapters 1-14 *Final Mastery Test page 2*

Final Mastery Test, Continued

Part B Identify the part of speech for each bold word. Write *Noun, Pronoun, Adjective, Action Verb, State-of-Being Verb, Adverb, Preposition, Conjunction,* or *Interjection.*

1) ______ Calico cats are **beautiful** animals.

2) ______ Trudy and **I** like to dance.

3) ______ We **chose** the blue balloons for the party.

4) ______ Isaiah **and** Ned are shooting baskets.

5) ______ Please bring me a **pencil**.

6) ______ The food **tastes** delicious.

7) ______ The dog is barking **at** the door.

8) ______ Portland and Los Angeles **are** west coast cities.

9) ______ Some friends are coming over **today**.

10) ______ **Whew!** That feels better.

Part C Write these sentences on your paper. Capitalize the proper nouns and proper adjectives.

1) ahmad has a cat named may.

______

2) julia likes dutch chocolate.

______

3) frank is taking spanish and computer I.

______

4) sherry read *a raisin in the sun* on her trip to arizona.

______

5) chuck is taking monday, august 15, off.

______

 Basic English Grammar

Final Mastery Test Page 2

Name Date Period

Chapters 1-14 *Final Mastery Test page 3*

Final Mastery Test, Continued

Part D Identify each kind of sentence. Write *Simple, Compound, Complex,* or *Compound-Complex.*

1) ______ Paddy, Dino, and Grant had enjoyed high school.

2) ______ They knew their lives would be different now, but they looked forward to it.

3) ______ They planned to keep in touch, although if they were going keep contact, they would have to work at doing it.

4) ______ They could write letters, and they also could leave messages for each other on e-mail.

5) ______ Paddy learned that he had been accepted at the local technical college.

6) ______ Grant got a scholarship to Washington State University, which was his first choice.

7) ______ He will major in physical education, and because of what he has been told, he knows WSU is a good school for PE majors.

8) ______ Dino is going to art school.

9) ______ He will start at the state university, and then he will transfer to the Kansas City Art Institute.

10) ______ All three hope they will be successful at their schools.

Part E Write whether each group of words is a phrase (*P*), a dependent clause (*DC*), or an independent clause (*IC*).

1) ______ When you finish the job.

2) ______ They ate supper.

3) ______ Seeing you is fun.

4) ______ Using the computer.

5) ______ Before we move.

6) ______ Unless it snows.

7) ______ After the winter.

8) ______ In the morning.

9) ______ Ken walked home.

10) ______ Whenever you go.

 Basic English Grammar

Final Mastery Test Page 3

Name Date Period

Chapters 1-14 *Final Mastery Test page 4*

Final Mastery Test, Continued

Part F Identify the purpose of each sentence. Write *Statement, Question, Command/Request,* or *Feeling.*

1) Who knows how to use this software? ______

2) Bring in the newspaper. ______

3) I am so excited! ______

4) The Yankees play the Athletics next week. ______

5) Tell me about your new apartment. ______

Part G Write whether the bold verb is transitive (*T*) or intransitive (*I*).

1) ______ Glen **reads** short stories.

2) ______ Birds **fly**.

3) ______ She **found** the number in the telephone book.

4) ______ Toni Morrison **writes** poems.

5) ______ Jim Thorpe **lived** in Oklahoma.

Part H Circle the verbal in each sentence. Write whether it is an *Infinitive, Gerund,* or *Participle.*

1) ______ Ms. Jones was at home watching television.

2) ______ She enjoys relaxing after a busy day.

3) ______ Tonya had gone to her room to study.

4) ______ They heard someone knocking at the door.

5) ______ Kirby had come to tell Tonya about his job.

6) ______ "Working in a bank is fun," he told Ms. Jones.

7) ______ Wondering what Tonya would like to do, Kirby asked her about her plans.

8) ______ Tonya thought she might get a job painting.

9) ______ Mr. Lee wanted Tonya to paint his house.

10) ______ Tonya wanted to paint his picture!

 Basic English Grammar

Final Mastery Test Page 4

Final Mastery Test

Name Date Period

Chapters 1-14 *Final Mastery Test* *page 5*

Final Mastery Test, Continued

Part I Write whether the bold word or words is a predicate adjective (*PA*), a predicate noun (*PN*), or a predicate pronoun (*PP*).

1) ______ That boy is my **brother**.

2) ______ Cardinals are **red**.

3) ______ Who is **she**?

4) ______ Kally will be **vice president**.

5) ______ Brothers all are **we**.

6) ______ Is he **scared** or **unsure**?

7) ______ Her workshop is usually **messy** but **clean**.

8) ______ Before two months pass, he will be **president**.

9) ______ Tran is **teacher** of the year.

10) ______ Gareth felt **calm** and **sure** about his test scores.

Part J Write whether the bold words are an adjective clause (*AC*), an adverb clause (*AVC*), or a noun clause (*NC*).

1) **After the sun sets,** the temperature drops. ______

2) She does **whatever pleases her**. ______

3) **Whenever you are ready** will be a good time to go. ______

4) The person **who lost the kitten** was upset. ______

5) The tree **that fell on the roof** was huge. ______

6) Gina knew **what the plans were**. ______

7) We got in the back way **because we knew the owner**. ______

8) Drew bought a laptop computer **that he travels with**. ______

9) He disagrees about **what we should do**. ______

10) She goes biking **whenever she has time**. ______

 Basic English Grammar

Final Mastery Test Page 5

Name Date Period

Chapters 1-14 *Final Mastery Test* *page 6*

Final Mastery Test, Continued

Part K Write these sentences on your paper. Add the necessary punctuation.

1) Because Elsas mother is working Elsa watches her sister Kim.

____

2) Len bought ten dollars worth of gas but he still did not fill the tank.

____

3) Hello Is anybody home?

____

4) Monica made supper however her father brought Chinese food.

____

5) Shira left the back door open therefore she had to catch the bird that flew inside.

____

Part L Write in the blank the word in parentheses that correctly completes each sentence.

1) Neither Larry nor his friends ______ in the play. (is, are)

2) Chris wants to leave, ______ her car is stalled. (and, but)

3) The restaurant has a ______ menu. (children's, childrens')

4) Husbands and ______ can attend the meeting. (wifes, wives)

5) Have you ______ your breakfast yet? (eaten, ate)

6) I had ______ by the time they got there. (gone, went)

7) ______ sister goes to our class. (Zoe's, Zoes')

8) The boys were on time for ______ game. (their, them)

9) Each girl brought ______ own baseball glove. (their, her)

10) My aunt is ______ than my mother. (tall, taller, tallest)

 Basic English Grammar

Final Mastery Test Page 6

Teacher's Resource Library Answer Key

Activities

Activity 1–Concrete Nouns

Answers will vary. Suggested answers are given.

1) a) motorcycle **b)** car **c)** wagon **d)** truck **e)** bus **2) a)** magazine **b)** road sign **c)** billboard **d)** newspaper **e)** mail **3) a)** rose **b)** daffodil **c)** carnation **d)** violet **e)** tulip **4) a)** library **b)** hospital **c)** store **d)** apartment **e)** warehouse **5) a)** teacher **b)** friend **c)** neighbor **d)** brother/sister **e)** dentist **6) a)** desk **b)** table **c)** sofa **d)** bed **e)** dresser

Activity 2–Abstract Nouns

Answers will vary. Suggested answers are given.

1) a) anxiety **b)** anger **c)** hunger **d)** thirst **e)** joy **2) a)** ounce **b)** pint **c)** quart **d)** dozen **e)** liter **3) a)** Monday **b)** hour **c)** year **d)** second **e)** August **4) a)** program **b)** trust **c)** walk **d)** plan **e)** cleaning **5) a)** love **b)** trust **c)** obedience **d)** faith **e)** loyalty **6) a)** track meet **b)** horse show **c)** party **d)** Olympics **e)** World Series

Activity 3–Find the Nouns

1) swimmers, pool **2)** cost, house, agent **3)** 1960s, Beatles, entertainers **4)** George, quarter, sidewalk **5)** Carlos, sweater, game **6)** Mrs. Edwards, Sam, kindness **7)** Kim, aunt, Monday **8)** Annie, books, week **9)** type, book, mystery **10)** president, James Madison **11)** Dolley Madison, wife, president, ice cream, White House **12)** courage, team, difficulties, game **13)** Bill, football **14)** kitten, bed **15)** team, Salina

Activity 4–Singular and Plural Pronouns

1) Our–P **2)** her–S **3)** We–P **4)** we–P **5)** their, us–P **6)** We–P **7)** we, their, we, them–P **8)** them–P **9)** Their–P **10)** their–P **11)** they–P **12)** They–P; You–S or P; it–S **13)** we, our, our–P **14)** us–P

Activity 5–Personal Pronouns

1) you **2)** their **3)** its **4)** it, she **5)** They **6)** We **7)** They, them **8)** it

Activity 6–Indefinite Pronouns

A	N	O	T	H	I	N	G	M	G	H	I
N	A	O	B	C	D	A	E	U	F	N	J
Y	Q	P	B	O	N	N	M	C	L	O	K
B	R	S	S	O	M	E	T	H	I	N	G
O	T	V	T	W	D	X	F	Y	Z	E	A
D	D	H	E	N	O	Y	R	E	V	E	B
Y	E	C	E	I	K	N	A	L	W	K	E
R	F	G	H	J	B	A	L	B	L	B	R
W	E	I	N	N	O	M	G	W	K	B	W

Sentences will vary. Each one should include one of these words.

1) nobody **2)** none **3)** another **4)** something **5)** anybody **6)** much **7)** many **8)** everyone **9)** nothing **10)** few

Activity 7–Locating Adjectives in Sentences

1) smart, loyal, fun–Alex **2)** tall, handsome–James Melcher **3)** her, sweet–puppy **4)** warm–weather **5)** tart, cold–lemonade **6)** lovely, sweet-tempered–Laura; popular–girl **7)** big, heavy–book **8)** tired, thirsty–Dina **9)** that, loud–noise **10)** bright, red–cardinal; tall, oak–tree **11)** thick–woods **12)** Young–children; wild–birds; cold, winter–months

Activity 8–Adjectives Are Words of Power

Suggested answers are given. Accept reasonable alternatives.

1) energetic **2)** chilly **3)** shining **4)** round **5)** favorite **6)** dull **7)** praiseworthy **8)** undependable **9)** one-of-a-kind **10)** unbelievable

Activity 9–Comparing With Adjectives

1) positive **2)** superlative **3)** comparative **4)** comparative **5)** superlative **6)** superlative **7)** comparative **8)** comparative **9)** positive **10)** superlative **11)** comparative **12)** comparative **13)** positive **14)** positive **15)** comparative **16)** positive **17)** positive **18)** positive

Activity 10–Irregular Verb Forms

1) seen **2)** giving **3)** chose **4)** go **5)** eaten **6)** chosen **7)** broke **8)** doing **9)** taught **10)** began **11)** done **12)** gave

Activity 11–Verb Tense

1) past **2)** past **3)** present perfect **4)** present **5)** present **6)** present perfect **7)** past perfect **8)** past **9)** present **10)** future perfect **11)** future perfect **12)** present perfect **13)** past **14)** future **15)** past

Activity 12–Conditional and *Do* Verbs

1) must have gone **2)** might have gone **3)** should have exercised **4)** Did know **5)** might win **6)** must leave **7)** can sing **8)** might come **9)** Do like **10)** must rake **11)** Did finish **12)** did trim **13)** must do **14)** Do like

Activity 13–Finding State-of-Being Verbs

1) are **2)** is **3)** tastes **4)** smells **5)** tasted **6)** had become **7)** seemed **8)** appeared **9)** Have become **10)** have grown **11)** felt **12)** should look **13)** is **14)** could be **15)** remained **16)** tasted **17)** gets **18)** looks

Activity 14–State-of-Being Verbs Express Tense

1) felt–past **2)** is–present **3)** has been–present perfect **4)** will be–future **5)** looks–present **6)** became–past **7)** keeps–present **8)** was–past **9)** will be–future **10)** had looked–past perfect **11)** will be–future **12)** felt–past **13)** Have looked–present perfect **14)** is–present **15)** will be–future **16)** grew–past **17)** have been–present perfect

Activity 15–Using the *Be* Verb

1) be **2)** is **3)** be **4)** is **5)** been **6)** be **7)** be **8)** been **9)** been **10)** been **11)** is **12)** been **13)** been **14)** was **15)** is **16)** been

Activity 16–Adverbs Answer Questions About Verbs

Answers will vary. Sample answers are given below. All of the responses must answer the question *How?*

1) carefully **2)** gracefully **3)** gladly **4)** beautifully **5)** loudly **6)** rapidly **7)** briskly **8)** carefully **9)** loudly **10)** slowly **11)** quickly **12)** slowly **13)** sharply **14)** happily **15)** softly **16)** fast **17)** straight **18)** well

Activity 17–Adverbs of Degree

A. **1)** very **2)** too **3)** so **4)** rather **5)** very

B. **1)** sometime **2)** very **3)** much **4)** very **5)** quite

Activity 18–Comparing With Adverbs

A. **1)** brightly **2)** faster **3)** better **4)** less happily (or more happily) **5)** more comfortably (or less comfortably) **6)** hard **7)** most loudly (or least loudly) **8)** best **9)** most quickly **10)** more sweetly

B. **1)** clearly, more clearly, most clearly (or less, least) **2)** loudly, more loudly, most loudly (or less, least) **3)** fast, faster, fastest **4)** nicely, more nicely, most nicely (or less, least) **5)** gracefully, more gracefully, most gracefully (or less, least)

Activity 19–Understanding Prepositions

Answers may vary. Possible answers are given.

1) of **2)** in **3)** beside, near, with **4)** with **5)** in, from, on **6)** beside, on, under **7)** from **8)** in **9)** on **10)** on **11)** across, at, beside, near **12)** for, from, to

Activity 20–Prepositional Phrases as Modifiers

A. **1)** to a class–went **2)** through her notebook–looked **3)** to page 72–textbook **4)** from the chapter–reading **5)** about the material–question **6)** to her room–went **7)** to the children's playroom–went **8)** with the children–talked **9)** to Katie–talked **10)** of young children–teacher

B. Responses will vary. Sentences should include the preposition *to*.

Activity 21–Finding Prepositional Phrases

1) of Beethoven–adjective **2)** up a tree–adverb **3)** During the summer–adverb **4)** on my street–adjective **5)** after next–adjective **6)** on the telephone–adjective **7)** to the north–adjective **8)** through the woods–adverb **9)** down the sidewalk–adverb **10)** at Boston College–adjective **11)** on the beach–adverb **12)** for the concert–adjective **13)** at noon–adjective **14)** over the water–adverb **15)** next to Chuck and Justin–adverb **16)** at the supermarket–adverb **17)** after the long meeting–adverb **18)** Across the dusty field–adverb **19)** on your paper–adverb **20)** near a busy highway–adverb **21)** across the bed–adverb **22)** During the storm–adverb **23)** on a hot summer day–adverb **24)** in North Carolina–adverb

Activity 22–Dependent Clauses

The subordinating conjunction is in bold.

1) **Because** margarine and butter are mostly fat, **2)** **until** I finish **3)** **When** April arrives, **4)** **Since** the party was over, **5)** **In order that** everyone might get home safely, **6)** **Whenever** I am sad, **7)** **Although** it was raining, **8)** **while** they watched the movie. **9)** **If** Jennifer is late again, **10)** **Because** an education leads to a better job, **11)** **In order that** the workers look the same, **12)** **Unless** you save your money,

Activity 23–Punctuating Compounds

1) hurry; otherwise, **2)** shopping, . . . house, and **3)** today; however, it **4)** tea; therefore, the **5)** afternoon; nevertheless, he **6)** fish; nevertheless, it **7)** tomatoes, cucumbers, green peppers, but **8)** Tulips, daffodils, and **9)** drinks, chocolate, coffee, and **10)** properly, avoid **11)** *Hamlet, Romeo and Juliet,* and **12)** Apples, Ataris, and IBM **13)** Janet, Katie, and **14)** movie, but

Activity 24–Words That Connect

Conjunctions are in bold.

1) Vanilla **or** chocolate **2)** **Either** milk or cream **3)** coffee **or** tea **4)** Jane, Katie, **and** Laura **5)** rained, **but** on **6)** **Neither** Jackie **nor** Bobby **7)** summer **and** in **8)** bow **and** accepted **9)** hitter, **but** he **10)** Hamburgers **and** hot dogs **11)** well, **but** the **12)** fell, **and** the **13)** piano, **but** she **14)** raspberry, orange, **and** lemon

Activity 25–Recognizing Interjections

1) Wow **2)** Hush **3)** my goodness **4)** Hurry **5)** Well **6)** Hum; Now **7)** What a loss **8)** Ouch **9)** Brr **10)** Stop **11)** Thanks

Activity 26–Punctuating Interjections

Responses may vary. There must be a mark of punctuation after each interjection and at the end of the sentence.

1) Uh, oh! That nurse is going to give me a shot. **2)** Wow! What a great car. **3)** So, you finally got here. **4)** Goodness! Why are you always late? **5)** No, no! I will not take that medicine. **6)** Whew, that tastes awful. **7)** Alas, no one seems to care about me today. **8)** Really? I hadn't heard that before. **9)** Oh, do you really mean that? **10)** Hush, hush. Don't you cry. **11)** Say, do you know where Carla lives? **12)** Nonsense! That will never work. **13)** Ouch! That hurt! **14)** Sorry, I didn't mean to step on your foot.

Activity 27–Interjections in Sentences

Answers will vary. Each sentence should have an interjection.

Activity 28–Finding Subjects

1) People **2)** The beach **3)** He **4)** Several of my friends **5)** Teachers **6)** One of the students **7)** It **8)** The black cat under the table **9)** All of us **10)** This restaurant **11)** The principal **12)** Young children **13)** My sister **14)** You **15)** we

Activity 29–A Sentence Has Two Parts

The predicate is in bold.

1) The teacher **opened the package.** **2)** Where is **my homework?** **3)** Everyone on the trip **was ready for lunch.** **4)** The mailbox **was entirely full of letters.** **5)** (You) **Stop that right now!** **6)** Both Heather and I **were late for class.** **7)** My exam for English **is scheduled to be at 1:00 p.m.** **8)** The bus driver **missed our bus stop today.** **9)** Two candy bars **were left.** **10)** Ice cream **will melt fast in warm weather.** **11)** The awards committee's final decisions **were made.** **12)** I'**m very excited about college.** **13)** We **should go out to dinner tonight.** **14)** **Did** any one of you **see that movie?** **15)** They **ran off in a hurry.**

Activity 30–Interrogative Sentences

The predicate is in bold.

1) Is this **your book**? **2)** Who **can help me**? **3)** **Have** you **seen that show**? **4)** **Why are** you **so concerned**? **5)** **Will** you **be home for dinner**? **6)** **Has** anyone **finished the project**? **7)** **Do** you **feel tired**? **8)** **When is** the game **going to be over**? **9)** **Where did** everyone **go**? **10)** **Is** your car **still in the garage**?

Activity 31–Direct Objects of Transitive Verbs

1) softball **2)** pie **3)** movie **4)** ground **5)** competition **6)** spaghetti **7)** sewing machine **8)** clouds **9)** thousands **10)** car **11)** articles **12)** lesson **13)** ball **14)** heater **15)** exercises

Activity 32–Understanding Intransitive Verbs

1) being **2)** being **3)** being **4)** action **5)** action **6)** action **7)** being **8)** action **9)** being **10)** action **11)** being **12)** action **13)** action **14)** being **15)** being

Activity 33–Transitive and Intransitive Verbs

1) intransitive **2)** intransitive **3)** transitive, competition **4)** intransitive **5)** transitive, dog **6)** intransitive **7)** transitive, bars **8)** intransitive **9)** transitive, car **10)** intransitive **11)** transitive, letter **12)** transitive, uniforms **13)** transitive, cookies **14)** transitive, me **15)** transitive, movie

Activity 34–Object or Predicate Nominative?

1) predicate nominative **2)** direct object **3)** predicate nominative **4)** predicate nominative **5)** direct object **6)** predicate nominative **7)** direct object **8)** predicate nominative **9)** predicate nominative **10)** predicate nominative **11)** predicate nominative **12)** direct object **13)** direct object **14)** predicate nominative

Activity 35–Complements of Linking Verbs

1) skiers–noun **2)** tall–adjective **3)** cook–noun **4)** difficult–adjective **5)** person–noun **6)** nice–adjective **7)** long, boring–adjectives **8)** ready–adjective **9)** score–noun **10)** 78%–noun **11)** actress–noun **12)** student–noun

Activity 36–Linking Verbs: Yes or No?

1) no–joined **2)** yes–is **3)** yes–looks **4)** no–felt **5)** yes–felt **6)** yes–are **7)** no–bucked **8)** yes–is **9)** yes–was **10)** yes–is

Activity 37–Finding Dependent Clauses

1) After it snows **2)** Before Jennifer went to bed **3)** that she couldn't attend **4)** that has just been picked **5)** Because Amy didn't want to leave **6)** after she plays tennis **7)** who just transferred to our school **8)** who drives that car **9)** who moved to Texas **10)** if you want to go **11)** that the cookout was nice **12)** that cut his leg **13)** Whenever you want to leave **14)** before she graduates from college **15)** that bite

Activity 38–Phrases and Clauses

1) dependent clause **2)** prepositional phrase **3)** independent clause **4)** independent clause **5)** dependent clause **6)** independent clause **7)** prepositional phrase **8)** dependent clause **9)** independent clause **10)** prepositional phrase **11)** dependent clause **12)** dependent clause

Activity 39–Dependent Clauses

1) exactly what I wanted–noun clause **2)** because we were thirsty–adverb clause **3)** Whoever wins the lottery–noun clause **4)** that was against her arch rival–adjective clause **5)** that we did not recognize–adjective clause **6)** what you wrote–noun clause **7)** that has a broken seat–adjective clause **8)** whenever the radio is on–adverb clause **9)** that is playing at our theater–adjective clause **10)** when he was finished eating–adverb clause **11)** that no one can ride–adjective clause **12)** what they are doing–noun clause

Activity 40–Recognizing Infinitives

1) prepositional phrase **2)** infinitive **3)** infinitive **4)** infinitive **5)** prepositional phrase **6)** prepositional phrase **7)** infinitive **8)** infinitive **9)** infinitive **10)** prepositional phrase **11)** infinitive **12)** infinitive

Activity 41–Infinitive Phrases

1) to go skiing in the Alps **2)** to be an engineer or a scientist **3)** to see the dolphins **4)** To be or not to be **5)** to clean his room **6)** to eat steak with corn and potatoes **7)** to be alone **8)** to be happy **9)** to fish for catfish **10)** To invest in the company **11)** to explore spooky buildings **12)** to decide on a topic for our report **13)** to count his fingers and toes **14)** to go to the movies tonight **15)** to be honest with me

Activity 42–Find the Verbals

1) to jog–infinitive **2)** to see–infinitive **3)** reading–gerund **4)** Watching–gerund **5)** to go–infinitive **6)** Eating–gerund **7)** to make–infinitive **8)** Growing–participle **9)** to get–infinitive **10)** Listening–gerund **11)** dancing–gerund **12)** to stay–infinitive **13)** Relaxing–gerund **14)** Weight lifting–gerund **15)** eating–participle **16)** painting–gerund

Workbook Activities

Workbook Activity 1–Finding Common and Proper Nouns

A. and **B.** Answers will vary.

Workbook Activity 2–Find the Nouns

1) Mrs. Parham, George, politeness **2)** Cindy, family, Kansas **3)** José, book, couch **4)** audience, violinist **5)** soldier, medal, bravery **6)** horse, fence **7)** crowd, game, pleasure **8)** Yoshi, mother, car **9)** hikers, Blueberry Mountain **10)** Henry, newspaper, porch **11)** price, coat **12)** Walter, knowledge, baseball **13)** waters, Long Pond, sunlight **14)** Mr. Wilson, idea, party **15)** Alice, dictionary, shelf **16)** The Doors, group **17)** John Adams, president **18)** Cora, dream, cat **19)** Peter, ring, stone **20)** speed, Tom, race

Workbook Activity 3–Finding the Plural Forms

1) boxes **2)** boys **3)** calves **4)** children **5)** chiefs **6)** geese **7)** keys **8)** knives **9)** ladies **10)** men **11)** mice **12)** shelves **13)** spies **14)** teeth **15)** wives **16)** women

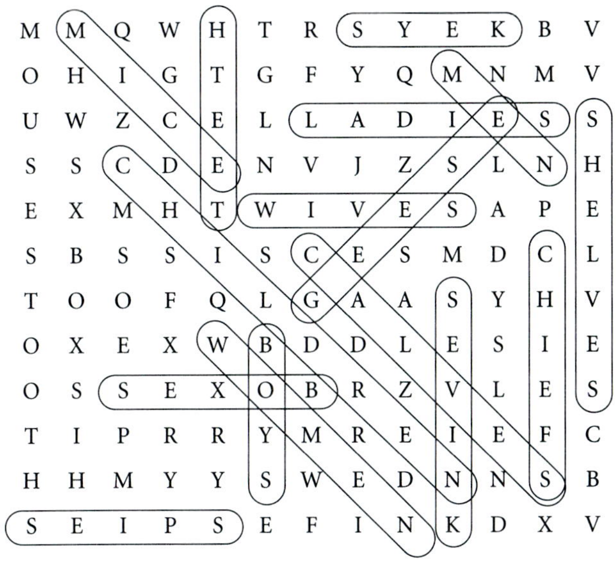

Workbook Activity 4–Selecting the Correct Possessive Form

1) trees' **2)** team's **3)** fire's **4)** plant's **5)** band's **6)** children's **7)** cats' **8)** mouse's **9)** hikers' **10)** books' **11)** men's **12)** snake's **13)** friend's **14)** Jean's **15)** coach's

Workbook Activity 5–Using Nouns Correctly

1) York City **2)** brother **3)** city's **4)** Building **5)** tickets **6)** City Music Hall **7)** zoo **8)** men's **9)** Janet's **10)** trees'

Workbook Activity 6–Singular and Plural Pronouns

1) They–P **2)** Our–P **3)** Those–P; my–S **4)** My–S; his–S **5)** We–P **6)** you–S, P; your–S, P **7)** he–S; we–P; them–P **8)** Our–P **9)** he–S; them–P **10)** they–P; ours–P **11)** this–S; your–S, P **12)** That–S; my–S; he–S **13)** Somebody–S; her–S **14)** Us–P **15)** He–S; nobody–S **16)** All–P **17)** herself–S **18)** My–S; us–P; we–P **19)** we–P; ourselves–P **20)** her–S

Workbook Activity 7–Selecting the Correct Pronoun

1) "May I have a sandwich?" he asked. **2)** "Here are my books," said Janet. "Where are yours?" Janet said to Ted. **3)** "I want you to help," she said to him. **4)** I put my papers right here. Have you seen them? **5)** "I invited him for dinner," Ted said to Janet. **6)** "We are hungry," said Ted. **7)** "This is my chair; that one is yours," said Ted. **8)** "We are happy that you could have dinner with us," said Janet.

Workbook Activity 8–Find the Pronouns and Their Antecedents

1) she–Tina **2)** their–Terry and Paul **3)** me–Sue **4)** I–Mrs. Parsons **5)** she–Ellen **6)** it–vase **7)** she–Pam **8)** they–boys **9)** she–Lucy; it–pin **10)** his–Lee **11)** I–Joe; you–Bob **12)** she–Mrs. Carson **13)** It–game **14)** his–Mr. Wardrop **15)** We–Meg and Sally **16)** that–house **17)** he–Larry; whom–boy **18)** it–day **19)** which–cat **20)** he–Tony

Workbook Activity 9–Finding Pronouns

1) I–personal; nothing–indefinite **2)** Who–interrogative; your–personal **3)** This–demonstrative **4)** that–relative **5)** whom–relative; I–personal **6)** few–indefinite **7)** Which–interrogative; you–personal **8)** none–indefinite **9)** Those–demonstrative; my–personal **10)** that–relative **11)** some–indefinite **12)** what–interrogative; your–personal **13)** him–personal **14)** Who–interrogative **15)** several–indefinite; us–personal **16)** who–relative

Workbook Activity 10–Using Pronouns Correctly

1) who **2)** her **3)** no errors **4)** whose **5)** Which **6)** It's **7)** my **8)** We **9)** that **10)** those **11)** its

Workbook Activity 11–Words of Power

Answers do not include articles.

1) impossible, his, eighth **2)** thoughtless **3)** sawlike **4)** grim, horrible **5)** my, shiny, blonde **6)** curious **7)** bright **8)** her, wedding, priceless **9)** unconquerable **10)** complicated

Workbook Activity 12–Proper Adjectives

A. 1) Swiss **2)** Palm Beach **3)** German **4)** Spanish **5)** European

B. Students will use Swiss, French, Democratic, Shakespearean, and Spanish in sentences.

Workbook Activity 13–Finding Adjectives

First paragraph: television, cable, their, The, cable, free, the, company's
Second paragraph: a, television, the, most, exciting, the, television
Third paragraph: That, first, the, the, county, the, heavy, the, tape, a, difficult
Fourth paragraph: a, good
Fifth paragraph: their, the, finished, the, cable, The, their, the, free, access

Workbook Activity 14–Comparisons With Adjectives

1) positive **2)** comparative **3)** comparative **4)** comparative **5)** superlative **6)** superlative **7)** superlative **8)** comparative **9)** comparative **10)** positive **11)** comparative **12)** positive, comparative **13)** superlative **14)** positive **15)** superlative **16)** superlative **17)** comparative **18)** comparative **19)** positive **20)** comparative

Workbook Activity 15–Find the Adjectives

1) a, big–garden; this–year **2)** her, French–class **3)** Ted's–car; a, good–radio **4)** the–winter **5)** American–literature **6)** his–money's; money's–worth **7)** Ted's, full–refrigerator **8)** Sixteen–people; the–party **9)** Most–people; vanilla–ice cream **10)** Last–Sunday; the, football–game **11)** That, chocolate, good–cake **12)** friendly–I **13)** those, two, larger–buildings **14)** The–Wildcats; their, first–game; last–Saturday **15)** a, shooting–star **16)** a–pencil **17)** Several, late–people **18)** Andy's, interesting, hard–class **19)** The, gold, expensive–chain **20)** his, final–decision

Workbook Activity 16–Irregular Verb Forms

1) writing **2)** found **3)** ridden **4)** had **5)** grown **6)** wrote, had written **7)** broken **8)** makes, made, had made, is making **9)** making **10)** done **11)** speak, spoke, have spoken, are speaking **12)** makes, made, has made, is making **13)** taken

14) bought **15)** written **16)** found **17)** rides, rode, has ridden **18)** breaks

Workbook Activity 17–Verb Phrases

1) was spent **2)** died, was **3)** had studied **4)** lived **5)** would build **6)** was surveying **7)** began **8)** went **9)** caught **10)** had **11)** died **12)** had willed **13)** started **14)** had sent **15)** was engaged **16)** married

Workbook Activity 18–The Irregular *Be* Verb

1) is **2)** was **3)** was **4)** were **5)** is **6)** been **7)** is **8)** is **9)** is **10)** were **11)** is **12)** is **13)** been **14)** is **15)** is **16)** is **17)** were **18)** are

Workbook Activity 19–Verbs and Helping Verbs

1) been **2)** will do **3)** Has *or* Had **4)** is *or* will be *or* was **5)** is **6)** Did **7)** doing **8)** did **9)** were **10)** done **11)** is *or* will be **12)** done **13)** did **14)** be *or* have been **15)** Has **16)** had **17)** having **18)** doing **19)** been **20)** Are

Workbook Activity 20–Active and Passive Verbs

1) passive **2)** active **3)** passive **4)** passive **5)** passive **6)** active **7)** passive **8)** active **9)** passive **10)** active **11)** active **12)** passive **13)** passive **14)** passive **15)** active **16)** active **17)** active **18)** passive **19)** passive **20)** active

Workbook Activity 21–Find the Linking Verb

1) is **2)** is **3)** are **4)** were **5)** Have felt **6)** are **7)** feel **8)** smells **9)** Have felt **10)** appear **11)** feel **12)** appeared **13)** seemed **14)** felt **15)** felt **16)** smelled **17)** looked **18)** remained **19)** looks **20)** seem

Workbook Activity 22–Rename the Subject

A. 1) Dawn–subject; was–linking verb; friend–predicate noun **2)** Adverbs, adjectives–subjects; are–linking verb; parts–predicate noun **3)** Pat–subject; is–linking verb; athlete–predicate noun **4)** C-SPAN–subject; is–linking verb; station–predicate noun **5)** Princeton–subject; is–linking verb; university–predicate noun **6)** marigold–subject; is–linking verb; flower–predicate noun **7)** birthday–subject; is–linking verb; event–predicate noun **8)** car–subject; is–linking verb; Ford–predicate noun **9)** dessert–subject; is–linking verb; strawberries–predicate noun **10)** apple–subject; is–linking verb; snack–predicate noun

B. Answers may vary. Suggested answers are given: **1)** network **2)** capital **3)** movie **4)** musician **5)** president **6)** fruits **7)** vegetables **8)** kinds **9)** movie, book **10)** parties

Workbook Activity 23–Describe the Subject

A. Answers may vary. Suggested answers are given. **1)** friendly **2)** spicy **3)** clean **4)** terrific **5)** expensive **6)** tall, handsome **7)** rested **8)** tasty **9)** fresh **10)** juicier

B. 1) will be **2)** felt **3)** will have been **4)** has been **5)** turn **6)** appeared **7)** gets **8)** are **9)** tasted **10)** were

Workbook Activity 24–Action or Being?

1) being **2)** action **3)** action **4)** being **5)** being **6)** being **7)** action **8)** being **9)** action **10)** action **11)** being **12)** action **13)** action **14)** action **15)** being **16)** being **17)** action **18)** being **19)** action **20)** being

Workbook Activity 25–Adverbs Answer Questions

1) never **2)** loudly; yesterday **3)** again; just **4)** quickly; sometimes **5)** comfortably; now **6)** carefully; weekly **7)** there **8)** upstairs; usually

Workbook Activity 26–Finding Adverbs

1) softly **2)** extremely **3)** quietly **4)** often **5)** well **6)** here **7)** not **8)** finally **9)** unusually **10)** happily **11)** very, gracefully **12)** too, lightly **13)** suddenly **14)** breathlessly **15)** not **16)** crossly **17)** almost **18)** never **19)** not, now **20)** quite, fast

Workbook Activity 27–Add an Adverb

Answers will vary.

Workbook Activity 28–Adverbs and Adjectives

1) adverb **2)** adjective **3)** adverb **4)** adverb **5)** adjective **6)** adverb **7)** adverb **8)** adjective **9)** adjective **10)** adverb **11)** adverb **12)** adjective **13)** adjective **14)** adverb **15)** adjective **16)** adjective **17)** adjective **18)** adverb **19)** adjective **20)** adverb **21)** adjective

Workbook Activity 29–Choosing the Correct Adverb

1) gave **2)** will arrive **3)** will visit *or* visited **4)** fix **5)** enjoy **6)** comes *or* came **7)** sing *or* will sing **8)** is **9)** is **10)** sent **11)** will be **12)** agreed **13)** go *or* will go *or* went **14)** has been **15)** trim

Workbook Activity 30–Prepositional Phrases as Adjectives

1) in England–tournament **2)** of the world's best players–Most **3)** from West Germany–man; to win the tournament–man **4)** of racket–kind **5)** of his matches–All; in the tournament–matches **6)** by Boris Becker–play **7)** of his points–Many **8)** with their grass surfaces–courts **9)** with a powerful serve–man **10)** with the smile–boy; on his face–smile **11)** with red hair–player **12)** on center court–finals; at Wimbledon, England–court

Workbook Activity 31–Adding Prepositional Phrases

A. and **B.** Answers will vary.

Workbook Activity 32–Prepositional Phrases

1) with chocolate sauce–adjective **2)** on the tree–adjective **3)** with Victor–adjective **4)** of the students–adjective; in the fall–adverb **5)** in school–adverb **6)** on his hamburgers–adverb **7)** at the end–adjective; of the line–adjective **8)** After the party–adverb; with Ted–adverb **9)** to the game–adverb; on Saturday–adverb **10)** in our garden–adjective **11)** with cream and sugar–adjective **12)** with Janet–adverb; for new shoes–adverb **13)** on Friday–adjective **14)** around the corner–adverb **15)** with the white markings–adjective

Workbook Activity 33–Prepositions and Their Objects

1) to–Bob **2)** on–rug **3)** with–friends **4)** near–mountain **5)** for–Rick **6)** on–porch **7)** down–hill **8)** of–hers **9)** in–town **10)** about–flags **11)** around–room **12)** over–creek **13)** from–me **14)** Above–fireplace **15)** into–ocean **16)** off–shelf **17)** behind–door; for–boots **18)** In–minutes **19)** over–bridge; past–woods **20)** with–friends; at–movies

Workbook Activity 34–Preposition or Adverb?

1) preposition **2)** adverb **3)** adverb **4)** preposition **5)** adverb **6)** preposition **7)** adverb **8)** preposition **9)** adverb **10)** preposition **11)** preposition **12)** adverb **13)** preposition **14)** adverb **15)** preposition

Workbook Activity 35–Using Conjunctions to Connect

Answers will vary. Possible answers are:

1) My favorite baseball players are Cal Ripkin and Kirby Puckett. **2)** John Steinbeck wrote *The Red Pony* and *The Grapes of Wrath.* **3)** My garden has zinnias, marigolds, and weeds. **4)** For the picnic, we bought hot dogs and rolls. **5)** Betty likes hot dogs but not hamburgers. **6)** This soda is sugar-free and caffeine-free. **7)** My older brother, Casey, and my little brother, Jimmy, play soccer. **8)** I have two poodles named Velvet and Coco. **9)** Velvet is black, and Coco is champagne. **10)** Our telephone is Touch-Tone and yellow.

Workbook Activity 36–Punctuating With Conjunctions

1) home, it **2)** beans, carrots, and **3)** movie, but **4)** chicken; also, she **5)** hurry, we **6)** busy; moreover, she **7)** flute, piano, and **8)** now, or **9)** began, the **10)** lunch, I **11)** snows, Tina **12)** sheep, a goat, and **13)** airport, for **14)** well; therefore, they **15)** fell, we **16)** quiet, for

Workbook Activity 37–Finding Conjunctions

1) Unless–subordinating **2)** Either . . . or–correlative **3)** however–coordinating **4)** when–subordinating **5)** since–subordinating **6)** whether . . . or–correlative **7)** and–coordinating **8)** both . . . and–correlative **9)** Whenever–subordinating **10)** but–coordinating **11)** Because–subordinating **12)** but–coordinating **13)** and–coordinating **14)** or–coordinating

Workbook Activity 38–Using Interjections

Answers may vary. Suggested answers are given.

1) goodness, **2)** what! Who **3)** Well, **4)** down! You **5)** gift! It's **6)** Brr! **7)** Ummmm, **8)** Oh, no! **9)** Hurry! We **10)** Oh, **11)** Nonsense! You **12)** Hello. Are **13)** Hey! Is **14)** Alas, **15)** Oh, woe is me, **16)** Oh, boy! That

Workbook Activity 39–Words of Feeling

Answers will vary. Suggested answers are given.

A. **1)** Wow! I need help. **2)** Hey, you are late! **3)** Oh, I am so happy! **4)** Boy! I love your new car. **5)** Hurrah! Our team won the game.

B. **1)** Oh, boy! That was fun. **2)** Whew! I am tired. **3)** Hey, buddy! You're in my way. **4)** Wow! What a great hit. **5)** Ha! Ha! That's too funny!

Workbook Activity 40–Expressing a Complete Idea

1) no **2)** yes **3)** no **4)** no **5)** yes **6)** yes **7)** yes **8)** no **9)** no **10)** yes **11)** no **12)** yes **13)** no **14)** yes **15)** yes

Workbook Activity 41–Finding Subjects

1) Soap operas **2)** People **3)** Many of the sponsors **4)** Daytime dramas **5)** One famous soap opera **6)** Your grandmother **7)** Another popular program in the 1940s **8)** My grandfather's favorite **9)** "One Man's Family" **10)** It **11)** That program **12)** people **13)** You **14)** The soap opera stars **15)** People

Workbook Activity 42–A Sentence Has Two Parts

The subject of each sentence is given here. The rest of the sentence is the predicate.

1) All of the students **2)** Victor, (you) **3)** (You) **4)** The lady at the end of the line **5)** Everyone **6)** No one **7)** The whole class **8)** The best hitter on the team **9)** Both Sue and Janet **10)** Spring and fall **11)** Darleen's dog, Tiny, **12)** Twelve dozen chocolate chip cookies **13)** any one of you **14)** it **15)** my gloves

Workbook Activity 43–Purposes of Sentences

1) ?–question **2)** .–statement **3)** ?–question **4)** .–request **5)** ?–question **6)** . *or* !–command **7)** .–statement **8)** ?–question **9)** .–request **10)** . *or* !–command **11)** .–statement **12)** ?–question **13)** . *or* !–command **14)** .–request **15)** . *or* !–command **16)** .–statement

Workbook Activity 44–Interrogative Sentences

1) you–subject; Have seen Billy–predicate **2)** Who–subject; is that–predicate **3)** that–subject; Isn't the new puppy's name–predicate **4)** your friend–subject; Will be staying for lunch–predicate **5)** anyone in this house–subject; has seen my other tennis shoe–predicate **6)** you–subject; Do think the puppy dragged it under the sofa again–predicate **7)** you–subject; Why don't ask the dog–predicate **8)** you–subject; Can't ever give me a straight answer–predicate **9)** this–subject; Is your shoe–predicate **10)** I–subject; How can ever thank you–predicate

Workbook Activity 45–Simple and Compound Sentences

1) S **2)** C **3)** C **4)** S **5)** S **6)** C **7)** C **8)** S **9)** S **10)** C **11)** S **12)** S **13)** S **14)** C **15)** C

Workbook Activity 46–Understanding Intransitive Verbs

1) being **2)** action **3)** action **4)** action **5)** being **6)** action **7)** being **8)** being **9)** being **10)** action **11)** being **12)** action **13)** action **14)** being **15)** action

Workbook Activity 47–Transitive and Intransitive Verbs

1) fell–intransitive **2)** cheered–intransitive **3)** Stop–transitive; noise **4)** should see–transitive; movie **5)** will win–transitive; contest **6)** laughed–intransitive **7)** Write–transitive; letter **8)** named–transitive; puppy **9)** Give–transitive; message **10)** made–transitive **11)** Have read–transitive; book **12)** Spend–transitive; money **13)** left–intransitive **14)** will stay–intransitive **15)** listened–intransitive **16)** Have seen–transitive; book **17)** is–intransitive **18)** rode–transitive; bus **19)** is walking–intransitive **20)** give–transitive; ride

Workbook Activity 48–Sentences to Diagram

1)
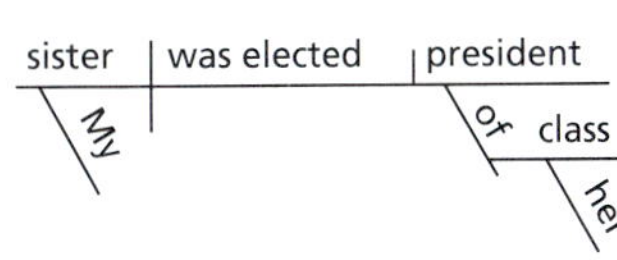

2)
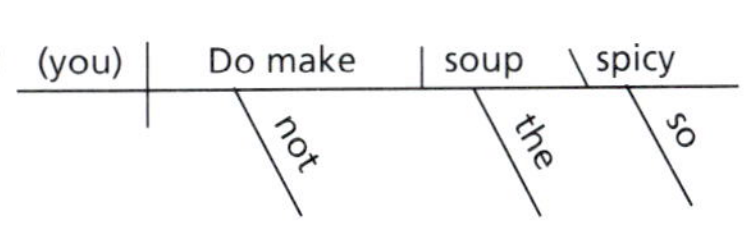

3)

4) 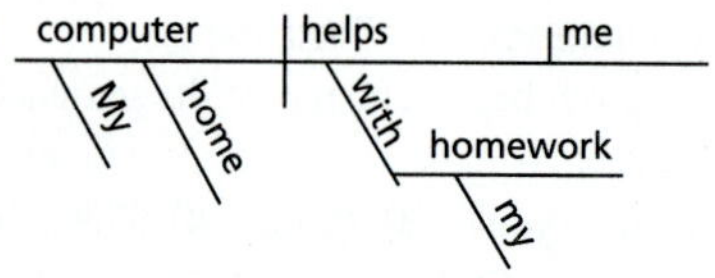

5) 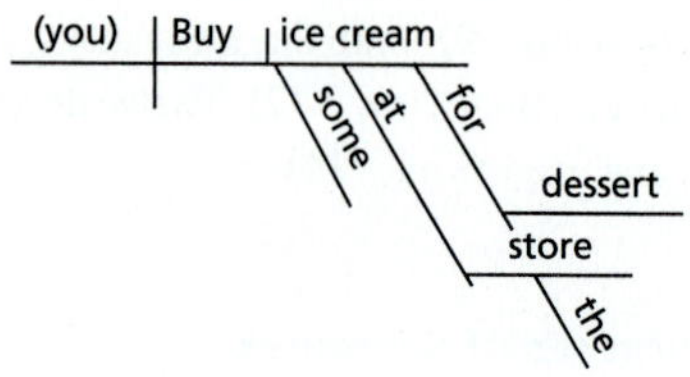

6) 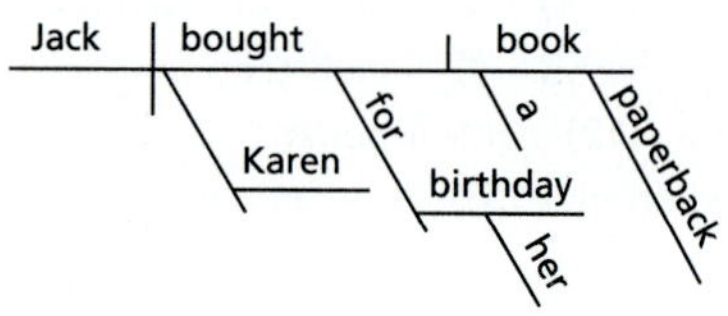

7) 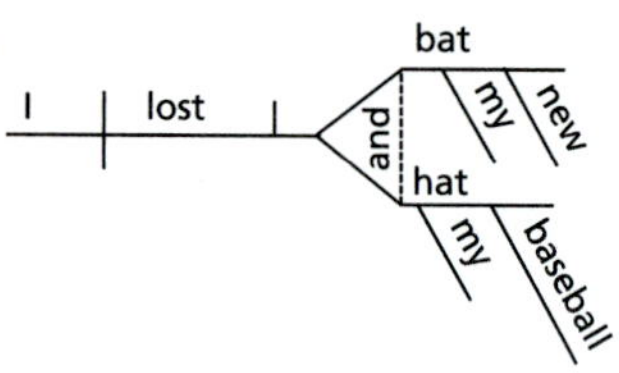

Workbook Activity 49–Object or Predicate Nominative?

1) predicate nominative **2)** direct object **3)** direct object **4)** predicate nominative **5)** predicate nominative **6)** direct object **7)** predicate nominative **8)** predicate nominative **9)** predicate nominative **10)** direct object **11)** predicate nominative **12)** direct object **13)** predicate nominative **14)** predicate nominative **15)** predicate nominative

Workbook Activity 50–Complements of Linking Verbs

1) pleased–adjective **2)** cook–noun **3)** big–adjective **4)** friendly–adjective **5)** ready–adjective **6)** difficult–adjective **7)** nice–adjective **8)** beige–adjective **9)** cheerleader–noun **10)** enthusiastic–adjective **11)** president–noun **12)** James Madison–noun **13)** name–noun **14)** Dolley Madison–noun **15)** book–noun

Workbook Activity 51–Linking Verbs: Yes or No?

1) no–are going **2)** no–graduated **3)** yes–has been **4)** yes–feels **5)** no–named **6)** no–won **7)** yes–became **8)** yes–is **9)** yes–was **10)** no–watched **11)** yes–looks **12)** no–have

Workbook Activity 52–Diagram the Sentences

1) Hamlet–subject; is–linking verb; play–noun

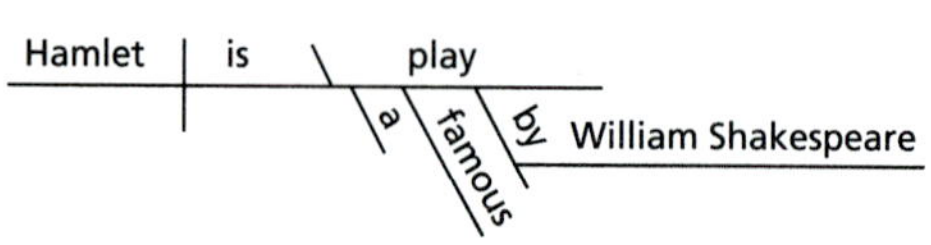

2) weather–subject; is–linking verb; hot and humid–adjective

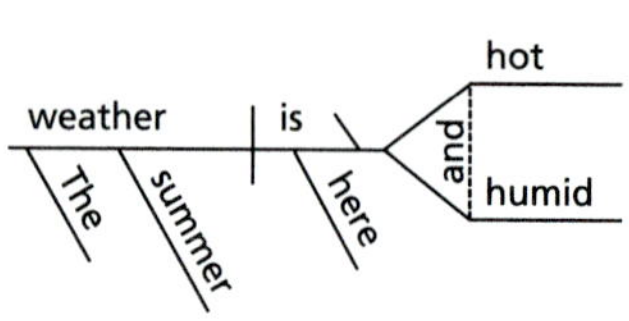

3) today–subject; does seem–linking verb; pleasant–adjective

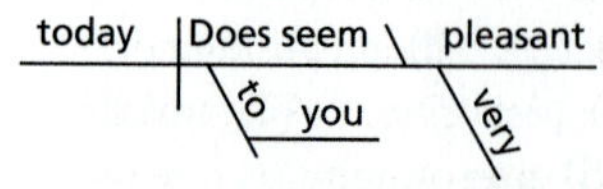

4) Maryland–subject; is–linking verb; state–noun

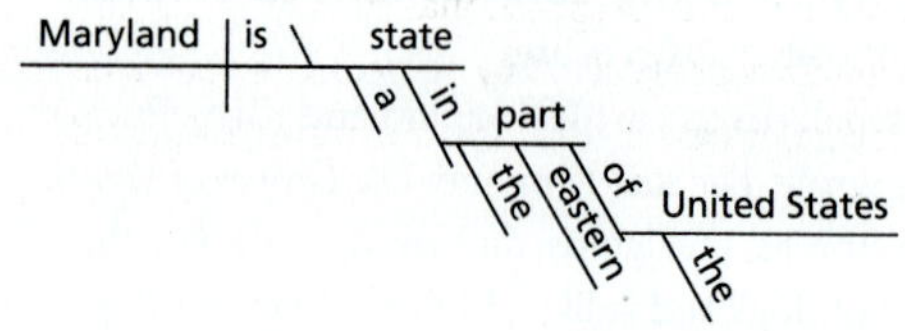

Workbook Activity 53–Phrases and Clauses

1) prepositional phrase **2)** dependent clause **3)** dependent clause; independent clause **4)** prepositional phrase **5)** dependent clause; independent clause **6)** prepositional phrase **7)** prepositional phrase; prepositional phrase; independent clause **8)** dependent clause **9)** independent clause; dependent clause **10)** dependent clause **11)** prepositional phrase **12)** dependent clause **13)** dependent clause; independent clause **14)** dependent clause **15)** prepositional phrase

Workbook Activity 54–Finding Dependent Clauses

1) when it rains **2)** Before James arrived **3)** that she would be late **4)** that the party was nice **5)** that come in a can **6)** Because Janet was graduating from high school **7)** after he runs **8)** who visited us last week **9)** What I said **10)** what she said **11)** Whoever is hungry **12)** if you want to **13)** Because it rained **14)** who moved to Cleveland **15)** who live in that house

Workbook Activity 55–Dependent Clauses

1) what I need–noun clause **2)** because we were hungry–adverb clause **3)** Whoever finds the clues–noun clause **4)** that was his favorite–adjective clause **5)** whom she did not know–adjective clause **6)** what you said–noun clause **7)** that has a hole in it–adjective clause **8)** whenever he has time–adverb clause **9)** that escaped from the zoo–adjective clause **10)** Wherever Megan goes–adverb clause **11)** whose garden is so beautiful–adjective clause **12)** which Robert hoped to buy–adjective clause **13)** Whenever you have time–adverb clause **14)** that is gray and white–adjective clause **15)** that a hurricane is coming this way–noun clause

Workbook Activity 56–Find the Dependent Clause

1) adjective clause, adjective clause **2)** adverb clause, adjective clause **3)** adverb clause **4)** adverb clause **5)** noun clause **6)** adverb clause **7)** noun clause **8)** adjective clause, adverb clause **9)** adverb clause, adjective clause **10)** adjective clause, adverb clause

Workbook Activity 57–Recognizing Infinitives

1) prepositional phrase **2)** infinitive **3)** infinitive **4)** infinitive **5)** prepositional phrase **6)** prepositional phrase **7)** infinitive **8)** infinitive **9)** infinitive **10)** infinitive **11)** infinitive **12)** infinitive **13)** infinitive

Workbook Activity 58–Infinitive Phrases

1) to sit–infinitive; on the beach–prepositional phrase **2)** to see–infinitive; dolphins–direct object **3)** to count–infinitive; them–direct object **4)** to walk–infinitive; on the beach–prepositional phrase **5)** to get–infinitive; sunburn–direct object **6)** to prevent–infinitive; burn–direct object **7)** to fish–infinitive; for flounder–prepositional phrase **8)** to eat–infinitive; flounder–direct object **9)** to clean–infinitive; fish–direct object **10)** to solve–infinitive; today–adverb **11)** to be–infinitive; on the beach–prepositional phrase; again–adverb **12)** to walk–infinitive; barefoot–adjective; in the sand–prepositional phrase **13)** to feel–infinitive; breeze–direct object **14)** to decide–infinitive; on a restaurant–prepositional phrase **15)** to taste–infinitive; good–predicate adjective

Workbook Activity 59–Three Kinds of Verbals

A. **1)** to use the boat **2)** to have steak for dinner **3)** to eat **4)** to leap to the next tree **5)** To join the country club

B. **1)** Barking **2)** Finding the right house **3)** swimming **4)** Camping **5)** auto racing

C. **1)** broken **2)** Fixing the bike ourselves **3)** riding the bike **4)** Shouting happily **5)** squeaking loudly again

Workbook Activity 60–Find the Verbals

1) infinitive–to work out **2)** infinitive–to watch **3)** gerund–Hitting **4)** gerund–Listening **5)** gerund–Relaxing **6)** gerund–Weight lifting **7)** participle–weight-lifting **8)** infinitive–to go **9)** gerund–Working **10)** participle–needed **11)** gerund–snacking **12)** participle–stewing **13)** infinitive–to stew **14)** infinitive–to improve **15)** gerund–writing

Diagramming

At the end of each worksheet, students write and diagram three of their own sentences. Check that their sentences fit the pattern. Check their diagrams for accuracy.

Pattern 1 Sentences

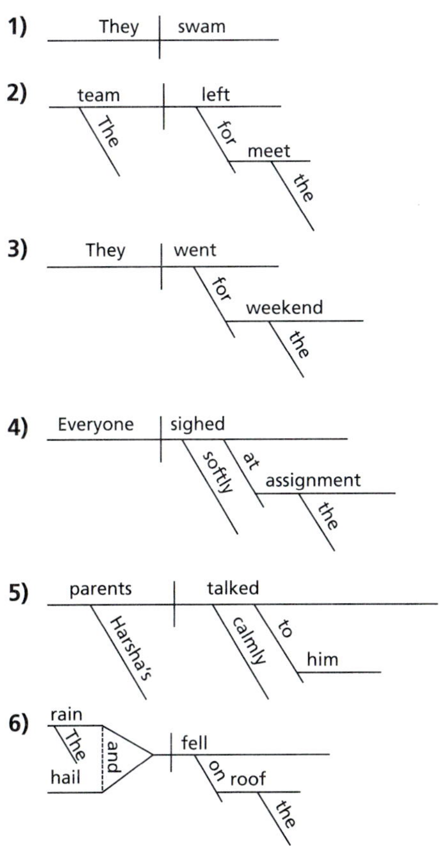

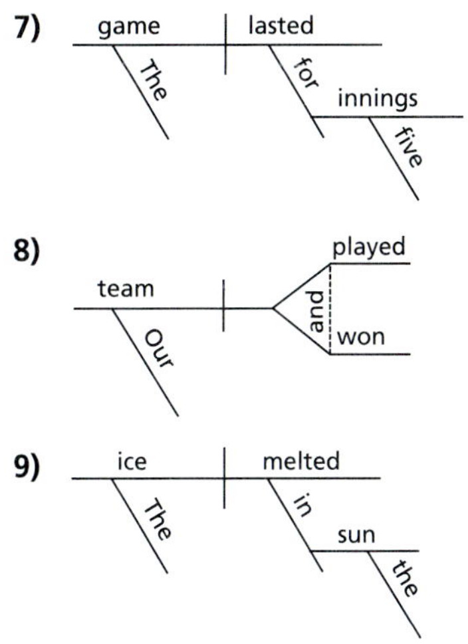

Pattern 2 Sentences

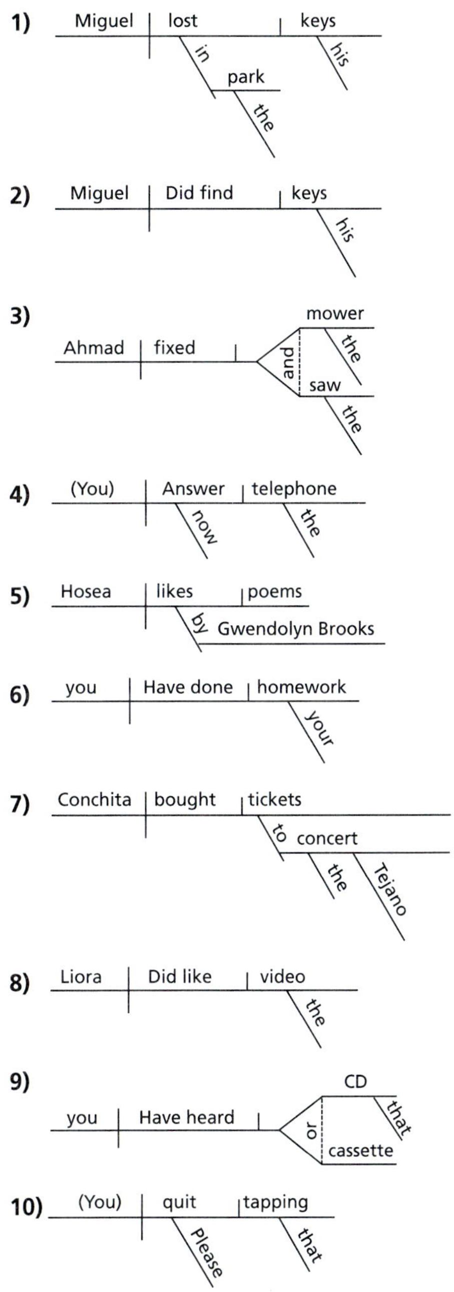

Pattern 3 Sentences

1)
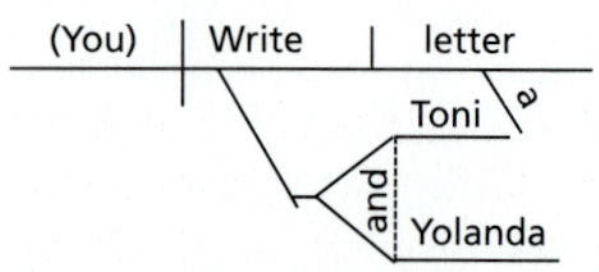

2)
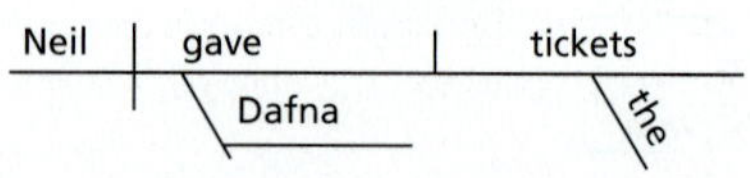

3)
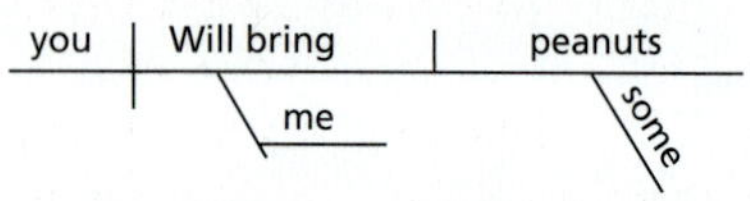

4)
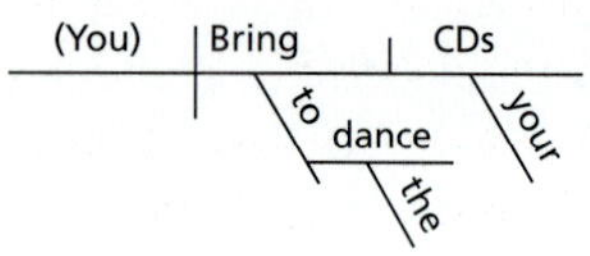

5)
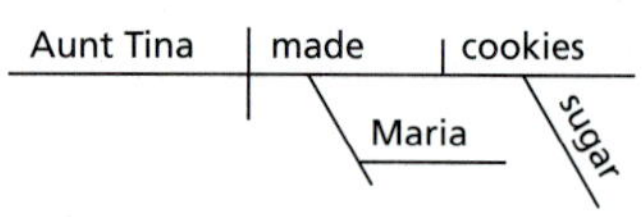

6)
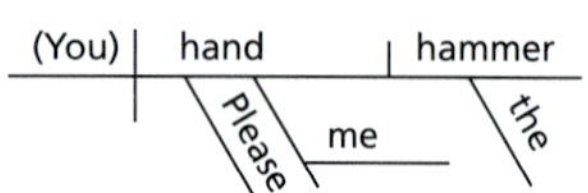

7)
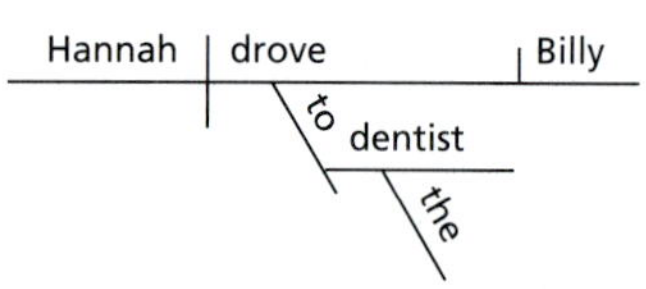

8)
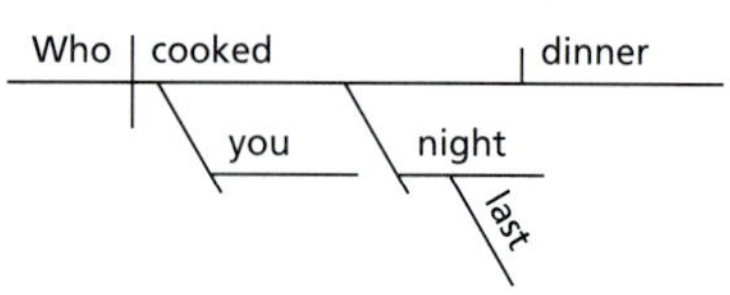

9)
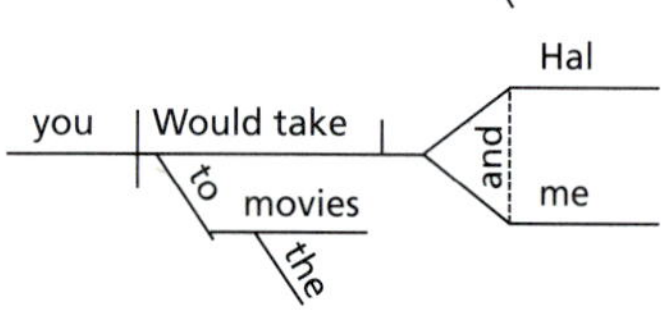

10)
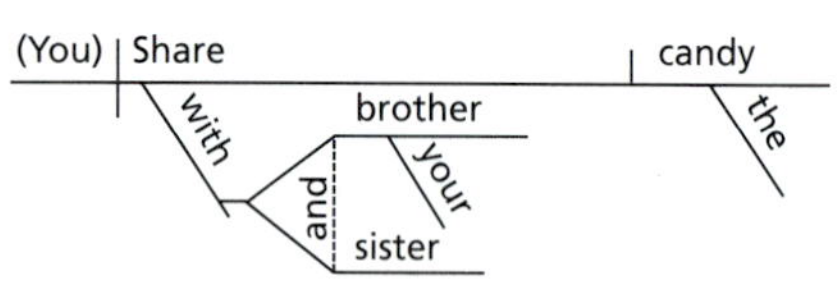

Pattern 4 Sentences

1)
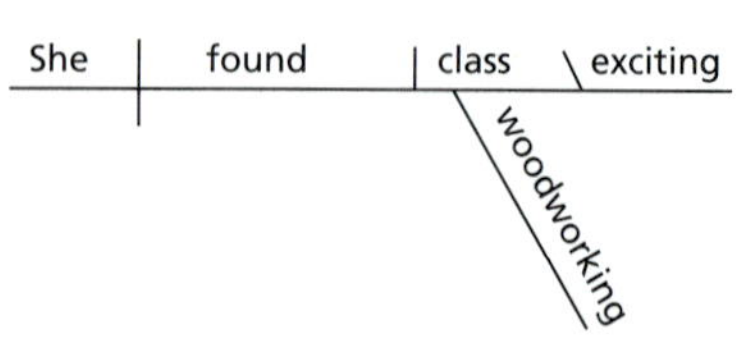

2)
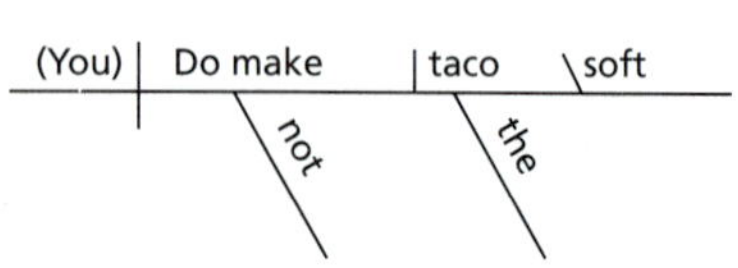

3)
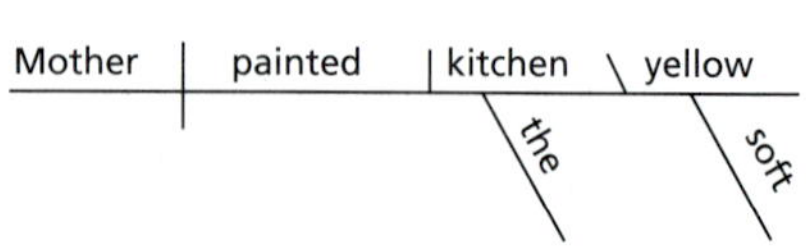

4)
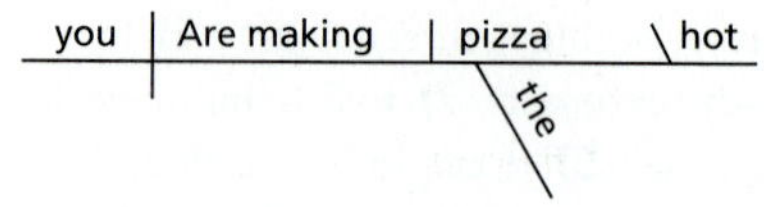

5)
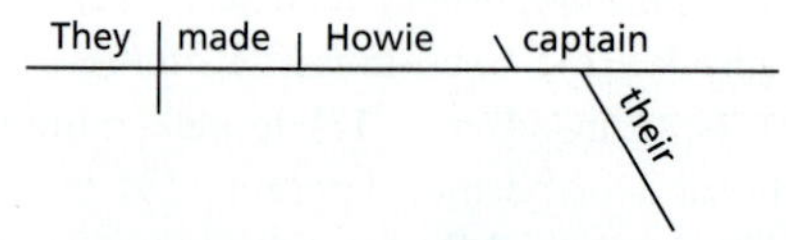

6)
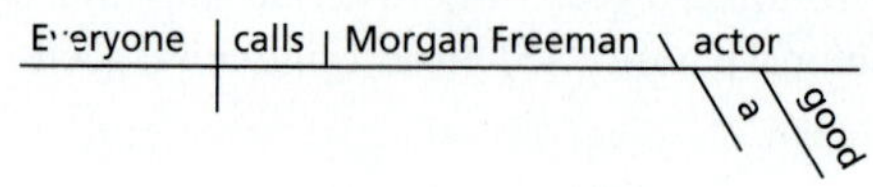

7)
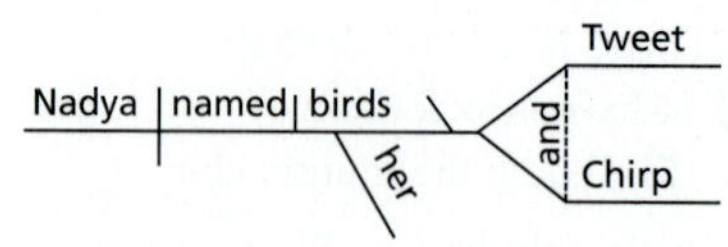

8)
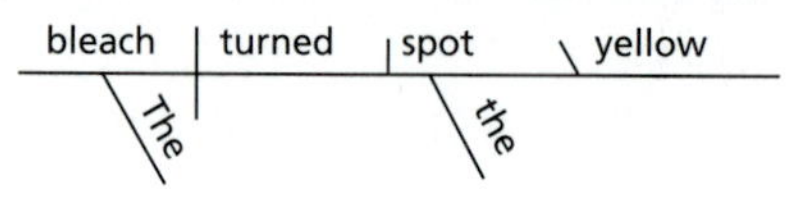

9)
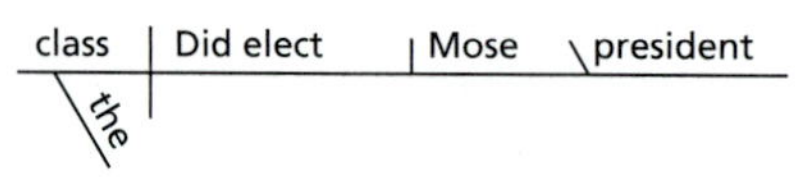

10)
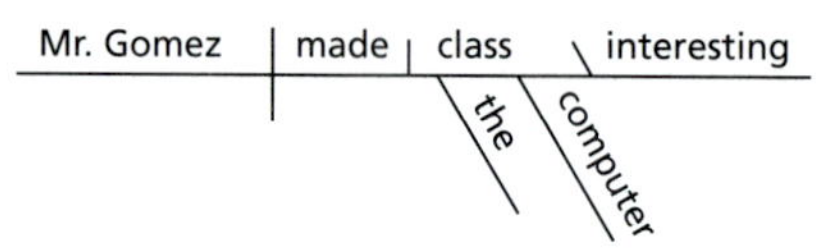

Pattern 5 Sentences

1)
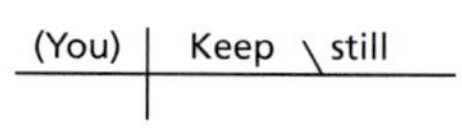

2)
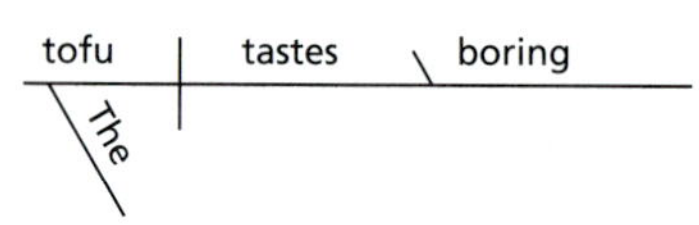

3)
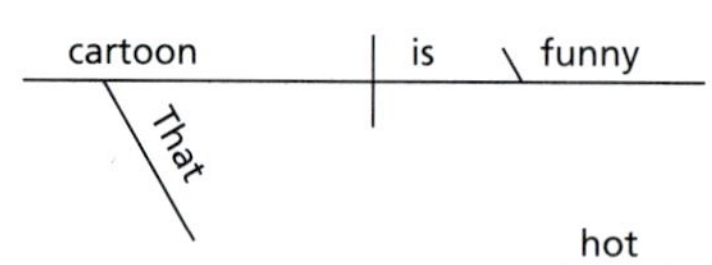

4)
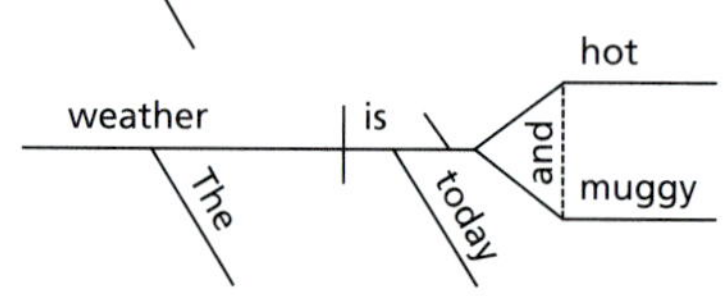

5)
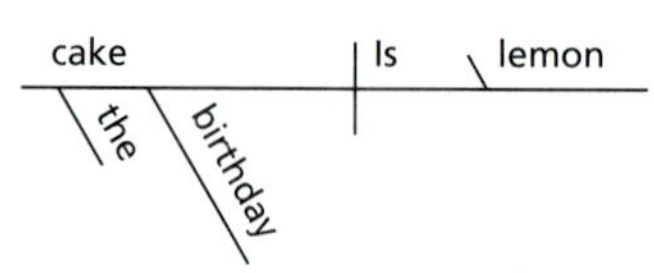

6)
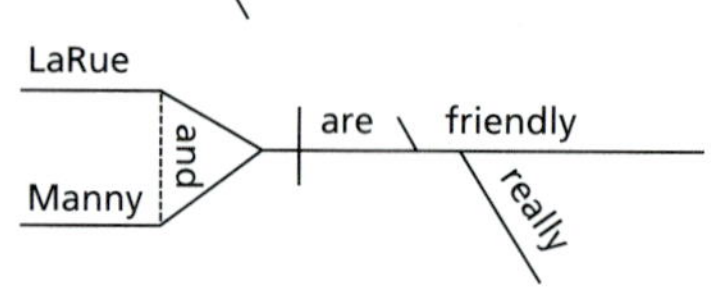

7)
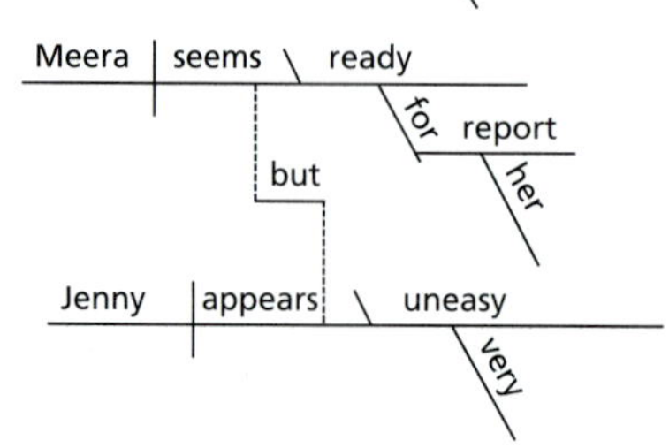

8)
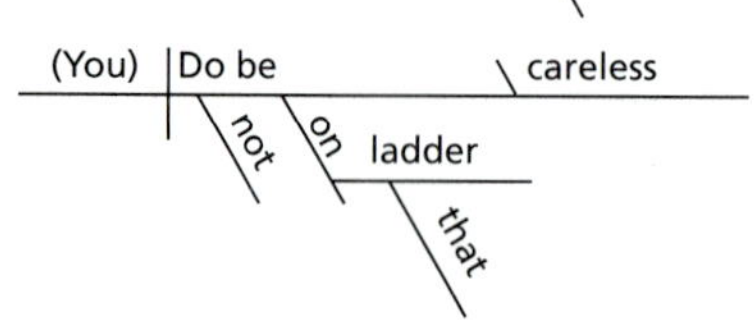

9) 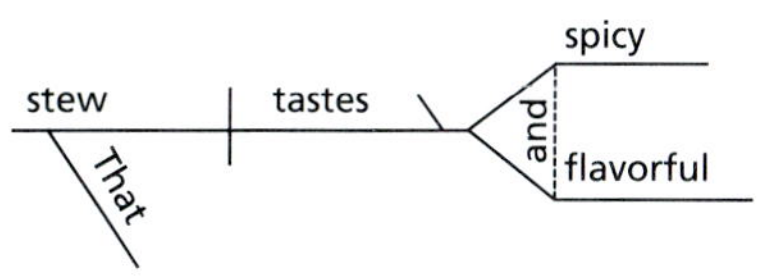

10) 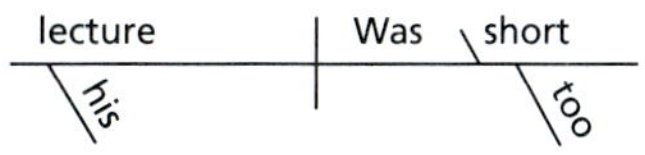

Pattern 6 Sentences

1) 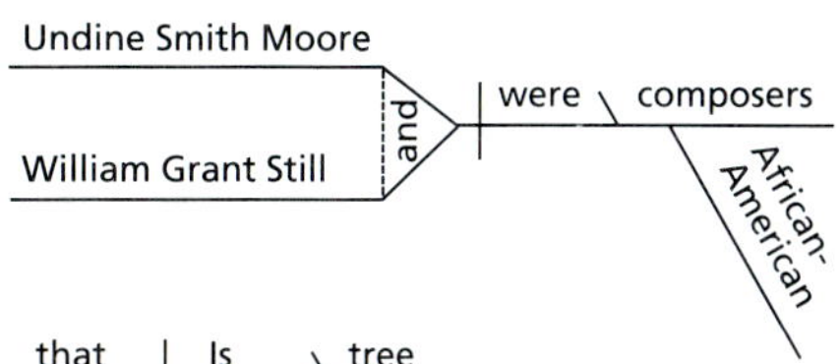

2) 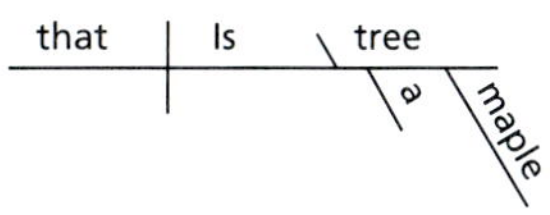

3) 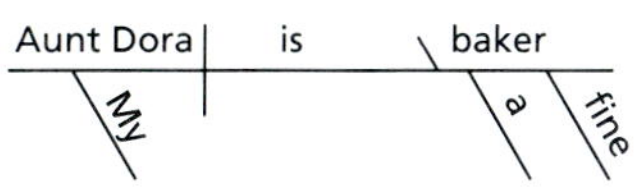

4) 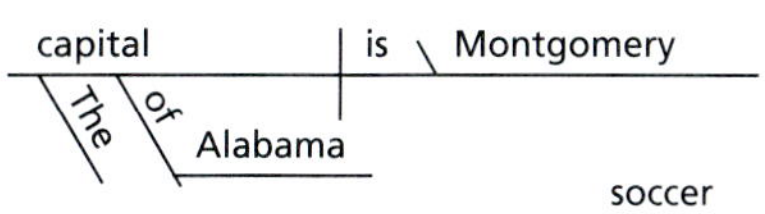

5) 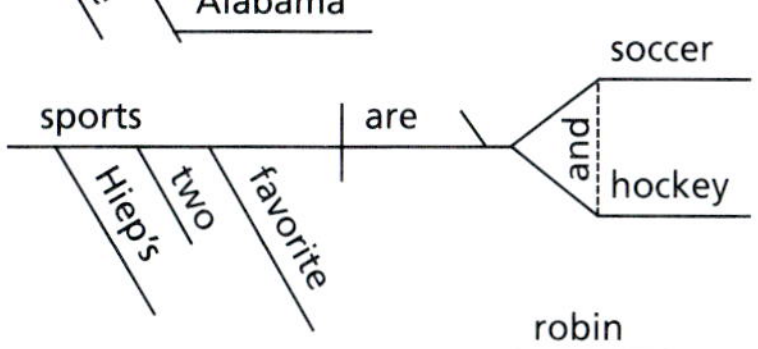

6) 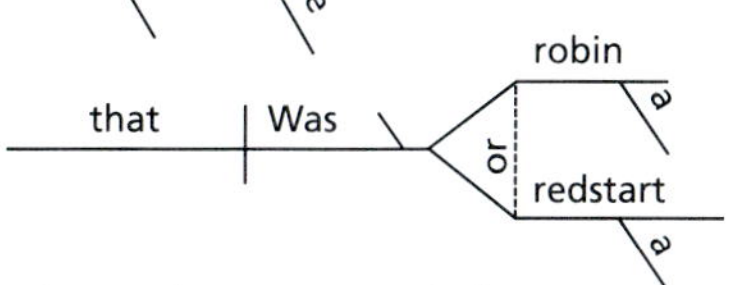

7) 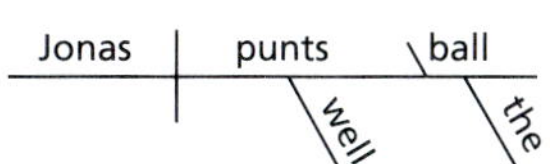

8) 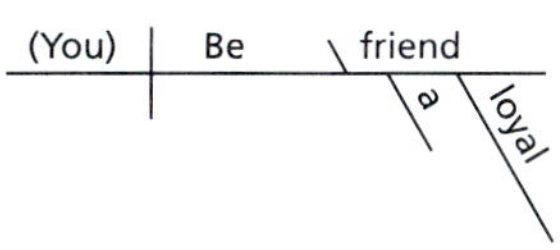

9) 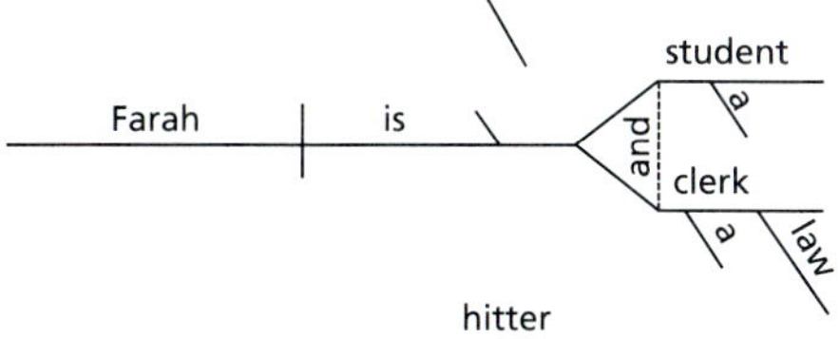

10) 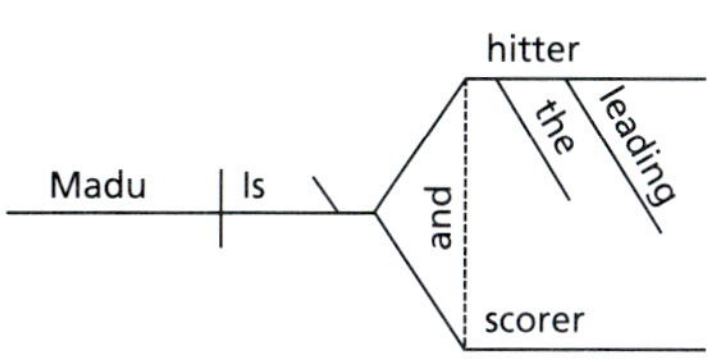

Community Connection

Completed activities will vary for each student. Community Connection activities are real-life activities completed outside of the classroom by the students. These activities give students practical learning and practice of the skills taught in *Basic English Grammar.* Check completed activities to see that students have followed directions, completed each step, filled in all charts and blanks, provided reasonable answers to questions, written legibly, and used proper grammar and punctuation.

Tests

Chapter 1 Mastery Test A

Part A: 1) Cy Young, games, pitcher, baseball **2)** record, wins, person **3)** Old Hoss Radbourn **4)** Old Hoss, games, career **5)** year, pitcher, baseball, award **6)** Cy Young Award **7)** person, Cy Young Award, Don Newcombe **8)** Jim Palmer, pitcher, Baltimore Orioles **9)** Palmer, Cy Young Award, times **10)** year, player, league, prize

Part B: 1) We saw Cal Ripken play baseball at Camden Yards in Baltimore. **2)** Next year Henry plans to take Spanish and Algebra I. **3)** Jackie visited the Midwest last August. **4)** In June Robert has an appointment with Dr. Welsey. **5)** For many years "60 Minutes" has been a popular news program.

Part C: 1) bunches **2)** cities **3)** foxes **4)** spies **5)** keys **6)** radios **7)** deer **8)** roofs **9)** countries **10)** photos **11)** knives **12)** reports **13)** feet **14)** women **15)** mice **16)** churches **17)** chiefs **18)** tomatoes **19)** teeth **20)** injuries

Part D: 1) book's **2)** dollars' **3)** children's **4)** churches' **5)** dish's **6)** students' **7)** Sharon's **8)** computer's **9)** bread's **10)** ships'

Chapter 1 Mastery Test B

Part A: 1) clock, wall **2)** computer, homework **3)** radio, table, sofa **4)** Roger, mother, CD, birthday **5)** brother, flowers, table **6)** Mickey, George, golf, afternoon **7)** turkey, dinner **8)** People, road, deer **9)** Kirby Puckett, hitters, baseball **10)** Tom, account, bank

Part B: 1) In June we went to Disney World in Florida. **2)** This fall Sally plans to take Computer Basics I and English. **3)** One of my favorite books is *Robinson Crusoe.* **4)** My aunt Marie lives in the South. **5)** On Wednesday we visited the Empire State Building in New York.

Part C: 1) guesses **2)** ladders **3)** counties **4)** wolves **5)** paths **6)** geese **7)** dishes **8)** sheep **9)** bodies **10)** moose **11)** men **12)** potatoes **13)** calves **14)** parties **15)** mice **16)** navies **17)** rodeos **18)** leaves **19)** series **20)** heroes

Part D: 1) month's **2)** dollars' **3)** teacher's **4)** team's **5)** town's **6)** sheep's **7)** nights' **8)** Jane's **9)** writers' **10)** flowers'

Chapter 2 Mastery Test A

Part A: 1) himself **2)** We **3)** Which **4)** themselves **5)** who **6)** her **7)** I **8)** their **9)** his **10)** that

Part B: 1) their–Howard and Mike **2)** who–fellow **3)** her–Joellen **4)** my–Sara **5)** whose–friend **6)** themselves–Fred and Gail **7)** our–Carol and Jane **8)** his–Jerry **9)** herself–Lora **10)** whom–woman

Part C: 1) They, someone, who **2)** She, her **3)** We, whose, that **4)** What, they **5)** anybody, those **6)** Whatever, you, what, we **7)** Who, your, **8)** This, we, that **9)** you, that, I **10)** We, ourselves, this

Part D: 1) Personal **2)** Indefinite **3)** Demonstrative **4)** Personal **5)** Relative **6)** Interrogative **7)** Indefinite **8)** Relative **9)** Demonstrative **10)** Interrogative

Chapter 2 Mastery Test B

Part A: **1)** himself **2)** that **3)** themselves **4)** who **5)** his **6)** I **7)** who **8)** her **9)** Which **10)** those

Part B: **1)** who–friend **2)** himself–Gary **3)** I–Gary **4)** whose–friend **5)** themselves–boys **6)** their–Karl and Gary **7)** That–meadowlark **8)** What–name **9)** my–Karl **10)** his–Karl

Part C: **1)** What, they, their **2)** He, himself, it **3)** Everyone who, that **4)** No one, anything, this **5)** They, it, those **6)** Our, its, that **7)** Which, this **8)** They, each, that **9)** Whose, our **10)** whichever, you

Part D: **1)** Indefinite **2)** Personal **3)** Indefinite **4)** Demonstrative **5)** Personal **6)** Relative **7)** Demonstrative **8)** Relative **9)** Interrogative **10)** Interrogative

Chapter 3 Mastery Test A

Part A:

Adjectives	Nouns
1) a, large	breakfast
2) Clare's	mother
a, big	breakfast
3) her	mother
a, tall	glass
cold, orange	juice
4) six, fluffy	waffles
four	pieces
French	toast
5) Those	waffles
that, French	toast
very, tasty	waffles, toast
6) The, Vermont, maple	syrup
their	waffles
7) an, enormous	breakfast
her	mother
8) The, spring, bright, cheerful	day
9) a, good	day
a, brisk	walk
10) That, perfect	exercise
our, huge	breakfast
Clare's	mother

Part B: **1)** My Spanish class comes before my English class. **2)** The parade on Thanksgiving Day is always fun. **3)** My friend Lek was born in Thailand. **4)** We went to New York City to hear Latin music. **5)** Is Kenya an African country?

Part C: **1)** shorter **2)** best **3)** more careful **4)** strong **5)** most wonderful **6)** heaviest **7)** easy **8)** larger **9)** most/least successful **10)** faster

Part D: **1)** Proper **2)** Possessive **3)** Demonstrative **4)** Article **5)** Number **6)** Article **7)** Number **8)** Proper **9)** Demonstrative **10)** Possessive

Chapter 3 Mastery Test B

Part A:

Adjectives	Nouns
1) his	brother
the, nature	park
their	home
2) Dale's	brother
two, red	squirrels
the	park
3) a, fresh	peanut
an, approaching	squirrel
4) The, lively	squirrel
a, large, bushy	tail
5) That	squirrel
hungry	squirrel
6) The, nearby, oak	tree
the, squirrel's	home
7) Those, two	birds
that	branch
English	sparrows
8) that	tree
the	hill
a, Chinese	elm
9) The	brothers
a	toad
the, small	pond
10) The, slippery, contented	toad

Part B: **1)** His father came from San José, the Costa Rican capital. **2)** It was cold and rainy over the Memorial Day weekend. **3)** Tom likes his German class better than his English class. **4)** Does Panama touch the South American continent? **5)** Earthquakes are common but frightening for California citizens.

Part C: **1)** greener **2)** taller **3)** worst **4)** larger **5)** more excited **6)** most/least generous **7)** oldest **8)** bright **9)** most/least expensive **10)** late

Part D: **1)** Proper **2)** Demonstrative **3)** Possessive **4)** Demonstrative **5)** Number **6)** Article **7)** Article **8)** Possessive **9)** Number **10)** Proper

Chapter 4 Mastery Test A

Part A: **1)** rides/rode **2)** pass **3)** doing **4)** sanded **5)** studied **6)** broke **7)** priced **8)** finished **9)** eating **10)** been

Part B: **1)** would like **2)** may come **3)** must plant **4)** Do know **5)** plays **6)** will be trimming **7)** Do like **8)** might have finished **9)** Did hear **10)** Would have gone

Part C: **1)** cleared **2)** will have finished **3)** have gone **4)** had called **5)** are planning **6)** will close **7)** was practicing **8)** will have been lasting **9)** will be selling **10)** rake

Part D: **1)** passive **2)** active **3)** passive **4)** active **5)** passive **6)** passive **7)** active **8)** passive **9)** passive **10)** active

Chapter 4 Mastery Test B

Part A: **1)** flew **2)** go **3)** teaching **4)** found **5)** taken **6)** saving **7)** lock **8)** fished **9)** plays/played **10)** walk

Part B: **1)** has gone **2)** may visit **3)** had purchased **4)** Do know **5)** has been acting **6)** will be making **7)** Do like **8)** may have eaten **9)** Did read **10)** Would have made

Part C: **1)** warned **2)** will rise **3)** are using **4)** was writing **5)** will have worried **6)** will be working **7)** have liked **8)** will have been continuing **9)** had ended **10)** dream

Part D: **1)** active **2)** passive **3)** active **4)** passive **5)** passive **6)** active **7)** passive **8)** passive **9)** active **10)** passive

Chapter 5 Mastery Test A

Part A: **1)** had felt–past perfect **2)** is–present **3)** appeared–past **4)** will have been–future perfect **5)** has become–present perfect **6)** is–present **7)** keep–present **8)** will be–future **9)** felt–past **10)** grew–past **11)** Are–present **12)** was–past **13)** seems–present **14)** will taste–future **15)** had become–past perfect

Part B: **1)** be **2)** is/was **3)** was **4)** are/were **5)** is/will be **6)** am/will be **7)** being **8)** be **9)** been **10)** were

Part C: **1)** state-of-being **2)** action **3)** action **4)** state-of-being **5)** state-of-being **6)** action **7)** action **8)** state-of-being **9)** state-of-being **10)** action **11)** action **12)** state-of-being **13)** state-of-being **14)** state-of-being **15)** action

Chapter 5 Mastery Test B

Part A: **1)** will remain–future **2)** is–present **3)** felt–past **4)** turned–past **5)** taste–present **6)** had seemed–past perfect **7)** will have been–future perfect **8)** became–past **9)** Will be–future **10)** felt–past **11)** looks–present **12)** has gotten–present perfect **13)** seems–present **14)** had stayed–past perfect **15)** smells–present

Part B: **1)** be **2)** is **3)** are **4)** been **5)** is/was/will be **6)** being **7)** were **8)** be **9)** Was **10)** am

Part C: **1)** state-of-being **2)** state-of-being **3)** action **4)** state-of-being **5)** state-of-being **6)** action **7)** action **8)** state-of-being **9)** state-of-being **10)** action **11)** state-of-being **12)** action **13)** state-of-being **14)** action **15)** action

Chapter 6 Mastery Test A

Part A: **1)** dances **2)** climbed **3)** shone **4)** picked up **5)** easy **6)** fast **7)** finished **8)** will go **9)** walked **10)** flew **11)** left **12)** well **13)** ready **14)** quickly **15)** beautiful

Part B: **1)** better **2)** most/least quickly **3)** slowly **4)** best **5)** more/less brightly **6)** most swiftly **7)** gladly **8)** more/less clearly **9)** most/least rapidly **10)** noisily

Part C: **1)** never, again, angrily **2)** loudly, when **3)** immediately **4)** Please, now **5)** up, down, almost, constantly **6)** never, too **7)** very **8)** forward, quickly **9)** higher, nearly **10)** here, cheerfully **11)** not, alone, around **12)** squeakily, when, strongly **13)** boldly, ahead **14)** Quietly, now **15)** eagerly, twice

Chapter 6 Mastery Test B

Part A: **1)** sings **2)** turned **3)** glistened **4)** retreated **5)** easy **6)** slowly **7)** exhausted **8)** went **9)** ran **10)** will talk **11)** exercise **12)** well **13)** can see **14)** well **15)** were frozen

Part B: **1)** clearly **2)** warmly **3)** more/less comfortably **4)** faster **5)** most/least easily **6)** well **7)** most/least skillfully **8)** more/less calmly **9)** most/least quickly **10)** hardest

Part C: **1)** Yesterday, early **2)** softly, when **3)** well, together **4)** Please, today **5)** soon **6)** always, immediately **7)** During, extremely **8)** more, slowly, when, very **9)** very **10)** unusually **11)** probably not, very, late **12)** never, alone, later **13)** noisily, when, forcefully **14)** proudly, today **15)** Peacefully, now

Chapter 7 Mastery Test A

Part A: **1)** In, into, over **2)** off, around **3)** for, from **4)** about, of **5)** at, behind **6)** to, through, near **7)** of, across, under **8)** with, on, of **9)** beside, during **10)** beneath, after

Part B: **1)** me **2)** him **3)** her **4)** their **5)** us **6)** it **7)** you **8)** them **9)** her **10)** our

Part C: **1)** adjective **2)** adverb **3)** adverb **4)** adjective **5)** adjective **6)** adjective **7)** adjective **8)** adverb **9)** adverb **10)** adverb **11)** adjective **12)** adverb **13)** adjective **14)** adverb **15)** adjective **16)** adjective **17)** adverb **18)** adverb **19)** adverb **20)** adjective

Chapter 7 Mastery Test B

Part A: **1)** During, in, down, by **2)** For, with **3)** about, on **4)** at, before **5)** of, beside, near **6)** from, for **7)** from, off, during **8)** under, behind **9)** into, beneath **10)** to, after

Part B: **1)** my **2)** us **3)** it **4)** them **5)** him **6)** me **7)** you **8)** our **9)** her **10)** their

Part C: **1)** adjective **2)** adjective **3)** adjective **4)** adjective **5)** adjective **6)** adverb **7)** adjective **8)** adverb **9)** adjective **10)** adverb **11)** adverb **12)** adjective **13)** adverb **14)** adverb **15)** adverb **16)** adjective **17)** adverb **18)** adjective **19)** adverb **20)** adverb

Chapter 8 Mastery Test A

Part A: **1)** and **2)** and **3)** for **4)** Both, and **5)** yet **6)** but **7)** however **8)** Because **9)** Either, or **10)** nevertheless

Part B: **1)** or **2)** nor **3)** Neither **4)** but also **5)** and **6)** or **7)** either **8)** whether **9)** Both **10)** not only

Part C: **1)** and **2)** consequently **3)** however **4)** so **5)** otherwise **6)** also **7)** nevertheless **8)** furthermore **9)** instead **10)** but

Part D: Possible answers are given. Accept any other sentences that include a logical subordinating conjunction.

1) Since my mom is working, I have to watch my little sister.
2) After Greg flew on an airplane, he lost his fear of flying.
3) Although the sky was cloudy, it was warm and comfortable.
4) Sue and Gil will clean this week, so we will clean next week.
5) Rita went to the store, because she needed groceries.

Chapter 8 Mastery Test B

Part A: **1)** however **2)** so **3)** yet **4)** otherwise **5)** Neither, nor **6)** and **7)** because **8)** Although **9)** unless **10)** but

Part B: **1)** nor **2)** or **3)** but also **4)** Either **5)** and **6)** whether **7)** not only **8)** neither **9)** or **10)** both

Part C: **1)** however **2)** otherwise **3)** instead **4)** but **5)** so **6)** and **7)** consequently **8)** furthermore **9)** also **10)** nevertheless

Part D: Possible answers are given. Accept any other sentences that include a logical subordinating conjunction.

1) Although we had just eaten breakfast, we went to the brunch anyway. **2)** We had been leading until the other team got three baskets. **3)** I was asleep when the storm blew down a tree.
4) After Gretta looked everywhere, she found her lens beside the sink.
5) While Joe waited for the doctor, he reviewed his questions.

Chapter 9 Mastery Test A

Part A: Possible answers are given. Accept any other logical interjections.

1) My goodness, **2)** Ouch! **3)** Well, **4)** Oh boy, **5)** Hooray! **6)** Wow! **7)** Whew, **8)** Gosh, **9)** Gee, **10)** Ha!

Part B: Possible answers are given. Accept any other logical punctuation.

1) So! Who cares? **2)** Wow! That dessert is good. **3)** Quick! Help me! **4)** Stop! That noise is bugging me. **5)** Hey, what's going on?

Chapter 9 Mastery Test B

Part A: Possible answers are given. Accept any other logical interjections.
1) Wow! **2)** Brr! **3)** Ah, **4)** Quick! **5)** Really! **6)** Nonsense! **7)** Yes, **8)** Hey! **9)** Hello! **10)** Sorry,

Part B: Possible answers are given. Accept any other logical punctuation.
1) Oh boy! What a nice day. **2)** Wow! I love that outfit. **3)** Ouch! My sunburn is sore. **4)** Hush, I am trying to concentrate. **5)** Oh, no! I lost my contact lens.

Chapter 10 Mastery Test A

Part A: **1)** NS **2)** S **3)** S **4)** NS **5)** NS **6)** S **7)** NS **8)** S **9)** S **10)** NS

Part B: The complete subject is given. Nouns and pronouns are underlined.
1) Irene and I **2)** Neither the television nor the radio **3)** Grandfather and the entire family **4)** Our friends Howard and Heidi **5)** Everything in the freezer

Part C: The complete predicate is given. The verb or phrase is underlined.
1) had knocked out the electrical power **2)** had electricity or telephones for three days **3)** fly casts in summer and ice fishes in winter **4)** are working day and night to plow the roads **5)** have been married for years

Part D: **1)** Question **2)** Command/Request **3)** Statement **4)** Feeling **5)** Question **6)** Command/Request **7)** Feeling **8)** Command/Request **9)** Question **10)** Statement

Part E: **1)** Jo | plays the drums, and her mother | plays the banjo. **2)** A motorcycle | is not as expensive as a car, but it | is trusty transportation. **3)** We | stopped at the mall, and we | came home after that. **4)** Donna | has not had any piano lessons, but she | plays very well. **5)** Deion | is coming for dinner, and he | is bringing the salad. **6)** The roads | looked dry and clear, but the black ice | fooled us. **7)** Talk radio | is popular in America, and many people | listen. **8)** Listeners | call the stations, and they | express their opinions. **9)** I | like Elton John's music, but Mike | prefers Bobby McFerrin's. **10)** English | is Andrea's favorite class, but her twin sister's favorite class | is math.

Chapter 10 Mastery Test B

Part A: **1)** S **2)** NS **3)** NS **4)** S **5)** S **6)** NS **7)** S **8)** NS **9)** NS **10)** S

Part B: The complete subject is given. Nouns and pronouns are underlined.
1) Mr. Alwin and his English class **2)** Either the shovel or the hoe **3)** Lucy and all her children **4)** The boys in the scout troop **5)** All of the trees

Part C: The complete predicate is given. The verb or verb phrase is underlined.
1) had blown over all of the lawn furniture **2)** will be planting tomatoes spinach and carrots **3)** composes music and writes the words for songs **4)** are volunteering our time at the food shelf last week **5)** got together and visited with her friends from France

Part D: **1)** Command/Request **2)** Question **3)** Feeling **4)** Statement **5)** Feeling **6)** Question **7)** Command/Request **8)** Statement **9)** Command/Request **10)** Question

Part E: **1)** Kirby | plays right field, and Kent | plays first base. **2)** We | were going to the beach, but we | got company. **3)** Hoa | has a computer science degree, and she | got a job with a software company. **4)** The sky | is clear and sunny, but the temperature | is below zero. **5)** Akin | had a cold, and he | stayed home. **6)** The rent | went up, but we | didn't hear about it for a month. **7)** CDs | are popular, and they | are better than tapes. **8)** Good cooks | try new recipes, and their efforts | please their guests. **9)** Shana | likes the beach, but her family | likes the mountains. **10)** I | wanted to go to a movie, but I | had to work.

Chapter 11 Mastery Test A

Part A: **1)** I **2)** I **3)** T **4)** T **5)** T **6)** I **7)** T **8)** T **9)** I **10)** T

Part B:

S V IO DO
1) James asked Mr. Cohen a question.
S V DO OC
2) Everyone calls Emma Thompson a great actress.
S V DO OC
3) Anne named her cat Jemima.
S V DO
4) Angus wrote his boss a memo.
S V IO DO
5) His boss gave everyone a reward.

Part C:

1) 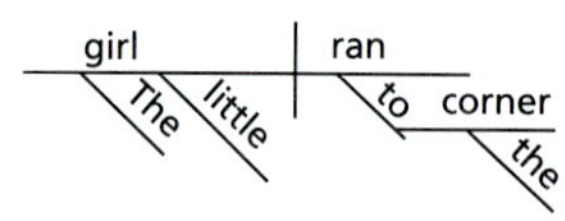

2) 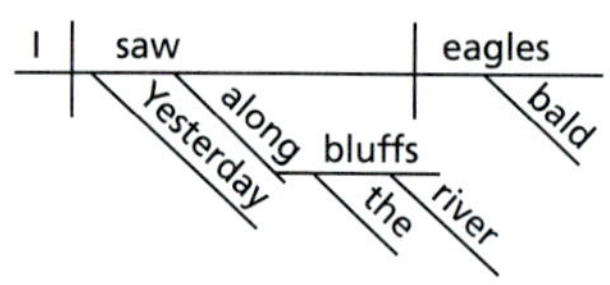

3) 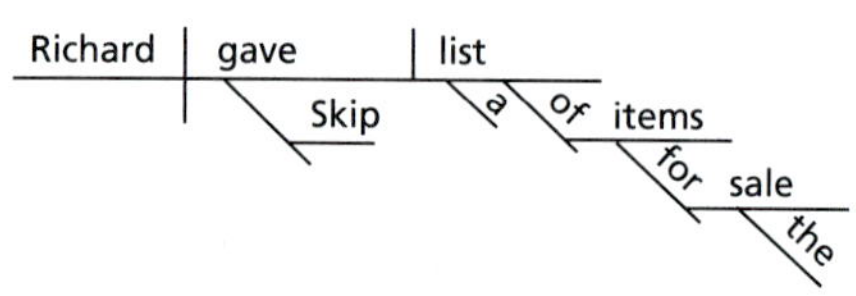

4) 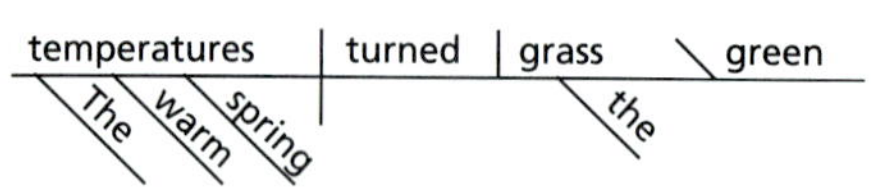

5) 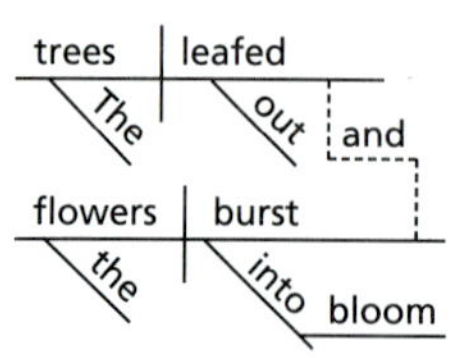

Chapter 11 Mastery Test B

Part A: **1)** T **2)** I **3)** T **4)** T **5)** I **6)** T **7)** T **8)** T **9)** I **10)** I

Part B:

S V IO DO
1) Juan gave his brother a gift.
S V DO OC
2) The frost turned the leaves red.
S V DO OC
3) The Hansons painted their shutters green.
S V IO DO
4) Gerald sent his friend a fax.

S V IO DO
5) His friend sent Gerald a reply.

Part C:

1) 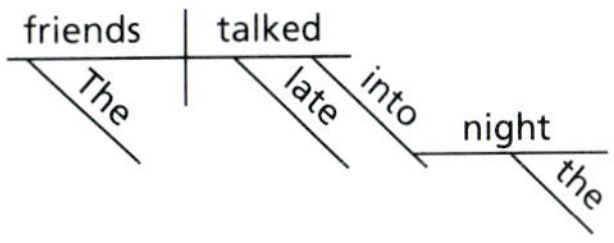

2) 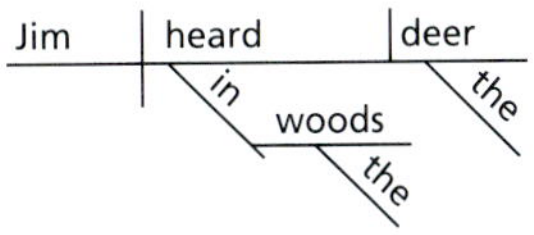

3) 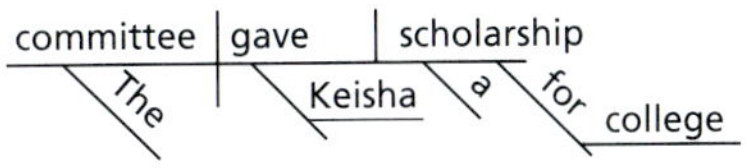

4) 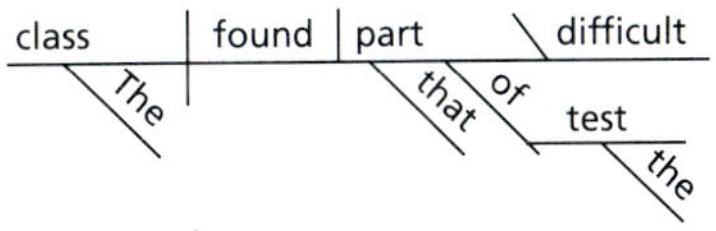

5) 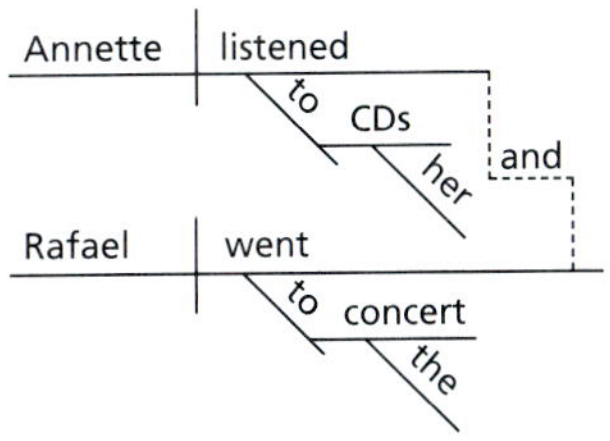

Chapter 12 Mastery Test A

Part A:

S LV Adv PA
1) Loretta is always friendly.

S LV PA Adv
2) Chip seems distracted today.

S LV PN
3) Marian Anderson was a marvelous singer.

S LV PN
4) Tom and Jane are outstanding athletes.

S LV PN S LV Adv PA
5) George Burns was a comedian and he was very lasting.

Part B: **1)** PN **2)** PA **3)** PP **4)** PN **5)** PP **6)** PA **7)** PA **8)** PN **9)** PN **10)** PA

Part C:

1) 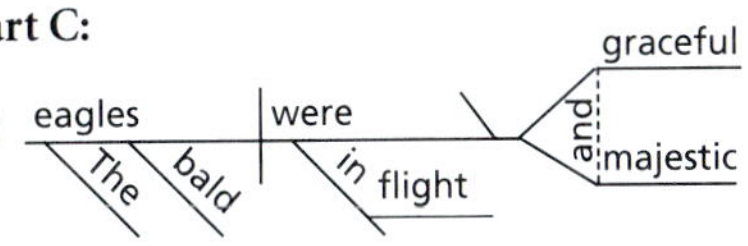

2) 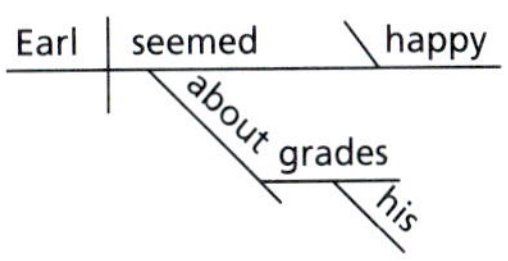

3) 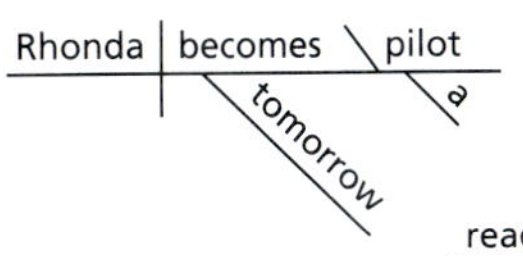

4) 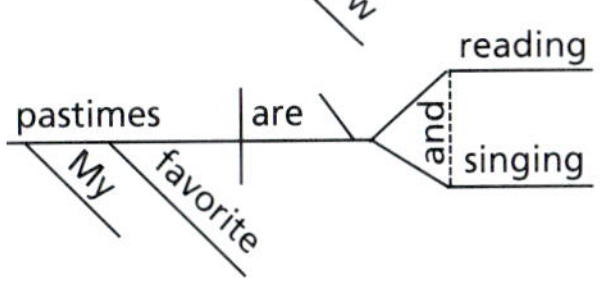

5) 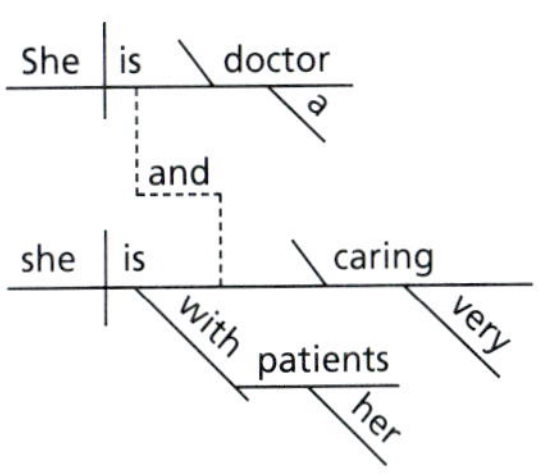

Chapter 12 Mastery Test B

Part A:

S LV Adv PA
1) Sharon seems very kind.

S LV PA Adv
2) Glen and Rita felt disappointed yesterday.

S LV PN
3) The weather system was an Alberta clipper.

S LV PN
4) Rudy is a naval officer.

S LV Adv PA S LV PN
5) Eileen was very bright, and she became an electrical engineer.

Part B: **1)** PA **2)** PN **3)** PN **4)** PP **5)** PA **6)** PN **7)** PN **8)** PA **9)** PA **10)** PP

Part C:

1) 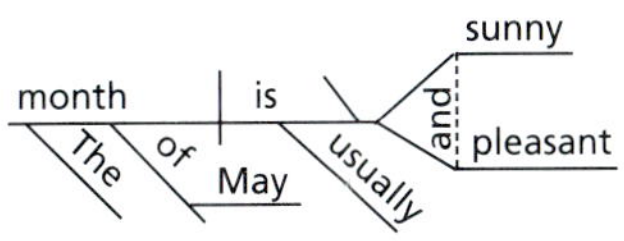

2) 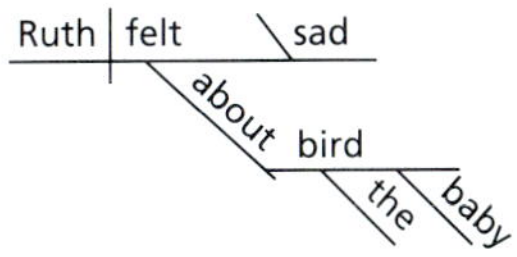

3) 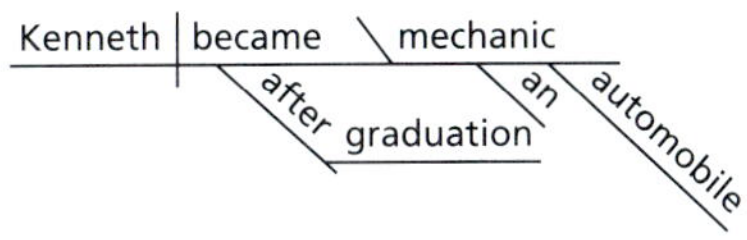

4) 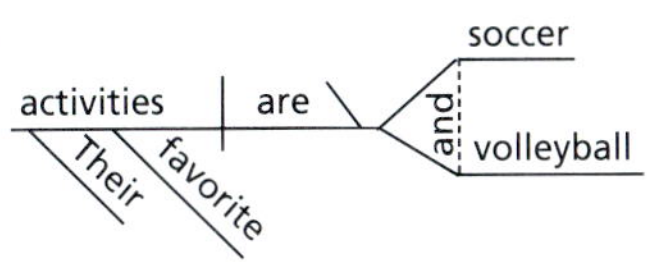

5) 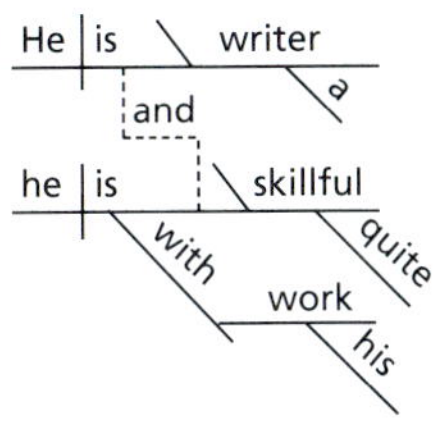

Chapter 13 Mastery Test A

Part A: **1)** IC **2)** P **3)** DC **4)** P **5)** DC **6)** IC **7)** DC **8)** IC **9)** DC **10)** P

Part B: **1)** AVC **2)** AVC **3)** NC **4)** AC **5)** AC **6)** NC **7)** AVC **8)** AC **9)** NC **10)** AVC

Part C: **1)** Simple **2)** Complex **3)** Compound **4)** Compound-Complex **5)** Compound **6)** Simple **7)** Complex **8)** Compound-Complex **9)** Complex **10)** Simple **11)** Complex **12)** Compound **13)** Compound **14)** Compound-Complex **15)** Simple

Chapter 13 Mastery Test B

Part A: **1)** IC **2)** DC **3)** P **4)** DC **5)** IC **6)** P **7)** DC **8)** P **9)** IC **10)** DC

Part B: **1)** AC **2)** AVC **3)** NC **4)** AC **5)** NC **6)** AVC **7)** AVC **8)** AC **9)** NC **10)** AVC

Part C: **1)** Simple **2)** Complex **3)** Simple **4)** Compound-Complex **5)** Compound **6)** Compound **7)** Simple **8)** Complex **9)** Compound-Complex **10)** Simple **11)** Compound **12)** Compound **13)** Complex **14)** Complex **15)** Compound-Complex

Chapter 14 Mastery Test A

Part A: **1)** Infinitive **2)** Participle **3)** Gerund **4)** Infinitive **5)** Gerund **6)** Participle **7)** Gerund **8)** Infinitive **9)** Participle **10)** Gerund

Part B: **1)** GP **2)** IP **3)** PP **4)** IP **5)** PP **6)** GP **7)** IP **8)** GP **9)** GP **10)** PP

Part C: Answers will vary. Sample answers are given. Each verbal should be used as indicated.
1) I like to run. **2)** To watch a sunset is one of life's pleasures. **3)** We had four rooms to paint. **4)** She had a reason for going home late. **5)** At 15, Tom began driving a car. **6)** Knowing how to type is a useful skill. **7)** Rosie's favorite sport is bowling. **8)** The howling wind blew through the trees. **9)** They were worried about the whining puppy. **10)** The cracked bowl was leaking.

Chapter 14 Mastery Test B

Part A: **1)** Participle **2)** Gerund **3)** Infinitive **4)** Infinitive **5)** Participle **6)** Gerund **7)** Gerund **8)** Participle **9)** Infinitive **10)** Gerund

Part B: **1)** GP **2)** IP **3)** IP **4)** GP **5)** GP **6)** PP **7)** GP **8)** IP **9)** PP **10)** PP

Part C: Answers will vary. Sample answers are given. Each verbal should be used as indicated.
1) The butterflies were hard to catch. **2)** Judy and Fred like to see the sunrise. **3)** We have many trails to climb. **4)** They got lost after leaving late. **5)** Fidel started riding a bike at a young age. **6)** Learning how to ski is my goal. **7)** My hobby is fishing. **8)** The leaves softly moved in a whispering breeze. **9)** The sound of the laughing child cheered me. **10)** A chipped tooth was the result of his fall.

Midterm Mastery Test

Part A: **1)** Adverb **2)** Preposition **3)** Adjective **4)** Pronoun **5)** Action Verb **6)** Conjunction **7)** Noun **8)** Interjection **9)** State-of-Being Verb **10)** Noun **11)** Preposition **12)** Action Verb **13)** State-of-Being Verb **14)** Conjunction **15)** Adverb **16)** Interjection **17)** Pronoun **18)** Action Verb **19)** Conjunction **20)** Adverb

Part B: **1)** Valerie has a French poodle named Mimi. **2)** Tim likes to eat Swiss cheese. **3)** We studied the Native American tribes of New Mexico. **4)** My friend Hanna is learning Spanish with her computer. **5)** Karl enjoys his English and Basic Computer II classes. **6)** Samantha is reading *Sense and Sensibility.*
7) We plan to see a play on Friday, April 21. **8)** Loren had an African family visit him over summer vacation. **9)** I would like Italian dressing with my salad. **10)** On vacation, Tracy went to the Rocky Mountains in Colorado.

Part C: **1)** Because Tim is Eliza's friend, he bought her a birthday gift. **2)** Sharon bought four dollars' worth of stamps, but she needs more to mail the package. **3)** That coat is Jack's, and this one is yours. **4)** Ouch! That hurt. **5)** Peter wanted to be on the wrestling team; therefore, he lifted weights every day. **6)** Kip's sister Dionn has three children named Jasper, Alf, and Evon.
7) Connie wanted to go biking; instead, she went fishing.
8) Wow! I got an A on my test. **9)** If at first you don't succeed, try, try again. **10)** Dave shut the closet door; however, he didn't know the cat was inside.

Part D: **1)** is **2)** are **3)** but **4)** however **5)** mice's **6)** girls' **7)** ladies' **8)** wives **9)** eaten **10)** gone **11)** Moe's **12)** their **13)** Which **14)** her **15)** taller **16)** tricky **17)** best **18)** eating **19)** taken **20)** better

Final Mastery Test

Part A:

1) Amanda (S) went (V) to Howard University.

2) Jimmy (S) won (V) a scholarship (DO).

3) He (S) would play (V) baseball (DO) for his school.

4) The college (S) gave (V) Jimmy (IO) a uniform (DO).

5) Jimmy (S) is (V) a good athlete.

6) Nadya (S) was excited (V) about her new job.

7) The new baby (S) made (V) the family (DO) happy (OC).

8) Only Ed (S) is doing (V) something (DO) special (OC) tonight.

9) The spring weather (S) was (V) beautiful.

10) The voters (S) arrived (V) at the polls early.

Part B: **1)** Adjective **2)** Pronoun **3)** Action Verb **4)** Conjunction **5)** Noun **6)** State-of-Being Verb **7)** Preposition **8)** State-of-Being Verb **9)** Adverb **10)** Interjection

Part C: **1)** Ahmad has a cat named May. **2)** Julia likes Dutch chocolate. **3)** Frank is taking Spanish and Computer I.
4) Sherry read *A Raisin in the Sun* on her trip to Arizona.
5) Chuck is taking Monday, August 15, off.

Part D: **1)** Simple **2)** Compound **3)** Compound-Complex **4)** Compound **5)** Complex **6)** Complex **7)** Compound-Complex **8)** Simple **9)** Compound **10)** Complex

Part E: **1)** DC **2)** IC **3)** IC **4)** P **5)** DC **6)** DC **7)** P **8)** P **9)** IC **10)** DC

Part F: **1)** Question **2)** Command/Request **3)** Feeling **4)** Statement **5)** Command/Request

Part G: **1)** T **2)** I **3)** T **4)** T **5)** I

Part H: **1)** watching–Participle **2)** relaxing–Gerund **3)** to study–Infinitive **4)** knocking–Participle **5)** to tell–Infinitive **6)** Working–Gerund **7)** Wondering–Participle **8)** painting–Gerund **9)** to paint–Infinitive **10)** to paint–Infinitive

Part I: **1)** PN **2)** PA **3)** PP **4)** PN **5)** PP **6)** PA **7)** PA **8)** PN **9)** PN **10)** PA

Part J: **1)** AVC **2)** NC **3)** NC **4)** AC **5)** AC **6)** NC **7)** AVC **8)** AC **9)** NC **10)** AVC

Part K: **1)** Because Elsa's mother is working, Elsa watches her sister Kim. **2)** Len bought ten dollars' worth of gas, but he still did not fill the tank. **3)** Hello! Is anybody home? **4)** Monica made supper; however, her father brought Chinese food. **5)** Shira left the back door open; therefore, she had to catch the bird that flew inside.

Part L: **1)** are **2)** but **3)** children's **4)** wives **5)** eaten **6)** gone **7)** Zoe's **8)** their **9)** her **10)** taller

AGS

Teacher Questionnaire

Attention Teachers! As publishers of *Basic English Grammar,* we would like your help in making this textbook more valuable to you. Please take a few minutes to fill out this survey. Your feedback will help us to better serve you and your students.

1) What is your position and major area of responsibility? ____________

____

____

2) Briefly describe your setting:

____ regular education ____ special education ____ adult basic education

____ community college ____ university ____ other ____________

3) The enrollment in your classroom includes students with the following (check all that apply):

____ at-risk for failure ____ low reading ability ____ behavior problems

____ learning disabilities ____ ESL ____ other ____________

4) Grade level of your students: ____________

5) Racial/ethnic groups represented in your classes (check all that apply):

____ African-American ____ Asian ____ Caucasian ____ Hispanic

____ Native American ____ Other

6) School Location:

____ urban ____ suburban ____ rural ____ other ____________

7) What reaction did your students have to the materials? (Include comments about the cover design, lesson format, illustrations, etc.)

____

____

____

8) What features in the student text helped your students the most?

____

____

____

OVER ➤

9) What features in the student text helped your students the least? Please include suggestions for changing these to make the text more relevant.

____

____

____

10) How did you use the Teacher's Edition and support materials, and what features did you find to be the most helpful?

____

____

____

11) What activity from the program did your students benefit from the most? Please briefly explain.

____

____

____

12) Optional: Share an activity that you used to teach the materials in your classroom that enhanced the learning and motivation of your students.

____

____

____

Several activities will be selected to be included in future editions. Please include your name, address, and phone number so we may contact you for permission and possible payment to use the material. Thank you!

▼ fold in thirds and tape shut at the top ▼

Name: ______________________

School: ______________________

Address: ______________________

City/State/ZIP: ______________________

Phone: ______________________

NO POSTAGE NECESSARY IF MAILED IN THE UNITED STATES

BUSINESS REPLY MAIL

FIRST-CLASS MAIL PERMIT NO.12 CIRCLE PINES MN

POSTAGE WILL BE PAID BY ADDRESSEE

AGS

ATTN MARKETING SUPPORT
AMERICAN GUIDANCE SERVICE, INC.
4201 WOODLAND ROAD
PO BOX 99
CIRCLE PINES MN 55014-9923